DK ESSENTIAL MANAGER'S MANUAL

DK ESSENTIAL MANAGER'S MANUAL

ROBERT HELLER & TIM HINDLE

DK PUBLISHING, INC.

A DK PUBLISHING BOOK

www.dk.com

Editor David Tombesi-Walton
Project Art Editor Ellen Woodward

Senior Editor Jane Simmonds
Senior Art Editor Tracy Hambleton-Miles

DTP Designer Jason Little
Production Controller Silvia La Greca

Managing Editor Stephanie Jackson
Managing Art Editor Nigel Duffield

First American Edition, 1998
4 6 8 10 9 7 5 3

Published in the United States by
DK Publishing, Inc.
95 Madison Avenue
New York, New York 10016

Library of Congress Cataloging-in-Publication Data
Heller, Robert, 1932–
    The essential manager's manual / by Robert
Heller and Tim Hindle. -- 1st American ed.
    p.   cm.
    ISBN 0-7894-3519-5
    1. Management.   2. Time management.
    3. Decision-making.   4. Communication in
management.   I. Hindle, Tim.   II. Title.
    HD31.H444   1998
    658.4--DC21   98–6507
                                                CIP

Reproduced by Colourscan, Singapore
Printed in Hong Kong

CONTENTS

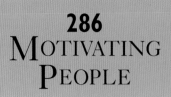

INTRODUCTION

KEEPING UP WITH CHANGE

In today's fast-moving business world, organizations are constantly evolving, and the role of the manager is becoming ever more diverse. Many organizations have undergone radical change, often prompted by economic pressure and the twin demands of increased efficiency and productivity, and also by information technology, which has enabled tasks to be carried out in seconds rather than days. In an aggressively competitive marketplace, organizations are often under pressure to deliver better and better results, and managers are naturally in the front line. At the same time, corporate mergers and acquisitions have inevitably led to reorganization and rationalization on a wide scale, forcing many people to change their jobs, or even their careers, and to undergo retraining. Organizations are also becoming much less hierarchical, with promotion increasingly based on genuine merit rather than length of service. In this climate, the most successful business

managers are those who have recognized the need to adapt to change by continually reexamining the way they work, by developing as wide a range of skills as possible, and by keeping these skills up to date.

HELPING ALL MANAGERS

The *Essential Manager's Manual* is a comprehensive guide to the most important areas of business life, covering interpersonal and professional skills vital to those who hold, or seek to hold, management positions in any organization, large or small, in both the public and private sectors. It makes essential reading for managers at all levels, whether they are new to their jobs and need to learn the necessary skills from scratch, have many years' experience and want a refresher course in current business practices, or are running their own operation. Certain sections, especially those on communication, time management, and dealing with stress, contain advice that is applicable outside a conventional office environment and will therefore be useful to students, first-time jobholders, the self-employed, and anyone else coping with an unfamiliar work situation. The *Manual* also provides useful information on the range of new technology to be found in today's offices, which in recent years has revolutionized the working lives of hundreds of millions of people around the world.

MANAGING TODAY

The extent and scope of the manager's role will depend, of course, on both the industry and organization within which he or she works, as well as on the present level of seniority. However, most managers need to supervise the work of more junior employees and to ensure that staff function effectively. A full understanding of what makes people perform well and of the problems that may affect performance in the workplace is therefore essential for any manager. He or she will need to employ a wide range of skills, both interpersonal and professional, in order to resolve these problems. In a single working day, a manager may be required to chair a meeting to look at ways of improving departmental efficiency, conduct staff appraisals, and delegate a task to an employee. The same manager may also need to use specialized skills in which his or her own performance may be scrutinized by superiors, for example when giving a presentation or acting as a member of a negotiating team. Throughout the day, the manager is likely to need to take and make phone calls; write and receive letters, faxes, and e-mails; and deal with many different types of people, ranging from customers and clients to suppliers and sales representatives. Naturally, he or she will also communicate within the organization.

IMPROVING SKILLS

The main aim of the *Manual* is to help the reader perfect his or her management techniques in a range of key areas, either by acquiring new skills or by improving existing ones as necessary. The *Manual* forms a complete guide to basic business practice and provides would-be and new managers with the confidence to handle the situations and problems they are most likely to encounter, while enabling more experienced managers to examine their performance and brush up their skills. It is organized in concise, clearly defined sections to enable busy managers to access specific information as quickly as possible. Readers may also wish to focus on an individual section in detail, in which case advice is given to help them research their subject and plan a strategy for action, anticipate any problems they are likely to encounter, and achieve their objectives efficiently.

USING THIS BOOK

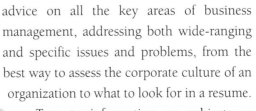

The *Essential Manager's Manual* contains sound, practical advice on all the key areas of business management, addressing both wide-ranging and specific issues and problems, from the best way to assess the corporate culture of an organization to what to look for in a resume. Turn to information on subjects as diverse as greeting overseas business contacts, setting an agenda for a meeting and taking the minutes, reorganizing the layout of an office, and holding a brainstorming session. The individual sections of the *Manual* have been arranged to deal first with interpersonal skills (Communicating Clearly and Managing Time), then to address five basic yet important areas of management practice (Making Decisions, Delegating Successfully, Motivating People, Managing Teams, and Managing Meetings). These are followed by three sections on specialized techniques that form part of many managerial functions today (Presenting Successfully, Negotiating Successfully, and Interviewing People). The book's last two sections (Managing Change and Minimizing Stress) look at ways of coping with the hectic pace of modern business life.

Fully illustrated with annotated photographs, charts, and flow diagrams, the *Manual* is written in jargon-free language and packed with commonsense advice to help anyone solve even the most challenging management predicaments. It also presents information in a clearer and more accessible format than any other business guide and features more than

1,200 quick-reference power tips, covering every management situation in the book and serving as handy memory aids. Other unique features include Checklists, Points to Remember, and Do's and Don'ts, summarizing key information; Questions to Ask yourself and others; Case Studies focusing on real-life management problems; Cultural Differences, describing business practices around the world; and expertly prepared charts that present essential information in a clear, concise form. Each section of the book includes a self-analysis exercise to enable readers to assess their performance in that particular management area.

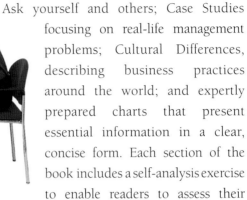

Covering all key aspects of management, the *Essential Manager's Manual* shows readers how they can analyze and improve their professional performance, whether they are first-time managers or the chairperson of a large organization. Its clear, no-nonsense approach gives all managers the confidence to act expertly in any work situation. Above all, the *Manual* allows good managers to become outstanding ones, making it an invaluable source of day-to-day reference in any office or organization.

COMMUNICATING CLEARLY

INTRODUCTION

T he art of getting your message across effectively is a vital part of being a successful manager. Whether you want to make presentations with confidence or to negotiate with ease, this section of the book will help you improve your communication skills. All the key aspects of business communication are clearly explained, from understanding body language to writing reports and proposals. Also included is practical advice on using public relations, advertising, information technology, and media techniques, while 101 concise tips scattered throughout give you further vital information. As you begin to communicate more effectively, this section will help you consolidate and build on your new skills. Finally, a self-assessment exercise allows you to evaluate how good you are at communicating.

LEARNING THE BASICS

Everybody communicates in one way or another, but few managers deliver their messages as well as they can. Learn some basic rules to help you get your message across clearly.

WORKING TOWARD BETTER COMMUNICATION

Good communication is the lifeblood of organizations. It takes many forms, such as speaking, writing, and listening, though its purpose is always to convey a message to recipients. Use it to handle information and improve relationships.

1 Encourage your company to improve all types of communication.

BEING EFFECTIVE

Effective communication (and therefore effective business) hinges on people understanding your meaning, and replying in terms that move the exchange forward – preferably in the direction you would like it to go. Communicating is always a two-way process. In management, you communicate to get things done, pass on and obtain information, reach decisions, achieve joint understanding, and develop relationships.

2 Note that good communicators make much better managers.

RECOGNIZING BARRIERS

There are always at least two parties involved in any communication, each of whom may have different wants, needs, and attitudes. These wants and needs can present barriers if they conflict with those of the other party, and such barriers may stop you conveying or receiving the right message. Any communication must overcome such barriers if it is to be successful, and the first step is to recognize that they exist.

▼ COMMUNICATING POSITIVELY
Breaking down barriers is one of the first steps toward good communication. Maintaining eye contact, listening to what the other person is saying, and mirroring body language all help you to communicate successfully.

Facing person you are talking to shows you are not afraid to listen to what is said

Tilting your head slightly shows you are listening

Break down barriers by adopting other person's pose and actions

Maintain eye contact with other person

ACHIEVING CLARITY

The three rules that govern good communication are all associated with clarity:
● Be clear in your own mind about what you want to communicate;
● Deliver the message succinctly;
● Ensure that the message has been clearly and correctly understood.
Good communication means saying what you mean – and fully comprehending any feedback.

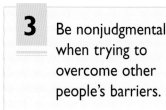

3 Be nonjudgmental when trying to overcome other people's barriers.

CHOOSING A METHOD

It is essential when communicating a message that you give serious thought to the medium you choose. For many, this choice is often between the spoken and the written word. If you decide that you want speed and convenience, you may well choose speech as the best form of communication. Alternatively you may want something more permanent and orderly – a typed document, for example – which will attract a considered reply.

Electronic media have generated even more possibilities by creating a hybrid form of speech and writing. Thus e-mails have the speed and informality of a phone conversation, yet they are in letter form and can be filed. The purpose of the message will dictate which method to choose. Decide on your message first, and then select the best method to convey it, making sure that you have mastered its technique.

CULTURAL DIFFERENCES

Broad generalizations are often made about a culture's use of word and gesture. Some Japanese and other Asians find it easier than some Europeans to be silent. The Germans, Nordics, and British, generally less voluble than many people in the Latin nations, are often more restrained in gesture. Some British seem to avoid saying what they mean, while Australians may disconcert others by forcefully saying exactly what they mean. Many Americans can be very straightforward.

4 Match your medium to your message with great care.

5 Wherever possible, use visuals to communicate.

COMBINING METHODS

Methods of communication can be grouped into five main types: the written word, the spoken (and heard) word, the symbolic gesture, the visual image, and a combination of these. Though the first four methods work well individually, it is now known that using two or more different communication methods together increases interest, comprehension, and retention. Methods are more potent when combined with others.

Examples of a combined approach include communicating via commercial media and electronic technology, such as multimedia and video conferencing. Multimedia allows better use of visual elements, and is increasingly the medium of choice when it comes to communicating with large numbers of people, especially employees in a big organization.

CHOOSING METHODS OF COMMUNICATION

TYPE OF COMMUNICATION	EXAMPLES	USEFULNESS
WRITTEN WORD In any language and in various media, the written word is basic to literate societies.	Letters, memos, reports, proposals, notes, contracts, summaries, agendas, notices, regulations, minutes, plans, discussion documents.	The written word is the basis of organizational communication, and is used because it is relatively permanent and accessible.
SPOKEN WORD Communication that is effective only when it is heard by the right people. 	Conversations, interviews, meetings, phone calls, debates, requests, debriefings, announcements, speeches.	Verbal exchanges in person and by phone are used because of their immediacy; they are the chief means by which organizations work on a day-to-day basis.
SYMBOLIC GESTURES Any positive or negative behavior that can be seen or heard by the intended target.	Gestures, facial expressions, actions, deeds, tone of voice, silence, stance, posture, movement, immobility, presence, absence.	Actions and body language profoundly but unconsciously affect people – propaganda depends on the manipulation of positive and negative signs.
VISUAL IMAGES Images that can be perceived by a target group.	Photographs (slides and prints), paintings, drawings, illustrations, graphics, cartoons, charts, videos, logos, film, doodles, collages, color schemes.	Visual images are used because they convey powerful conscious and unconscious messages.
MULTIMEDIA A combination of the different methods above, often involving IT (information technology).	Television, newspapers, magazines, leaflets, booklets, flyers, posters, Internet, intranet, World Wide Web, video, radio, cassettes, CD-ROMs.	Media are especially useful when they can be participative. The more professional the use of multimedia, the more effective and productive they are likely to be.

UNDERSTANDING BODY LANGUAGE

Your body language – a huge range of unconscious physical movements – can either strengthen communication or damage it. Even if you are sitting completely still, you may be unknowingly communicating a powerful message about your real feelings.

6 When standing with people, leave a personal space of about 1 yd (1 m).

COMMUNICATING ▼ BY BODY LANGUAGE

Posture is all-important in body language. On a first meeting, these three postures would create very different impressions. The positive posture might have the best effect on the outcome by encouraging open communication, while the negative one would make communication difficult.

READING BODY LANGUAGE

Because of its subtlety and range, body language is difficult to read – and to control. However, a broad understanding of body language is one route to understanding the real opinions of others. For instance, if people are inwardly feeling uncomfortable because they are lying, their awkward body language will betray the lie.

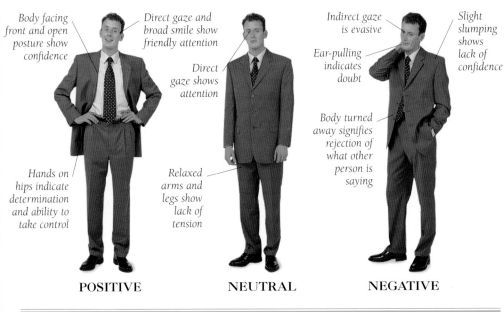

Body facing front and open posture show confidence

Direct gaze and broad smile show friendly attention

Hands on hips indicate determination and ability to take control

Direct gaze shows attention

Relaxed arms and legs show lack of tension

Indirect gaze is evasive

Ear-pulling indicates doubt

Body turned away signifies rejection of what other person is saying

Slight slumping shows lack of confidence

POSITIVE　　　　**NEUTRAL**　　　　**NEGATIVE**

CONQUERING NERVES

The nervousness people feel before making a presentation or attending an interview is very natural. Their minds prepare them for action via their nervous system, so nervousness is due in part to glands pumping the hormone adrenaline into their blood. Use body language to appear more confident than you feel by making a conscious effort to smile and to relax your arms. Look people in the eye while you are talking or listening to them, keep your posture comfortably straight, and do not fiddle with your hands.

CULTURAL DIFFERENCES

Britons and Americans tend to leave more personal space around them than other nationalities, and are more likely to move away if they feel that their space is being invaded. People who live in rural areas may also stand farther apart than city dwellers.

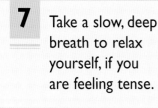

7 Take a slow, deep breath to relax yourself, if you are feeling tense.

KEEPING YOUR DISTANCE

Leaving an acceptable distance between people is part of body language, and this distance changes depending on situation. For instance, guests at a social gathering stand closer to one another than strangers in a business situation. Always take care not to intrude into another's personal territory in case you arouse defensive or hostile reactions.

CREATING AN IMPRESSION

First impressions are very important. It is thought that the initial five seconds of any first meeting are more important than the next five minutes, so attention to detail can make a huge difference. Think about grooming and appropriate clothing, and err on the conservative side. Even if an informal look is required, ensure your garments and shoes are in impeccable condition. Before going into a meeting, check your appearance in a mirror to make sure that your hair is neat.

MAKING AN IMPACT ▶
Grooming and posture always create an impression. This woman looks much more confident and capable when she has made an effort to neaten her appearance.

Neat hair

Messy hair

Upright posture

Crumpled T-shirt

Neatly buttoned jacket

Slovenly stance

Shining shoes

Dirty shoes

WRONG **RIGHT**

UNDERSTANDING AND USING GESTURES

Gestures, together with other nonverbal communication such as posture and facial expressions, are an important part of body language. Knowing how to gesture for effect, on public platforms or in face-to-face meetings, will help to convey your message.

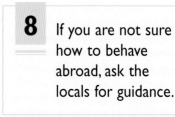

8 If you are not sure how to behave abroad, ask the locals for guidance.

9 Make sure you are not unintentionally wearing a hostile expression.

CULTURAL DIFFERENCES

The nonverbal language of gestures varies from country to country. Some to watch for include the North American thumb and forefinger gesture for OK (may insult a Dane); pointing with a finger (considered rude in China); the French enthusiasm for shaking hands (excessive to Britons); shaking your head meaning "no" (means "yes" to Indians); and hugging in public (unacceptable in Singapore).

RECOGNIZING GESTURES

All skilled public speakers use gestures for emphasis. For example, John Kennedy used a chopping motion, while Bill Clinton points his finger. Devices like smacking your fist into an open palm and spreading your palms can reinforce points you make verbally. Remember that over-assertive gestures, such as banging a table, or other signs of anger, can alienate people. Also, if you do bang a table, take care not to drown your words.

Single gestures may combine to form complex patterns. For instance, in a private meeting, you may recognize that a colleague is appraising you while listening to you, by the position of their fingers on their cheek or chin. However, to know whether the appraisal is positive or negative, you need to observe other signs, such as whether their legs are crossed defensively, or if their head and chin are lowered aggressively.

10 Practice a range of gestures in front of a mirror to find those that look natural for you.

GIVING BODY SIGNALS

Supportive gestures, such as making eye contact and nodding while somebody is talking, create empathy – unless the person you are speaking with can tell that you are concealing your true feelings. Everyone can control their body language to an extent, but not totally. Choose your words with care, being as honest as possible; otherwise, your body language may contradict you.

Gesturing with your hand adds emphasis

Hand on chin indicates appraisal

Raised eyebrows indicate interest

▲ LISTENING WITH APPROVAL

Approving listening is shown here by the slight tilt of the head together with friendly eye contact.

▲ PAYING ATTENTION

Eyes making contact and the body leaning forward show alertness and readiness to assist the speaker.

▲ EMPHASIZING A POINT

Using a hand to gesture emphatically is one way of reinforcing a verbal point.

Indirect gaze adds to sense of uncertainty

Arm wrapped around body is a form of self-comfort

Knitted brow and closed eyes show doubt

▲ SHOWING UNCERTAINTY

Pen-biting is a throwback to the need to be nursed. This shows fear and a lack of confidence.

▲ NEEDING REASSURANCE

One hand around the neck and the other around the waist show a need for reassurance.

▲ EXPERIENCING CONFLICT

The closed eyes and nose-pinching reveal inner confusion and conflict about what is being heard.

LEARNING TO LISTEN

The two-way nature of communication – so that both sides understand each other – is widely ignored. Listening techniques are vital, since how you listen conveys meaning to the other person and helps to make the exchange successful.

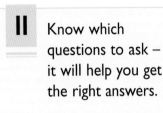

11 Know which questions to ask – it will help you get the right answers.

SHOWING ATTENTIVENESS

12 Use silence confidently as a tool to encourage hesitant speakers.

When you are in search of information, consensus, or a working relationship, the more obviously you listen attentively, the better. You may need to speak to get a response, but show you do not wish to dominate the conversation. Ask open questions, which lead to discussion, and keep your responses brief. Repeat key words silently as you hear them to help you to remember what is said.

USING LISTENING SKILLS

TYPE OF LISTENING	PUTTING METHODS INTO PRACTICE
EMPATHIZING Drawing out the speaker and getting information in a supportive, helpful way.	Empathize by imagining yourself in the other person's position, trying to understand what they are thinking, and letting them feel comfortable – possibly by relating to their emotional experiences. Pay close attention to what the person is saying, talk very little, and use encouraging nods and words.
ANALYZING Seeking concrete information and trying to disentangle fact from emotion.	Use analytical questions to discover the reasons behind the speaker's statements, especially if you need to understand a sequence of facts or thoughts. Ask questions carefully, so you can pick up clues from the answers and use the person's responses to help you form your next set of questions.
SYNTHESIZING Proactively guiding the exchange toward an objective.	If you need to achieve a desired result, make statements to which others can respond with ideas. Listen and give your answers to others' remarks in a way that suggests which ideas can be enacted and how they might be implemented. Alternatively, include a different solution in your next question.

POINTS TO REMEMBER

● Confidence is inspired in a speaker if you listen intently.

● What you are told should be regarded as trustworthy until proved otherwise.

● Misunderstandings are caused by wishful listening – hearing only what you want to hear.

● Constant interruptions can be very off-putting for people who find it difficult to get across their point of view.

INTERPRETING DIALOGUE

Take statements at face value without reading hidden meanings into what is being said. Test your understanding by rephrasing statements and repeating them to the speaker. It should then be clear that you have understood each other – or they may correct you and clarify their statement. However, watch for physical signs, such as evasive eye contact, and verbal signs, such as hesitation or contradiction, that provide clues to the truthfulness of the message. Be careful not to hear only what you want to hear and nothing else.

USING NEURO-LINGUISTIC PROGRAMMING (NLP)

One basic theory behind neuro-linguistic programming (NLP) is that the way in which people speak shows how they think. Thinking preferences can be categorized by choice of phrase. Categories include the visual, which is indicated by phrases such as "I see where you're coming from," and the auditory, indicated by phrases such as "This sounds like a problem to me." By listening attentively, you can harmonize a conversation by "mirroring." That is, you can reply to visual language with visual, auditory with auditory, and so on. This all helps you to establish rapport with the other person. At the same time as listening intently and mirroring thinking preferences, you can also physically mirror the person. Adopting a similar posture and using the same gestures can create empathy.

Direct eye contact

Lightly clasped hands

Closed-mouth smile

Attentive posture

▲ LISTENING AND MIRRORING

NLP techniques can be used to take the tension out of a situation. For example, if you strongly disagree with someone seated opposite you, listen to them speaking, then speak yourself, using similar imagery and phraseology. If they are sitting defensively, subtly mirror their posture, then slowly change it into a more open one, as above, to encourage them to be less defensive.

RECOGNIZING PREJUDICE

When what you see or hear only fulfills your own expectations, you probably have an inflexible mind-set. Most people have this problem and are unconsciously influenced by stereotypical views. We are also influenced by others, and often adopt their opinions without thinking. Prejudices block good communication: If you can recognize your prejudiced ideas, you will be a better listener.

13 Think about the words you hear, not the person saying them.

OVERCOMING PREJUDICE

Personal prejudices may be difficult to eradicate because they are inbuilt and exist regardless of the behavior or character of other people. A frequent mistake is to assume that you know what someone is going to say, and not to listen to the actual message. However, people do not always behave according to stereotype or expectation. Listen very carefully to what people are saying to you, and do not let your prejudices get in the way.

AVOIDING ▼ FAVORITISM

In this example, a manager is asking three subordinates for their views on a new strategy. He has personal prejudices about each of them. So, if the meeting is to be successful, he must overcome these prejudices and listen to what they are saying without making assumptions.

Manager has several preconceived opinions

Open-necked shirt not considered appropriate by manager

Confident woman causes manager to act defensively

Clothing mirrors what manager is wearing and gains approval

CHECKING YOU UNDERSTAND THE MESSAGE

Use phrases such as these when you need to clarify what has been said, or if you think that your own message might have been misunderstood. Take responsibility for finding out the things you need to know, and listen to the answers you are given.

I'm afraid I didn't quite catch what you said. Would you mind repeating it, please?

I'm aware that this isn't your field, but I would be very interested to hear your opinion.

I can't have explained myself clearly. What I meant to establish was...

RESPONDING TO SOMEONE

The first step in responding to what you hear is to listen properly. If you are preparing an answer or are thinking about what to say next while you should be listening, you are not giving your full attention to what is being said. In your response, outline what you have understood so far. If you need repetition, further explanation, or extra information, do not hesitate to ask for it.

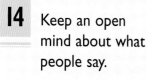

14 Keep an open mind about what people say.

 Listen → **Respond** → **Act**

ACTING ON WHAT YOU HEAR

In some cases, communication is an end in itself – an update on progress, for example. In others, action is vital – clearing a bottleneck, say. What you must never do is promise an action and fail to deliver. A classic example is the employee attitude survey, which always raises expectations of action to remedy management errors. Failure to act on the survey findings means you have not listened and instead delivers a harmful message. Keep your promises – and take action as soon as possible.

▲ **LISTENING FIRST**
The three steps to successful communication are: listen carefully to what is said; respond (if necessary, ask for clarification); finally, take action.

15 Put promises in writing as soon as you can to avoid misunderstandings.

ASKING QUESTIONS

How you ask questions is very important in establishing a basis for good communication. Why, what, how, and when are very powerful words. Use them often to seek, either from yourself or from others, the answers needed to manage effectively.

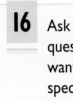

16 Ask a specific question if you want to hear a specific answer.

17 Use open questions to gain insight into the other person's character, and to invite a response.

KNOWING WHAT TO ASK

The right questions open the door to knowledge and understanding. The art of questioning lies in knowing which questions to ask when. Address your first question to yourself: If you could press a magic button and get every piece of information you want, what would you want to know? The answer will help you compose the right questions. If you are planning a meeting, prepare a list of any answers you need to obtain. As the meeting progresses, check off the answers you receive. If new questions occur to you while others are talking, note them down and raise them later.

CHOOSING QUESTIONS

When preparing questions in advance, always look at the type of question that best meets your aims. You may want to initiate a discussion, obtain specific information, attain a particular end, or send a command cloaked as a query. However, be aware that prepared questions will rarely be enough – answers to them may be incomplete or may prompt a whole new line of questioning. Keep asking questions until you are satisfied that you have received the answers you require. When asking prepared questions, watch out for clues in the answers that you can follow up later with a new set of questions.

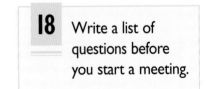

18 Write a list of questions before you start a meeting.

19 Do not be afraid to pause while thinking of your next question.

CHOOSING QUESTIONS FOR DIFFERENT RESPONSES

TYPES OF QUESTION	EXAMPLES
OPEN Question does not invite any particular answer, but opens up discussion.	Q What do you think about the company setting up a canteen for all staff members? A I think it is a good idea for a number of reasons.
CLOSED Question is specific and must be answered with a yes or a no, or with details as appropriate.	Q Do you ever read the company magazine or newsletter? A No.
FACT-FINDING Question is aimed at getting information on a particular subject.	Q What percentage of staff has replied to the employee attitude survey? A Out of 2,000 questionnaires we got 1,400 replies – that's 70 percent.
FOLLOW-UP Question is intended to get more information or to elicit an opinion.	Q Is this a good response compared with last time? A Two-thirds is average, so this indicates reasonably good morale.
FEEDBACK Question is aimed at getting a particular type of information.	Q Do you think that communications within the company have improved? A Yes. I find it is useful being able to talk to my manager in our new weekly meetings.

STRIKING THE RIGHT TONE

Your tone of voice is a part of communication in itself – for example, you may convey anger by speaking harshly or sympathy by speaking softly. The wrong tone may generate a counter-productive response, so work on improving your ability to manage your tone of voice. Using a tape recorder, play back your voice. Is there any unintentional sharpness? Is it too conciliatory? Practice until you are happy with how you sound. You can often steer people toward agreement by using an optimistic and confident tone of voice.

20 Speak in as natural a tone as possible to create a warm environment.

READING EFFICIENTLY

The more you read and understand, the better informed you are. You can improve the speed and efficiency of your reading by using several easy techniques. Concentration is the key to all methods of reading faster and understanding more.

21 Use associations – especially striking ones – to enhance your memory.

22 Make sure reading conditions – such as the lighting – are acceptable.

READING EFFECTIVELY

The two most common methods used to read and fully understand a passage are to read it slowly, or to read it and then go back over it. Both methods are inefficient. Reading slowly has no effect on comprehension. The second method – known as regression – halves speed, but improves comprehension by only 3–7 percent. Eliminate regression, and your reading speed will rise from the average of 250–300 words per minute (wpm) to 450–500 wpm with no loss of comprehension.

LEARNING TO SKIM

Skimming can help you manage your time and reduce hours spent reading. In normal reading, the eyes make small, swift movements (known as saccades) between groups of words, "fixing" briefly on each group. To read faster, you enlarge the groups and accelerate the move from one group to another. Before reading a book or proposal, if it has a contents, introduction, conclusion, and index, glance at these to decide what you need to read and what you do not.

A comfortable posture aids concentration

Book is flat on desk

IMPROVING YOUR SPEED ▶
When you are practicing, read in bursts of about 20 minutes. Eliminate distractions when reading, and make sure that you are comfortable. Sit upright, in good lighting, with your book flat.

IMPROVING MEMORY

On average, it takes about seven hours to read a reasonably long book of about 100,000 words. You could halve this time with skimming. The object of learning how to read more quickly is to raise your maximum speed of reading by up to 80 percent, without lowering your standard of comprehension. But reading and understanding at a faster rate do not help if you promptly forget what you have read, so you may need to improve your memory skills.

Memory is strongest after a few minutes, and 80 percent is lost within 24 hours. An effective way to learn from books is to study for an hour, wait for a tenth of the time spent studying (6 minutes), review what you have studied, and then wait for 10 times the study period (in this instance, 10 hours) before you review again.

POINTS TO REMEMBER

- Powers of comprehension are usually overestimated.
- Lots of information can be picked up at a glance from illustrations and other visual material.
- Speed-reading can be learned in a course or from books.
- Pages should be scanned down the center, or diagonally, to achieve the most sense quickly.
- Time can be saved by looking at a book's contents, introductory pages, conclusion, and index, to check if it is worth reading.
- Memory can be improved by changing the way you learn and reviewing knowledge regularly.

TESTING YOUR COMPREHENSION

There are about 300 words on these pages under the headings "Reading Effectively," "Learning to Skim," and "Improving Memory." To check how much you have taken in, read these again (it should take about a minute), then answer the questions below.

QUESTIONS:

1. What is regression?
2. What is the gain in comprehension from regression?
3. What is the average reading speed?
4. What is the objective of a speed-reading course?
5. What is the fast-reading speed range?
6. What is the main result of reading everything twice?
7. How much of your memory is lost within 24 hours?
8. What length is a reasonably long book?
9. How long should a reasonably long book take to skim?
10. When is memory strongest?

ANSWERS: 1. Going back over material again. 2. About 3–7 percent. 3. 250–300 words per minute. 4. To raise maximum speed by up to 80 percent without loss of comprehension. 5. 450–500 words per minute. 6. Reading everything twice merely halves your potential reading speed. 7. 80 percent. 8. About 100,000 words. 9. About three-and-a-half hours. 10. After a few minutes.

TAKING NOTES

There is no need to rely on memory if you have mastered efficient methods of recording speech or condensing written communication. There are several different ways to make written records; experiment, and use whichever method suits you.

23 Read your notes while what you have recorded is fresh in your mind.

24 Mark passages in books, and make notes afterward.

TAKING LINEAR NOTES

If you are taking notes while people are speaking, do not try to write their words in longhand and in sequence, or you will fail to keep up. Instead, listen to what is being said and note down the key points in your own words. Try writing a succinct explanation of each point, and use headings and numbers to structure your notes.

USING SPEED WRITING

There are classes for learning shorthand and speed writing, but you can also teach yourself, and double your writing speed. In general, drop all vowels unless they begin a word, use numerals for numbers, and use standard abbreviations such as an ampersand (&) for "and." Use special abbreviations for common words or word parts, such as tt (that), th (the), t (to and it), r (are), s (is), v (very), f (of), g (-ing), and d (-ed).

TAKING NOTES USING ▶
SPEED WRITING
Space your notes in short paragraphs. Afterward, read through quickly to check that everything makes sense to you.

Word is obvious from its context: this is "notes" not "nuts"

In th sm wy tht spdwrtg cn incrs th spd at whch y wrt nts wth a pn or pncl, y cn gtly incrs th spd at whch y mk nts usg a wrd prcssr or typwrtr, if tht s hw y prfr t wrk.

Whn y spdwrt, th shp f th wrds s unffctd by th dltd vwls, & y hv an entrly smpl & prctcl systm.

Y my fnd tht evn whn y r sklld at spdwrtg, t s snsbl t spll unusual or dffclt wrds in fll. Als, f yr spdwrttn wrd cld b mstkn for 1 or 2 othr wrds, thn t s a gd pln t wrt th wrd in fll.

Short words, like "at," can be written in full

Words are still easy to recognize when they are spelled without vowels

Words that are difficult to shorten or which may be hard to decipher are spelled out in full

USING MIND MAPS

Mind Maps®, which were devised by Tony Buzan, are a way of making visual notes. To make a Mind Map, write down a key word or phrase, or draw an image in the middle of a page. This is the subject of the Mind Map. As you make notes, create "branches" from this central point. Each branch can have sub-branches (one idea leading to another), and different branches may link to one another. Use color and images to illustrate points and to make the Mind Map easier to recall.

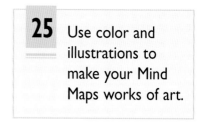

25 Use color and illustrations to make your Mind Maps works of art.

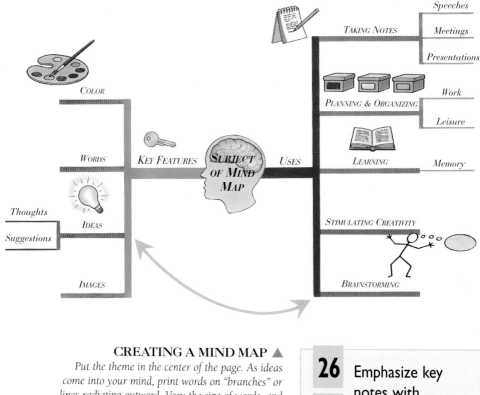

CREATING A MIND MAP ▲
Put the theme in the center of the page. As ideas come into your mind, print words on "branches" or lines radiating outward. Vary the size of words, and use lots of color and images since both help memory. Link related ideas with arrows.

26 Emphasize key notes with highlighter pens.

EXCHANGING INFORMATION

Face-to-face, phone, or written communications can range from open warfare to perfect agreement. In every case, choose the right communication method to achieve your aim.

MAKING CONTACT

A satisfactory end to an encounter can never be guaranteed, but a good start is always possible. Your words and demeanor significantly affect the reactions of others, so use welcoming words to help start all proceedings on a positive note.

 27 Stand up to greet or say good-bye to people – it is rude to stay seated.

POINTS TO REMEMBER

- Initial greetings should be as welcoming as possible.
- All attendees at a meeting need to be introduced to each other at the outset.
- Meetings are best ended courteously, even if they have involved disagreement.
- Behavioral and cultural differences (like whether it is customary to shake hands) should be respected at all times when traveling.

GREETING PEOPLE

The words used to greet people you know will be governed by the relationship. If the relationship is an equal one, you will almost certainly use first names and an informal salutation such as "Good morning," "How are you?" or "Nice to see you." With strangers, the greeting also acts as an introduction, so you announce your name ("I'm Mary Black") and follow up with an expression of polite pleasure ("It's good to meet you"). This implies friendly intent. Even if hostilities are possible, a civil verbal start is always wise.

USING BODILY CONTACT

If you are greeting a person with whom you are familiar, you may or may not shake hands, though it is more likely in a formal situation. In most situations, meet strangers with an extended hand, and offer a firm shake. Avoid offering a limp handshake, which may give an impression of weakness. Be aware of cultural rules that affect greetings between sexes. For example, it may be inappropriate for men and women to make any physical contact. Watch your posture, too: rise to your feet when receiving guests, and stand straight.

CULTURAL DIFFERENCES

In greetings, Spanish, French, Italian, and Latin American male colleagues may embrace each other. In contrast, the Japanese usually bow from a distance, perhaps shaking hands when better acquainted. They and the Chinese always accompany introductions with visiting cards.

Face each other and make eye contact

Use a two-arm good-bye to show more warmth than a handshake on its own

Stand up when saying good-bye

ENDING MEETINGS

When an agreement has been reached or a productive meeting is ending, make a point of emphasizing its success with your body language. If you are the host, remember to thank the other party or parties for their contribution and show them not just to the door of the meeting room but to the exit of the building. You may wish to say good-bye with a handshake, which will probably be warmer and more prolonged than when you greeted them. In other words, treat them as if they are your guests. The same analogy applies to the meeting's attendees – if they are on your territory, they should behave with courtesy. If the meeting has not been easy, remain courteous and civil, but without glossing over the failure.

◀ SAYING A WARM GOOD-BYE

Saying good-bye is likely to be a warmer experience than saying hello, especially if the encounter has been productive. In some countries, people are more likely to use physical contact, such as holding one of your arms when shaking hands.

PASSING ON INFORMATION

Managers spend much of their time delivering and receiving messages in person. This can be the most critical – and satisfying – arena of communication. Honesty and feedback are both essential if you are to achieve clarity and progress.

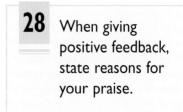

28 When giving positive feedback, state reasons for your praise.

29 Let staff know what efforts you are making to relay information.

FINDING INFORMATION

The workforce's need to obtain information and the ability of its managers to provide all types of information in the right way are crucial elements in any organization. Start by finding out which areas people most want to know about. Job security, working conditions, reward, location, and benefits are all important, and you should communicate any changes affecting these as soon and as directly as possible.

BEING UNDERSTOOD

Delivering a message that may be misunderstood is all too easy. It may happen because you are not clear about what you want to say; or because your language is vague even though your objectives are clear; or because your body language very subtly contradicts your verbal message. Another reason why it may happen is that you are communicating with someone who has decided in advance what the message is – without listening to you and regardless of what you are actually trying to say.

A useful way to avoid misinterpretation is to rehearse your message with an objective critic. Alternatively, get the recipients to repeat your message – you can then use their feedback to try to correct any misapprehensions. Use positive body language to emphasize your verbal message.

30 If in doubt about whether or not you should pass on information, do so.

GIVING FEEDBACK

Feedback is essential to communication – to check that you have understood the other person's message, and to react to what they have said and done. It can be difficult to give negative feedback, but remember that it is bad management to avoid doing this. When giving negative feedback, follow these simple rules to avoid any antagonism:

- Show an understanding of exactly what went wrong, and why;
- Draw out ways in which poor performance or behavior can improve;
- Use questioning rather than assertions to let the staff member know what you think, and why;
- Aim to express your negative opinions honestly, but in a positive manner;
- Above all, take negative feedback away from the emotional zone by being objective, not personal.

31 Waste no time on people who refuse to understand you.

▼ **HANDLING CONFLICT**
Do not allow negative body language directed toward you to put you off. Sit up straight, make nonhostile eye contact, and give your message unambiguously.

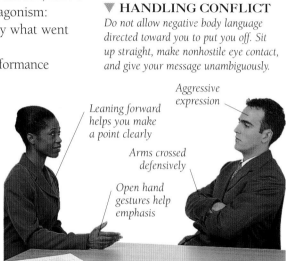

Leaning forward helps you make a point clearly

Aggressive expression

Arms crossed defensively

Open hand gestures help emphasis

REACTING HONESTLY

It is vital that you react honestly to the statements or actions of your employees. Give reasons for positive feedback, and use questions rather than assertions when giving negative feedback. Below are some examples that you can use:

" *I especially like how you backed up your argument with relevant facts, information on our competitors, and up-to-date statistics.* "

" *You are the right person for this job because…* "

" *Would you agree that this report is very unsatisfactory?* "

USING THE PHONE

Phones are very strong communication tools because they make people at a distance – and even total strangers – immediately accessible. Use the phone to create opportunities that otherwise would be much harder to exploit.

32 Keep a clock on your desk to monitor the time you spend on calls.

33 Use features such as "call waiting" to increase your effectiveness.

IMPROVING TECHNIQUE

Many people tend to take their phone skills for granted. However, phone skills can be improved by know-how and practice. Telemarketers, who use the phone for cold calls to people they do not know, are experts. Telemarketing tips include:

● Write down in advance what you want to cover and in what order;
● Speak slowly and pace yourself with the other person;
● Always be polite and friendly;
● Smile – a smiling face encourages a smiling voice and invites a positive response.

Smile – it raises your voice and makes it warm and friendly

Follow a script so that you do not lose track

Time your calls to make sure you do not run long

◀ **READING FROM A PREPARED SCRIPT**
When making an important phone call, it is easy to be sidetracked. One way of avoiding this is to write a list of all the things you need to discuss and then check them off as you go. Similarly, if you think a conversation might be difficult, write out useful phrases before phoning.

34 If you say you will return a call, make sure you do.

LEAVING MESSAGES

If you have answering machines and voice mail, deal with incoming messages waiting for you as soon as you can, and always within 24 hours.

When leaving a message for someone else, start with your name, phone number, and the time of your call. Speak slowly and clearly, or your name, number, or both may be lost. When leaving an outgoing message, keep it brief and businesslike. If you can be specific about your time of return, or who should be contacted in your absence, change your outgoing message accordingly.

35 End telephone messages by repeating your name and number.

MANAGING TELEMARKETING

Telemarketing is a specialized form of communication. If you are involved with a sales team, make sure the staff follow these golden rules:

● Work from a script;
● Do not pause or stop once you have started;
● Use "please" and "thank you" copiously;
● Put a mirror on the desk to check that you are smiling;
● Use "I" very sparingly.

GETTING THROUGH

You will not be able to communicate effectively if you fail to get through to the correct person. Do your research thoroughly to find the name of the person appropriate to your needs, and then, even if the person is a total stranger (and an important figure), adopt an intimate, confident approach when you phone them. For instance, when making the initial phone call, use the person's first name, and announce yourself by saying "This is so-and-so" (never "My name is so-and-so"). If the person in question is "in a meeting," ask when he or she will be free, and say when you will call back. Then phone later, and say your call is expected.

When you get through to the right person, never put down the phone without making your point – repeatedly, if possible. As with any verbal exchange, check that your message has been correctly understood by the other party.

36 Change your recorded phone message as and when your circumstances change.

USING INFORMATION TECHNOLOGY

New technology has greatly increased the choices for communicators. The personal computer, in both desktop and portable form, is a superb message center for managers receiving and relaying information quickly all around the world.

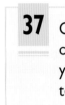 **37** Get expert advice on the best use of your information technology (IT).

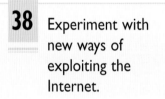 **38** Experiment with new ways of exploiting the Internet.

USING THE FAX

Despite the advent of electronic mail (e-mail), facsimile (fax) is a useful form of communication that can help you manage your time. For example, if you have to pass on information to someone who wastes your time on the phone, using e-mail or fax will bypass this problem. The fax is very valuable for documents that need delivery and response faster than is possible by mail.

USING E-MAIL

E-mail is fast, user-friendly, and versatile. It is a prime medium of communication within businesses, and accounts for more and more external messages. Keeping staff informed by e-mail also saves paper. However, e-mail can be abused, so follow these rules of "netiquette":

- Use meaningful subject titles;
- Be as brief as possible;
- Distinguish business from nonbusiness mail;
- Be selective in the recipients of your e-mails;
- Avoid attaching extra files to your e-mail if you are mailing to a lot of people at once;
- Never use obscene language or insults, and shun any racist or sexist mail.

POINTS TO REMEMBER

- Faxes can be either freestanding and paper-fed or linked to a personal computer.
- Managers without laptops or notebook computers can consider themselves underequipped.
- The World Wide Web is the future of communications for most purposes.
- The Internet is a powerful communications tool mainly because of its ability to mix all media in real time.
- Cutting out communication waste helps everybody.

USING THE INTERNET

The Internet is transforming communication, as are internal networks, groupware, intranets (in-company internets), and the Extranet (which connects suppliers with customers). Use basic Web sites on the Internet to carry up-to-date information about your own organization for both customers and employees. Similarly, look at the Web sites of other companies for information on your competitors. The Internet is a valuable tool for all kinds of research, and for interactive dialogues. You can also use the Internet for buying and selling products.

▲ MAKING THE MOST OF TECHNOLOGY

Computers and information technology give staff immediate access to information of all kinds – from financial transactions to scientific data – throughout the world.

| Send only essential messages | → | Keep messages short | → | Avoid delays in replying |

CONTROLLING ▲ INFORMATION FLOW

To keep communication by electronic means fast and efficient, do not send irrelevant messages. Write succinctly and to the point, and reply to incoming messages as soon as possible.

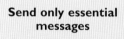

39 Use e-mail's "reply" feature to respond swiftly.

SPEEDING COMMUNICATION

The most effective way to improve the speed and quality of communication and information flow is to control the quantity. Whenever you send a message, ask yourself whether you really need to – if not, do not send it. Keep messages brief, because the shorter they are, the faster they can be processed. Check regular reports to see if anything can be shortened or eliminated – will anyone really notice if some regular communications are no longer made? Finally, do not procrastinate over responses; it is better, faster, and more efficient to answer immediately and keep your desk clear.

WRITING LETTERS

Documents that are written well, easy to understand, and keep to the point are composed by people who have clarified their thoughts before writing. Make your letters effective by thinking before you write, and always writing what you think.

40 Visualize the reader when you are writing a letter or report.

41 Delegate writing routine replies to an assistant.

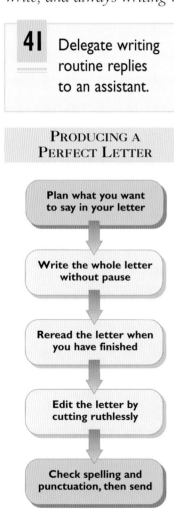

PRODUCING A PERFECT LETTER

Plan what you want to say in your letter

Write the whole letter without pause

Reread the letter when you have finished

Edit the letter by cutting ruthlessly

Check spelling and punctuation, then send

WRITING FOR RESULTS

All business letters have a purpose. The first rule of letter writing is to make that objective perfectly clear to your recipient. The second rule is to include all the information that the reader needs in order to understand your aim. Resist the temptation to write too much – try to fit your letter on one side of paper if you can. Ask a friendly critic to read any letters dealing with problematic situations.

COMPOSING CLEAR TEXT

The key to writing any business letter clearly and concisely is to keep your words simple and to the point. Use short words and sentences in preference to long, and active verbs rather than passive. Avoid double negatives, jargon, and archaic terminology (such as "notwithstanding" and "albeit"). Use natural, unforced diction: in other words, write as you talk, not as you think you should write. Do not revise until you have finished, and then cut fearlessly – editing always improves the impact of a letter.

42 Avoid using complicated, unusual words or abstract terms – they may obscure your meaning.

STRUCTURING LETTERS

When structuring letters, apply the principles of direct mail. These are as follows:

- Attract the *attention* of the reader by stating why you are writing. Use humor if appropriate;
- Engage the reader's *interest* by arousing his or her curiosity about what you are saying;
- Provoke *desire* in the reader by making your proposal or product sound attractive;
- *Convince* the reader that your letter rings true by supplying references or guarantees;
- Stimulate *action* on the part of the reader by explaining what you expect him or her to do.

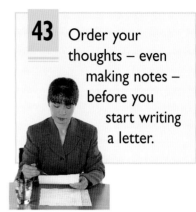

43 Order your thoughts – even making notes – before you start writing a letter.

◀ **GETTING THE WRONG RESULT**

This letter lacks clarity. It has not been thought through, it is badly spelled and punctuated, and unnecessarily wordy.

Dear Sir/Madam,

I have heard on the grapevine that you are seeking a company which is capable of installing new computers for all your departments. I believe that my company can be safely appointed as one in which you might have complete confidence. Notwithstanding our somewhat limited experience in your industry, I have been advized by some one who used to work for you that we would be just right for the job. I am most enthousiastic, about the possibilities to mete you except please be advized that I will unfortunateley be unable to visit your office on Mondays, Tuesdays or on Friday afternoons. This is because at

Writer has not bothered to find out a contact

Meaning is unclear

Grammar and spelling are poor

Writer gives irrelevant details

Letter is on more than one page

GETTING THE ▶ RIGHT RESULT

This letter is clear, optimistic, and to the point. The writer has made an effort to be positive about the potential business relationship with the company.

Has written letter on just one page

Knows to whom to send the letter

Shows positive outlook

Suggests next step

Explains reason for letter

Today's date

Ms. Jeanette Martin
Planning Company
Street Name
Big Town

Dear Ms. Martin:

Further to our phone conversation last week, I am pleased to enclose a recent brochure.

You confirmed that your company is interested in installing new computer software, and I am sure we will be able to supply your needs.

I look forward to hearing from you and to meeting you in the near future.

Yours sincerely,

Signature

ACQUIRING MORE SKILLS

The best communicators succeed in getting written
and verbal messages across to both individuals
and larger audiences, with understanding on all sides.

BRIEFING EFFECTIVELY

*Conveying to people the purpose, means,
and extent of a task entrusted to
them is a basic exercise in communication.
Learn how to brief effectively – whether
a client, colleague, or supplier – and you
will help a project on the way to success.*

44 Lean toward
giving too much
autonomy rather
than too little.

Good eye
contact helps
retain
attention
as brief
is given

▲ **GIVING PEOPLE INFORMATION**
*If you are providing a colleague or client with a written
brief, talk through this to expand or clarify any points
and to check that the brief is completely understood.*

SELECTING A BRIEF

There are a number of different types
of brief. Briefs may be about action to
be taken in the future, or they may be
debriefing reports that explain what
has happened and why. If a client is
involved, the brief may be partly a
report and partly an action plan, in
which you give details of what you
propose, including what role the
client is to play. Get feedback from
the person you are briefing to check
you have given enough information.

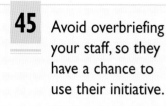

45 Avoid overbriefing your staff, so they have a chance to use their initiative.

▼ STRUCTURING A BRIEF
A written brief should be a clear document, setting out exactly what has to be done, when, and how. If relevant, state the budget allowance, plus the dates of any approval stages.

COMPILING A BRIEF
When briefing someone verbally, agree which of you will follow up with written confirmation of the brief. When compiling a briefing document:
- Put the aim at the top;
- Give the resources available;
- Provide a time horizon;
- Describe the method;
- If the brief is to produce a document, identify to whom this should be sent.

Even if you are delegating straightforward tasks, if you are specific, errors are less likely to be made.

BRIEFING DOCUMENT

Objective is clearly stated —— • *Produce a questionnaire to find out what staff think of the canteen.*

• *Use company typist and get in quotations for photocopying.* —— *Available resources and advice on budget are noted*

Deadline is given —— • *Complete by noon on Friday.*

• *Interview one person from each floor before compiling the questionnaire.* —— *Action necessary to achieve objective is outlined*

People who should receive questionnaire are noted —— • *Give questionnaire to me for approval, then circulate to heads of departments.*

DELEGATING POWER
Most briefs involve delegation of power. If you are responsible for seeing that a task is completed and choose to nominate someone else to execute it, you are handing over power to that person and must outline their areas of responsibility in a brief. You should state how much you expect to be kept informed, and whether you will issue further instructions. If the project has a long time span, remember to include the timing of reviews.

46 If you feel a project as briefed is not working out, do a rebrief fast.

COMMUNICATING ONE TO ONE

A meeting with a staff member can be formal (part of the way the unit is run) or informal (arranged to deal with a particular issue raised by either side). Use one-to-ones to check performance and find out if coaching or counseling is needed.

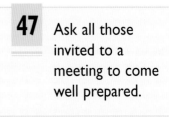

47 Ask all those invited to a meeting to come well prepared.

THINGS TO DO

1. Try to meet staff for formal one-to-one meetings at least monthly.

2. Stick to an agenda, and make sure you agree on any decisions.

3. Remember to listen to what is being said, and do not dominate the meeting.

MEETING FORMALLY

There are no fixed guidelines for informal get-togethers, but for formal one-to-one meetings the rules are the same as for any other meeting. Get to the point quickly, stick to the agenda, sum up at the end, and make sure that the other side agrees with the summary. In any one-to-one meeting the relationship between a manager and subordinate has a tendency to move into one of dominance and submission. To make meetings productive, listen to the other person, aim for rational discussion, and be courteous. Remember, however, that a certain degree of confrontation may be perfectly healthy – and also unavoidable.

BEING PREPARED

For regular meetings, preparation can make all the difference between a satisfactory or unsatisfactory outcome. Some companies stage one-to-ones between superiors and subordinates every two weeks to discuss any problems, define objectives, and deliver written performance reviews. For these one-to-ones, the managers distribute the reviews a few days beforehand. This preparation time gives the staff a chance to consider their response.

48 Remember that a "good meeting" is one that has produced results.

COACHING STAFF

Good managers must be good coaches who know how to encourage staff to raise their performance at work, improve their knowledge, and realize their full potential. Coaching is inherent in the whole management process and should not be confined simply to performance reviews and annual appraisals. As a manager, take the initiative by setting staff goals, by regularly encouraging staff to achieve higher standards, and by discussing any strengths or weaknesses. As the people being coached gain in confidence and performance, they will take on more responsibility for setting personal targets for improving at work.

49 Listen to your staff. Coaching or counseling may provide solutions to discontent.

COUNSELING STAFF

Problems that arise either from work or from personal life can be helped by counseling. But unless you are a trained counselor or have considerable experience, leave this to a professional, who will help people to confront and resolve their problems. If an employee has become unhappy over a situation, offer to arrange a counseling interview, and be sympathetic. The counselor will try to help the individual get to the root of any problem. Give practical support when you can. If time off work will help, for example, make sure that it is available.

▼ **EXPLORING SOLUTIONS**
Before you suggest professional counseling to a staff member, check that they agree they have a problem that needs help. Meet on neutral territory, where you will not be interrupted by people or phone calls.

50 Be aware of your staff's problems, because they affect performance.

CHAIRING MEETINGS SUCCESSFULLY

Most managers feel they spend too much time in meetings. However, a well-run meeting can be a productive way to communicate. When you are chairing a meeting, stay in control of the proceedings, and never let arguments get out of hand.

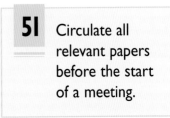

51 Circulate all relevant papers before the start of a meeting.

PREPARING FOR A MEETING

When preparing for a meeting, ask yourself four key questions: What is the meeting for? Why is it being called? How will I know if it has been successful? Who should attend? These questions will determine whether the meeting is necessary. All meetings should have a purpose that will be achieved by their end. If final decisions are not made, there should at least be a plan of action. The most effective meetings are usually small, with only vital people attending.

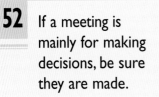

52 If a meeting is mainly for making decisions, be sure they are made.

OPENING A MEETING

After making any necessary introductions, remind all those present of the meeting's purpose, what outcome it is expected to deliver, and when it will end. If there are ground rules, state them right away. Check that everybody has any relevant papers and that the agenda is approved. If there has been a previous meeting, minutes may need approval and discussion, but do not discuss anything that already features on the agenda. Instead, go straight into the first item, preferably calling upon another participant to initiate the discussion.

53 If you are acting as chairperson, do not manipulate the meeting to your own advantage.

54 Use humor when appropriate to help produce a consensus.

CONDUCTING A MEETING

Strike a balance between keeping the discussion process moving briskly forward and ensuring that everyone who wants to speak has a chance to state their opinion. The custom of debating an issue until a decision is made can be time-consuming and lead to tension. To prevent this, act as a timekeeper. (Make sure you have a watch or clock on hand.) Set time limits to discussions in order to end the meeting at the appointed time.

CLOSING A MEETING

Allow yourself enough time for winding up a meeting. Summarize the discussion and check that others agree with your account; make decisions about unfinished business (which may include nominating someone to deal with it); and, finally, run through the implementation of any decisions taken, that is, the actions that will be the result of the meeting. Assign each action to a person, and attach a time target for completion.

55 Make sure you stick to the time limits for each item on an agenda.

COMMUNICATING BY SCREEN

Video conferences are not a substitute for face-to-face meetings, but they may usefully complement them. They can be much more effective than phone conferences because participants like (and sometimes need) to see what is going on. Use video conferencing especially if you have far-flung offices that make regular meetings impractical.

◀ USING VIDEO CONFERENCING
Video conferencing, where everyone involved can see each other's body language and expressions while they talk, is a useful way of holding a meeting, and saves on travel time and costs.

REACHING AN AUDIENCE

I*t pays to take care over preparing and delivering speeches, whether for presentations, seminars, conferences, or training. Audiences find it easier to absorb information by eye than by ear, so use audiovisual (AV) techniques when possible.*

56 Finish your speech before the allotted time rather than long after it.

PREPARING SPEECHES

Give yourself enough time to compose and rehearse your speech, including a final review. If you write out the full text for a 30-minute speech, you will need about 4,800 words, and the writing will take many hours. Notes are obviously quicker. Plan the 30 minutes around linked themes. Summarize each theme, then add material for each in note form. Allocate about 3 minutes per theme if you are using AV aids (making 10 themes in 30 minutes), otherwise 1–2 minutes for each.

57 Keep physical (or at least mental) backups in case your AV aids fail.

MAKING YOUR POINT

Repetition, often a fault on the page, is essential in oratory. Any speech is a performance. If you plan to use notes, make them brief. By glancing at a single word, you should be able to recall several complex ideas. Refer to your notes, but do not read straight from them. The brain's recall of heard information is poor, so make your speech as accessible as possible. Keep your language clear, your sentences short, and preserve a smooth flow, with a logical transition between points. The last point you make should relate to the first.

58 Ask questions of the audience if it is slow to ask questions of you.

▼ GETTING THROUGH
The three crucial steps in getting your message across are to tell the audience what you are going to say, say it, and then repeat what you have said.

| Introduce the message | Convey the message | Repeat the message |

ENCOURAGING REACTION

If you can, speak without any notes and move confidently around the stage. This removes the psychological barrier of the podium and makes you and your speech more accessible. As you speak, focus on the center of the audience, about two-thirds of the way back. People listening will usually be inclined to feel positive toward you rather than hostile, so allow their support to give you confidence. Make eye contact, and encourage the audience to participate – asking people questions, either en masse or individually, works well. Making them laugh also breaks the ice.

59 Speak for 20–45 minutes maximum – this is the length of the average person's attention span.

USING VISUAL AIDS

The most commonly used visual media are probably still the 35-mm slide projector and the overhead projector. For smaller audiences, the flip chart and writing board are effective. The most powerful AV media use color and images, including moving ones. Technology has made this easy, fast, and cheap, linking PCs to projectors. Whatever you use, make sure that the technical operation is foolproof and that the visual material is the best possible. If appropriate, support your speech by giving the audience copies of notes and visual materials.

▼ **PRESENTING SUCCESSFULLY**
Make your body language positive. Use gestures to reinforce your points – but sparingly. If you are fluent and confident without notes, do not use them.

Speak clearly, and not too rapidly

Keep expression positive

Use open-palm gestures for emphasis

Stand straight and face audience

Use a pointer to illustrate what you are saying

Check that material on overhead projector is ready in order

53

TRAINING FOR RESULTS

Leading a training session for staff is a vital form of communication. Speak to trainees as you would to any audience: be confident, make eye contact, and invite questions. Training courses are often most effective when they are intensive and are held over a few days away from the office. By talking to staff in informal discussion groups or in conversation outside training sessions, you will also be able to get valuable feedback on all aspects of the organization. Feedback on the training itself is vital to check that the process is worthwhile.

60 If possible, invite a famous speaker to a seminar or conference.

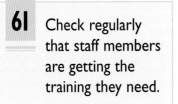

61 Check regularly that staff members are getting the training they need.

HOLDING A SEMINAR

Internal seminars and workshops provide training in areas that are important to an organization. They are working events, practical, informal, and focused on specific aims. If you are running an internal event, invite only relevant personnel; it is often valuable for senior management to attend. Use external seminars to introduce changes to customers and suppliers, or to provide a selling opportunity. Invite top management to contribute to these seminars with an introductory or concluding speech, or a nonselling lecture.

SPEAKING AT A SEMINAR

If you are speaking at either an internal or external seminar, ask the organizer what subjects other speakers will be covering to make sure you do not repeat each other. Check how long you will be expected to talk, and whether there will be a question-and-answer session afterward. If you are speaking without a microphone, make sure the audience can hear you at the back of the room (ask them, if necessary). Do not talk too quickly, and keep an eye on a watch or clock to ensure that you speak only for the allotted time.

62 Ask other managers if they would like to speak at seminars.

PLANNING A CONFERENCE

Conferences are more formal and larger than seminars. In the same way that meetings must have a purpose, all conferences should have objectives. These will be the basis of any agenda, and will provide a springboard for discussions. Internal sales conferences, in particular, are usually motivational events. Like all conferences, they require first-class settings, professional presenters, excellent sets and audiovisuals, and careful planning. Well in advance, decide who will address the conference. If you can arrange for a guest speaker to liven up the proceedings, it will help maintain the audience's interest and enthusiasm. Make sure that all speakers know when they are expected to make their speech and for how long they are scheduled to talk.

POINTS TO REMEMBER

● The more planning and thought that go into an event, the more it is likely to achieve.

● Any message will usually be reinforced if accompanied by good audiovisual technology.

● Staff at seminars or conferences should be treated with as much respect and care as suppliers.

● Show-business or professional speakers can be hired (at a price) to talk at company events.

● Conferences and seminars always need to be followed up, or they may be of little benefit.

63 Get some recommendations if selecting a new conference site.

CHOOSING A LOCATION

The location is part of the message, and speaks volumes to those who are attending. When you are deciding where to hold a conference or seminar, think carefully about what is required, and always choose a site that is suitable for the scale and type of event. For a large conference, you need a space that easily accommodates everyone. However, for a workshop, you may only need one medium-sized room plus a few smaller ones, where trainees can work together in groups or teams. Before booking a site, check that everything you require will be available, such as electronic and other equipment (like microphones and projectors), comfortable seating for all attendees, and catering.

DO'S AND DON'TS

✔ Do check attendees know how to get to the site and have transportation.

✔ Do plan a schedule of events, including refreshment breaks.

✔ Do be ready to adapt the agenda in case proceedings run long.

✘ Don't expect people to make impromptu, unprepared speeches at a conference.

✘ Don't invite people to seminars if their presence is not vital.

✘ Don't forget to obtain feedback to check on an event's success.

COMMUNICATING TO SELL

Selling is basic to business, and not only in persuading external customers to buy. In all business situations, you can use established sales techniques to gain the agreement of others, enlist support, obtain resources, and overcome any opposition.

64 If you want to "soft sell," make your point in the form of a question.

SOFT SELLING

All good selling is "soft": you seek to establish a need and promise to fulfill that need. You can use this approach at work, and adapt your "sales pitch" to suit the situation. Techniques include:

- Exploring a situation by using questions and listening, rather than making statements;
- Letting others reply, even at the price of pauses;
- Showing sympathetic understanding if you encounter resistance – but persevering until the other person accepts your view.

Non-threatening smile

Open-palm gesture

◀ **USING SOFT-SELLING TECHNIQUES**
Smiling and using upturned hands with open palms are soft-selling techniques. Both are friendly, persuasive, and non-threatening. The hand gesture also adds emphasis.

HARD SELLING

The old-fashioned hard-sell method works by putting people on the spot and forcing them to make a decision. If you are trying to implement an idea at work, be positive and use hard selling when you get close to a deal. Hard-sell tactics include:

- Making a "final, final" offer;
- Stressing loss of opportunity;
- Emphasizing a competititve situation;
- Making a hard, clear proposition;
- Pressing for immediate agreement.

65 Listen to objections from potential customers – they may give clues to help you make the sale.

SELLING BY WRITTEN WORD

Using written documents to sell – whether you are trying to sell a product by mail or are "selling" a proposal to colleagues – follows some apparently paradoxical rules. For instance, in direct marketing to outsiders, long letters markedly outsell short ones. However, when sending internal memos, short documents are more effective. Long or short, explain at the beginning of the document why you are writing. Gain the readers' interest, keep to the point, make your case convincing, and end with a concise, clear and positive summary.

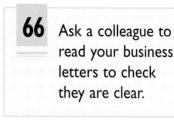

66 Ask a colleague to read your business letters to check they are clear.

67 Approach any sale as a joint exercise between you and the buyer.

UTILIZING COMPUTERS

The personal computer has evolved as a powerful sales aid. For example, you can store the names and addresses of potential customers in a database, and even call up files relating to a client while you are talking to them on the phone. Having facts on screen can make you more efficient and help you close a deal. Computers are particularly useful for selling financial services; when details of a buyer's finances are input, many programs will generate personalized proposals.

SELLING IDEAS AND CONCEPTS

Basic sales techniques are applicable to many essential management tasks. Mastering "the patter" can be crucial to success inside your organization, as well as outside. Try some of the soft- and hard-sell phrases below next time you want to sell an idea.

I developed this from something you said to me the other day.

This is what you've been looking for. If we don't do it, one of our competitors will for sure.

We haven't got long to consider this latest proposal – it's basically now or never.

Nobody else could do this as well as we could.

NEGOTIATING TO WIN

All negotiation requires first-class communication skills. You need to be able to put forward proposals clearly and to understand exactly what the other side is offering. Such skills are vital in all kinds of management, so try to improve them.

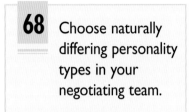

68 Choose naturally differing personality types in your negotiating team.

STAGES OF NEGOTIATION

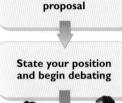

Plan your strategy and tactics

Put forward your proposal

State your position and begin debating

Bargain with the other side

Sum up and ratify agreement

PREPARING FOR TALKS

The better prepared a negotiation, the greater its chances of success. Start by deciding on your objectives. Next, decide who will conduct the negotiation. Will it be one person or a team? If it is a team, who will form the best partnerships? Ensure the team thoroughly researches the issues and their positions. The research will help to determine the agenda agreed with the other side. Have the team do at least one role-play beforehand. Finally, develop your minimum position – that is, the least you will settle for.

MASTERING TECHNIQUES

Negotiating experts usually base their approach around needs – generally the needs of the other side. When you enter negotiations "working for the other side's needs," you are taking maximum control with minimum risk. Good timing is crucial. During the debating and bargaining stages, you need to judge what the other side is thinking and pick your moment to raise or alter your offer, reject a proposal, or introduce a new element. Always try to shift the opposition from an adversarial stance towards an alliance. Asking leading questions, such as "Are you ready to sign?" is one way to soften your stance while gaining attention, getting and giving information, and stimulating thought.

NEGOTIATING TO BUY

Two things are essential when you are negotiating to buy. Firstly, decide exactly what you need (not what you want). Remember that the seller's job is to persuade you that your needs and their offer are one and the same. Secondly, decide how much you are prepared to pay. Set yourself an upper limit, and do not exceed it. In such a negotiation, the first person to name a price is at a disadvantage, so try to persuade the other side to be the first to make a financial offer.

69 Think about your ideal outcome – and how you can achieve it.

70 Share helpful information with suppliers – long term, it may help you win a better deal.

WORKING WITH SUPPLIERS

The traditional way to negotiate with suppliers is to get a number of quotes in from more than one supplier (to create healthy competition), listen to the quotes, bargain hard, ask for substantial cuts, raise your offer a little, and settle for the lowest possible price. If the supplier fails on quality or delivery, you negotiate again.

A newer, better approach is to choose the best suppliers, and negotiate in a way that achieves lower costs and shared profits for both sides. With this approach, instead of making price the only issue, you first negotiate reliability and other nonprice issues before discussing actual costs.

BARGAINING WITH STAFF

One-to-one meetings can be useful for individual negotiations with staff on issues like quality of work and productivity. When you conclude an agreement, remember that it helps if the other side thinks that they have won something, even if they have not. If you ever have to deal with hostile professional negotiators (perhaps when a union is involved), and if their demands are above your maximum position, keep calm and concentrate on securing a result within your limits.

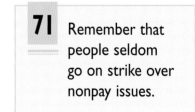

71 Remember that people seldom go on strike over nonpay issues.

COMPILING REPORTS

Reports are formal documents that will be read by others. They must always be accurate and well laid out, finishing with a definite conclusion. If you have been asked to write a report, make sure that it fulfills all the requirements of your original brief.

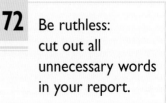

72 Be ruthless: cut out all unnecessary words in your report.

73 Tailor reports to suit what you know about the recipients.

RESEARCHING A REPORT

If you are reporting on an activity of your own, check every fact to ensure accuracy. If you have been asked to report on a subject – say, a new market for a product – write down what you need to know as a series of points. Then note the sources you can tap and match them to the points, making sure everything is covered. Before finalizing, get information supplied by one source confirmed by at least one other reliable authority.

DO'S & DONT'S

✔ Do make each report interesting.

✔ Do use verbatim quotes from interviewees.

✔ Do emphasize your most important findings and facts.

✔ Do use numbered paragraphs to make cross-referencing easier and to keep points separate.

✔ Do use headings for changes of subject and subheadings for related themes.

✘ Don't waffle or write unbroken, long paragraphs.

✘ Don't overuse the first person singular ("I") or allow your personal prejudices to show.

✘ Don't indulge in digressions or go off on tangents.

✘ Don't draw conclusions from insufficient evidence.

✘ Don't print your report without thoroughly checking your sources.

STRUCTURING A REPORT

Write the purpose of a report and summarize its main conclusions in your opening paragraphs. In the body of the report, support your findings with evidence, set down in a logical sequence, in numbered paragraphs. Use headings, sub-headings, and bullet points, all of which are effective structural aids, drawing attention to key facts. Use underlining and bold type for emphasis. End the report with recommendations for action in summary form.

ENSURING CLARITY

Reports are not works of literature, but good ones follow the rules of good writing. Avoid ambiguities. If you are unsure about your conclusions, state the alternatives and invite readers to make up their own minds. Express yourself in short sentences. Above all, put yourself in the readers' shoes. Will they understand what you mean? If you can, get a friend or colleague to read the report before you distribute it.

74 Seize opportunities to present your report in person to an audience.

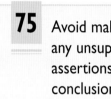

75 Avoid making any unsupported assertions or conclusions.

BEING CONCISE

If you are concise, you will reinforce the clarity of your report. Never use two words where one will do, or three where two are enough. Use short words rather than long ones. Spend time on the report's main conclusion, and place smaller summaries at the start of each section. When reading through the report, cut where you can. This should improve the sense of the text.

PRESENTING A REPORT

If you are going to make a verbal presentation of your report, ask yourself what matters more: deliberation or impact? If you are putting a case forward at a meeting, you should distribute your report then, and give a summary using AV aids if possible. Where your position is more neutral – with a feasibility study, perhaps – distribute the report in advance. Then make sure you come to the meeting well prepared for likely questions and objections.

▲ **PRESENTING USING AV AIDS**
Presenting your conclusions with excellent AV aids and speaking skills increases the impact of a report handed out at a meeting. Visual messages sell a report in an immediate way.

WRITING PROPOSALS

A proposal differs from a report in that it is a selling document, which should persuade readers to commit to whatever you are proposing. You could use an internal proposal, for example, to argue for extra company investment in computers or staff.

76 Enlist allies in preparing and lobbying for your proposal.

DRAFTING A PROPOSAL

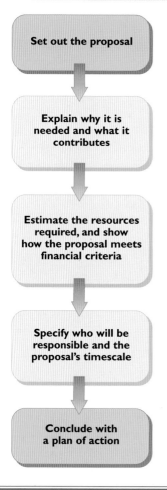

Set out the proposal

Explain why it is needed and what it contributes

Estimate the resources required, and show how the proposal meets financial criteria

Specify who will be responsible and the proposal's timescale

Conclude with a plan of action

RESEARCHING A PROPOSAL

To be successful, projects must be consistent with the overall aims of an organization. Before you write a proposal, research whether and how it fits into the wider scheme of the organization. When planning your research:

- Find out how the proposal would fit company strategy, and if there are any conflicting relevant activities that are either under way or planned for the future;
- Find out which aspects (such as finances, human resources, and legal implications) must be taken into account, and what repercussions these might possibly have for the organization;
- Ask those in a position to make decisions what objectives they would like to achieve in the form of short-term, medium-term, and long-term results;
- Gather together all necessary information to support the proposal, in readiness to go on to the next stage: planning.

77 Ask yourself honestly why one proposal might fail and another might succeed.

PLANNING A PROPOSAL

Structure a proposal following the same basic format as a report. State the proposal in a summary at the beginning; use headings as you develop your argument; then repeat your main points in a conclusion at the end. Make your approach upbeat – your enthusiasm should convince others of your ability to deliver the proposed outcome. If any risk is involved, explain that you have already fully considered potential drawbacks, and concentrate on positive benefits.

78 Use soft-sell techniques to get your proposal accepted.

QUESTIONS TO ASK YOURSELF

Q How much will the proposal cost, and who will be involved?

Q What will be the benefits – economic, marketing, quality – if the proposal is accepted?

Q How will the proposal be implemented?

Q Why is it being put forward at this time?

Q Why do you believe the proposed plan will succeed?

FOLLOWING UP

When you distribute a proposal, make sure that the recipients know when and how you plan to follow it up, or whether you expect a written response. Whether the proposal is to colleagues within your company, or to an outside supplier or customer, it is useful to follow up with a meeting where the proposal can be discussed. If possible, make a presentation at the meeting using AV aids, since the more visual impact a proposal has, the greater its chances of success. Remember, though, that no matter how strong the presentation, it will not sell a definitely weak proposal.

WRITING AN EFFECTIVE BUSINESS PLAN

If you require funding in order to set up a business, potential finance lenders will want to see a business plan. Write this document with a clear proposal, discussion, and conclusion. Support your proposal with detailed facts and figures projected over a relevant period (usually at least three years). The business plan must show that you have a good grasp of financial matters, that you have considered all factors, making best and worst case assumptions, and that there is a good chance of profit if the plan goes ahead.

CREATING PLANS
Make sure your business plan looks professional. Include title and contents pages, and bind the plan securely between covers.

MAKING A VISUAL IMPACT

Even the most promising proposal or report can suffer from poor layout, graphics, or typography. Similarly, a brilliantly designed document carries greater – perhaps decisive – impact. If practical, use professionals for this kind of work.

79 Add meaningful headlines and captions – people read them first.

ASSESSING DESIGN NEEDS

Whatever the document, aim for the highest practicable design standards, but vary the approach to meet the need. For example, the design of external sales documents must complement your corporate image and "advertise" the organization, using its logo properly and projecting high quality. Internal documents have more freedom. Unless you have been trained in design, you may need to employ a professional designer to give documents extra visual impact. Choose someone experienced who specializes in this type of work.

80 Use color images, graphs, and charts in documents when possible.

USING A DESIGNER

If you decide to employ a professional designer, how do you find someone whose work fits the style you are looking for? Always look at a designer's portfolio, since their previous work is a good indication of what they can do. Give the designer a clear brief at the outset. Explain fully what you want designed, ask for roughs if appropriate, and give dates for any review stages and deadlines. Do not be afraid to reject preliminary work, and rebrief to ensure that ultimately you get what you want. Remember that your judgment should not just be based on whether or not you "like" the design, but rather on whether it meets the business aims.

81 Keep an eye on design work as it progresses so you can head off errors or rebrief early.

DESIGNING FOR CLARITY

One of the most important design decisions is the choice of font (typeface). Modern software programs offer a fantastic range, but the main font must be clear and highly readable. If your budget allows the use of color, by all means make the most of it. However, avoid printing words over color or illustrations, since this may affect legibility. White type on a black background is also hard to read. Resist gimmicks; keep the design simple and suited to its purpose.

POINTS TO REMEMBER

● Using many different fonts at the same time can lead to a confusing overall look.

● Legibility is very important – the type should not be too small.

● A well-designed document is one that you enjoy looking at, but that also serves its function.

Type layout is very unprofessional   *Colored paper is a bad choice*

Aligned type is easy to read   *Aim of proposal is in clear bold type*

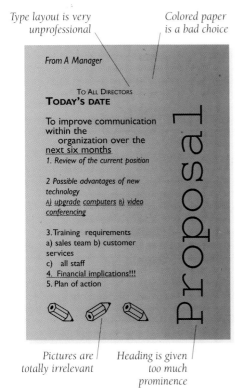

From A Manager

TO ALL DIRECTORS
TODAY'S DATE

To improve communication within the
   organization over the
next six months
1. *Review of the current position*

2 *Possible advantages of new technology*
A) *upgrade computers* B) *video conferencing*

3. Training requirements
a) sales team b) customer services
c)   all staff
4. Financial implications!!!
5. Plan of action

Proposal

From A Manager
To All Directors   Today's date

PROPOSAL
To improve communication within
the organization over the next
six months

1 Review of the current position

2 Possible advantages of
new technology
● upgrade computers
● video conferencing

3 Training requirements
● sales team
● customer services
● all staff

4 Financial implications

5 Plan of action

Pictures are totally irrelevant   *Heading is given too much prominence*

Numbers and bullets help legibility   *Type is well spaced on neutral paper*

▲ GETTING IT WRONG

This document looks messy for a number of reasons: it has too many type styles, uneven spacing, and unnecessary illustrations. Its appearance suggests it was written in a hurry.

▲ GETTING IT RIGHT

Using bold numbers and bullets for different subjects, aligning the type, and spacing the items consistently make the first page of this proposal look professional. It sends a positive message.

COMMUNICATING FOR RESULTS

The challenge to managers today lies in knowing how to exploit different types of media and use them to influence the public most effectively.

CREATING AN IDENTITY

A corporate identity is what enables an organization to be easily recognized by the public and within industry, and helps to establish its position in the market. If your budget allows, enlist the services of a designer or consultant to create an identity.

82 Get the opinion of trusted outsiders before finalizing a new logo.

83 Keep vision and mission statements short and action oriented.

CONSIDERING IMAGE

The type of corporate identity you choose influences the way your organization is perceived. The right image will strongly influence audience perceptions in your favor. Similarly, the wrong image gives an undesirable message to employees and the public. Ideally, a corporate identity should make a visual impact – perhaps including a striking logo or the use of colors – since this is a key element of effective communication. Before you brief anyone to design a new identity, decide what image you wish to convey, and check that you have your colleagues' support and agreement.

CHANGING AN IDENTITY

84 Check large corporate Web sites to see what others are doing.

Every organization has an identity – meaning how it is perceived by others – but many leave that identity to chance. However, if you do this you are neglecting a powerful marketing and recruitment tool. To create an effective corporate identity, you should decide on a central purpose and strategy (a "vision" and "mission"), as well as the image that you want to convey. Compare that desired image with current perceptions, and act to close the gap.

USING AN IDENTITY

Having settled on an identity, aim to use every piece of design, from the organization's reports to letterheads, from interiors to logos, to deliver a coherent message. You can also stamp an identity on internal documents, like memos, to emphasize the organization's image. Ensure that the identity is consistent in all of your communication media. Monitor the ways in which the identity is used. Occasionally, you may need to revise this use, to ensure that perceptions match your strategic need.

▼ USING LOGOS ON PRODUCTS

Coca-Cola's distinctive logo and the use of red and white on its packaging make the product instantly recognizable. This strong identity helped to make Coca-Cola a market leader worldwide.

Plastic bottle echoes shape of glass bottle

Traditional glass bottle distinguishes Coca-Cola from other cola drinks

Bright red cans carry logo

USING WEB SITES

The World Wide Web is a major source of corporate information, and often provides product and service news as well. Anybody can develop a site, but it is valuable to remember the following points:

● Professionals will always do a better job of developing a Web site. Ask them to cut down the preliminaries (the welcoming pages of your site) to the minimum; wading through page after page is irritating, time-wasting, and off-putting to site visitors.

● If you come across an effective site, do not hesitate to copy the elements that make it work, or adapt them to suit your organization.

● Watch out for bad habits, such as overusing graphics. This slows down access.

USING PUBLIC RELATIONS

*A*ll *managers have to consider the public impact of their actions. Public relations (PR) is the term used to describe the way issues and messages are communicated between an organization and the public. Handle PR internally, or employ experts.*

 **85** Get your PR people to handle potentially difficult media situations.

 **86** If you meet a hostile journalist, keep your cool; say nothing that could damage good PR.

RAISING YOUR PROFILE

An organization's reputation is one of its most critical assets. The role of public relations is to build and enhance a good reputation, and to prevent or mitigate damage to that reputation. Expert PR practitioners work to a plan that is linked to the organization's overall long-term strategy. They will use a number of techniques to supplement paid advertising campaigns and increase public awareness. The most effective advertising is favorable word-of-mouth; this free promotion should be one of PR's main objectives.

WORKING WITH PR

In small companies, PR may be handled by management or by employees who are not necessarily specialists in dealing with press or publicity. In larger organizations, internal PR departments are indispensable, mainly for the routine tasks of keeping in touch with and responding to the media and interest groups. If you have a PR department or employ a PR company, make sure that the relevant people are informed about things likely to generate public interest – from new products to the latest company results.

 87 If bad news breaks, admit the reality to everyone – especially yourself.

EMPLOYING CONSULTANTS

▼ BRIEFING CONSULTANTS
When you initially employ a PR company, introduce the PR consultants to the relevant personnel in your organization. Explain the brief, and check that the consultants know whom to contact in the future if necessary.

Generally, if you have a new message to relay to the public, it makes sense to use specialist PR consultants. Even large corporations with dedicated internal departments are likely to employ consultants occasionally. These range from multinational empires to one-person bands. They should be expert in everything from crisis management to arranging conferences, from launching products to introducing a new manager. Their contacts are usually extensive, and they should be capable of original ideas as well as effective execution. Always look at past work and take up references. Remember, too, that however able the PR company, it can only be as good as its client, and relies heavily on the brief.

USING PR EFFECTIVELY

The main thing to remember in using PR is that the quantity of coverage is less important than quality. PR is naturally cheaper than advertising, but you get what you pay for, so set aside a reasonable budget. Also, remember that publicity is double-edged and unpredictable, and PR officers are not to be blamed automatically if the media take a hostile turn. Nor can PR officers compensate for the lack of a proper brief. You need them to work with you to devise a PR strategy, but as in any supplier relationship, you must outline their duties and your expectations clearly. Agree on a plan of action, and review progress of the campaign at regular intervals.

POINTS TO REMEMBER

● PR departments and consultants must be kept informed about the organization's public actions.

● Staff should be trained and told when to speak to the media, and how to deal with enquiries.

● PR consultants need to be properly briefed so that they know what is expected of them.

● PR can be used as a valuable complement to advertising.

● Using PR to project the image of an organization can improve overall public perceptions.

USING PRINT MEDIA

Published articles that mention your organization or products can be more credible to the public than straightforward advertising. Take advantage of opportunities for you or your PR consultant to get features and news stories into print at both national and local level. Editors are usually hungry for copy, so do not be shy about making a direct approach to them. Some editors can be extremely demanding, so check that you know exactly what the paper or magazine wants, and hire professional help if necessary. In the same way, ensure that your press releases are clear and well written.

88 Buy and read the newspapers and magazines you want to influence.

POINTS TO REMEMBER

● News releases should be tailored to the needs of the press.

● Your company will benefit if you find time for media people.

● It is always safer to stick to the truth – the facts are sure to be uncovered eventually.

● The more accessible you are to the media, the more coverage you will be given.

USING RADIO

The numerous radio programs at local and national level can be a valuable asset to any publicity campaign. Radio provides companies with an alternative, immediate way to reach large target audiences. Before agreeing to take part in a program, check on the size and type of audience it will reach. You do not want to find yourself talking only to a few night owls. Talk to radio personalities on equal terms, and give honest answers. Try to control the interview so that you talk the most and can get your message across.

USING TELEVISION

Television is an extremely powerful and seductive medium, so accept any invitations to appear on TV, as long as you are confident in front of a camera. Get training in how to handle an interview beforehand. The technique is to look and be natural, and to answer questions as you would away from the camera. Managers can get valuable practice for appearing on real TV by taking part in video conferences, especially if they are exposed to unexpected questions.

89 Treat cameras and microphones as if they were friendly people.

TALKING TO JOURNALISTS

It always pays to cultivate good relations with the press and journalists who work in radio and TV. However, remember that journalists are not interested in serving your ends, but in getting a good story – preferably one that beats their competitors. Play fair; giving exclusives to one journalist will irritate the others – and you do not want journalists as enemies. If journalists contact you for your comment on something, and you are not confident about what you should say, ask if you can phone them back with a statement.

90 If you have a good relationship with the press, exploit it to the fullest.

▼ **CONVEYING THE RIGHT MESSAGE**
When talking to journalists, think before you make a response; give straightforward answers, and speak with confidence.

Eye contact shows lack of anything to hide

Journalist takes occasional notes to support taped conversation

Open body language conveys willingness to be helpful

Taping interview ensures you should be quoted accurately

USING STATISTICS

Readers, TV viewers, and radio listeners are always impressed by statistics, even when they cannot check their relevance or accuracy. Indeed, the more statistics you can muster in support of an argument, whether in a newspaper article or during an interview for broadcasting, the more convincing it will appear to an audience.

One feature of statistics is that the same data can be presented in a favorable or an unfavorable light, depending on how you handle the figures. For example, if statistics show an increase of, say, 258 percent, this may not be as good as it sounds. If the previous period was barely profitable, you may still really be showing poor results.

ADVERTISING EFFECTIVELY

The creative ideas and designs of good advertisements (which can be in any medium) must always be linked to a clear, measurable selling purpose. Ensure that your advertising gives potential customers a good reason to buy your product or services.

91 Make sure your product matches the promise, or advertising will fail.

92 Target your advertising for maximum impact.

93 Be as creative as possible – you can succeed on a small budget.

PLANNING ADVERTISING

Whether you are embarking on an expensive long-term campaign or placing a single advertisement on the recruitment pages of a newspaper, plan your advertising carefully. All advertisements convey a public message about your organization. What you are advertising and the size of your budget will influence the media you choose. Will you use TV, radio, newspapers, magazines, posters, billboards, the Internet, or direct mail, for instance? If you use more than one, the messages in different media should reinforce each other. For a big campaign, you should employ a specialized advertising agency.

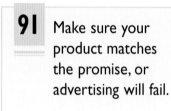

◀ USING A
TARGET GROUP
In this case study, the campaign was successful because the agency knew its target group well. It realized that it was not the quantity of advertising that would affect the target group most, but the quality of the publication in which the advertising was found.

CASE STUDY
A shoe company wanted to launch a brand of distinctive fashion boots. The company employed an advertising agency, whose customer research showed that the market for such boots was limited. The agency felt that the brand could not support a heavy advertising campaign aimed at everyone who might buy the boots. Instead it decided to target its efforts at a smaller group of what it termed "style leaders."

The desire to buy would trickle down from this select group to other purchasers. The agency placed advertisements in a trend-setting magazine to attract the style leaders, even though research showed the magazine was read by few potential purchasers.
The strategy worked: the style-leaders bought the boots followed by thousands of buyers who had never seen the advertisement. Sales multiplied more than fivefold.

MEASURING AWARENESS

Researching the market is crucial, because the information provides a yardstick for judging whether advertising is working. If necessary employ market research specialists to provide valuable feedback. For example, a survey can reveal the extent of public awareness about an advertised product before, during, and after a campaign. If appropriate, adapt any follow-up advertising to reach a new target audience.

94 Use panels of consumers to test advertisements before release.

USING THE INTERNET

An increasing number of organizations are successfully advertising on the World Wide Web. One big computer company achieves 10 percent of its sales from its 24-hour, 7-day-a-week Web "store." There are various reasons why advertising on the Internet is so popular:

● You can advertise products and direct-sell simultaneously;
● Images can move, which adds to effectiveness;
● Costs are quite low compared with other media;
● The Web is potentially the largest single medium for advertising many goods and services, in industrial products, as well as in consumer areas.

▲ **COMPANY WEB SITES**
Use your site on the World Wide Web to sell products, advertise, and provide information. You may take spots on other people's sites, even if you have your own.

USING DIRECT MAIL

The beauty of a direct mail campaign – when you try to sell your product or services to selected customers by mail – is that the marketing message goes straight to a target group. This means that the response and cost-effectiveness of your direct mailing can be accurately measured. For maximum effectiveness, you must have the right list for mailing – compiled by your own staff or bought from a mailing-list company. Add the right offer, and a direct mailing should work well. Research shows you are more likely to get a response if there are a number of items in the envelope. If your target group is small, you may be able to handle your mailings without the need for a dedicated department or direct mail specialists.

COMMUNICATING AT WORK

The techniques used for external communication can also be used effectively inside an organization, though on a much smaller scale and budget. Exploit these methods to ensure that messages reach your staff with real impact.

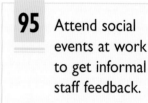

95 Attend social events at work to get informal staff feedback.

96 Get professional advice on media techniques you can use internally.

WINNING OVER EMPLOYEES

Employees are people who depend vitally on their management's services for their livelihoods. They are, in fact, an organization's most important "customers." Similarly, each department inside an organization is a "customer" of another; they all depend on each other to provide their services effectively. All lines of communication should be open between departments.

Good employers take every opportunity and use every transaction with employees to show that they really believe that people are valuable assets. Communication is important to get this message across. Target employees for offers tailored to their needs: continuing education, community projects, and sports facilities, for example.

MARKETING FROM INSIDE

In-company marketing can operate as efficiently as external marketing in catching the attention of people, engaging their interest, arousing their wish to participate, convincing them to follow your lead, and encouraging the behavior you want. Various devices – from competitions to "consumer" panels – can all be used effectively to put across the management message in direct and powerful terms. Remember not to talk down to the audience, and always tell the truth.

97 Use logos on all stationery to promote company awareness.

USING DIFFERENT MEDIA INSIDE AN ORGANIZATION

TYPE OF MEDIUM	FACTORS TO CONSIDER
HANDOUTS Including questionnaires, notices, and memos.	● These are useful to explain and report issues affecting employees, for example, results of attitude surveys. ● Even if kept as brief and concise as possible, handouts create an unavoidable buildup of paper, and are frequently tossed in the trash basket unread.
MEETINGS AND SOCIAL EVENTS Including team meetings, sales conferences, and product launches.	● These are ideal opportunities for generating motivation within the organization or team. ● Functions can be expensive because they need careful planning, preparation, and follow-up. Larger events also often require professional help and first-class locations.
PUBLICATIONS Including glossy magazines and desktop-published news sheets.	● Take care to match publications to employees' likes, dislikes, and needs. Use research, such as inviting readers' comments, to ensure the effort is paying off. ● These require a lot of effort for what may be low readership.
ELECTRONIC Including Web sites, intranets, and other electronic networks.	● The biggest advantage is that these can be updated continually and give an instant response to questions. Information can be sent worldwide in seconds. ● The biggest drawback is potential abuse, including use for personal – not business – needs.
TELEVISUAL Including videos, closed-circuit TV, and multimedia.	● This is a fast-growing modern approach which often uses interactive elements for optimum effect. ● These communication methods can be expensive because they require professional input and training.

TALKING UP THE TEAM

One of your responsibilities as a manager is the "advertising" of your team's image among peers and superiors. To do this, make sure you credit staff for their work, strive to have senior managers present at celebrations and in training or strategy sessions, make sure that good news about the department is covered in corporate journalism, and show off any inside achievements in outside presentations.

98 Find out which colleagues are most skilled at communicating.

CHECKING YOUR MESSAGE GETS THROUGH

If you are communicating to improve perceptions, you need to check how your message is received. Managers are often very bad judges of this. Remember, there is only one reliable source of information on perceptions: the recipients of the messages.

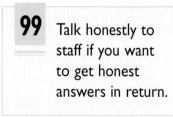

99 Talk honestly to staff if you want to get honest answers in return.

EVALUATING PERCEPTIONS

GETTING ▼ USEFUL FEEDBACK

How feedback is transmitted, and what happens in response to it, is basic to effective communication. Always act promptly when you get feedback. Also, hold team meetings regularly to check that feedback is well used.

The acid test of whether internal and external communications are successful is what the recipients perceive. An unfavorable perception is either merited, or the intended message did not get through. Whichever the case, you must take action. Honest analysis of the reasons will provide a basis for effective communication in the future.

LISTENING TO STAFF

The most important feedback is in individual, informal conversations between managers and those managed. However, you can also check how management is perceived by using a more formal approach, such as conducting attitude surveys, although these are sometimes expensive to carry out. Other ways to get useful information include more limited surveys, sample polling, suggestion boxes, and focus groups. For example, try polling your employees twice yearly to discover how they rate management. Targeted inquiries like this will raise issues, and give more general indications of morale. As with all feedback, what matters most is how you respond to what you hear.

QUESTIONS TO ASK STAFF

Q How do you get most of your information about the organization?

Q Does your manager communicate with you constantly, often, sometimes, or hardly ever?

Q What do you understand about the company's strategy?

Q What would you like to know that you are not being told?

Q Which type of communication is most effective for you?

100 If more than one or two make the same complaint, it may be widespread.

GETTING OUTSIDE VIEWS

If problems are revealed by internal questionnaires or through focus groups, one-to-one employee interviews, or any other meetings, the chances are that the external perceptions of the company also need to be improved. Get feedback by talking to your suppliers, clients, and customers, or perhaps by conducting a survey of target groups. Also, check the general response to recent advertising or PR campaigns. If the feedback suggests any dissatisfaction, you need to find remedies fast.

IMPROVING COMMUNICATION

To improve internal communications, involve all managers, stressing their responsibility for communicating clearly and consistently at all times. Decide whether other staff also need to improve their communication skills. For external communications, agree on a plan of action with all the relevant people. You must get to the root of any problem, strengthen your effectiveness, and shift perceptions, or mistakes will be repeated.

101 If you get only positive feedback, it may well not be the whole truth.

ASSESSING YOUR COMMUNICATION SKILLS

*E*valute how well you communicate by responding to the following statements. Mark the options that are closest to your experience. Be as honest as you can: if your answer is "never," mark Option 1; if it is "always," mark Option 4; and so on. Add your scores together, and refer to the Analysis to see how skilled you are at communicating. Use your answers to identify the areas that need improvement.

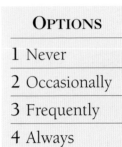

OPTIONS
1 Never
2 Occasionally
3 Frequently
4 Always

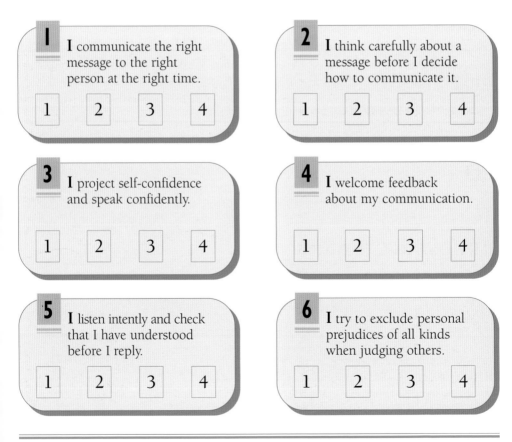

1 I communicate the right message to the right person at the right time.

| 1 | 2 | 3 | 4 |

2 I think carefully about a message before I decide how to communicate it.

| 1 | 2 | 3 | 4 |

3 I project self-confidence and speak confidently.

| 1 | 2 | 3 | 4 |

4 I welcome feedback about my communication.

| 1 | 2 | 3 | 4 |

5 I listen intently and check that I have understood before I reply.

| 1 | 2 | 3 | 4 |

6 I try to exclude personal prejudices of all kinds when judging others.

| 1 | 2 | 3 | 4 |

7 I am constructive and civil when I meet others.

1   2   3   4

8 I take time to give people the information they need and want.

1   2   3   4

9 I use one-to-one meetings for reviews of performance and coaching.

1   2   3   4

10 I question people to find out what they think and how they are getting on.

1   2   3   4

11 I hand out written briefs that give all pertinent information on a task.

1   2   3   4

12 I use professional phone techniques to improve my communication.

1   2   3   4

13 I communicate via all available electronic media.

1   2   3   4

14 I apply the rules of good writing to external and internal communications.

1   2   3   4

15 I use an effective system of note-taking for minutes, interviews, and research.

1   2   3   4

16 I test important letters and documents on reliable critics before finalizing.

1   2   3   4

17 I use fast reading techniques to speed up my work rate.

1 2 3 4

18 I prepare speeches carefully and deliver them well after rehearsal.

1 2 3 4

19 I take an active and highly visible role in internal training.

1 2 3 4

20 I plan important events, such as conferences, to high professional standards.

1 2 3 4

21 I apply the rules of soft and hard selling to put across my points of view.

1 2 3 4

22 I enter negotiations fully primed on issues and on the other side's needs.

1 2 3 4

23 I make my reports accurate, concise, clear, and well structured.

1 2 3 4

24 I research thoroughly before putting forward a written proposal.

1 2 3 4

25 I try to understand how all relevant audiences react to the organization.

1 2 3 4

26 I consider how skilled advisers can help on public relations issues.

1 2 3 4

27 I make useful contacts with journalists and other media people.

1 2 3 4

28 I make sure specialist work such as design is done by qualified professionals.

1 2 3 4

29 My briefs to advertising agencies are based on clearly defined business targets.

1 2 3 4

30 I give priority to communicating regularly with employees.

1 2 3 4

31 I receive and react positively to feedback from employees and others.

1 2 3 4

32 I have a strategy for communication and check activities against this plan.

1 2 3 4

ANALYSIS

Now that you have completed the self-assessment, add up your total score and check your performance by reading the corresponding evaluation. Whatever level of success you have achieved when communicating, it is important to remember that there is always room for improvement. Identify your weakest areas, and refer to the chapters in this section where you will find practical advice and tips to help you to hone your communication skills.

32–64: You are not communicating effectively or enough. Listen to feedback, and try to learn from your mistakes.
65–95: Your communications performance is patchy. Plan to improve your weaknesses.
96–128: You communicate extremely well. But remember that you can never communicate too much.

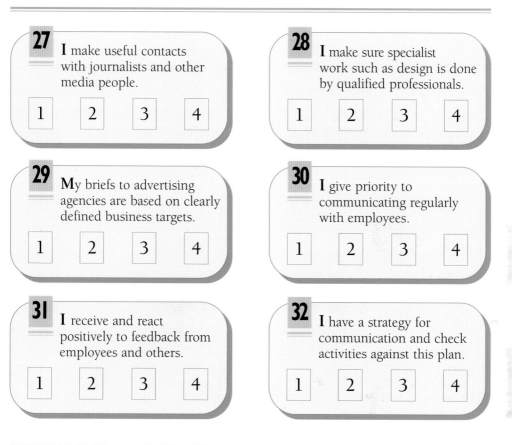

MANAGING TIME

INTRODUCTION

At home and at work, everybody can benefit from finding new ways to use time as efficiently as possible. Setting aside the time to analyze how you work can be an invaluable time-saver in itself, helping you make your day more productive and less stressful. This section takes you stage by stage through a quick and easy program designed to improve your use of time. It shows how to isolate aspects of your time management that are in need of improvement and how to set long- and short-term goals to prioritize your workload. It looks at how to save time in meetings and on business trips and how to avoid interruptions at work. This section also includes 101 concise tips covering vital time-saving tools such as diaries and planners, filing systems, and information technology. Finally, practical guidance is given on how to interact with subordinates, colleagues, and seniors to get the most out of your working life.

UNDERSTANDING TIME

Time is our most valuable resource. By analyzing time usage on a regular basis, it is possible to understand the most efficient ways to use time, both in and out of the workplace.

ANALYZING TIME

People's attitudes toward time are complex and variable. If you want to use your time efficiently to accomplish all that you need to do at work and at home, you need to be aware of the current habits and attitudes that shape your use of time.

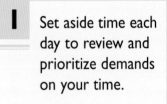

1 Set aside time each day to review and prioritize demands on your time.

CULTURAL DIFFERENCES

Perceptions of time and its usage vary worldwide. Differences are often reflected in the average number of hours worked per day or week, the importance of punctuality, or time spent on leisure activities. Be prepared to adapt to others' practices and timetables when working abroad.

CHANGING ATTITUDES

Our attitudes to time are constantly changing. Many of these changes are due to the advent of new technology, which affects our work, travel, and communication. The Internet, e-mail, and modems have made the exchange of information almost instantaneous. Travel, especially over long distances, has become faster and more affordable. The increase in options available has made it possible for us to do more in a day but has also increased the pressure on our time. This makes it all the more important to use time in the most efficient and productive way.

USING TIME WISELY

Everybody is increasingly aware of the cost of time. Individuals and departments are held accountable for their use of time: goals are clearly defined and financial penalties are incurred for missed deadlines. Company culture can have an important influence on how employees use their time. In too many organizations, working long hours is equated with working hard; if you leave on time, others may think you are not pulling your weight. In fact, long hours often decrease efficiency and productivity. Ways of using time become habitual, so make an inital investment of time to rethink and improve these habits. The rewards will be the ability to control your workload and more time to focus on the most important aspects of your job.

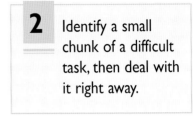

2 Identify a small chunk of a difficult task, then deal with it right away.

▼ **MANAGING QUESTIONS**
A manager who is constantly interrupted has little time for substantial tasks, while staff who must always consult their manager for decisions and information are held up. Use planning and delegation to minimize time-wasting at every level.

Subordinates waste time waiting for manager's attention

Colleague needs clarification and authorization from manager

Manager neglects own tasks while dealing with questions from other staff

ANALYZING USE OF TIME

F*ew of us will readily admit that large parts of our working day are wasted. The only way for you to make better use of your time is to analyze how you use it now and then to consider ways in which you can reallocate it in a more effective way.*

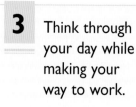

3 Think through your day while making your way to work.

ASSESSING YOUR DAY

There are always competing demands on your time. It is very easy to spend too much time on routine things, such as reading mail, at the expense of high-priority, productive tasks. How do you divide up your day at the moment? Do you prioritize your work so that you tackle important and urgent projects first? Or do you concentrate on completing enjoyable tasks first? Are you distracted by phone calls, or do you have a system for dealing with them? Do you waste a lot of time?

4 Always delegate tasks which are not time-effective for you to do.

COSTING YOUR TIME

It is a sobering exercise to calculate exactly how much your time costs and then realize how much of it is not being spent effectively. Use the calculation on the right to work out how much your time at work costs per hour and per minute, and then use these figures to analyze the relative cost of a few activities typical of your day, such as arranging a meeting yourself rather than asking your assistant to undertake that task. Always consider whether you should delegate tasks to others: it is generally more cost-effective to give routine tasks to more junior staff rather than doing them yourself, since your cost to the company will be higher.

▼ ESTIMATING VALUE
To find out the cost of each minute of your time, multiply your annual salary by 1.5 – to include overhead – and divide the total by the number of working hours in a year (working hours per week times working weeks per year). Divide this total by 60.

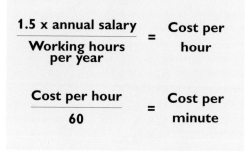

$$\frac{1.5 \times \text{annual salary}}{\text{Working hours per year}} = \text{Cost per hour}$$

$$\frac{\text{Cost per hour}}{60} = \text{Cost per minute}$$

KEEPING A TIME LOG

Maintaining a daily log of how much time you spend on particular activities is fundamental to managing your time more effectively. You may be surprised at how much time you spend chatting and at how little time you spend working and planning. Your time log provides you with a starting point from which you can assess areas to improve. How long you should keep a time log is dependent on the nature of your work. If you work on a monthly cycle, keep the log for a couple of months. If your work cycle is weekly, a two- or three-week log should suffice.

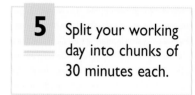

5 Split your working day into chunks of 30 minutes each.

▼ TIMING TASKS
Compile a simple time log by dividing your day into 30-minute chunks and recording exactly how you spend your time. This will help you determine how much time you spend on useful and unnecessary tasks.

Time	Monday
8:30	*Train to work – looked at papers and stared out of window.*
9:00	*Went through mail. Chatted with Steph over coffee.*
9:30	*Read some e-mails.*
10:00	*Regular Monday progress meeting – started 10 minutes late.*
10:30	*Continuation of meeting. Phoned Mary to confirm lunch.*
11:00	*Started writing up list of things to do.*
11:30	*Read more e-mails and responded to a few.*
12:00	*Phoned suppliers about late deliveries.*
12:30	*Traveled to Mary's office for working lunch. Bus late. Wasted 15 minutes.*
1:00	*Had working lunch with Mary to discuss her promotion prospects. Got distracted.*

Time	Monday
1:30	*Lunch with Mary continued. Did not talk about work.*
2:00	*Traveled back to office.*
2:30	*Organized desk. Made cup of coffee. Read more e-mails and responded to Alec's.*
3:00	*Called Jim about Thursday's meeting. Started to write two letters. Robert called.*
3:30	*Phoned Anna about international sales. Talked about her family for 15 minutes.*
4:00	*Discussed today's progress meeting with Ken and Anne.*
4:30	*Started to write up progress reports, including data from today's meetings.*
5:00	*Checked e-mails again. Refiled some documents on screen.*
5:30	*Reserved table for tomorrow's lunch with Susan.*
6:00	*Took work home on train. Fell asleep.*

REVIEWING A TIME LOG

To analyze your time log, allocate all of the 30-minute time chunks that you have recorded into categories according to the nature of each task, then calculate the amount of time spent on each type of task, such as meetings, reading and replying to mail, helping colleagues, or making phone calls. Now calculate the percentage of your time spent on each task. This will give you a better picture of your working day and will enable you to assess how you can allocate your time more effectively.

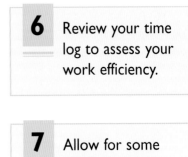

6 Review your time log to assess your work efficiency.

7 Allow for some thinking time in your schedule.

8 Estimate how much time a task will take, then see how accurate you were.

BREAKING DOWN TASKS

Look at the categories into which you have allocated your tasks, then divide them into groups: routine tasks (for example, writing a regular report), ongoing projects (for example, organizing a meeting), and tasks that would further develop your job (for example, making new contacts). Work out the percentage of time spent on each group.

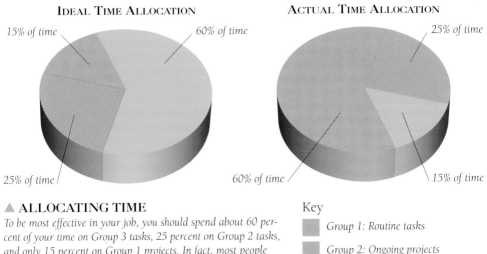

IDEAL TIME ALLOCATION

15% of time
60% of time
25% of time

ACTUAL TIME ALLOCATION

25% of time
60% of time
15% of time

▲ **ALLOCATING TIME**
To be most effective in your job, you should spend about 60 percent of your time on Group 3 tasks, 25 percent on Group 2 tasks, and only 15 percent on Group 1 projects. In fact, most people allocate their time in the opposite proportions: 60 percent on Group 1, 25 percent on Group 2, and 15 percent on Group 3.

Key
- ■ *Group 1: Routine tasks*
- ▨ *Group 2: Ongoing projects*
- ▧ *Group 3: Planning and development*

LOOKING FOR PATTERNS

Now that you have established how your time is being allocated, ask yourself if the breakdown meets your expectations of your working day. Are you spending too much time on Group 1 tasks rather than concentrating on important Group 3 jobs? Look at the distribution of these tasks throughout your working day. Are there times when you are very busy and others when you are slack? If so, try to find ways to reorganize your working day so that you are able to work more consistently and efficiently, and achieve more.

9 Update your time log as often as possible – memory is often unreliable.

QUESTIONS TO ASK YOURSELF

Q Do I do work that should be done by somebody else?

Q Are there patterns that repeat themselves in my time log? Am I always involved in Group 1 tasks in the morning?

Q Do jobs frequently take longer than I expect them to?

Q Do I have enough time to be creative and innovative?

ESTIMATING EFFICIENCY

How close is your work pattern to the ideal 60:25:15 time distribution ratio shown on the facing page? If you find you are spending too much time on one group of tasks to the detriment of others, work out how you can reorganize your daily schedule so that your time is distributed more efficiently. For example, if you find you are spending time on tasks that could easily be done by a junior, delegate them. This way you can concentrate your energies on the areas in which you are not spending enough time.

REVIEWING YOUR USE OF TIME

SHORT TERM

Once you have analyzed your use of time, there are several time-saving strategies you can implement immediately:

● Make a list of things to do, and update it several times a day;

● Look on your time log at wasted time and think of ways to fill those time slots more constructively in the future.

LONG TERM

If you find you have long-term problems, try changing your work patterns more radically:

● Pinpoint all the work patterns you are unhappy with. In particular, look for any bad habits you have slipped into.

● Once you have identified these problem areas, set aside time to rethink and improve your approach.

Assessing Your Ability

The key to successful management is the possession of good time-management skills. Think about how well you manage your time by responding to the following statements, then mark the options that are closest to your experience. Be as honest as you can: if your answer is "never," mark Option 1; if your answer is "always," mark Option 4; and so on. Add your scores together, then refer to the Analysis to see how you scored. Use your answers to identify the areas that need the most improvement.

Options	
1	Never
2	Occasionally
3	Frequently
4	Always

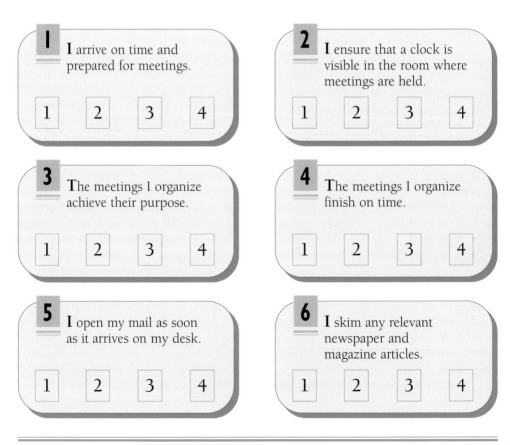

1 I arrive on time and prepared for meetings.

1 2 3 4

2 I ensure that a clock is visible in the room where meetings are held.

1 2 3 4

3 The meetings I organize achieve their purpose.

1 2 3 4

4 The meetings I organize finish on time.

1 2 3 4

5 I open my mail as soon as it arrives on my desk.

1 2 3 4

6 I skim any relevant newspaper and magazine articles.

1 2 3 4

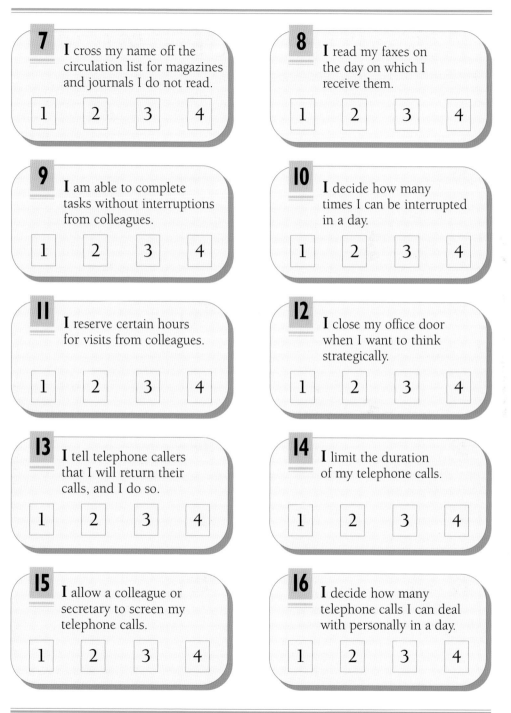

7 I cross my name off the circulation list for magazines and journals I do not read.

1   2   3   4

8 I read my faxes on the day on which I receive them.

1   2   3   4

9 I am able to complete tasks without interruptions from colleagues.

1   2   3   4

10 I decide how many times I can be interrupted in a day.

1   2   3   4

11 I reserve certain hours for visits from colleagues.

1   2   3   4

12 I close my office door when I want to think strategically.

1   2   3   4

13 I tell telephone callers that I will return their calls, and I do so.

1   2   3   4

14 I limit the duration of my telephone calls.

1   2   3   4

15 I allow a colleague or secretary to screen my telephone calls.

1   2   3   4

16 I decide how many telephone calls I can deal with personally in a day.

1   2   3   4

17 I skim internal memos as soon as I receive them.

1 2 3 4

18 I read internal memos thoroughly later.

1 2 3 4

19 I keep the contents of my in-box to a manageable size.

1 2 3 4

20 I clear my desk of all paperwork.

1 2 3 4

21 I delegate tasks to colleagues that I could do myself.

1 2 3 4

22 I follow up on the work I have delegated.

1 2 3 4

23 I encourage subordinates to limit their reports to one side of paper.

1 2 3 4

24 I consider who needs to know the information I am circulating.

1 2 3 4

25 I achieve the right balance between thinking time and action time.

1 2 3 4

26 I make a list of things to do each day.

1 2 3 4

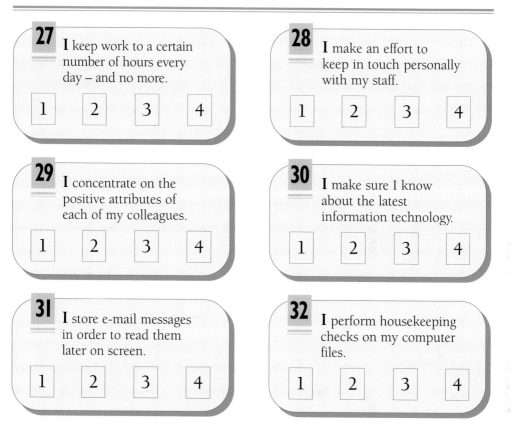

27 I keep work to a certain number of hours every day – and no more.

1　2　3　4

28 I make an effort to keep in touch personally with my staff.

1　2　3　4

29 I concentrate on the positive attributes of each of my colleagues.

1　2　3　4

30 I make sure I know about the latest information technology.

1　2　3　4

31 I store e-mail messages in order to read them later on screen.

1　2　3　4

32 I perform housekeeping checks on my computer files.

1　2　3　4

ANALYSIS

Now that you have completed the self-assessment, add up your total score and check your performance by reading the corresponding evaluation. Whatever level of successful time management you have achieved, it is important to remember that there is always room for improvement. Identify your weakest areas, then refer to the chapters in this section where you will find practical advice and tips to help you establish and hone those skills.

32–64: Learn to use your time efficiently, then reduce the time you spend working in unproductive and labor-intensive ways.
65–95: You have reasonable time-management skills, but they could improve.
96–128: You use your time very efficiently; keep looking for new ways to further streamline your work practices.

PLANNING FOR SUCCESS

You cannot decide what to deal with today unless you know where you want to be tomorrow. Any plan to improve your use of time depends on being clear about your goals.

ANALYZING YOUR GOALS

Long-term personal and professional goals are essential when it comes to setting overall targets. But in the short term a personal goal, such as starting a family, may take temporary precedence over long-term aims such as running a business.

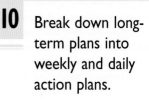

10 Break down long-term plans into weekly and daily action plans.

BALANCING GOALS

Short-term professional goals

Long-term professional goals

Short-term personal goals

Long-term personal goals

SETTING GOALS

Write down all your goals and then divide them into short and long term, personal and professional. Consider whether your goals are realistic: while you cannot change your physical attributes, you can learn new skills at any time. Think about which skills you need to acquire to achieve the goals you have set. As the traditional idea of one job for life disappears, you may need to update certain skills in order to remain employable, and this means your professional goals can be richly varied. Finally, set a timetable – decide when you would like to achieve each of your goals.

PLANNING CAREER GOALS

To help you achieve your goals, it is important to make long- and short-term career plans that you can bear in mind as you plan your use of time from day to day. You may find it useful to write down your experience, skills, and qualifications. As well as work, you may have acquired valuable management experience from running the home or looking after siblings. Looking at these skills and experience, list all the careers to which they would be relevant.

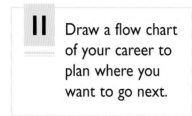

11 Draw a flow chart of your career to plan where you want to go next.

CHARTING YOUR WORKING LIFE

Start first job or apprenticeship

Work in finance or accounting

Take evening classes

Start a family

Join the company's biggest customer

Meet students in other lines of work

Take maternity or paternity leave

Work in sales and marketing

Take a management course

Broaden horizons

Gain work experience abroad

Apply for promotion

Cultivate useful contacts

Set up and run own business

WORKING OUT PRIORITIES

Once you have listed your long- and short-term professional goals, you need to arrange them in priority order. Each goal will involve the successful completion of a number of tasks. Decide which tasks are the most important and need urgent attention.

 12 Ask for a second opinion if you cannot prioritize competing tasks.

POINTS TO REMEMBER

- Your employer's priorities may not be the same as your own.
- Priorities change. They may need to be reassessed at the beginning of every day.
- The closer you are to achieving your goal, the more important it is to prioritize and concentrate on the tasks in hand.

13 Identify conflicts of priority between you and your boss.

ANALYZING YOUR WORK

Be as honest as possible about your current job. How much of your time is spent doing the wrong task at the wrong time and missing the goals you have set for that day? If you have 10 objectives to achieve each day, ranging from the mundane and routine to the urgent and complex, which of these takes priority? Analyze your working day, then decide which of your projects are routine, which concern ongoing or mid- to long-term projects, and which are extremely urgent and important or due for imminent completion. Whatever your position within your workplace, the careful planning and organization of your day will make all the difference to your efficiency at work and how successful you are at achieving your goals.

ANALYZING TASKS

Make a list of all your current, upcoming, and routine goals and tasks. Then divide them into three categories – Type A, B, or C:
- Type A: tasks that are important and urgent;
- Type B: tasks that are either important or urgent, but not both;
- Type C: tasks that are neither important nor urgent, but routine.
If you are in any doubt about how to categorize a specific task, consider it a C-task or discard it.

14 Find out whether your colleagues' priorities conflict with your own.

PRIORITIZING AND DELEGATING WORKLOAD

To work out your specific priorities, look again at your task list. Now make three separate lists – one each for A-, B-, and C-tasks. Starting with the A-tasks, work through the lists, deciding which tasks need input from others, which ones only you can do, and which can be delegated. Consider whether any tasks are unnecessary; if so, discard them. Involve people with the tasks that require outside input, and hand over jobs that can be delegated immediately. This will leave you with three shorter lists of A-, B-, and C-tasks that only you can do, enabling you to go to the next step: planning your day. By estimating how long it might take you to complete each of these tasks (noting down timings next to each item), you will be better placed to begin coordinating contributions from colleagues, fitting your tasks around organized meetings, and planning longer-term projects.

15 Classify all work engagements in your diary according to their importance.

16 If your schedule is full of A-tasks, then delegate or redefine them.

BALANCING DAILY TASKS

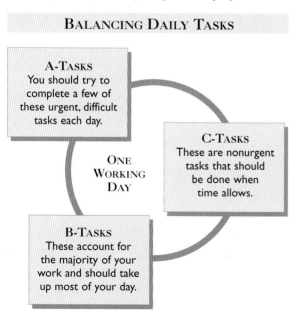

A-TASKS
You should try to complete a few of these urgent, difficult tasks each day.

ONE WORKING DAY

C-TASKS
These are nonurgent tasks that should be done when time allows.

B-TASKS
These account for the majority of your work and should take up most of your day.

PLANNING YOUR DAY

Any working day should include a mixture of A-, B-, and C-tasks. Plan a selection of tasks that you can realistically achieve in one day, while making sure that the working day does not stretch to 20 hours. Spread the three types of tasks throughout the day, rather than working in sequence through all the A-tasks followed by B-tasks, and so on. This way, you can intersperse blocks of intense concentration (devoted to A-tasks) with periods of less demanding B- and C-tasks.

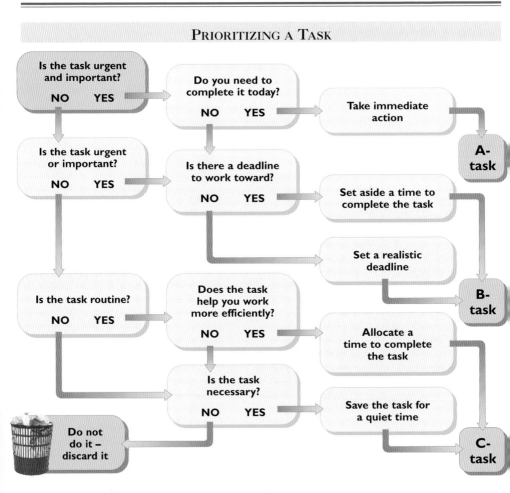

PRIORITIZING A TASK

Is the task urgent and important?
NO   YES

Do you need to complete it today?
NO   YES

Take immediate action

A-task

Is the task urgent or important?
NO   YES

Is there a deadline to work toward?
NO   YES

Set aside a time to complete the task

Set a realistic deadline

B-task

Is the task routine?
NO   YES

Does the task help you work more efficiently?
NO   YES

Allocate a time to complete the task

Is the task necessary?
NO   YES

Save the task for a quiet time

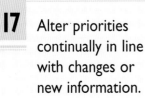

Do not do it – discard it

C-task

BALANCING DEMANDS

Priorities change all the time because we receive information all the time, whether from the Internet, the telephone, or a colleague popping their head around the door. New information may change a task's importance or urgency. It may push an urgent job off your critical list. Why prepare a report for a meeting scheduled for tomorrow when it has been postponed for three days? When you receive any new information, quickly reassess your list of priorities.

17 Alter priorities continually in line with changes or new information.

- Time spent on drawing up a plan is never a waste – it will save you time in the long run.
- Avoiding burnout is achieved by pacing yourself for a working life, not just a working day.
- Time management is doing things more effectively, not just more quickly.
- Food is vital for concentration levels and health – regular refreshment breaks are important.
- Quiet times in the office, such as before everyone has arrived, can be used to great effect.

18 To keep discussions short, avoid open-ended questions.

BEING REALISTIC

There are few things more stressful than exaggerated expectations, so be realistic about what you can achieve in a given period of time. You will not benefit yourself or your colleagues by embarking upon a punishing and overambitious schedule that you cannot maintain. Learn to recognize the limits of your capabilities, and do not undertake a project that you know you cannot complete successfully. Likewise, try to be realistic in your expectations of others. Do not demand too much from your colleagues, or you will be frustrated by their inability to complete the jobs you have given them, and they will soon become exhausted and demoralized. Once you have established what is reasonably achievable – whether for yourself or for others – stretch your expectations from time to time. People sometimes need to feel stretched and challenged at work, and they want to enjoy the satisfaction of having achieved something that is a little bit beyond their expectations and experience.

BOOKING QUIET TIME

You need some time to yourself – time to collect your thoughts, assess priorities, and concentrate on difficult or high-priority tasks. This quiet time will not become available unless you schedule it into your day. Do not feel guilty about shutting yourself off from your colleagues. Explain that they can have your full attention once you have had a short period of time free from interruptions and distractions. This is particularly important if your workplace is noisy and chaotic. Try to be self-disciplined, and use this time constructively to tackle A- or B-tasks that need your undivided attention. Remember that even a short period of quiet time will help you work more efficiently.

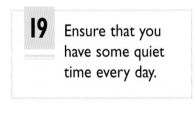

19 Ensure that you have some quiet time every day.

20 Do not be afraid to leave the phone off the hook.

ASSESSING WORK PATTERNS

Everybody has a natural daily rhythm to their energy patterns, rising to peaks of mental and physical performance, then experiencing troughs of low energy. Become familiar with your personal rhythm so that you can work with it rather than against it.

21 Time your physical and mental peaks so that you know how long they last.

22 Save some energy for home life and leisure activities after work.

TIMING TASKS

It is important to allocate the most demanding tasks of the day to the times when you are at your physical and mental peaks. If you are the sort of person who gets up early and goes jogging at dawn, you should make sure that you complete most of your A-tasks early in the day. On the other hand, if you have difficulty with getting out of bed before 9 a.m., you should leave your A-tasks until the late morning or early afternoon.

TAKING BREAKS FROM CONCENTRATED WORK

It is important to schedule relaxation time into your day, because your concentration levels and productivity start to decline as you tire. Plan breaks in your personal work pattern to match the times when your energy levels are low. Remember, the average person can concentrate intensively on work for only one hour without a break.

RELAXING AT WORK ▶
When you take a break, let your mind and body rest. Relax at your desk by lowering your head and closing your eyes. Rest your hands on your thighs, and breathe deeply.

MAXIMIZING EFFICIENCY

Your performance levels will fluctuate according to when you feel energetic and alert and when you feel tired. You need to understand the mental and physical cycles that your body follows each day in order to prioritize and plan your workload effectively. Note down the times at which you feel most tired or alert over a few days, then record the tasks you were performing at these times. If you were performing difficult tasks when you were tired, you were not working efficiently. In the future, try to schedule C-tasks for energy dips.

Because individual energy patterns can vary enormously, many companies now operate more flexible working hours. This allows employees greater control over their daily timetables and the opportunity to use time more efficiently by fitting work around their mental and physical cycles.

23 Suggest working flexible hours to improve company productivity.

▼ **CHARTING PEAKS AND TROUGHS**
Draw up a chart to show how your energy levels vary during a typical working day. Assign a number between 5 and -5 to your performance at every hour during the day (0 represents an average level of performance), and mark it on a graph as shown below. Join the marks to illustrate your energy cycle. Use this as a guide when scheduling your A-, B-, and C-tasks.

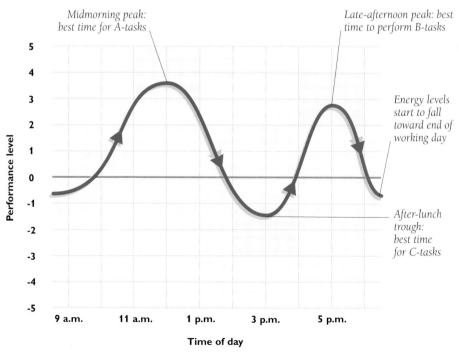

Midmorning peak: best time for A-tasks

Late-afternoon peak: best time to perform B-tasks

Energy levels start to fall toward end of working day

After-lunch trough: best time for C-tasks

Performance level

9 a.m.   11 a.m.   1 p.m.   3 p.m.   5 p.m.

Time of day

USING TIME PLANNERS

Keeping a reliable and precise record of forthcoming events, appointments, and obligations is crucial for efficient time management. There are many different types of planner available, so shop around to find the one that suits your needs best.

 24 Choose a diary that looks good and that you will enjoy using.

CHOOSING A SYSTEM

The traditional way to record future plans by hand is in a diary. Increasingly sophisticated personal planners and electronic organizers, with address books and accounting systems, are now available and are useful for keeping information at hand. The type you choose should depend on the work you need to organize. You may need a whole page for each day, or it might be more important to be able to see a week at a glance.

 25 Always keep a pen in your diary for noting information and dates.

CHOOSING A TIME PLANNER

The type of time planner you choose will largely be a matter of personal choice. Each type, from the traditional diary to the high-tech electronic planner, has specific features to recommend it, so it is up to you to find which one suits you best.

▲ **STANDARD DIARY**
Record events and appointments in a diary as and when they are scheduled. It is a good idea to keep old diaries for future reference.

▲ **PERSONAL ORGANIZER**
Use a personal organizer as a diary, address book, weekly or monthly planner, and notebook.

▲ **ELECTRONIC PLANNER**
Store names, telephone numbers, addresses, appointments, and personal details in digital form.

PLANNING WITH A DIARY

Using a diary takes discipline. The first thing you need to do is to get used to taking the time to record appointments and scheduled events as and when they are made. Make a note of how long the preparatory steps prior to your meetings take, and remember to build in the time needed for preparation and travel before appointments, as well as for any followup or reporting afterward.

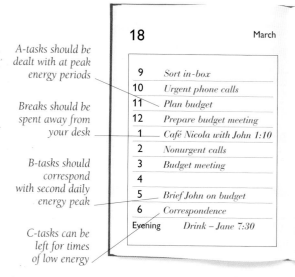

A-tasks should be dealt with at peak energy periods

Breaks should be spent away from your desk

B-tasks should correspond with second daily energy peak

C-tasks can be left for times of low energy

	18	March
	9	Sort in-box
	10	Urgent phone calls
	11	Plan budget
	12	Prepare budget meeting
	1	Café Nicola with John 1:10
	2	Nonurgent calls
	3	Budget meeting
	4	
	5	Brief John on budget
	6	Correspondence
	Evening	Drink – Jane 7:30

26 Use colored pens to denote tasks of varying importance.

▲ **USING A DIARY EFFECTIVELY**
Take a look at the events scheduled for each day in your diary. Make sure that you have planned the right balance of tasks and taken into account a realistic assessment of your personal, mental, and physical energy patterns.

MAINTAINING A DIARY

If somebody other than yourself is responsible for the upkeep of your diary, let them know of any appointments as soon as you make them to ensure maximum efficiency and productivity. Make sure that you have access to the latest version of your diary and that you check it at regular intervals to confirm your arrangements. Consider using an intranet system that can provide simultaneous access to a single electronic organizer from a number of different locations.

Each day, schedule important A-tasks around planned events, and make sure you complete them within a specified time. Remember to leave yourself enough slack time each day to deal with any unexpected situations that may arise.

ACCESSING INFORMATION

Take advantage of the speed with which electronic organizers can access data through their search facilities. By using key numbers and/or words, any information in the database can be called up almost immediately. Similarly, you can add a series of tabs to a personal organizer to help you open it quickly at particular days or letters of the alphabet.

MAKING A MASTER LIST

Having categorized all your A-, B-, and C- tasks according to urgency and importance, there may still be occasions when you feel confused about and overwhelmed by the number of projects that you face and the time you have in which to complete them. This is a good time to take a few minutes to make a master list, writing all your tasks on it, great and small, plus their deadlines. The very act of listing these important tasks is therapeutic and will take a weight off your mind. In addition, a list gives you a better overview of the whole situation than does a daily view of scheduled tasks. Certain solutions will suggest themselves; you may realize, for example, that the marketing plan for a new product that seemed to be far behind schedule can be postponed because the assembly line for the new product is itself running late.

▲ KEEPING UP TO DATE
Remember to add new items to your master list as soon as you receive them, and cross off any tasks once you have completed or delegated them.

POINTS TO REMEMBER

● Your master list should be consulted at the beginning of every day.

● Items should be crossed off your master list as and when they are done: it is very satisfying to see a list get shorter.

● At the end of each day, new items that have been added to a master list should be assessed and categorized as A-, B-, or C-tasks.

● Your master list can enable you to combine related tasks.

● When time is allocated for tasks on a master list, extra time should be left for unscheduled items.

● A master list of things to do at home should be kept, as well as a master list of work-related tasks.

USING LISTS EFFECTIVELY

Your master list should feature all your A-, B-, and C-tasks. Make the list living and ever-changing, crossing items off as you complete them, adding new tasks as they arise, and highlighting items as your priorities change. If you wish, group similar tasks together, for example, putting a star next to phone calls, a cross next to important letters to be written, and highlighting meetings to be arranged. This will help you see at a glance what has to be done and may encourage you to complete all similar tasks at the same time. You may save time at home if you also make a list of domestic tasks.

 27 Set realistic deadlines. A deadline is meant to be helpful, not a major cause of stress.

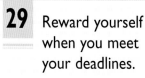

28 Delegate enjoyable tasks as well as unpleasant ones.

29 Reward yourself when you meet your deadlines.

DOING UNPLEASANT JOBS

Tasks of different types suit different personalities. A job that you find particularly unpleasant, such as dealing with a difficult customer, for example, may be regarded as an enjoyable challenge by a colleague. There is nothing to be gained from performing unpleasant tasks for the sake of it, so if you can delegate appropriately, do so.

When it is unavoidable, try to do a difficult job when you are in a positive frame of mind. Do not put it off until the end of the day, when you may be tired, or wait until just before the deadline.

LONG-TERM PLANNING

Many tasks on your master list will not disappear when they are done. Tasks in the working year often recur in cycles – for example, you may want to aim a certain product at certain customers at the same time every year. To allocate regular time to recurring tasks, you need a long-term backup to your short-term planner, such as a color-coded wall chart. Use bright colors to map out regular events so that you can see how busy you are at a glance and can plan ahead accordingly.

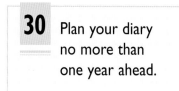

30 Plan your diary no more than one year ahead.

▼ **PLANNING THE YEAR**
List all regular events on a color-coded wallchart, like the example below. Allocate the time needed for each in a different color. This allows you to see if any events are overlapping and need to be rescheduled.

Budget deadlines occur regularly

March is busiest time of year

Additional time is allowed when tasks overlap

October is free month

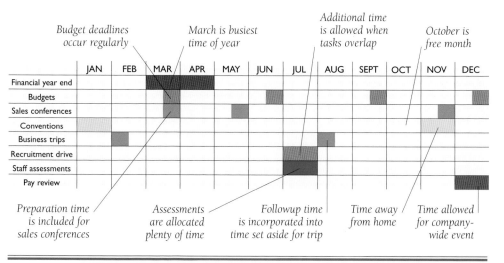

	JAN	FEB	MAR	APR	MAY	JUN	JUL	AUG	SEPT	OCT	NOV	DEC
Financial year end												
Budgets												
Sales conferences												
Conventions												
Business trips												
Recruitment drive												
Staff assessments												
Pay review												

Preparation time is included for sales conferences

Assessments are allocated plenty of time

Followup time is incorporated into time set aside for trip

Time away from home

Time allowed for company-wide event

THINKING POSITIVELY

Time can sail past for some people and drag for others. Which of the two applies to you depends mostly on your attitude. Use the power of positive thinking to make your plans successful, and even the most distasteful of tasks will seem painless.

 31 Make sure you do at least one thing every day that you enjoy.

ENJOYING LIFE

Different people have different ways of enjoying themselves, but if you do not make time to do the things you genuinely enjoy, your whole outlook can be adversely affected. Be aware of the tasks at work that give you particular pleasure, and make sure that they are well spread throughout your schedule. Plan regular leisure outings – to the movies, music festivals, or local park. In addition, try to cultivate a positive outlook, even when not engaged in the tasks that give you particular pleasure.

 32 Read a passage by your favorite author last thing at night.

LIVING WELL

The beginning and end of each working day are particularly important times. Start the day with a healthy, unhurried breakfast, and sit down while you are eating to allow you to relax and enjoy it more. Make sure that you leave yourself enough time to get to work without feeling rushed. At the end of the day, leave your workplace in a positive frame of mind. This will help prevent the difficulties of the day from carrying over into your personal life. Make a conscious effort to relax and stop thinking about work at least two hours before you intend to go to bed.

◀ **EATING HEALTHILY**
Think carefully about what you are eating, and at what time of day. Ideally, your day should start with fresh fruit and cereals or bread and finish with a light meal. Too much heavy food late at night can lead to insomnia, fatigue, and irritability.

DEALING WITH PROBLEMS

With a positive attitude to life, it is much easier (and quicker) to manage your time and solve problems at work. Start focusing on feeling good about yourself and your life, and you will be less likely to interpret the problems of others as your own. This will help you to be objective and constructive in coming up with methods of dealing with tight deadlines and budgets, and resolving conflict.

33 Concentrate on your colleagues' and clients' positive attributes.

CASE STUDY

Anthony, a sales executive, had been asked to attend a high-pressure meeting, which included staff from other departments among its participants.

A week before the meeting, Anthony realized that he had been convincing himself that it would go badly. He decided it was time to try to change his pattern of negative thinking into positive thinking.

First, he used various prioritizing techniques to ensure his material would be prepared

well. Then, he set about positively visualizing the meeting and its outcome. He "saw" himself stand up, clear his throat, and give the report he had prepared. He then imagined himself successfully answering all of the questions that came from the other participants at the meeting. Finally, he visualized the approval on the faces of his colleagues, especially the ones that he usually felt intimidated by.

The meeting went just as Anthony had imagined – and this boosted his confidence.

◀ **TAKING POSITIVE STEPS**
Anthony was creating a cycle in which his negative thinking was producing a negative outcome. His decision to change negative aspects into positive ones was conscious, but not easy to effect at first. Each success made it easier, and eventually the habit of positive thinking became automatic.

34 Use an organizer to list weaknesses, then plan how to combat them, one by one.

AVOIDING STRESS

By definition, busy people do not seem to have time to plan their future. It takes determination to find time in a busy schedule to think about how to use the next few hours productively. Psychologically, however, it is good practice to plan your activities because it enables you to be in command of your time, putting you back "in the driver's seat" of situations that look as if they might go out of control. When you take the time to plan, you can consciously be positive – and this will help you avoid stress as well as achieve your goals.

MAKING INSTANT CHANGES

There are many practical things that you can do to improve your efficiency over the short and long term – from clearing a desk and keeping it neat to streamlining computer systems.

CLEARING YOUR OFFICE

Efficient organization of your work space can make an enormous difference. Starting with your desk, set up a system to ensure that nothing is lost among growing piles of papers. Then tackle filing cabinets, bookshelves, and your general surroundings.

35 Keep your desk clear of everything but the current job in hand.

 36 Beware of self-sticking notes. They are easily lost.

 37 Clean up daily. Never leave a mess for the morning.

PROJECTING AN IMAGE

You can tell a great deal about the occupant of an office from the arrangement of items on the desk, the use of color, and the general level of neatness. Superiors, colleagues, and subordinates alike will form their first impressions of you from the state of your work space – so ensure that the impression you give is positive. If you regularly receive visitors at your desk, make sure that the image you are projecting is the one that you want them to see. You will never convince a well-organized outsider that a messy work space reflects anything other than a disorganized mind.

Memos and junk mail cover computer

Reading material is stuffed into file and forgotten

Files are bulging and not kept up to date

Filing cabinets overflow with irrelevant information

Important contact name is stuck on side of computer

Papers obscure telephone

Waste paper covers floor

Trash can needs emptying; papers are overflowing

▲ WORKING IN CHAOS
The longer you delay straightening your desk, the more difficult the job becomes and the more likely it is that time will be wasted.

PROCESSING DOCUMENTS

Think of your desk as an assembly line. Raw materials (mostly in the form of paper) come in at one end to be processed by a machine (your mind) before they are sent off to the next stage. The just-in-time logistics that companies apply to manufacturing processes can also be applied to your desk. This means being aware of how urgent papers are and where they need to go. Glance at documents as soon as they come in: if they are urgent, take action or delegate at once. Place nonurgent papers that are waiting for something else before they can be processed into a pending tray, and put all other nonurgent papers into your in-box to be processed next time you go through it.

THINGS TO DO

1. Keep work surfaces as clear as possible at all times.

2. Neaten desk drawers, and keep them ordered.

3. Keep pens, pencils, glue, and rulers together in a single, accessible container.

4. When not in use, place the computer keyboard out of the way to create more working space.

111

ORGANIZING PAPERWORK

Set up a system for keeping up to date with all the paperwork that appears on your desk. Deal with urgent items immediately. For nonurgent items, set aside some time each day to go through your in-box. If you need to take any action, write it down on your master list of things to do. File away other items to read later (or keep them for reference), and throw away anything that you do not need or have already dealt with.

38 Highlight key points on paperwork to speed up rereading.

▼ PROCESSING PAPERS
Take time to process all incoming papers daily. Be disciplined, and follow this simple system to keep your desk clear.

Note action you need to take	→	Handle, file, or delegate	→	Throw away everything else

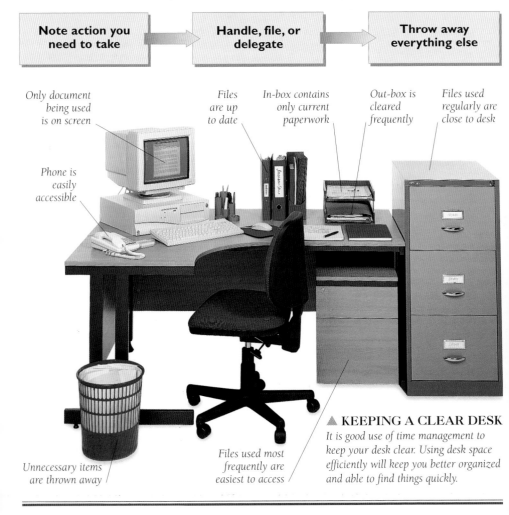

Only document being used is on screen

Files are up to date

In-box contains only current paperwork

Out-box is cleared frequently

Files used regularly are close to desk

Phone is easily accessible

Unnecessary items are thrown away

Files used most frequently are easiest to access

▲ KEEPING A CLEAR DESK
It is good use of time management to keep your desk clear. Using desk space efficiently will keep you better organized and able to find things quickly.

ORGANIZING WORK SPACE

The objects in your work space (desks, chairs, tables, filing cabinets, lamps) should be organized to suit you. Think about your work patterns and what you use your office for. If you have a lot of visitors, place your desk so that you can see the door and be aware of people approaching. If you regularly hold meetings in your office, arrange the furniture so that visitors can sit comfortably.

If possible, your work space should contain only those files to which you refer regularly. Keep these near your desk, preferably so that you do not need to stand up frequently to reach them. The files that you look at rarely should be put in a special storage space or, if this is not available, in an out-of-the-way corner of the office.

39 Position a clock in your office so it is visible to you and to visitors.

40 Review your filing system at least every few months.

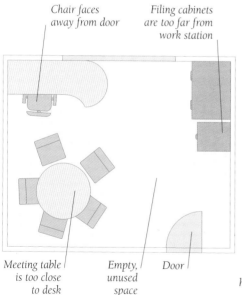

Chair faces away from door

Filing cabinets are too far from work station

Meeting table is too close to desk

Empty, unused space

Door

▲ **WASTING SPACE**

The furniture in this office is arranged so that it is cramped in some areas and empty in others. The room must be crossed to reach the filing cabinets, while the meeting table is too close to the desk.

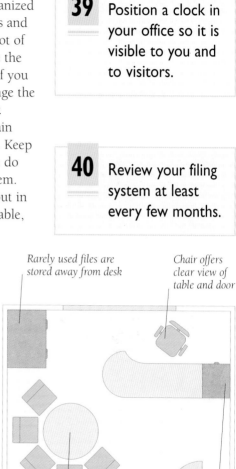

Rarely used files are stored away from desk

Chair offers clear view of table and door

Meeting table has ample space

Regularly used files are next to desk and give extra work space

▲ **CREATING SPACE**

This arrangement makes a more efficient use of the space available. The table is well placed for meetings, and there is a good view of approaching visitors. Frequently used files are next to the desk.

FILING PAPERWORK

*I*t is well worth taking time to set up an *efficient filing system – think of the hours you can waste looking for something that has been stored at random. No one filing system is ideal. Choose one that is designed to suit the materials you need to store.*

 41 Set up a filing system that will grow with you and your business.

42 Go through your files regularly and discard documents that you no longer need.

ORGANIZING YOUR FILING

A filing system needs to work in the same way as a computer's search function. Key words need to trigger thought sequences in your brain that lead you easily to the place where a paper is filed. Such sequences will be determined by the nature of your work. If you are an exporter with markets in 70 different countries, your basic classification may be along geographic lines, so you might have five big filing cabinets – one for each continent. If you are a sales manager for a small company producing stationery products, you may divide your customers into two filing cabinets – one for domestic customers, the other for overseas. Each customer will be allocated their own folder.

BREAKING SUBJECTS DOWN

If you have large categories in your files, it is a good idea to subdivide them to make them more manageable. For example, a development manager who is responsible for overseeing numerous projects could group files by individual project and then subdivide each project into different sections, each with a separate file.

▼ SORTING FILES
Divide your files into categories on the basis of need, then store them accordingly. Keep those that you use all the time nearest to you and those that you refer to occasionally a little farther away. The rest should be archived elsewhere or thrown away if they will not be used again.

Often need	Sometimes need	Archive

LABELING CLEARLY

It is helpful to have a system that indicates immediately, by means of color or typography, the level or classification of each file. For example, a sales manager could file documents relating to export customers in red files tagged with red labels and those relating to domestic customers in blue files with blue labels. Each label would be annotated with the name of a customer. Whatever system you adopt, it must be easily understood by you and any other users, so keep a printed list of the sections, subsections, and their contents for easy reference.

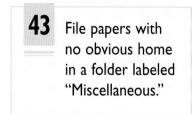

43 File papers with no obvious home in a folder labeled "Miscellaneous."

▼ **COLOR CODING**
Using a system of color coding allows you to locate files of a particular type at a glance. This reduces the time you spend searching for documents, thus increasing the efficiency of your working practices.

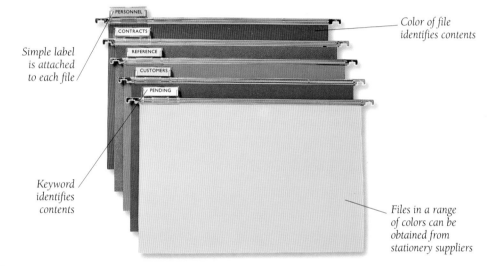

PERSONNEL

CONTRACTS

REFERENCE

CUSTOMERS

PENDING

Color of file identifies contents

Simple label is attached to each file

Keyword identifies contents

Files in a range of colors can be obtained from stationery suppliers

FILING REGULARLY

Set aside a regular time for filing – either at the end of every day or at the end of each week. Do not always delegate the task of filing to someone else – it is useful for everyone to update their knowledge of the filing system. Decisions about what to keep and what to throw away are critical, so take an active part in deciding which documents are no longer required and should be discarded, and which are to be kept for future use.

44 File only essential documents that will be referred in the future.

AVOIDING INTERRUPTIONS

*S*ometimes interruptions are welcome, but everyone needs to work undisturbed at certain times. Make your working day as productive as possible by discouraging interruptions by colleagues and reorganizing your office so that you are less visible.

LISTING INTERRUPTORS

To reduce the number of unnecessary interruptions you receive, first draw up the following lists:
● People who may interrupt you at any time, such as your boss or important customers;
● People who may interrupt you when you are not particularly busy, such as colleagues;
● People who may not interrupt you at all.
Keep these lists in mind, and give copies to your support staff and relevant colleagues. Ask them to follow these lists as much as possible.

 45 Ask your secretary or a colleague to screen incoming phone calls for you.

 46 Pick up the phone to indicate the end of a meeting.

Visitor stands to one side of chair and must work hard to gain attention

DISCOURAGING ▶ INTERRUPTIONS
Use negative body language to fend off unwanted intrusions. Turn your head, but not your whole body, toward the visitor. Use signals such as glancing at your watch.

Head turns toward visitor

Arm and shoulder form a barrier, discouraging long discussion

Holding pen signals an unwillingness to be interrupted

RETHINKING WORK SPACE

You are especially vulnerable to interruptions if it is easy for passersby to catch your eye. Position your desk so that you can see who is approaching the door. Keep your office door closed when you do not want to be interrupted. Even if you work in an open-plan office, you can minimize interruptions by making changes to the layout of your work space – repositioning your desk behind filing cabinets, for example, or placing your computer monitor directly in front of you. Once you make yourself less visible to staff and colleagues, they are less likely to disturb you unnecessarily.

47 Do not sit down if you are followed into your office.

48 Place your chair out of view if your door is open.

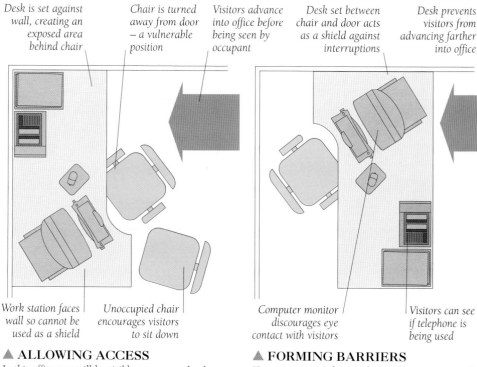

Desk is set against wall, creating an exposed area behind chair

Chair is turned away from door – a vulnerable position

Visitors advance into office before being seen by occupant

Desk set between chair and door acts as a shield against interruptions

Desk prevents visitors from advancing farther into office

Work station faces wall so cannot be used as a shield

Unoccupied chair encourages visitors to sit down

Computer monitor discourages eye contact with visitors

Visitors can see if telephone is being used

▲ ALLOWING ACCESS

In this office you will be visible as soon as the door is opened. You are seated with your back to the door and have to turn to see who is coming in, making you unable to preempt unwelcome visitors.

▲ FORMING BARRIERS

Here, a computer forms a barrier between you and anyone entering the room. Your chair faces the door, so you can see approaching visitors. The lack of a spare chair will discourage visitors from staying too long.

FILTERING INFORMATION

Most people receive hundreds of different pieces of information every working day, and processing them takes up large amounts of time. Take time to work out a systematic way of handling all the incoming information that ends up on your desk.

49 Throw away any information that you think you do not need.

50 Keep all chance meetings short by standing – it will then be easier to get away.

GAINING INFORMATION

Information comes to you in increasingly diverse forms, including the following:
- On paper (for example, via mail, faxes, memos, newspapers, magazines, journals, reports);
- Electronically (for example, via e-mail, intranet);
- By voice (for example, via face-to-face meetings, television, radio, telephone, voice mail).

Remember that some forms of information appear to be more urgent than others – but this may not be a true reflection of their importance. For example, phone calls often take precedence over mail because they are more immediate.

PROCESSING INFORMATION

Try to establish a routine for processing set information. For example, if you know that the external mail arrives at 10 a.m. and that internal messages are distributed at 11 a.m., set aside a time just before lunch for sorting through the mail. Read your electronic messages at the same time and, if you have not already done so, make some time to skim newspapers and magazines.

You will need to repeat the same process toward the end of the day to straighten your desk and to prepare yourself for the following morning. It is often a good idea to let information "stew" overnight before taking any action on it.

POINTS TO REMEMBER

- Messages arrive all the time and should not disrupt the work flow.
- Messages should be skimmed until their main information content is absorbed.
- If a message requires action, a note should be made and added to a master list.
- For ease of filing, a printed piece of information can be immediately coded with a folder name.
- Messages should be discarded once they have been dealt with.

CIRCULATING MATERIAL

Much of the information that comes your way can be passed directly on to colleagues or staff. Divide information into three categories:

- That which you amend or add something to before passing on – this is typical of the general internal memo or report;
- That which you read, digest, then pass on to someone else. This is typically what happens with journals and magazines;
- That which you copy and distribute – you may do this with a thank-you letter from a happy, satisfied customer about which colleagues should be informed.

51 Copy information only to those who need to know.

52 Stop subscriptions to magazines you no longer read.

HANDLING DIFFERENT TYPES OF INFORMATION

INFORMATION SOURCES

HOW TO HANDLE THEM

INTERNAL MEMOS AND REPORTS
Information contained in internal memos and reports can be specific to an individual, work team, department, committee, or other group.

- Timing is the critical element when circulating information of this type.
- Decide by when and by whom your comments or actions are needed.
- Plan to fit any action into your schedule.

EXTERNAL MAIL AND FAXES
The range and importance of incoming information is very wide. Mail is usually delivered at regular intervals, but faxes can arrive at any time.

- Decide what action is needed and when.
- Ascertain whether you should distribute the information and, if so, in what form.
- Ensure that any information that needs filing is filed and anything that is not needed is thrown away.

INTRANET AND E-MAIL
Electronic messaging systems are being increasingly used for rapid communication and dissemination of information to individuals or groups.

- Electronic messages can be created and distributed easily, so check if they are relevant to you.
- Do not open messages that are not relevant to you.
- Once you have acted on a message or added it to your master list, delete it.

NEWSPAPERS AND MAGAZINES
Much information on specific areas of a trade or profession can be sourced from a selective subscription list of newspapers and magazines.

- Skim articles and decide whether you want to keep them for future reference.
- Make a photocopy before passing a magazine on.
- Cut out information, mark relevant sections with red ink, and file in the appropriate place.

DEALING WITH REFERENCE

What should you do with material (both paper and electronic) that you want to read at a later date? One option is to keep it all in a separate "pending" file, dipping in and out of the file as and when you have time for background reading. However, one of the problems with files such as these is that they have a tendency to become unmanageably large, so they need to be cleared out as regularly as possible. You should therefore try to clear the file of any outdated and irrelevant material each time you dip into it.

53 Remove magazine and newspaper articles you wish to keep, then file them for reference.

54 Keep only essential reading on your desk.

READING REFERENCE ▼
Read through relevant magazines and newspapers regularly to source up-to-date reference material. Build up a filing system to deal with this reading matter.

DELEGATING YOUR WORK

It is very daunting to return from time away, for example at meetings or on business travel, to find your desk covered in unprocessed messages and information. If you are often away from your desk, organize someone to filter these for you. The person to whom you delegate this responsibility should be able to sift through your messages and mail, distributing items to staff who can deal with them in your absence. Explain which matters can be handled at once and which are best saved for your return.

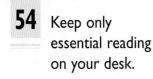

Useful articles can be torn from magazines for future reference

Reference and information can be stored in a reading file

KEEPING UP TO DATE

The relevance of information changes as time marches on. As most of today's news is history tomorrow, so our perspective of what is relevant alters over time. Some people believe that what is useless today may come in useful at a later date and consequently tend to hoard all sorts of information. Generally, however, remember that it takes time and space to process written information, so always carefully consider the relevance of any reference material to your work before filing it away.

55 Assess each piece of information for its relevance to current projects.

PROCESSING INFORMATION

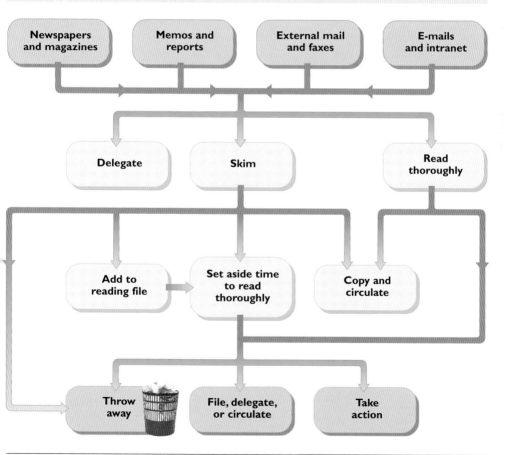

121

WORKING WITH OTHERS

The best-laid plans for managing time are always to some extent in the hands of others. Nobody works entirely alone. An unexpected telephone call can throw a day's plans into chaos. Learn to reconcile other people's time management with your own.

> **56** Think before you interrupt anyone. Their time is as valuable as yours.

QUESTIONS TO ASK YOURSELF

Q Do I consider others' plans when making my own?

Q Do I write too many unnecessary memos?

Q Do I organize too many rambling meetings?

Q Do I always arrive on time for appointments?

Q Do I frequently interrupt other people?

My colleagues spend too much time discussing rather than working

My colleagues do not work long enough hours

My colleagues waste time and money on lunches

My colleagues are not busy enough

My colleagues take too many days off

▲ **MAKING FALSE ASSUMPTIONS**
If you are guilty of looking at your workmates and making false assumptions about how they manage their time, rethink your attitude. Are they really being unproductive, or do they achieve results from spending time in meetings, discussions, and lunches?

ASSESSING WORK ROLES

The extent to which you compromise your plans for somebody else depends on your relationship with that person. Consider, for example, whether you should call an urgent meeting that includes your boss without discussing it first. Your boss may resent being involved in a meeting without prior consultation – perhaps he or she may have information that alters the agenda or makes the meeting unnecessary. It is essential always to think through the decisions you make when dealing with colleagues at all levels of seniority.

REVIEWING YOUR ASSUMPTIONS

Many people make erroneous judgments about what constitutes good management of time – it is easy to confuse someone seeming to be busy with them working hard and managing their time well. When working with others, analyze their work practices before making assumptions about their productivity. Consider whether you could save time by adapting your work methods to mirror theirs, or vice versa.

ANALYZING MOTIVATION

Everyone is motivated by different aspects of their job. If you think your workmates could make better use of their time, consider whether they are demotivated. This could be because:

- They do not get enough work to do – in which case, redistribute work around the department to ensure everyone has busy schedule;
- They feel frustrated because they are not interested in the work they are doing – discuss a more fulfilling program of work;
- They feel overworked – help them develop their time-management skills or consider whether they can reduce their workload.

57 Call a meeting only after considering other options.

58 Do not make assumptions about work colleagues.

HANDLING MEETINGS

You work with others most often when attending meetings. Organizing a meeting between busy people can be complex and time-consuming. It takes time to set up, prepare an agenda, travel to and from a meeting, and follow up. Remember that meetings take up time that participants could spend on other activities. Always ask yourself if it is really necessary to bring people together. You might be able to save time by not calling a meeting but instead speaking to individuals by phone, for example. If all the participants work for the same organization, it will be to your mutual benefit if time spent in meetings is kept to a minimum.

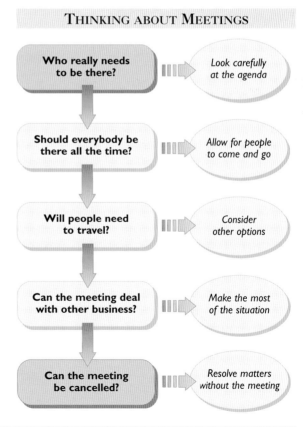

THINKING ABOUT MEETINGS

Who really needs to be there? → Look carefully at the agenda

Should everybody be there all the time? → Allow for people to come and go

Will people need to travel? → Consider other options

Can the meeting deal with other business? → Make the most of the situation

Can the meeting be cancelled? → Resolve matters without the meeting

MAKING PHONE CALLS

There is hardly a business in existence that does not depend on the phone and, increasingly, voice mail for rapid and direct communications. Their effective and appropriate use can dramatically improve your efficiency and performance.

59 Take a deep, relaxing breath before you make a phone call.

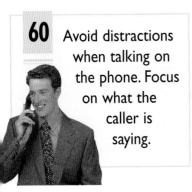

60 Avoid distractions when talking on the phone. Focus on what the caller is saying.

CHOOSING WHEN TO CALL

Set aside a specific time of day for making phone calls, and list all the calls that you need to make every day. Be clear about the purpose of each call, and draw up a brief agenda for each as if the call were a meeting. Then make sure that you cover all the items on the agenda during the conversation. Prioritize your calls in order of importance to ensure that you concentrate your time and resources on the most important and urgent calls.

KEEPING ON TRACK

Do not let a phone conversation stray too far from your agenda unless there is a good reason, such as dealing with an unexpected problem. Take notes and check off items on your agenda as they are covered. You may find it easier to lead your conversation if you stand up or walk around.

It is easy to lose track of time when speaking to someone whose conversation you enjoy, but try to keep this in check. Assess the purpose of the call – for example, can you be brief, or do you need to spend time building up a rapport or placating an angry customer? As an exercise, use a timer for a week to monitor the length of time you spend on each call. This can be sobering, both because of both the cost of the call itself and the cost in terms of your time.

THINGS TO DO

1. Prepare yourself for a phone conversation as you would for a meeting.

2. Bunch calls together. If a number is busy, try it after completing other calls.

3. Choose an order of priority in which to make your calls.

4. Use a speaker phone so that you can do other work while waiting for an answer.

5. If you use a pager, put aside time to return all your calls.

USING A VOICE-MAIL SYSTEM

Corporate answering machines, also known as voice mail, are becoming commonplace. Some people dislike the impersonal nature of voice mail, but you need to understand how the system works and how to make efficient use of it. It is an ideal tool for arranging internal meetings or eliciting a response from a busy colleague. Avoid bargaining or making deals by means of a seemingly endless series of voice-mail messages, since you need to speak directly to customers or suppliers to gauge reactions and find areas of compromise and agreement.

61 When making a phone call, have another project at hand to work on in case you are kept waiting.

DO'S AND DON'TS

✔ Do introduce yourself. "This is Brian Smith. I'm calling about...".

✔ Do be aware of the amount of time you spend on each call.

✔ Do be clear about the points you want to discuss every time you make a call.

✔ Do leave short, concise messages on answering machines.

✘ Don't start a call with "Hello" and expect to be recognized.

✘ Don't put off urgent, difficult calls to deal with easier and less important ones.

✘ Don't continue a call if you have a bad line. Hang up and call back.

✘ Don't make important calls unless you are fully prepared.

CHOOSING A TELEPHONE TO SUIT YOUR NEEDS

Telephones now have a tremendous range of optional extras; look into the choices to see whether they can be used to help you work any more efficiently. Facilities available include call forwarding, speed-dialing, desk speakers, conference lines, and small screens that show an incoming caller's number and name before you pick up the receiver. There is no point, however, in having a host of buttons and features that you do not use. Choose a telephone system with features that you actually do need.

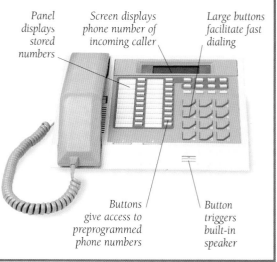

Panel displays stored numbers

Screen displays phone number of incoming caller

Large buttons facilitate fast dialing

Buttons give access to preprogrammed phone numbers

Button triggers built-in speaker

TAKING PHONE CALLS

Receiving phone calls is very different from making calls. Incoming calls can take you by surprise and interrupt you when you are unprepared. Develop techniques to reduce the time wasted and enable you to deal with callers when you choose to do so.

 62 Tell people when they can call you, and note the time in your diary.

POINTS TO REMEMBER

- It is easy to decide if a person should call back by making your first question "How long is this conversation likely to take?"

- People you would like to call back should be asked to do so at a time that is convenient to you.

- It is not impolite to take an easy way out. "Is this an inconvenient time?" invites the answer "Yes."

- A direct line enables you to give your number to those you want to reach you at once; you can divert other calls.

MAKING TIME FOR CALLS

Phone callers have the upper hand in deciding when they want to make a call, but modern technology is shifting the balance of power between caller and called. To some extent you can now dictate the time when you receive calls, enabling you to arrange your working day as you prefer. If you have an answering machine or voice-mail system, leave a short message on it saying when you will be in your office and that callers should call back at that time. If you have a secretary, route all your calls via him or her, with instructions regarding to whom you wish to speak and when it would be most convenient.

SIGNALING THE END OF A PHONE CALL

It can be difficult to end a phone conversation initiated by somebody else, but do not assume that it is up to them to close. If you are too busy to talk, tell the caller just that, and explain your reasons politely. Try one of the following phrases:

66 *Is there anything else we need to discuss before I go?* 99

66 *I have a call on my other line. Is it okay to call you back another time?* 99

66 *Perhaps we can discuss this further next time we speak.* 99

66 *I must go. My boss is signaling to me to join her from the other end of the room.* 99

DEALING WITH COLD CALLERS

If you have secretarial staff, brief them not to transfer cold callers through to you. If a persistent caller does succeed in getting through, politely but firmly inform him or her that you are not interested in what they are offering. Remember that, however annoying it may be to have interruptions from cold callers, they are only doing their job, and you should always treat them courteously.

DO'S AND DON'TS

✔ Do be polite.

✔ Do keep an open mind. Cold callers may have information that is useful to you.

✔ Do suggest someone who may be interested in the product or proposal being offered.

✔ Do get a phone that shows a caller's number as they call. If you do not know the number, you need not take the call.

✘ Don't ask cold callers to call back. They will, and it may be at a less convenient time.

✘ Don't say you will call back if you have no intention of doing so.

✘ Don't ask a caller to send details unless you are genuinely interested.

✘ Don't answer questions with long rambling sentences. Keep to the point.

RECORDING MESSAGES

Use a recorded message on your answering machine or voice-mail system to influence the replies you receive. A crisp, brief message invites a crisp, brief reply. If your machine allows you to limit the lengths of incoming messages, use this feature to force callers to leave short messages. Messages will then take you less time to listen to, and this will free your time. Set aside a time each day to play back and make a note of all your messages.

63 Reroute your calls when you want to avoid interruptions.

▼ NOTING MESSAGES
Play back your messages, noting any action required. Add these tasks to your master list.

READING AND WRITING

Many people spend a significant proportion of their working lives reading and absorbing information, as well as providing it in the form of memos, letters, and reports. Learn how to cope with these well, and you will save a great deal of time.

 64 Never delay dealing with any written material – it will just mount up.

 65 Underline key phrases in reports you need to read.

 66 Skim the headlines in your daily newspaper.

LEARNING TO SKIM

Everybody wastes time reading sentences that link the important points made in text. Learn to skim from paragraph to paragraph, identifying the key words in each. Effective skimming requires practice. Start with a piece of text and read every word. As you go along, underline one key word in each paragraph, then go back over the text and see if you can reconstruct the sense from the key words you have chosen. Repeat on new pieces of text until eventually you can identify key words quickly and easily.

ASSESSING MATERIAL

When reading reports and articles, try to get an overview of their contents first. Read any introduction or summary, and take time to look at the list of contents. If you have a long report to read, start by glancing through it from beginning to end, noting the headings and the lengths of different sections. When you read the report in full – either immediately or later on – you will then find you have a good idea of its content and structure, helping you read it quickly and efficiently. The same also applies to newspapers and magazines. If you do not have enough time to read your daily paper, make a mental note of the main headlines and skim the digest section.

POINTS TO REMEMBER

- The main purpose when reading is to understand the material.
- Not everything can be understood fully after one read. It takes time to absorb a long list of points, so relevant documents must always be read carefully.
- Skimming is generally suitable for documents such as memos, not for more detailed material.
- Readers need to be led through a report, so directional signposts should be included.
- A document should always be written with the reader in mind.

COPING WITH WRITER'S BLOCK

If you have trouble starting to write, vary your approach until you find the system that works for you. A report does not need to be written in its final order, and may be less daunting if you divide it into small sections. Introductions and conclusions can be difficult, so try starting wherever inspiration strikes – the important thing is to get something down in writing from which to work. It is often easiest to "top and tail" a report after writing the main text.

FACING A ▶
BLANK SCREEN
Even experienced writers are sometimes at a loss for words. Instead of staring blankly at a screen, try writing the first thing that comes into your head – you may find that this unblocks your thoughts and allows your ideas to flow more freely.

DO'S AND DON'TS

✔ Do prepare an outline before you write.

✔ Do read your work as if it is new to you.

✔ Do keep in mind the point you are making while you write, and use clear language.

✘ Don't stare at a blank computer screen – write anything.

✘ Don't make your text too complex or too simple for your reader.

✘ Don't pad your work with irrelevant facts.

REDUCING PAPERWORK

To cut down on the amount of writing you need to do, learn to deal effectively with incoming correspondence such as memos and faxes. Your response may merit a lengthy reply, but it may be more appropriate to add a quick, handwritten note on the original before passing it on; this is much quicker and saves on paper. Delegate the opening of your mail to your assistant or a junior member of your team. Brief them about what they can deal with themselves and how to prioritize items for your attention. This way you can reduce the volume of paper that you handle yourself.

67 Keep essential reference material separate from your other documents and papers.

USING TECHNOLOGY

F*ew people today can make effective use of their time if they do not understand the basics of information technology (IT) – the convergence of telecommunications and computing. IT puts libraries in our offices and a postal service at our beck and call.*

68 Clear unwanted documents from your computer once a month.

69 Consider carefully your computing requirements.

▼ STORING INFORMATION
Keep your documents and folders well organized. If you do not, the desktop will become a mess of icons labeled with names that no longer mean anything to you. Take half an hour each month to go through your computer, keeping folders up to date and deleting things you no longer need.

FILING ON A COMPUTER
Design a system for storing information along the same lines as a filing system for paperwork. Create a method of classification that suits your business, and label your documents clearly and logically. Keep your data in documents stored in folders on a hard disk (the computer's memory) or on removable floppy disks (the equivalent of a series of filing cabinets). Electronic data can be corrupted by magnetic fields, and an electricity surge can result in the loss of data on a hard or floppy disk, so make a backup copy of important material on a separate disk and label it clearly.

BEFORE FILING

AFTER FILING — *Folder is labeled clearly*

budgets

letters

Folder is unlabeled

Randomly located document can accidentally be deleted

All related documents are grouped together in one folder

USING E-MAIL

There are two types of e-mail system: intranets within companies, used mainly to relay messages between colleagues, and Internet-based e-mail, which allows for international communication. E-mail is easy to use and can be a channel for more than just simple messages. You can send any document on a computer as an attachment to an e-mail, so you will not need to import or retype as long as the recipient has the right software to read it. Because of its immediacy, e-mail is an informal medium, and strict rules of grammar and formal written language tend not to be used. But remember that confidentiality is not guaranteed.

70 Keep your e-mail messages short, and address them accurately.

SEARCHING ON THE INTERNET

The Internet has a number of search engines – systems that enable you to search for information speedily. To ensure a successful search, carefully choose the keywords for which you ask the search engine to look. If you do not, you will be given an unmanageable number of references, many of which will be irrelevant. If your choice is too narrow, the search engine may not find anything.

**USING A ▶
WEB-SITE PAGE**
In Internet language, a Web page is what you see on a computer screen. A Web site may be elaborate and contain many pages and will usually provide links to many other related sites.

Internet address of Web-site page currently accessed

Icon for searching Internet

Icon for accessing e-mail service

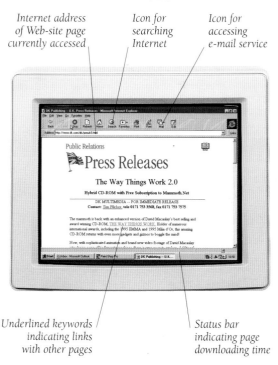

Underlined keywords indicating links with other pages

Status bar indicating page downloading time

HOLDING MEETINGS

Meetings consume a large proportion of the average working week. Typically, a manager spends up to half of each week in meetings. Making sure that meetings run smoothly and achieve their purpose is an essential ingredient of time management.

71 Encourage people to express views, even if they are contrary to yours.

72 Keep meetings short by listening rather than talking.

MEETING ONE TO ONE

One-to-one meetings are more flexible than large, formal gatherings, and their duration is more easily controlled. Nevertheless, you need to achieve a delicate balance between cutting a meeting too short, leaving the other person feeling frustrated, and allowing it to go on so long that both parties feel their time is being wasted.

ASSESSING STAFF ▼
Staff assessments are a sensitive example of one-to-one meetings. They should be of fixed duration and free from interruption to allow frank communication.

Manager talks encouragingly and directly

Subordinate responds in receptive and confident manner

Subordinate notes key points

TIMING SMALL MEETINGS

Some one-to-one meetings have a very specific purpose, such as recruitment or staff assessment, and in these cases there usually tends to be a well-understood format and duration. Less formal one-to-one meetings tend to be either short and focused, in response to a particular situation (such as a reprimand), or more general and of indefinite duration. In these latter cases, avoid unnecessary time-wasting for both parties by deciding informally on an agenda and time frame for the meeting beforehand. Be disciplined in adhering to it. This way, both parties' expectations of the meeting's purpose will be clarified, minimizing the need to spend time resolving misunderstandings afterward.

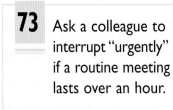

73 Ask a colleague to interrupt "urgently" if a routine meeting lasts over an hour.

▼ **REPRIMANDING STAFF**
Reprimands should be brief, without anger, and as close as possible to the offending event; try to ensure that the issue is dealt with and resolved in a single meeting. Use assertive body language to emphasize and reinforce your message.

Subordinate's head is tilted downward, but he maintains eye contact with manager

Manager assumes dominant position by standing and leaning across desk

PLANNING LARGE MEETINGS

Make sure that everybody attending a meeting knows its purpose and their roles in advance. Circulate an agenda well beforehand to tell participants which subjects are to be discussed. This will allow them to prepare any necessary information and gain an idea of the duration of the meeting. It will be easier for the chairperson to control time-wasting tactics if everybody is aware that the agenda must be covered within the set time limit. Your agenda will also help define the amount of time allocated to individual items.

 **74** Allocate a specific amount of time to each subject on an agenda.

75 Encourage people to attend only the parts of a meeting that concern them.

CULTURAL DIFFERENCES

Different cultures view meetings in different ways, so the handling of a meeting depends to some extent on the nationalities of those present. The Japanese consider it an insult if you appear alone at a meeting – they honor their hosts by appearing in numbers. In Arab countries, it is not usual to be told how long a meeting will last. It will finish when all the guests are ready to leave.

PREPARING AN AGENDA

The order in which items appear on an agenda can have a powerful effect on a meeting's timing. Avoid heading an agenda with a contentious subject, since the participants in the meeting may spend too much time discussing it instead of moving on to the next item. Instead, begin with routine and straightforward business, which offers easy decisions. This gives the meeting a feeling of achievement and the impetus to progress rapidly.

AVOIDING TIME-WASTING

Time-wasting in meetings costs more than just the participants' time; the monetary cost of a meeting may be considerable when the combined salaries of those present are taken into account. So it is imperative that time is not lost by people attending unnecessary meetings, by meetings being disrupted, or by meetings failing to achieve their objectives. Do not tolerate tactics such as lengthy, irrelevant speeches by fellow participants, or the endless revising of points. If you are the chairperson, it will be your role to recognize such tactics and ensure that the meeting is kept moving.

KEEPING TO SCHEDULE

Meetings should start punctually: begin without latecomers, and do not waste time recapping for them when they arrrive. Keep a careful track of time throughout a meeting to ensure the agenda is covered in the allotted time. In general, defer overrunning items until the end of the meeting so that other items can be dealt with on schedule.

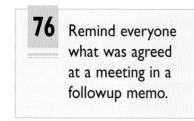

76 Remind everyone what was agreed at a meeting in a followup memo.

KEEPING A MEETING ON COURSE

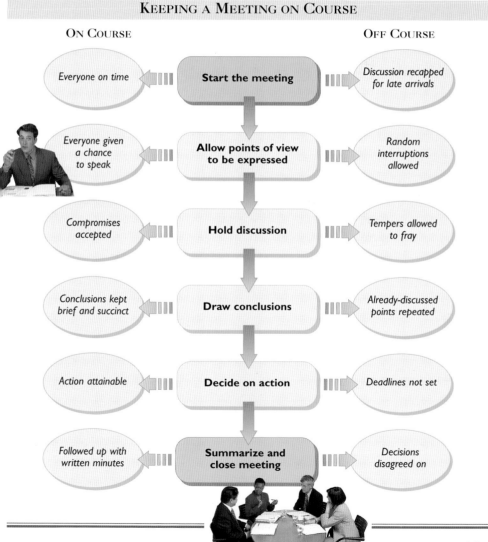

ON COURSE		OFF COURSE
Everyone on time	**Start the meeting**	Discussion recapped for late arrivals
Everyone given a chance to speak	**Allow points of view to be expressed**	Random interruptions allowed
Compromises accepted	**Hold discussion**	Tempers allowed to fray
Conclusions kept brief and succinct	**Draw conclusions**	Already-discussed points repeated
Action attainable	**Decide on action**	Deadlines not set
Followed up with written minutes	**Summarize and close meeting**	Decisions disagreed on

TRAVELING FOR WORK

With the development of the global marketplace, a growing number of people are finding that travel is an integral part of their job. Organizing business trips effectively is now an essential part of time management for many managers.

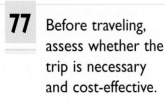

77 Before traveling, assess whether the trip is necessary and cost-effective.

78 If possible, fit everything you need to take into one small piece of hand luggage.

ASSESSING NEED

Before making plans to travel, ask yourself a number of questions about the trip. Am I making the best use of my time by going on this trip? Will a phone call or letter suffice instead? Can I send someone else? Can I persuade the people I need to see to come to me? Can I meet them half way? If the answer to any of these is yes, seriously question the time-effectiveness of your trip.

PACKING EFFICIENTLY

Effective packing requires you to make an accurate assessment of your needs based on the duration of your trip. For a short trip, take just enough clothing and accessories with you to cover the number of days you anticipate being away. This way you do not need to spend money on laundry services. However, if you are going to be away for more than a few days, it may be better to take only one or two changes of clothes and have them cleaned on the trip, rather than burdening yourself with heavy suitcases.

79 Take work to do in an airport lounge in case of delays.

▼ PACKING A BRIEFCASE

Be selective about what you take. Assess which documents and equipment you will need for any meetings you have planned and for staying in touch with your office.

Background material

Mobile phone eases contact with office

Diary contains detailed travel itinerary

Files necessary for trip

MANAGING YOUR TRAVEL TIME

BEFORE YOU TRAVEL

- Carefully plan your route and itinerary.
- Combine numerous visits within the same country or region if possible.
- Draw up a precise daily schedule. Leave a copy with colleagues at the office so that you can be contacted if necessary.
- Gather together all the documents you will need for your meetings while you are away.
- Always confirm arrangements before you set out in case a meeting needs to be rescheduled or is no longer necessary.
- Prepare a permanent general file containing essential information that you can use each time you visit a particular area.
- Reserve seats in advance when traveling by train so that you can avoid lines and arrive at the station just before the train departs.

WHILE YOU ARE AWAY

- Keep in touch with your office so that you can update them on your progress and keep abreast of any new developments that will affect your plans.
- Use a recorder for memos or notes, or use a laptop for e-mails or other work that can be done on-screen.
- Use your own alarm clock as a backup in case the wakeup-call service in your hotel proves to be unreliable.
- At your destination, travel at off-peak times if possible; it is less stressful – and may be quicker – than battling through the rush-hour commuters.
- Combine meals with business meetings to save time and create a more informal and congenial working atmosphere.

COPING WITH JET LAG

Your daily life is governed by an internal body clock that regulates sleep patterns. Jet lag occurs when you travel through different time zones and disrupt this clock. If you are traveling to a time zone with a 2- or 3- hour difference from your own, try going to bed when it is time to sleep at your destination on the day before you travel. This allows your body to adopt the new sleep pattern. For places with a larger time difference, ensure you are well rested before you travel and allow rest time upon arrival.

80 Set your watch to the local time at your destination.

◀ **TRAVEL LIGHT**
Today's bags and suitcases are better designed and more ergonomic than ever before. Use a bag with wheels to save lifting a heavy case. Carry a suit carrier and small wheeled bag onto a plane as hand luggage to save time on arrival at your destination.

Hard-cased wheeled bag

Suit carrier

STAYING IN TOUCH

While it is important to work out how you are going to keep in touch with your office when traveling, try to be realistic about it. There are many methods of communication you can use, with varying levels of complexity. Choose the method best suited to your needs. In some situations, your absence from work may cause practical difficulties. For example, your signature may be required to validate important documents. In such circumstances, it may be appropriate to use an overnight courier to get the documents to you and to take them back to the office.

POINTS TO REMEMBER

- A fax is faster than a mailed letter and often cheaper.
- Modems can be attached to portable computers, enabling you to send faxes or e-mail.
- Mobile telephones do not work in all parts of some countries.
- International call costs can vary, so options such as calling cards and pay phones should always be checked before any telephone calls are made from overseas.

COMMUNICATING WHILE TRAVELING

Communicating with colleagues at your office while on a business trip is now more convenient and reliable than ever. Use any one of the following methods according to your location and the type of communication you want to send or receive.

MOBILE ▶ PHONE
Most mobile phones now offer overseas communications. They are useful in areas where there are no public telephones.

▲ TELEPHONE
Leave a contact number with your office. Note that most hotels charge large premiums to use the phones in the rooms.

▲ FAX MACHINE
Send messages by fax if you want a fast reply. Some hotels have machines in their rooms or a central fax in reception.

◀ E-MAIL
Send documents and communications that need instant attention by e-mail. To access e-mail you will need a computer set up with a modem link.

◀ MAIL
Use guaranteed delivery services for sending original documents or those that require a signature. Air mail can be used for less urgent items.

KEEPING ON TOP OF WORK

Before you travel, draw up a schedule that utilizes your time to the optimum; this will minimize the time you are away and reduce the cost of the trip. Many people think that they can carry on with their normal job while on a business trip, but this is not possible in the majority of cases – nor is it always necessary. Ensure that your business trip has a specific purpose, and keep free time to a minimum. Use any time you have available to concentrate on the purpose of your trip.

81 Check how much your hotel charges for phone calls before making any.

82 Find out whether you need adapters for your electrical equipment abroad.

UPDATING YOUR NOTES

Most of your time on business trips will be spent attending meetings; the longer the trip, the more meetings you will attend. It is crucial to update your notes every day; otherwise, all your meetings will have merged into each other by the time you return to your office, and you will not be able to recall who agreed to what and when. Allow time each day to write up the day's meetings, noting any decisions made and action to be taken.

◀ **WORKING IN YOUR ROOM**
Take advantage of the peace and quiet of a hotel room to write up the day's events and prepare for the next day's meetings. Use a laptop computer to record the proceedings and results of your meetings and to correspond with your office. As an alternative, have the details of your your meetings typed up and sent back to your office electronically by hotel business center staff.

SCHEDULING TIME OFF

Managing your time successfully involves more than just organizing your workload. Work will suffer if you do not schedule regular breaks to recharge your batteries. Try to make time for family and friends, hobbies, and leisure activities.

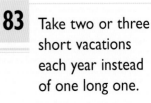

83 Take two or three short vacations each year instead of one long one.

TAKING DAILY BREAKS

Some business leaders include a regular period in their day when they briefly take time off. Similar to the siesta, it is often taken after lunch. Their doors are closed to interruptions, allowing them to take a short period of semisleep (only about 10 minutes), which has a recuperative effect on the body. Schedule a set time each day to switch off; pick a quiet period that fits in with your personal energy rhythm and work obligations. With practice, you will be able to reduce this rest time.

It can be difficult to find a suitable place to take such a break. Open-plan offices lack privacy and are noisy, making it difficult to relax. Try to find a vacant room or office away from all disturbances.

84 Schedule regular time off to pursue your hobbies and leisure interests.

◀ **TAKING TIME FOR YOURSELF**
Do not rush straight back to work after a hectic meeting – take a break in a café or go for a walk. Time out will allow you to clear your head and restore your energy.

Recharging Batteries

To recharge your batteries you must lead a well-balanced life and take time off. Spend this time with family and friends, exercise regularly, eat properly, learn new things, and take vacations. If you do not have school-age children, plan breaks to coincide with quiet periods at work. Off-season vacations can also provide relaxation, since destinations are less crowded.

▲ GETTING AWAY

A change of scenery can provide a breathing space from work and help you relax. Vacationing with your family or friends allows you to take a break from the pressures of your daily routine. Even a short break away can be beneficial.

Planning Ahead

Good time management means planning ahead. Scheduling vacations in advance allows you to organize your workload around your breaks. At the start of each year, take the time and effort to organize your diary. Work out when you are likely to be busy and when your workload will be lightest. Look ahead at the year as a whole, and plan your vacations accordingly. Ask everybody in your office to do the same with their own schedules, and you will soon be able to see if any conflicts of time are going to arise.

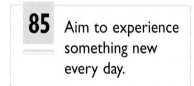

85 Aim to experience something new every day.

▼ ORGANIZING TIME OFF

Estimate the time needed to complete your work commitments over the year, and block it out on a wall chart. You will then be able to assess the best times to take vacations.

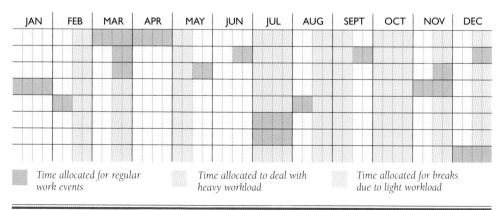

JAN	FEB	MAR	APR	MAY	JUN	JUL	AUG	SEPT	OCT	NOV	DEC

Time allocated for regular work events	Time allocated to deal with heavy workload	Time allocated for breaks due to light workload

Managing the Time of Others

To make the best use of your time, you also need to manage that of your staff, colleagues, and seniors. Learn to delegate well, share tasks, and manage upward as well as down.

Communicating Well

To manage others so that you all make the best use of available time, you first need to master the art of communication. This is not just a matter of deciding what your message is; it is also about deciding how to communicate that message.

 86 Maintain high expectations, and people will live up to them.

Cultural Differences

Hierarchy is deeply embedded in the cultures of most Eastern countries, and age still matters. If you are a young manager, do not expect to be listened to in China, for instance. Deference will be awarded to a consultant with gray hair, even if you both give exactly the same message.

Spreading Information

Today, companies are evolving in a way that makes it easier for the people within them to communicate with each other. A gradual cultural change has meant that organizations are more open. You can use this new openness to save time, for example by spreading information verbally rather than writing a memo. Spoken communication has the added advantage of being two-way, encouraging the involvement of staff and allowing refinement of detail. But any important points covered verbally should also be noted in writing to minimize later uncertainties.

REVISING METHODS

Intranets and e-mail systems allow rapid, widespread dissemination of information. They can also make working at home without losing touch with colleagues a more practical and attractive option than it used to be. However, beware of information overload: the volume of data may make what is effectively junk e-mail seem more important than it is, and the ease of electronic communication can make it tempting to send messages that are not strictly necessary. Remember, too, that as organizations become less hierarchical and lines of communication open out, recipients may lack necessary background information, so always be clear and precise to avoid time-wasting misunderstandings.

87 Persuade others of your case using facts, not emotions.

88 Take an interest in what others are trying to achieve.

▶ **ANALYZING INFORMATION FLOW**
Certain communication lines in any organization are better developed than others. For instance, sales staff spend more time in contact with the production department than with colleagues in administration.

KEY

◀▬▬▶ *Communicates frequently*

◀▬▬▶ *Communicates occasionally*

◀▬▶ *Communicates rarely*

89 Hearing is not the same as listening. Learn to listen.

SALES
DIRECTOR

ACCOUNTS
MANAGER

PRODUCTION
MANAGER

SALES
MANAGER

ACCOUNTS
ASSISTANT

PRODUCTION
ASSISTANT

SALES
REPRESENTATIVE

DELEGATING EFFECTIVELY

One of the keys to effective management is delegating work to others – no one can do everything for themselves. Learn to delegate aspects of your work properly, and you will have time to complete the most important elements of your job successfully.

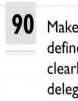
90 Make sure you define objectives clearly when you delegate a task.

91 Reserve some time for the tasks that you alone can do.

POINTS TO REMEMBER

- When you delegate, you are not delegating the right to perform an action, you are delegating the right to make decisions.

- It is important to be flexible; the person to whom you delegate may have a better and faster way of completing a job than you.

- A brief can be misinterpreted, so it is a good idea to ask for it to be repeated back to you.

- Overall responsibility for a delegated task remains with you.

- It is helpful to others if you can provide constructive feedback on their performance.

- Too much criticism is far more harmful than too much praise.

LEARNING TO DELEGATE

The process of delegation consists of the decision to delegate, the briefing, and the followup. At each of these points, anticipate the potential problems.

- The decision: persuade yourself to delegate. You will not benefit if you work to the assumption that it takes longer to teach somebody else to do a job than to do it yourself. Delegation has its own rewards – once someone has learned a particular task, they will be able to do it in the future without repeated briefings. However, be sure to delegate each job to a person with the appropriate skills and knowledge.

- The briefing: make sure that the person to whom you are delegating clearly understands the brief – what you want them to do and by when. Offer ongoing support and guidance.

- The followup: during the course of the project, check the standard of work produced. Provide positive feedback, but beware of overdoing it – there is a narrow line between helpful supervision and debilitating interference.

92 Keep a checklist to help you monitor the progress of tasks that you have delegated to others.

REINFORCING A BRIEF

In addition to providing a clear brief when delegating, you must provide all the information necessary for someone to complete the task successfully. To avoid any misinterpretation of the facts, take time to explain exactly what you expect and how the project fits into your overall plan. Discuss any difficulties that may occur and how they could be tackled, and answer queries as they arise during completion of the task.

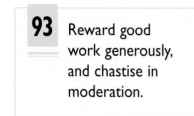

93 Reward good work generously, and chastise in moderation.

94 Set precise and realistic deadlines for tasks that you delegate.

STRENGTHENING RESPONSIBILITY

Delegation does not mean handing over control of a project, but handing over responsibility for certain tasks. Encourage individuals to work using their own methods, providing they stick to the brief. This allows you to exploit their specialized knowledge or to provide them with an opportunity to develop a new area of expertise. One of the common contentions arising out of delegation is conflict over responsibility, so it is vital to define exactly what the delegate is responsible for.

DELEGATING CHOICES

Someone who has done similar work	⇦ **Delegate to whom?** ⇨	A novice
By memo, fax, or e-mail	⇦ **How to brief?** ⇨	By meeting face to face
As and when needed	⇦ **How to check progress?** ⇨	Daily

MANAGING COLLEAGUES

One of the most difficult things to get right is managing interruptions from colleagues. Either you become too available to each other, in which case you lose control of your time, or you are too distant and fail to take advantage of each other's abilities.

 95 Try not to allow colleagues to distract you with unimportant issues.

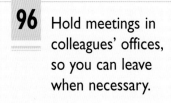 **96** Hold meetings in colleagues' offices, so you can leave when necessary.

WORKING TOGETHER

Traditional corporate hierarchies are gradually being flattened, and more tasks are now being assigned to teams designed and brought together for single projects. This means that you need to be able to work side by side with a variety of individuals and find ways of agreeing with them about work priorities and time management.

SHARING YOUR TIME-MANAGEMENT SKILLS

TASKS	WAYS TO SHARE SKILLS
PRIORITIZING WORK	● Talk through the principles of dividing work into A-, B-, and C-tasks and allocating a set number of each to do every day. ● Use examples from your colleagues' workload.
USING DIARIES AND PLANNERS	● Ask your colleagues to keep a time log, then review and analyze it with them to discover their various working patterns. ● Help your colleagues set up an appropriate planning system.
FILTERING INFORMATION	● Encourage your colleagues to assess every item of information they receive to decide what action is required. ● Provide hints on faster reading based on your own experience.
DELEGATING AND FOLLOWING UP	● Discuss specific, related examples from the past to determine the best course of action in this instance. ● Be prepared to review any new systems that are set up.

FOCUSING ON OBJECTIVES

A good time-saving habit for you and your colleagues to get into is always to ask yourselves what you expect when you meet to discuss an issue. There is a useful mnemonic – AID – that helps in classifying the options available to you. Is it Advice you need from each other, is it Information, or is it a Decision? At the beginning of each discussion, indicate exactly what you are expecting from each other and you will all be more aware of the demands that the exchange will make on your time. You can also use the AID technique to help you decide how to respond to colleagues seeking your attention.

USING AID OPTIONS

ADVICE
If you are going to give advice to a colleague, make sure that you do it when you have plenty of time available. It is best to give advice only when you are not in a hurry.

INFORMATION
Dispensing information is a one-way process – in most cases it does not require any feedback. Set aside a short amount of time in your day for giving out information.

DECISION
Reaching a decision may well take some considerable time. It is important that you do not allow yourself to be hurried into an overhasty decision by an anxious colleague.

ENCOURAGING OPINIONS

The unique thing about most colleagues is that they can give you dispassionate, on-the-job feedback, which you often cannot get from further up or lower down the organizational hierarchy. Unlike colleagues, seniors and subordinates may think too much in terms of job assessments.

Encourage your colleagues to give you their opinions of your performance. They may raise some helpful points that will save you time in the future. For example, they may let you know that your meetings last too long or are disorganized, or that you appear to be inaccessible to others when they need you. Listen to their advice, and adopt any useful time-saving techniques.

97 Set aside special times when your office is open to all.

98 Visit colleagues only when you have more than one issue to discuss.

MANAGING YOUR MANAGER

Everyone should know how to manage their managers if they want to be able to make the best possible use of their own time. Learn to do this discreetly so that your seniors do not feel as though they are being undermined or manipulated.

99 Be aware of your boss's working patterns, and try to adapt to them.

100 Ask about your boss's home life – it will help build up a relationship.

BUILDING A RELATIONSHIP

The first thing you need to know is exactly what your manager expects of you. Do you have the sort of manager who delegates a task to you and then gives you the freedom to get on with it, or are you expected to report back every day and to wait around until they are free to hear you? Discuss this matter tactfully with your manager early on. That way you can tailor the way you work to fit in with your boss's expectations.

If you decide you would like more autonomy, persuade your seniors to trust you by establishing a strong relationship with them. When you have a good relationship with your manager, you can be less formal; communication becomes easier, more direct, and therefore more efficient.

Bring more than one thing at a time to discuss with your boss

◀ **SORTING OUT QUESTIONS**
Take the initiative to arrange a time to see your manager, rather than waiting for your manager to see you. They may be so involved with their work that they do not realize that you need help from time to time.

COMMUNICATING EFFICIENTLY

In any relationship with your seniors, there is an implicit assumption that they are busier than you and that the claims on their time are more pressing than the claims on yours. When you have something to discuss, make your communication brief. Get to the point quickly, and try to anticipate any queries that your seniors may raise. Keep your conversations high on factual content and low on your personal opinions.

DO'S AND DON'TS

✔ Do arrive at meetings well prepared and with any relevant documentation.

✔ Do take relevant notes, and give your boss a copy.

✔ Gather questions up to avoid constantly interrupting your manager.

✔ Do work out whether your manager prefers written or spoken information, and supply it in that way.

✘ Don't volunteer your opinions unless they are requested or you feel they are important or relevant.

✘ Don't present any problems without offering some viable solutions to them.

✘ Don't be late for meetings with your manager.

✘ Don't mistake your boss's occasional thoughtless action for maliciousness.

GETTING YOUR OWN WAY

As you build up a personal relationship with your manager, you will learn what it takes to get your own way – and thus work more efficiently and with a greater amount of satisfaction. Of course, the priorities of your manager will alter all the time (as will your own), and it is your job to keep abreast of those changes and adapt sensitively to fluctuating demands. Remember that there is little to be gained in being abrasive toward your seniors. This will simply irritate them, making them feel defensive, less willing to listen to you, and unsympathetic to your viewpoint. Try to be aware of the pressures that your manager is under, and be sympathetic.

101 Remember that time is perfectly democratic. Nobody has more or less of it than you.

KNOWING WHEN TO OFFER ADVICE

It is a useful tool to think of communication with your manager in terms of the AID acronym: Advice, Information, and Decision. Offer your boss advice either when it is asked for or when you feel it would be welcomed. However, you should give relevant or important information without constraint. It is often possible to influence your boss to make a different decision to the one he or she was going to make. Remember, though, that there may be reasons behind a decision of which you are unaware.

MAKING DECISIONS

INTRODUCTION

Decisions are an essential part of life – in and out of a work environment. Decision makers are those who are responsible for making a judgment – sometimes a crucial judgment – between two or more alternatives. This section of the book takes you through the whole process of making good, effective decisions, from initial deliberation to final implementation. It is suitable for anyone making work-related choices, whether they are new to decision-making or are seasoned managers. Information is provided on generating ideas, forecasting, assessing risks, and dealing with personnel issues. The section includes a self-assessment exercise, which allows you to judge your own decision-making abilities, and has 101 practical tips containing further vital information.

ANALYZING DECISION-MAKING

Part of a manager's role is needing to make a series of large and small decisions. Reaching the right decision in every situation is an ambition that is well worth striving to achieve.

DEFINING DECISIONS

A decision is a judgment or choice between two or more alternatives, and arises in an infinite number of situations, from the resolution of a problem to the implementation of a course of action. Managers of people, by definition, must be decision makers.

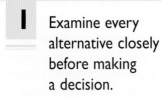

1 Examine every alternative closely before making a decision.

2 If you find that previous decisions are still workable, make use of them.

WHO MAKES DECISIONS?

A decision is a choice between a variety of alternatives, and a decision maker is whoever makes such a choice. A decision can be made instantly but more often involves the decision maker in a process of identification, analysis, assessment, choice, and planning. To arrive at a decision, a manager must define the purpose of the action, list the options available, choose between the options, and then turn that choice into action. Decisions and the process of decision-making are fundamental to all management processes – just as they are to everyday life.

CATEGORIZING DECISIONS

The various types of decision a manager has to make include routine, emergency, strategic, and operational. Many decisions are routine: the same circumstances recur, and when they arise you choose a proven course of action. Some situations, however, are without precedent – you make the decision on the spot as events unfold. This is emergency decision-making and can take up most of a manager's time. The most demanding form of decision-making involves strategic choices; deciding on aims and objectives, and converting these into specific plans, or subdecisions, is a manager's most important task. Operational decisions, especially those concerned with "people problems" (including hiring and firing), require particularly sensitive handling.

3 Make long-term decisions with the short term in mind.

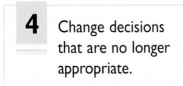

4 Change decisions that are no longer appropriate.

▼ **REACHING DECISIONS BY CONSENSUS**
Discussing a problem with colleagues is often the best way to move toward a decision. When people get together, they often come up with unexpected solutions.

Colleague's contribution adds to creative process

Manager explains alternative solutions

Colleague pays close attention to proceedings

BREAKING DOWN THE PROCESS

Reaching a decision involves a methodical thought process. The first step is to identify the exact issue that is being tackled, and to prioritize objectives. An analysis of the situation will reveal those options that are impossible or impractical to implement, leaving a manageable range of alternatives for more detailed assessment. At this stage – if not earlier – others' views may be enlisted. The advantages and disadvantages of each course of action should be carefully evaluated, always keeping the ultimate goal in the forefront. Finally, a plan can be devised to show exactly how the decision will be carried out.

ANALYZING THE DECISION PROCESS

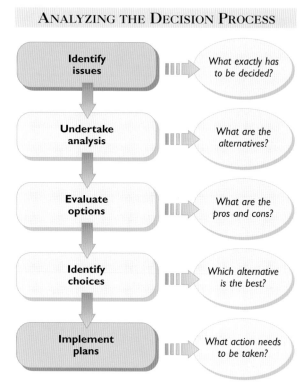

Identify issues	What exactly has to be decided?
Undertake analysis	What are the alternatives?
Evaluate options	What are the pros and cons?
Identify choices	Which alternative is the best?
Implement plans	What action needs to be taken?

5 Consider the implications of each decision – they can be huge.

6 Try to foresee and prepare for any changes in a situation.

COMPARING SOLUTIONS

Most decision-making involves problem-solving, and managers arrive at their answers in a wide variety of ways. For example, there might be a clear and correct answer (based on facts and figures); there might be an insight that feels right (based on experience); there might be a solution that you need to test by carrying it out (or carrying out a simulation of it); there might be a solution that works in the short term but not in the long term (such as throwing money at a scheduling problem); or there might be a fuzzy solution – one that seems to work but does not have clear boundaries (such as launching a new product and waiting to see if it changes the parameters of the marketplace).

7 Always ask what can go wrong when you are making a decision.

UNDERSTANDING RISKS

Most decisions involve an element of risk, though some are less risky than others. Sometimes, even when theoretical options exist, their disadvantages are so great that there is no real alternative. This may arise from a bad original decision. For example, an organization has overstretched itself financially by deciding to invest in a new factory. It could decide to halt the project, but only at the risk of immediate financial collapse. That may be averted if the new plant eventually meets its targets. Therefore, to retreat is riskier than to proceed. Also, remember to watch for side effects. Cutting staff may seem a safe decision, but not if it risks deterioration in customer service.

EVALUATING SOLUTIONS

Sometimes the risks involved in a decision can be reduced by testing, either in the marketplace or by simulation. For example, if a new product on the market has a problem – such as if it has missed its target and is losing money – you can look at some possible solutions and simulate the financial outcome of each:

- Closing production down at once to prevent further financial loss;
- Carrying on marketing the product with renewed vigor but along the same lines;
- Replacing the management team and having the new team review the marketing campaigns;
- Redesigning the product and starting the campaign again from scratch;
- Selling the product to another company and developing a new product.

The correct decision in any case must be the one that offers the best prospects for the long-term future, because long-term success is naturally the ultimate aim of any manager.

QUESTIONS TO ASK YOURSELF

Q What are our short- and long-term objectives?

Q Will we make money with this product/service/idea?

Q How much energy do we need to put into marketing?

Q Do we need to recruit new people?

Q What happens if the marketplace changes?

Q What are our worst-case scenarios, and how would we deal with them?

8 Always consider all the possible outcomes when making a decision.

IDENTIFYING DECISION-MAKING STYLES

People have individual styles of making decisions. Whether your style is logical or creative, your method should also be rational and straightforward. Good decision makers do not allow personality to control the decision process or its outcome.

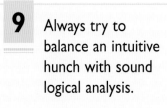

9 Always try to balance an intuitive hunch with sound logical analysis.

10 Assess your decision-making abilities, and strive to improve them.

ASSESSING THE ▼ THINKING PROCESS
Whether the intuitive or rational side of your brain dominates your thinking processes, both can contribute to forming a balanced picture.

USING HUNCH AND LOGIC

One side of the brain is believed to be the location of emotion, imagination, intuition, and creativity; the other is the site of logic, language, math, and analysis. Though people tend to have a dominant side, this does not mean that decision makers fall into two separate categories: the intuitive decision maker deciding creatively and spontaneously, versus the logical decision maker working rationally on fact-based judgment. Whichever side your natural decision-making style leans toward, always aim to achieve a balance between both sets of faculties.

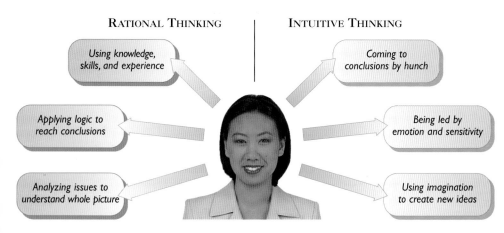

RATIONAL THINKING

Using knowledge, skills, and experience

Applying logic to reach conclusions

Analyzing issues to understand whole picture

INTUITIVE THINKING

Coming to conclusions by hunch

Being led by emotion and sensitivity

Using imagination to create new ideas

TAKING RISKS

Risk-taking is not just for the intuitive – any decision with an uncertain outcome involves some element of risk, and even people who are totally logical in their thinking take risks. Much of the difference between the two methods of reaching a decision lies in the mental approach: intuitive thinkers back an option that they are convinced is a certainty, although it may seem to others to be a long shot, while logical thinkers calculate all the odds and only then make their decision to go for the best option. Either way, seek to minimize the degree of risk involved.

BEING SYSTEMATIC

Whatever your decision-making style, there are advantages in being systematic. Systematic methods of reaching a decision ensure that all the correct issues are addressed: necessary information is gathered, all alternatives are properly considered and compared, difficulties are identified and feasibility assessed, and consequences are taken fully into account. A systematic approach enables you to prepare a logical and effective plan of action so that your decision process can be explained clearly to any colleagues or clients who are affected.

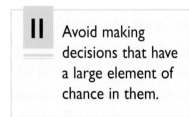

11 Avoid making decisions that have a large element of chance in them.

12 Follow a precedent when it works – but not when it doesn't.

REVIEWING PRECEDENTS

People often repeat what has previously worked well. This can lead to very good performance, since repetition improves effectiveness. At some point, however, needs may change, and a previously correct decision becomes wrong or less appropriate. The antidote is to approach your decision like a first-time choice. What would a newcomer decide? If, after putting yourself in this position, it feels wrong to follow precedent, it is probably time to innovate.

KNOWING YOUR CORPORATE CULTURE

A powerful ingredient in decision-making is the corporate culture of your organization. This affects the issues and options available to you when making a decision. Learn what is acceptable to your organization and what is always ruled out.

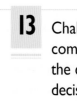

13 Challenge the company culture in the cause of good decision-making.

14 Make sure that you are known for coming up with good, creative, innovative ideas.

ANALYZING DIFFERENT CORPORATE STYLES

Decisions are affected by, and impact on, the surrounding organization. If your corporate culture is authoritarian and conformist, you are probably bound by bureaucracy, and your ability to make dynamic decisions will be restricted. In contrast, an innovative and progressive company will expect you to be more adventurous, making decisions on your own initiative. With companies that alternate between being risk-averse and ambitious, try to sense the prevailing climate and act accordingly.

OVERCOMING RESISTANCE

The artful decision maker learns to manipulate the system when necessary. For example, the risk-taking organization's bold decisions may have to be curbed if they outrun the available resources, and the risk-averse company may sometimes need to be coaxed into taking unprecedented action in order to stay ahead of the competition. In either case, try to identify the levers of power and influence and form firm alliances with those individuals who are best placed to overcome the various obstacles you may encounter.

15 Marry intellect with intuition in decision-making.

16 Be aware of the politics behind decision-making.

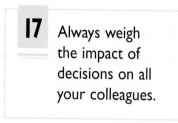

17 Always weigh the impact of decisions on all your colleagues.

◀ **ENCOURAGING CREATIVITY**
Creativity flourishes and individuals use their initiative confidently in an atmosphere of equality, where team spirit exists between staff at all levels.

WHAT CULTURE DOMINATES YOUR ORGANIZATION?

To assess whether your organization tends to be risk-averse or adventurous or is a mixture of the two – overcautious some of the time and overconfident the rest – read through the statements in the columns below and see which of them best fit the company culture.

RISK-AVERSE:
- New ideas are often dismissed.
- The organization is not always driven by external needs.
- The emphasis within the organization is on dealing with problems.
- Stability and experience are the most valued attributes of the organization.
- The good of the company is put before the success of the individual.
- Command and control appear to be the dominant processes.
- It is almost impossible to change the corporate mind-set.

If you agree with most of the definitions above, your company is definitely averse to taking risks. Decisions involving new ideas and technologies are not welcomed readily.

ADVENTUROUS:
- New and creative ideas are welcomed.
- The organization focuses mainly on the needs of the customer.
- The corporate emphasis is on taking advantage of new opportunities.
- Motivation and innovation are among the most valued characteristics.
- Corporate and individual aims are largely aligned.
- All staff are allowed autonomy and are able to show their initiative.
- Minds and policies are frequently changed, according to circumstances.

If you agree with most of the definitions above, your company is forward-thinking, not afraid of change, and happy to accept bold decisions that create success.

ANALYZING YOUR RESPONSIBILITY

Top-down decision-making leads to the delegation of work to subordinate levels. This is natural in hierarchies, but you must decide which decisions to make yourself and which to delegate to others. The best decision makers share responsibility widely.

18 Avoid clinging possessively to a decision that you have delegated.

19 Always give your reasons if rejecting a decision made by a delegate.

MAKING YOUR OWN DECISIONS

It is up to you to decide which decisions are yours alone. Assess what decisions your subordinates are capable of making. If the answer is none, either your assessment of the situation or your initial recruitment must be at fault. Assess which aspects of your role have the greatest impact on outcomes. Retain decisions concerned with these aspects yourself and delegate the rest. Retaining a decision does not mean monopolizing the process – allow your delegates to participate in the decision-making while accepting that you have the final choice.

DELEGATING DECISIONS

Remember that you remain responsible for the decisions you delegate, so oversee the delegation, particularly in sensitive areas. Use that overview for coaching and monitoring; try to build up the confidence of the people you delegate to, maintain a two-way flow of information, and encourage people to develop their own initiative. Do not second-guess or countermand unless absolutely necessary. If you are occasionally forced to reject a decision, explain why in detail.

20 Build up your trust in the ability of other people to make decisions.

PUSHING DECISIONS DOWN

When analyzing responsibilities, it is clear that those closest to the point of action should also make the decisions. For example, mortgage applications are best approved at branch level, plant modifications are best decided on the factory floor, recruitment is best done by those with whom the recruit will work, and so on. Information at the sharp end is likely to be specific and up-to-date. Those who have to live with decisions should participate in them. Sending decisions upward causes delays – the more hierarchical layers there are, the greater the delays. Pushing decisions down pays off in speed and efficiency. Though delegates need to be monitored, they will soon grow into their roles.

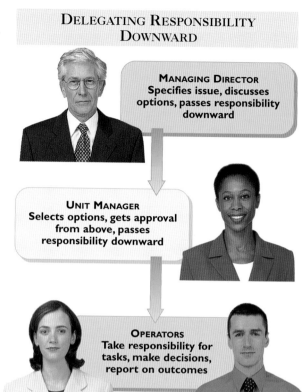

DELEGATING RESPONSIBILITY DOWNWARD

MANAGING DIRECTOR
Specifies issue, discusses options, passes responsibility downward

UNIT MANAGER
Selects options, gets approval from above, passes responsibility downward

OPERATORS
Take responsibility for tasks, make decisions, report on outcomes

LETTING PEOPLE ▶ MAKE DECISIONS

In this example, people were delegated to make decisions, initiated action, and implemented their decisions. Things became unworkable in the face of unhelpful interference from others. Given permission to handle their own decisions once again, the team moved ahead successfully.

CASE STUDY

John, an engineering boss, sent a shop-floor team to one of his competitors to see what improvements could be made to part of his operation. The team came back enthusiastic about several innovations and was told to go ahead with decisions on changes required to improve productivity and then to implement them.

Performance began to deteriorate immediately, and a subsequent investigation revealed that managers and senior engineers, hearing about the changes, had descended on the unit, second-guessing decisions that had been made by the shop-floor team.

John was incensed and ordered everybody to stay away from the operation. The shop-floor team was allowed to implement its original decisions, the decline in production was reversed, and the promised gains in productivity were achieved.

BEING DECISIVE

The ability to make timely, clear, and firm decisions is an essential quality of leadership. But the type of decision needed will vary according to the circumstances. As a manager, you need to recognize the implications of making different decisions.

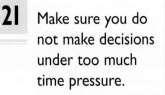

21 Make sure you do not make decisions under too much time pressure.

BEING POSITIVE

Taking decisive action does not mean making decisions on the spur of the moment. Although that may sometimes be necessary in emergencies, and occasionally desirable for other reasons – for example, if the right decision is obvious – the correct definition of "decisive" in this context is "positive." The true leader must approach decisions confidently, being aware of what must be taken into account and fully in command of the decision-making process. Understand what kind of decision is required from you, and do not be afraid to change the decision if circumstances subsequently alter.

Decision maker assesses all his options

▲ **TAKING YOUR TIME**
Do not make a decision immediately unless the solution is obvious. Study all the options open to you and weigh up all the pros and cons.

22 If and when decisions misfire, take fast action.

23 Never postpone vital decisions – make them quickly.

MAKING FAST DECISIONS

It often seems that the most important aspect of a decision is whether it can be made quickly or whether it can wait. For example, if a customer demands an instant discount, you have to decide on the spot whether it is worth conceding for future goodwill. On the other hand, if you are considering a program of price cuts, you can offer discounts to valued customers in a more considered way. Good decision makers often make instant decisions – but they then assess the long-term implications.

TYPES OF DECISION-MAKING

CHARACTERISTICS	IMPLICATIONS
IRREVERSIBLE The decision, once made, cannot be unmade – such as when signing an agreement to sell or buy a company.	● Commits you irrevocably when there is no other satisfactory option to the chosen course. ● Should never be used as an all-or-nothing instant escape from general indecision.
REVERSIBLE The decision can be changed completely – either before, during, or after the agreed action begins.	● Allows you to acknowledge a mistake early in the process rather than perpetuate it. ● Can be used when you see that circumstances may change, so that reversal may be necessary.
EXPERIMENTAL The decision is not final until the first results appear and prove themselves to be satisfactory.	● Requires positive feedback before you can decide on a course of action. ● Useful and effective when correct move is unclear but general direction of action is understood.
TRIAL-AND-ERROR Taken in knowledge that changes in plans will be forced by what actually happens in the course of action.	● Allows you to adapt and adjust plans continually before full and final commitment. ● Uses positive and negative feedback before you continue with a particular course of action.
MADE IN STAGES After the initial step, further decisions follow as each stage of agreed action is completed.	● Allows close monitoring of risks, as you accumulate evidence of outcomes and obstacles at every stage. ● Permits feedback and further discussion before the next stage of the decision is made.
CAUTIOUS Decision allows for contingencies and problems that may crop up later. Decision makers hedge their bets.	● Limits the risks inherent in decision-making, but also may limit the final gains. ● Allows you to scale down projects that look too risky in the first instance.
CONDITIONAL Decision altered if certain foreseen circumstances arise. An "either/or" decision, with options kept open.	● Prepares you to react if the competition makes a new move or if the game plan changes radically. ● Enables you to react quickly to the ever-changing circumstances of today's competitive markets.
DELAYED Put on hold until decision makers feel the time is right. Go-ahead given when required elements are in place.	● Prevents you from making a decision at the wrong time or before all the facts are known. ● May mean that you miss opportunities in the market that needed fast action.

Reaching a Decision

Mastering the processes and methods involved
in making decisions goes a long way toward maximizing
your effectiveness and efficiency as a manager.

Identifying Issues

*It is crucial to diagnose problems correctly.
Before any decision can be made, identify
and define the issue and its boundaries
clearly. This also means identifying who else
needs to be involved in the issue, and
analyzing what their involvement means.*

24 Approach different
types of decision
in different ways
for good results.

25 If you are having
problems making a
decision, change
your perspective.

Understanding Why a Decision Needs Making

Most managerial decisions are prompted by one
of four different types of event, each requiring a
particular decision-making style:

- Disturbances – manager decides on the best way
  to solve problems, emergencies, and upheavals;
- Opportunities – manager decides which new
  openings to pursue and how;
- Resource allocation – manager arbitrates in the
  distribution of money, personnel, or supplies;
- Negotiations – manager makes decisions as a
  representative of an organization or individuals.

QUESTIONS TO ASK YOURSELF

Q Have I looked at all the issues involved in the scenario?

Q Have I looked at problematical issues objectively?

Q Are my decisions approached rationally or emotionally?

Q Are my decisions suited to each individual issue?

Q Have I identified issues that tend to recur?

TACKLING WHOLE ISSUES

Decisions that tackle only one specific part of a problem tend to fail. Any decision affects a component or components in an entire business system. Consider whether the issue in question is company-wide or an isolated incident. For example, you can remove one difficult employee, but if the problem is caused by bad management or a bad recruitment policy, nothing has been truly resolved. Do some research; dig deep to find out why a decision is required. This establishes the correct boundaries – and leads to superior results.

CONSULTING OTHERS

In addition to identifying issues, as a decision maker you need to identify the individuals involved. List everybody who would be significantly affected by a decision, such as those in higher management with decision powers of their own; other departments whose work would be affected; and clients and suppliers. Assess who you need to consult to ensure support and goodwill. When you reach a decision, make sure that everybody on your list knows what you have decided and why, whether you have consulted them or not.

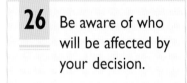

26 Be aware of who will be affected by your decision.

▼ INFORMING COLLEAGUES
Any workplace decision will affect other people in other parts of the organization. Ensure that departments are working together by keeping colleagues informed of proceedings.

IDENTIFYING A TIMESCALE

When you are making a decision, be aware of the timescale involved, but remember that the quality of thinking and execution, rather than the time available, must be the key factor. You should reach your decision without undue haste but also without unnecessary delays. The right time to make your decision is when all the information is in and all the issues have been addressed. Delay is beneficial only if you need to obtain more vital information or if circumstances change and issues have to be reassessed. Time pressure can, in fact, be helpful – it concentrates the mind, rules out procrastination, and reduces the number of alternatives that can be considered.

27 Once a decision is clear, make it quickly rather than slowly.

28 Avoid rushing an important decision just because others expect it.

▼ PARETO ANALYSIS

Applied to problem analysis, Pareto's law suggests 80 percent of a problem results from 20 percent of the factors involved (A), so 80 percent of the factors involved account for 20 percent of the problem (B).

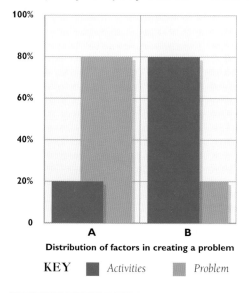

Distribution of factors in creating a problem

KEY ▮ *Activities* ▮ *Problem*

PRIORITIZING FACTORS

When making a decision, prioritize significant factors. Common sense suggests that some factors in a process are more important than others – and analysis supports this. In reality, only 20 percent of activities may account for up to 80 percent of results. This is known as Pareto's law, the "80/20 rule," or the principle of the "vital few and the trivial many." When decision-making, use Pareto's law to sort your priorities. Giving every factor affecting a decision equal weight makes sense only if every factor is equally important; Pareto's law concentrates on the significant 20 percent and gives the less important 80 percent lower priority. When decision-making, divide relevant factors into categories. Prioritize them correctly, and allocate time and effort accordingly so that vital aspects of a decision are not rushed and immaterial aspects do not consume too much time.

THINKING STRATEGICALLY

Before you make a strategic decision, you must first gain a full understanding of the current situation. Get to know the general environment, comparative performances, external requirements, root causes of any performance gaps, and the price of inaction. This five-stage "business case" works for both giants and small units. In any organization, there are questions you can ask yourself, such as:

- What is happening in the marketplace, and how does it work against us?
- Where and why are we underperforming when compared with our competition?
- What do our customers demand that we are unable to supply?
- What causes shortfalls in our performance?
- What negative results will follow if we do not take action immediately?

29 Be optimistic – but remain realistic – when planning your future objectives.

---

30 Be honest and objective when describing the current situation.

▼ IDENTIFYING PROBLEMS

The first half of making a strategic plan is seeking the positive side of a negative situation. Only after you have identified and analyzed any shortfalls can you make the decisions that will take the organization to where you want it to be.

DECIDING WHERE TO GO

In an ideal situation, you work out where you want your organization to be, and then you make the necessary decisions to get there. Do this firstly by identifying shortfalls and setting them in context, and secondly by setting out the actions necessary to close the gaps. These actions will include:

- Correcting underperformance;
- Meeting customers' requirements;
- Removing the causes of shortcomings;
- Replacing threatened negative results with large benefits.

Each of these actions requires further decisions, all of which are made within the overall decision to get from A (unacceptable) to B (excellence).

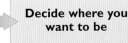

| Identify the problem | → | Find out where you are | → | Decide where you want to be |

DECIDING WHOM TO INVOLVE IN A DECISION

Whom to involve, and how, is your very first decision as a decision maker. The number of people you can involve ranges from none, when you make a decision single-handedly, to all, when you lead a whole team searching for consensus.

31 Involve as many people as you need in making a decision.

POINTS TO REMEMBER

● Superiors and subordinates alike enjoy expressing their views.

● People implement decisions more willingly when they have participated in them.

● Collective decisions need not be slow decisions.

● The role of superiors should be clarified before the decision-making process is started.

USING ADVISERS

The arguments for making collective decisions are powerful. The saying that "Two (or more) heads are better than one" is a good one, although this can be countered by the maxim that "Too many cooks spoil the broth." However, in most cases, advisers supply expertise and experience – so there is a clear need for other "cooks." For example, a computing decision will need an IT expert. Ideally, this specific expertise would be supplemented by the experience of a person who has dealt with similar issues.

However, the decision maker, having weighed the advice of the experts and the experienced hands, must then use authority to ensure that a decision is seen through.

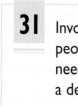

◄ CHOOSING CAREFULLY
This method of decision-making was successful because, although the manager made the final decision, she consulted both outside experts and colleagues with relevant experience.

CASE STUDY

A manager wanted to remove a production bottleneck by reorganizing one of her departments. After thinking extensively about whom to involve in the process, she decided to call on outside consultants because of their expertise in the department's processes. She also asked the advice of her colleagues Ali, who had several years' experience of working in the department, and Marty, who had led change teams successfully in the past and had considerable authority. She also involved her own team members in a planning group to win cooperation.

The advice and input of Ali, with his in-depth view of the project, Marty's experience in planning the project, the contribution of the staff, plus the technical expertise of the outside consultants, meant that the reorganization was successfully completed.

VETTING DECISIONS

If you do not have full autonomy to proceed, make sure you consult the relevant authority – not just for the ultimate blessing, but also for input. It is always in your interest to have your plans vetted by any senior colleagues whose judgment and experience you trust. Even if you do not need to have your decision sanctioned by your managers, remember that they are much more likely to lend valuable cooperation if they have been kept fully informed all the way along the decision path.

32 Ask an objective critic to look at your decision and give you feedback.

INVOLVING OTHERS IN DECISION-MAKING

METHODS	CHARACTERISTICS	WHEN TO USE THEM
LOW INVOLVEMENT These decisions are made by senior management and are low on consultation.	Telling: manager makes unilateral decision without consultation.	When there is a tight deadline, or in an emergency situation.
	Selling: manager makes decision, but others may question validity.	When a hard sell is needed because consensus is impossible.
	Presenting: staff are allowed to hear the progress of discussions.	When a manager has strong views but wishes to inform colleagues.
MEDIUM INVOLVEMENT Although the final decision is made by the manager, staff are consulted for their input.	Suggesting: manager puts forward choices for discussion and may be willing to change opinion.	When the views of colleagues can contribute useful options for discussion and decision.
	Consulting: colleagues' views are sought before any input from above, but manager has final say.	When a decision needs specialist input or other contributions that a manager needs to have.
HIGH INVOLVEMENT Decision-making is a democratic process, with all staff being invited to participate.	Asking: manager establishes parameters to be discussed, but responsibility rests with team.	When the best decision requires the input and full involvement of the team.
	Participating: all staff come together to discuss options and make decisions by consensus.	When commitment to the decision is of vital importance to the success of the plan.

CONSULTING EFFECTIVELY

Consulting with team members can improve the effectiveness of a decision in two ways: first, the people you approach for their opinions should be able to make a real contribution to the process. Second, the chances of implementing your decision successfully are always increased if people know what they are doing and why; most people operate better if they feel totally involved in a project. Take care to demonstrate that the contributions and opinions you sought have been taken into account in your final decision.

CULTURAL DIFFERENCES

Different consulting traditions exist in different cultures across the world. *Ringi* is the formal mode of consultation in Japan and has deep cultural roots. Despite their innate respect for seniority and authority, the Japanese do argue their cases with their superiors, but once a consensus decision has been reached, conformity and support is total – as is the tendency throughout Southeast Asia. Americans and the British still have a tendency toward "order-and-obey," or top-down management, even within the top echelons, although a more consultative decision-making system has become increasingly popular in the US and the UK. Though consultative at the top, European corporations remain hierarchical further down the organization and in their decision-making processes.

AVOIDING PITFALLS

Consulting others, in some cases, can have more disadvantages than advantages. First, there is the time factor: the more people consulted, however qualified they are to comment, the longer the decision-making process will take, and the greater the number of people approached, the higher your chances of being confused by contradictory opinions. Second, you may lose control over the entire process if too many people become involved. To avoid these pitfalls, make sure you keep a tight grip on proceedings, and limit the number of opinions you seek to those that are really essential. When you involve others in your decision, explain the whole picture. Telling half a story can lead very quickly to rumors, with a subsequent drop in staff morale. Token or partial consultation does not succeed.

33 Be prepared to accept people's advice if you have asked for it.

34 Encourage people to participate in decisions to get better results.

LISTENING TO OTHERS

The manager who reverses a decision after hearing the contrary views of a meeting is strong rather than weak. Positive listening means not just hearing the words but understanding their significance and recognizing their sense. You do not want unthinking endorsement of your decisions. Encourage those you consult to speak their minds, and ensure that you have a representative spread of interests and perceptions. Advocate a background of continuous consultation, using every device you can, from team meetings to suggestion boxes. This will enable you to make decisions based on a real understanding of the attitudes of others. Remember that consulting others does not necessarily mean inviting endless debate. Seek views and information and listen to what is said, but decide on the best course of action yourself.

QUESTIONS TO ASK YOURSELF

Q Am I presenting my own view in the most rational, understandable way?

Q Am I changing my mind because of fluent argument, or is there a sound reason?

Q Have I ever ignored attempts to consult with me about a problem before?

Q Am I listening properly to others and hearing what they are really saying?

Q Do I give colleagues the chance to express their own opinions?

SOLICITING OPINIONS INFORMALLY ▼
To understand the opinions of your colleagues fully, it is important to built up a strong and open rapport. Take time away from the office to discuss matters informally and without constraint – the results will be honest and positive.

Leader reassures colleagues that conversation is confidential

Open body language shows colleagues feel at ease together

USING ANALYTICAL METHODS

To reach a sound decision, you need to analyze all the relevant facts. There are several analytical tools that are both useful and simple to employ. Use analysis to lead to strong conclusions, and therefore good strategic decision-making.

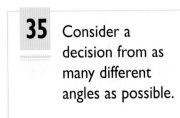

35 Consider a decision from as many different angles as possible.

36 Know your three largest rivals as intimately as your own company.

USING SWOT ANALYSIS ▼
The chart below highlights key questions to be asked. By identifying an organization's Strengths and Opportunities, and pinpointing its Weaknesses and Threats, effective strategies can be made for the future.

ANALYZING YOUR SWOT

SWOT analysis helps establish where an organization, team, or product stands in the marketplace. Your organization's SWOT – an acronym for Strengths, Weaknesses, Opportunities, and Threats – holds the key to future strategic decision-making. Make an honest and realistic list under the above headings. As you do, you may unearth valuable facts – often the analysis alone highlights areas that you may have overlooked – and realize that your organization's weaknesses may be as important as its strengths. Having analyzed your own SWOT, analyze that of your competitors.

UNDERSTANDING YOUR ORGANIZATION'S SWOT

STRENGTHS
What is the organization competent at? What is it really good at?

WEAKNESSES
Is the organization short of key resources or capabilities? Is it vulnerable to competition?

OPPORTUNITIES
Can the organization sell more, or find new markets, products, or services?

THREATS
Can the organization's products or technology be overtaken? Are its markets deteriorating?

RELATING PRICE TO QUALITY

A key decision is where to position a product in the market. Use a price/quality matrix to relate price to quality. If your ultimate aim is high price/high quality, you still may want to use another strategy initially, such as selling your product at medium price/medium quality, as a stepping stone to get there. If analysis shows that lower profit margins can be offset by winning a larger share of the market, you can still profit by selling top-quality products at medium or even low prices.

Organizations frequently aim at placing a high price/high quality product on the market

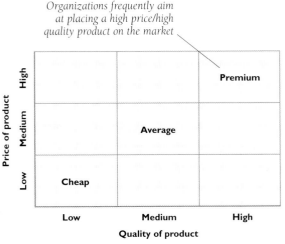

▲ USING THE PRICE/QUALITY MATRIX
This matrix shows that the rising quality of products can accompany a corresponding rise in price to give the best profit margins within the market. The matrix gives nine alternatives for positioning the overall stance of a product in the market.

COMBINING ANALYSES

A single piece of analysis may well need to be combined with other approaches to gain a view of the complete picture. Analysis ensures that you understand the problems and can safely make decisions that will markedly improve results. Combining different types of analysis is a way of strengthening the analysis – and the stronger it is, the stronger the pointers to the correct decision, and the better the chances of getting it right. For example, the price/quality matrix can be combined with a study of market growth rate and relative market share, or RMS. RMS represents sales as a percentage of the combined sales of your three largest rivals. The best RMS is 100 percent or more. If it is less, you should not reduce the high price of your high quality product to medium, because you do not have a large enough market share.

CULTURAL DIFFERENCES

The phenomenon of "paralysis by analysis" refers to an over-reliance on analysis in business situations that can lead to an inability to reach decisions. It does occur in the American business community, which can be obsessed with numbers. At the other extreme, the British have a tendency for inadequate analysis, while other Europeans fall between the two extremes. The Japanese are thorough analysts but avoid "paralysis" by acting fast once decisions are final.

GENERATING IDEAS

The creation of new ideas is vital to bringing fresh light to the decision-making process. When looking for ideas, try to achieve a balance between imagination and practicality. Your first hurdle lies in generating the ideas with others.

37 Be disorganized when generating ideas, organized in developing them.

38 Promote lateral thinking, but try to develop ideas in a logical fashion.

CHALLENGING TRADITIONS

When making decisions, do not blindly accept tried-and-tested "conventional wisdom." Try it yourself; be ruthless in its application and open-minded about alternatives. It is not wrong to use a conventional approach, but do so only after you have fully and fairly examined other new and more innovative ideas. Compare the obvious and easy with the unorthodox and difficult, and you may well find the latter the better solution by far.

BRAINSTORMING FOR IDEAS

Brainstorming meetings are held specifically to generate new ideas. Gather a group of people – three to eight ideally – and ask each to submit an idea (or list of ideas) relevant to the decision being made. As each idea is produced, the group facilitator should record it. Be democratic. Do not reject any ideas, and be sure to value a junior's idea as highly as that of a senior. The more ideas generated, the better, but do not judge or analyze them, or make any decisions, during the session.

▲ ENCOURAGING PARTICIPATION
New ideas help people to look outside the confines of their own jobs. Brainstorming is useful for breaking creative logjams, but you need more disciplined methods for actual decision-making.

PRODUCING NEW IDEAS

When setting up any group to generate ideas, choose the participants to reflect differences in expertise and experience. Define the issues and the relevant criteria clearly, and make sure that all ideas are recorded. It is useful to have a facilitator, who does not contribute ideas, to keep the session on course. Part of the facilitator's role is to promote lateral thinking. If a seemingly absurd proposition is offered, he or she should use it to provoke fresh thinking. When enough ideas have been presented, end the meeting. Select the ideas that are worthy of further investigation, and follow up promptly. You could use the same group of people to evaluate the analyses and advise on the best alternative.

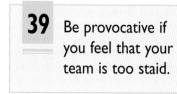

39 Be provocative if you feel that your team is too staid.

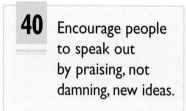

40 Encourage people to speak out by praising, not damning, new ideas.

ENCOURAGING THE CREATIVE PROCESS

Generating a relaxed environment in which individuals feel comfortable and unthreatened helps to draw out new ideas. The more closely a set of people work together, the easier it is for them to relax and build up trust in one other.

If you are leading a meeting intended to generate new and creative policies, consider using some of the following methods:

- Ask all the attendees to come to the meeting prepared to present two or three ideas each.
- Give everybody at the meeting the chance to air their views in turn.
- Do not allow the creative flow of ideas to be ruined by imposing too many constraints or making assumptions.
- Do not allow interruptions or discussions to wander too far off the subject in question, but encourage the free, creative flow of ideas and associations.

- Try asking your colleagues to circulate ideas in advance of the meeting – this may help those who like to work alone to develop their ideas.
- Provide the group with a few ideas of your own – this will help to direct discussions and act as stimulation if inspiration seems to be running dry.
- Try to encourage lateral thinking as well as logical thought to break down and challenge any long-held preconceptions.
- Put together all the ideas generated into clusters so that you end up with groups of related ideas. At this point, start to create a shortlist of the best ideas.
- Above all, never criticize any of the ideas in front of your colleagues.

DEVELOPING CREATIVE THINKING

There is a common misconception that creative thinking, and therefore the ability to make innovative decisions, is an inborn talent that cannot be learned. Try to develop the quality and originality of your ideas by adopting new methods of thinking.

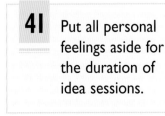

41 Put all personal feelings aside for the duration of idea sessions.

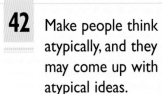

42 Make people think atypically, and they may come up with atypical ideas.

EMBRACING NEW IDEAS

People – and organizations – form habits of thinking just as they form other habits. Many organizations that reject new thinking outright do so because they view change as risk. There are, however, ways to defeat this negativity and encourage an acceptance of the new. For example, in any type of ideas meeting, forbid the use of the response "Yes, but..." – a classic idea killer – until a predetermined number of new ideas have been explored and discussed.

THINKING POSITIVELY

If you are cautious by nature, you are not very likely to think adventurously, but if you are highly creative, you may be impatient with skeptics who see only the objections in a discussion. Do not allow colleagues to get locked into these or any other mind-sets that prevent them from listening to other points of view with an open mind. If you think that a debate is becoming too negative, say so and ask everybody to try and make a positive, creative contribution. This will help you avoid sterile debates in which everyone defends their own fixed position and attacks all others.

43 Always encourage new, unexplored ways of thinking.

44 If using a multistage approach, work through the stages one at a time.

DECIDING ON ACTION

The object of generating new ideas is to find the best one and act on it. Expert Mark Brown uses a five-stage model (given the acronym AGISA) for the group thinking process. It starts with Analysis, in which you seek to uncover the issues affecting the decision. That enables you to set Goals – either "opportunities" (coded white) or "problems" (gray). Then you search for Ideas, which are either "conventional, mildly original" (light blue) or "unconventional, needing further discussion" (blue). At the Selection (red) stage, ideas are examined for weakness and solutions are discarded or adopted. Those adopted call for Action (green), in which the accepted decision is implemented.

POINTS TO REMEMBER

- Assumptions should always be challenged.

- Conventional thinking should not be rejected just because it is conventional.

- New ideas are as valuable as any others but should not be adopted simply because they are new.

▼ GATHERING IDEAS

In the AGISA thinking model, you must complete each stage of idea generation before moving on. In any given situation you may need to follow either one or both of the possible routes shown here.

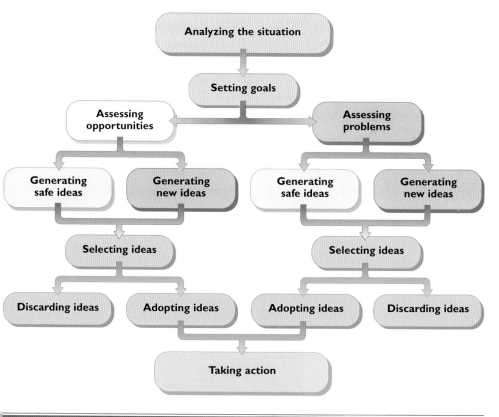

ASSESSING THE VALIDITY OF IDEAS

After you have generated a range of ideas, you need to assess them. Apply objective criteria and use rational methods to narrow down the range of choices, and keep an open mind when deciding which ideas you want to take forward to the next stage.

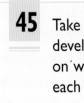

45 Take the time to develop criteria on which to base each decision.

46 Make sure that ideas are able to rise up your organization.

NARROWING THE OPTIONS

Use "What if?" analysis when the time comes to assess the value of ideas. Ask yourself what would be the likely consequences of adopting decision A, B, or C. Discuss and establish the answers in group debates that consider the situation from all angles. Make the most of these meetings by asking people to present their views one at a time rather than descending into a free-for-all debate.

OVERCOMING RIGID THINKING

There are several methods of overcoming rigid thinking. First, ensure that the structure of your organization will not inhibit the adoption of innovative ideas. Second, ask people to spend time thinking about ideas before meetings, and third, use multiskilled teams that can cut across departmental boundaries to expose people to different disciplines and experience.

▼ **BEING OPEN-MINDED**
In this encounter, one person's defensive seated posture shows a defensive attitude toward his colleague's ideas.

Open posture

Defensive posture

LISTING ▶ THE OPTIONS

When assessing a range of new ideas, write down the problem, all suggested solutions, and the potential outcomes of each.

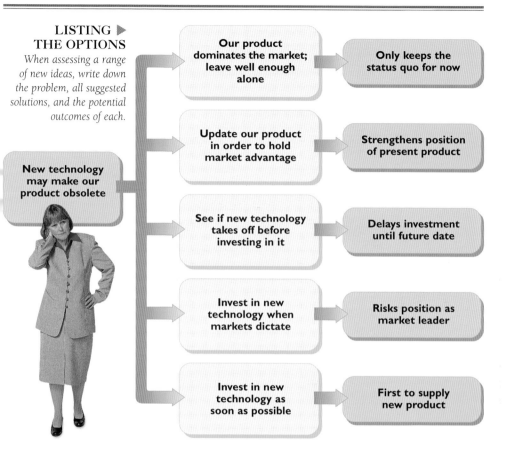

New technology may make our product obsolete

- **Our product dominates the market; leave well enough alone** → **Only keeps the status quo for now**
- **Update our product in order to hold market advantage** → **Strengthens position of present product**
- **See if new technology takes off before investing in it** → **Delays investment until future date**
- **Invest in new technology when markets dictate** → **Risks position as market leader**
- **Invest in new technology as soon as possible** → **First to supply new product**

NARROWING DOWN IDEAS

The best way to reduce a long list of options to a manageable size is to have clear criteria. For example, for an investment decision, the criteria could relate to the maximum investment, payback period, return on capital, and strategic fit. Having selected criteria, you can then safely discard ideas that fall outside them. If this type of test is unsuitable – for example, on recruitment issues – list the pros and cons of each alternative, and then attribute scores of up to plus 10 for each pro and minus 10 for each con according to importance. Discard the lowest minus-scoring alternatives.

QUESTIONS TO ASK YOURSELF

Q How well do the alternatives fit the criteria?

Q What is the balance between the disadvantages and advantages of the solution?

Q What will be the consequences of each solution?

Q Have I canvassed all relevant views and opinions?

Q Do I know which solution has the widest support?

GATHERING INFORMATION

Once you have narrowed down all your ideas, you may need to research them in more detail in order to check out their viability and understand their implications. Think carefully about the questions you need to ask to evaluate the situation properly.

47 Work to a realistic but demanding timetable when getting information.

POINTS TO REMEMBER

● Your requirements should be assessed thoroughly before embarking on any research.

● The Internet provides an excellent source of all kinds of information and data.

● Using the wrong methodology for research will lead to the wrong results being produced.

● A clear, concise, and accurate interpretation of the data that you have acquired is the most crucial factor in its usage.

RESEARCHING PROPERLY

Vast amounts of information are now available from more sources than ever before. Focus your research by asking yourself what information you would ideally obtain in order to make your decision. Write down the contents of this "ideal information pack," and check how much is available and where. Stick to your ideal, and try to glean as much of it as possible, taking care not to exclude anything that is relevant. Sometimes, it can be easy to overlook important details that might sway your choice – especially if you are not being sufficiently objective.

UTILIZING RESOURCES

Start with your company's own resources. Look for data that has not been analyzed. One accountant found that toothpaste sales to pharmacies were far less profitable than those to chains. The outcome was a profit of millions. Consulting electronic media brings in a whole world of information, but printed media may be more accessible. The information industry has grown enormously, and consulting firms can give invaluable guidance, especially on competitive activity. Conferences and seminars are vital for networking, and be sure not to neglect your colleagues inside the company.

48 When delegating information-gathering, use your brightest people.

49 Do not throw away source material – you may find you need it later.

HANDLING INFORMATION

Before you feed information into the decision-making process, organize and check it thoroughly. Reports from outside consultants or internal sources should come properly organized, with all the conclusions clearly stated at the beginning of the report, supporting data arranged in a logical order, and all relevant information gathered into logical sections. Treat reports exactly like all other information – never take anything for granted. If the data comes from too small or unrepresentative a sample, or the questions were loaded, you will not be able to rely on the information. Can it be cross-checked? If so, do it. When satisfied, organize your research along similar lines to the consulting reports for consistency. Use this information as the basis for your decision and for any plan of action.

THINGS TO DO

1. Look out for interesting information, and file it away for future use.

2. Establish good relations with in-house librarians, finance departments, and other information sources.

3. Build your own library of reference books, press clippings, and reports.

4. Keep looking at the overall problems as well as the specific details when searching for material.

LOCATING INFORMATION

SOURCES	FACTORS TO CONSIDER
COMPANY RESOURCES Includes company library, internal statistics, finance department, colleagues, and researchers.	● A good starting point for most information-gathering. ● Can be time-consuming if much unwanted data must be searched through to find something relevant. ● Is dependent on cooperation of colleagues.
INDIVIDUAL SOURCES Includes friends, outside contacts, competitors, seminars, press reports, and publications.	● Useful ideas and contributions can come from people at any level of any business. ● Many informal, individual sources of information may be difficult to exploit fully.
EXPERTS Includes management and other consultants, market and economic research, and academic experts.	● Level of expertise should be high and broadly based. ● May take time for experts to find relevant information. ● Quality of the service is likely to be high, though proposals and references will need careful checking.
ELECTRONIC MEDIA Includes Internet, intranet, PC and other computer networks, and all on-line information services.	● The World Wide Web and other such services provide a wealth of useful information – perhaps too much. ● Global links are slow at busy times of the day. ● Information may not always be accessible or correct.

ASSESSING COMPETITION

Before implementing any decision, spend some time looking at how it will affect the market and what reactions it might cause among your competitors. It is essential to carry out extensive market research if you want to understand and counteract competitive activity. So, find out from your customers how they rate both your product and your competitors', and act on these findings. Another way to approach your competition is by applying what is known as "game theory".

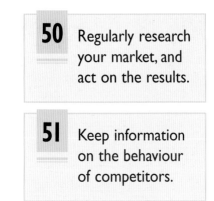

50 Regularly research your market, and act on the results.

51 Keep information on the behaviour of competitors.

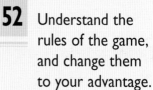

52 Understand the rules of the game, and change them to your advantage.

KNOWING THE SYSTEM

According to game theory, an organization and its competitors all form part of the same "business system", which has boundaries, players, and a set of rules – all of which you must learn as you play. Also you must understand the key relationships between cause and effect. Any change in one part of the system will be reflected throughout it. Players in the game never make a decision without considering all foreseeable effects.

CHANGING THE RULES

Traditionally, beating the competition involved offering better goods or services, and doing so at lower costs. However, in today's marketplace, this has become much harder, and is not always possible. An alternative method is to change the rules of the game. To gain the advantage, think of how your products or services are currently being supplied, and look for radically different ways to reach the market – by selling directly to customers, or opening a 24-hour, seven-days-a-week "shop" on the Internet. To be a successful player, go for moves that other players either will not or cannot follow, and attack their weaknesses by developing and exploiting unique strengths of your own.

THINGS TO DO

1. Always be aware of exactly what your competition is doing in the marketplace.
2. Look for innovative, new ways to attract people to your product or service.
3. Keep one step ahead of the competition.
4. Once you have researched the market, change your sales policy as necessary.

FORMING ALLIANCES

In sport, opposing teams have common interests, such as getting the largest possible attendance at their games. Business players also have common interests – they may compete for market share, but they all want to maximize the total market. Look for organizations complementary to your own, and form alliances allowing you to play on the same side in one sector of the market, yet compete in others. Such supplier-customer alliances can mean improved performance and lower costs, with everyone sharing the benefits.

53 Anticipate competitors' actions in order to compete successfully against them in the marketplace.

▲ WORKING TOGETHER

Competing sports teams have mutual interests. It is to their advantage to create as big a "market" as possible (in this case, spectators) to create revenue. Both sides strive to play a great game, thus pleasing their fans and increasing their "market".

QUESTIONS TO ASK YOURSELF

Q Are there areas of common ground with our competitors?

Q How can we co-operate in each area of common ground?

Q Would our competitors benefit the most?

Q Would our company benefit the most?

Q How can we maintain competitive vigour?

185

FORECASTING THE FUTURE

Decision-making rests on predicting the future and assuming that events will unfold following an established action plan. Develop methods of improving the accuracy of your own forecasts and ways of using forecasts made by others to best effect.

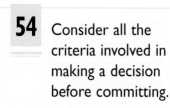

54 Consider all the criteria involved in making a decision before committing.

55 Check forecasts by your own intuition and experience.

56 Make the future happen – this is the most effective way of forecasting.

SELECTING METHODS

Most forecasting is based on extrapolation of figures. For example, when budgeting, you will look back at the costs and sales for the previous year, and base the estimates of the next year's sales and costs on the increases and decreases that you anticipate. This method of forecasting is also used as the basis for longer-term planning. As a more dynamic alternative, work back from the future: envisage your desired outcome, then plan the action required to achieve it. This is an exercise in creating, rather than merely predicting, the future, and is the key to making progressive, proactive decisions.

TAKING A WIDER VIEW

When making a forecast, you need to consider criteria both internally, within your organization, and externally, in the outside market. For instance, if you are proposing a full-scale program to develop a new product, you should forecast the following:

INTERNAL CONSIDERATIONS:
- Financial – how will you raise the cash?
- Structural – where will the operation be based?
- Staff – who will manage the operation?
- Development – how long will this take?
- Timing – at what time of year will the product be launched?

EXTERNAL CONSIDERATIONS:
- Customers – where is the market?
- Market – how strong will the market be at the launch date?
- Competitors – how will they react?
- Promotion – what will be required and how much will it cost?
- Investors – will you need more money?

USING FORECASTS

The most important element in forecasting is judgment. Use your experience and intuition to estimate the value of predictions. Ask "what if" questions – "what happens if the sales forecast is raised by 50 percent?" – and treat the forecast as dynamic, updating it as information comes in. For example, revise your annual budget in the light of performance over the first quarter. In this way forecasting becomes a flexible tool for controlling, monitoring, and planning the future.

57 Question every assumption before making your forecast – and then check them again.

ASSESSING SUCCESS

The future rarely imitates the past exactly, so some degree of error is inevitable when making forecasts. Refine your forecast using "probability theory" to reduce the element of error. Assess the likelihood of an event occurring on a scale of 0 ("no chance") to 1 ("certain"), with a 50 percent chance of success scoring 0.5. For example, two potential investments are forecast to show profits of $20,000 and $40,000, rating 0.5 and 0.4. Multiplying outcomes by probabilities gives these figures: $20,000 x 0.5 = $10,000; $40,000 x 0.4 = $16,000. So, even with a lower probability of total success, the $40,000 project is clearly the better option.

▼ **FORECASTING TO WIN**
This company wanted to triple its market share within a specific time limit. The chief executive worked backward from this outcome to find out what steps were needed to achieve it. Strategists worked with forecasts to produce detailed plans that would turn ambition into reality.

CASE STUDY
A company selling its product at premium prices was hit by the introduction of low-priced competition. Forecasts confirmed that this trend would continue in a market showing strong growth. Extrapolating figures from its own results showed that the company would lose its market share and profit over a very short period of time.

The chief executive decided to look for a future in which the company became so competitive on costs and prices that it would triple its market share within four years.

To achieve this, the company planned a rise in production and sales figures. Working back from that high ambition, the strategists worked out the forecasts and targets for costs, margins, production, and the introduction of new products. With careful targeting, the chief executive's vision of a tripled market share was realized two years ahead of schedule.

USING MODELS

As a decision maker, you should become familiar with "modeling," such as simple spreadsheets or computer-generated graphics. Use these vital tools to test variables, test relationships between data, and predict the consequences of alteration in any factors.

58 Simulate and predict the future rather than waiting for it to happen.

USING COMPUTERS

Processes of any kind can be simulated mathematically to imitate real-life causes and effects. Many computer programs go beyond simple spreadsheets to explore and illustrate what would happen if certain decisions were made, and to anticipate the long-term effects of competitors' reactions. Ask an expert's advice on which program to use, and be sure that everybody working with it is properly trained. Good computer graphics are easy to access and understand, and forecasting in this way may save the pain of real-life trial and error. Decision-making in once-complex areas like distribution logistics and inventory control has now become routine with the advent of more and more powerful computer programs. These can quickly deal with complex calculations and produce user-friendly statistics.

▼ RAISING PRICES

*This equation helps you decide if you can raise prices, by showing how far sales can fall before profitability declines. In this example where **c** equals 25, if the product price is raised by 20 percent, profits will not fall until sales drop by more than 44 percent (Critical Volume Loss), making this a risk worth taking.*

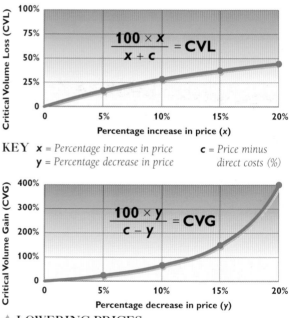

$$\frac{100 \times x}{x + c} = \text{CVL}$$

KEY x = *Percentage increase in price*
y = *Percentage decrease in price*
c = *Price minus direct costs (%)*

$$\frac{100 \times y}{c - y} = \text{CVG}$$

▲ LOWERING PRICES

*This equation helps you decide if you can cut your product prices, by showing how far sales must rise at the new price in order to sustain profits. If the product price is dropped by 20 percent when **c** equals 25, sales must rise by 400 percent (Critical Volume Gain) to maintain profit levels. This is clearly not a viable strategy.*

USING CONSULTANTS

Specialist techniques are best applied by specialists. If in-house resources are inadequate for a particular task, it makes sense to use outside consultants. There are many consulting firms with specific experience in highly refined forecasting, modeling, and computer simulation techniques – but such expertise does not come cheap. To make the most of this specialist knowledge, always provide a thorough brief.

GETTING HELP ▶

As a manager, you have to make decisions, some of which may be based on forecasts and models. To use time efficiently, hire consultants and provide them with a detailed brief of your modeling requirements.

HANDLING RESULTS

No matter how experienced the forecaster, his or her results can only be as good as the information they are given to work with. Bear in mind the acronym GIGO – "Garbage In, Garbage Out." Make sure that all relevant data is gathered as comprehensively and accurately as possible. If the results of modeling seem hard to believe, check the validity of any assumptions that have been made, and the methodology used, before acting on the forecasts. Never ignore disconcerting modeling results, however. You may well find that they have arisen because vital information has been overlooked, or important consequences have not been properly taken into account.

59 Do complex calculations yourself only if you have the skills.

60 If the model contradicts your beliefs, check and double-check.

MINIMIZING RISKS

Most decisions contain a degree of uncertainty. Use your own judgment and experience to remove as much doubt as possible from a situation. Think through the consequences of your actions, be prepared to compromise, and consider timing carefully.

 61 Use both judgment and calculation to get the optimum value from each.

ASSESSING CONSEQUENCES

Making a decision usually results in some form of action being taken at some point in the future. Minimize risks by listing the possible effects of any action, and assessing the likelihood of each negative event, as well as how much damage it could inflict. Also, assess consequences in terms of time – immediate, short term, or long term – and consider the long-term results of a decision rather than looking exclusively at short-term effects. Look for external factors that could affect your decision, and try to quantify the likelihood of – and reasons for – your plan failing. Itemizing such factors is a step toward making contingency plans to deal with any problems. This will reduce the chance of failure and optimize your chances of success.

 62 Never sacrifice the future for the short-term unless there is no option.

 **63** Make competitive decisions earlier rather than later.

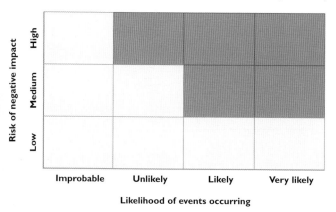

◀ **ASSESSING RISKS**
This matrix combines the chances of an event occurring with the severity of its impact on a decision. If it is very unlikely that an event may occur, a high risk of negative impact may be sustainable. A very likely to occur/high negative impact result needs rethinking.

KEY

▮ *High risk of negative impact*

Low risk of negative impact

QUESTIONS TO ASK
YOURSELF

Q Have I fully considered all the alternatives?

Q Have I fully considered and analyzed each alternative?

Q Have I assessed and compared the probabilities?

Q Do any of my proposed trade-offs endanger the objectives?

Q Have I built enough leeway into the timing?

Q Does my team support the choice between alternatives?

64 Keep a list of the trade-offs you are making.

USING TRADE-OFFS

Successful management involves trade-offs and compromises to reach the best decision when several factors are involved. The aim of trade-offs is to keep short- and long-term risks as low as is possible. You cannot maximize investment and profits at the same time – short-term profit is sacrificed for long-term success. Equally, ambitious plans for expansion may be trimmed to achieve satisfactory current returns. Products are similarly affected – you cannot simultaneously maximize a car's acceleration and minimize its fuel usage.

To make decisions satisfactorily, work out your priorities and assess those of your opposition. Establish which features matter most to customers to compile an order of priorities – you can then trade off the less important features against the significant ones. Although some trade-offs involve reducing costs, few customers will be willing to accept the sacrifice of quality to profit.

TIMING IMPLEMENTATION

Many projects fail because their timing is wrong – they start too early or too late. When dealing with the launch of a new product, for example, a trade-off may be needed between having all the necessary elements securely in place and moving swiftly in order to beat your competitors to the market. Although the latter seems the riskier alternative, you may lose out to the competition altogether if you delay for too long. Have the confidence to decide and implement quickly, and delay only if there are convincing reasons for waiting.

▼ PLANNING AHEAD
Use wall charts that show all information relating to a decision to help you plan your time well in advance and to calculate the optimum time for implementing a decision.

USING FAIL-SAFE STRATEGIES

Decision makers need to take a broad view and consider the impact of different outcomes. Having assessed the risks, try to build in safety nets to minimize them. This will enable you either to succeed in full confidence or fail in relative safety.

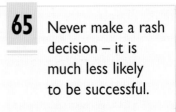

65 Never make a rash decision – it is much less likely to be successful.

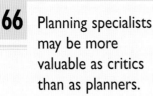

66 Planning specialists may be more valuable as critics than as planners.

▼ CHOOSING A STRATEGY
Of the three outcomes shown below, the "best case" scenario is the outcome to be hoped for, but considering alternatives and preparing to meet all eventualities allows contingency plans to be made.

PLANNING SCENARIOS

When assessing the potential risks involved in a decision, always ask yourself "What is the best combination of consequences ("best case") that I can reasonably expect from the decision? And the worst ("worst case")?" The key word here is "reasonably." Neither optimism or pessimism should be taken to extremes, but this simplest form of scenario-planning shows whether the "best case" payoff justifies taking "worst case" risks.

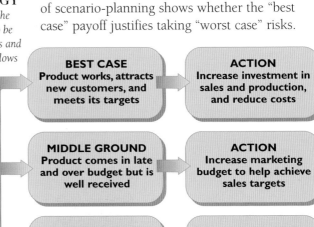

THE DECISION
Proceed with plan for new technology product via new operation, reviewed at regular intervals

BEST CASE
Product works, attracts new customers, and meets its targets

ACTION
Increase investment in sales and production, and reduce costs

MIDDLE GROUND
Product comes in late and over budget but is well received

ACTION
Increase marketing budget to help achieve sales targets

WORST CASE
Operation runs over budget and into loss, and product fails

ACTION
Scale down operation and invest in new technology

- Differences should never just be split between best and worst case scenarios – there is always middle ground to be found.

- Big risks should not be taken if the rewards are small.

- While planning for the best, it is important to be prepared for the worst.

- A broad range of people should take part in scenario-planning.

- If none of the scenarios seems attractive, there should be a major rethinking of ideas.

DEVELOPING SCENARIOS

So-called "single-point forecasts" that predict only one eventuality are more risky than plans that consider a range of possible outcomes. Work out alternative scenarios for yourself, filling in as much detail as possible, so that you are better prepared for actual events. For example, you could forecast prices in your industry on the basis of increases by competitors, no change, or price cuts. The three alternatives will lead to three alternative strategies. Pick the strategy that best fits the scenarios as a whole, or select as your goal the most attractive scenario outcome and make decisions that optimize your chances of reaching that target.

DISCUSSING ALTERNATIVES

Producing scenarios is an ideal way of bringing colleagues into the decision-making process. You can examine key questions objectively and use the answers to react effectively when the situation occurs in real life. What are the main variables? What happens to them in each scenario? Are assumptions or subjective thinking affecting the issue? What are your best responses if and when a particular scenario materializes?

67 Check any action plans against the desired outcome.

Colleague wants to make an informed decision

Colleague requests more detail of various plans of action

Leader outlines potential outcomes

TALKING ▶ FREELY
Discuss a variety of scenarios with colleagues, and consider all options before you move toward consensus for a final decision.

ASSESSING THE CONSEQUENCES FOR STAFF

While assessing ideas in order to make a decision, consider the options for your staff. They may feel unhappy about imminent change if they are not consulted, or if you need to recruit new people with the necessary skills to implement your decision.

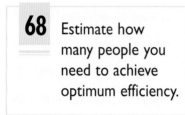

68 Estimate how many people you need to achieve optimum efficiency.

69 Ensure that staff have access to information whenever possible.

ASSESSING REQUIREMENTS

Most decisions made within an organization will have consequences for existing staff. Once you have made a decision, consider the number of people required to execute it with optimum efficiency. In addition, decide which skills are needed to fulfill the plan, and at what stages of the plan they will be deployed. Always inform existing staff of decisions made on recruitment issues, which are often highly sensitive. If you do need to recruit new skills, explain your reasons, basing them on your objectives and action plan.

REVIEWING STAFF SKILLS

Examine the strengths and weaknesses of the existing workforce before making a final decision on their deployment. You may find that their numbers and skills match exactly those required by your decision and any subsequent plan of action. However, it is much more likely that you will need to change some roles or give some people more responsibility. There may be overlap in responsibility, and some people may no longer be needed. Others may require specialist training to upgrade or augment their skills.

70 Consider existing skills when deciding future action.

71 Be objective when making staffing decisions.

REDEPLOYING PEOPLE

There will often be quite a considerable degree of emotional resistance among staff if your decision demands substantial recruitment of new people, reorganization, changing roles, or losing roles altogether. Keep staff informed, and consult them at every stage of the decision-making process so that they will be better prepared for the outcome. The impact of redeploying people or them experiencing job loss, however, can still be traumatic and will require diplomatic handling. Take care to explain all the reasons if you have to replace existing staff, and handle any necessary layoffs with tact, generosity, and sympathy – especially over money matters.

▼ DISCUSSING ROLES
When discussing role changes with staff, always be honest yet tactful. Prepare for the meeting by noting down possible responses to their objections to help you deal with them calmly and diplomatically.

Manager anticipates objections and lists some solutions

INVOLVING A NEW TEAM

Once a new team is in place, act swiftly to involve people fully in making your decision effective. See that everybody has a concise job description and knows exactly how they fit into the team. Give new recruits an introduction to your organization, and ensure that they are quickly integrated into the team. Explain both the reasons that led to your decision and the action required to implement it clearly so that everybody knows the common aims. Provide stretching goals to encourage team members to work hard toward fulfilling these aims and executing your decision.

QUESTIONS TO ASK YOURSELF

Q What qualities do I want in the staff who will help to implement my decisions?

Q What qualities are already available in the people I can call upon?

Q Will I need to recruit more people with fresh skills to cover the tasks required?

Q Have I told existing staff I may have to recruit new skills?

MAKING YOUR DECISION

W*hen your preparations are completed and the moment of decision finally arrives, double-check that you are making the right decision. Reassess your options and seek other opinions to reinforce your point of view. Once you are fully convinced, go ahead.*

72 Make a checklist of the main issues before finalizing any decision.

Q How likely am I to change my mind if given more time or information?

Q Has the decision-making process been thorough and sensible?

Q Have other minds made a large enough contribution to this decision?

Q Am I pleased and happy with this decision?

ASSESSING A DECISION

You have taken all possible care and every reasonable step to ensure that the decision is correct. Now, the die must be cast. Somebody must be hired or fired. An order will be placed, or a supplier dropped. An advertising campaign will be approved or rejected. Before setting action in motion, take time out to run over and assess the decision. What will it achieve? Why make it now? Will it be understood? How will it be received? The object is not to raise doubts in your mind, but to make yourself confident that a rational process has reached a reasonable decision.

ESTABLISHING YOUR COMMITMENT

In very rare cases, you may wish to avoid making what appears to be the best decision because you suspect that the action involved may expose you to risk and blame. This is avoiding responsibility, and may well do more harm than any personal risk involved in going ahead with a plan. When making a decision, ask yourself whether you are really committed to it, are prepared to take full responsibility for your actions, and are ready to face the consequences if you are proven to be wrong in the long term. Go ahead only if you can give a positive answer to all three questions.

73 Note that over-cautious decisions may stem from self-protection.

74 Try to uncover any hidden flaws before finalizing your decision.

REINFORCING DECISIONS

The most confident solo performer needs the comfort of talking through what they have decided, or are deciding, to do. Even when your mind is made up, it helps to talk over your final decision with a colleague or friend. Such a discussion, assuming that it is supportive, eases the stress of making the decision and provides another opportunity to go over the process, the pros and cons, and the reason for your choice. If in the course of discussion you uncover a vital flaw in the decision, so much the better. You can amend your decision while there is still time.

DEALING WITH DOUBT

The greatest single fear is that of getting it wrong. This is often combined with fear about the consequences for your job, your reputation, and your rewards. Do not bury such fears. Accept that every decision in life has a chance of error and that no individual or organization can make progress by being negative. Your fear of making a mistake can be eliminated completely only if you never make a decision at all. Instead of falling into this trap, take positive steps to strengthen your confidence. Remind yourself of what the worst case scenario is, assess what the chances are of the worst happening, and what the impact of this outcome would be. If you decide you can live with even the worst result, what is there to fear?

▲ **AIRING OPINIONS INFORMALLY**
An informal chat with a close colleague is one way of helping you over the stress of the decision-making process – and there is always a chance that they may uncover a flawed area that needs more work.

75 Write down all your predecision fears on paper, then throw them in the trash.

GETTING APPROVAL FOR YOUR FINAL DECISION

Once you have made your decision, it may need official sanction. If your superiors are fully informed of your progress, this may come readily. If not, try producing a written report or presentation – this can be a vital tool in gaining a positive response.

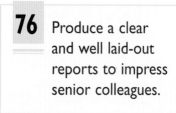

76 Produce a clear and well laid-out reports to impress senior colleagues.

77 Find a sponsor to improve chances of gaining approval for your decision.

OBTAINING APPROVAL

The fewer approvals required, the easier and better for the decision maker. The ideal is a one-stop approval; always try to limit the number of approval stages involved. However, in multi-layered hierarchies, with managers at each level needing to approve lower-level decisions, the decision-making process can be slow and even frustrating. Employ patience and persistence to win the day.

PREPARING A REPORT

To proceed with some decisions, you may need to prepare a report detailing your recommendation and how you reached it. To be convincing, reports should state the following clearly:
● Why the decision is required;
● What action is recommended;
● How the action will be implemented;
● Who will be involved;
● When the action will happen.
Provide all the answers to these questions in a forceful opening summary, preferably on a single sheet of paper. Prepare the report as if you were writing a newspaper story – try using arresting headlines and bold type to emphasize key points.

THINGS TO DO

1. Always look at your decision hypercritically.
2. To make sure you have covered everything, go over your objectives again before starting your report.
3. List all the benefits reaped from your decision – as well as all the negatives.
4. Name the deadline by when approval is required.

PROVIDING EVIDENCE

The single page summarizing your decision and its rationale should be supported by the data that has led to your conclusion. Think about who will read your report, and anticipate the questions they may ask, including some that are nit-picking and even obtuse. Remember that you have lived with this issue for some time, while other people are starting from scratch. Resist the temptation to cram the report so full of facts that readers will give up. Instead, provide the significant data organized in the same logical order as the summary.

78 Regard hostile questioning as a technique, not a personal attack.

PRESENTING YOUR IDEAS

If you have to present or explain your report in person, prepare for the meeting as for a major speech. Go over your material carefully and be prepared for counterattacks. Your seniors may believe that a "trial by fire" tests a team leader's case by teasing out any flaws. Even if your decision is subjected to brutal questioning, keep your cool and reaffirm your belief in your proposals. Remember that you have given great thought to this issue from all angles and have reached the best possible decision in the circumstances.

Open body language is used to instill confidence in a decision

MAKING A ▶ PRESENTATION
Use visual aids to support your report, incorporating clear, good-quality diagrams as required. They may help win approval for a decision more quickly.

79 Ensure that you have covered all objections.

IMPLEMENTING A DECISION

Decisions are valueless until they are translated into positive action, which in turn involves the decision maker in making a series of operational decisions and choices.

DEVELOPING A PLAN

A plan of action will begin to evolve naturally as options are narrowed and their feasibility is studied during the decision-making process. Once you have made your final decision, concentrate on developing plans for its implementation.

80 Be sure of your decision before beginning to plan a course of action.

MAKING AN ACTION PLAN

When developing a plan to implement your decision, involve others in the plan. Use those with relevant abilities. Make sure that everybody fully understands the decision and the reasons for it. With their help, analyze the overall task, determine what actions should be taken, and decide when to implement the decision. Every activity should have start and stop dates, milestones for key events, and specified outcomes. The plan also specifies break points at which action can be reviewed and revised.

DELEGATING ACTION

Implementing some decisions – such as arranging meetings – can be handled by one person. More complex decisions, such as the creation of an advertising campaign or the launch of a new product, involves a number of tasks and the work of a team. Break these tasks into manageable chunks and delegate responsibility for planning each one to individuals within the team. Give these individuals freedom to act independently, and hold them personally accountable for their delegated activity. Remember that they are also responsible for their contribution to achieving the overall purpose of the decision. Your job is to ensure that accountability is clear and monitored, and that people are managed in a supportive way.

81 Consider the mix of skills needed when you are setting up a team.

82 Encourage team members to take part in making a plan.

▼ BRIEFING A TEAM

When explaining a decision to a team, describe the context in which it was made and what will make it effective. Use visual aids to get the message across.

Team member raises a point

Leader explains decision

SETTING UP A PROJECT TEAM

In organizing a project team you must provide for all technical needs and cover all activities. Include team members in setting up; this will produce better plans and will also foster team spirit. As decision maker you will probably continue in the roles of coordinating all activities and building the team. Your functions will include ensuring that shared values are developed and that the team swiftly finds the best way of working as a group – from the first team meeting onward. You must also think about the roles the individual members will play. Make sure that everybody contributes to teamworking.

COMMUNICATING A DECISION

Once a decision is made and planned, relay it to those colleagues who need to know. Listen and respond to the reactions of staff at all levels, and keep everybody as closely involved as possible with your decision to avoid potential resistance.

83 Be as honest as possible when communicating a decision to staff.

CLARIFYING A DECISION FOR COLLEAGUES

Break down your decision into its component parts

Discuss the key objectives of each part of the decision

Explain the actions required to complete each objective

Delegate responsibility for completion of each action

Give colleagues the deadline for completing each action

Agree on points to monitor the progress of each action

RELEASING INFORMATION

The release of information to everybody concerned in the implementation of a decision is part of the decision-making procedure. When done properly, it ensures that people understand exactly what has been decided and why, and it encourages their support. When you make your decision, explain which alternative action you have considered and the reason why you opted for your choice. Specify what the effects of your decision will be upon individuals. Be open to questioning, and try to remove doubts by making changes in response to genuine objections and concerns. Welcome contributions from anybody who will be affected.

MAINTAINING CONTACT

It is vital to keep everybody informed of progress as well as of changes in policy at all stages of the implementation of a decision. Team meetings, whether formal or informal, are ideal situations in which to discuss work-related problems, brainstorm new solutions to specific aspects of a decision, and air any general grievances. Encourage staff to speak to you in confidence about any interpersonal problems they may have, and, where appropriate, take action on their behalf.

AVOIDING SECRECY

When communicating a decision, lean toward releasing rather than suppressing information – and toward telling everyone involved, not just a chosen few. In traditional hierarchies, decisions are often reached behind closed doors, with the result that rumors may abound. This creates anxiety and uncertainty, and it lowers morale. Sometimes it may be necessary to keep good news under wraps, perhaps for reasons of security, but delaying bad news, understandable though it is, is always counterproductive. If you need to delay the release of information for any good reason, tell people when you expect to be able to give them details.

84 Spot check a few individuals within your organization to ensure that everyone has the right message.

SELLING DECISIONS

To "sell" your decision to colleagues who are unconvinced of its viability you will need to:
- Ensure that you understand the needs of your colleagues;
- Present your decision in a way that matches these needs;
- Stress the advantages of the decision to the organization and individuals involved;
- Let colleagues do most of the talking, and try to turn all objections in your favor;
- Try to convince colleagues that they would have made the same decision as you when closing your "sale."

LETTING OTHERS KNOW OF YOUR DECISION

DECISION MAKER
As a decision maker, you need to inform colleagues throughout the organization of your decision and the actions required to fulfill it. You should use different approaches for different levels of staff.

INFORMING SUPERIORS
You may need to sell your decision to your superiors, since they usually have the ultimate power of veto over any course of action.

INFORMING COLLEAGUES
You may need to work to gain the support and trust of your colleagues, especially if they are suspicious of your motives.

INFORMING JUNIOR STAFF
You may need junior staff to help implement your decision, so invite them to contribute any specialized knowledge they have.

DISCUSSING THE PROGRESS OF A DECISION

Many meetings have no purpose but to discuss and inform. Some, however, are held specifically to discuss progress in the implementation of a decision. For the best results, be clear about what is expected from such meetings and who should attend.

 85 As chairperson, control a meeting and do not become sidetracked.

 86 Make sure the agenda for every meeting is clear to everyone present.

AVOIDING TIME-WASTING

It is important to avoid time-wasting when meeting to discuss the implementation of a decision. Prepare yourself by anticipating and obtaining all the facts that you require. Do you need to provide further evidence of the validity of your plans? Send the agenda, and any supporting papers, to participants in advance so that they can familiarize themselves with the issues. If any vital personnel are unable to attend, consider using telephone or video-conferencing facilities to provide a linkup.

CONDUCTING A MEETING

Keep a tight rein on the proceedings of meetings called to discuss any points raised or problems arising during the implementation of your decision. Make sure that each issue is properly tackled and that all the relevant data concerning your decision are included in the discussion. If necessary, you should guide the participants toward a consensus decision on how to improve an action plan. Try to streamline working procedures and to involve all those present at the meeting. Avoid arguments at all costs – they waste time that would be better spent in discussing and resolving the issues.

POINTS TO REMEMBER

● The fewer people who attend a meeting, the better.

● Agendas should be distributed as far in advance of a meeting as possible.

● Any new information to be provided in a meeting should be prepared well and presented as briefly as possible.

● Each person at a meeting must be given the chance to express their views; otherwise, there is no point in their being present.

FOLLOW-UP MEETINGS

Decisions taken at progress meetings should result in an action agenda, with designated people responsible for seeing that the agenda is kept. Follow-up meetings are as important as the original discussions and must be treated as such. Each action should have a deadline, and the chairperson or a delegate should take charge of seeing that target dates are kept. If you are holding a series of meetings on a project, review the action agenda at each meeting. Discrepancies, variances, and delays should be explained and any consequent decisions taken. The follow-up may indicate a need for radical change to the original decision or decisions. Do not hesitate to act accordingly.

DO'S & DON'TS

✔ Do produce an agenda laying out decisions to be reached in a meeting.

✔ Do make a note of who is following up each course of action.

✔ Do review any action planned at a meeting.

✔ Do face up to change if it proves necessary.

✘ Don't ignore what your team members have to say.

✘ Don't let deadlines drift – keep a tight rein on them.

✘ Don't neglect to prepare properly for each meeting.

✘ Don't be afraid to change your mind.

87 Always take into account the individual skills and personalities in the team you choose for action.

▼ DISCUSSING PLANS OF ACTION

Use meetings to discuss any problems that have occurred during the implementation of a decision. Monitor failure, but focus mainly on receiving constructive input from each participant and discussing improvements to future action plans.

Team member listens to new idea

Chairperson listens to comments by participant

Participant has new idea for solving problem

OVERCOMING OBJECTIONS

Decisions are likely to attract varying degrees of opposition, from mild dissent to outright resistance. Rather than feeling aggrieved, view opposition as a valuable part of decision-making, and respond with intelligence and care.

 88 Always look for an underlying emotional cause for any objections.

LISTENING TO OBJECTIONS

Even if you need to push a decision through, never simply ignore objections or brush them aside – this is guaranteed to let misunderstanding fester. If you feel that those raising objections do not understand your position, remember it is likely that you do not fully understand theirs. Talk to people honestly, one to one, to find out what their complaints are – and the underlying causes. Having decided to reduce staff from 60 to 15, one boss asked those remaining for their views on the issue. It transpired that, although they had agreed with the decision in principle, they feared further dismissals. The boss reassured them that they were good workers, and indispensable. As a result of this two-way openness, morale improved and resentment ended.

 89 Do not be belligerent – it is counterproductive.

▼ SPOTTING SIGNALS

It is crucial to observe and act on non-verbal signals. Recognizing resistance, doubt, or even cool appraisal can help you tackle objections in the best way.

Arms crossed defensively show lack of willingness

Face-cupping shows need for reassurance

RESISTANCE

DOUBT

Hand on chin shows appraisal is unemotional

Open, direct gaze indicates desire to be helpful

ASSESSMENT

SUPPORT

▲ DELIVERING NEWS
Whether the news is good or bad, tell it swiftly to forestall rumors and to canvass support. Create a relaxed atmosphere where people feel that you are willing to listen to any reservations they may have.

90 Involve your colleagues in any decision-making as much as possible.

RESPONDING TO STAFF

If you feel that a decision has raised a number of objections among the workforce, call a meeting to talk about the issues and clear the air. Even where a decision is final, and will be implemented, allow people to air their views freely, and listen carefully to what they have to say. You can often overcome opposition simply through listening, discussing, and reassuring. Your first need is to establish any specific complaints. Are the objections specific, and can they be removed by acceptable changes? If so, inform colleagues that these changes will be made.

FOCUSING ON BENEFITS

Sometimes a decision involves making changes that will have a negative impact on some staff. For example, if you are combining two departments, roles may change or become redundant. Reassure those affected that they are valued, either verbally or through financial compensation. To avoid hard feelings, explain fully why the decision was made. Outline the harm of maintaining an inefficient status quo, and always be positive as you describe the long-term benefits that the decision will bring.

POINTS TO REMEMBER

● People are most likely to accept unpleasant decisions when facts are presented in a positive light.

● If people feel able to come forward with objections, they tend to do so calmly.

● Irate people may make reasonable points that deserve answers.

● Even final decisions can be modified if there is good reason.

MONITORING PROGRESS

After a decision has been put into action, plans rarely go smoothly. There are usually unforeseen eventualities, such as poor performance from key people. Monitor progress to make sure you spot problems and can devise effective remedies.

91 Always identify the reasons for any deviation from planned action.

92 If you overturn a subordinate's decision, explain the reasons for doing so.

MEASURING PROGRESS

The progress of an action plan based on your decision can be measured in time and cost. To monitor financial performance, compare actual expenditure with the budget. Accompany this with an updated forecast of final costs and of any revenue being generated. Set up an annual progress chart mapping the actual performance of the project, and compare this with the original plan to see where problems are arising. If you need to modify a plan, record in a log any changes, why they were made, who authorized them, and the outcome.

SELECTING BREAKPOINTS

You need to check progress of a project regularly, either at natural breakpoints or at specific intervals, to see whether your initial decision still holds good. This is particularly necessary when a decision affects a whole project. Drastic action may be required to put the project back on course, with parts or all of the action plan changing. Always make contingency plans in case the project needs to be abandoned – for example, if a business plan has weakened or staff performance is inadequate. Consider taking a "Go/No-go" decision at selected breakpoints – for example, when research into the validity of a decision is completed or when the project has reached prototype stage.

POINTS TO REMEMBER

- Action agendas should be distributed to everyone who needs them.
- No-go decisions should mean starting again from scratch.
- Making the "best of a bad job", rather than giving up on an entire project, can sometimes be a wise decision.
- A subordinate's decision should be countermanded only if there is no alternative.
- Monitoring progress involves looking at implementation from several different angles.

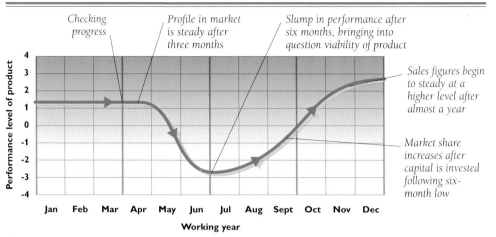

Checking progress

Profile in market is steady after three months

Slump in performance after six months, bringing into question viability of product

Sales figures begin to steady at a higher level after almost a year

Market share increases after capital is invested following six-month low

Performance level of product: 4, 3, 2, 1, 0, -1, -2, -3, -4

Jan Feb Mar Apr May Jun Jul Aug Sept Oct Nov Dec

Working year

▲ WATCHING PROGRESS

This bar chart shows the progress of a new product in the marketplace. Since the performance was monitored and reviewed every three months, the dip in sales at six months was easily rectifiable – a further decision was taken to inject more capital.

93 If your decision to go ahead is half-hearted, cancel it.

MODIFYING DECISIONS

When reviewing decisions, ask yourself: "With the benefit of hindsight, would I make the same decision again?" If the answer is "No," review your decision and change the elements that are at fault. This may mean investing further capital or changing personnel. One manager launched a new product on the basis of market information that proved inaccurate. After a progress review, the product concept was radically altered and the staff in charge replaced – with great success.

OVERTURNING DECISIONS

Monitoring progress may spotlight decisions that are working badly or have been overtaken by events. If you find yourself obliged to overturn a decision made by somebody else, tread carefully. Be diplomatic, but remember that you need to put the good of an organization and the welfare of its people first. If a decision threatens the future or financial status of an organization or its people, react at once. Speak to all the people involved in implementing the original decision. If you are unable to find a way of solving the problem, consider restarting the whole process from scratch.

94 Redefine your decisions if they are not working.

95 Record all changes if you deviate at all from the agreed plan.

Handling Other People's Decisions

Most decisions are delegated downward and involve subordinates. Although final responsibility remains with the delegator, remember that you are responsible for the success of your own performance when asked to undertake and complete a task.

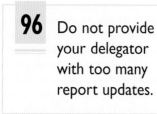

96 Do not provide your delegator with too many report updates.

97 When asked to advise, think what you would do if a decision were yours alone.

Coping with Delegation

If a superior delegates a decision to you, you need to know whether you have total responsibility or whether the delegator wants to retain the ultimate power of approval. If delegation is total, you are required to keep the delegator informed only on a "need-to-know" basis, both for the decision process and on its implementation. If the delegator interferes heavily, either obey unquestioningly or try your powers of argument and diplomacy to do things your way. Consider the delegator's personality in order to judge which course of action is best.

Making a Contribution

If you are invited to help a decision maker, you may be required to draw up a scenario, consider competitive response, explore technical limitations and opportunities, and so on. Remember that your mission is to assist rather than usurp, but take full advantage of the opportunity to influence the decision in whatever way you think is best. State your opinion without fear or favor: pulling punches does not help anyone. Do not be tempted to trim your views to fit those of the decision makers – you will be letting everybody down.

Points to Remember

● You need to understand every aspect of a problem if you are being asked to advise on the best way to solve it.

● Outside advisers should be providing helpful solutions rather than seeking to contradict.

● If it is difficult to agree fully with a decision, the use of tact and honesty is more helpful than a silent submission.

SEEKING CLARIFICATION

It is vital to be clear about any task delegated to you. If you are not sure that you have fully understood your boss at the briefing, note down any points needing clarification. Whether the reason is a failure to convey the brief clearly on the boss's part or simply that there is a lot of information to process at once, you must seek to clarify unanswered questions. Do not seek clarification too often; gather all the points on which you are unclear, and request one session to clear them all up.

Delegate queries points on written brief

▲ UNDERSTANDING A BRIEF

If you have received an unclear brief for a task, it is acceptable to ask your boss to write down exactly what is expected of you. Otherwise, you may fail to produce the desired result.

DO'S AND DON'TS

☑ Do question a superior's decision if it seems wrong.

☑ Do keep asking questions until you understand the brief.

☑ Do feed back your understanding to any colleagues involved in carrying out the brief.

☑ Do protest politely if interference from above is excessive.

☒ Don't try to take over a superior's decision.

☒ Don't just accept a decision for the sake of keeping the peace.

☒ Don't forget that decisions need to be "sold" to the people making the ultimate decisions for you.

☒ Don't forget your responsibilities to those working with you.

98 Gain an understanding of every detail of the brief so that you can carry out your task successfully.

UNDERSTANDING ACCOUNTABILITY

To carry out a task successfully, check what you are accountable for. What are you expected to do, how, and by when? To enable you to monitor and execute your task satisfactorily, devise your own action plan. However, there is a wider issue of responsibility – sticking to your accountable requirements may not be enough. Think carefully about your relationship with other people and other tasks, and keep these shared goals firmly in mind. Your aim should be to deliver a small success as part of a wider, overall success.

BUILDING ON DECISIONS

F ew decisions stand completely alone. In
most cases, one decision leads to others,
forming a continuing process of feedback
and analysis. To build successfully on a
decision, learn your lessons from previously
successful (and unsuccessful) plans of action.

99 Always be prepared
for unexpected
events to affect
your plans.

100 Limit the number
of your goals to
keep them clear.

101 Be prepared to
change your plan
of action to suit
new circumstances.

REVISING OBJECTIVES

At regular intervals, check that decisions are being
made with final goals in mind. Are the original
goals still valid? If so, which new decision can you
take to augment those original aims? If not, revise
your objectives and think again. For example,
if you decide to sell a product direct to retailers,
bypassing the wholesale trade, reaction from the
middlemen may be bad, threatening heavy loss
of business. Do you retreat, or seek a compromise
with the wholesalers? You must
decide how best to react to
overall objectives.

PRIORITIZING DECISIONS

Do not delay badly needed decisions while you
wait for the annual budget or the planning round.
The regular budget and planning cycles cannot
allow for the unexpected, such as the appearance
of a revolutionary new product serving the same
purpose as your own, but in a more effective
way. Recognize that a disruptive event like this
will demand radical steps outside the normal,
predictable procedures of budgeting and planning.
In this case, priority may be given to combating
the revolutionary technology with major new
investment, starting immediately, even though
neither budget nor plan allow for the new strategy.

*Recording
observation
is crucial*

BUILDING ON SUCCESS

Postmortems in management, like those in medicine, usually follow disasters, while success is often neglected. However, it is always as important to know why a decision has succeeded as it is to explain a failure. The exact circumstances of the decision and its action plan may never recur, but a successful methodology could hold important lessons for use in the future. An "action review" technique, such as that employed by the US Army, is helpful. After every decision is implemented, sit down and review what went right and what went wrong, and why. Do not leave it at that. Record the lessons so that they can be absorbed and applied by others – and by you – in the future.

▼ **REVIEWING AN ACTION PLAN**
Use meetings to review action plans. Look at both positive and negative aspects of a situation so that successful outcomes can be repeated and any problems ironed out for the next time.

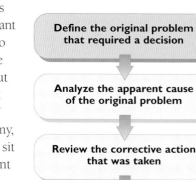

ASSESSING A DECISION'S EFFECTIVENESS

Define the original problem that required a decision

⬇

Analyze the apparent cause of the original problem

⬇

Review the corrective action that was taken

⬇

Consider the effectiveness of the corrective action

⬇

Learn from the result of the action taken

Active listening encourages participation

Giving positive feedback improves morale

ASSESSING YOUR ABILITY

M aking the right decision every single time is practically impossible. However, employing the right processes, techniques, and tools can improve your chances of making the correct choices. Use the following self-assessment to test your decision-making abilities. Be as honest as you can: if your answer is "never," mark Option 1; if it is "always," mark Option 4; and so on. Add your scores together, then refer to the Analysis to see how you scored. Use your answers to identify the areas that need improving.

OPTIONS

1 Never

2 Occasionally

3 Frequently

4 Always

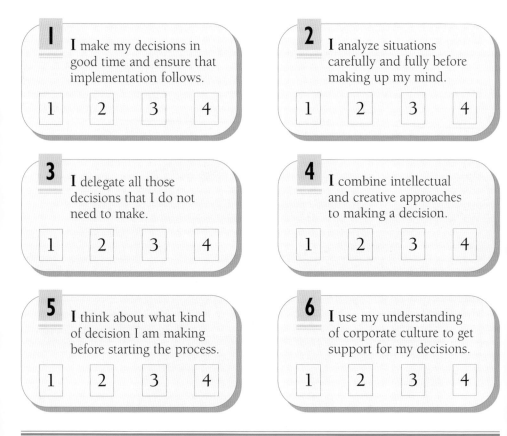

1 I make my decisions in good time and ensure that implementation follows.

1 2 3 4

2 I analyze situations carefully and fully before making up my mind.

1 2 3 4

3 I delegate all those decisions that I do not need to make.

1 2 3 4

4 I combine intellectual and creative approaches to making a decision.

1 2 3 4

5 I think about what kind of decision I am making before starting the process.

1 2 3 4

6 I use my understanding of corporate culture to get support for my decisions.

1 2 3 4

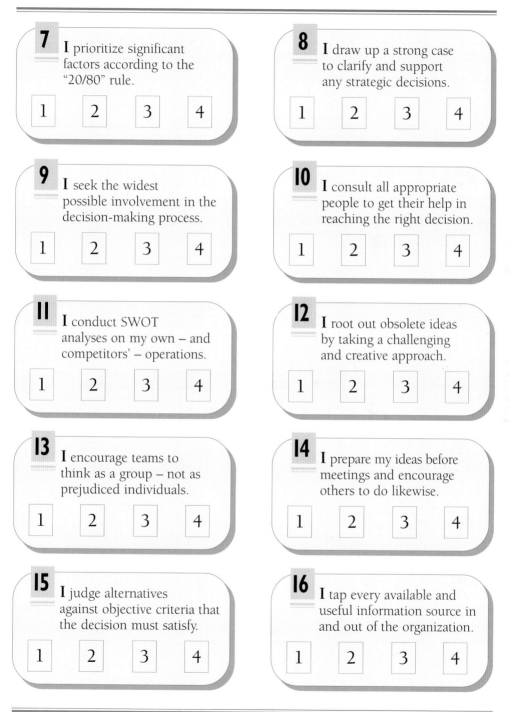

7 I prioritize significant factors according to the "20/80" rule.

1   2   3   4

8 I draw up a strong case to clarify and support any strategic decisions.

1   2   3   4

9 I seek the widest possible involvement in the decision-making process.

1   2   3   4

10 I consult all appropriate people to get their help in reaching the right decision.

1   2   3   4

11 I conduct SWOT analyses on my own – and competitors' – operations.

1   2   3   4

12 I root out obsolete ideas by taking a challenging and creative approach.

1   2   3   4

13 I encourage teams to think as a group – not as prejudiced individuals.

1   2   3   4

14 I prepare my ideas before meetings and encourage others to do likewise.

1   2   3   4

15 I judge alternatives against objective criteria that the decision must satisfy.

1   2   3   4

16 I tap every available and useful information source in and out of the organization.

1   2   3   4

17 I consider the actions and reactions that affect and follow from my decisions.

1 2 3 4

18 I weigh up probabilities when considering forecasts and planned outcomes.

1 2 3 4

19 I use computers where appropriate to assist in decision-making.

1 2 3 4

20 I seek to minimize risks, but I take necessary ones with confidence.

1 2 3 4

21 I use different scenarios to improve forecasts and test plans for their viability.

1 2 3 4

22 I make decisions on their merits and without fear for my own position.

1 2 3 4

23 I take care to canvass support for my decisions at all stages of the process.

1 2 3 4

24 I involve the whole team in drawing up plans for implementation.

1 2 3 4

25 I ensure that a named person is accountable for each stage of an action plan.

1 2 3 4

26 I communicate my decisions openly, honestly, and as quickly as possible.

1 2 3 4

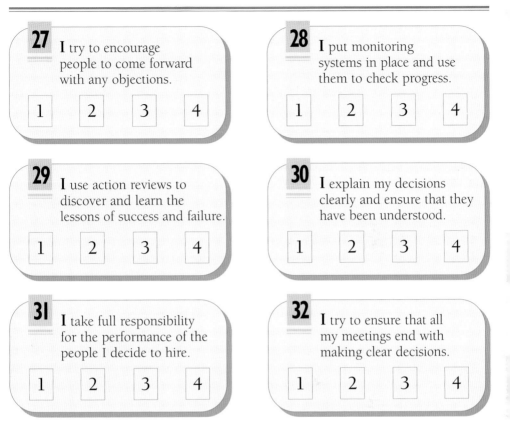

27 I try to encourage people to come forward with any objections.

| 1 | 2 | 3 | 4 |

28 I put monitoring systems in place and use them to check progress.

| 1 | 2 | 3 | 4 |

29 I use action reviews to discover and learn the lessons of success and failure.

| 1 | 2 | 3 | 4 |

30 I explain my decisions clearly and ensure that they have been understood.

| 1 | 2 | 3 | 4 |

31 I take full responsibility for the performance of the people I decide to hire.

| 1 | 2 | 3 | 4 |

32 I try to ensure that all my meetings end with making clear decisions.

| 1 | 2 | 3 | 4 |

ANALYSIS

Now that you have completed the assessment, add up your total score and check your performance by reading the corresponding evaluation. Whatever level of success you have achieved, or have the potential to achieve, there is always room for improvement. Identify your weakest areas, then refer to the relevant chapters of this section, where you will find practical advice and tips that will enable you to hone your decision-making skills.

32–64: Your decision-making is poor. Look at the areas in which you scored badly, then adopt methods you have not tried before.
65–95: Your decision-making skills are basically sound; build on them.
96–128: Your decision-making skills are strong, but do not become complacent – look to improve.

DELEGATING SUCCESSFULLY

INTRODUCTION

D elegation is an essential element of any manager's job. Used effectively, it provides real benefits for everyone involved. This section will enable you to achieve the best possible results from each delegation you make – from small everyday tasks to major leadership appointments. The section covers every aspect of this process, from deciding and prioritizing which tasks to delegate and choosing the right person for the job to recognizing and overcoming barriers and anticipating risks. Practical advice on how to motivate and develop staff, build loyalty, and give and receive feedback will increase your confidence and help you become a skilled and trusted delegator. Included are 101 practical tips that summarize key points and a self-assessment exercise that provides insight into your performance as a delegator.

UNDERSTANDING DELEGATION

Effective delegation is an essential managerial skill.
To achieve the best results, you must be aware of its benefits
and recognize the barriers that can hinder its success.

DEFINING DELEGATION

As organizations grow increasingly complex, duties and responsibilities across the workforce can become less well defined. Often it seems as though everyone is doing everyone else's job. Delegation is the manager's key to efficiency, and benefits all.

1 Use delegation to benefit you, your staff, and your organization.

▲ **DELEGATING FOR MANAGERIAL SUCCESS**
An effective manager must monitor a delegated project, assuming responsibility while allowing the delegate autonomy.

EXPLAINING DELEGATION

Delegation involves entrusting another person with a task for which the delegator remains ultimately responsible. Delegation can range from a major appointment, such as the leadership of a team developing a new product, to one of any number of smaller tasks in the everyday life of any organization – from arranging an annual outing to interviewing a job candidate. Examining the overall structure of an organization will reveal a complex web of delegated authority, usually in the form of management chains, providing a mechanism for reporting and control.

222

EXPLORING THE FUNDAMENTALS

The basic issues involved in delegation are autonomy and control. How much authority is the delegate able to exercise without referring back to the delegator? How far should the delegator exercise direct influence over the delegate's work? When you choose a delegate you are assessing whether a particular person is fully capable of performing the task within available resources. Having appointed a delegate, you must ensure that they are allowed sufficient autonomy to undertake the task in their own way, subject to an initial briefing and regular reports on progress.

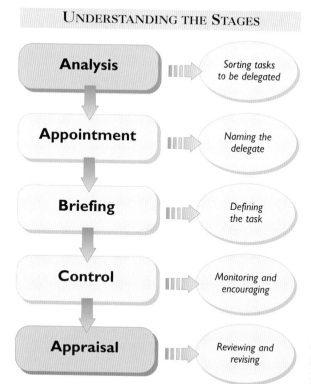

UNDERSTANDING THE STAGES

Analysis → Sorting tasks to be delegated

Appointment → Naming the delegate

Briefing → Defining the task

Control → Monitoring and encouraging

Appraisal → Reviewing and revising

DEFINING THE PROCESS

The unending process of delegation is integral to the manager's role. The process begins with the analysis – selecting the tasks that the manager could, and should, delegate. When the tasks are selected, the parameters of each should be clearly defined. This will help the delegator to appoint an appropriate delegate and to provide as accurate a brief as possible. Whatever the role, proper briefing is essential – you cannot hold people responsible for vague or undefined tasks. Monitoring of some kind is also essential, but should be used for control and coaching rather than interference. The final stage is appraisal. How well has the delegate performed? What changes, on both sides, need to be made to improve performance?

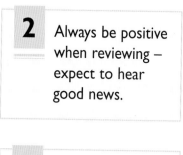

2 Always be positive when reviewing – expect to hear good news.

3 Show faith in your chosen delegate, even if others have reservations.

WHY DELEGATE?

*D*elegation has a number of benefits. When you streamline your workload, you increase the amount of time available for essential managerial tasks. Your staff feel motivated and more confident, and stress levels decrease across the workforce.

4 Delegate to boost staff morale, build confidence, and reduce stress.

INCREASING YOUR TIME

Managers commonly claim that the short-term demands of operational and minor duties make it impossible to devote sufficient time to more important, long-term matters. Strategic planning, control, and training are among the higher level activities which will suffer under the burden of undelegated, routine tasks which you wrongly attempt to do yourself. To create more time for yourself, more routine work must be handed down by delegation. Also, the more frequently you delegate, the more experienced staff become, and the less time you need to spend on briefing.

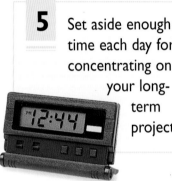

5 Set aside enough time each day for concentrating on your long-term projects.

REDUCING STRESS

The pressure on managers to perform under demanding conditions can lead to a marked increase in stress levels. The symptoms are visible in erratic and sometimes disorientated personal behavior, mounting paperwork on desks, and overcrowded calendars. Clearing your desk and your calendar is best accomplished through delegation. Fully effective delegation not only eases the pressure on the delegator, but can benefit the delegate and the team or department as a whole. Before delegating, consider carefully the task requirements, and make a realistic assessment of your proposed delegate's abilities.

QUESTIONS TO ASK YOURSELF

Q Am I devoting enough time and resources to strategic planning and overall monitoring?

Q Is my desk overflowing with uncompleted tasks?

Q Are staff enthusiastic and sufficiently motivated?

Q Am I delegating routine but necessary tasks to staff?

Q Is staff training given priority to ensure effective skills for future delegation plans?

DELEGATING TO MOTIVATE

A sense of achievement is central to any employee's job satisfaction. Effective delegation involves the stimulus of increased responsibility and can provide a delegate with an enriched level of satisfaction as well as a greater sense of worth. Delegation is empowerment, and that is the mainspring of better work. Your staff will not develop unless they are given tasks that build their abilities, experience, and confidence. They will perform best in a structured environment in which everyone is aware of delegated duties and responsibilities and each has the necessary skills and resources to carry out tasks efficiently. Use regular and effective feedback sessions as tools for maintaining a delegate's motivation.

6 Make sure you have the right experience to coach others.

7 If delegation is not working, ask yourself, "What am I doing wrong?"

THE COSTS OF AVOIDING DELEGATION

Delegation takes time to organize and prioritize, but the costs of avoiding it are high. The manager who does not delegate or delegates inefficiently will not only seem disorganized, but will spend many hours each week completing low-priority tasks. This can result in excessive hours worked by senior managers, low morale among underemployed staff, basic processes slowed down by bottlenecks, poor quality of work, and missed deadlines. Together, all of these factors will have a detrimental effect on long-term performance.

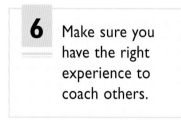

▼ **DELEGATING INEFFECTIVELY**
A manager who avoids delegation cannot possibly hope to complete effectively all of the tasks that find their way onto his or her desk.

RECOGNIZING AND DEALING WITH BARRIERS

Managers often find delegation difficult. Barriers preventing delegation are often based on negative feelings of insecurity and mistrust. The gains achieved through overcoming these feelings and beginning to trust will far outweigh any possible losses.

8 Avoid keeping work because you do it better – that is bad management.

DOING IT YOURSELF

As a manager, you will probably be more efficient at many tasks than your staff. But if you attempt to do everything because you are quicker, surer, and more proficient you will inevitably find yourself overburdened. As a result you will not have sufficient time to spend on the higher-level tasks that only you can do. Moreover, how will your staff become proficient if they are not given the opportunity to learn and perform more tasks?

MISUSE OF A ▼ MANAGER'S TIME
Here the manager is not only doing his own job, but is wasting time that should be spent on more important work by performing the routine, nonmanagerial tasks that could and should be delegated to appropriate subordinates.

Manager works on appropriate, high-level task

Menial tasks waste time and energy

Faxing does not need to be done by a manager

OVERBURDENING STAFF

The fear of overburdening staff is a strong barrier to delegation – it is natural for conscientious managers to want to ensure that staff workloads are not excessive. If staff members appear to be working to full capacity, how can you delegate tasks without overburdening them? One solution is to keep back tasks and find time to do them yourself. A more sensible approach is to make employees analyze their own use of time and free capacity for more work. If staff shortage is truly the problem, the answer is to take on more staff. It is important not to allow the overburdening argument to result in overwork for yourself.

QUESTIONS TO ASK YOURSELF

Q How much of my time is spent on things that I should be delegating to colleagues?

Q Can I learn from the way my own boss delegates to me?

Q Have I got my paperwork under control?

Q Why should it upset me if a subordinate performs part of my job brilliantly?

Q How much spare work capacity is there in my unit?

9 Delegate efficiently to strengthen your own performance.

10 Be loyal to your staff, and they will be loyal to you.

BEING INEXPERIENCED

The basic mechanics of the delegation process involve common management skills that delegators should develop, including skills in controlling and reviewing. The challenge for managers with limited experience of delegation is to master the more complex aspects of the process, such as attaining an effective and appropriate leadership style. Delegation is a self-teaching activity – you develop and perfect skills through the process itself, and your confidence and abilities increase the more you delegate.

LOSING CONTROL OF TASKS

The desire to be in total control is a common human trait. Delegation involves the loss of direct control, and this loss is a potential barrier to the delegation process. When delegating, the manager passes on responsibility for completion of the tasks to the chosen delegate – but the delegator retains overall control by appointing the right person, having a clear idea of how the task should progress, and exchanging regular feedback.

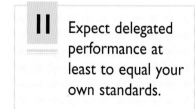

11 Expect delegated performance at least to equal your own standards.

DEALING WITH FEAR

Fear is a major barrier to delegation. Sometimes managers fear that delegates will perform so well that they will challenge the delegator's own position. A parallel fear is that "losing" part of the job diminishes personal importance. These fears may underlie a third – that the delegate will do badly. Tackle the fears by asking yourself four questions: Is the task suitable for delegation? Is the delegate competent to perform the task? Will I brief them fully and correctly? Will I give them all proper support, authority, and resources? If the answers are positive, then there is nothing to fear, and the delegation should succeed.

POINTS TO REMEMBER

- Possessive feelings about work are negative and unproductive.
- Keeping hold of minor tasks impedes the development of effective management.
- Analysis of staff work time is sure to reveal spare capacity.
- It is self-defeating and wastes time to attempt to manage without the use of schedules.
- Delegation involves the loss of direct control but the retention of overall responsibility.

12 Encourage people who claim to be overworked to keep a time log.

FEELING INSECURE

Insecure managers who do not take advantage of delegation underuse employees and actually endanger their own security. But if you enlist skilled and motivated people to carry out the delegated work, there is no need to feel insecure. The use of delegation, far from being a threat to a delegator's position at work, actually enhances performance and therefore increases job security. That is why many top managers have remarkably clear desks – they concentrate on a small number of priority tasks, and delegate everything else.

BEING SUSPICIOUS

Managers can still be unsure even when their staff have proved their competence. The bad delegator believes that a job, particularly one that is important, must be done "their way." This leads to very restrictive briefings that give the delegate little space for initiative. Resist any urge you may have to interfere more than necessary, as this will only create more work and worry for you, thus defeating the object of the delegation.

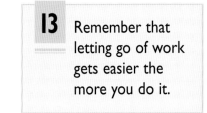

13 Remember that letting go of work gets easier the more you do it.

14 Use the delegation of tasks as an effective means of training your staff.

15 If you often say "I don't have enough time," you are badly organized.

BEING TOO BUSY

Planning your own daily and weekly schedule is an essential precondition of effective delegation. An overworked manager, with a disorganized and overloaded schedule, is both the villain and the victim of inadequate delegation. It is all too easy to establish a vicious circle. You do not delegate enough because you lack the time to explain or monitor the tasks which should be delegated, therefore you are always busy doing the tasks that should have been delegated – which means that you lack the time to explain or monitor the tasks which should be delegated, and so on. Organize your schedule to ensure that you have enough time available to plan and manage delegation properly, including writing effective briefs and the actual monitoring of your delegates.

LACKING TRUST

If both sides in the delegation process do not trust each other, the process will be hindered. A manager must have complete confidence in a delegate's ability to perform the task, and delegates should feel that their managers are consistent and fair in their approach. Subordinates must feel assured about their manager's integrity, competence, and loyalty. On both sides, the trust is conditional. Trust is not blind, and its continuation depends on good performance. Maintain trust by showing respect to your delegate and by giving honest and constructive feedback during the delegation.

Uses schedules when planning

Has confidence in subordinates

Knows the value of delegating

Does not feel insecure

Ensures staff are trained

THE EFFECTIVE DELEGATOR

▲ OVERCOMING BARRIERS
When you recognize the barriers that are preventing you from delegating effectively, you are more than halfway toward dealing with them: Once you have overcome your initial fears, your efficiency as a delegator and manager will be greatly increased.

Building a Relationship

Frankness, openness, and effective communication are essential to successful delegation, helping to build and sustain trust and overcome many personal barriers. You can reinforce trust and nurture mutual esteem through careful management.

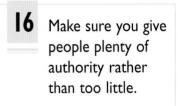 **16** Make sure you give people plenty of authority rather than too little.

Communicating Well
When managers keep knowledge to themselves, communicate sporadically and incompletely, or even make no attempt to tell the truth at all, mistrust and other negative feelings in their staff will build rapidly. But misunderstandings and unjustified suspicions can result even when people believe they are discussing matters openly and honestly. Some managers hear only what they want to hear, and employees may be afraid to contradict them. To be a good communicator, you must express your ideas clearly and develop your listening skills. This will encourage others to share their thoughts and opinions with you.

 **17** Always deal swiftly and positively with idle and unjustified rumors.

Comparing Perceptions
When assessing whether you are a helpful and accomplished delegator, you must always bear in mind the delegate's point of view. You may uncover a surprising gulf in the way a situation is perceived. Make it clear from the start that you want and expect honest opinions about your delegating style. If the feedback you receive indicates that you are thought of as interfering and distrustful, act immediately to correct the situation. The more delegates realize that they have real responsibility and will not be second-guessed, the better they will do.

 18 If you do not trust a staff member, do not keep them.

 19 Treat your own perceptions as facts and analyze them objectively.

RESPECTING OPINIONS

Treat everyone with the same respect that you expect yourself, because your staff are allies in the job of management. When you delegate, you show respect by entrusting part of your work to another because you believe in their capability and their suitability. To build mutual respect, ask your delegates for their opinions on how the work should be done, and show you are listening to their suggestions.

DO'S AND DON'TS

✔ Do use all means to communicate with your staff.

✔ Do strive to regard your associates as competent people.

✔ Do remind delegates that you respect and appreciate them.

✔ Do show your delegates loyalty and support.

✔ Do allow delegates the opportunity to give their opinions.

✘ Don't be dismayed by differing perceptions – they are natural.

✘ Don't forget that trust is a two-way process that can take time and effort to establish.

✘ Don't ask people to do things that you wouldn't do yourself.

✘ Don't use delegates as scapegoats when things go wrong.

✘ Don't dissuade staff from speaking out.

LOOKING AT TRANSACTIONAL ANALYSIS

Understanding how people behave with each other helps build successful delegating relationships. Transactional Analysis is a systematic approach to interpersonal behavior that defines three "ego" systems:

● PARENT: Directive, rigid, controlling, supportive.
● ADULT: Rational, objective, fact orientated.
● CHILD: Self-centered, dependent, stubborn.

By observation it is possible to recognize which system is dominant in an individual. For example, people may dominate others by using their PARENT mode to provoke the other's CHILD. Or the CHILD may take a "poor me" stance to control others. Productive delegation depends on mutual trust and respect, and Transactional Analysis suggests that this is best achieved if the ADULT system is most active.

USING THE RIGHT ATTITUDE ▶

The interpersonal process of delegation is greatly enhanced if relationships are conducted in an honest and open ADULT to ADULT way.

DELEGATING EFFECTIVELY

The most successful delegators are expert, self-disciplined managers who are efficient at choosing tasks to delegate and able to monitor and provide positive feedback to each delegate.

SELECTING TASKS

Before you can improve your delegating technique you must decide which tasks you could, or should, be delegating. The selection process involves assessing your time and that of your subordinates, and grouping and prioritizing activities.

20 Do not allow people to create unnecessary work for you.

21 Review and revise your detailed time log every three to six months.

ANALYZING YOUR TIME

The way you, as a manager, distribute your work and how much time you allocate is probably under your control. A useful exercise is to determine how your actual expenditure of time matches the areas or tasks for which you are responsible. Start the analysis by keeping a detailed time log for at least two weeks; note all activities you undertake and the time taken. You will probably find that only a small amount of your time has been spent on the high-level activities that only you can do. Far more time will have been taken up by routine activities that could have been delegated.

BREAKING DOWN YOUR TASKS

After analyzing how much time is spent, analyze the tasks you are undertaking. Do this by dividing the tasks listed in your time log into the three groups outlined by the management writer Peter Drucker: those that do not need to be done at all – by you or anyone else; those that you could and should delegate; and those that you are not able to delegate and must do yourself. Use this breakdown as a basis for reducing any unnecessary activities, delegating more tasks, and concentrating on tasks that only you can complete.

EVALUATING YOUR ACTIVITIES

What tasks am I doing that need not be done at all? → Do not complete them yourself or delegate them.

What am I doing that could be done by someone else? → Delegate these tasks to subordinates.

What tasks am I doing that can only be done by me? → You cannot delegate these, so prioritize them.

CONSIDERING OTHER IMPORTANT FACTORS

When you come to choose which tasks to delegate, there are several points that you must consider. Some of the most important of those factors are:

- That unnecessary activities are eliminated from the task list altogether;
- That you are able to concentrate your attention on the tasks that only you can do;
- That there are enough suitably qualified delegates for the tasks to be delegated;
- That, where necessary, the delegation has been cleared with your own superior.

Obviously, these are not the only points you need to think about, but once you have considered and acted upon them – along with any others that you think are important – you can move on to the next stage of the delegating process: prioritizing.

22 If possible, attend only the meetings directly relevant to your work.

23 If you cannot fix a meeting for weeks ahead, you are not delegating enough.

PRIORITIZING TASKS

Having decided which tasks to delegate and which to handle yourself, your first concern is to deal with the allocation of tasks. Prioritize the remaining tasks according to their importance or urgency. Start each day by listing these tasks, and tackle them one by one in order of priority. If circumstances allow, always complete a task before starting a new one. The closer you keep to this system, the more effective you will be.

 24 Do not prioritize easy tasks over those that are more arduous.

ESTIMATING TIME

When delegating tasks you need to have a fairly accurate idea of how long each task will take to complete. Base this estimate either on your own experience or the experience of others. Try not to tie your delegates to an excessively tight schedule, but always encourage them to improve their own time management and the time spent on a task. This approach is essential and invariably effective. You and they will find that the time spent on tasks – especially routines that go unchallenged for years – can often be greatly shortened by cutting out any unnecessary stages, or by radically changing processes and working methods.

 **25** Do not attempt to undertake more than seven tasks in one day.

GROUPING TASKS

Your list of tasks to be done – either by yourself or a delegate – will produce activities that are related to, or have affinities with, each other. Study these carefully and group them under specific headings: administration, human resources, or financial, for example. You can then consider delegating each group of related tasks to one person. More importantly, if you have a potential delegate who particularly enjoys and is good at administrative tasks, say, it makes perfect sense for that person to deal with all of them.

26 Make a habit of challenging long-standing routines.

MAKING CHOICES

Ultimately, the choice of what you delegate, however logical the analysis has been, will have an element of subjectivity. Some jobs that could be delegated will be especially dear to you. For example, you may choose to retain close day-to-day contact with suppliers whom you have known for a long time – suppliers who could be dealt with by a subordinate. Provided these tasks have no adverse impact on general effectiveness, this is perfectly acceptable. However, do not allow your choice to be dictated by dislikes – you cannot always delegate the tasks you do not like. So periodically revise the list of activities only you can do and consider whether the list could be cut down, perhaps by training somebody to do a task.

POINTS TO REMEMBER

- Tasks should be listed in order of priority based on their urgency and importance.
- Undertaking work that you cannot carry out shows willingness but is counterproductive.
- Every moment of your day should be used efficiently, and time-wasting should be eliminated from your schedule.
- Responsibility for an entire task should be given to one employee whenever possible.
- New opportunities for the delegation of tasks should be sought continuously.

AN EXAMPLE OF TASK GROUPING

THE PROJECT

THE TASKS TO BE DELEGATED

THE DELEGATOR
A senior employee is asked to organize the manufacture and launch of a new product. While retaining overall responsibility, he decides to list what needs doing and group the work into three key areas for delegation.

STAFF RECRUITMENT
The delegator asks one person to produce a human resources strategy that will supply multiskilled staff in advance of deadlines and will operate within the agreed financial constraints.

PRODUCT MANUFACTURE
He asks another person to produce a work flow chart, a layout of the manufacturing process, a program to meet deadlines, and details of quality-control procedures.

MARKETING
He asks a third person to calculate a budget to cover the total costs of marketing the new product to both established and new customers, including mailings and sales trips.

DECIDING WHICH TASKS TO KEEP

As a manager you should delegate as many of the lower-level operational tasks as possible. But you cannot delegate such areas as strategic planning, occasional crisis management, and sensitive matters such as salaries and promotion.

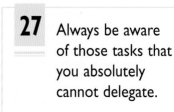

27 Always be aware of those tasks that you absolutely cannot delegate.

28 Plan your thinking time as a meeting, with an agenda and timetable.

RETAINING TASKS

Tasks that you cannot delegate include key areas such as controlling overall performance, and confidential human resources matters – how people are rewarded, appraised, promoted, informed, coached, and counseled. You may also need to manage all dealings with important customers. Make these tasks your priority and ensure that you allocate ample time to them.

SETTING ASIDE THINKING TIME

Tasks that you cannot delegate have common themes – meeting the strategic objectives of the organization, the team, and you the manager. Typically, a manager is immersed in operational detail, such as gathering information or organizing meetings, and spends only 20 percent of the workweek in high-level thinking. By delegating effectively you can reorganize your time to allow strategic planning, or thinking, to occupy the largest segment of your time. Delegation and effective use of information technology could triple the time available for thinking to about 60 percent of the workweek.

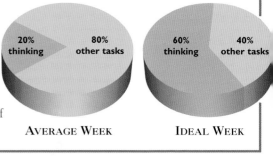

| 20% thinking | 80% other tasks | 60% thinking | 40% other tasks |

AVERAGE WEEK   **IDEAL WEEK**

TASKS MANAGERS SHOULD RETAIN

RESPONSIBILITIES	FACTORS TO CONSIDER
LEADERSHIP Providing the drive and stewardship for a project or an organization.	A leadership task is one that is essential for leading a group or project to success. Because of its importance to control, it cannot usually be delegated to a subordinate but can be shared with one or two senior colleagues.
REWARD Setting and maintaining parameters for salaries and bonuses.	The setting of general and individual levels of pay and other remuneration is so basic to motivation that it clearly falls within the manager's duties. The same is true of any significant nonfinancial rewards.
CONTROL Achieving optimum performance in the working environment.	Day-to-day working discipline, accurate systems, quality procedures, and efficient execution do not have to be the manager's operational tasks. But the responsibility for seeing that controls are effective cannot be delegated.
PERSONNEL Controlling human resource matters, conduct, and discipline.	The manager must take a close interest in staff careers and performance, personally conducting reviews and appraisals and making sensitive and confidential decisions on promotions, reviews, hirings, and dismissals.
KEY CUSTOMERS Maintaining key relationships that rely on personal and social skills.	The continued success of a business is closely tied to continued good relationships with key customers. The manager must never endanger these relationships by delegating ultimate responsibility for these contacts.
STRATEGY Establishing key targets and the means of fulfilling them.	Planning for the future (short-, medium-, and long-term) is a task that must be originated and led from the top, but which depends for full success on enlisting committed contributions from all levels of the team.
COMMUNICATIONS Ensuring the efficient internal transfer of information.	Making sure that good channels of communication exist and are used continuously cannot be delegated. The manager ensures that on both a personal and group level, a smooth flow of relevant information is maintained.
RESULTS Assessing outcomes and the application of lessons learned.	The manager sets the goals, in agreement with all staff, and monitors the successful progress toward these goals. When any targets are endangered, the manager steps in and immediately acts to improve the situation.

PLANNING A STRUCTURE WITH DELEGATION

D*elegation is a planned and organized sharing of responsibility that requires careful structuring. Once you have decided which tasks to delegate and which to keep, set up a structure and devise an overall plan for all the individual delegations involved.*

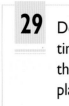

29 Devote sufficient time and effort to the organizational plan and structure.

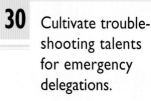

30 Cultivate trouble-shooting talents for emergency delegations.

PLANNING A STRUCTURE

A planned delegation on any scale, from a few individuals to an entire company, provides the basis for a structure that resembles a set of building blocks, each representing a specific responsibility, and each with a specific person in charge. The stability of the whole structure depends on the individual blocks; remove any and the edifice may tumble down. For added stability, ensure that delegated tasks are directly relevant to the delegate's overall job responsibility, and that every delegate has a direct reporting line to the delegator.

▼ USING A FAULTY STRUCTURE
An organizational structure in which any key part is missing, or the whole is badly planned, is a weak and unstable edifice liable to collapse in times of crisis.

SETTING UP A STRUCTURE

When setting up a structure, your priority will be to ensure that the organizational framework is balanced and responsive to any of the inevitable changes that can occur. Do this by ensuring that each delegate has sufficient support and backup when unforeseen problems arise and that, as far as possible, adequate coverage will always be made available in any absence. Inform each delegate of the support structure you have devised so that each knows where they can go to seek assistance immediately in a crisis. When planning the structure, remember that it is your responsibility as the delegator to ensure that the structure remains relevant, stable, and effective.

THINGS TO DO

1. Draw up a delegation plan.
2. Inform delegates of your plans well in advance.
3. Consider the overall structure when delegating.
4. Ensure that delegates know to whom they are reporting.
5. Monitor the progress of each task to make sure that no gaps or overlaps appear.

31 Start considering possible delegates when planning the tasks to be done.

AVOIDING DUPLICATION

When planning a structure, delegating, and distributing tasks, avoid giving the same task to more than one person or overlooking a task so that it is not done at all. To prevent confusion, create a chart with all key activities listed on the left-hand side, and the names of those with delegated responsibility along the top line. Check off each box in the chart with both a task and a delegate to reveal any gaps or overlaps in the distribution and structure of the tasks.

DELEGATING IN ADVANCE

It is inappropriate to treat delegation as simply a way for a harassed manager to shed excessive work during busy periods. As the start date of a project for which you are responsible draws near, plan and make any delegated appointments as early as possible. This will give you sufficient time to prepare a detailed brief, and will allow you and your delegate to discuss task requirements fully and arrange any training that may be needed.

32 Ensure you provide enough support and backup to each delegate.

CONSIDERING ROLES

Unless you are intending to delegate the management of an entire project, you will need to consider the various roles that could be delegated. Assess these in relation to potential team members and consider the contribution each individual could make.

 33 Ensure that you have an informed assessment of a delegate's abilities.

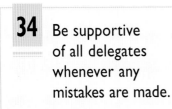 **34** Be supportive of all delegates whenever any mistakes are made.

DEFINING THE TASKS

To delegate effectively, you need to define the tasks and also have a good understanding of a proposed delegate's abilities. So for each task in your planned delegation, work out a clear definition, including the skills required and the range of responsibilities to be delegated. Go through this process whether you are delegating a large project with a number of parts requiring different skills or a simple, one-time task.

TRAINING DELEGATES

When you are planning delegations in advance, consider which skills will need to be taught or developed to enable the potential delegates to undertake tasks successfully. Remember that even a skilled and highly experienced delegate may well require help in mastering a new role. Specific training will not only provide delegates with invaluable knowledge about the task they are to be involved with, but will also complement their other abilities. Additionally, teaching will motivate delegates and strengthen their self-confidence.

35 Do not give advice if delegates can manage without it.

▼ DEVELOPING STAFF
Training serves two purposes: strengthening skills needed in new roles, and motivating staff as they become more competent.

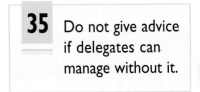

Teach ➤ Strengthen ➤ Motivate

ASSESSING INDIVIDUALS

Having clearly defined the tasks involved, carefully consider the qualities of all members of your team and begin thinking about which roles may suit each individual, bearing in mind their strengths and weaknesses. For example, when assessing the role of cost controller for a project, the manager will be looking for a delegate with good numerical skills and sufficient self-confidence to initiate any cost-cutting measures that may prove necessary.

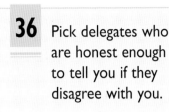

36 Pick delegates who are honest enough to tell you if they disagree with you.

LOOKING FOR INITIATIVE

Initiative is an ideal quality in any potential delegate, so look at your team to see who acts on their own initiative, and bear them in mind for more responsible and challenging roles. Remember that a person who has strong ideas and opinions of their own may sometimes disagree with their manager. An employee who is prepared to do this is showing self-confidence – a desirable quality that should be encouraged. Disagreement is not insubordination, and must not be treated as such.

ENCOURAGING ▼ INITIATIVE

Here the manager appreciates the initiative the delegate has shown in preparing in advance all he needs to put his ideas across as clearly as possible.

A confident approach to manager

Manager is impressed by delegate's approach

Delegate presents ideas clearly

UNDERSTANDING ACCOUNTABILITY

Accountability is at the very heart of delegation, so before you finally select your delegates, consider who you are going to make responsible for what. Accountability must be strictly defined so that there is no doubt over where it lies and what it covers.

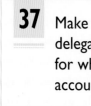

37 Make clear to delegates the areas for which they are accountable.

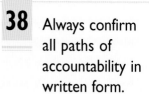

38 Always confirm all paths of accountability in written form.

SETTING GUIDELINES

Delegation operates within guidelines, and the most important of these is an understanding that each delegate will be accountable for a specific task. It follows that you must define the task very clearly, and the delegate must confirm that they fully understand what the task involves. However clear the delegation, and however much you wish to avoid interference, there are likely be occasions when the delegate does not know what to do. The guideline here is: when really in doubt, ask.

AVOIDING OVERLAPS

To avoid any confusion over which delegate is accountable for what part of a task, break down delegated tasks into specific elements and allocate each element to a named person. Within the overall structure of responsibility, make each delegate accountable for his or her own particular component of the task – for example, controlling expenditure or processing contracts with outside suppliers. This "single-point accountability" is not only very precise, it will also greatly reduce the risk of you giving more than one delegate responsibility for the same task or part of a task.

39 Encourage staff with shared tasks to form effective partnerships.

SHARING ACCOUNTABILITY

In general, delegation is most effective when accountability for a task rests with one individual. This avoids confusion and the tendency for one party to blame another for a mistake or failure. A pooling of accountability, however, is natural in self-managed teams or project groups where leadership is shared by the members. In these groups all decisions relating to a project are reached through collective effort, and all team members are jointly accountable for the outcome of their work; that is one of the basic strengths of teamwork. For shared accountability to work effectively, it should follow the same principles as for individual accountability – a clear and agreed definition and breakdown of tasks into very precise, individually allocated "single-point" elements to eliminate any possible overlaps.

40 Establish a culture that recognizes success and avoids blame for failure.

41 Ensure that written documents are circulated to all relevant staff.

▲ INDIVIDUAL ACCOUNTABILITY
Each member of this four-person sales and marketing team is individually accountable to a sales director for a specific area. The director plans strategy and has responsibility for the performance of the team.

▲ SHARED ACCOUNTABILITY
In this self-managed sales team each member shares equal responsibility for planning and implementing a strategy for the unit, for the attainment of targets within a set budget, and for the team's efficiency.

Choosing the Right Person

*I*t is very important to choose the right person for the task at hand. The first few times, it will be a case of trial and error, but before long you should learn how to better assess the skills, and therefore the person, needed for every situation that arises.

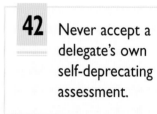

42 Never accept a delegate's own self-deprecating assessment.

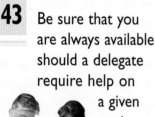

43 Be sure that you are always available should a delegate require help on a given project.

Making Quick Decisions

If a job must be completed in a hurry and you can resist the impulse to do it yourself, you may be tempted to commandeer the nearest available person. Occasionally these sudden demands can reveal unsuspected talents, but sometimes not – with negative consequences. If circumstances force you to make a quick decision and you have any choice at all, pick the person whose overall experience is most relevant. Bear in mind that the monitoring will have to be closer than usual.

Being Objective

For more considered, structured delegation, it is important that your assessment of a person's suitability for a particular task is not clouded by irrational factors. For example, a predecessor or colleague may have influenced you by making an erroneous judgment based on prejudice, or you yourself may have gained a negative impression of somebody based on a single unrepresentative incident. To ensure that you make your decision fairly and objectively, always use your written job definition to match the candidate's skills and abilities to the requirements of the task.

Cultural Differences

In countries such as the US, with strong hire-and-fire cultures, managers delegate more freely than those in Japan, who are likely to be highly selective since failure is considered shameful. In highly structured cultures, like Germany, managers retain more control of tasks, delegating less.

EVALUATING STAFF

Choosing the right person for a task requires careful assessment of experience and specific abilities. Different types of tasks require different skills. For example, a job may demand speed over accuracy, or vice versa. The ideal candidate for a specific delegation may not exist – in which case, your choice will necessarily involve an element of compromise. Remember that delegation can be used to train and develop a valued employee's range and depth of skills with a view to future promotion.

44 Ensure that your staff do not take on too much.

COMPARING STAFF ATTRIBUTES

POSITIVE	NEGATIVE
● Mary is analytical in her approach and can get to the root of a problem quickly. ● She has a great grasp of the details of a task.	● Mary cannot handle the pressure of urgent deadlines. ● It often takes her some time to grasp the whole picture.
● Gordon is capable of tackling most delegated tasks with confidence. ● He is an excellent all-around performer.	● Gordon tends to delegate too few tasks himself. ● He finds it hard to apply himself to a long-term project.
● Jane is good at organizing schedules and budgets. ● She is an enthusiastic and cooperative team player.	● Jane does not show enough initiative. ● She is not confident when working without supervision.

TRAINING STAFF

If you cannot find enough suitably experienced or qualified staff, and new hirings are ruled out, the soft option is not to delegate at all. That choice is negative and self-defeating. It reflects failure to provide enough continuous staff training and development to fill identified future needs. Good training enables you to build people's capability, which will often have remarkable results. The more skills each staff member has, the greater your choice of potential delegates. Training also has beneficial effects on motivation, since people feel more valued when you invest in their futures.

QUESTIONS TO ASK YOURSELF

Q Is there anybody who could, and should, be doing more important work?

Q Do my staff each have at least one task that will develop and improve their skills?

Q Are all my staff multiskilled, and, if not, what am I doing to make them so?

Q Am I doing anything just because nobody else can?

PREPARING A BRIEF

When planning a brief, first define your objective and compile a full checklist to ensure that all the individual aspects of a task are included. The more complete the final brief, the more confident you can be that the task will be successfully executed.

 45 Make all the objectives as precise as possible when briefing.

 **46** Do not set too many controls when you are writing a delegate's final brief.

DEFINING THE OBJECTIVE

The most important part of the briefing process is defining the overall objective clearly. As far as possible, outline the aims in terms of required outcomes. For example, ask a delegate to "reorganize stationery purchasing by March 31 to achieve 10 percent savings on present costs," rather than to "sort out the stationery." Here, the saving in costs could be included in the brief as a subobjective within a broader project for improving office efficiency and administration.

USING A CHECKLIST

Your delegation should be based on breaking down a task into all aspects, naming the person who is responsible for each item, and eliminating overlaps of responsibility. This provides the basis for making a checklist. Use this list to ensure that nothing significant has been omitted from the brief, and that component tasks have an explicit timetable. If the task is to improve the efficiency of repairs carried out on a customer's premises, for example, the key factors are likely to include identifying faults and their root causes, preventing recurrence of shortcomings, speeding up response and repair times, and assessing and raising the degree of customer satisfaction. Make sure that the checklist and the brief dovetail precisely.

THINGS TO DO

1. Keep objectives as clear and concise as possible.
2. Build a certain amount of flexibility into the brief.
3. Base the objectives on required outcomes.
4. Make a checklist to avoid overlaps and omissions.
5. Ensure that the delegate is fully aware of the aims.
6. Allow the delegate to comment on the brief.

STRUCTURING A BRIEF

PARTS OF A BRIEF	FACTORS TO CONSIDER
OBJECTIVES Defines the task, listing the major objectives and subobjectives in clear and concise language.	List all the objectives and discuss them with the delegate before finalizing any agreement. Ensure that this list is referred to continually.
RESOURCES Specifies what personnel, finance, and facilities are available or need to be obtained.	Finalize resource needs after the objectives have been set. Ensure you include the limits to spending authority in the delegate's budget.
TIMESCALE Sets out the schedule with review points, stage completion dates, and final deadlines.	Use the schedule to motivate the delegate and to provide the basis for a critical path analysis showing all the completion stages.
METHOD Describes procedures, as agreed with the delegate, and summarizes the key points.	Devise and agree on a thorough plan that will provide the delegate with a concrete but flexible methodology within which to work.
LEVELS OF AUTHORITY Specifies the range of the delegate's authority and to whom they will report.	Apply authority limits that tell the delegate when it may be appropriate to refer to you, and when they should use their own initiative.

ALLOWING FLEXIBILITY

Do not regard your brief as sacrosanct, but as a framework within which delegates can use reasonable flexibility in order to achieve their objectives. Be very precise about what delegates are expected to achieve, what financial and other resources will be available, when the role begins and what its deadlines are, and what delegates may or may not do on their own authority. Keep the brief tightly focused on the results you want, but leave delegates as much flexibility as possible in following the brief, especially in deciding what procedures to use. You should expect them to seek review and revision of the brief as events demand.

 Incorporate a reporting plan into each brief.

 Ensure that the delegate fully understands and agrees to the brief.

SECURING AGREEMENT IN PRINCIPLE

Agreeing in principle on a brief with your proposed delegate involves contributions from both sides. You must motivate the delegate and confirm their suitability, while the delegate has to understand the brief and consider whether they can take on the task.

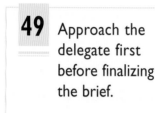

49 Approach the delegate first before finalizing the brief.

USING THE RIGHT APPROACH

It is frustrating to present a final brief to a delegate only to have them raise doubts about the task. Always obtain an agreement in principle before finalizing, as the delegate's collaboration is essential if the brief is to be fully workable. Your choice of time, place, and method for negotiating with a chosen delegate can make the difference between a positive and negative response. Location is determined by the level of the appointment. For a high-level delegation, you might take the individual to lunch; for routine tasks, the office will suffice. Whatever setting you choose, approach all potential delegates with their needs in mind, encouraging questions and giving full information.

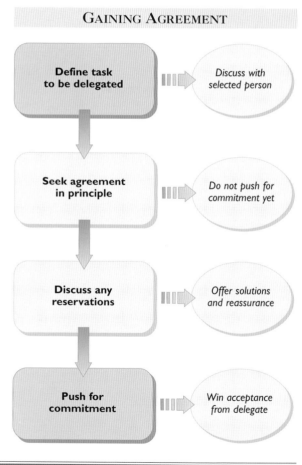

GAINING AGREEMENT

Define task to be delegated → Discuss with selected person

Seek agreement in principle → Do not push for commitment yet

Discuss any reservations → Offer solutions and reassurance

Push for commitment → Win acceptance from delegate

AIRING RESERVATIONS

If your chosen candidate is reluctant to undertake an assignment, try to discover and understand what their actual reservations are. A common objection, and a major cause of demotivation, is a perceived lack of autonomy. Do not fudge this issue, or any other areas that have given rise to objections. Give honest reassurances, and ensure that your body language reinforces your words to show confidence in the assignment and the potential delegate. By presenting the task as an opportunity to develop skills and experience further, you place the delegate in the role of a partner rather than a subordinate. If you cannot overcome the candidate's reluctance by persuasion, do not try to force acceptance. Cut your losses and look for someone else.

Manager appears confident and positive

Delegate questions certain points

DISCUSSING A BRIEF ▶

Before you finalize the brief and formally appoint a delegate, discuss its contents with your potential delegate and give him or her the opportunity to raise any reasonable reservations they may have.

50 Do not hesitate when delegating – be positive.

51 Consider positive and negative comments when finalizing the brief.

PROVIDING SUPPORT

Most people react anxiously when offered new responsibility, and many doubt their ability to perform well. To boost your chance of securing a positive response from a chosen delegate, always discuss the support, both formal and informal, that they will be able to call on during the period of delegation. Reasonable doubts can be partially dispelled by carefully considering and naming the people to whom the delegate can turn. Suggest close colleagues or staff from other departments who could provide valuable help, and discuss any training that may be appropriate. Make clear what level of support you as manager are prepared to give to ensure the delegate's success.

Briefing Effectively

Once you have reached an agreement in principle, refine the brief and organize a detailed briefing meeting. Select your approach carefully, since the outcome of this meeting is vital to the success of the partnership between delegator and delegate.

52 If a delegate is negative at the briefing, reconsider the assignment.

53 Keep on encouraging delegates after they have taken on a task.

Communicating a Brief

The delegator's primary task at the briefing is to communicate effectively and ensure the delegate's full understanding of the assignment. You can achieve this by adopting a methodical approach. Explain the task objective clearly and state your expectations in terms of deadlines and levels of measured achievement. List the steps that you think will have to be taken to complete the task successfully, and ask if your delegate understands. Be clear about which areas of the brief are flexible and which must be followed to the letter.

Securing Agreement

Even the most carefully prepared and well-communicated brief can result in misconceptions. You can avoid misunderstandings by asking relevant questions throughout the meeting and inviting the delegate to do the same. Pay attention to body language; a lack of eye contact may indicate that your delegate is not absolutely in agreement with you or is having trouble taking it in. If you suspect any disagreement, encourage the delegate to repeat what they have heard to ensure that they understand and agree. Make it clear that you expect the delegate to use their own initiative when appropriate, and ensure that there are no doubts over the extent of their authority.

Being Briefed

If you are taking on a task, the briefing session may be your only chance to discuss it in detail, so ensure that you clarify the major objectives. It is also your opportunity to discuss the allocation of resources and the flexibility of the schedule. Find out the extent of your personal autonomy, and if you feel it is inadequate, argue for more at the start – before it is too late.

SELECTING A BRIEFING METHOD

BRIEFING STYLES	FACTORS TO CONSIDER
INFORMAL "I would like you to take this on for me when you have the time."	For people you know well, and for delegating less important, simpler tasks. Verbal instruction is sufficient, although some formal follow-up may be required.
FORMAL "I have decided to put you in charge of budgetary control."	When the task is important to the group and to you. Usually accompanied by a written brief stating the task objective and how and when it should be accomplished.
COLLEGIATE "We all think you are the best person for the job."	When recognizing the particular skills of an individual within a team or task force, and singling them out for special responsibility. The whole group decides the brief.
LAISSEZ-FAIRE "I am not going to tell you how to do this job. I'll leave it up to you."	An ideal approach for experienced staff. You rely on your delegate to assume complete control of a task and to make key decisions without supervision or follow-up.
TROUBLESHOOTING "We have a problem at the main office that I want you to sort out."	A rewarding form of delegation. Your candidate is creative and is able to communicate ideas effectively. Outline the problem – he or she will know what is required.
RIGHT-HAND MAN/WOMAN "I would like you to take this off my shoulders, and improve it."	Used when you delegate part of a key task to a trusted individual whose fresh approach may provide some new solutions. You are regularly informed of progress.

ENDING A BRIEFING

Draw the briefing session to a conclusion by summarizing the key points of the delegation. End the meeting by thanking the delegate for taking on the task and communicate your confidence that the assignment will be carried out successfully – it is important to emphasize that you have appointed this delegate because you trust his or her abilities. Finally, establish a date for a follow-up meeting to review progress.

54 Ask for any new ideas when your delegate reports on task progress.

MONITORING PROGRESS

For delegation to be successful it is vital to have an effective and responsive system of controls. Use them to monitor delegates and the progress of assignments.

WORKING WITH CONTROLS

A good monitoring system consists of a light rein and a tight hand. You can always exercise more control if you feel it is necessary, but you should do so with tact and sensitivity. This is especially the case if your delegate is inexperienced.

 55 Give inexperienced delegates special attention when monitoring tasks.

CULTURAL DIFFERENCES

In German-speaking countries, delegates traditionally stay under tight control at all times. Japanese delegates often have autonomy, but are expected to discuss all matters with their managers. In the US and UK, the culture of delegation is encouraged, but, in practice, controls can be rigid.

SUPERVISING EFFECTIVELY

The level of experience of your delegate will help you to decide whether to adopt a hands-on or hands-off approach when controlling a delegated assignment. A person with a considerable amount of experience at handling similar tasks will require less supervision and control than someone with little or no experience. But remember that the learning process has to begin somewhere, and inexperience can be overcome by good leadership. The monitoring process provides an opportunity for you to assess and extend any delegate's abilities and to supply specific skill training.

DO'S AND DON'TS

✔ Do encourage all delegates to make their own decisions.

✔ Do move from hands-on to hands-off as soon as possible.

✔ Do intervene when absolutely necessary, but only at that time.

✔ Do ask delegates if they feel thoroughly prepared for the task.

✘ Don't say or hint that you doubt the delegate's ability.

✘ Don't miss any stage in the briefing process.

✘ Don't surreptitiously take back a task.

✘ Don't place seniority above ability.

✘ Don't deny a delegate the chance to learn by interfering too much.

GUIDING A NEW DELEGATE

Assigning a task to a first-time delegate requires careful briefing and close supervision during the early stages. Help to build confidence by focusing on, and praising, good work. If an error is made, show how it could have been avoided, but try not to dwell on mistakes. You may ask an experienced colleague to help you oversee the delegate at the start of the assignment.

AVOIDING INTERFERENCE

Managers who can maintain a distance between themselves and their delegates are more likely to see positive results. Nobody will work in exactly the same way as you, so resist the temptation to intervene the moment you suspect the task is not being performed your way. Instead, set up a system of regular checks, meetings, and reports, either formal or informal, to ensure that the task objectives are being met. Heavy intervention, in which the delegator makes all the decisions, will frustrate the delegate and deny him or her the chance to gain experience. It will also save very little of the delegator's time.

DENYING AUTONOMY ▼
A manager who constantly interferes with a delegate once a task is assigned is not only denying the delegate the chance to learn new skills and gain experience, but is also not delegating effectively.

Insensitive invasion of delegate's space creates hostility

Delegate's well-ordered paperwork is needlessly disrupted

CHOOSING A MONITORING SYSTEM

TYPE OF SYSTEM	FACTORS TO CONSIDER

INVOLVEMENT IN ALL CORRESPONDENCE
You retain the greatest share of authority and may expect to sign memos, invoices, and so on.

- Keeps you fully informed of developments and allows you to anticipate and avoid any bad errors of judgment.
- Could indicate that you do not trust the delegate fully.

WRITTEN REPORTS
The delegate supplies a written commentary regarding actions, results, and any figures that are regularly updated.

- Encourages delegates to organize their thoughts clearly and give a full account of how the delegation is progressing.
- Can prove to be too remote.
- Can be used to mask problems.

PERSONAL REPORT
You arrange for the delegate to meet with you to discuss the assignment at regular intervals.

- Provides an opportunity for regular, informal updates and early airings of any potentially problematic situations.
- May encourage you to become overinvolved in making decisions and taking action.

OPEN-DOOR POLICY
You encourage the delegate to bring you his or her day-to-day problems at any time for help or clarification.

- Enables you to give support and show encouragement, and stresses the collaborative aspect of delegation.
- Delegates may rely too heavily on your input, rather than use their own initiative.

ACCESS VIA COMPUTER
You use information technology systems to check directly on what is happening at any time.

- Very discreet and diplomatic and enables you to become involved only when a major decision is required.
- If used alone, may give an inaccurate or incomplete picture of the actual situation.

MEETINGS
You discuss the delegated task in a meeting which includes you, the delegate, and other staff involved in the assignment.

- Allows issues to be debated in a wider forum, and emphasizes that delegation also involves coherent teamwork.
- Can lessen the delegate's perception of personal responsibility for the task.

QUESTIONS TO ASK YOURSELF

Q Have I ensured the delegate is adequately trained?

Q Is the delegate looking at the task with a fresh eye?

Q Are too many handovers involved in delegated tasks?

Q Is the delegate delivering according to plan?

Q Are defects being picked up and corrected quickly?

Q What savings, if any, have been made by the delegate?

ELIMINATING STAGES

You can markedly reduce the amount of time spent reviewing progress by encouraging your delegates to streamline or simplify procedures. Reforming ill-conceived processes reduces the workload and cuts down on the number of stages that require monitoring. With the final objective in mind, ask delegates to work back through all the stages currently employed to the starting point of the task. With this chain of activities mapped out, look for any stages that could be combined or not done at all. In particular, ask delegates to eliminate wasteful handovers of incomplete pieces of work from one individual or department to another.

REVIEWING PROGRESS

Once a task is underway, you will need to review its progress and the performance of the delegate. There are a number of ways in which you can keep tabs on proceedings, including face-to-face discussions with the delegate, written reports, and personal observations. Choose a system that suits you, is appropriate to the task, and gives you all the information you need to review what has been achieved so far. It must also enable you to check that you are on course to achieve the objective and pinpoint any corrective action that may be required.

56 Operate on the assumption that every process can be improved.

CHECKING ▶ PROGRESS

When delegates are actively involved in every stage of the process, and managers encourage them to share their views, delegation is a two-way system making the best use of everyone's skills.

Manager listens to reports from delegates

Delegate details latest progress

MINIMIZING RISKS

Understanding the risks involved in delegating a task will help you to anticipate problems and monitor progress. So form contingency plans, take action to reduce risks, and intervene in good time before minor problems lead to major failure.

 57 Ensure that bad news is not kept from you by a worried delegate.

58 Never gamble when taking risks; act on judgments based on probabilities.

MONITORING RISKS

When monitoring a delegate's progress, keep an eye on those areas of the task that you consider to be of high risk. For example, you may delegate the control of customer credit limits. Here, there is a risk of too high a level of credit being given to customers whose credit history is either unknown to you or who have been late payers in the past. This task will therefore require much more careful and consistent monitoring than a lower risk task, such as the maintenance of office equipment. Keep a list of all risks, and periodically check whether any of them can be eliminated.

USING MANAGEMENT BY EXCEPTION

Management by exception is a highly effective control method whereby a delegate informs their manager only of those exceptional events that require major decisions. You should not expect to hear about actions that proceed as planned, only of deviations from the plan. For example, a sales executive is asked to handle key accounts. As long as sales targets and profit margins are maintained, the delegator need not be involved in decisions. But if a customer suddenly asks for a higher discount, with a resulting drop in margins, the delegate must seek a decision from the manager.

 59 Try to anticipate problem areas for the delegate.

 60 Make contingency plans just in case things go wrong.

BUILDING IN CONTROLS

Key controls, such as a scheduled time frame or specific budgetary limits, can be used as efficient constraints to guide and monitor a delegate. If tasks start missing deadlines or overrunning on cost, you must talk to the delegate immediately in order to identify the root causes of the problem as soon as possible. Ask the delegate to supply you with regular reports, both written and verbal, to gauge whether your initial brief was at fault or if the failures or deficiencies are a result of poor performance by the delegate. If the brief is at fault, revise it at once. If the problem lies with the delegate, consider providing further training or, if necessary, reassign the task to another delegate.

THINGS TO DO

1. List all possible risks in order of importance.
2. If possible, reduce a risk at the briefing stage.
3. Monitor all risks during the delegation.
4. Deal with the root cause of problems quickly.
5. Have contingency plans ready for immediate implementation.

61 Speedily remove delegates who make several serious mistakes.

TAKING FAIL-SAFE ACTION

In order to ensure achievement of the objective stated in the brief, it is prudent to build in an alternative course of action in case events do not follow expectations. For example, you may be using a bright but inexperienced delegate to maintain sufficient stock levels to keep one of your most important customers regularly supplied with a particular item. Here, you can minimize risk by ensuring that contingent stock is always available if the delegate underorders or if the customer increases the units ordered unexpectedly.

◀ **REDUCING RISK**
Here, the risk of the level of returns becoming too high is eradicated by setting a strict limit beyond which the matter is referred to a director.

CASE STUDY

Jane was marketing manager at a company producing garden furniture. Directors had set tolerance levels for customer complaints and returns at 3.5 percent. This margin was accepted and planned for, and it was agreed that any increase should be brought to the attention of the marketing director.

When Jane became aware of a rise in returns, she suspected a problem at the factory. As instructed, she informed her supervisor, who then discussed the problem with his opposite number in production. It transpired that some of the machinery was worn out, but the finance department had vetoed its replacement.

The directors assessed the situation and decided that profit losses from returns would quickly outweigh the cost of new equipment, and ordered immediate purchase.

REINFORCING A DELEGATE'S ROLE

When appointing delegates, always introduce them to team members, clearly stating the delegates' responsibilities. This will help delegates feel part of a team and encourage them to accept ownership of the tasks for which they are responsible.

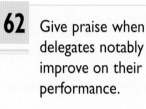

62 Give praise when delegates notably improve on their performance.

INTRODUCING A ▼ NEW DELEGATE

Introduce a new delegate to existing team members, and inform any customers or suppliers who need to know the relevant responsibilities the delegate will have.

ESTABLISHING DELEGATES

For delegation to be effective, the delegator must always make a new appointment known. Having delegated a task, ensure that all relevant people who may be affected, including all colleagues, customers, and suppliers, are informed. If the appointment is high profile, make an occasion of the announcement – so boosting the delegate's prestige, pride, and confidence. Ensure that the exact nature of a delegate's responsibility is fully understood by all, as confusion could be counterproductive.

Manager introduces new delegate

New delegate uses open body language

ACCEPTING IDEAS

When you delegate a task you are also delegating the right to make decisions. Openly encouraging delegates to use their own initiative at all stages of a task or project will give them an added interest in the task and will boost their self-confidence. Unless there are good reasons for not doing so, accept ideas even if you consider the benefits to be marginal. Demonstrating openness to others' ideas will also motivate all members of a team.

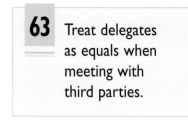

63 Treat delegates as equals when meeting with third parties.

64 Take action to get delegates to come forward with new ideas.

DELEGATING OWNERSHIP

The highest form of delegation is the transference of "ownership" of an entire project to a trusted individual. However, this delegation of ownership should extend to all delegated tasks, small or large, as it is one of the most effective of all incentives. You will encourage ownership by allowing delegates to plan and execute a task in their own way, and by suggesting that delegates find their own solutions to problems that arise.

COMPARING MANAGEMENT TECHNIQUES

UNDERMINING OWNERSHIP

COUNTERMANDING
The manager asks what decision has been made, or what action has been taken, and countermands the decision or action.

INTERFERING
The manager demands to be informed of any progress, expressing approval or disapproval, and does not allow the delegate ownership.

TAKING OVER
The manager does not trust the delegate, or is unable to relinquish control, and reclaims the day-to-day performance of the task.

REINFORCING OWNERSHIP

HANDS-OFF
The manager does not interfere during the performance of a delegated task, but is fully informed to ensure good execution.

ADVICE AND CONSENT
The manager takes on the role of an adviser to the delegate. Major decisions on issues raised by the delegate are agreed on jointly.

COACHING
The manager uses the delegated task as an opportunity to develop delegates' skills and broaden their range of experience.

PROVIDING SUPPORT

Delegates will often need positive support and encouragement in the early stages of an assignment. You can help them to succeed by providing all the information, time, and resources they need, and by being prepared to secure extra help if necessary.

65 Be aware that a helpful attitude may be perceived as interference.

66 Meet at regular times for feedback sessions, but not too frequently.

ASSESSING PROGRESS

It is a good idea to schedule meetings with your delegate before they embark on an assignment. If you are firm about deadlines and checks in the first place, you will be able to maintain regular contact and avoid the risk of your input being seen as an intrusion. Make it clear that you are available between those dates, and that you expect to be informed if any difficulties arise. When results deviate from expectations, examine the problem together from every angle, to find out whether it stems from a lack of resources, time, supervision, experience, or effort. You will then know what to do to put things back on course.

CHECKING PROGRESS WITH DELEGATES

When discussing progress with delegates, always use positive questions, like those below, that will encourage delegates to suggest their own solutions to problems. Avoid questions that may discourage or demoralize the delegate.

❝ *Is there anything you want to bring to my attention?* ❞

❝ *We failed to meet that deadline. Any suggestions as to how that happened?* ❞

❝ *I see that costs are over-running. What steps are you taking to bring them back in line?* ❞

❝ *How do you think we can avoid making this mistake again?* ❞

CONTRIBUTING ADVICE

Throughout the monitoring process, make it clear to delegates when you expect to be told about problems, and when not. The safest policy is to encourage them to seek advice when in doubt. If they fail to do this, problems may arise that could have been avoided. Always be sympathetic and encouraging when delegates ask for help, but be firm in delivering your verdict if you think the delegate could have dealt with the issue unaided.

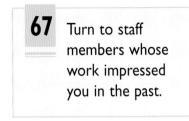

67 Turn to staff members whose work impressed you in the past.

68 Consider using outside sources of help if necessary.

UTILIZING CONTACTS ▼
Keep an up-to-date list of experienced contacts on hand so that you can quickly find help when required.

SUPPLYING ASSISTANCE

At some stage your delegate may claim that he or she needs help from others in order to meet the task objective. Use your judgment to establish whether this is a legitimate claim. Then, with your delegate, work out how much assistance is needed and for how long. If no other staff are available, consider outside sources of help. Keep the names of qualified people on hand, but do not call on them too readily. Commit extra resources only if the project is at risk. Always try to keep to the brief that was agreed at the outset.

Manager quickly locates known and trusted contact

Details of contacts kept on desktop index card system

MAINTAINING THE BOUNDARIES

When monitoring progress, ensure that the boundary between yourself and the task remains clear. Your delegate is now responsible for doing the work. If there are difficulties, the line may have to be crossed, but you should step back as soon as possible.

 69 Having delegated a task, do not interfere with how it is done.

STEPPING BACK

 70 If you have to take back a task, start looking for a new delegate at once.

As a delegation proceeds, you should gradually reduce the frequency of review meetings. This is especially the case when dealing with first-time delegates who may require more intensive supervision at the outset. Meeting very frequently defeats the object of delegation and reduces the available time of both you and the delegate. Never refuse a request for a meeting, but make it clear to the delegate that the aim is self-management.

ENCOURAGING SOLUTIONS

When a delegate runs into difficulties, it could give you great satisfaction to "magic" the problem away. But unless he or she learns how to deal with similar situations in the future, no progress is being made. Discourage delegates from arriving at your door before thinking an issue through. Instead, ask them to consider why the situation may have arisen, and insist that anyone coming to you with a problem should also come with two solutions and a stated preference between them. In this way, delegates will get used to working out solutions themselves and never form the habit of relying on you to come up with all the answers.

QUESTIONS TO ASK YOURSELF

Q Do I avoid interfering unless absolutely necessary?

Q Am I keeping the number of meetings to a minimum?

Q If a delegate is struggling, am I inclined to complete the task for them to save time?

Q Do I express confidence in my delegate in words and actions?

Q Do I encourage my delegates to work independently of me, and find their own solutions?

IDENTIFYING PROBLEMS

When an otherwise competent delegate leaves aspects of a task incomplete, look for the possible causes. Are you checking, interfering, or worrying too much, or even taking work back because you are dissatisfied? If your behavior is the cause of the trouble, make changes immediately. If the problem lies with the delegate, consider all the possible causes. It could be that the delegate is overwhelmed by responsibility, is lacking in confidence, or is not coping well with criticism. Restate why they were appointed, reassert your confidence in them, and stress that criticism can identify opportunities to improve skills.

71 Keep all review sessions brief and well organized.

72 Do not let a delegate become discouraged when problems arise.

DIFFICULTIES WITH MAINTAINING BOUNDARIES

TYPICAL PROBLEMS	POSSIBLE SOLUTIONS
CONTINUAL INTERRUPTIONS You are continually asked questions and have to make decisions.	The delegate may mistakenly believe that everything must be double-checked by you. Explain that you expect them to act on their own initiative whenever possible.
DELEGATED TASKS REBOUND The delegated tasks, or parts of them, reappear on your desk.	Consider whether the task as a whole may be altogether too complex. Go through it with the delegate to see if it can be broken down into more manageable elements.
EXCESSIVE WORKLOAD Although you have delegated all you can, your workload has increased.	Over time you may have reclaimed small elements of many delegations, so your work consists of a series of unrelated tasks. Ensure that delegates retain complete tasks.
GIVING TOO MUCH SUPPORT You help out in order to save time and eliminate the risk of mistakes.	This could be a genuine misdelegation. Consider whether, for this particular assignment, you may have overestimated the abilities of your delegate, and act accordingly.
INSECURE DELEGATES You are constantly asked to check progress and give your approval.	Your delegate may feel intimidated by the responsibilities involved in completing the task. Overcome their anxieties by stressing your own confidence in their abilities.

GIVING FEEDBACK

*T*he most effective way to review staff
performance is to provide delegates with
constructive feedback sessions after each task.
Use these meetings to recognize and analyze
achievements, and to discuss problems and
solutions. But be sure to avoid laying blame.

73 Make sure that review sessions are conducted in a constructive way.

BEING POSITIVE

One-to-one review meetings between delegator
and delegate can achieve either constructive or
negative results. To establish a positive environment,
treat the session as a discussion between partners:
air and discuss problems openly, and acknowledge
achievements readily. Unless it is necessary, do not
use the meeting to assert your authority, and
ensure that any criticisms of the delegate's work
are as constructive as possible with a view to
improving performance.

74 Use positive and polite language when managing all delegates.

▼ **DISCUSSING PROGRESS**
*When reviewing a delegate's performance,
be positive both in your praise and in any
criticism you provide. Use the meeting as
an opportunity to encourage
a delegate who may be
experiencing difficulties with
a particular assignment.*

*Delegate provides
progress report*

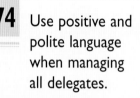

*Manager chooses
informal seating
arrangement to put
delegate at ease*

REVIEWING PERFORMANCE

For a final performance review to be effective you should systematically work through a clearly established agenda. Look especially at whether the final objective has been achieved. Consider:

- Did the delegate encounter any problems that meant revising the initial brief?
- Were the task's allocated resources adequate?
- Was it necessary to take drastic action following poor handling by the delegate?

Even if no problems were encountered, consider and discuss whether there are any changes that could be made that would improve general performance and efficiency in the future.

QUESTIONS TO ASK YOURSELF

Q Am I adopting a positive and helpful attitude during review meetings?

Q Is the delegate presenting me with all the essential facts?

Q Am I encouraging delegates to provide their own solutions?

Q Do I avoid allocating blame when mistakes occur?

Q Am I using review sessions to develop delegates?

75 Hold impromptu review sessions only when it is really necessary.

AVOIDING BLAME

From time to time, events will not proceed as planned: projects will go over budget, schedules will not be kept, or a particular task will have to be done again. When things go wrong, avoid the temptation to apportion blame – this may discourage the delegate. Instead, use a feedback session to analyze what has gone wrong to ensure that lessons are learned and that similar mistakes are avoided in the future.

OFFERING FEEDBACK TO YOUR MANAGER

When reporting on progress to your manager, try to be selective about the information you offer. There is little need to report back on every single aspect of a task. Your manager should neither need nor want to know every detail in order to assess your progress. If you are presenting either verbal or written information, report only on essential developments. Avoid the temptation to exaggerate those aspects that are going well, or to gloss over what is going wrong. If you have encountered problems or difficulties you wish to discuss, explain the causes, and state what action you propose to take. End the meeting by asking whether you have covered every issue of concern to your manager.

PRAISING AND REWARDING

Always acknowledge a delegate's exceptional performance, and give credit where credit is due. Identify all faults and errors, but remember that praise and reward play an important part in motivating and encouraging future achievements.

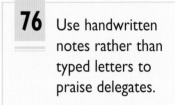

76 Use handwritten notes rather than typed letters to praise delegates.

THANKING A TEAM

PRAISING PUBLICLY ▼
Choose an appropriate time when team members are together to thank a specific delegate for exceptional performance.

When a task or project is successfully completed, an effective manager ensures that all the delegates who contributed to its success are duly and fairly credited. A delegator who takes little interest in a task and then assumes the majority of the credit is guilty not only of bad management, but also of bad manners. If you are presenting the finished task, consider involving your colleagues, and stress the contributions made by all members of the team.

Manager thanks delegate for his contribution to project

Delegate

Team members attend meeting

RECOGNIZING EFFORT

Never take satisfactory performance of a delegated task for granted – you will probably have set the delegate a reasonably stretching task. To achieve ambitious objectives, the delegate probably had to overcome several difficulties and cope with unforeseen events. He or she may have had to work long hours and will certainly have learned much during the assignment. Show that you are fully aware of what has been achieved and of the effort required, even if you also have to draw attention to various errors and omissions. Remember that pride in achievement is a prime motivator – perhaps the most important of all. Recognizing that achievement will help to ensure that a delegate's good performance continues.

CULTURAL DIFFERENCES

Reward practices vary greatly worldwide. In Japan, for example, exceptional performance is regarded as part of an employee's commitment to the job and is not rewarded separately. In the US and the UK, and increasingly in the rest of Europe, payments based on performance (with bonus payments for special achievements) are becoming much more common.

77 Always recognize the effort that was put into a task, and reward it.

PRAISING DELEGATES

The most effective way to praise a delegate is either in person or by letter – both methods will have a major motivational impact. Equally, failure to praise tends to undermine confidence rapidly. Remember that praise will be most welcome from a fair and honest critic, so do not devalue praise by using it excessively. Rewards in the form of salary increases, bonus payments, and non-financial benefits will all reinforce praise.

REWARDING EXCELLENCE

Delegates who excel in the performance of a task should always be appropriately acknowledged and rewarded. Any reward plan you set up should recognize really exceptional performance with an appropriate reward, and should stimulate an expectation of future performance-based rewards. However, do not give special rewards to delegates who perform to expectation – that was part of the initial agreement when taking on the task.

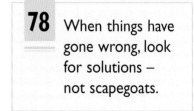

78 When things have gone wrong, look for solutions – not scapegoats.

ANALYZING DIFFICULTIES

Both the delegator and delegate need to analyze, and learn from, any difficulties encountered during a delegation. The first step toward finding a solution to a problem is to ascertain whether it stems from you, your delegate, the task brief, or procedure.

79 Try to give a delegate another chance if a task is mishandled.

QUESTIONS TO ASK YOURSELF

Q Was I too hasty in making the appointment?

Q Is there somebody available who would do better?

Q How can I prevent this problem from recurring?

Q What would I do differently if I could start again?

Q What are the delegate's proven strengths and weaknesses?

QUESTIONING YOURSELF

If a delegated task has not been performed to your satisfaction, look first at your own actions. Perhaps you should have kept this particular task yourself, or been more selective when choosing the delegate. Go over the brief to find out if you could have made it clearer, and examine your monitoring procedures to be sure that they were adequate for the task. Maybe you made yourself too remote, or did not provide sufficient guidance when problems arose. Be as objective as possible in this self-examination so that you can identify and deal with your own weaknesses.

REASSESSING A DELEGATE

If your delegate is not performing as well as you expected, examine why and how you made the selection in the first place. If you systematically matched the needs of the task with available staff, then either the system, the task specification, or your assessment of the person is at fault – maybe a combination of all three. A delegate's failure may not necessarily mean that your choice was wrong – your own mistakes or circumstances beyond your control could be hindering the work. Do not let the issue drag on; discuss the matter with your delegate promptly, then take action. Consider reallocating a task only as a last resort.

80 Analyze your own actions if difficult problems arise.

81 Consider all the implications before you radically alter an agreed brief.

REVISING A BRIEF

As a task progresses, discuss the brief and make any minor alterations at regular review sessions. If major difficulties reveal serious defects, consider whether a more rigorous monitoring process could have highlighted the problem sooner, or if a sudden change in circumstances has invalidated some of the brief's assumptions. Think carefully before you implement any changes, since an alteration of plans at this stage could solve one problem while creating several more. If the brief requires revision, remember that any really radical changes may require the choice of a new delegate.

THINGS TO DO

1. Look at your own role.
2. Consider whether the brief or the delegate is at fault.
3. Replace a delegate if absolutely necessary.
4. Review problems regularly.
5. Deal with any known difficulties at once.

82 Be open and constructive when discussing the performance of a task with a delegate.

LOOKING AT PERFORMANCE

Results alone will not necessarily tell you all you need to know about the performance of a task. More accurate indicators can be gathered from your feedback sessions with the delegate, and other personal observations. However, remember that you cannot maintain a delegate's trust if you make inquiries behind his or her back. Be open about seeking relevant information from trusted colleagues and inviting comments from those who are affected by the delegation. If any defects come to light, it is your responsibility to take steps to improve the delegate's performance.

HANDLING DIFFICULTIES WITH A DELEGATED TASK

Understanding the process of delegation will help when you are the delegate, rather than the delegator. When matters do not proceed as planned you have a chance to show your initiative and resolution. Analyze the causes of problems, and take corrective action if you can – and keep your manager fully informed throughout. If correction is beyond your reach, say so at once, and work with your manager to find a solution. Remember that the successful outcome of a task is all-important and is the major factor by which your performance will be judged.

RECTIFYING PROBLEMS

As a manager, you must be able to identify and help to rectify any errors a delegate makes while undertaking an assignment. When a delegate makes a mistake and you have to make criticisms, phrase these tactfully and positively, addressing the actual problem rather than castigating the delegate. This positive guidance will encourage the delegate and help to prevent the same or similar errors from happening again.

 83 Be firm with delegates who conceal errors or do not admit them.

 84 Use mistakes as learning tools to improve your managerial skills.

85 Consider whether a project brief was the cause of any serious error.

LEARNING FROM FAILURE

Knowing how to deal with failure may be as valuable as the successful outcome of the task. Take the opportunity when things go wrong to extract as many useful lessons as possible. Naturally, managers and delegates alike will be tempted to come up with excuses rather than explanations when a failure occurs, but excuses elucidate very little and are usually smoke screens that obscure the real causes of error. When you have identified a failure, carefully analyze the causes and discuss these with the delegate. Always stress that the sin is not to fail but to make the same mistake twice.

CORRECTING ▶ PROCEDURES

The account supervisor's error was certainly avoidable and should not have occurred. However, the mistake offered the managing director a useful opportunity to pinpoint weaknesses in procedures and to change working methods.

CASE STUDY

When the Smith Printing Company lost money after underquoting a client's job, the managing director's first concern was to find out how such a mistake could have been made. The account supervisor admitted that she had failed to notice that the cost of folding and binding had not been included in the estimate. She had been working on other projects at the time and had been under pressure, but was otherwise unable to account for the oversight. It was essential to identify the factors that had led to the error, so time was spent looking at procedures. It emerged that in the estimate, folding and binding was simply listed as "finishing" and the client had been charged only for trimming. To avoid future errors, it was agreed that all future quotations should include a more specific breakdown of each job.

REVIEWING PROJECTS

An "action review" is a systematic approach to identifying and correcting mistakes. It involves regularly comparing actual progress made against the objectives in a brief. This allows you to analyze and explain deviations from the intended plan of action. Keep a record of the lessons learned from failures and successes so that you can revise procedures and provide a report for the benefit of other managers and delegates.

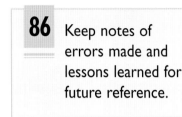

86 Keep notes of errors made and lessons learned for future reference.

ASSESSING DIFFICULTIES IN A PROJECT

ASPECTS OF PROJECT	FACTORS TO CONSIDER
OBJECTIVES The goal of a project, and interim targets that should be met.	● The long-term objective may not be reached if the initial brief was faulty and needs constant amendment. ● A project can flounder if interim targets are missed.
RESOURCES The people, finances, information, and equipment required.	● If in doubt, it is wise to overestimate the costs involved in a project to cover any unforeseen expenses. ● Inadequate facilities will impede even very able staff.
TIMESCALE The planned schedule for completion of the project.	● The risk of running over schedule can be minimized by detailing when each stage is to be completed. ● Unexpected problems can undo the best-laid plans.
METHOD The strategy for achieving a project's ultimate objective.	● To reach the desired outcome you must have a clear vision of the route you will take to get there. ● If initial plans alter, methods may also have to change.
AUTHORITY The responsibility for the decisions relating to a project.	● An inadequate level of autonomy for delegates hinders decision-making and can lead to avoidable delays. ● If authority is withheld, staff will be demotivated.
FEEDBACK The essential communication between delegator and delegate.	● A project that is in difficulty will fail unless there is a structured process of communication in place. ● Body language can reinforce or contradict your words.

ASSESSING YOUR ABILITY

*D*elegation requires a broad range of managerial abilities, from communication skills to the use of monitoring systems. Evaluate your performance by responding to the following statements, and mark the options that are closest to your experience. Be as honest as you can: if your answer is "never," mark Option 1; if it is "always," mark Option 4; and so on. Add your scores together, and refer to the Analysis to see how you scored. Use your answers to identify which areas need improving.

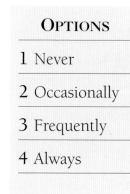

OPTIONS

1 Never

2 Occasionally

3 Frequently

4 Always

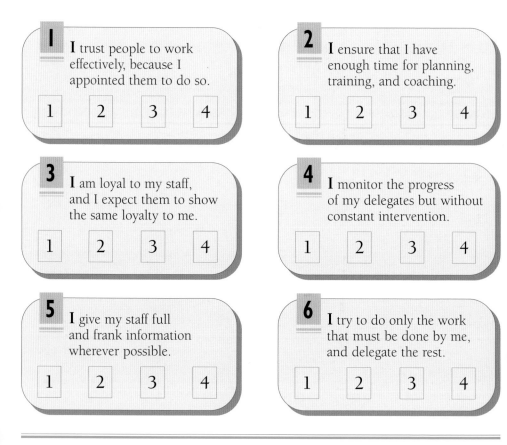

1 I trust people to work effectively, because I appointed them to do so.

1　2　3　4

2 I ensure that I have enough time for planning, training, and coaching.

1　2　3　4

3 I am loyal to my staff, and I expect them to show the same loyalty to me.

1　2　3　4

4 I monitor the progress of my delegates but without constant intervention.

1　2　3　4

5 I give my staff full and frank information wherever possible.

1　2　3　4

6 I try to do only the work that must be done by me, and delegate the rest.

1　2　3　4

7 I prioritize and devote time to personnel management.

1   2   3   4

8 I take great care over the structuring and reviewing of delegation.

1   2   3   4

9 I treat my subordinates as equals when establishing the best course of action.

1   2   3   4

10 I ensure that delegates understand the extent of their accountability.

1   2   3   4

11 I ensure that there are no overlaps in responsibility between delegates.

1   2   3   4

12 I am able to appoint or replace delegates quickly when required.

1   2   3   4

13 I evaluate staff by looking at both positive and negative aspects.

1   2   3   4

14 I appoint the best person for the job, irrespective of age, experience, or seniority.

1   2   3   4

15 I involve my delegate in the process of preparing a full and detailed brief.

1   2   3   4

16 I make sure that there is adequate backup available for delegates when needed.

1   2   3   4

17 I encourage delegates to use their initiative when confronted with problems.

1 2 3 4

18 I do not reprimand someone who fails while trying something new.

1 2 3 4

19 I gauge all delegates' performance, concentrating on significant indicators.

1 2 3 4

20 I ensure that I provide positive feedback to my delegates at all times.

1 2 3 4

21 I see to it that processes are examined regularly and adapted if needed.

1 2 3 4

22 I use an agenda when reviewing progress with a delegate or team.

1 2 3 4

23 I keep an up-to-date log of which tasks I have delegated, and to whom.

1 2 3 4

24 I make myself available to see my staff and deal with any problems they have.

1 2 3 4

25 I consider all possible alternatives before reclaiming a delegated task.

1 2 3 4

26 I make a special point of recognizing all outstanding achievements.

1 2 3 4

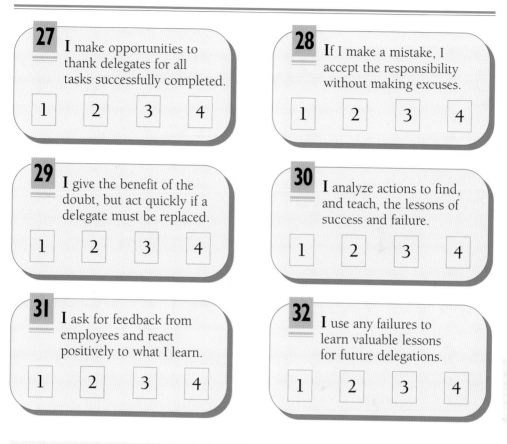

27 I make opportunities to thank delegates for all tasks successfully completed.

1 2 3 4

28 If I make a mistake, I accept the responsibility without making excuses.

1 2 3 4

29 I give the benefit of the doubt, but act quickly if a delegate must be replaced.

1 2 3 4

30 I analyze actions to find, and teach, the lessons of success and failure.

1 2 3 4

31 I ask for feedback from employees and react positively to what I learn.

1 2 3 4

32 I use any failures to learn valuable lessons for future delegations.

1 2 3 4

ANALYSIS

Now you have completed the self-assessment, add up your total score and check your performance by reading the corresponding evaluation. Whatever level of success you have achieved when delegating tasks, it is important to remember that there is always room for improvement. Identify your weakest areas, and refer to the relevant chapters in this section where you will find practical advice and tips to help you to develop and refine your delegating skills.

32–64: You are neither delegating effectively nor enough. Learn to prioritize appropriate tasks and to select the most suitable delegates.

65–95: Some of your delegation works well, but there are gaps. Identify and improve your weakest areas.

96–128: You delegate very well. Do not become complacent – continue to use your skills to achieve success.

IMPROVING SKILLS

The process of delegation provides an ideal opportunity
to raise skill levels in your staff and in yourself. Use it
to assess staff and motivate them at all levels.

DEVELOPING DELEGATES

*To allow delegates to develop their skills,
you need to offer them support and
help. This includes making available the
resources and facilities for staff to be trained
on a continuous basis, setting achievable
targets, and providing effective appraisals.*

87 Train your staff
so that they
can undertake
a variety of tasks.

88 Set an example to
your staff by being
trained yourself.

89 Try not to
underestimate a
delegate's qualities.

COMBINING TASKS

By broadening a delegate's skills, you can appoint
that delegate to handle a complete task whose
individual elements would previously have been
done by a number of people. For example, the
financing of customer purchases at one company
was split between five people and took seven
working days to complete. It was calculated that
most of this time was spent handing the project
between staff who also had higher priority work
to finish first. A decision was made to assign the
whole task to one person backed up by a special
team. The completion time was cut to four hours.

TRAINING STAFF

It is ineffective and demoralizing to delegate a task to someone who lacks the necessary skills. Never place people in new or changed roles without first providing the training they need, and always keep the option of further training available. Ask suitably skilled delegates too if there are any areas that need developing – this can be highly motivational. Always build delegation on a foundation of ongoing training at all levels so that suitably qualified people will be available whenever you need them.

▲ CHOOSING A TRAINING PROGRAM
Consider budgeting for a certain amount of staff training each year. Compare course details, and remember that the cheapest training program may be a false economy in the long term.

REASSESSING ABILITIES

Delegating a task will give you the opportunity to assess a delegate's abilities. If the delegate has worked for you before, you will have a chance to reassess his or her performance in the light of any new demands and challenges. Always keep delegates' performances under constant review, since new tasks are likely to reveal either hidden talents or areas in which deficiencies become apparent. Reassessment of delegates sometimes reveals that a staff member is being used for tasks that are far beneath his or her potential abilities.

▼ TRAINING TO COMMUNICATE
When the manager realized that problems in the workshop were the result of poor communications, he initiated a training program for one of his key staff.

CASE STUDY
The efficiency and reputation of a major auto service center was being weakened by interdepartmental conflict. When promises were made to customers that could not be fulfilled, the counter staff and the mechanics blamed each other. To build an understanding between the two teams, the manager decided to develop head mechanic Ryan's communication skills and give him an opportunity to work with the counter staff. Ryan was then able to discuss some of the customer service issues with staff in the shop and vice versa. When required, he was also able to assist in situations where customers had technical questions.

Being in contact with the whole job gave Ryan great satisfaction. Customers benefited from his expert knowledge, and the conflict between the teams ended.

COACHING DELEGATES

When delegating, a manager takes on the role of a coach, talking to staff and encouraging their development. One of the most important points to discuss with delegates is whether they are tackling tasks in the most efficient way. Delegates who are eager to impress may not wish to ask for help, so ensure that they are working within their skill levels. If they are not, provide the appropriate training or backup to improve their abilities.

90 Set aside some of your working week for coaching your key delegates.

Display shows structure of project

Delegate notes down information

Manager explains developments

▲ **FINDING TIME TO DEVELOP STAFF**

Consider setting aside some regular time every week to keep your staff informed of any new developments and to concentrate on developing skills in the specific areas in which you are eager to delegate work.

SETTING TARGETS

One of the most effective ways of developing delegates is through setting targets. However, set targets at levels that both you and the delegate consider attainable through good performance. This will enable both of you to anticipate and focus on areas of the task in which the delegate's skills need to improve. This type of on-the-job training will help the delegate to complete the task and move on to more difficult ones.

278

BEATING EXPECTATIONS

Staff can exceed expectations if you set them ambitious but achievable targets and let them make their own decisions about how to attain them. This hands-off approach has two major benefits: delegates are motivated by being given the freedom to use their initiative and improve their own performance, and the organization as a whole benefits through the improved efficiency demonstrated by the newly motivated workforce.

DO'S AND DON'TS

✔ **Do** ensure that employees are aware that training is available if needed.

✔ **Do** thank those who have performed well.

✔ **Do** tell delegates that they should ask others for help when needed.

✔ **Do** ask people what additional skills they feel they require.

✔ **Do** encourage delegates to use their own initiative to achieve objectives.

✘ **Don't** forget that financial reward is not always the most effective motivator.

✘ **Don't** stifle creativity by emphasizing rules over results.

✘ **Don't** assume that all criticism is always discouraging.

✘ **Don't** set obscure targets that could seem unattainable.

✘ **Don't** neglect a delegate who may be struggling with a task.

91 If people appear dissatisfied by the reward system, find out why.

PRAISING EFFECTIVELY

Deliver praise to a delegate as soon as possible after the occasion that merits it. Be genuinely warm, but not effusive, and be specific about the aspects you have most admired. Comparisons are sometimes beneficial; if the delegate has outshone others in certain ways, make that a point of admiration. The object of praise is to thank and to motivate, and thus to establish a foundation on which to build still better performance.

OFFERING REWARDS

People are paid for meeting expectations, so avoid incentive schemes that pay bonuses for expected performance. Remember that the delegator and the delegate share the same goals. You want the job to be done well, and they want to do the job well. Their earnings are likely to improve as they continue to develop their skills. So try to ensure that performance meets or exceeds expectations, and reward exceptional performance separately.

92 Set realistic targets, and be flexible in case events force a change of plan.

Appointing Deputies

The development of deputies is a major part of a manager's task. This involves encouraging the appointment of deputies, sharing authority by promoting the most qualified candidates, and considering all means of training for potential leaders.

 93 Ask a senior to keep an eye on a deputy when you are absent.

Developing Deputies

As a manager it is important for you to assess your staff continually for potential deputies. Remember that there will be times when you are absent and someone will have to deputize for you. Delegation to cover your absence, or to take over part of your work temporarily, will provide an opportunity for potential future leaders to step into your shoes. Develop reliable deputies by deputizing as much and as often as you can. This will free you to concentrate on high-level tasks.

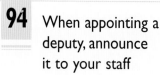 **94** When appointing a deputy, announce it to your staff with confidence.

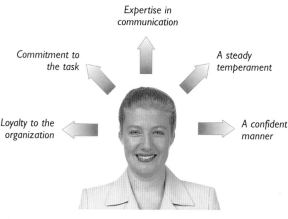

Expertise in communication

Commitment to the task

A steady temperament

Loyalty to the organization

A confident manner

▲ **WHAT TO LOOK FOR IN A DEPUTY**
When selecting a person for a leadership position, consider all the qualities that a potential candidate will bring to the role. Look for relevant experience and reliability combined with excellent communication skills, confidence, and enthusiasm.

Delegating Authority

You, as leader, are ultimately responsible for appointing or removing deputies, altering instructions, or changing levels of responsibility. However, the more authority that you give your deputies to exercise on delegated tasks, the more they will develop their own skills – including those of delegation. Always encourage deputies to follow your example and share as much authority as possible with their own delegates.

Promoting on Merit

To avoid negative reactions following a promotion to a leadership position, you must be careful to choose your candidate solely on the grounds of merit. People who are promoted beyond their capabilities will feel inadequate, and their insecurity will make them less effective. Others, especially those who have been passed over, may feel that they have been unfairly treated and will be demotivated. Even with a deserved promotion, the attributes that you have recognized may not be immediately appreciated by others. So show that you have confidence in your delegate/deputy as the right person for the job. A genuinely deserving delegate will not take long to fulfill your expectations and justify the appointment.

Providing Training in Leadership

There are plenty of leadership courses from which to choose, and effective ones will teach specific skills and reinforce the personal characteristics and expertise needed by a deputy. Leadership training is often run in combination with other programs, such as quality management. However, learning the theory of management is not enough. Leadership is an interpersonal skill and has to be practiced in a real environment. So consider providing opportunities for subordinates occasionally to lead a team. The role need not be permanent, nor need it depend on status. Rotating the leadership of task forces or similar sub-groups is an excellent means of showing people, through their own experiences, what the requirements of leadership are.

▲ **DEVELOPING LEADERS**
Management training can take place away from the workplace. Outdoor activity courses will assess and develop team-working and leadership abilities.

DEVELOPING YOURSELF THROUGH DELEGATION

You should never become so busy developing others through delegation that you neglect your own development. While the delegating process is an education in itself and will free your time, it can be reinforced through formal instruction.

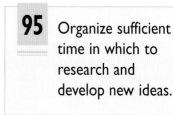

95 Organize sufficient time in which to research and develop new ideas.

96 Set yourself a weekly or monthly reading plan and try to stick to it.

IMPROVING PERFORMANCE

Delegation involves some of the most important aspects of the manager's job: selection, planning, and operating through others to achieve results. These activities are such an intrinsic part of the management process that the delegator is able to improve his or her efficiency simply by delegating well. But good performance can always be better. There is no absolute level of attainment, even in settled conditions. To be a successful manager you must undergo routine self-assessment, and look for ways to develop new and improved skills.

REASSESSING TASKS

As you develop your delegating skills, your staff will naturally progress, improving and increasing their own skills and gaining in confidence and experience. Reassign those individuals who have outgrown their initial task, and are ready to take on more, or higher-level, work. Also, monitor the performance of your team as a whole, to assess whether they are capable of undertaking higher-profile projects. This will improve the structure and balance of your workload, allowing you to take on other tasks and achieve still better results.

QUESTIONS TO ASK YOURSELF

Q Am I up to date with current management issues?

Q Have I become complacent about my own performance?

Q Do I invest enough time in looking for new ways to deal with familiar problems?

Q When I am guiding others, how often do I stop to listen to my own advice?

DEVELOPING YOUR SKILLS

Use the delegation process to free yourself from structured work, such as administration, so that you can undertake more demanding and unstructured tasks, such as managing people, solving problems, and researching new ideas. It is by constantly developing these special skills that you as a manager can raise your performance from the adequate to the exceptional.

97 If you are aware of a gap in your management education, fill it.

98 Reinforce your skills by taking the opportunity to learn from others.

UTILIZING TRAINING

Seek relevant training even if you feel you have reached the top. Consider taking advantage of courses that teach skills that you have not yet mastered in order to increase your area of expertise, or use them to update your knowledge and develop new ideas. Remember that many trainers and approaches are available to meet your own specific needs, so your options are limitless.

EDUCATING YOURSELF

An American pizza multimillionaire has the world's biggest library of self-help books. Whether or not the books contributed to his success, the principle is powerful. Every one of those books contains ideas or techniques designed to make the manager's job easier and improve performance. Although managers acquire knowledge and know-how as they carry out their tasks and communicate with others, there is much to be gained from an organized approach to self-education. Take time to study and absorb books, journals, and other media, and the payoff will be incalculable.

▼ STUDY TO SUCCEED
Make use of correspondence courses if you cannot spare the time during the day or evening to attend a "live" course.

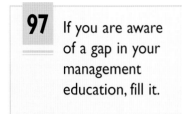

Take notes of important points

DEVELOPING YOUR BOSS

Although you may have developed effective delegation skills, your own manager's approach to delegating tasks to you may be deficient. Ask yourself if this is because your manager has not fully understood your abilities, or if it is because he or she feels threatened by you. Consider saying to your manager that you feel underused and are able to take on more responsibilities. Adapt your manner to the situation, and always be polite.

> **99** Develop the habit of speaking frankly to your manager at all times.

MANAGING YOUR CAREER

When planning your career, actively seek ways to make progress – do not wait for your rise to be dictated by events. Use your delegating skills to give yourself time to think about your aims and ambitions. Consider writing a career plan, complete with target dates, for advancing from one stage to the next. Working toward these targets will give you a positive attitude that will help you to identify and make the best of any career opportunities that arise.

John is promoted to project leader and is introduced to members of his team

John's poor delegation skills rapidly lead to inefficiency and delays

▲ MAKING PROGRESS BY DELEGATING

This manager realizes that his under-use of delegation adversely affects his performance. Improving his delegating skills enables him to use his time more productively, develop and pursue a career plan, and achieve promotion.

BEING PROACTIVE

In today's fast-changing world, managers are expected to be highly independent and proactive. Showing initiative, making up one's own mind, and taking charge of one's destiny are all qualities valued by organizations that recognize that they need managers with these skills to survive in a competitive climate with fast-moving markets. To be effective, managers must be able to act rather than react under pressure, and delegate efficiently. So strive to stretch yourself and use your abilities to the fullest in your present position, and look for and take any chances to exercise responsibility. If the organization denies you the opportunity to develop, the best response may be to move on.

100 Ask where you want to be in ten years time, and plan your route.

John develops career targets and achieves promotion

Effective delegation allows John to become a successful manager

Having taken steps to improve his delegating skills, John starts using his team members much more productively

101 Do not keep quiet about your ambitions – let your superiors know what you want to achieve.

MOTIVATING PEOPLE

INTRODUCTION

Today's increasingly competitive business world means that a highly motivated workforce is vital for any organization seeking good results. Therefore, learning how to motivate others has become an essential skill for managers. This section shows you how best to put effective motivational theories into practice to create and sustain a positive environment in the workplace. The section contains a wealth of practical advice, including 101 quick-reference tips, while all of the most important motivational techniques are comprehensively explained – from analyzing the needs of individual staff members to offering incentives and using multiskilling and training to increase job satisfaction. A self-assessment test at the end of this section evaluates your motivational skills, helping you raise levels of performance and get the most from both yourself and your staff.

ANALYZING MOTIVATION

To inspire people to work – individually or in groups –
in ways that produce the best results, you need to tap into
their own personal motivational forces.

WHAT IS MOTIVATION?

*T*he art of motivating people starts with
learning how to influence individuals'
behavior. Once you understand this, you are
more likely to achieve the results that both
the organization and its members want.

I If you do not know
what motivates a
person, just ask.

▲ **BEING MOTIVATED**
For an employee, the chief advantage of
being motivated is job satisfaction. For the
employer, it means high-quality work.

DEFINING MOTIVATION

Motivation is the will to act. It was once assumed
that motivation had to be injected from outside,
but it is now understood that everyone is motivated
by several differing forces. In the workplace,
seek to influence your staff to align their own
motivations with the needs of the organization.

To release the full potential of employees,
organizations are rapidly moving away from
"command and control" and toward "advise and
consent" as a way of motivating. This change of
attitude began when employers recognized that
rewarding good work is more effective than
threatening punitive measures for bad work.

MOTIVATING LONG TERM

Self-motivation is long-lasting. Inspire self-motivated staff further by trusting them to work on their own initiatives and encouraging them to take responsibility for entire tasks. For demotivated staff members, find out what would motivate them and implement whatever help you can. Highly motivated individuals are vital to supply organizations with the new initiatives that are necessary in the competitive business world.

2 Assess your own motivation levels as well as those of your staff.

WHOM TO MOTIVATE?

Motivation used to be considered only in one direction: downward, the superior motivating the subordinate. That is no longer enough. In well-managed organizations, in which subordinates do far more than take orders, superiors may need motivating to act accordingly. Encourage colleagues to share your ideas and enthusiasm at work. Use motivation to achieve both collaboration and cooperation from everyone with whom you work.

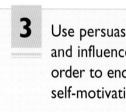

3 Use persuasion and influence in order to encourage self-motivation.

MOTIVATING DIFFERENT PEOPLE IN DIFFERENT WAYS

MANAGER
As a manager, it is important to remember that you should use your motivational techniques to influence not only subordinates, but also your colleagues and managers senior to yourself.

SENIOR MANAGER
Motivate superiors to perceive that what you request suits their own purposes: for instance, improving management information with a new system.

COLLEAGUE
Motivate colleagues to feel that by helping and supporting you they are pursuing their own ends: for example, putting together a joint plan for office economies.

SUBORDINATE
Motivate subordinates to think that following your wishes will bring them satisfaction: for instance, taking over responsibility for an entire job.

RECOGNIZING NEEDS

Since the 1940s, research into human behavior has suggested that people are motivated by a number of different needs, at work and in their personal lives. Recognizing and satisfying these needs will help you to get the best from people.

4 Establish what the needs of your staff are, and assist in meeting them.

UNDERSTANDING MOTIVATION

Several motivation theories work on the assumption that given the chance and the right stimuli, people work well and positively. As a manager, be aware of what these stimuli or "motivational forces" are. Theorist Abraham Maslow grouped them into five areas. The first is physiological needs, and they are followed by further needs, classed as "safety," "social," "esteem," and "self-actualization." According to Maslow, the needs are tackled in order: as you draw near to satisfying one, the priority of the next one becomes higher. Also, once a need has been satisfied, it is no longer a stimulus.

SELF-ACTUALIZATION
Realizing individual potential; winning; achieving

ESTEEM NEEDS
Being well regarded by other people; appreciation

SOCIAL NEEDS
Interaction with other people; having friends

SAFETY NEEDS
A sense of security; absence of fear

PHYSIOLOGICAL NEEDS
Warmth; shelter; food; sex – a human being's "animal" needs

5 Remember that making work fun does not mean making it easy.

▲ **THE MASLOW HIERARCHY**
Abraham Maslow believed that satisfying just physiological and safety needs is not enough to motivate a person fully. Once these needs have been appeased, there are others waiting to take their place. The Maslow hierarchy can be applied to every aspect of life, and the more ambitious and satisfied the personality, the greater the potential contribution to the organization.

MEETING NEEDS AT WORK

The Maslow hierarchy is particularly relevant in the workplace because individuals need not just money and rewards, but also respect and interaction. When designing jobs, working conditions, and organizational structures, bear in mind the full range of needs in the Maslow hierarchy. Doing this will cost no more, but it will undoubtedly generate higher psychological and economic rewards all around.

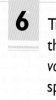

6 Try to motivate through the use of *voluntary* social and sports activities.

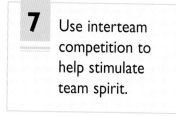

7 Use interteam competition to help stimulate team spirit.

BALANCING GROUP NEEDS

Individuals acting as part of a group have needs that differ from those of the group. However, it is important for individuals to feel they belong. Find a way to balance the needs of the group with those of individuals. For example, tell staff that if the group meets its major objectives, you may be able to satisfy individual requirements. Do not, of course, promise what you cannot deliver.

MOTIVATION OUTSIDE THE WORKPLACE

One of the areas in which individuals tend to satisfy their motivational needs outside work is sports activities. It is interesting to note the effort that people put into such endeavors, for which they are unlikely to gain material reward. Try to motivate your staff to apply as much effort in the workplace as they would in a team sports event by making work as much fun as possible. A shrewd motivational strategy is to encourage your staff to take up team activities outside the workplace in order to improve their teamwork skills.

▲ **HIRING SPORTS PEOPLE**
Some companies find that staff who are involved in regular sports activities are more likely to enjoy cooperative teamwork in the workplace.

SATISFYING BASIC NEEDS

Psychologist Frederick Herzberg developed a "two-factor" theory for motivation based on "motivators" and "hygiene factors." Hygiene factors – basic human needs at work – do not motivate, but failure to meet them causes dissatisfaction. These factors can be as seemingly trivial as parking space or as vital as sufficient vacation time; but the most important hygiene factor is money. A manager should try to fulfill staff members' financial needs. People require certain pay levels to meet their needs, and slow income progression and ineffective incentives quickly demotivate. Insecurity in a job also greatly demotivates staff.

POINTS TO REMEMBER

- The effects of getting hygiene factors right are only temporary.
- The results of getting hygiene factors wrong can cause long-lasting problems.
- The more choice people can exercise over both hygiene factors and motivators, the better motivated they will be.
- Job insecurity undermines motivation at all levels.
- Recognizing good work is as important as rewarding it.

ESTABLISHING BASIC NEEDS AT WORK

HYGIENE FACTORS	DEFINITIONS
SALARY AND BENEFITS	These include basic income, fringe benefits, bonuses, vacation time, company car, and similar items.
WORKING CONDITIONS	These conditions include working hours, workplace layout, facilities, and equipment provided for the job.
COMPANY POLICY	The company policy is the rules and regulations – formal and informal – that govern employers and employees.
STATUS	A person's status is determined by rank, authority, and relationship to others, reflecting a level of acceptance.
JOB SECURITY	This is the degree of confidence that the employee has regarding continued employment in an organization.
SUPERVISION AND AUTONOMY	This factor concerns the extent of control that an individual has over the content and execution of a job.
OFFICE LIFE	This is the level and type of interpersonal relations within the individual's working environment.
PERSONAL LIFE	An individual's personal life is the time spent on family, friends, and interests – restricted by time spent at work.

ENSURING MOTIVATION

The second of Herzberg's two factors is a set of motivators that actually drive people to achieve. These are what a manager should aim to provide in order to maintain a satisfied workforce. How much a person enjoys achievement depends purely on its recognition. The ability to achieve, in turn, rests on having an enjoyable job and responsibility. The greater that responsibility, the more the individual can feel the satisfaction of advancement. Motivators are built around obtaining growth and "self-actualization" from tasks. You can raise motivation in your staff by increasing their responsibility, thereby "enriching" their jobs.

8 Keep the number of supervisors to a minimum.

9 Remember that different people are motivated in different ways.

HEIGHTENING WORKPLACE MOTIVATION

MOTIVATORS	WHY THEY WORK
ACHIEVEMENT	Reaching or exceeding task objectives is particularly important because the "onward-and-upward" urge to achieve is a basic human drive. It is one of the most powerful motivators and a great source of satisfaction.
RECOGNITION	The acknowledgment of achievements by senior staff members is motivational because it helps enhance self-esteem. For many staff members, recognition may be viewed as a reward in itself.
JOB INTEREST	A job that provides positive, satisfying pleasure to individuals and groups will be a greater motivational force than a job that does not sustain interest. As far as possible, responsibilities should be matched to individuals' interests.
RESPONSIBILITY	The opportunity to exercise authority and power may demand leadership skills, risk-taking, decision-making, and self-direction, all of which raise self-esteem and are strong motivators.
ADVANCEMENT	Promotion, progress, and rising rewards for achievement are important here. Possibly the main motivator, however, is the feeling that advancement is possible. Be honest about promotion prospects and the likely timescale involved.

UNDERSTANDING BEHAVIOR

*A*ctual behavior is very important, but so are the reasons behind it. In most cases, the only way to know how motivated your staff members are is through the ways in which they behave. This includes what they say, their gestures, expressions, and stance.

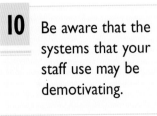

10 Be aware that the systems that your staff use may be demotivating.

11 Look for positive responses to any criticisms – they are good signs of motivation in staff.

READING BEHAVIOR

When trying to read behavior, recognize that while body language can give clues to motivation levels, it can also be misread. More concrete signals will be provided by the ways in which individuals perform their tasks: this is likely to give you the clearest indication of their motivation. People who work cheerfully and efficiently are unlikely to be hiding anything if they greet you with a smile. Likewise, a dour facial expression should be interpreted adversely only if combined with a grumpy "That's-not-my-job" attitude to work.

SEEING ENTHUSIASM

Positive motivation is often signaled by positive gestures: a smile, an eager pose, and a relaxed manner. When people carry out a task in which they are interested or enthusiastic, they may have a "sparkle" in the eyes, since their pupils actually enlarge. Confident eye contact is also important as a measure of motivation: demotivated people are less likely to look you straight in the eye. Blushing can indicate pleasure, while an increased rate of breathing can indicate enthusiasm – both of these are good signs of motivation.

12 Maintain eye contact with your staff whenever you speak with them.

RECOGNIZING MOTIVATION

Motivation can be recognized in a number of ways – look particularly for signs that your staff feel useful, optimistic, or able to take opportunities. A team in which each member looks after the others' interests is likely to be a good source of motivation. Look for evidence that your staff are satisfied in their jobs rather than anxious or frustrated. If you find no such signs, ask them whether they are satisfied. You can also establish a good idea of an individual's level of motivation by his or her attitude toward work. The statements below are all indicative of motivated staff members:

- They freely volunteer effort and ideas, as well as other contributions;
- They always react well to requests and new assignments;
- They work to achieve, not "to rule";
- They seem to be happy at work;
- They always respond frankly to questions.

13 Ask your staff if any changes at work would help motivate them.

14 Learn to see the difference between work problems and personal ones.

▼ **RECOGNIZING A MOTIVATED WORKER**

A tidy, organized work space and a well-groomed appearance can indicate a positive attitude to work. A neat desk is a sign of a motivated worker who wishes to be able to find the things they need easily, while attention to personal appearance suggests a high level of commitment to the job.

Cheerful expression is combined with smart appearance

Paperwork is kept neatly

Only task at hand is on desk

Tidy in-box shows that work is up-to-date

REDUCING DEMOTIVATION

Workplace demotivation for many people tends to be caused by poor systems or work overload. Very clear signs of demotivation include high levels of absenteeism and quick turnover of staff. Recognizing demotivation is pointless unless you intend to eradicate its causes. Remember, too, that poor behavior and underperformance are not necessarily signs of workplace demotivation. If demotivation remains even when the situation is improved, it may be due to personal problems.

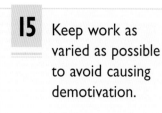

15 Keep work as varied as possible to avoid causing demotivation.

SEEING NEGATIVE SIGNS

Demotivation may not always be obvious, but look out for defensive, protective actions, such as folding the arms when seated or clenching the fists involuntarily. Inattention, the first sign of demotivation, may be seen in facial expressions, though tapping fingers and restlessness are also negative indicators. A sloppy, "couldn't-care-less" attitude and a lack of enthusiasm for work may also be observed. A monotonous tone of voice may tell of boredom, but be aware also of signs of aggression, such as chopping motions of the hand or pointing a finger in an accusatory manner.

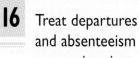

16 Treat departures and absenteeism as warning signs of demotivation.

NOTICING NEGATIVE ▼ APPEARANCE

This person seated at his work station conveys a very negative impression. The disheveled appearance and disorganized desk suggest a careless attitude to work, while the head propped on his hand is a classic sign of boredom.

Hand propping up head may indicate lack of motivation

Untidy pile of papers points to inefficiency

MEASURING MORALE

It is important to measure workplace morale on a regular basis to discover if and why staff are experiencing problems. However, if you notice a rise in departures, suspect that motivation is low, or find that absenteeism is increasing, do not wait to take the workplace "temperature": do it now. You may wish to try using employee attitude surveys; these give a broad indication of morale but can be lengthy and costly. Read the signs from your own talks with people, such as annual appraisals, or set up focus groups or one-to-one interviews. Another way to measure morale is to take a random opinion poll. Remember, however, that if you investigate staff attitudes you must act on the findings, or risk causing further demotivation.

POINTS TO REMEMBER

● Measuring the workplace morale of your staff should be a continual process.

● Lack of motivation may have many causes – do not jump to conclusions about them.

● Inquiring into attitudes carries with it an implicit promise of reform, which must be kept.

● You may not always get honest responses when questioning demotivated staff about their motivation levels.

● Exit interviews with departing staff can give valuable clues as to what is right or wrong with your motivational management.

WAYS OF MEASURING MORALE

METHODS	FACTORS TO CONSIDER
ATTITUDE QUESTIONNAIRES Providing questionnaires to be filled in by all staff members at regular intervals.	● Must be sent to home address to ensure individual attention. ● Follow-up required to obtain satisfactory reply rate. ● Questions need expert drafting, which may be expensive. ● Better for trends rather than showing entire situation.
OPINION POLLS Surveying attitudes on a sample basis (that is, a random selection of the workforce).	● Can be repeated more often than full-scale surveys. ● Lacks the motivational impact of asking everybody. ● Lacks depth, but can be continually revised or refined. ● Good for follow-up on management reforms.
UNSTRUCTURED INTERVIEWS Arranging for employees to meet an outside interviewer one-to-one to talk about the company.	● Can elicit buried concerns and shared difficulties. ● Seems unscientific, but results match questionnaires'. ● Process itself generates improvement in staff morale. ● Interviewer must be careful to avoid overinfluence.
FOCUS GROUPS Arranging for employees to meet an outside interviewer in small groups to discuss company issues.	● Useful insights surface more than in attitude surveys. ● Needs experienced handling by the outside interviewer. ● If too structured, may prevent real concerns from arising. ● Problems tend to be either exaggerated or understated.

BUILDING UP MOTIVATION

Before staff can be receptive to your motivational techniques, you must make sure that the environment in which they work meets a number of important human needs.

ASSESSING YOUR ATTITUDE

It is important that you understand your attitude toward your subordinates. Your thinking will be influenced by your experience and will shape the way in which you behave toward all the people you meet.

17 Be sure staff know their role and its importance.

18 Demonstrate your competence at every opportunity.

19 Improve order and control by using collaborative management.

KNOWING YOUR STYLE

The forces that drive managers will strongly influence motivational behavior. It is important, therefore, to understand your own assumptions and priorities, paying particular attention to your personal and corporate ambitions, so you can motivate others effectively. If you put your job first, you are probably highly motivated and know your career will benefit from success. However, success is not just about meeting task objectives, but also about building an efficient, creative team that will succeed even in your absence. For this, a "share-and-collaborate" style may be more effective than an authoritarian "command-and-control" method.

EVALUATING YOUR TENDENCIES

Theorist Douglas McGregor defined two sets of management styles, which he labeled Theory X and Theory Y. Theory-X managers believe their staff respond mainly to the rewarding carrot and the disciplinary stick. Theory-Y managers, however, believe their staff find work to be a source of satisfaction and will strive to do their best at all times. Most people are not entirely X or Y, but fall somewhere in between. The X and Y theories apply not only to individuals but to organizations as well; indeed, Theory-X managers and habits will often be found in Theory-Y organizations, and vice versa. Study the statements below to judge which of the theories best describes you and your organization.

THEORY X

- If I did not drive my people constantly, they would not get on with their work.
- I sometimes have to fire somebody or tongue-lash them to encourage others.
- Leaders have to lead by making all key decisions themselves.
- I find that most people are unambitious and must be forced to raise their sights.
- I keep my distance from the team since it is necessary for effective command.

THEORY Y

- If somebody falls down on the job, I first ask myself what I did wrong.
- I should sometimes take a back seat at meetings and let others take the lead.
- If I ask someone for their opinion on an issue, I try to do as they suggest.
- People should appraise their bosses as well as be appraised by them.
- Anyone can have creative, innovative ideas if they are encouraged.

▲ MANAGING BY THEORY X

A typical Theory-X manager is likely to keep away from his or her workforce much of the time. In fact, the only time the two meet is when orders or reprimands are to be given.

▲ MANAGING BY THEORY Y

Collaborating with staff over decisions to be made, and getting feedback before implementing decisions, are traits that tend to be typical of a Theory-Y manager. This approach is often more motivating than that of Theory X.

BEING A GOOD MANAGER

Managers often take courses to learn leadership, but good leaders are not necessarily good managers. Leadership is only one part of being a manager, and while a successful manager needs leadership skills, other abilities are equally important.

20 Do not just assume you are "visible" – make sure that you are.

21 If bad results occur, review your own motivation as well as employees'.

ASSESSING QUALITIES ▼
There are a number of important qualities that a manager must possess in order to motivate staff effectively. If any one of these qualities is absent or deficient, staff will quickly lose their motivation.

MANAGING TO MOTIVATE

An essential foundation for motivation is a positive workplace environment created by you, the manager. Employees have the right to expect fair treatment and understanding. They also expect professional competence, part of which includes delegating tasks in order to increase staff members' self-management and participation.

Establish a system that is constructive – not obstructive – in which people can hope to perform at their best. Ascertain where your employees' strengths and interests lie, and then delegate responsibilities that will both exploit these and meet the needs of the organization.

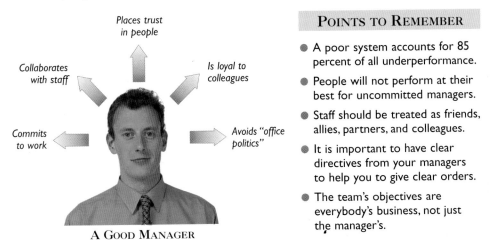

Places trust in people

Collaborates with staff

Is loyal to colleagues

Commits to work

Avoids "office politics"

A GOOD MANAGER

POINTS TO REMEMBER

● A poor system accounts for 85 percent of all underperformance.

● People will not perform at their best for uncommitted managers.

● Staff should be treated as friends, allies, partners, and colleagues.

● It is important to have clear directives from your managers to help you to give clear orders.

● The team's objectives are everybody's business, not just the manager's.

TREATING STAFF WELL

When considering how best to treat your staff remember the old adage, "Do unto others as you would be done by." Demonstrate trust in your staff, and prove yourself worthy of trust. This trust includes, on the part of the manager:

- Never making promises that you are not able or are not intending to keep;
- Never asking others to do anything that you would not do yourself;
- Letting your people know that they can count on your respect and your loyalty, unless and until they prove to be undeserving.

To the best of your ability, see to it that working conditions, pay and status issues, job security, and working atmosphere are managed promptly and in a way that is comfortable to employees. Deal with personal problems, which arise from time to time, in a sympathetic and positive manner.

CULTURAL DIFFERENCES

The command-and-control style of management still prevails in the US, despite the more relaxed style found on the West Coast. Japan uniquely combines domination with participation. Collaborative ideas have gained more ground in the UK than in the rest of Europe.

22 Show respect to your staff, and they will show it to you.

CALCULATING YOUR MOTIVATION

Staff will not commit to an uncommitted manager, so it is important that you motivate yourself as well as others. Consider the question, "Am I committed to my objectives and my staff?" The amount of energy you put into your work will indicate your level of motivation. If you are reluctant to begin necessary tasks, unable to make decisions, or prefer office politics to achievement, these are all signs that you are demotivated.

HARNESSING MOTIVATION

Motivation depends on having clear objectives, which will be achieved with good management. Since motivation is personal, aim to align staff's individual drives with the company's purposes in general and your unit's in particular.

In "Management by Objectives" (MBO) systems, objectives are written down for each level of the organization, and individuals are given specific aims and targets. The principle behind this is to ensure that people know what the organization is trying to achieve, what their part of the organization must do to meet those aims, and how, as individuals, they are expected to help. This presupposes that the organization's programs and methods have been fully considered. If they have not, start by constructing team objectives and asking team members to share in the process.

IMPROVING COMMUNICATION

Not communicating at all conveys a very powerful message – the last one that a committed manager wants to deliver. You can never communicate too much, but be careful about the content and delivery of a message so that it inspires motivation.

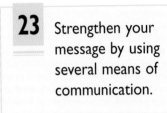

23 Strengthen your message by using several means of communication.

24 Deliver internal communications as soon as possible.

25 Encourage your staff to participate in decision-making.

PROVIDING INFORMATION

The ideal approach when providing information is that everybody should know about everything that concerns them directly or indirectly, in full and accurate detail, as soon as possible. Always aim for the ideal: overkill is better than underprovision. Preselect the information that your staff have told you they want – responding to demand is motivational – as well as the information that you want them to know. Once these lists of requirements are established, supply regular updates. Set up a help desk for "other queries," and always inform before rumors arise.

USING OPEN MANAGEMENT

The open system of management, which encourages the exchange of information and views between team members, allows managers and staff to work together creatively. Problems can be discussed and decisions reached quickly and easily. To achieve this, try to make your office open-plan – this will facilitate collaboration. You may also wish to leave your office door open whenever you are available to speak to staff; if this is not practical, make appointments with staff and keep them.

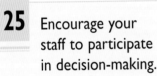

26 Keep staff informed wherever possible – uncertainties are very demotivating.

CHOOSING EFFECTIVE METHODS OF COMMUNICATION

METHODS	FACTORS TO CONSIDER

ELECTRONICS
The variety of methods made possible by the computer age, such as e-mail.

- These are highly effective means of quickly reaching those with whom you are communicating.
- Interaction and participation are possible – and often simple – for all involved parties.
- Their ease of use means that they pose a possible risk of communications overload.
- The seemingly endless possible combinations of words, images, and color are very powerful.

MEETINGS
The basic means of direct people management.

- If used properly, meetings can build relationships and mutual trust.
- Meetings enable instant feedback.
- Meetings facilitate mutual understanding.
- Responses can often be gauged through eye contact.
- Preparation, planning, and openness are required.

JOURNALISM
Takes many forms, from newsletters to full magazines.

- In-house publications enable a wide range of messages and editorial techniques.
- It is possible to facilitate some interaction through readers' letters and contributions.
- The content of most organizations' journals tends to be bland, resulting in low readership.

INTERNAL MARKETING
Consumer techniques applied internally.

- This is a powerful method of "selling" change to the organization's own staff.
- Detailed written documents and colorful posters help explain and simplify complex messages.
- These techniques are able to elicit very strong, immediate motivational responses.

BULLETIN BOARDS
The easiest way of messaging in an organization.

- Bulletin boards can be either official information givers or for general use by employees.
- Bulletin boards provide a central location on which to make information accessible to all employees.
- There is no real possibility of interactive response, and employees may feel uninvolved.

TELEPHONE
A critical tool for one-to-one communication.

- The telephone is not suitable for lengthy or complicated discussions.
- The lack of physical presence may lessen the speakers' understanding of each other.

PROMOTING DISCUSSION

Motivational management encourages and guides discussion about further involvement and contribution. Even issues that are dealt with by formal channels have probably been discussed informally. To this end, it is just as important to have informal talks with your staff as formal team meetings. Invite discussion by posing questions and seeking opinions. Treat contrary views with respect, and when you disagree, explain why fully.

27 Encourage disagreement – it often paves the way to consensus.

MAKING TIME AVAILABLE

Communicating and thinking are important activities in motivational management. Try to avoid becoming so preoccupied with your workload that you run out of time for these activities. Keep a diary in which you analyze your workweek. Eliminate or shorten activities where possible, in order to leave more time for communication and thought. Set aside time for at least one face-to-face discussion or coaching session each week. Remember that to motivate your staff fully it is important to be visible, approachable, and unhurried at all times.

28 Make time to stop and chat rather than simply greeting staff.

Staff member is given opportunity to speak freely

Manager listens to what is being said and offers advice as necessary

◀ TALKING FACE TO FACE
You should regularly take the time to talk with each member of your staff. Ask if anything would make his or her job easier, and try your best to fulfill requests.

COMMUNICATING WELL

To motivate team members, engage them in decisions that might affect them, instead of merely informing them after the fact. If people express concern about a new policy, ask how you can allay their concerns. Undertake to report back on any problems that they pinpoint, and let them know how you plan to proceed, using their input. Involving staff from an early stage encourages all members to feel that they can make a difference.

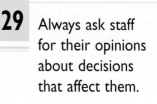

29 Always ask staff for their opinions about decisions that affect them.

POINTS TO REMEMBER

- If the manager does not play favorites, favors are less likely to be sought.
- Honest disagreement can be fruitful, but only if those in dispute share an objective.
- Hidden agendas arouse suspicion.
- False rumors should be quashed as soon as they are heard.
- Ignoring the efforts of "office politicians" often discourages further attempts.

30 Be aware of office politics, and set an example by never taking part yourself.

AVOIDING OFFICE POLITICS

Many work groups are highly political. Members jockey for position, form cliques, spread rumors, curry favors, and backbite. Do not get involved in office politics; indeed, discourage them at every opportunity. Any personal advantage that you may gain will be outweighed by the long-term damage to the organization as energies are diverted away from business. The motivational manager must concentrate on clearly communicated purposes and not allow any deviation from the behavior that promotes those goals.

Manager intervenes to prevent an angry exchange between two staff members

INTERVENING IN ▶ OFFICE POLITICS
If staff become involved in political games, intervene quickly. Make it clear that nobody will win from the exchange, and insist that differences be settled.

CREATING A NO-BLAME CULTURE

*A*nyone with responsibility – including *yourself – must accept their failures. However, to motivate effectively you need a culture in which no blame is laid for failure. Errors should be recognized, then used to improve chances of future success.*

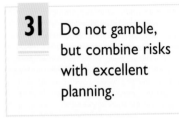

31 Do not gamble, but combine risks with excellent planning.

32 Praise work well done, even if some targets are missed.

33 Take risks only when the chances of success are high.

ACCEPTING RISKS

Management by motivation hinges on delegation and runs two risks: the delegate entrusted with the mission may fail; and the task may fail. To maximize chances of success, you must understand the nature of true risk. This should be a calculated step, not a gamble. Make sure that the delegate is fully briefed before starting the task. Assess the situation, and take action only when the possible and probable outcomes have been systematically weighed and success appears extremely likely. Anything less is generally poor management.

LEARNING FROM MISTAKES

The lessons of failure are valuable, not only to the individuals involved, but also to the organization. Discuss the reasons for failure, so that you can eliminate them and strengthen the platform for success. Taking a constructive and sympathetic attitude to failure will motivate and encourage staff. If you choose to punish failure or motivate by fear, you will not create lasting success. However, make it clear that tolerance of error has its limits. Repetition of the same error is inexcusable, since it shows an inability to learn from mistakes.

QUESTIONS TO ASK YOURSELF

Q What precisely went wrong, when, and where?

Q What were the root causes of the failures?

Q When were the deviations first signaled?

Q Why were the warning signals not acted upon?

Q What could have prevented the failures from occurring?

SOLVING PROBLEMS WITHOUT ATTRIBUTING BLAME

POSITIVE   NEGATIVE

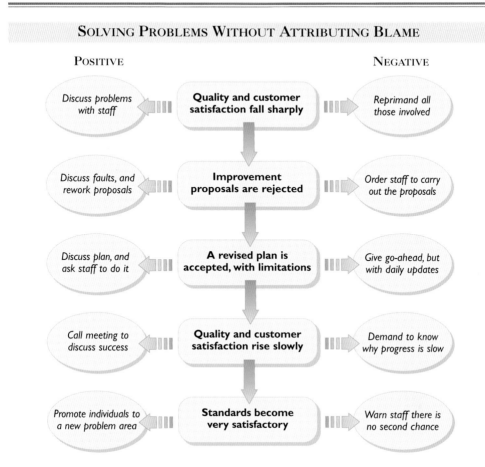

POSITIVE		NEGATIVE
Discuss problems with staff	Quality and customer satisfaction fall sharply	Reprimand all those involved
Discuss faults, and rework proposals	Improvement proposals are rejected	Order staff to carry out the proposals
Discuss plan, and ask staff to do it	A revised plan is accepted, with limitations	Give go-ahead, but with daily updates
Call meeting to discuss success	Quality and customer satisfaction rise slowly	Demand to know why progress is slow
Promote individuals to a new problem area	Standards become very satisfactory	Warn staff there is no second chance

USING ACTION REVIEW

Action review is the process of systematically reviewing the success or failure of a project in order to learn from mistakes. The participants in the review agree on the lessons to be learned. They are put on the record and circulated to everyone involved in the project, helping establish what went right and what went wrong, and the reasons why. Use action review to inform staff what they should and should not do in the future and to spotlight the parts of the system that need reform.

34 Be firm but fair when you are drawing attention to error, and do not pull any punches.

WINNING COOPERATION

The basic component of a motivational environment is cooperation, which you must give to your staff, as well as expect from them. It is still essential to be in control and to support your staff while doing so, but be sure not to damage workplace motivation.

 35 Find the root cause of repeated complaints, and eradicate it quickly.

HELPING STAFF

Two key motivational questions to ask your staff are: "What do I do that stops you from doing a better job?" and "What should I do to help you perform better?" If you cooperate by acting on the answers – for example, by investing in new tools or training if requested – you can bring about major improvements in motivation. Not acting on such feedback will demotivate. The prime objective is to help staff to help themselves.

DO'S AND DON'TS

✔ Do follow up on suggestions, requests, and comments made by others.

✔ Do get feedback to ensure that what you say has been fully understood.

✔ Do ask a critic to judge your voice and body language and their impact on audiences.

✔ Do remember that the best discipline is self-discipline.

✘ Don't ask for advice unless you respect the potential adviser.

✘ Don't neglect to provide the right resources if you want the right results.

✘ Don't try to do somebody else's job – even if you are better at it.

✘ Don't leave people without clear instructions and guidelines to follow.

MOVING CONTROL LEVELS

Levels of control vary from an insistence on checking and approving every action, to laissez-faire, in which people are free to perform as they wish and be judged only by the results. Increase motivation by moving toward less rather than more control. To do this, discuss and agree on tasks, objectives, and methods; then allow the implementation to proceed independently, subject only to reports on progress and major deviations. In case of problems, do not rebuke, but consider potential remedies.

36 Always check that your wishes have been understood.

 37 Inform staff of the use of their ideas – and success rates.

BEING GENUINE

Feigning a cheerful manner to help you win cooperation can backfire. For example, you may feel that you are successfully hiding the fact that you are tense, but those around you can tell – by your body language and voice tones – that you are faking. A forced smile is often easily recognizable. Try to be open in your appearance and behavior.

38 Have a good reason and an explanation for refusing a request.

Open stance

Welcoming, friendly expression

Tense expression

Hunched shoulders and crossed arms

▲ HOW YOU SEE YOURSELF
It is quite possible that you think of yourself as a relaxed, friendly manager, who always welcomes your staff with a smile on your face.

▲ HOW OTHERS SEE YOU
Your inner view can differ greatly from external perceptions. Your staff may read your expression as grim and think of you as a grumpy person.

USING VOICE TONE

Always match your tone of voice to the message you are delivering. A genuine smile is audible in the voice, and staff will be more willing to cooperate with a friendly manager. Do not drop your voice at the end of a sentence: it can be dispiriting. Try not to sound worried, or everyone listening will worry. Before an encounter, ask another person to listen as you rehearse and give you advice, if necessary, on how to sound positive.

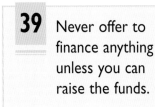

39 Never offer to finance anything unless you can raise the funds.

40 Consider ideas from staff at all levels of seniority.

41 Make use of the positive elements of each person.

SUPPORTING YOUR STAFF

If your staff believe that you are standing in their career path, they will rapidly become demotivated. Part of your job is to foster their careers, so you must repress the urge to keep very good people for yourself. Support and encourage your staff, and make the case for them to your seniors if necessary. Remember, though, not to agree to anything that you cannot deliver, and never make promises and then renege. Actions such as these can undermine your authority and inflict a level of motivational damage that cannot be recouped.

TAKING AN OVERVIEW

When analyzing staff motivation, stand back and look at the overall situation. Do not concentrate solely on one set of needs – whether they are team, individual, or task needs. Think about atmosphere, team complaints, and results achieved. Above all, ask lots of questions – you will then form a picture of how the system operates and how well it works.

TASK NEEDS
Determine the task objectives, and consider the problems involved.

TEAM NEEDS
Encourage team members to share ideas and to support one another.

INDIVIDUAL NEEDS
Monitor working conditions, and help staff develop their full potential.

▲ JUGGLING NEEDS

As a manager, there are three "needs" that you must juggle constantly and ensure are equally met: those of the task at hand, of the team, and of the individuals. The needs always overlap and, at times, may conflict.

USING FREE INCENTIVES TO WIN COOPERATION

Free or easy-to-supply incentives are a simple and essential way to win and maintain cooperation. Start by thanking people for a job well done, and follow this up with a written acknowledgment. This is hard for many managers, but is an essential counterweight to criticism. Other ways to increase cooperation include acknowledging staff achievements publicly and holding specific meetings for the purpose of boosting morale. Be friendly and polite at all times – bad manners demotivate – and deal sympathetically with personal requests, such as time off for a special purpose. Play the helpful friend, not demanding employer, in these circumstances.

▲ PUBLIC RECOGNITION
If you are with senior managers or clients and notice a member of your team, introduce her to those with you and, if possible, mention her achievements. This type of gesture makes people feel valued.

Manager uses visual aids to show progress achieved

WRITTEN ▶ PRAISE
Always follow up a verbal thank you with a written note. This will emphasize your appreciation while increasing motivation and cooperation levels. Handwritten notes tend to be the most effective.

▲ MORALE-BOOSTING MEETINGS
Try to hold regular morale-boosting meetings, especially if your work is full of deadlines and stress. The meetings support staff and help put everyone's minds at ease.

Encouraging Initiative

A sure sign of high motivation is a lot of initiative. The ability to take the initiative depends on empowerment and an environment that recognizes contribution. The more you expect of people, the more they will give, as long as you support them.

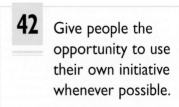

42 Give people the opportunity to use their own initiative whenever possible.

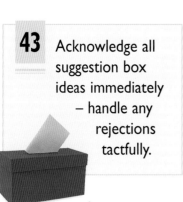

43 Acknowledge all suggestion box ideas immediately – handle any rejections tactfully.

Asking for Suggestions

The results from one survey showed that in the typical company only 4 percent of the ideas for improvement ever reach the top. Do not let that happen. Invite suggestions via a suggestion box, or hold brainstorming meetings. Respond positively to all volunteered ideas. Use marketing devices such as "Idea of the Month" to recognize and encourage good contributions. If at all possible, accept each suggestion, even if it must be modified. If you must reject any ideas, explain to the staff why – and do it with sincere regret.

Using Individual Efficiency Projects

When you find a suggestion that you want to implement, allow the person from whom it came to see it through to fruition. The idea behind this action is that the staff member whose suggestion it was is likely to have the most enthusiasm for it and be very motivated to ensure that it is a success. He or she should be free to delegate the whole task or any of its parts, but it remains that person's responsibility. Use this as one of your chief motivating factors when requesting ideas from your staff, and you are likely to be encouraged by the increased enthusiasm that will result.

▲ **WORKING ALONE**
If a staff member is eager to take his ideas further, allow the time and allocate the resources to do so.

SETTING HIGH TARGETS

If you think small, that is how you are likely to end up. Set high expectations, and you will find that people rise to the challenge. If you let present performance become your benchmark, your team may never achieve its full potential. However, high expectations must be realistic or demoralization will result. Encourage continual improvement, until it becomes second nature to the organization.

 44 Encourage staff to achieve by setting high but realistic targets.

CASE STUDY

A high-growth company reported the first losses in its history, so a new chief executive, Sue Wilde, was promoted from within the organization.

Sue was set the seemingly impossible target of making the company the largest in the business within a four-year period. This meant tripling market share against powerful competition. She considered that a massive communication program was a vital requirement. At one mass meeting, Sue asked the staff for suggestions for substantially reducing production costs and underpricing outside suppliers.

Having considered all their ideas, Sue allowed her staff to put the most promising ones into practice. As a result, the company went on to reach its market-leading target two years ahead of schedule.

◀ **ACHIEVING THE IMPOSSIBLE**
Sometimes it is possible to achieve what may seem, at first glance, to be impossible. In this example, the new chief executive successfully motivated the organization's workforce, who took a challenge to its heart and turned around an entire market. It is quite possible that without the extra efforts the organization would have collapsed, with disastrous results for all.

45 Do not be too fast in accepting "No" for an answer.

46 Give your staff a say in the setting of targets.

REVIEWING SYSTEMS

Once you have encouraged initiative and set targets, performance should improve. If there is no discernible improvement, look more closely at the present system, since it may be blocking progress. If so, sweep it away, start afresh, and set new, higher benchmarks. Ask colleagues with high performance records what systems they suggest, and implement the best practice. Both the investigation and the implementation will score high motivationally. A high target set by the staff themselves is a great incentive.

GETTING THE BEST FROM PEOPLE

People are capable of remarkable achievement, significantly ahead of previous performance, if they are provided with the right environment and given the right motivational leadership.

MOTIVATING INDIVIDUALS

Trying to motivate individuals is always tricky because of the variations between them and the way they interact with your own personality and motivation. Remember at all times to serve your ultimate interest – obtaining the right outcome.

47 Stretch people with goals that push them to perform better.

48 Make the most of new staff by first making them feel welcome.

49 Form your own opinions of your colleagues and staff.

ASSESSING INDIVIDUALS

To motivate well, start by assessing the individuals on your team. Once you have done so, you will have a far better idea of the best ways in which to motivate them to achieve their maximum potential.

Always approach people without preconceptions, and concentrate your attention on performance – not on personality, habits, or physical appearance. Liking people is a valuable quality in a good leader; favoritism is not. It demotivates the unfavored and may make the favorite unpopular within the team. Avoid accepting a third party's judgment of a staff member; make up your own mind.

RECOGNIZING DIFFERENCES

To achieve the best results from each individual, it is important that you recognize his or her specific motives and treat people on their own merits. Differences in behavior may be influenced by age, gender, and position on the career ladder.

Give tasks to the most suitable people. For example, a gregarious person will be best at a task that involves meeting people, while someone with a quiet personality may appreciate being given a task that mainly involves working alone. Do not shy away from giving tasks that may develop skills and increase motivation.

CONSIDERING NEEDS ▶
People at different stages in their careers are motivated by different elements of their work. These examples show some typical motivational factors that may influence two very different individuals.

Good basic rates of pay

Plenty of free time to enjoy personal life

High level of interest and job satisfaction

Recognition for good work

Regular promotions

NEEDS OF YOUNG WORKER

Reward in form of annual bonuses

Responsibility for tasks

Advancement on regular basis

Status within team

Security of post

NEEDS OF EXPERIENCED WORKER

50 Be as natural as possible, but tailor your approach to each individual.

TAILORING YOUR ACTIONS

Different people want their managers to play different roles. One may seek a parent figure, while another wants to prove his or her capability. A third may be looking for reassurance. If the role makes sense in management terms, play it. You have to be both soft and hard. Use the appropriate management style for each individual. It is not necessary for everyone on the team to like you, but they must like working for you. Achieve this through firmness as well as friendliness.

OFFERING INCENTIVES

There are many incentives you can offer to help motivate people, and each has different effects. Some of those most commonly used include recognition, money, health and family benefits, and insurance. There tends, however, to be a dividing line between financial and nonfinancial incentives. If you are not in a position to offer financial incentives like pay raises and bonuses, it is still possible to motivate staff by ensuring that the non-financial incentives you offer are attractive to the potential recipient. For example, you might allocate a parking space to someone who drives to work. Think about the general and specific requirements of your staff.

51 Remember that what you measure and reward is what you get.

TAKING A BREAK ▶
Travel incentives – overseas trips, discounts on flights, or just a weekend break, especially when there is no work involved – are all highly motivational. Additionally, the staff member returns to work refreshed.

CASE STUDY
Barbara, a human resources manager, had interviewed two internal candidates for a vacancy and had to decide between them. She considered both to be suitable but, after much deliberation, felt that Liz had the advantage over Tony.
Instead of simply appointing Liz and letting Tony hear the news from other sources, Barbara arranged a meeting with him before announcing Liz's appointment. Barbara felt that an e-mail or a memo, however tactfully composed, was the wrong way to inform Tony of her decision, and would intensify any stress that he may feel. She explained the reasons behind her decision, emphasizing that Tony was a valued employee, and that the decision had been very difficult to reach. Tony appreciated Barbara's honesty and accepted her explanation. Because he was treated with respect, Tony suffered no loss of motivation in his existing job.

◀ MOTIVATING BY FEEDBACK
When delivered in the right way, even bad news need not demotivate. In this example, Tony is motivated by the knowledge that Barbara thought him to be a valuable staff member. He felt that she was honest with him and that he could still make a positive contribution to the team.

SETTING REALISTIC GOALS

Motivate both teams and individuals by involving them in deciding on budgets, targets, and other goals. Find the right combination of target and reward – one that will maximize effort and achieve economic returns for the company – remembering that no scheme linking rewards to goals can work well unless both aims and thresholds are realistic and fair. For example, if you are trying to reduce costs, advise the team of present cost levels, give them a target figure to work toward, and tell them the figure for the company as a whole. Offer a proportion of their target savings as a reward.

THINGS TO DO

1. Offer a variety of fringe benefits, allowing people to choose from several options.
2. Look for projects in which cash savings can be shared.
3. Use gifts as incentives when cash is not possible.
4. Set realistic timescales if goals are very demanding.

52 Do not put a ceiling on incentives – it limits motivation.

MAKING INCENTIVES WORK

If your staff are earning good salaries and have interesting and responsible jobs and recognition from you as their manager for work well done, they should perform well without constant offers of new incentives. Reserve exceptional incentives for occasions when exceptional effort is required to meet demanding targets. Do not allow staff to expect special rewards for simply doing their jobs.

CHOOSING FROM INCENTIVE OPTIONS

There are many ways in which you can provide incentives to motivate your staff. Try some of the following:

- If you have large enough numbers, group staff into teams and offer a reward to the "winning" team;
- Divide staff into three teams, and split the total reward into first, second, and third "prizes" to reward all the teams;
- Do not set any limits on incentives – devise individual targets for each person;
- Allow people to set their own goals, and link the incentives to ambitions as well as successes;
- Set a threshold – nobody gets anything unless the benchmark is passed;
- Run a lottery in which every 10 percent improvement wins a ticket that enables people to compete for prizes;
- Devise extra incentives for performance early in the financial period in order to get a fast start.

MOTIVATING GROUPS

Peple behave differently in groups. Mob hysteria is one example. Its benevolent opposite is the spirit of togetherness that can animate groups of any size. Motivate staff by mobilizing support for their group aims and setting strategies for tackling objectives.

53 Ambition dictates achievement, so be sure to encourage big ambitions.

54 Confront trouble-makers as soon as you become aware of their presence.

LEADING A TEAM

Within any group, one person is usually singled out as the team leader. That may be you, but if several teams are working for you, nominate a leader for each. Always be positive with the leaders. Meet regularly with them and the team, and keep motivation levels high by involving everyone in decision-making, praising them for their team's good work, and pointing them in the right direction when things go astray. However, remember that if motivation is poor, it is the leader who is at fault. He or she should be aware of any problems within the group and should be the one responsible for keeping things in check.

CHANGING SYSTEMS

Sometimes, if your system fails, say, the only solution may be to start afresh. It should not be necessary to get rid of a whole team or even any individuals. Indeed, these courses of action may demotivate further. The problem is usually that good people are trapped in a bad system, rather than vice versa. Listen to your staff's problems. Once the initial period of complaint is over and the genuine causes start to surface, they will point the right way to reform. The more the "brave new world" is their own, the better the individuals will feel about – and perform under – the new system.

POINTS TO REMEMBER

- People in groups produce better ideas, since they can bounce ideas off one another.
- Asking staff members to contribute to planning heightens their levels of motivation and feelings of value.
- Staff criticisms should be taken seriously – do not automatically think of critics as troublemakers.
- Meetings, celebrations, and milestones can raise team spirits.

STRETCHING GOALS

A positive state of mind is crucial to reaching goals, so try to instill this in your team. The group that is motivated by a shared vision and that has translated it into practical objectives will notice – and take – more opportunities than one lacking that double focus. Join with others in shaping the vision and the plan. Then encourage and enthuse, so that the reality matches up to the dream. It is important when setting goals not to stop short of the group's capability; indeed, you should go slightly beyond it. For example, a sports coach may set a goal for his or her team to reach the final of a tournament and urge the players to believe in the aim. The danger is that once in the final the group will feel the goal has been reached, whereas they should strive to win that game, too.

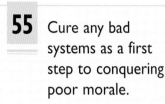

55 Cure any bad systems as a first step to conquering poor morale.

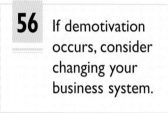

56 If demotivation occurs, consider changing your business system.

▼ **ACHIEVING "IMPOSSIBLE" GOALS**

In order to achieve "impossible" goals, first set yourself or your team a target that you deem to be "perfection"; this is a goal that you will probably never reach. Make this "impossible" goal less daunting by setting another goal: to be halfway to perfection by the end of the first year. This halfway point, once achieved, then becomes the starting point for year two, so set another halfway goal. Motivate staff by celebrating each halfway achievement.

KEY

Current year's progress

Previous progress

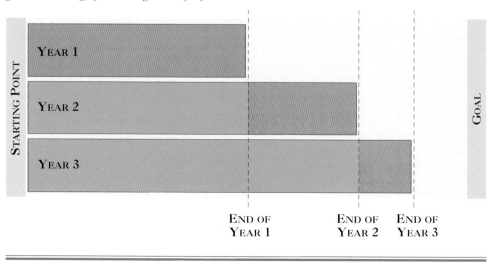

PREVENTING DEMOTIVATION

The course of people management seldom runs smooth, and emotions often run high on both sides of the process. The most valuable technique you can use for preventing demotivation is a sympathetic and understanding human response.

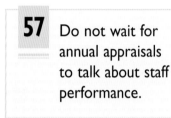

57 Do not wait for annual appraisals to talk about staff performance.

58 Talk about work-related problems to prevent them from becoming more intense.

USING INTERVIEWS

If you find it difficult to motivate staff members, try to establish whether they feel – and are being utilized fully as – part of the team. Arrange interviews with the people involved, leaving them in no doubt about its purpose. Eliminate any fears they may have by striking a positive note at once. Ask them whether they are happy with their working conditions and whether there are any aspects of their jobs they would like to change. Do what you can to improve the situation, and keep any promises you make at the interviews.

TALKING FACE TO FACE

During the interviews, interviewees will hardly ever reply just as expected. However emotional they are, stay calm and collected. Try to establish the reasons for their dissatisfaction as fully as possible. Listen carefully to what they have to say, and try to agree on a resolution. Always be sure to get feedback from interviewees before they leave the room, in order to avoid further misunderstandings by either party. As they depart, remind them that they can come directly to you to talk about any future problems.

59 Allow people to talk about what demotivates them, and listen carefully.

TACKLING PROBLEMS

Personal difficulties and workplace problems are both potential causes of demotivation at work. Never ignore your staff's emotional strains, even if performance is going well, because there is a high probability that the personal troubles will eventually affect work. Your first responsibility must be to the job. At the same time, you must also look after the individual. Approach emotional upsets in the same way as workplace difficulties. First, get the problem clearly defined; then seek the root cause. See if there is a solution that the individual will accept. If so, act upon it. It is important not to let the situation worsen. If you are unable to provide enough help, make sure that you find someone who can.

60 Bad news always travels fast, so deliver it as quickly as possible.

CASE STUDY

A new manager took over the running of a factory and, acting on instructions from above, concluded a long-term contract for the plant's lower-priced output to be supplied by an overseas factory. Rumors about the proposed move had been rife for some time. Once the contract was approved, the manager immediately announced the layoffs that would follow. However, the bad news was coupled with information about an intended major strategic revamp, in order to prevent demotivation caused by the layoffs and the change of management. The manager promised that the new system would increase sales, and announced the introduction of a profit-sharing plan.

Although skeptical, the workforce was motivated enough to give the new system all the effort necessary. As the manager had expected, productivity soared.

DO'S AND DON'TS

✔ Do move away from the desk, which acts as a barrier.

✔ Do show sympathy, however much you feel problems are self-inflicted.

✔ Do make your criticism constructive – you want the person to succeed.

✔ Do keep interviews as short as possible by sticking to the point.

✘ Don't confuse the roles of manager and counselor.

✘ Don't seek to blame individuals for errors.

✘ Don't allow staff members to harbor unfounded fears.

✘ Don't hesitate to discuss difficult personal cases with both colleagues and superiors.

▲ COMMUNICATING TO PREVENT DEMOTIVATION

This case study shows the principles of communicating change and bad news. Deliver bad news quickly, counteracting it with incentives if possible. Tell everyone what is happening, why, and what results you expect, placing emphasis on benefits. This will help prevent demotivation.

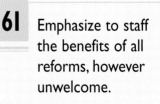

61 Emphasize to staff the benefits of all reforms, however unwelcome.

DEALING WITH
DEMOTIVATED PEOPLE

However hard you try to prevent staff demotivation, you will not always succeed. Ways of dealing with demotivated people depend on the situation. A personality clash between staff members needs different treatment than demotivation caused by stress.

62 Assess the reasons for demotivation before considering any action.

IDENTIFYING CAUSES

Demotivation must be analyzed before you can do anything about it. It may be caused by stress, emotional problems, or physical illness. Alternatively, there may be something wrong with the job itself or with the person's approach to it. Talk to the demotivated person in order to identify where the problem lies, and tailor the remedy to the cause – for example, by getting secretarial help for someone who is overworked.

▼ **SOLVING PROBLEMS**
In this example, the manager discovers that two of his staff members are not working well together. He steps in to try to correct the problem. His follow-up actions determine whether there will be an improvement in the situation or complete refusal to collaborate.

Two staff members are incompatible and often clash at work

Manager steps in to calm situation

ENCOURAGING TEAMWORK

When two members of your staff seem to be constantly at loggerheads, masterly tact is usually required to replace the element of confrontation with collaboration. One course of action is to move the two into a larger team, insisting that they cooperate with and not ignore each other. Another approach is to have the two people swap roles for a while, so that each can gain an understanding of the other's workload. If all else fails, separate the two warring parties permanently to avoid disrupting the work of the entire team.

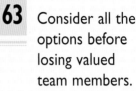

63 Consider all the options before losing valued team members.

Manager suggests new ways to work together, and staff members' professional relationship starts to improve

Manager leaves both parties to their own devices, and relationship breaks down

COUNSELING STAFF MEMBERS

To cope with the trauma that follows job loss, counseling has become more commonly available in organizations, allowing workers to discuss their reactions to a difficult situation with an impartial, sympathetic listener. You might consider providing counseling as a service even to those whose jobs are secure. They may need to discuss workplace or personal problems that are causing them to feel demotivated. Ideally, a person's counselor will be somebody from outside the company. If there is no option but to use a counselor who is also a staff member, he or she must not have direct or indirect responsibility for the work of the person who is being counseled. Older or more experienced staff members may prefer to talk with a counselor of comparable age and experience.

APPRAISING EFFECTIVELY

Opportunities to motivate your staff will vary according to the current tasks at hand, but appraisals are one way to ensure regular feedback. However, you must remember to follow up properly once the staff appraisals are over.

64 Keep the appraisal relaxed and friendly – do not make it an inquisition.

65 Take the chance to improve yourself by asking staff to appraise you, too.

STAYING RELAXED ▼

In this appraisal, both manager and interviewee are sitting in a relaxed manner, using reciprocal body language and maintaining strong eye contact.

CONSIDERING AIMS

The true objective of appraisal systems is not to blame, reward, or praise, but to develop. In some progressive organizations, the appraisal is not labeled as such, but is called a "personal development plan" or something similar. Conduct your appraisals properly, and you will help people form an objective view of their past performance. More important, you will also be equipped to encourage better staff performance as well as to enable and assist the interviewee to take on greater responsibility in the future.

Staff member holds eye contact, indicating he is relaxed in his manager's company

Manager sits next to staff member to avoid seeming confrontational

QUESTIONS TO ASK
YOUR STAFF

Q Can I do anything to help you perform better?

Q Am I doing anything that hinders your performance?

Q What do you see as your key strengths and weaknesses?

Q Have you any ideas about how you can improve or develop yourself as a team member?

Q How could your job or the system be improved?

DISCUSSING WEAKNESSES

In appraisals, emphasize what the people being appraised have done well – their strengths. You must, of course, also remark on and discuss their weaknesses, but only for improvement's sake. Eliminating weaknesses strengthens performance. However, it is not just staff performance that should be discussed. How does the person being appraised perceive the contribution of the appraiser? Has the manager's conduct throughout the year been helpful and motivating? If not, the appraiser has just as great a responsibility to improve performance as those he or she appraises.

LISTENING TO OPINIONS

Appraisal interviews provide a chance to talk widely over external and internal matters, so do not confine them to issues of personal performance. Remember that all employees are sources of ideas and opinions. Discuss them throughout the year, not just at appraisals. Note the ideas and opinions that you think the organization could benefit from, and consider implementation. The appraisal is ideal for constructive question-and-answer sessions, and you, as the manager and appraiser, should do more listening than talking.

66 Always start appraisals by discussing the progress made and success achieved.

67 Find out about the quality of support given in the job.

ASSESSING MOTIVATION

The appraisal provides a good opportunity to assess staff motivation levels. Be on the lookout for telltale signs of failing interest, such as a lack of enthusiasm for the organization or personal career ambitions. If such signs appear, you must decide how to reverse the process and reinstate a feeling of motivation. You may be able to act before demotivation has a chance to set in fully. Remember that a competent performer will do better at a task that engages his or her full enthusiasm.

FOLLOWING UP AFTER APPRAISALS

The fact that formal appraisals tend to take place annually does not mean that appraisal is only a once-a-year process. In particular, the formal appraisal contains elements that need to be followed up more regularly – perhaps monthly or quarterly. For instance, if a weakness was diagnosed and training followed, has it been effective? Is the person now confident with that element of his or her job and able to use the new-found knowledge effectively at work? Follow up any interpersonal problems on a quarterly basis. Such follow-up is essential for maintaining the high level of motivation that the appraisal should have triggered. If an appraisal did not motivate, use the follow-up to find out why, and how to get better results.

Review records regularly to make sure improvement is made

Store appraisals in a filing cabinet that you can lock

REFERRING TO RECORDS ▶

Keep appraisal records safely for later reference, in case of any problems. It is also useful to reread the previous appraisal form just before starting on the next one, to see if anything discussed was not implemented.

GIVING FEEDBACK

Appraisal feedback can be positive or negative, one-way or two-way. The result should always be to alter or reinforce behavior. Positive feedback is always welcome, but never give negative personal feedback in public – that is bound to have a demotivating effect. Nor should negative feedback ever be abusive. Focus on one issue at a time, and be highly specific about the past behavior that has generated the feedback and the new behavior that is now wanted. You should also get feedback on your feedback. Make sure your message has been received and understood, and make a mental note of the type of response it provoked.

68 Provide training in small, regular doses rather than one long course.

69 Follow up on any courses to check their quality and staff responses.

DEVELOPING ABILITY

The concept of critical success factors – the elements that organizations need in order to succeed – applies to people, too. Write a list of the key qualities that are needed for a particular task, and assess how they match the qualities of the jobholder. If you feel there is a mismatch – especially one that is likely to cause demotivation – do not reallocate the task, but take immediate action to develop the missing attributes. Abilities are learned and rarely inborn. In almost every case it is possible to be taught a necessary skill, and where abilities are weak they can nearly always be developed. If you feel certain qualities need to be acquired, be sure to provide the training.

PLANNING A CAREER PATH

The appraisal is only one step in a carefully constructed program of planning an individual's career path. It helps both staff and manager to work out the next move and to ensure that training and development are provided before the move, and not after. Appraisals – and their place in the career-planning process – should never be a waste of time and effort, which are precious in every type of organization. Send staff on any necessary training courses before, or as soon as possible after, appointing them to a new task or position; do not allow them to embark on a job for which they are not properly trained. Discuss and agree on a career plan when you make the appointment, and ask the staff member to sign off what you have agreed. Don't let this be something that is handed down from your superiors to your subordinates via you.

70 Give staff chances to use and increase their expertise.

71 Sit in on training courses to ensure the quality is high.

▼ **DEVELOPING STAFF**
There is a simple yet powerful three-point system that you can apply when you begin developing your staff. Using the system will enable you to focus skills and keep staff motivated.

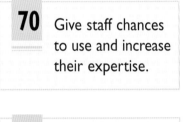

| Evaluate strengths and weaknesses | Ensure job makes full use of strengths | Provide training to improve weaknesses |

Evaluating Each Job

As well as looking at ways to motivate your team as a whole, you need to look at ways to develop individuals and their jobs. Conduct a thorough evaluation of all aspects of each job as well as of the organization's overall system.

72 Regard grading and similar systems with caution – not as sacred.

Points to Remember

- The right pay for the right contribution is the perfect pay system.
- If grades are necessary, they should not be encumbered with bureaucratic rules.
- If it is possible, people will turn grades into status symbols.
- Performance must be analyzed from all angles to get a full picture.
- Job specifications should be clearly defined without being overly restrictive.

Using Grading Systems

Your organization may run its job and reward system in a rigid, graded way. And you may be in a situation where almost all the factors are outside your control. If that is the case, make the most of the rewards that you are able to distribute. If you are in a position to make such decisions, remember that grading jobs and their holders, and assigning to each grade a salary range, may be useful. However, aim to keep the number of grades as small as possible (in extreme cases, a large organization can have a huge number), the pay ranges as wide as possible, and the importance to staff of the grading system as low as possible.

Putting the Job First

The key point to remember when evaluating jobs is that the job is more important than the grade, which is merely an administrative convenience. The lure of rising one or two grades may well be motivational, but rules for how many grades staff can advance at any one time, or stating that "a lower grade cannot be the manager of a higher grade," are nonsensical and unnecessary. Get the right person in the right job, and make it clear that the grade goes with the job, not vice versa. If you ask someone about his or her job and the reply is "I'm an 8," take corrective measures.

73 Pay your staff members for responsibility and contribution, not for seniority and status.

DESIGNING JOBS

Jobs exist to fill roles. If you are in the position of designing a job, your first task is to assign and clarify the job's role and its relationship to the overall task. Be as clear as possible about what the job entails. Every job has its own skills, necessary knowledge, and attributes, so be sure to specify them. There may also be certain legal requirements, terms and conditions of service, and other company stipulations with which the job must comply. Finally, remember that both jobs and their holders need regular modification – and sometimes radical change – over the course of time.

Multiskilling · Variation · Interest · Targets · Prospects · Accountability · Ownership

▲ **ANALYZING JOB CONTENT**

Whatever level of job you are designing, it must be of interest and give satisfaction to the worker. In other words, it must be motivational. Including the factors above will help to make any post more appealing in the long term and motivate the jobholder to perform more effectively.

DEFINING PERFORMANCE

Part of the process of evaluating an existing job – or defining the ideal for a new job – involves looking at past performance levels and deciding what new qualities or tasks are needed to improve them. Arriving at a single measure of performance is difficult. Financial results are the best all-inclusive measure, but do not rely solely on them, since they will convey the wrong message – that only profit counts. They also neglect to show that good short-term results can be gained through bad management, such as cutting back on investment or understaffing. To measure quality, rather than just quantity, include staff morale, customer satisfaction, interteam collaboration, and specific project results as measures of performance.

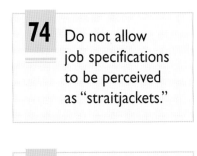

74 Do not allow job specifications to be perceived as "straitjackets."

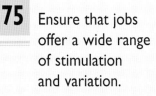

75 Ensure that jobs offer a wide range of stimulation and variation.

CONSIDERING PAY

When staff members are asked what would raise their motivation, many say, "More money." But money has only a short-term motivational effect. Use pay to reflect good performance, and remember that other motivators may be more effective. The key phrase is "individual circumstances." When you ask a special effort of an individual, however, offering a cash reward in return may work well.

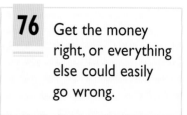

76 Get the money right, or everything else could easily go wrong.

ANALYZING PAY SYSTEMS

REASON FOR PAYMENT	FACTORS TO CONSIDER
TIME Work has been carried out for a specific number of hours.	● It is difficult to monitor the use of working time. ● Payment for fixed hours is not an efficient motivator. ● Effort and hours spent are much less important than individual expertise and quality of contribution.
EXPERTISE Skills possessed by the individual are essential to the job at hand.	● Achievement and recognition are key motivators for staff with expert knowledge. ● Levels of payment are directly related to the amount of demand for specific skills.
INPUT Individual has made a significant contribution to the project, unit, or organization.	● Staff who produce good work should be highly valued. ● It can be difficult to measure an individual's input. ● A good organization encourages innovation, does not penalize mistakes, and rewards creativity imaginatively.
QUALITY OF OUTPUT Work has been of a consistently high standard, enhancing quality of the final product.	● Quality of output is more important than quantity. ● Payments made on this basis result in increased competitiveness among team members. ● Achieving quality standards is motivational.
ACHIEVEMENT Objectives have been met to the satisfaction of those who commissioned the task.	● Rewards offered to project leaders are often linked to the success of the project. ● As workloads are increasingly divided into tasks, more pay is becoming achievement-based.

CONSIDERING PAY PACKAGES

Basic salary raises can dominate pay negotiations. However, wise employers (and wise employees) look at the value of the total package when recruiting and promoting. The other elements, in addition to the basic salary, can be decisive. Profit-sharing and pension plans are very attractive, and non-financial benefits can also be valuable. Be sure that the package you offer compares well with industry and other norms. A competitive pay package can be a highly effective motivating tool.

Salary

Flextime

Paid vacations

Shares

Car

Pension

Insurance

Health care

▲ ANALYZING PACKAGES

A pay package is not just about salary, though that is how most people tend to think of it. Other elements come into play, not all of them directly cash related. Check out packages offered by rival companies, and make sure what you have to offer is comparable.

77 Watch costs of fringe benefits – unwatched, they tend to soar.

78 If you are the highest payer, be sure to get the highest results.

AVOIDING SECRECY

Secrecy is one factor that makes pay a managerial minefield. Usually, people do not know what other people in a unit – or an organization – earn. They tend to make wrong guesses, or else they find out and then feel aggrieved by what they discover. Openness is a great way to promote a sense of fairness. People can accept the principle of unequal pay for unequal achievement, but only in an atmosphere of consensus and cohesion. Encourage both by ensuring that pay levels are discussed openly and with full information. The feelings involved can be painful and deep, though, so treat perceptions of unfairness accordingly. Be sympathetic with people who feel unfairly paid, even when nothing can or should be done.

Enriching Jobs

One way to improve motivation is to enrich jobs. The "scientific" management school divided work into component parts, at which each worker, by repetition, became proficient – and bored. Aim for variety, multiskilling, and high interest levels.

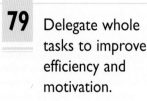

79 Delegate whole tasks to improve efficiency and motivation.

Raising Interest Levels

The interest in a job depends on the content of the work, its complexity, and the sense of achievement generated by successful completion. You will not raise an assembly line worker's interest, for example, by adding one more repetitive task. Instead, put staff in a manufacturing cell with six people, say, each with interchangeable skills, and make that group responsible for an entire subassembly. That will raise interest levels in the same way as giving a wine-shop assistant expertise in the wines carried. Ideally, give difficult, yet doable jobs to somebody whose personal drive will be engaged by the task.

80 Give staff every opportunity to use newly acquired skills once training has finished.

Developing Skills

The more varied the job content, the greater the need for new skills. Try to apply multidisciplinary, cross-functional working in teams. This helps develop new skills, which may require formal training. Although training may take staff members away from their workloads, it is beneficial in adding to variety and is essentially motivational. Encourage everybody to think of portable skills as their personal capital. Consider making the acquisition of new skills an element in bonuses and pay raises. With good management, the acquired skills of each staff member will more than justify the extra rewards.

Points to Remember

- Real job enrichment produces cost savings as well as increasing motivation.
- Training is both a means to and a form of job enrichment.
- Staff members prefer a difficult job to a boring one.
- Employees like to be considered as experts in their jobs and to be treated accordingly.
- People who have kept valuable suggestions quiet for years should be helped to "open up."

Manager splits a three-part task among three staff members – one task each

Team member is bored with her single task

TEAM

MANAGER

Staff member is happier having three varied tasks

STAFF MEMBER

Manager gives the whole task to one staff member to provide variety

PROVIDING VARIETY

If you give a whole task to one person, instead of splitting it among several, it will add more variety and responsibility to the job. It is also a good way to increase staff involvement and commitment levels as well as develop otherwise unused skills. Provide variety by giving people new tasks, making them members of quality-control and other project teams, sending them on customer visits, and so on. The guiding principle is to stimulate enthusiasm.

EXTENDING SKILLS
When delegating work that is divided into two or more parts, try to give the whole task to one person, providing training where necessary. This saves time on handovers, relieves monotony, and raises motivation for the staff member.

ASKING FOR SUGGESTIONS

Encouraging people to use their initiative to improve efficiency enriches jobs and increases variety. Ask staff for suggestions, and, if possible, act on the answers you receive. Feeling comfortable making suggestions is enriching in itself. Constantly looking to see how a task can be improved adds to the variety. Beware, though, that an atmosphere that has been unresponsive in the past may inhibit people from volunteering ideas.

81 When an idea is accepted, let its creator implement the suggestion.

Empowering Staff

Most organizations run on rulings that are passed down to the staff from top management; this is demotivating. In contrast, delegating powers traditionally kept at the top not only motivates, but also raises everyone's levels of performance.

82 Make sure that your staff do not suffer under outside limitations.

83 Find out about a job from the person doing it.

USING TEAM MEETINGS ▼
People who want to do a job well are most likely to offer the best advice on improving the system in which they work. Ask your staff to discuss their opinions with you, and listen to what they have to say.

Encouraging Input

In most cases, people are experts in their jobs, having improved their skills over time, and they are perfectly capable of both suggesting improvements and implementing those changes. Use these people when seeking improvement. If their knowledge is ignored, staff become demotivated by the neglect and resistant to change imposed from outside. Consult with those affected before making changes, and encourage them to take full responsibility for redesigning their jobs.

Staff member offers advice to senior manager

Senior manager makes full notes of proposed changes

DELEGATING AUTHORITY

Being managed is not in itself a motivating experience. If you are a wise, stimulating manager, those who work for you will be well motivated. However, the more authority is retained at the top, the lower motivation will be. Staff become used to depending on their manager's decisions and authorization, blunting their own initiative and making them dependent. Exercise authority, but not unnecessary force, to achieve desired results. Sharing authority helps develop people's own talents. Delegate downward any tasks that you do not have to do yourself. Look also for whole areas of authority that can be delegated, but always retain overall control.

▼ **RAISING ISSUES**

Encourage your team to come to you with changes they would like to make to work procedures; discuss their proposals with your superior if necessary. This system is known as "bottom-up" management.

KEY

 Team suggests to manager a change in work procedures

Senior manager, via manager, allows team to try new system

Team reports results to manager, who discusses them with senior

Senior approves new system to be implemented permanently

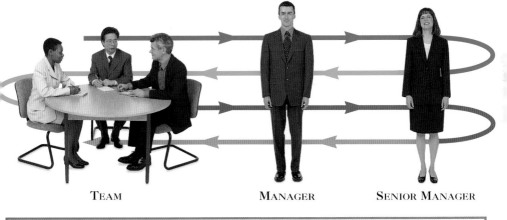

| TEAM | MANAGER | SENIOR MANAGER |

USING UPWARD APPRAISAL

Appraisal of superiors by their subordinates has achieved wide publicity. It has been installed in many organizations, either by itself or as part of a system in which everyone appraises one another. Do not regard this type of appraisal as a cure-all; use it instead to draw attention to areas of potential improvement and to give a different perspective to the manager-staff relationship. Do not allow the process to be used to settle old scores, or people may find it too embarrassing to use properly. A constructive working environment should support and exploit upward appraisal.

BUILDING CAREERS

The ideal career path is smooth and clear of obstacles. Such a path can be highly motivating: encourage your staff to follow it by offering them the support they need to develop the abilities that will ultimately take them on and up.

84 Find an assignment for anyone who has not had one in the past year.

85 Encourage your staff to enroll for regular training – it will pave the way to future success.

USING ASSIGNMENTS

One of the best ways of helping staff in their career progress is by issuing short-term "assignments," which give people the chance to show both their mettle and their ability. Opportunities of this kind are fewer under the old-style, hierarchical methods of career development in which people stay in one job for a set length of time before moving up the ladder. Look out for any chance to broaden staff confidence and experience by giving people tasks, either singly or in a group, that lie outside their normal work. Take an interest in their progress, and debrief often. While your staff are learning, you learn what they can do.

CASE STUDY
Andrea Morgan, a clever and hard-working manager, was swiftly promoted as her abilities grew, but soon her work began to fall below acceptable standards. She had personal difficulties to cope with at home, but this did not fully explain the decline in her performance. A new senior manager made it clear that Andrea had a choice: either improve performance or leave the organization.

In an interview between them, it emerged that Andrea felt frustrated by the underuse of some of her abilities and also by poor leadership from the head of her department. After some consideration, her senior manager promoted Andrea to that post, in which she succeeded admirably. She paid special attention to – and utilized fully – the abilities of every member of her workforce.

◀ **MOVING CAREER-PATH OBSTACLES**
There are many reasons why a person's performance might suffer, so do not pass judgment until you have taken the time to talk through any problems. You may find, as in this case, that the career path is being blocked by what the person sees as an immovable obstacle. Find out what it is and move it, or you risk losing valuable staff members.

WIDENING PERSPECTIVES

Most people – possibly unconsciously – undergo a process of self-actualization, moving by trial and error toward the field that suits them best and in which they can achieve to the utmost of their ability. As they grow out of one "phase," they move on. Most people start out with a narrow range of skills and interests; as that broadens, so will their career path. Perspectives will shift, too, from short term to long. As confidence increases, so will self-control and self-awareness. Watch for these signs, and accentuate the positive through regular communication. Be sure that personal goals and the job remain in step, or the person will lose motivation and you will probably lose the person.

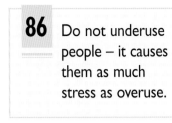

86 Do not underuse people – it causes them as much stress as overuse.

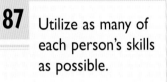

87 Utilize as many of each person's skills as possible.

GETTING THE MOST FROM TRAINING

Training can be an end in itself. Learning to learn develops the mind and objectivity. It is useful, as well, in terms of personal development, offering a sense of growth. However, the day-to-day work of an organization also provides plenty of practical reasons for training people. For example, if your company is moving from selling commodities to marketing consumer goods, try to ensure that you and your staff are fully trained in modern marketing techniques. Make sure that skills acquired in training can be used directly in the job. This will overcome the familiar "reentry" problem of the trained individual, bursting with newly acquired knowledge, who meets resistance when trying to implement the new-found information, gets frustrated, and gives up. This is most demotivating.

▲ **LEARNING SKILLS**
No matter what the job or situation, it is imperative that an individual is taught the necessary skills before you encourage the next career move. For example, a staff member who has the opportunity to work abroad may need to be sent on a language course.

REWARDING ACHIEVEMENT

For rewards to motivate, make sure you encourage competition among staff by acknowledging individual achievement and giving appropriate recognition to highfliers.

RECOGNIZING EXCELLENCE

In the achievement-led style of modern business, outstanding contributions from individuals further careers and earn rewards. Any rewards, however, must be motivational. Reward appropriately any contributions that are of genuine benefit to the organization.

88 Seek early chances to promote able, younger members of your staff.

89 Use monetary rewards as flexibly as possible to get the most of their motivational value.

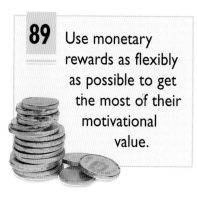

EMPHASIZING ACHIEVEMENT

The Japanese have one of the most hierarchical societies, and respect for one's elders is built into their culture. However, age does not come before ability in their organizations. Seniors earn respect, but the best-qualified person gets the job, irrespective of age. The system in the West, too, is becoming less age-led. For example, a project could be given to a young manager to command without upsetting the hierarchy or anyone within it. To make sure talent is allowed to develop, some seniors may have to be moved "sideways" to make room for more able juniors on their way up.

BREAKING WITH TRADITION

The traditional, hierarchical system was ideal for maintaining order within large organizations. Command and feedback flowed through the same channels, via each member of the hierarchy. It was an orderly method for an orderly world, but this system is no longer appropriate. Today, quick completion of tasks is more important than obedience to rules, and high achievers may earn more than their nominal superiors. Encourage staff to accept the new approach, but introduce it gradually to those who are used to the old way.

90 Use task forces to develop your best people.

▼ **COMPARING ATTITUDES**
One of the main differences between people who take a traditional attitude to work and those with a more modern outlook is the length of time that they expect to stay with a company. Traditionalists are more likely to feel that a job is for life.

TRADITIONAL ATTITUDE

Thinks maturity equals seniority

Expects to receive a good pension

Feels an allegiance to the organization

MODERN ATTITUDE

Feels achievement leads to seniority

Expects to be headhunted regularly

Puts own interests equal to the company's

USING A TASK FORCE

A task force is a high-performance, high-morale team set up to undertake a clearly defined task. It fosters leadership qualities and places paramount importance on achievement. Its criteria include:

● A task that is demanding in both time and standards of achievement;

● A single leader, whose role is defined in terms of the task;

● A full-time "core" of staff, who must be completely dedicated. They will be aided as necessary by part-time and temporary team members;

● A special privilege for the leader, who reports directly to top management, bypassing the usual hierarchy;

● Disbandment after the completion of its mission.

MOTIVATING THROUGH CHANGE

Change is a good way to raise levels of achievement, and few things increase staff morale more than successful change. There are two ways to improve – gradually and radically. You must decide which system is best for you in each situation.

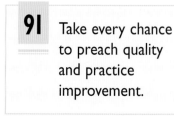

91 Take every chance to preach quality and practice improvement.

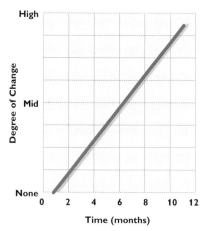

High

Degree of Change

Mid

None

0   2   4   6   8   10   12

Time (months)

CHANGING GRADUALLY

The concept of continual, gradual change (known as *kaizen*, from the Japanese) has become attractive to Westerners and essential to those who adopt Total Quality Management (TQM), which is about constantly improving every process and product by progressive methods. *Kaizen*, however, is more a way of life in which all staff members are urged to look constantly for ways to improve any element of their performance and to believe that nothing is the best it can be.

▲ USING KAIZEN

When using kaizen, set out your planned improvements in the form of a chart showing projected changes over a period of 12 months. Aim for a constant degree of gradual change.

MOTIVATING ▶ THROUGH KAIZEN

The motivational effect of kaizen, applied to an organization that was underperforming, was such that staff redoubled their efforts.

CASE STUDY

An organization whose products had acquired a bad reputation in the marketplace decided to adopt *kaizen* as its "religion." Staff members received full training in the techniques of continual improvement and were given specific, measured targets to meet. In addition, they were told that if they felt any elements in their working environment would benefit from change, they should propose a new option. The motivational effect of this was striking, since everyone felt in control of his or her own situation. As soon as one target was met, another higher one was put in its place. Quality improved by leaps and bounds, and the company moved from threatened failure to large profits and a rapidly growing market share.

CHANGING RADICALLY

Another method of change is *kaikaku* (Japanese for "radical change"). *Kaikaku* redefines an organization's entire business, looking at its ultimate purpose and examining every process to see what each contributes to the final goal. It also takes into account how that contribution can be radically improved or, in cases where the process serves no purpose, eliminated.

The problem with *kaizen*, and the reason why many Western companies gave up early with their TQM programs, is that major breakthroughs in one part – or even in several parts – of the system may not add up to a sizable achievement for the organization as a whole. *Kaikaku* forces you to concentrate on only those activities that add value. Having tracked down these activities, you then fix targets far in excess of current levels of achievement. The motivational impact of *kaikaku* is enormous, but staff may be slow to accept its necessity.

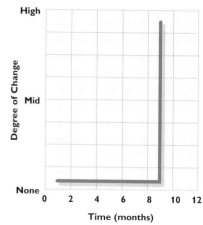

▲ USING KAIKAKU

The projected level of change for an organization using kaikaku *is a period of stability followed by an immediate acute change of direction. As long as staff are properly briefed and each member knows what level of change to expect and what the goal is, it is a highly effective way to implement change – especially in a crisis.*

COMBINING TECHNIQUES

The techniques of *kaizen* and *kaikaku* are not mutually exclusive. The former is a way of life, "the way we do things round here." Everybody accepts the principle that every operation and product or service can always be improved, and that an increase in efficiency will generally result in a rise in profit. The principle of *kaizen* is still applied when an organization is going through radical change. To get the full benefit of *kaikaku*, you will also have to use *kaizen* techniques in the initial revamping and refocusing of activities. Encourage acceptance of radical change in your staff through strategy meetings. At these meetings, it is important to make it clear that no holds will be barred, and to encourage staff to discuss and offer suggestions on any issues.

92 Make one major change, while also going for many small ones.

93 Ensure that all staff members are involved in quality-improving schemes.

REWARDING EXCEPTIONAL PERFORMANCE

S taff members are paid for the work they do, but many employers have incentive schemes for exceptional performance. When considering these as an option, work out what constitutes expected performance, and plan a sliding scale for anything above it.

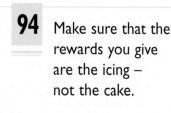

94 Make sure that the rewards you give are the icing – not the cake.

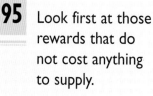

95 Look first at those rewards that do not cost anything to supply.

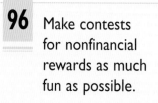

96 Make contests for nonfinancial rewards as much fun as possible.

DEFINING EXCEPTIONAL PERFORMANCE

The term "exceptional perfomance" is not a fixed, scientific measure. It varies from task to task, job to job, and organization to organization. As a manager, it is important that you recognize and reward what you consider to be genuinely exceptional. To do this, carefully work out, and fix solidly, the levels at which both financial and nonfinancial rewards are triggered off. Seek to ensure not only that good work gets good rewards, but also that top standards are not so high as to be impossible to achieve. You will find that a certain amount of trial and error is inevitable in this process.

REWARDING ACHIEVEMENT

Most incentive schemes tie rewards to sales or profits, or both. Do not reward for achieving budget. Instead, offer rewards at, say, 10 percent intervals above budgeted levels, and inform staff of this. The extra profit should handsomely cover the cost of the reward. You can choose to reward cost reduction, quality improvement, innovation, or customer satisfaction. Rewards must motivate, so monitor the scheme to be sure that they do.

97 Do not let sliding-scale cash rewards become a source of demotivation.

OFFERING NON-FINANCIAL REWARDS

Achievement is its own reward – but it is never enough. Achievers also want recognition. Even a simple "thank you" is an important, underused reward that costs nothing. Staff also value inclusion in events like seminars to discuss company strategy. Such events fit into development programs that are central to sustaining job satisfaction, increasing responsibility, and enhancing career progress and personal growth. Other non-financial rewards such as gifts and vacations may prove cheaper than cash rewards – and everyone loves to receive presents. However, these provide less motivation than individual recognition and are not substitutes for good, year-round management.

CULTURAL DIFFERENCES

Nothing differs more across industry and commerce than the use of money as reward and motivation. Managers in the US may expect large bonuses and stock options, although in Japan, straight salary is dominant and financial motivators are little used. Europe falls in between: mainland Europe being nearer to the Japanese model and Britain closer to the US.

CONSIDERING NONFINANCIAL REWARDS

REWARD	FACTORS TO CONSIDER
RECOGNITION Handwritten note, engraved trophy	● An often-overlooked form of reward that is personal as well as effective in both the short and the long term.
GIFTS AND PRIVILEGES Vacations, sports events, merchandise	● Immediate, and stimulating in the short term. ● May not meet long-term motivational needs.
SPECIAL EVENTS Weekends away, parties, theater trips	● Involve staff from all levels. ● Can stimulate, relax, bond, and motivate staff.
PROFESSIONAL TRAINING On- or off-site courses	● Effective, focused training brings high returns. ● Company gains a qualified employee, who feels valued.
SELF-DEVELOPMENT Personal, nonvocational training	● Very high motivational value. ● Enhancing self-image raises performance levels at work.
EQUIPMENT Company car, laptop computer	● Expensive equipment is highly motivational. ● Need to ensure that equipment is fully utilized.

OFFERING CASH REWARDS

Use rewards in the form of pay increases or financial benefits to recognize achievement, prevent a high-flying staff member from leaving the organization, or encourage an individual to take a greater level of responsibility in his or her job. Remember, however, that this type of reward often has only short-term motivational value. It can also lead to resentment among other staff members and discourage interaction within a team.

 98 Give performance-related rewards, not just pay raises, where possible.

CONSIDERING FINANCIAL REWARDS

REWARD	FACTORS TO CONSIDER
SALARY INCREASES Increases in basic rate of pay.	● Money is a powerful short-term motivator: the bigger the raise, the higher the motivation. ● The impact wears off relatively quickly.
COMMISSIONS AND BONUSES One-time payments linked to targets.	● Increases motivation and job satisfaction. ● There can be difficulties in fixing rates and relating these rewards to base pay.
PERFORMANCE-RELATED PAY Regular wage increases based on target-linked performance.	● Is motivational and can be a tax-effective incentive. ● There may be a delay between earning and receiving performance-related pay, thus weakening its impact.
SHARES/STOCK OPTIONS Gifts of shares, or the chance to buy shares at a fraction of actual value.	● Encourages long-term loyalty and sense of involvement. ● A highly effective motivator, as pay-off can be substantial. ● Reward is not immediate, and initial benefit may be small.
SPECIAL RATES Help with mortgage/rent, insurance, and other items within tax limits.	● Has considerable staff-retention value and can act as "golden handcuffs." ● Has low motivational value.
FAMILY HEALTH BENEFITS Paid or subsidized plans offering a wide range of health-care options.	● It is in an organization's interest to have healthy staff. ● Has low motivational value because health-care provision is expected from organizations.

CELEBRATING SUCCESS

Personal thanks for exceptional performance are powerfully reinforced by being repeated or given at a public celebration. Celebrate success, and you can motivate everybody in the unit, not just the achiever. External awards and dinners have proliferated, and few industries are now without them. Pay for entries and tables at these events, and make a fuss of any winners. The same format applied internally is also effective. If a whole team, rather than an individual, is involved, celebration is highly appropriate. Parties give you the chance to motivate by words and by singling out special contributions. Ensure, however, that any event of this type is carefully planned and well staged. Skimping on any elements, especially the catering, is a false economy in terms of motivation.

99 Use certificates and engraved presents as reminders of high achievement.

THROWING A PARTY ▷
A staff party is a great way to show your appreciation to all the people who work for you. It is also the ideal setting for rewarding or speaking about exceptional performers.

SETTING PERSONAL TARGETS

Set yourself personal career targets in order to achieve exceptional performance. Ask yourself the following questions:

- What do you want to have achieved in one, three, and five years from now?
- What developments, knowledge, and experience can make your aims possible?

- What can you do to acquire the necessary skills to attain your targets, and how long will it take you to master each of these skills?
- Are there any midway points in your program that will allow you to check progress and make revisions if necessary?

KEEPING MOTIVATION HIGH

Once you have successfully raised the motivation levels of your staff, it is important that they stay raised. Varying working conditions, improving management systems, and placing a high value on your employees should all be top priorities.

 **100** Change your own working methods if it will improve staff motivation.

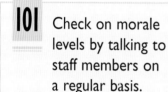 **101** Check on morale levels by talking to staff members on a regular basis.

MONITORING MOTIVATION

People want to feel good about their work and their organization. Encourage and nurture this natural drive – do not spend your time cracking whips and shouting slogans. Use surveys, research, and polling to check on morale and find out when and where new initiatives are needed. Select trusted people to talk to you informally about general mood, developments that affect motivation, and potential problem individuals.

MODIFYING PRACTICES

In 1927 psychologist Elton Mayo discovered that output increased every time a change was made in working conditions. Also, absenteeism declined during the period of change by 80 percent. The explanation he gave is that people respond to attention. Taking part in experiments and cooperating in changes heightens interest, team spirit, and self-esteem, regardless of the change. Any aspect of motivational practice is open to change. Look for ways to engage all staff in reviewing processes and practices, and in devising ways of changing them. If you find any current practice demotivates, correct it immediately.

Amy is regularly turning up late for work and showing other signs of demotivation – she is asked by her manager to be more prompt

REVIEWING SYSTEMS

Underperformance is expensive, yet 85 percent of all recorded underperformance is thought to result from the system imposed by managers. Do not let that be yours. Review every aspect of your business system regularly. All business systems are capable of demotivating staff, and all are open to improvement. Poor systems generate poor morale. Regularly test your system, and ask for improvement suggestions from those who are on the front line. Remember that the act of reform itself improves morale. Even if your system was motivational when it was originally set up, changing conditions mean that you should always be open to revisions – whether the initiative comes from you or from your staff. Above all, treat seriously all comments on the system – staff will often bring matters to you as a last resort.

THINGS TO DO

1. Look for areas suitable for experimental changes.
2. Use inspiring names for your motivational projects.
3. Keep track of staff morale.
4. Ask staff to inform you of any system problems.
5. Modify or drop any changes that do not work.
6. Give low performers plenty of encouragement.

Amy's timekeeping starts to improve but she continues to underperform – her manager asks her why

A vacancy arises in Amy's new field and she is promoted to it, raising her motivation level further

Amy reveals that poor job prospects are making her feel demotivated – she is sent on a skills-development course

◀ INVESTING IN STAFF

This staff member has become demotivated, and her attitude to work has plummeted. Instead of issuing a reprimand, her manager decides to invest in her future career by offering her training with a view to promotion.

ARE YOU A GOOD MOTIVATOR?

*G*auge your ability as a motivational manager
by responding to the following statements, and
mark the options closest to your experience. Be as
honest as you can: if your answer is "never," mark
Option 1; if it is "always," mark Option 4; and
so on. Add your scores together, and refer to the
Analysis to see how you scored. Use your answers
to identify the areas that need improving.

OPTIONS
1 Never
2 Occasionally
3 Frequently
4 Always

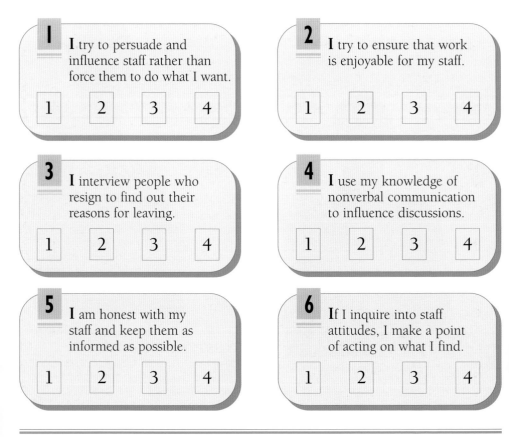

1 I try to persuade and influence staff rather than force them to do what I want.

1   2   3   4

2 I try to ensure that work is enjoyable for my staff.

1   2   3   4

3 I interview people who resign to find out their reasons for leaving.

1   2   3   4

4 I use my knowledge of nonverbal communication to influence discussions.

1   2   3   4

5 I am honest with my staff and keep them as informed as possible.

1   2   3   4

6 If I inquire into staff attitudes, I make a point of acting on what I find.

1   2   3   4

7 I apply Theory-Y management principles rather than Theory X.

1   2   3   4

8 I avoid office politics and discourage others from politicking.

1   2   3   4

9 I involve people in issues at the earliest possible opportunity.

1   2   3   4

10 I give reasons for my actions and for any disagreements with people.

1   2   3   4

11 I seek consensus and encourage others to do the same.

1   2   3   4

12 I react to failure not by blame but by analysis and correction.

1   2   3   4

13 I seek a balance between firm control and giving people independence.

1   2   3   4

14 I make conscious efforts to improve my motivational skills.

1   2   3   4

15 I change benchmarks to keep targets at stimulating heights.

1   2   3   4

16 I revise the system in order to remove obstacles to performance.

1   2   3   4

17 I look at more than just financial results when assessing staff performance.

1 2 3 4

18 I encourage people to be open about how much they and others are paid.

1 2 3 4

19 In appraisal interviews, I request and receive appraisals of myself.

1 2 3 4

20 I get full, clear feedback from people whose behavior I have had to criticize.

1 2 3 4

21 I organize work so that one person can complete an entire task.

1 2 3 4

22 I look at assignments and moves as ways to develop people.

1 2 3 4

23 I encourage people to act on their own initiatives.

1 2 3 4

24 I delegate work that does not have to be done by me.

1 2 3 4

25 If difficult "people decisions" are needed, I make them willingly.

1 2 3 4

26 I act to avert or settle disputes and personality clashes.

1 2 3 4

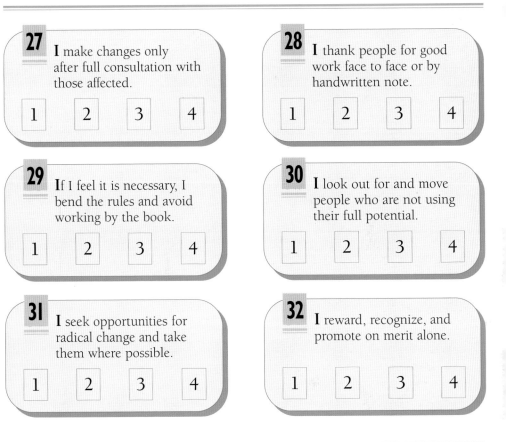

27 I make changes only after full consultation with those affected.

| 1 | 2 | 3 | 4 |

28 I thank people for good work face to face or by handwritten note.

| 1 | 2 | 3 | 4 |

29 If I feel it is necessary, I bend the rules and avoid working by the book.

| 1 | 2 | 3 | 4 |

30 I look out for and move people who are not using their full potential.

| 1 | 2 | 3 | 4 |

31 I seek opportunities for radical change and take them where possible.

| 1 | 2 | 3 | 4 |

32 I reward, recognize, and promote on merit alone.

| 1 | 2 | 3 | 4 |

ANALYSIS

Now you have completed the self-assessment, add up your total score and check your performance by reading the corresponding evaluation. Whatever level of success you have achieved in motivating people, it is important to remember that there is always room for improvement. Identify your weakest areas, and refer to the relevant chapters in this section where you will find practical advice and tips to help you to develop and refine your skills.

32–64: You are demotivating rather than motivating people. Find actions that work and practice them often to achieve results.
65–95: Your motivational skills are fairly sound, but your weak points need to be addressed.
96–128: You are a great motivator. Be careful not to become complacent or to let your high standards slip.

MANAGING TEAMS

INTRODUCTION

Working with teams, whether as leader of a single team or manager of several, is an essential part of a manager's job. Teamworking is rapidly becoming the preferred practice in many organizations as traditional corporate hierarchies give way to flat, multiskilled working methods. This section is an indispensable and practical guide to leading teams with expertise, covering subjects such as defining the skills required to complete a project, establishing trust between individuals within a team, and maximizing the performance of that team. The section is vital reading for anyone involved in teamwork, whether as a novice or as an experienced team leader. A self-assessment exercise allows you to evaluate your own leadership abilities and potential, while 101 concise tips offer practical advice.

UNDERSTANDING HOW TEAMS WORK

Teamwork is the foundation of all successful management. Managing teams well is a major and stimulating challenge to any manager, from novice to experienced hand.

WHAT MAKES A GOOD TEAM?

A true team is a living, constantly changing, dynamic force in which a number of people come together to work. Team members discuss their objectives, assess ideas, make decisions, and work toward their targets together.

WORKING TOGETHER

All successful teams demonstrate the same fundamental features: strong and effective leadership; the establishment of precise objectives; making informed decisions; the ability to act quickly upon these decisions; communicating freely; mastering the requisite skills and techniques to fulfill the project at hand; providing clear targets for the team to work toward; and – above all – finding the right balance of people prepared to work together for the common good of the team.

Team member has idea prompted by presentation

Team leader assesses new idea

1 Remember that each member has something to add to your team.

2 Formulate team objectives carefully, and always take them seriously.

ANALYZING TEAM TASKS

Successful teams can be formed by 2 to up to 25 people, but much more important than size is shape – the pattern of working into which team members settle to perform their given tasks. There are three basic methods of performing a task:

- Repetitive tasks and familiar work require each team member to have a fixed role, which is fulfilled independently, as on assembly lines.
- Projects that require some creative input require team members to have fixed roles and working procedures, but also to work in unison, as when generating new products.
- Work that demands constant creative input and personal contributions requires people to work very closely as partners. This style of working is prevalent among senior management.

Colleague introduces new idea to group

Listener watches reactions of all team before delivering opinion

One member of team questions all new ideas

◀ WORKING WELL TOGETHER

A team of managers discusses a new idea that has been put forward by a member of the team. All the members of the team are free to join the discussion. Later, the team leader will assess their contributions.

359

ACHIEVING POTENTIAL

There is no limit to the potential of a good team. Given an "impossible" task, team members will reinforce each other's confidence as they seek to turn the impossible into reality. The collective ability to innovate is stronger than that of the individual because the combined brainpower of a team, however small in number, exceeds that of any one person. By harnessing this power, a team can go beyond simple, useful improvements to achieve real breakthroughs. For example, in one company an engineering team was asked to double machine reliability. They thought it impossible, but went on to produce a plan that tripled performance.

3 Remember that team members must support each other.

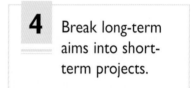

4 Break long-term aims into short-term projects.

WORKING COLLECTIVELY

To harness and take full advantage of team-power, the individual brains and personalities involved must be encouraged to collaborate. This process is vital in generating results. Giving stretching goals to a team will encourage it to work collectively and introduce a sense of urgency – potentially eliminating bureaucracy as it concentrates on getting positive results in the shortest possible time. The impact of a single team breakthrough can, by its example, galvanize an entire company.

▼ **WORKING TOWARD UNDERSTANDING**
Encouraging open communication and the free flow of information within a team ensures that each member is fully aware of the talents and experience available within the group.

KNOWING TEAM GOALS

Once a team has been formed, the next major step is to establish its goals. There is little point in having a team that is raring to go if its members are all pursuing disparate aims. Goals may well change over the course of a team's existence; for example, if a new product is being launched onto the market, the first priority will be for the team to concentrate on research into its competition. If the aim is to improve customer satisfaction, the first goal will be to find ways of providing a higher standard of service. According to the circumstance, teamworking goals might include:

- Increasing the rate of productivity in a manufacturing company;
- Improving the quality of production;
- Involving all employees in the decision-making process to increase job satisfaction;
- Looking at working systems and practices to reduce time wastage;
- Working together with customers to build closer relationships so that the needs of the market can be better understood.

5 Allocate a clear deadline for each of your projects.

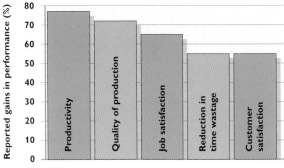

Areas in which team performance was measured

Reported gains in performance (%): 80, 70, 60, 50, 40, 30, 20, 10, 0

Productivity · Quality of production · Job satisfaction · Reduction in time wastage · Customer satisfaction

▲ IMPROVING PERFORMANCE

In a survey of 230 personnel executives, the American Society of Training and Development found that teamworking led to a substantial rise in performance in key areas.

CULTURAL DIFFERENCES

Cross-functional, multi-disciplinary, interdepartmental teams are spreading fast in the West, having been established in Japan for many years. The democratic attitudes of many North Americans have helped them to adapt well to this way of working, and in some British companies, managers already spend half their time working in such teams. Continental Europeans still tend to be more comfortable with the traditional hierarchical systems, but increasing competitive pressures and the need for speed-to-market are now forcing change on managers in many industries.

Matching Team to Task

There are numerous types of team, formal and informal, each suited to fulfilling particular tasks. Team leaders need to understand the objectives and goals of their team clearly in order to match tasks to the most appropriate style of team.

6 Decide early on what style of team is appropriate for your objectives.

7 Try to form strong bonds with other team members of formal or informal teams.

FORMAL TEAMS

Formal teams are fundamental to an organization – whether internal audit units or supermarket counter staff. They are often permanent, carry out repetitive work, and have a defined mandate:

- Cross-functional executive teams exist at director level to pool high levels of expertise;
- Cross-functional teams at all levels pool their knowledge to solve problems and run projects;
- Business teams at all levels of an organization place people with similar expertise in long-term teams to oversee specific projects;
- Formal support teams provide internal expert administrative backup in their own fields.

INFORMAL TEAMS

Casual groupings of people come together to work on an informal basis throughout all organizations. Informal teams can be formed on an ad hoc basis to deal with many needs:

- Temporary project teams stay together for the duration of a specific task;
- Change teams discuss strategy or troubleshoot when a particular, one-time problem occurs;
- "Hot groups" brainstorm creative projects while retaining autonomy and spontaneity;
- Temporary task forces deal informally with specific short-term tasks and issues.

8 Find a sponsor – a senior individual who can promote the team's work.

9 Remind members that they are all team participants.

Cross-functional executive
team heads organization

Business teams
utilize expertise in
particular fields

Cross-functional teams
can exist at any level
in a company, forming
a permanent part of
its structure

"Hot groups" come
together temporarily to
tackle creative tasks

Formal support
teams provide
backup services

◀ TEAM FUNCTIONS

This diagram shows how teams can function at all levels within an organization. The colors represent the various departments, which have traditionally worked separately from each other. Many organizations now encourage departments at all levels to work closely together to pool their expertise.

Change teams discuss
strategy off site

Project team deals
with specific issues

Finance team forms
temporary task force

KEY

	Production
	Support
	Sales
	Finance
	Marketing

COMPARING FORMAL AND INFORMAL TEAMS

The more formal the team, the more disciplined its leadership tends to be: company rules and procedures have to be followed, reports made, progress noted, and results obtained on a regular basis. By the same token, informal teams follow informal procedures. Ideas and solutions to problems can be generated on a more casual basis and procedures are less stringent. However, it is important to remember that team leadership always has to be results-oriented, whether in a formal or informal team. For example, the temporary, casual nature of a "hot group" brainstorming a project should not be an excuse to do away with team discipline altogether.

POINTS TO REMEMBER

● A team member is still an individual and should always be treated as such.

● Cross-functional teams offer people the chance to learn about the roles and work of others.

● Interdepartmental teams break down costly barriers.

● Formal teams sometimes need informal elements to stimulate and refresh their work.

● Teams cease to be teams if one member becomes dominant.

● All team members should make sure that they are working toward the same goals.

CHOOSING TEAM MEMBERS

One of the secrets of successful team leadership is matching the skills of team members carefully to the type of task they are required to perform. For example, if a product launch requires the generation of new ideas, a team should be cross-functional, comprising people from different disciplines who can apply their varied expertise and creativity to a project from several different angles. If, however, a task requires specialist knowledge of accounting procedures, it makes sense to recruit specifically among the leading minds of a financial division. As the demands of a project change, it may be necessary to introduce different talents into a team and replace members whose roles are no longer relevant.

10 Fix goals that are measurable to keep your team focused.

11 Make use of the great power of friendship to strengthen a team.

BUILDING ON FRIENDSHIPS WITHIN A TEAM

It is important to generate an easy, friendly atmosphere in a formal team meeting, even though the imposition of official procedures contrasts with the casual, occasionally even disorderly tone of an unofficial or informal team meeting. Try to create an atmosphere in which all ideas get a respectful hearing and conversation is open. This is easier if team members can relate to each other as people rather than simply as colleagues, so encourage members of both formal and informal teams to spend time together outside their official meetings. Arrange social events and celebrate a team's successes to help maintain a friendly atmosphere. Encourage people to spend time together outside working hours – real friendships between individuals have a unifying effect on a team as a whole.

◀ **TALKING INFORMALLY**
Talking to colleagues outside office hours or in an informal environment helps build up a bond within the team. Encourage informal gatherings as good opportunities to exchange views and opinions in a relaxed atmosphere.

MATCHING TYPES OF TEAM TO CERTAIN TASKS

TYPES OF TEAM	TASKS AND CHARACTERISTICS
EXECUTIVE TEAM A cross-functional group headed by chief executive. Members chosen by role; for example, finance director.	● Manages organization or divisional operation on day-to-day basis. Meets regularly, with agenda and minutes. ● Depends on information from lower levels. If badly controlled, can be forum for personality battles.
CROSS-FUNCTIONAL TEAM A multidisciplinary, inter-departmental team, found at any level in an organization.	● Removes obstacles to exchange of ideas in a variety of specific tasks – for example, a new product launch. ● Team members bring their different areas of expertise and skill to a problem or task.
BUSINESS TEAM A group of people in charge of the long-term running of a project or unit within their organization.	● Runs a unit and optimizes its results. ● Depends on the leader, who may change too often for the group to settle into optimal team-working. Usually subject to fairly close supervision.
FORMAL SUPPORT TEAM A team providing support and services, such as finance, information systems, administration, and staffing.	● Carries heavy load of routine work, such as the postal system, whose efficiency is indispensable for success. ● Depends on processes, offering scope for raising productivity by teamwork. Tends to be clannish.
PROJECT TEAM A team selected and kept together for the duration of a project, such as the construction of a new facility.	● Requires a large number of subgroups, subtasks, and detailed planning, plus tight discipline. ● Depends on close understanding among members and well-organized work practices.
CHANGE TEAM A group of experts briefed to achieve change. Value depends on collective ability. Sometimes starts off site.	● Influences corporate cultures to achieve radical improvement in results by applying new methods. ● Led by believers in change, with a high level of dedication to their organization.
HOT GROUP An autonomous body set apart from the rest of an organization, often in a remote site.	● Concentrates on tasks such as moving into new markets or creating new product programs. ● Flexible, independent, and high-achieving groups of people who question assumptions and get fast results.
TEMPORARY TASK FORCE A short-term body set up to study or solve a specific problem or issue and report back to management.	● Establishes new IT systems, removes production bottlenecks, or involves itself in similar tasks, usually working under intense time pressure. ● Uses informal processes and generates alternatives.

ANALYZING TEAM ROLES

In an effective team, all members know their roles thoroughly. While having their own strengths, skills, and roles, they must also contribute to the "togetherness" of the team. It is the role of either team leader or senior manager to see that this happens.

12 Always choose leaders on merit, regardless of other considerations.

ASSESSING LEADERSHIP QUALITIES

All leaders need strong personality traits to assert influence and function. Some of these attributes are internal, such as vision, but they always have to be complemented by external qualities, such as high visibility, to produce the utmost from team members. A team leader needs to be both facilitator and inspirer – a business team depends upon its leader to provide it with the facility to make decisions and the support to grow.

13 Look for a strong team commitment from a leader.

▼ EVALUATING LEADERSHIP QUALITIES
The analysis of leadership qualities shown below was developed by the UK's Insights consultants and is influenced heavily by the example of famous sports stars. The model indicates the five internal and five external skills that should be present in a successful leader of teams.

KEY

Inner strengths

Outer signs

Communication

Vision

Self-belief

Commitment

Visibility

Results-focused

Integrity

Attentiveness

Courage

Teamwork

LEADING A TEAM

The performance of any team depends on the quality of its collective thinking. How good are its decisions? This reflects the quality of the decision-making processes. The leader should strive to achieve a positive atmosphere, free from rigidity and envy, in which people compete with ideas – not egos. Teamwork does not function if the leader consistently puts forward ideas before others have had the chance to speak. In the classic Japanese method, the leader listens silently until every team member has expressed an opinion before making the decision for the whole team. A true team leader will facilitate, inspire, and implement rather than control.

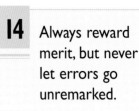

14 Always reward merit, but never let errors go unremarked.

▼ GIVING INSPIRATION
Team leaders play several roles: they are there to facilitate the making of decisions; to inspire lateral thinking, motivation, and hard work within the team; and to implement decisions made by the team.

Facilitate → **Inspire** → **Implement**

UNDERSTANDING LEADERSHIP FUNCTIONS

The main task and function of a leader is to achieve the goals of the team. If you are team leader, ensure your team goals are achieved via these processes:
● Planning roles to be filled and selecting appropriate individuals;
● Leading the team in meetings, starting with a discussion of team objectives and values;
● Ensuring that targets are met and that values – above all, the values of working collectively – are observed by the team;
● Analyzing and correcting failures swiftly and surely – but always remembering to celebrate the successes just as enthusiastically;
● Carrying the responsibility of representing the team loyally to others, both inside and outside the organization.

CULTURAL DIFFERENCES

Styles of leadership vary internationally. Americans are accustomed to blunt, assertive leadership, and the Japanese to a consensus, in which unanimous agreement is reached through a laborious process. British managers often conceal firm orders behind apparently woolly statements, while German leaders invite the views of their teams but retain control of all decision-making. True teamwork may bring these styles closer together.

Considering Roles

For a team to function most efficiently there are several key roles that should be filled. These include coordinator, ideas person, critic, external contact, implementer, team leader, and inspector. It is useful to bear these roles in mind when you are considering candidates for team membership, although you should also look for people with the ability to perform the specific tasks on which your team's operations depend. Never forget that the most important function of a team is to achieve the objective of the task in hand. Remember, too, that a friendly and open personality, and the ability and willingness to work with a group of people, are indispensable characteristics for a team player.

Dividing Up Roles

It does not make sense to fit anyone into a strait-jacket. You may find a perfectly equipped external contact or critic; you may not. Try to match roles to personality rather than attempting to shoehorn the personality into the role. It is not necessary for each person to perform only one function. If the team has only a small number of members, doubling or tripling up the roles is fine – as long as all the needs of the team are truly covered and the members feel comfortable with their roles.

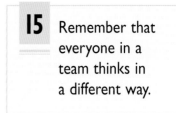

15 Remember that everyone in a team thinks in a different way.

Team leader also takes on roles of coordinator and inspector

Implementer also acts as team critic

Ideas person also deals with external contacts

◀ **SMALLER TEAMS**
Double or triple up roles when a team has only a few members, to ensure that all the key requirements for the successful completion of the task are catered for.

IDENTIFYING THE KEY ROLES WITHIN TEAMS

TEAM ROLES		CHARACTERISTICS

TEAM LEADER
Finds new team members and develops the teamworking spirit.

- Excellent judge of the talents and personalities of individuals within the team.
- Adept at finding ways of overcoming weaknesses.
- Is a first-class two-way communicator.
- Good at inspiring and sustaining enthusiasm.

CRITIC
Guardian and analyst of the team's long-term effectiveness.

- Never satisfied with less than the best solution.
- Expert at analyzing solutions to find the possible weaknesses within them.
- Merciless in insisting that faults be corrected.
- Constructive in pointing way to possible remedies.

IMPLEMENTER
Ensures the momentum and smooth running of the team's actions.

- A born time-tabler who thinks methodically.
- Anticipates threatening delays in schedule in time for them to be prevented.
- Has a "can-do" mentality and loves to fix things.
- Able to rally support and overcome defeatism.

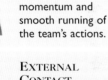

EXTERNAL CONTACT
Looks after the team's external relationships.

- Diplomatic, and good judge of the needs of others.
- Has a reassuring, authoritative presence.
- Has an effective grasp of the overall picture of the team's work.
- Discreet when handling confidential information.

COORDINATOR
Pulls together the work of the team as a whole into a cohesive plan.

- Understands how difficult tasks interrelate.
- Has a strong sense of priorities.
- Has a mind able to grasp several things at once.
- Good at maintaining internal contacts.
- Skilled at heading off potential trouble.

IDEAS PERSON
Sustains and encourages the team's innovative vitality and energy.

- Enthusiastic and lively, with a zest for new ideas.
- Eager for and receptive to the ideas of others.
- Sees problems as opportunities for successful innovation, rather than as disasters.
- Never at a loss for a hopeful suggestion.

INSPECTOR
Ensures that high standards are sought and maintained.

- Strict, and sometimes even pedantic in enforcing rigorous standards within the team.
- Good judge of the performance of other people.
- Unhesitating in bringing problems to the surface.
- Able to praise as well as to find fault.

BALANCING SKILLS WITHIN A TEAM

Acquiring the right mix of experience in a team can be more difficult than finding the basic skills, but is vital if the team is to be effective. Encourage each team member to make their own individual contribution, both on a technical and a personal level.

 **16** When recruiting people for a team, look for their growth potential.

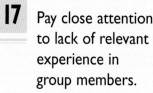 **17** Pay close attention to lack of relevant experience in group members.

FINDING THE RIGHT BALANCE OF SKILLS

Look for team members who possess one of the three major types of skill that are vital for the success of a team's task. These are:

- Technical expertise in disciplines (such as engineering and marketing);
- Problem-solving skills and the ability to make clear, informed decisions;
- Teamworking skills and an ability to cope well with interpersonal relationships.

MAINTAINING THE RIGHT BALANCE OF SKILLS

As a project proceeds, the range of skills needed within the team can change. For example, some specialist skills that were vital at the outset of a team's life may become superfluous as the project develops. To maintain the right balance of complementary skills, a team leader must be able to recognize any changes in project or team needs and act accordingly. This ability is as important in team leaders as their ability to evaluate the technical and analytical skills of potential team members. Both individuals and team need the power to grow.

 18 Take people out of the team if they do not perform.

 19 Find people with a good level of personal skill, and help develop them.

CHOOSING INDIVIDUALS FOR SPECIFIC ROLES

DO'S

DON'TS

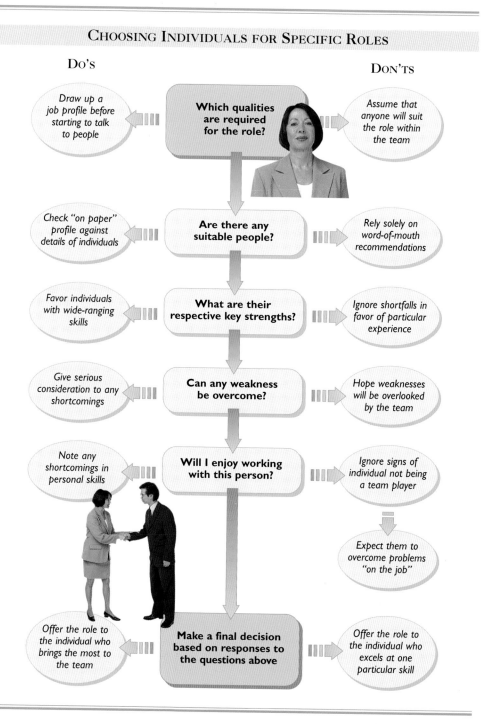

Draw up a job profile before starting to talk to people

Which qualities are required for the role?

Assume that anyone will suit the role within the team

Check "on paper" profile against details of individuals

Are there any suitable people?

Rely solely on word-of-mouth recommendations

Favor individuals with wide-ranging skills

What are their respective key strengths?

Ignore shortfalls in favor of particular experience

Give serious consideration to any shortcomings

Can any weakness be overcome?

Hope weaknesses will be overlooked by the team

Note any shortcomings in personal skills

Will I enjoy working with this person?

Ignore signs of individual not being a team player

Expect them to overcome problems "on the job"

Offer the role to the individual who brings the most to the team

Make a final decision based on responses to the questions above

Offer the role to the individual who excels at one particular skill

371

SETTING UP A TEAM

Establishing a team is the leader's prime task. Make sure your team has a clear purpose and sufficient resources to achieve it. Be open and impartial in your treatment of team members.

SETTING GOALS

What is your team for? The question may sound obvious, but time spent at the beginning of a project in defining team objectives is crucial to a successful outcome. Make sure that you have clearly established the issues that the team needs to resolve.

 20 Set challenging goals that are still realistic in view of your deadlines.

POINTS TO REMEMBER

- All team members need to agree on a precise definition of what they are working toward.
- Goals should not be set until you have discussed all possible approaches to the task.
- Although team members are needed to finalize team goals, the objectives of the team can also dictate membership.
- For best results targets should be challenging, with a combination of general and specific goals.

BUILDING A CONSENSUS

Meetings are an excellent way of fostering team spirit and the team-working habit in the early stages of a team's existence. Set up an initial series of meetings in which members can get to know each other and work toward a consensus about the goals of the team. Make sure that the task the team has been assigned and the issues it will be addressing are fully understood by everyone, and assess all the options available to the team before deciding how the team will be organized. Finally, discuss and decide on achievable deadlines for all the elements of the project.

ANALYZING GOALS

Goals will vary according to whether a team is there to recommend a course of action, to make or do something, or to run something. For example, a task force that makes a recommendation can measure its success rates against feedback from within the organization. A "doing" or "making" team, such as a manufacturing unit, has specific costs and customer satisfaction targets to work toward. A team charged with running a marketing drive has to work to strict budgets and schedules.

21 Consider the aims of individual team members when setting targets.

HARNESSING MOTIVATION

Ambitious, challenging goals are more motivational than smaller, specific ones. For example, aiming to be biggest and best in retail financial services is more motivational than trying to reduce average mortgage application approval to two days. If possible, set both general *and* specific goals, aiming high but remaining realistic. Ensure that everybody participates in setting their own goals, as well as the team's. Do not compromise on any teamwork needs. Look for the optimum combination of strong teamwork and technical capabilities.

22 Do not let failure of one part of a project jeopardize its overall success.

▼ **TAKING AN OVERVIEW**
Take into account all the aspects of your appointed task or project, and discuss them with team members when defining the team's overall goals.

Timescale
Work out realistic adlines for the team to complete its task

Subgoals
Break down targets and budgets for sub-groups and individuals

Constraints
Assess how much autonomy the team as, and its limitations

Vision
Set out attainable, but demanding, long-term goals

Priorities
Assess the order in which key elements in the project must be completed

Budget
Prepare the budget, allowing for staff salaries and any additional resources

PROVIDING SUPPORT FOR A TEAM

A degree of independence is essential in successful teamwork, but few teams are able to stand completely alone. Nurture good relations and support systems within your organization that satisfy both your team's needs and corporate requirements.

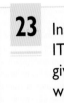

23 Insist on having IT support that gives you exactly what you want.

PROVIDING BASIC SUPPORT

Most teams are supported by the technical and administrative infrastructure of the organization to which they belong. It often makes little sense to set up an accounting system within a team, especially as external financial control can help to limit financial outlay. However, there are some exceptions, notably in information systems: the danger of relying on a centralized IT department is that your team will not receive the specific software support that it requires in order to complete a particular task successfully. To overcome this difficulty, some teams incorporate their own IT expertise. Think carefully about any specialist support your team is likely to need, and then discuss the options for acquiring it with all the team members.

PROVIDING SUPPORT FROM WITHIN AN ORGANIZATION

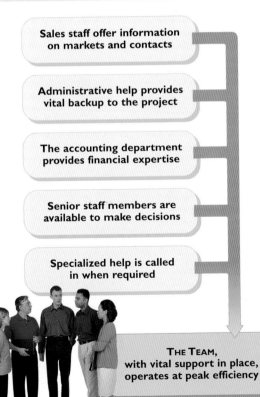

Sales staff offer information on markets and contacts

Administrative help provides vital backup to the project

The accounting department provides financial expertise

Senior staff members are available to make decisions

Specialized help is called in when required

THE TEAM, with vital support in place, operates at peak efficiency

SETTING UP LINKS WITH MANAGEMENT

All teams need to have the backing of the senior staff in the parent organization. The three key relationships a team needs are: the main team sponsor, the head of the department or operation to which the team reports, and whoever controls the team's budget. Their roles are to monitor and approve the team's activities, and to ensure that all necessary practical support is available. Keep strong lines of communication going with these managers. This becomes even more important if your team is based away from headquarters, for example in a factory or separate office building.

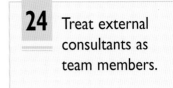

24 Treat external consultants as team members.

25 Keep your team sponsor informed of progress.

CHOOSING A LOCATION FOR A TEAM

LOCATION	IMPLICATIONS	EXAMPLE
HEAD OFFICE Team occupies space in company headquarters, near other related activities, with managers in separate offices.	● Close to management to liaise with decision makers. ● May be separate from main production source and thus some internal customers.	A group responsible for organizing distribution, working on plans for centralizing warehouses in a location overseas.
FACTORY Team is part of operational unit or attached to regional or local office; managers are on same site.	● Physical closeness to manufacturing is helpful. ● Distance from headquarters and decision makers can cause delays or problems.	Specialist marketing group for products made on site, with managers reporting back to marketing director at company headquarters.
"SKUNK WORKS" Special project team occupies make-do premises remote from other corporate activities. Management on site.	● Facilitates very high level of group dedication, team spirit, and teamwork. ● Can lose support, lack realism, or become isolated.	New product or business development where corporate mold needs to be broken, so that physical and managerial separation is vital.
"IVORY TOWER" Long-term project team is set apart from the rest of the organization in permanent offices. Management on site.	● Suits professional operation run to high standards. ● Remoteness from internal customers and market may promote arrogance.	Information systems team, responsible for planning, purchasing, maintaining, and controlling computer-based activities on all company sites.

ESTABLISHING TEAM TRUST

The most essential feature of successful teamwork is trust. Teams thrive on mutual trust, so it must be established early in the life of a team. Promote mutual trust through delegation, openness of conduct and communication, and a free exchange of ideas.

26 Keep tasks to yourself only if you know that no one else can do them.

27 Do not delegate any unnecessary work – scrap it.

28 Give your team the freedom to make its own decisions.

LEARNING TO DELEGATE

Delegation takes two forms: delegation of tasks and authority. Teamwork needs both for mutual trust to develop. Break down each project into single tasks or goals, and allocate them to individual team members. Leave things alone, intervening only if it appears that a goal will not be achieved. To delegate authority, share your power both with the team, consulting members on all issues, and with individuals, giving them full authority if their area of expertise is involved. Ask members to keep you informed of progress – and let them get on with it.

RECOGNIZING CHARACTER TYPES WHEN DELEGATING

CAN DO – WILL DO
The ideal delegate, happy to accept full responsibility for his specific task and also happy to consult others, acting on the advice that is given.

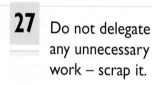

WILL DO – CAN'T DO
Initially the delegate may require encouragement and proper training to overcome inexperience before taking responsibility for the allotted task.

CAN DO – WON'T DO
A reluctance to learn or accept other opinions may mean that an individual is simply not a team player, and therefore not a strong delegate.

CAN'T DO – WON'T DO
Unless this person's lack of motivation and ability can be overcome, delegation will fail, and he may need to be moved to another environment.

PROMOTING OPENNESS

Teamwork and secrecy cannot live together, so a leader who is not open with team members will not get the best of their potential. Arrange regular formal and informal meetings: these are avenues to openness. As people get to know one another, they will relax and start to feel at ease with the team – and this will allow a sense of loyalty and cohesion to develop. Try to allow the team full access (where appropriate) to all facts and figures, agendas, and minutes relevant to their overall responsibilities for the project, but bear in mind that there will be times when you may have to maintain confidentiality.

CULTURAL DIFFERENCES

Attitudes toward teamworking vary around the world. A North American team is unlikely to have any such qualms, and may bounce ideas off each other from the time of their first meeting. Members of British teams may be inhibited about expressing themselves in front of others until a rapport has been established.

---

29 Encourage positive contributions from team members.

ENCOURAGING IDEAS

People have far more potential for creating ideas when working as a team than they do individually. Encourage the open discussion of ideas, and make sure that all suggestions are heard with respect. If an idea needs to be discounted, do so at a later date, and always give valid reasons for doing so. Alert team members to the expertise available within the group, and to all of its objectives, to promote the open discussion of relevant ideas.

CREATING ▼ NEW IDEAS
When holding a creative session, ask attendees to come with two or three prepared ideas to present to colleagues.

Record all ideas and evaluate them afterward

MAXIMIZING PERFORMANCE

It is vital that all members of a team work together to maximize team performance. Give people full responsibility for their jobs, and empower them to execute and improve their own work in ways that optimize their contribution to the entire team.

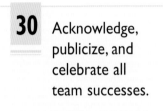

30 Acknowledge, publicize, and celebrate all team successes.

AWARDING RESPONSIBILITY

The first duty of any person working in a team is to attend to their own job. To make a team work together successfully, however, responsibility must go beyond the individual. Award your team total responsibility for achieving its own goals. Create a sense of responsibility in each individual so that they are happy to fulfill their allotted tasks to the best of their ability. Do this by delegating tasks efficiently and monitoring each team member's performance, as well as that of the team as a whole. In this way you will promote the sharing of responsibility among team members and encourage individuals to assist their colleagues and enhance the overall performance of the team.

POINTS TO REMEMBER

- Each team member should be able to cover the role of at least one other member.
- People should be given the responsibility to act on their own initiative within a team.
- A large task will be handled better if the entire project is handed over to a team.
- People need to be aware of where their own responsibilities begin and end.
- Each team member needs to be encouraged to find their own best method of working.

31 Find an easily accessible way of displaying team progress daily.

SHARING RESPONSIBILITY

Drawing up common aims and agreeing upon individual roles when a team is set up is only the beginning of a process that needs to last as long as the team does. A team must be responsible for implementing its policies, monitoring progress, and responding creatively and constructively where action is falling short of objectives. It is also the responsibility of the team as a whole to make sure there is a free flow of communication among members – everybody needs to be kept fully informed about progress and changes in policy.

ENSURING PEAK PERFORMANCE

As team leader, your role is to facilitate your team's efficiency. You can do this by taking responsibility for a number of different functions:

- Ensuring that all the members of your team are aware of their responsibilities and are challenged by their work;
- Encouraging team members to contribute their best to both the team and the task at hand;
- Overseeing the team's work practices to ensure that individual members work toward a common end;
- Assessing and setting team goals at the correct level to inspire continued motivation;
- Making sure that any overlap between team and individual responsibilities does not result in duplicated tasks.

Team works to common end to complete tasks

Challenging tasks maintain individual interest

Each individual contributes to team effort to complete task at hand

Needs of individual are addressed by team

KEY   Task   Team   *Individual*

▲ UNIFYING A TEAM

Most teams have a tendency to place too much focus on the task and not enough on the individual. This model shows an ideal situation in which the needs of the individual, the dynamics of the group, and the requirements of the task coincide at four strategic points to produce a unified, effective working team.

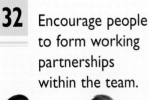

32 Encourage people to form working partnerships within the team.

BEING FLEXIBLE

Any team demands much of its members. While each member of the team has their own role and responsibility, they should remain flexible and willing to adapt to change. Some manufacturing groups require members to be able to fulfill every aspect of their team's work. Show flexibility by sharing aspects of your leadership role, and help team members by providing an assistant to share or take over some of their duties. As the team develops and progresses, look at individual roles, and modify them as and when the task requires it.

CREATING A SELF-MANAGED TEAM

*S*elf-managed teams (SMTs) are more independent than other teams. They are found increasingly in organizations that have flattened their structures and cut out layers of middle management and supervisory levels as they reform their working practices.

33 Encourage natural leaders to lead and develop their leadership skills.

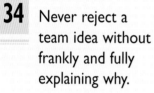

34 Never reject a team idea without frankly and fully explaining why.

DEFINING SMTS

Self-managed teams take on total responsibility for a specific project from inception to conclusion – for example, a manufacturing cell might take over the entire production process from an assembly line. Characteristics of these teams include the sharing of leadership roles, a high rate of autonomy, open discussion leading to democratic decision-making, control over team activities, and total self-accountability, which is based on individual and team results.

REAPING THE BENEFITS

When running properly, a self-managed team can be very productive. It can save on management costs, raise levels of quality and customer service, cut out process steps, reduce waste, and introduce more flexibility in the workplace. In addition to the economic benefits, such a team can provide a daily training ground for its members, who may need to develop their skills to take on the responsibilities of self-management. If the system works, expect to see a rise in employee morale and retention, and, with experience, more ability to react swiftly to changes in the marketplace.

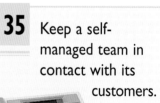

35 Keep a self-managed team in contact with its customers.

▲ RUNNING AN SMT

Allow a self-managed team to take full responsibility for its own actions. Give guidance only when it is specifically requested – so that members will be free to gain new experience and skills.

POINTS TO REMEMBER

● Teams usually respond well to having autonomy in all matters.

● SMTs should be responsible for setting their own high targets.

● Teamwork should focus on customer satisfaction.

● Consistent quality needs to be maintained at all times.

● The team should be able to ask for outside help when it is needed – but only then.

SUPPORTING SMTs

To work effectively, self-managed teams need full backing and support from a management that appreciates their need for autonomy. This means allowing team members a full say in any decision that affects them, including pay, performance measures, and personnel matters. Although a nominal team leader may be installed by senior management, that leader's position will be entirely dependent upon the consent of the others in the team. Aspects of leadership can change: a new talent may come to the fore, or the project may change direction. One of the more difficult aspects of working with SMTs is psychological: managers are required to surrender a major part of their right to manage the SMT while still monitoring its progress. Be flexible enough to accept that good decisions may be taken without you.

TAKING ON AN EXISTING TEAM

Taking on an established team is a testing experience. While you share the learning process with a team in a start-up situation, a takeover demands immediate evidence of your ability to take charge and recognize team strengths.

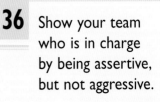

36 Show your team who is in charge by being assertive, but not aggressive.

BECOMING A TEAM LEADER

When a new leader joins an existing team, caution and doubt coexist with hope and interest on both sides. Try to make a favorable, positive first impression. Much may depend on the previous leader's standing and the cause of the change. If the team you have inherited has done well under good, strong leadership, recognize that – if not, presume that the members hunger for reform. Even if your predecessor was disliked and regarded as incompetent, or if the team is failing, never dwell negatively on past faults or poor performance. Demonstrate trust, promote team togetherness, and appear quietly confident. Insist on producing a competitive performance, achieved with the full support of your new team.

New leader's body language is open

▲ **MEETING FOR THE FIRST TIME**
When meeting a new team, be relaxed and confident without appearing arrogant. Keep your body language open and friendly so that you look both approachable and natural.

37 Think of ways to make an instant good impression on a new team – but without being overeager.

TALKING TO A NEW TEAM

Find out about your new team's background, purpose, progress, and membership before you meet them. Other people's input can be valuable at this stage, but trust your own judgment as you start to form an opinion of the team's abilities. Remember that your best chance to observe the team will come only once you have taken charge. Soon after taking on the team, set aside time to talk to each member, one-to-one, about their individual tasks and the project as a whole, their views of their own performance, whether they favor any changes in working practice, and, if so, why. From their ideas, you will gain a clear insight into each individual's character, motivation, and abilities. Avoid asking individuals to assess their colleagues – it is up to you to form your own opinion.

THINGS TO DO

1. Socialize with the team, at least occasionally, to show willingness and prevent being excluded later.
2. Show you appreciate the skills of the team to prevent any resentment.
3. Actively show your willingness to listen to team members.
4. Show your authority from the outset with confidence – otherwise you may find yourself being undermined.

BECOMING A TEAM MEMBER

The rules of being new to a team are simple. Form a clear idea of your personal goals, and work toward fitting them to the purposes of the team. If there is anybody you already know in the team, use them to ease your way into the group. Strive to make a good impression, but do not appear to be overconfident. Observe the culture of the team, and once you are comfortable with what you have learned about your colleagues and your new task, begin to show your own capabilities and initiative.

 38 If you ask people for their advice, be prepared not only to accept it but also to act upon it.

INTRODUCING A NEW TEAM MEMBER

When old team members are replaced by new staff, encourage and welcome the opportunity for new ideas and approaches, rather than expecting them to follow previous ways of working. Never leave new members to make their own introductions and find their own way around the team: instead, ensure that each new member has a guide to pilot them through their early weeks. At the first opportunity, such as during a team meeting, introduce new members to the group and ask the newcomers to say a few words about themselves – but prepare them beforehand!

IMPROVING TEAM EFFICIENCY

Teams are properly effective only when everyone learns to pull together. You must understand team dynamics in order to ensure the success of your team.

ANALYZING TEAM DYNAMICS

Good team leaders make the most of the human assets at their disposal. To do this, you need to understand each group member, how their behavior changes within the team, and how individual responses vary at different stages in the team's development.

39 Help your team find a way to change obstructive group behavior.

POINTS TO REMEMBER

● Teams should spend as much time together as possible within working hours.

● People need to be comfortable to work well together.

● Negative behavior within a team needs to be wiped out at the earliest opportunity.

● Insecurity is the enemy of team excellence and good management.

● The underlying causes of trouble should be dealt with at once.

ENCOURAGING TEAMWORK

Humans operate well in groups – a characteristic that can be seen in sports teams, in which people instinctively cooperate, voluntarily take on responsibility, and endorse decisions for the overall good of the team. To achieve the same cohesive behavior in a work environment, team members need to overcome any inclination to be defensive with each other. Encourage your team to spend as much time together as possible – humans are naturally gregarious creatures and will overcome any initial reticence as they grow to recognize each other's particular skills and strengths.

UNDERSTANDING TEAM DEVELOPMENT

A team grows and changes markedly during its lifetime. The process of development has been described as having four stages: forming, storming, norming, and performing. All teams pass through the initial stage of being brought together as a group. This is a tentative period that can easily develop into a "storming" phase in which people are unsure of each other and confused, and may become aggressive at times. With strong leadership, methods of working can be fully agreed in the "norming" stage, before the team goes on to perform at its best for the duration of its project.

40 Look for ways to use conflict constructively.

41 Remember that everyone deserves some fun during work hours.

DEALING WITH STAGES IN THE LIFE OF A TEAM

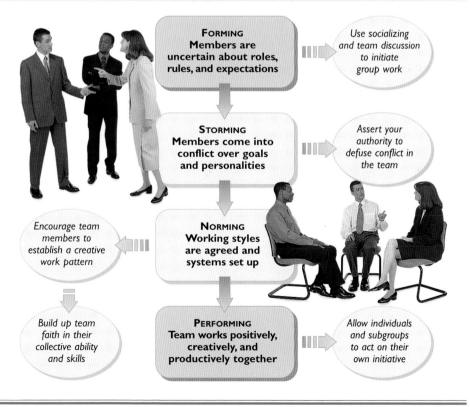

FORMING Members are uncertain about roles, rules, and expectations

Use socializing and team discussion to initiate group work

STORMING Members come into conflict over goals and personalities

Assert your authority to defuse conflict in the team

NORMING Working styles are agreed and systems set up

Encourage team members to establish a creative work pattern

PERFORMING Team works positively, creatively, and productively together

Build up team faith in their collective ability and skills

Allow individuals and subgroups to act on their own initiative

USING MANAGING TACTICS

There are various management styles, but often successful management – and improving team efficiency – hinges on your ability to adapt your style to the changing needs and dynamics within a team as it develops. Team management tactics may vary from the autocratic to the liberal, but even the most tolerant and sharing of leaders needs to be able to control their team. Firm leadership is the foundation of collaborative, cooperative, and efficient teamwork.

42 Always conduct a thorough, open analysis when projects go wrong.

43 Have an open-door policy if you want to be accessible.

44 Ask people who bring you problems to bring solutions.

FORMING A TEAM

The formative stage of any project is always slightly experimental, and a team can be an excellent testing ground for new ideas. Although experiments should be worked out with care to give them a fair chance of success, a major part of teamwork is knowing how to recognize mistakes early and then to move to correct defects without anger or recrimination. Dealing with failed experiments is part of the learning process summed up in the "forming to performing" progression. Remember that different solutions are required at varying stages of the team's development.

USING THE ▶ BEST PEOPLE
It is important to remember that the individuals initiating a project may not be the ones to see it through to the end. Here, different skills were introduced into the team at different stages, as one individual could not perform as implementer, salesperson, and producer. The result was success for the whole team.

CASE STUDY

Jenny headed up the new venture team within her company and came up with an idea for a line of stationery. She passed her idea to the marketing department, who seemed to get nowhere with selling the product internally. Jenny went to a colleague, Peter, who was known to be a good decision maker, and got him to further her cause. Peter joined up with Anna, a good implementer of ideas, and they formed a new venture team. Together they personally took the new stationery line around to all their senior managers, selling the idea and convincing the managers to put capital into the project. Before they went into production of the stationery, they realized that they needed a line manager whose management style they liked and who could keep costs down. They recruited James to set the team temporarily to set up the manufacturing process.

RESOLVING CONFLICT

In the "storming" part of the life of a team, conflicts can take place between:
- The leader and individual team members;
- The leader and the whole team;
- Individual team members.

These conflicts can be emotional, factual, constructive, destructive, argumentative, open, or suppressed. Try to resolve any disputes among team members by replacing emotive approaches to a problem with rational, open-minded ones.

45 Meet informally as well as formally to discuss your team's progress.

46 Use dispassionate fact-finding as the best method of defusing conflict.

ADAPTING YOUR ROLE

During the development of a team, changes in the management role occur. In the first instance, the team leader is predominantly an organizer who puts the team together. As the team settles, your role changes to that of counselor or trouble shooter. When the team is functioning – or "norming" – inspirational leadership is required to maintain momentum. During the final phase, "performing," act as facilitator to keep the team's wheels turning.

DEVELOPING MEMBERS' ROLES

It is not only the nature of teams that changes over time – so do the abilities of the members as they build on their personal skills. With experience, indivduals learn how to be team members, solve problems, and work together successfully. At each stage of the development of your team, set challenging goals, review its working methods, and question its achievements to improve overall performance.

DO'S AND DON'TS

✔ Do change your leadership style according to the needs of your team.

✔ Do stress and support the values established by your team.

✔ Do be seen to react positively to novel and creative ideas.

✔ Do encourage individual and group learning at every stage of the team's development.

✘ Don't always dismiss conflict as somebody else's fault – look to see if you are to blame.

✘ Don't shirk any issues in which you feel strong management is needed for success.

✘ Don't let "not invented here" kill promising new initiatives.

✘ Don't miss the times when your leadership qualities are needed by your team.

COMMUNICATING EFFECTIVELY

Strong communication links are vital to the well-being of a team. The most effective links occur naturally – for example, in casual conversation – but these will need supplementing by new technology. Choose the most appropriate method to suit your team.

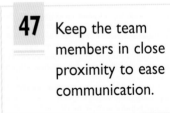

47 Keep the team members in close proximity to ease communication.

48 Set aside areas in which people can meet and talk informally.

ENSURING ACCESSIBILITY

How a team communicates internally depends on its size and the location of its members. The most effective method of communication is informal direct conversation: for this, ideally, team members should have easy access to each other at all times, preferably sitting close together. If certain members of a team are situated off site, establish efficient communication links, such as telephone, fax, e-mail, or video, between all the locations to ensure that dialogue can still flow freely between the parties concerned.

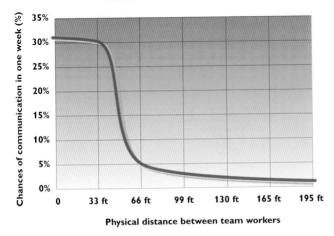

Physical distance between team workers

◀ **ENCOURAGING COMMUNICATION**
Physical distance has a great effect on levels of communication between team members. Research shows that if team members are seated less than 33 ft (10 m) apart, they have a 30 percent chance of communicating at least once a week. This probability dwindles to a mere 5 percent when people are seated more than 66 ft (20 m) apart and falls to virtually nothing when seated at a distance of 195 ft (60 m) or more apart.

COMMUNICATION METHODS

There are many ways for a team to communicate, whether formally or informally, within its own organization or externally. These include:

- Constant casual conversational links between colleagues. These create an informal "grapevine" throughout the organization;
- Traditional methods of communication such as paper memos, circulars, letters, reports, bulletin boards, faxes, and telephone calls;
- Electronic means, such as e-mail, intranet (internal e-mails), Internet, and groupware (software packages tailored to groups);
- Videoconferencing facilities and video telephones that can reach right across the international business world.

Whichever communication systems are utilized, remember that they are all a supplement to, rather than a substitute for, face-to-face meetings.

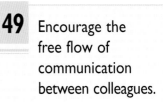

49 Encourage the free flow of communication between colleagues.

50 Invest in the most appropriate technology, and keep it up to date.

CHOOSING METHODS OF COMMUNICATION

In any organization, many modes of communication exist side-by-side. You cannot stop the "grapevine" from working – indeed, it is one of the faster and thus more efficient methods of communication – so use it to your advantage by talking informally to all colleagues. If you want to reach your team or your whole organization quickly, use electronic means, such as e-mail. Video communications emulate the collaborative, informal style of true teamwork closely: you can see the reactions of the people you are dealing with, so try these when your team is spread across a distance. Remember that traditional communications, such as memos and bulletin boards, still have their place. For example, anybody can use bulletin boards to share information that has not reached them personally.

RUNNING TEAM MEETINGS

Making team meetings effective is a major test of leadership skills. The key to holding a productive meeting is to actively involve everybody in the proceedings. Ensure that team members understand the purpose of each meeting and what is expected of them.

51 Change the chairperson at each meeting to involve everybody.

FULFILLING YOUR PURPOSE

Meetings should always have a clear purpose over and beyond the exchange of information. Determine the purpose of each meeting carefully – for example, is it to plan future action, or discuss a new recruit? Draw up an agenda listing the points to be discussed, and distribute this in advance of the meeting so that people know why they are attending and can gather their thoughts beforehand. Lead the discussion and make your purpose clear, but aim to achieve consensus within the team.

▲ KNOWING YOUR AIMS
Be clear about what you need to achieve in a meeting: draw up an agenda and follow it closely. Go armed with all relevant facts and figures, and encourage team members to do the same.

52 Try to delegate as much as possible to other members of the team.

CONSIDERING FREQUENCY

Team and progress meetings should be held at least once every two weeks, so that the group's plans and deadlines stay clear in everyone's mind and the lines of communication remain open. Other types of meeting, such as confidential one-to-ones, focus groups, and reporting meetings that are aimed at solving or discussing specific problems should be held as and when required.

PACING MEETINGS

When running a meeting, pace yourself with the aid of a preprepared agenda. Group similar topics together on the agenda to avoid repetition, allocate a time limit to each point to be discussed, and adhere to it strictly. Ask for ideas to be prepared in advance to save time in the meeting. Start proceedings promptly, and keep them moving – 75 minutes is enough to cover most agendas, and people lose concentration beyond that length of time. Encourage everybody to have their say, subject to relevance and reasonable brevity: the livelier a meeting, the more creative the ideas generated.

53 Distribute agendas in advance of the meeting to give your team time to prepare.

MATCHING PURPOSE TO MEETING TYPE

MEETING TYPE	CHARACTERISTICS
TEAM MEETING Regular update meeting for whole team.	● Indispensable for teamwork; allows everyone a chance to find out how other team members are progressing. ● Run freely by team leader to allow fruitful discussion.
FOCUS GROUP Meeting of subgroup with specific knowledge.	● Ideal for problem-solving, as all the people involved know the issues at stake and discuss them from an informed point of view. ● As everyone is well-informed, does not require a leader.
PROGRESS MEETING Regular update meeting for subgroup of team.	● To set agenda at start of day or week. ● Used to review and alter agenda for a set period of time. ● Run tightly by team leader to use time effectively.
ONE-TO-ONE Private meeting held between two people.	● Can be informal or formal. ● May cover any topic, work-related or personal. ● May cover confidential matters, which are not recorded.
METHOD MEETING Meeting of whole group to study work methods.	● For examining and improving work methods and processes. ● Involves a free discussion across the whole team. ● Generates practical, quick solutions to problems encountered.
REPORTING MEETING Meeting to spread specific information to team.	● Allows the spread of information among team members. ● Meeting is run by the presenter of the information. ● Team leader acts as chief inquisitor to verify the information.

Networking a Team

All teams, no matter what their purpose, depend to a considerable extent on good networking skills. Make full use of the formal and informal connections both inside and outside your organization to provide valuable support for your team.

54 Cultivate all relationships that may be useful to the team.

55 Try to keep all team relationships on an even keel.

Understanding the Need for Support

All teams need friends in high places – a network system. At the top end of an organization, a network may include a decision maker, such as a top executive; an influencer, who may have the ear of senior managers; one or more players, whose own tasks depend on your team's performance; and a consent giver – an individual whose consent is officially required for key purposes. Remember to network in and outside the organization to find the support your team needs to function efficiently.

UNDERSTANDING ▼ OUTSIDE INFLUENCES
Specific individuals can exert considerable influence on your team from outside. Be aware of their impact upon the team, and seek their support and approval.

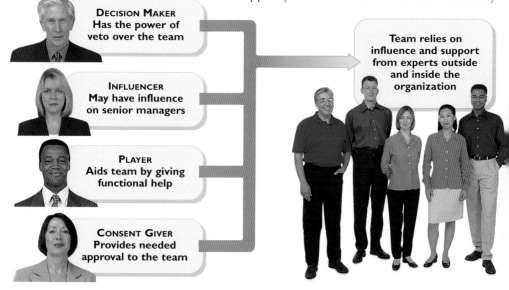

DECISION MAKER
Has the power of veto over the team

INFLUENCER
May have influence on senior managers

PLAYER
Aids team by giving functional help

CONSENT GIVER
Provides needed approval to the team

Team relies on influence and support from experts outside and inside the organization

FINDING SPONSORS

A team sponsor is usually a well-placed, well-disposed individual, working from either inside or outside an organization, who does not occupy any of the main four roles (decision maker, influencer, player, or consent giver) that affect a team. When a start-up runs into difficulties, or a crisis develops later in a team's life, your sponsor may have the ability to influence the four role fillers. The sponsor's function is to help resolve an impasse or head off conflict. Team life is much tougher without such mentors.

56 Make sure that good news is heard and clearly understood by all the relevant people.

57 If trouble is brewing in any team relationship, deal with it quickly.

REMOVING WORK-RELATED PROBLEMS

Barriers to the success of team performance can be caused by the inflexibility of corporate tradition. Be aware of any company rules, regulations, or procedures that can cause delays and difficulties for the team. Look to your sponsor and network of contacts in senior management to smooth the passage of team decisions and action through the organization. Such allies may be able to influence reticent colleagues and speed up approval processes.

DEALING WITH PROBLEM INDIVIDUALS

Watch out for the human factor: problems within the team can equally well be caused by external colleagues. Work pressures, conservatism, jealousy, self-protection, or stubbornness can all drive individuals outside a team to try to disrupt its efficiency. Although many such situations can be resolved informally, avoid head-on conflict if you can. Ask an influencer, decision maker, or team sponsor to deal with extreme cases personally. If troublemakers persist in causing problems, look to senior management to resolve the situation.

POINTS TO REMEMBER

- The higher-placed a team's allies, the better the chance of success for the team.
- Time should be allocated to maintaining a network of influencers and sponsors.
- Sponsors need to be informed of team progress and consulted regularly for their advice.
- Anyone with influence over a senior decision maker should be regarded with respect and caution.

SHARING INFORMATION OUTSIDE A TEAM

No person and no team is an island. Two-way information links between a team, the rest of an organization, and its external support are vital for efficiency. Remember that collaboration and cooperation are hindered by the absence of open communication.

58 Arrange social contacts with other parts of the organization.

COMMUNICATING FROM INSIDE

The natural tendency of teams is for their innate strength – their togetherness – to become a weakness: they may become clannish, keeping themselves and their information to themselves. Where work can be carried out in isolation, this may not matter, but most teams depend to some extent on other departments and functions within an organization, for example, for backup, such as computer support, or when needing specialist help in, say, production or engineering.

59 Find out which technology can keep you in touch with sponsors.

POINTS TO CONSIDER
BEFORE SPREADING INFORMATION

Is the information accurate?	Double-check all available facts and figures
Who needs to know this information?	Always inform more people rather than less
How is it best communicated?	Consider complexity of material to be communicated
Who communicates the information?	Choose a qualified, experienced person to spread message
Should any action follow?	Know the purpose of spreading information
Do you need to follow up afterward?	Set a deadline for follow-up to information

MAINTAINING CONTACT

Keep a list of key people in other departments and outside the organization, making sure that everybody who needs to know particular information is included. Update and refine this list constantly, as different people and skills will be required to support a team at differing stages of its life. Use memos, faxes, letters, e-mail, video links, or groupware – software that ranges from electronic mail to complete networking systems – to enable members of the team to stay in touch with each other and with the support system.

60 Keep a record of contacts with valuable people you meet outside the team or office.

61 Award team roles carefully so they do not overlap.

CONFIDENTIALITY

A truly efficient team should have no professional secrets between its members, and should keep confidential only those matters that members agree are in the best interests of the project. Before deciding what is confidential, ask "Who else needs to know this?" and "Would openness be damaging?" If the answers are *everybody* and *no*, then feel free to circulate the information. However, if there is a real need for secrecy, ensure that it is maintained absolutely.

AVOIDING DUPLICATION

Duplication of roles is a critical problem in large organizations. For example, two projects, each instigated by different departments for different reasons, may well overlap. To prevent this waste of resources, circulate a brief covering your team's function to all relevant people. The overlap will soon be discovered if information is circulating properly. In some cases, it may be possible for the separate projects to benefit by uniting their efforts, or it may be constructive to combine results when both teams have completed their work.

CASCADING INFORMATION

One popular method of passing information down the line is the cascade, in which a chief executive briefs an executive committee, who briefs divisional heads, and so on. The more layers there are, the greater the danger that the cascading message can be distorted. Even without any factual distortion, comprehension and perception may differ from the original intention, and this can confuse a team's aims and its efficiency. To prevent this, hold large meetings rather than many small ones, and then, if necessary, feed an agreed summary back upward.

THINKING CREATIVELY

Without new ideas, teams are unlikely to achieve the breakthroughs that generate real success. Creative thinking is a team responsibility in which all members should participate. Develop it in teams through plenty of training and practice.

62 Look for the good points in an idea, and never criticize ideas in public.

63 Look for people with experience when seeking problem solvers.

64 Analyze the roles that people play within your team.

ENCOURAGING CREATIVITY

Many people become locked into patterns of thinking drawn from their own experience and personalities. To unlock their creativity, do not allow yourself or your team members to become typecast as creative or noncreative. Everybody is capable of having or developing new ideas. Encourage people to think creatively by insisting that they come to appropriate meetings – to discuss new products, for example, or to solve a problem – with a number of ideas. Then all can play a creative role, which emphasizes that thinking is a team activity in which everybody shares. Always welcome diversity of views and ideas, but steer debate toward consensus.

◀ **TRYING A NEW PERSPECTIVE**
In this case, a company was in danger of losing money and face by not being able to complete an order. Drawing together people with different skills and ideas brought fresh solutions to the problem.

CASE STUDY
Harry is a clothing manufacturer. One of his best customers had placed a large order that seemed to be impossible to meet without diverting workers from jobs for other clients. He called together the whole executive team to look for a solution to the problem. Carlo, the head of manufacturing, wanted to hire tailors on a temporary basis to fill the order. The finance director, Jane, regarded this as costly and uncertain, and suggested subcontracting the work to another supplier. Ellen, from marketing, asked if anybody had contacted the customers to see if deliveries could be rescheduled. Carlo immediately saw that, given this leeway, he could organize production, and meet all the demands with little delay. All the customers agreed to the new schedules, the improved work flow actually cut costs, and everybody was satisfied.

Ideas are brought to meeting

Team member contributes

All ideas are recorded on flip chart

Leader

▲ WORKING TOGETHER

To achieve the most from a brainstorming session, make sure that the atmosphere between team members is amicable – more creative ideas will be produced if attendees are relaxed and have no qualms about speaking in front of each other.

POINTS TO REMEMBER

- Brainstorming is sometimes called "group action thinking."

- Criticism kills creativity. Ideas should never be scorned during a brainstorming session.

- Many seemingly foolish ideas can lead to sensible solutions.

- All ideas should be recorded – no matter how unconventional they appear to be.

- The joint creative input in these sessions will always be higher than individuals can provide alone.

GENERATING NEW IDEAS

Brainstorming sessions aim to generate as many ideas as possible, no matter how far-fetched. They can be used for many purposes, from new ways to market a product, to devising a new pay system. Brainstorming requires a leader and takes some organization – a session should be open-ended, but the leader should call a halt when it starts to run out of steam. All ideas should be recorded on a flip chart or white board so they can be seen by everyone. Methodically reject nonstarters, and produce a shortlist of feasible ideas. Use this as the agenda for a subsequent meeting to discuss and agree on the best idea and action plan.

65 Never dismiss brainstormed ideas out of hand – that is disheartening and stops the flow of creativity.

Dealing with Problems

Team members not only solve problems – they also create them. It is vital to build up loyalty between team members so that all difficulties, whether personal, work-related, or procedural, are tackled before they undermine the collective team spirit.

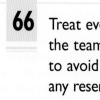

66 Treat everyone in the team equally to avoid causing any resentment.

Instilling Team Spirit

That indefinable quality known as team spirit can be encouraged in a number of ways:

- Let team members know why they were chosen for their particular task;
- Establish a common team purpose and specific goals to challenge the strengths of the team;
- Encourage the team to communicate well, and always praise wherever praise is due;
- Ask your team for its advice, and then be seen to act upon it;
- Take the time to respond in detail to reports and information coming from your team.

◀ **PROVIDING FEEDBACK**
Team spirit is encouraged by a feeling of mutual trust and open communication. Always be ready to give praise to team members, and listen carefully to what they have to say to you.

Identifying Problems

All teams have a latent difficulty. You want the individuals to act as a unit, but they may disagree with each other or with the direction of the team. Ask questions to establish whether problems are localized (one or two people) or a sign of general dissatisfaction. If the morale of the whole team is unsatisfactory and therefore damaging its work, there is no alternative but to rethink your strategy, how the team is structured, and who is in it.

67 Regard disruptive team members as innocent until they are proven guilty.

TALKING TO INDIVIDUALS

Once a problem is identified, it is an inevitable and important part of team leadership to discuss it with the people involved. This is preeminently a listening task – let them tell you how they see what is happening. At the same time, use your prior knowledge of them, and any observations made during meetings, to assess their attitudes and preconceptions. What they say and what they do and feel may be different things. Do they have hidden agendas? Are they withholding any information and/or emotions that run deep? Their reactions will tell you whether their commitment to the group and its objectives is strong. If it is, they will genuinely want to find the root of the problem as much as you do, and will be happy to cooperate with you fully. If an individual blames others and plunges into self-justification, confront and question this defensive reaction.

POINTS TO REMEMBER

● Personal problems between members of a team should be handled in a constructive way.

● It is not sensible to react to any difficulties until you are sure that you know the real cause.

● There are always new mountains for any team to climb.

● A "blame culture" must be prevented from developing – otherwise, it will kill team spirit.

68 Telling individuals they are doing a good job will build team morale.

LEADING TEAMS FROM THE FRONT

Your team looks to you to provide cohesion and inspiration. Be aware of this, and lead them from the front by:

● Raising team sights continually: the higher the realistic aims, the greater the shared excitement of the team hitting the target – which will instill a sense of urgency and drive in the members;

● Recognizing and celebrating group or individual successes as they occur;

● Using your own interpersonal skills to pull the team together. Be confident and highly visible. Develop an accessible style to which people can relate – this will promote ease of communication.

▲ ENCOURAGING PEOPLE
To instill and maintain confidence in team members, always make obvious your enthusiasm for the project in hand and your faith in the team.

DEALING WITH PROBLEM PEOPLE

After speaking to the people causing a problem within a team, further action may be needed. Be positive, and search for any common ground from which to start rebuilding relations. Are roles within the team unclear, causing overlap of responsibility? Is the workload fairly distributed, or are certain individuals feeling overburdened and stressed? In both cases, rethink the allocation of the workload. Experiment may find solutions to the problems, but remember to act in good time. You must remove people from a team if you find their disruptive behavior persists after all avenues have been explored.

70 Avoid direct conflict with team members.

71 Remember to be tough on the problems, not the people.

 69 Always treat team members with respect, even those who may be creating problems for you.

DO'S & DON'TS

✔ Do tell the truth about how you see a situation.

✔ Do try to see a problem from your team's angle.

✔ Do use the problem as a lever for change.

✔ Do be positive when handling problems.

✔ Do tackle problems head-on, rather than delaying your action.

✘ Don't persist with impossible people.

✘ Don't lose your own temper with any members of the team.

✘ Don't lose sight of the team's purpose.

✘ Don't hesitate to call on outside help where you feel it is necessary.

✘ Don't cause more problems by ignoring tensions in your team.

DEALING WITH CONFLICT

Head-on personal conflict between team members soon becomes a problem for the entire team. Address such situations as soon as they arise. Offer one or two team members the opportunity to tell you, in confidence, what they perceive as the root of the clash, and explore ways of defusing the situation. How many people are causing the conflict? Is one individual behaving badly? Talk to them personally. Has the team become divided? If so, insist on a truce between the warring parties. Is your management at fault? If so, talk to team members to see how you can redress the situation. The object of the exercise is to improve behavior, not parcel out blame and criticism. Do not rest until a solution has been found and agreed by all.

USING A PROBLEM LOG

Regard work-related problems as opportunities for team learning and improvement. Enter the issue in a log, and allow all team members access to it so that the lessons learned can be shared. Select an individual to resolve the problem, and give them the necessary authority and resources. Ask for a plan of action and regular progress reports. Record these reports in the log, noting any problems and the final resolution.

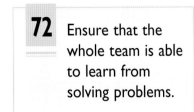

72 Ensure that the whole team is able to learn from solving problems.

LEARNING FROM PROBLEM-SOLVING

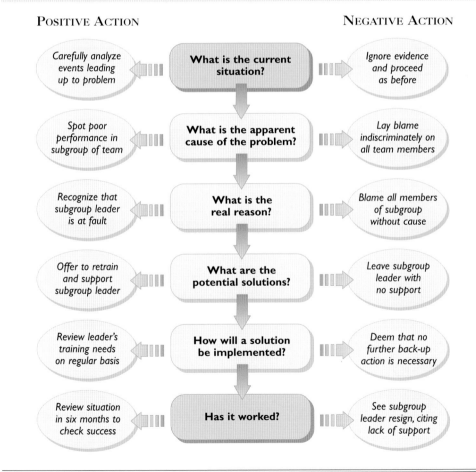

POSITIVE ACTION | | NEGATIVE ACTION

Positive Action	Question	Negative Action
Carefully analyze events leading up to problem	**What is the current situation?**	Ignore evidence and proceed as before
Spot poor performance in subgroup of team	**What is the apparent cause of the problem?**	Lay blame indiscriminately on all team members
Recognize that subgroup leader is at fault	**What is the real reason?**	Blame all members of subgroup without cause
Offer to retrain and support subgroup leader	**What are the potential solutions?**	Leave subgroup leader with no support
Review leader's training needs on regular basis	**How will a solution be implemented?**	Deem that no further back-up action is necessary
Review situation in six months to check success	**Has it worked?**	See subgroup leader resign, citing lack of support

IMPROVING STANDARDS IN A TEAM

Any systematic approach to improving performance needs to challenge existing ways of working. Teams looking to improve must learn to generate their own tasks, tackle problems, agree on solutions, and implement their decisions with confidence.

73 Go for some large, quick, quality wins to encourage further effort.

KNOWING THE PROJECT

People in true teams "own" their jobs – they are each responsible for finding the best methods of performing excellent work to the highest possible standard. A manufacturing cell goes one step beyond this: team members are multiskilled and know each team role well enough to take it over. Such flexibility can strengthen any team. Teams gain greatly by studying the progress of other people's jobs. Track your team's project "end-to-end" to gain a better understanding of the task, your role, other team roles, how to improve performance, and how such improvement will pay off.

▼ **KEEPING TRACK OF PERFORMANCE**
Track the progress of a team project from beginning to end to see what pitfalls and problems are encountered. Talk to individual team members to understand the problems they have faced and make a note of how these were solved.

Leader asks team member pertinent questions and notes answers

Team member describes problem and solution

IMPROVING SYSTEMS

The Japanese management technique of *kaizen* holds that everybody and every team can improve the quality of their work continually by valuable and quantifiable amounts. Even a small fall in the percentage of rejected products, for example, can mean big savings in production costs. Give teams complete responsibility for their task, so that they can set the improvement process underway by defining problems, analyzing the root cause, improving the situation – perhaps by bringing in external specialist help, if necessary – and, above all, preventing the problem from recurring.

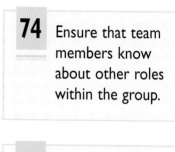

74 Ensure that team members know about other roles within the group.

75 Work out the cost of failure before the cost of quality.

76 Build significant improvement targets into every budget and every team action plan.

MAINTAINING A FRESH APPROACH

As teams develop and settle into a routine, they often fall into set patterns of behavior and group thinking. Avoid the temptation to leave a situation alone on the grounds that change serves little purpose: strive for continual improvement to challenge the viability of a team's assumptions and working practices. How can you improve team performance? Have you overlooked anything that can be improved? Do you need new blood in the team? Is the product still right for the market?

CHALLENGING COMMON ASSUMPTIONS

Challenge any perceived assumptions in order to improve team practice:

- "Tackling the symptom cures the disease." Bear in mind that problems will recur if not tackled at root level;
- "Problems and their solutions are always isolated." Remember: secondary effects can be worse than primary consequences;

- "Quality comes expensive." Remember that improving quality makes great economic sense when measured against both the direct and indirect costs of failure;
- "Quality applies only to products." Apply quality to every service and process in which your team is involved.

RATING TEAM LEADERSHIP

Team leadership is a many-sided process, as the following self-assessment shows. If you are currently leading a team, this will test the quality of your working methods and ability to manage people. If you are a team member, test your own leadership potential. Be as honest as you can: if your answer is "never," mark Option 1; if it is "always," mark Option 4; and so on. Add your scores together, and refer to the Analysis to see how you scored. Use your answers to identify the areas that need improving.

OPTIONS

1 Never

2 Occasionally

3 Frequently

4 Always

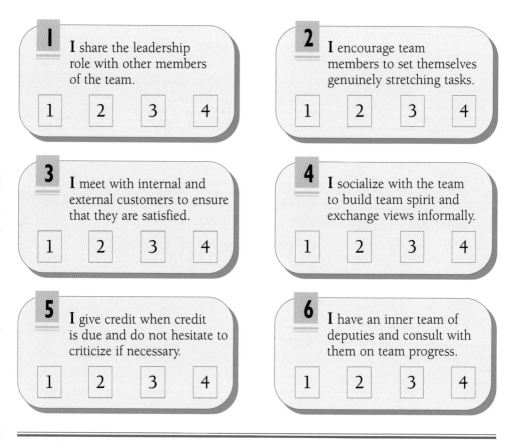

1 I share the leadership role with other members of the team.

1   2   3   4

2 I encourage team members to set themselves genuinely stretching tasks.

1   2   3   4

3 I meet with internal and external customers to ensure that they are satisfied.

1   2   3   4

4 I socialize with the team to build team spirit and exchange views informally.

1   2   3   4

5 I give credit when credit is due and do not hesitate to criticize if necessary.

1   2   3   4

6 I have an inner team of deputies and consult with them on team progress.

1   2   3   4

7 I give the team and its members precise goals and communicate them clearly.

1 2 3 4

8 I keep in touch with team sponsors to keep external relations smooth.

1 2 3 4

9 I try to show the members of my team that I trust them implicitly.

1 2 3 4

10 I explain why, if I need to reject a team member's idea on solving a problem.

1 2 3 4

11 I turn whole tasks over to the team to carry out as the members see fit.

1 2 3 4

12 I allow my team to have a say in any decision that affects it.

1 2 3 4

13 I ask individuals on the team what they think about current working methods.

1 2 3 4

14 I look for the underlying causes of any problems that arise within my team

1 2 3 4

15 I deliberately change my management style to suit changing situations.

1 2 3 4

16 I encourage team members to come to me with any problems.

1 2 3 4

17 I plan team meetings well in advance and provide an agenda.

1   2   3   4

18 I communicate with team members via every available means.

1   2   3   4

19 I pass on all information I receive to my team, as long as it is not confidential.

1   2   3   4

20 I try to eliminate unnecessary reporting levels from the team hierarchy.

1   2   3   4

21 I consult sponsors and other well-placed people to ease the team's work.

1   2   3   4

22 I encourage team members to think in innovative ways.

1   2   3   4

23 I run brainstorming sessions to generate new thinking within my team.

1   2   3   4

24 I run frequent checks on team spirit and individual morale levels.

1   2   3   4

25 I treat problem-solving as an opportunity for lasting improvement.

1   2   3   4

26 I eliminate conflict caused by overlap of role responsibility in the team.

1   2   3   4

27 I try to inspire my team by leading it firmly from the front.

| 1 | 2 | 3 | 4 |

28 I deal with personal problems within the team as and when they arise.

| 1 | 2 | 3 | 4 |

29 I use a log to record any way we find to improve working practice.

| 1 | 2 | 3 | 4 |

30 I am tough on problems, but not on the individuals in my team.

| 1 | 2 | 3 | 4 |

31 I track the projects being worked on by individual team members.

| 1 | 2 | 3 | 4 |

32 I seek all opportunities for long-term improvements in working systems.

| 1 | 2 | 3 | 4 |

ANALYSIS

Now that you have completed the assessment, add up your total score and check your performance by reading the corresponding evaluation below. Whatever level of success you have achieved (or have the potential to achieve), there is always room for improvement. Identify your weakest areas, then refer to the relevant chapters of this section, where you will find practical advice and tips that will enable you to establish and hone team leadership skills.

32–63: You are not keeping up with the pace of change. Look for ways to update your management style.

64–95: Some of your leadership qualities are good, so concentrate on improving weak areas.

96–128: This is the zone of excellence, but do not let that lull you into complacency – strive to improve.

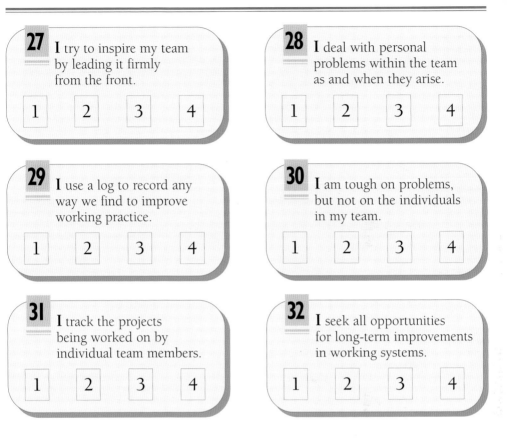

WORKING FOR THE FUTURE

Identifying new challenges for an established team is one of the most exciting aspects of teamwork. Use appropriate techniques to drive the team forward to bigger and better targets.

MEASURING PERFORMANCE

I f something cannot be measured, it cannot be improved upon. This basic principle applies to any job. Define individual and team standards – that they always meet deadlines, for instance – to give a targeted objective by which performance can be judged.

77 Tell each member of a team which measurements set the standards.

78 Ensure that all improvements and new targets are maintained.

CHOOSING MEASURES

Every team effort contains some elements that can be measured by performance. Look for wide-ranging measures when analyzing performance. Measure those standards whose improvement will ensure real economic benefits. For instance, if a call-center team is measured only by the number of calls handled per hour, the quality of response may suffer. Setting a quota of calls per hour and a waiting time target, monitoring a percentage of calls, and surveying customer satisfaction by making follow-up calls will be a more effective way of measuring team performance.

ASSESSING RESULTS

Teamwork can benefit from having performance measured by the team members themselves. They can generally be trusted to assess their own achievement levels accurately and understand the implications. Make sure that the data used is "robust" – that is, any measures you are assessing are meaningful and accurate. Input data onto appropriate computer software to save time and interpret the results effectively. Use independent outside assessors if you need specific facts, such as comparative market shares of products in competition with your own.

Leader asks for individual reaction to team performance

Team member gives his appraisal of team performance

▲ DISCUSSING TEAM RESULTS
When measuring the performance of a team, ask each member for their opinion of how targets were handled, if working methods could be improved, and whether the results are realistic.

MEASURING STAFF PERFORMANCE

WHOM TO MEASURE

WHOLE TEAM
Measure the progress of the whole team against the project objectives, schedules, and budgets.

LEADER
Measure the effectiveness of the team leader in providing support and direction to the team.

SUBGROUP
Evaluate the effectiveness of each subgroup within the main team in meeting the set objectives.

TEAM MEMBERS
Assess the contribution of each individual to the achievement of the objectives of the team.

ASPECTS TO MEASURE

- Finance: actual expenditure; profit versus forecasts.
- Time: physical output and tasks achieved versus schedule.
- Quality: accuracy; customer satisfaction.
- Development: investment in teamwork; technical skills.

- Control: achievement of results as planned or budgeted.
- Upward appraisal: performance as rated by team.
- Downward appraisal: performance as rated by superiors.
- Morale: ratings by team members, customers, or suppliers.

- Targets: actual results versus objectives.
- Quality: level as assessed by internal customers.
- Customer: performance as assessed by external customers.
- Improvement: plans for better results in the future.

- Output: performance against targets.
- Appraisal: rating by superiors, colleagues, and customers.
- Self-appraisal: own rating as individual and team member.
- Added value: contribution outside specific, defined duties.

TRACKING TEAM PROGRESS

A good team is aware of the need to remain dynamic. Review progress regularly to maintain momentum, provide an overview, and ask team members, singly or in groups, to define specific aspects of the project that could be improved in the future.

79 Circulate all relevant facts and figures before team reviews.

80 Never make personal attacks on individuals during reviews.

HOLDING TEAM REVIEWS

Regular team reviews strengthen teamwork and provide impetus for further progress. They can be conducted by the entire team or by key team members. Use them to check team performance against team objectives and any valid comparisons – such as the results of competitors. Check work methods to see if they are still appropriate, and consider what the next stages of action need to be. If necessary, delegate the development of any necessary action plans to experienced people.

Team communicates well at outset of project

REVIEWING PROGRESS ▲
This illustration shows two possible outcomes of the career of a team – negative and positive. Despite starting out well, it is easy for a team to let personal problems hinder its progress. To stay on course, maintain constant, open communication.

Team performance declines due to poor communication

Team fails to achieve target

HIGHLIGHTING OBSTACLES

As a team becomes established, every team activity can be seen as a distinct process. Tracking these processes almost always reveals ways in which time and money can be saved and quality improved. This is a valuable teamwork exercise, both for results and for the discussion involved in achieving them. For example, a team may draw up a flowchart showing how customer orders result in final delivery. Each activity and all decision points are marked on the diagram. If the flowchart reveals a bottleneck, the team draws a diagram of causes and effects, then solves or improves the situation.

81 Remember that relationships will change over time.

82 Avoid the trap of minimizing or ignoring bad news.

Team achieves targets

Team holds regular reviews

Individuals discuss ways of improving performance

ACTING ON INFORMATION

In addition to information from reviews and the team's own analysis, a team may receive information from outside, such as a falling share of a particular market. In other cases, a team itself seeks new information – for example, customer reaction to proposed changes in its services. Some of this data-gathering is analytical: which activities generate what costs, which products make money. To remain dynamic, the team needs to use this information to change and improve. Encourage team members to look at the information and discard some activities, reduce some costs, raise some prices – and obtain better overall results.

TRAINING A TEAM

Training helps to improve the technical skills of team members and develop the managerial and interpersonal relations within a team. Review and upgrade the skills of a team constantly to meet current and future challenges successfully.

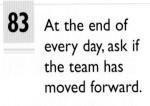

83 At the end of every day, ask if the team has moved forward.

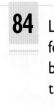

84 Listen to the feedback given by trainees about training courses.

ASSESSING COSTS

Despite the expense involved in training, it is cheaper than the cost of persisting without it, which will be damaging to performance. Calculate the costs of training, including training staff, materials, room rental, course fees, meals, travel, and loss of work hours. Weigh up these costs against the expected financial gains and improvements evident in team performance following training.

TRAINING TEAM MEMBERS

When trying to optimize the various skills in a team, involve the whole team in planning its own development. The aim is to reinforce the strengths and eliminate the weaknesses of all team members, and develop the skills necessary to seize future opportunities and face any threats. Discuss these aims with the whole team, draw up a training plan, and work out with each individual what his or her own needs are now and what will benefit projects and the team as a whole in the future.

Team member builds on existing skills

Team leader demonstrates new techniques

▲ **WORKING WITH TEAM MEMBERS**
Ask team members to evaluate their own skills and weaknesses. Encourage them to tell you where they feel they need more skills training – for example, in using specialized software. If you have relevant experience, set aside time to train them yourself.

TRAINING LEADERS

As a team leader, you should be exemplifying the qualities necessary to manage a team successfully. Ensure that you receive the requisite training to develop prioritizing, supervision, delegation, and motivating skills. Make these an integral part of your personal development plan, and ensure that team members – especially your deputies – also develop their own leadership skills. Listening carefully, criticizing constructively, being tolerant of error while correcting mistakes, and retaining objectivity are leadership qualities that members should use within a team and in future projects.

85 Find the best and best-equipped training facilities.

86 Use consultants to develop in-house training courses.

87 Use mealtimes on away days to plan informally.

▼ **OFF-SITE WORKING**
Meeting off-site enables team members to maximize their time together creatively, pool ideas, and concentrate on training without any of the usual distractions.

USING AWAY DAYS

From time to time, it can be helpful to take a team away from the workplace for a training session. Make sure that team members understand that you are planning a determined strategic work session and intend to keep firmly to the agenda. Bring in outsiders to give constructive criticism and advice. Leave the session with an agreed action plan, and make sure that individuals are accountable for each aspect of its implementation.

SETTING TARGETS

Targets are vital to the whole teamwork process. They ensure that a product is delivered to the satisfaction of the customer, schedules and budgets are adhered to, and that standards are met. They are also the yardstick on which rewards can be based.

 88 Involve everybody in target-setting to foster teamwork and consensus.

USING TARGETS TO MOTIVATE A TEAM

Successes, training, and learning are all highly motivational, and the same should be true of the way in which you communicate your expectations to your team. Motivate your team to reach specific goals by describing the ultimate set of targets as challenges that can be met through their own combined skills and effort. You can also increase team motivation by allowing members to form their own targets. Give them the opportunity to debate their aims in detail and discuss between themselves how aims can be met and possibly exceeded. It is highly motivational to set targets and succeed in outstripping them.

 89 Motivate teams by allowing them to decide how to meet targets.

CASE STUDY

Elaine was a vital backroom figure in setting up a new call center for dealing with customer inquiries. She was offered the chance to take on more responsibility, and given the option of three projects in which to become involved. She chose to work in a team monitoring the number, type, and handling of questions that came in from the public.

Having realized that some callers were not receiving the information they wanted, Elaine gave herself six months in which to reach the target of 90 percent customer satisfaction with response to the calls from the public. She began to reorganize the company's research facility and to speed up reaction times to the phone calls and improve the manner in which they were handled. She was highly motivated by the challenge she had set herself, and a marked improvement in customer satisfaction was soon obvious.

◀ **MOTIVATING INDIVIDUALS**
The challenge of being in a more responsible role, and the desire to see the project succeed, motivated an individual member of the team to set herself, and reach, an ambitious personal target.

STRETCHING TARGETS

The greatest challenge that you can present to a team is the "stretch" goal. This means setting a target that can be achieved only by using skills that extend the previous capabilities of the team. Even an already successful team can outperform its previous standards, as long as you provide them with appropriate backup. Set a stretch target with concise, well thought-out, practical, financial, and economic aims. This will provide a whole set of subsidiary targets which you should then break down into individual goals and tasks.

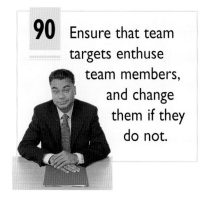

90 Ensure that team targets enthuse team members, and change them if they do not.

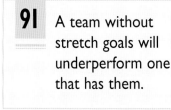

91 A team without stretch goals will underperform one that has them.

MODIFYING TARGETS

A target, stretch or not, involves a plan. If the plan is failing, and the targets are likely to be missed, find out why. Set up a meeting with the whole team to analyze the issue until you have pinpointed the problem. As a team, decide how to solve it, then do just that. Set new targets in line with the new situation. This may be more motivating than any previous plan, both because the team is solving the problem together and because, sometimes, the revised plan improves on the original.

PHRASES TO USE TO MOTIVATE A TEAM

Remember that everybody responds best to constructive leadership. Never voice any doubt about the abilities of a team, and always show confidence in their ability to reach their targets, making each team member feel appreciated.

" I know that I'm asking for the impossible – but I also know that this team can do it. "

" Thanks for a terrific job – I think you are ready for something even bigger now. "

" Why did we fail to meet that target – do you think we need to revise our original plan? "

" If we can just get through this minor setback, reaching that target will seem like smooth sailing. "

REWARDING PERFORMANCE

The object of a successful reward system is to motivate teams to improve their overall performance. Calculate rewards with care, and choose the most appropriate types. Financial and incentive-based plans – or a combination of both – are popular.

92 Allow your staff to have a say when it comes to setting reward levels.

CULTURAL DIFFERENCES

National cultural differences on rewards and performance are narrowing as companies continue to spread globally. In the US, share ownership has become common in some industries, but it is still rare in Japan. Large Europe-wide groups are now tending toward rewarding staff with performance-linked pay.

BROADCASTING FIGURES

When targets and results are used to encourage and reward performance, both sets of relevant figures must be known and accepted by all the team. Publicize the numbers – whether by fax, memo, bulletin board, electronic means, or newsletter – and explain to everyone exactly how the reward system will work. Make sure that each team member understands the bonus system, has access to the targets they are expected to reach, and can see their actual performance figures. Only then will they appreciate what they are working toward and how they will benefit – both as a team and in an individual capacity.

SETTING REWARD LEVELS

It requires judgment and experience to set a reward system at just the right level. Fix too low a rate, and team effort and morale fall off. Be too generous, and you will not stretch the team. When calculating rewards, work out what you can reasonably expect from your team by looking at their past performance, and that of similar departments and organizations. As the team gains in experience and skill, you may need to raise your sights by setting a higher reward base in order to encourage team members to continue stretching themselves and performing at their best.

93 Avoid using rankings – the team member at the bottom will become resentful.

CHOOSING REWARDS

REWARD	IMPLEMENTATION	BENEFITS TO TEAM
PAY RAISE Raise in salary not directly related to performance and with no direct teamwork element.	● Requires no extra action by the management above approval of overall salary scale and placing particular jobs within the scale. ● May go hand in hand with promotion up the job scale.	● Members of the team know where they stand financially. ● The uncertainty of variable payments is avoided. ● Can take away element of competition within team.
BONUS PAYMENT Can take several forms, including sharing of financial savings made as a result of team effort.	● Needs meaningful measures on which payments can be based. ● Can allow team to decide how gross sum should be divided. ● May reveal how members of the team regard each other.	● Members have incentive for cost-cutting and quality drives as the bonus paid out from team funds will increase. ● Acts as a good long-term motivator of individuals.
PROFIT SHARING Usually a given share of the profits is split between employees, on either corporate or divisional basis.	● Management must find a fair method of profit distribution. ● If of equal benefit to whole team, need to confront the fact that individual performances are not being singled out.	● Profit sharing is popular with employees and is a great motivator of individuals. ● Increases the sense of people belonging to a team working toward a common aim.
SHARE OWNERSHIP Rewarding team members with shares is moving down from senior levels in many corporations.	● Is directly linked to corporate results rather than individual staff performances. ● Helps to close the "us and them" gap between management and lower levels of staff.	● Pride of ownership encourages team spirit, but hinges on the share price, rather than team effort or success. ● Identifies team members with overall group results.
RECOGNITION REWARDS Possibilities are legion, ranging from formal prizes to holidays and parties.	● Management must be careful to avoid implying that doing a great job is the exception instead of the expectation. ● Encourages people to perform since rewards are motivational.	● Members love recognition, even if only verbal, and cost is often little or nothing. ● Can reward team or individual. ● The better these rewards, the better the team atmosphere.
COMPOSITE REWARDS Types of reward are often combined for maximum team and individual effect.	● Should always include and emphasize individual recognition. ● Allows management to combine individual with company-wide rewards, with elements tied to teamwork.	● Reward packages stimulate and motivate: variation helps keep interest fresh. ● All senior-level recognition of teamwork elements will help to boost team spirit and morale.

ADAPTING TO CHANGE

Managing change is fast becoming a dominant theme of management practice. The pace of change is accelerating as markets become more international and technological innovation increases. Ensure that teams adapt to external changes.

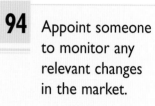

94 Appoint someone to monitor any relevant changes in the market.

95 Be prepared to change even the most fundamental elements of a plan.

ANTICIPATING CHANGE

Over the course of a team's life, it is inevitable that its tasks will change in terms of objectives, timescale, cost elements, or deadlines. To be successful, teams must be prepared to adapt quickly to new circumstances. External pressures may force changes within a team, and personnel may come and go. Make sure that team members recognize the need for change and are flexible enough to accept it, whatever form it may take.

ANALYZING TYPES OF CHANGE

TYPES OF CHANGE	EFFECTS OF CHANGE
STAFFING Team members leave and join; roles are reorganized.	● May involve a change in working practice, and a different set of objectives for the team as a whole. ● Provides an opportunity to demonstrate a fresh start.
MANAGEMENT New management strategies or policies affect team.	● Team may become responsible to a different department. ● External management supervision may intensify. ● Challenges team to prove its value by improved performance.
PROJECT Content of teamwork is radically altered.	● Internal or external circumstances force major change in the nature or timescale of project and undermine assumptions. ● Project may have to be restarted from scratch.
EFFICIENCY Leader takes a decision to improve team efficiency.	● Strengthens ability of team members to meet their targets. ● May require a new plan of action or restaffing. ● Emphasizes positive aspects of new approach.

KEEPING TEAMS INFORMED

▼ **MAKING PEOPLE AWARE OF CHANGE**

In order to avoid speculation and rumor about any upcoming changes, and to ensure that team members do not feel threatened, make a point of letting them know what is happening well in advance.

If you announce changes with enthusiasm, teams will develop a more positive attitude toward the new. Tell people about change as soon as enough detail is known for most questions to be answered, and be open with your opinions, but – as with all communication – make it a two-way exercise. Change affects every member of a team, so everyone should be given a chance to react. Listen carefully to your team's reactions – the more involved the team is in any decisions, the more likely it is to accept change, however difficult.

Leader responds to team questions when discussing change

SEIZING OPPORTUNITIES

Market fluctuations, technological advances, new competitors, or simply new tastes in the market may appear to pose a threat to teams, but even unwelcome changes can be used as a springboard for renewed progress. Try to analyze the proposed changes objectively. How can the drawbacks be offset or eliminated? How can the positive aspects be exploited? Follow this analysis by brainstorming alternative courses of action to deal with the change – and look for the plan that seems to offer the least disadvantage and the greatest opportunity for progress to everybody within the team.

96 Remember that some people are afraid of change.

97 Look for team members who can advance change.

PLANNING FUTURE GOALS FOR A TEAM

The vision that holds a team together does not end with the task at hand. Consider the future of the team both as a group and as individuals, as the career progress of each member is affected by their experience and success within the team.

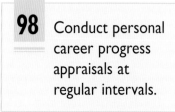

98 Conduct personal career progress appraisals at regular intervals.

DEVELOPING YOUR TEAM

The main objective of any team is to work together to succeed at a given task, and this is facilitated if individual members are constantly increasing their own skills base. Good team leaders understand that the future success of a team depends entirely on how individuals develop. Act as both coach and career counselor to the members of your team. Help to advance their careers by developing their natural talents and providing training and support, stretching challenges and realistic targets. This will be of benefit to them and also to your team.

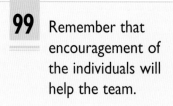

99 Remember that encouragement of the individuals will help the team.

LETTING PEOPLE GROW

The larger a team and the wider its mandate, the greater the chance for individuals to develop their careers by changing roles or being promoted within the team. While promotion is usually vertical, team careers tend to progress horizontally: people move to larger teams or those handling higher-profile projects. Do not discourage this. Help promising colleagues to find suitable positions elsewhere, internally or externally. Even in organizations where vertical promotion is harder, individuals can still progress as they move from team to team.

100 Agree on career plans and give team members any support they need.

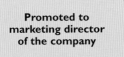

Promoted to marketing director of the company

Headhunted as manager in company making that product

Made team leader due to specialized product knowledge

Promoted to manager of sales team with a budget of $10 million

Promoted to director of sales team with a budget of $100 million

Begins career selling new product in specific market

◀ MAKING PROGRESS

This chart shows two options for career progress. Following the traditional, vertical path, progress is made by moving from one organization to another and being promoted upward. In the alternative, horizontal progress is made by moving to more powerful teams with bigger mandates.

QUESTIONS TO ASK TEAM MEMBERS

Q Where do you want your career to be in ten years?

Q Have you thought seriously about your career options?

Q Do you undewrstand that, ultimately, the smooth progress of your career is in your own hands?

Q Have you considered the experience that you need to acquire to follow your chosen career path?

Q Are you aware that your contribution toward the success of your team will help advance your career?

BUILDING CAREERS

However helpful you and other senior colleagues are, individual team members must be aware that they have the overall responsibility for their own careers. Encourage each member to regard working on the team as part of a learning process, in which all lessons can open up new opportunities, thus building up a body of qualifications to take to their next position – whether in another team, a different department, or outside the organization. Career-building, like good teamwork, will always be more effective if it is targeted. Where do team members want to be by a certain age? What do they need to qualify for that position? Help them to act on the answers to these questions, and you are providing them with a stepping stone to success.

101 Keep in touch with team members after they disperse – you may well want to work with them again.

MANAGING MEETINGS

INTRODUCTION

Meetings are a crucial element in business: many millions are held worldwide every day. Whether you are attending as a participant or as the chairperson, you can improve your handling of meetings so that they run more efficiently and effectively. The following section offers practical advice on all aspects of holding meetings, both formal and informal. Essential information is included on planning and preparing an agenda, choosing the location and arranging the seating, keeping on schedule, and closing the meeting. Throughout the section, 101 useful tips give clear and concise information to help you make a positive contribution toward achieving the objective of any meeting you attend. A self-assessment questionnaire allows you to evaluate your performance and chart your progress.

USING MEETINGS EFFECTIVELY

Meetings cost time and money, both of which are
valuable. Hold meetings only when necessary,
and ensure that they are concise and constructive.

DO YOU NEED A MEETING?

*Most managers feel pressurized by the
amount of time that they are expected
to spend in meetings. But how many meetings
really serve a useful purpose? If you were to
consider the true cost of meetings, you might
arrange – and attend – fewer of them.*

DEFINING MEETINGS

A business meeting consists of people coming
together for the purpose of resolving problems
or making decisions. A casual encounter in the
corridor between colleagues could be described
as a meeting. However, most meetings at work
are more formal, with a prearranged time and
place. They may be one-to-one meetings with a
senior manager, colleague, or client, but usually
they consist of more than two people. The
typical meeting has a clearly defined purpose
summarized in an agenda – a written list of issues
to be discussed – that is circulated in advance.

Sales manager helps
put information
in context

Sales representative
presents report

426

CONSIDERING COSTS

The best meetings save time and money by bringing together the right people to pool their knowledge for a defined purpose. However, many meetings are held unnecessarily – for example, the regular team meeting that once had a purpose then became a habit, or the meeting seen as a break from working alone. These are expensive luxuries. The biggest cost of any meeting is usually that of the participants' time – from reading the agenda and preparing materials to attending the meeting. If participants will need to travel, this time must also be taken into account. Finally, there is the "opportunity cost": what could the participants have been doing if they had not been in the meeting, and how much would that have been worth to their organization? Consider all these costs before calling a meeting.

ADDING UP COSTS

To work out a meeting's total cost, first calculate the combined salaries of all the participants. Add to this the annual cost of their respective organizations' overheads, and divide the sum by the number of working hours there are in a year (working hours per week multiplied by working weeks per year). Add any sundry hourly costs, such as room rent. This final total is the cost per hour of the meeting. Is the purpose of the meeting really worth that much money? It may well be, but you should always consider less costly but equally effective alternatives.

Managing director chairs meeting

Sales director puts questions to sales team

Secretary takes minutes

◀ **HOLDING A MEETING**

This meeting brings together members of a department and a managing director in order to resolve an issue. Based on their combined salaries of $270,000 a year, annual overheads of $150,000, and various sundry costs, the hourly cost of this meeting is $267.

427

KNOWING YOUR AIMS

Meetings can be held for any number of different reasons. The exact purpose of a meeting must always be made clear well in advance to both the chairperson and the participants. This helps everyone make the meeting a success.

1 Always be clear about the purpose of a meeting from the outset.

CONSIDERING PURPOSE

The purpose of most meetings will fall into one of the following categories. Decide in advance to which of these a particular meeting will belong, and ensure that all participants are aware of it:

2 If an issue can be resolved without a meeting, cancel the meeting.

- Imparting information or advice;
- Issuing instructions;
- Addressing grievances or arbitrating;
- Making or implementing decisions;
- Generating creative ideas;
- Presenting a proposal for discussion and, usually, for ultimate resolution.

SORTING OUT DETAILS

When you have decided what the main purpose of a meeting should be, you can begin to consider the other details. Think about how long the meeting should last, and bear in mind which issues need to be discussed and the amount of time that should be allocated to each. Remember to allow time for delegation of tasks, maybe a refreshments break, and summing up. Be sure to schedule the meeting so that the right people, with the requisite levels of authority, are able to attend. If they cannot, rearrange the meeting at a more convenient time. When it comes to meetings that are held regularly, check at frequent intervals that they continue to serve a useful purpose and do not waste time.

QUESTIONS TO ASK YOURSELF

Q Is the purpose of the meeting clear to everyone?

Q Does everyone need to attend the entire meeting?

Q Is there a better way of addressing the issues than having a meeting?

Q Are there other people who do not usually attend your meetings who might make a useful contribution this time?

Q Will the meeting benefit from the use of any visual aids?

ASSESSING PERSONAL AIMS

Whether you will be chairing a meeting or simply attending one, reflect in advance on the specific objectives of the meeting as well as on your own personal aims. There may be certain items on the agenda in which you have a particular interest, for example. Clarify in your own mind what outcomes you would consider acceptable. You can then start to prepare accordingly. Another question to consider is whether you can minimize the amount of time you spend at the meeting. If you do not need to attend the entire meeting and have decided to be present only for part of it, inform the chairperson in advance.

3 Consider carefully what makes a successful meeting and what is likely to make an unsuccessful one.

CONFIDENTIALITY ISSUES

All parties should know at an early stage in the proceedings if they will be dealing with any confidential issues in a meeting, since this may affect the approach of the participants. All confidential items must be handled appropriately, and confidentiality must always be respected outside the meeting room. If an agenda will contain a mixture of confidential and nonconfidential items, ensure that the status of each item is made clear to all of the participants in advance.

REINFORCING OBJECTIVES

If you are chairing a meeting, start the proceedings by summarizing its aims and objectives, so that all the participants can keep them in mind for the duration of the meeting. Remind the participants of the decisions to be reached and by when, and what information will be conveyed. If they stray from the point, draw their attention to the amount of time that has been allocated to the discussion of each issue. If you are simply an attendee at a meeting, ensure that you are well prepared for thorough discussion of any issues that particularly concern you.

4 Consider what would happen if a regular meeting were not held.

▼ YOUR CRITICAL PATH
Until you have decided upon your aims, you cannot decide the sort of meeting you need. Determine them and the length of the meeting, then invite the participants.

| Define the meeting's purpose | Decide how long it should last | Ensure the relevant people attend |

Meeting Informally

Informal meetings take several different forms and can be a useful forum for discussion. Whether they happen by chance or are organized in a casual manner, such as by word of mouth, make the most of these opportunities for resolving matters simply.

5 Remember that the presence of senior managers may inhibit discussion.

6 Hold meetings away from your work space so that you can leave easily.

▼ **RESOLVING ISSUES**
Use an impromptu meeting, for example with a colleague in a corridor, in order to attempt to resolve an issue immediately.

SETTING THE SCENE

Informal meetings, despite their casual nature, still benefit from well-chosen surroundings. A fruitful discussion is unlikely if participants feel uncomfortable or if they are attempting to discuss confidential issues in an open-plan office. Select the right surroundings to encourage the outcome you are seeking.

IMPROMPTU MEETINGS

Meetings called at very short notice, and those that happen in passing or on the spur of the moment, are termed "impromptu." They are ideal for discussing issues frankly and reaching decisions quickly without being impeded by the presence of large numbers of people. Use them to best effect in order to resolve minor problems simply by calling together a maximum of three or four people. Alternatively, use them to make urgent announcements. Between colleagues, impromptu meetings tend to be characterized by casual verbal style and relaxed body language. Set an informal atmosphere: this will help you interpret the reactions of other people in the meeting. Look out for facial expressions; because participants may be off their guard, their expressions are likely to be genuine.

SMALL INFORMAL MEETINGS

Useful for discussing, problem-solving, and giving feedback, small informal meetings are planned – therefore they allow for preparation time, in contrast to impromptu meetings. Even when running a small informal meeting consisting of just two or three people, keep the purpose of the meeting (and a time limit) in mind. Control the meeting properly, and you can keep the subject matter moving along while at the same time allowing for open conversation between participants. Encourage this by maintaining eye contact – the most expressive form of body communication – with them.

▼ DISCUSSING ISSUES
If you are leading a discussion, make sure that you make a lot of positive eye contact to help you retain control of the meeting.

▼ SHARING IDEAS
Small brainstorming meetings are a good forum for sharing ideas freely. If you are in control of a brainstorming meeting, ask someone to note ideas down as they are mentioned. This written record often sparks other suggestions.

BRAINSTORMING SESSIONS

Use informal brainstorming sessions to generate new ideas or elicit quick ideas for solutions to problems. For the best results, explain the purpose and time limit of the meeting in advance so that participants can prepare. Brainstorming is most effective with a small group of people who have a range of approaches and expertise, so ask everyone to contribute in turn. Avoid criticizing or judging the ideas during the meeting, since this inhibits suggestions; judge their feasibility afterward.

MEETING FORMALLY

*E*ach *of the various different types of formal meeting has different rules of procedure. Some meetings, such as annual general meetings, must be convened by law; others are voluntary and are called to make a particular decision or to discuss an issue.*

 7 Familiarize yourself with the different types of formal meeting procedure.

FORMAL MEETINGS

TYPE OF MEETING	CHARACTERISTICS
BOARD MEETING A board meeting is attended by the board of a company, usually consisting of its directors. In some countries, the board must exercise its powers collectively by law.	● Board meetings usually take place at regular intervals, perhaps once a month, to discuss company business. Meetings usually take place in a board room – traditionally a formal space with a large table. ● A board meeting is chaired by the chairperson, who is elected according to the rules of the company.
STANDING COMMITTEE A standing committee is a subgroup of a company board. It may be given responsibility for recurring tasks, such as the annual review of a chief executive's salary and performance.	● A standing committee meets regularly to fulfill its delegated tasks. ● The board of a company may authorize a standing committee to act in its place. ● A standing committee may report back to a company board, which will then implement any necessary action.
AD HOC COMMITTEE A company board may establish an ad hoc committee to look at an issue that needs particular attention. Such a subgroup may meet more regularly than the full board.	● Ad hoc committees can meet as and when necessary to discuss specific issues that require specialist expertise or to look at complicated problems in detail. ● Many company boards find it difficult to meet more than once a month; an ad hoc committee can meet regularly and need only involve the necessary individuals.
PUBLIC MEETING A public meeting is open to anyone. This type of forum may be used by local government or private action groups wishing to consult the public on various issues, or by companies wanting to discuss developments.	● All members of the general public are invited to attend public meetings, which are usually advertised in advance at local community centers, in public libraries, and in local newspapers or magazines. ● An agenda for a public meeting usually consists of only one main issue for discussion.

FOLLOWING THE RULES

The rules that govern formal meetings can be complicated and vary from country to country and organization to organization. Rules may dictate the amount of advance notice that must be given for a meeting, the rights of people to attend, or the procedures to be followed in the event of a vote. If you are involved in formal meetings, find out in advance which set of rules you should follow.

 8 Be aware of any legal requirements that are entailed in formal meetings.

TYPE OF MEETING

CONFERENCE
A conference is a meeting at which several presentations are given on one theme. Some conferences are open to the public; others are for a restricted group, such as company employees.

EXTERNAL MEETING
An external meeting consists of a group of people from one organization and another group from outside that organization – for example, visiting trade-union negotiators.

ANNUAL GENERAL MEETING (AGM)
An AGM is a yearly, often mandatory, gathering of a company's directors and shareholders to discuss business during the past year and future plans.

EXTRAORDINARY GENERAL MEETING (EGM)
An EGM is a meeting that can be called at any time between AGMs if shareholder approval is needed for immediate action.

CHARACTERISTICS

- This type of meeting is ideal for communicating information to a large number of people at once and in a short space of time.
- Due to their size, conferences allow little scope for discussion or audience participation, although speakers may hold question-and-answer sessions.

- Confidentiality is an important issue in external meetings. Participants should think carefully about which information must remain private and which may be disclosed in the meeting in order to achieve its ends.
- External meetings can be held on neutral ground.

- An AGM allows shareholders to question company directors and hold them accountable for the company's performance.
- Directors use this opportunity to seek approval of annual accounts, reappoint auditors, and to discuss future plans and policies.

- Shareholders should be given a certain amount of notice of an EGM. How much notice varies from country to country.
- The rules governing the procedure of an EGM are usually the same as those governing the procedures of an AGM.

REVOLUTIONIZING COMMUNICATIONS

Computer and communication technology (together known as information technology, or IT) is advancing so rapidly that fewer face-to-face meetings are needed. Use these sophisticated tools to reduce the time you spend attending meetings.

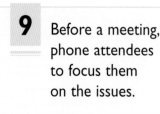

9 Before a meeting, phone attendees to focus them on the issues.

VIRTUAL COMMUNICATION

Digital technology is revolutionizing traditional methods of exchanging information, greatly reducing the need for travel. Digital alternatives to face-to-face meetings include telephone conference calls; real-time, on-line video conferencing; and e-mail and Internet messages. Consider these options before scheduling distant meetings.

10 Be selective with information, and avoid overload.

VIDEO CONFERENCING

The video conference, using real-time audio and video links, is now a widely used and increasingly user-friendly way of holding a meeting. Provided you have the required technology in place, you can use this method as you would use telephone conferencing to link individuals from all around the globe. Video conferencing has the advantage of revealing body language and facial expressions – often key elements in effective communication.

11 Take into account global time differences when organizing and setting up conference calls.

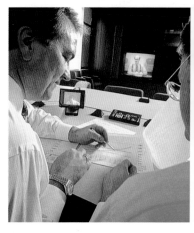

▲ VIDEO PARTICIPATION
Mix traditional and new approaches to suit your needs. For instance, let those unable to attend an meeting join in via video.

12 Optimize an on-line meeting by setting a time limit.

13 Repeat your name when you speak during a telephone conference call.

CULTURAL DIFFERENCES

Traditional barriers to cross-cultural business communication include different languages, different time zones, and traveling times between countries – as well as different cultural expectations. However, many of these difficulties are diminishing with the aid of information technology. E-mail provides a ready channel of communication, regardless of location or time zone. The widespread use of English, which can deter nonnative speakers from formal communication, is less of a problem when it comes to e-mail, since messages tend to be relatively short and informal, with little need for sophisticated use of language.

E-MAIL CORRESPONDENCE

Electronic mail (e-mail) facilitates the sending and receiving of written communication via the Internet at great speed and frequency. This can amount to a different kind of meeting, extending over days and even weeks, as participants join a "virtual" conference site and comment on a current issue or problem, or discuss a range of topics. Within organizations, this enables a wide cross-section of employees from different departments – and different sites – to participate in discussions without going to the trouble and expense of meeting physically. Unnecessary information, however, can quickly accumulate. Try to keep all messages short and to the point – this will help limit the agenda of the "conference."

▼ **EFFECTIVE LINKUPS**
Video conferencing allows you to communicate fully even when you cannot meet. Make the most of all tools available to you, including written material and the full range of body language.

CHOOSING THE RIGHT TYPE OF MEETING

There are many types of meeting – formal and informal – and each type suits a particular purpose. For this reason, you must decide which type is most likely to achieve your purpose before you begin to make arrangements and notify participants.

14 Always think carefully about the type of meeting you need to hold.

15 Keep meetings as small as possible to help minimize distractions.

CONSIDERING FACTORS

Once you have decided that you need to hold a meeting, the next step is to consider a number of factors, such as the urgency of the meeting. Should it be held immediately? Who needs to attend? What do you want to achieve from the meeting? Bearing in mind these questions and your core aim, choose the type of meeting that is most appropriate. For example, a one-to-one meeting or a formal committee meeting is usually best suited to decision-making, while brainstorming sessions may be good for sharing ideas.

DECIDING MEETING SIZE

The purpose of a meeting will influence its ideal size. There are advantages and disadvantages to both large and small meetings: large groups of people hold diverse opinions but the members are likely to split into cliques, whereas small groups can act together more productively but may have a narrower range of views. The popular meeting size of between six and nine participants is small enough to control, yet large enough to provoke debate. Meetings of this size encourage attendance since participants know that they will be heard.

16 Place a watch or clock in a prominent position so you are able to keep an eye on the time.

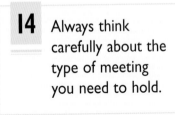

MATCHING THE PURPOSE OF A MEETING TO THE TYPE

PURPOSE	CONSIDERATIONS	MEETING TYPE
DEALING WITH INFORMATION For example, giving or receiving reports, issuing instructions, or announcing and explaining procedural change.	Concerns up to three people	Informal
	Concerns four or more people or a team	Formal
	Requires feedback and discussion	Informal or formal
	Keeps company directors up to date	Formal
	Involves shareholders	AGM or EGM
	Involves informing as many people as possible outside an organization, including the media	Public
	Involves speakers providing information	Conference
RESOLVING PROBLEMS For example, handling grievances.	Concerns only one person	One-to-one
	Requires input from several people or a team	Ad hoc committee
	Concerns urgent problem	Impromptu
MAKING DECISIONS For example, choosing between options, obtaining authorization, or committing to a course of action.	Needs quick discussion, or concerns nonstandard business matter	Impromptu
	Involves recurring business matters	Formal
	Requires discussion or authorization at the highest level of an organization	Board
	Requires authorization from the shareholders of a company	AGM or EGM
ENCOURAGING IDEAS For example, generating creative solutions.	Needs creative ideas to be discussed	Informal
	Needs fresh ideas to be generated quickly	Brainstorming
	Needs reports on issues to be considered, discussed, and prepared	Formal

KEEPING ON TRACK

There are various reasons why some meetings do not achieve their objectives. Attendees may have conflicting aims, the meeting may lose direction, or the agenda may be too long to cover in the time. Agreeing to goals in advance will help you reach them.

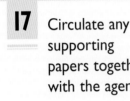

17 Circulate any supporting papers together with the agenda.

THINKING AHEAD

Before any meeting, it is important to think ahead and plan carefully to ensure that the meeting goes smoothly. First, circulate a clear agenda. Make sure that you allow enough time for the meeting so that you do not end up rushing through major items on the agenda. Identify people who may try to hijack your meeting, and anticipate their arguments. Seek out those who you think may share your opinions, and encourage them to support your case.

18 Canvass support from possible allies in advance of the meeting.

AVOIDING PITFALLS

Most of the pitfalls that arise in meetings can be avoided by good preparation and participation by all attendees. Be sure to always:

- Study all the material that has been circulated in advance of a meeting;
- Start and finish the meeting on time;
- Follow the agenda scrupulously;
- If chairing the meeting, involve others as much as possible in questions and answers;
- Make sure that participants are fully aware of the decisions that have been reached.

When the last item on the agenda – usually called "Any Other Business" – is reached, attendees may start talking over each other, raising minor points. If you are chairing the meeting, allow everyone to have their say in an orderly fashion.

19 Make sure the aim of a meeting is agreed before the meeting starts.

20 Remind people of the agenda whenever they stray from it.

RUNNING A MEETING

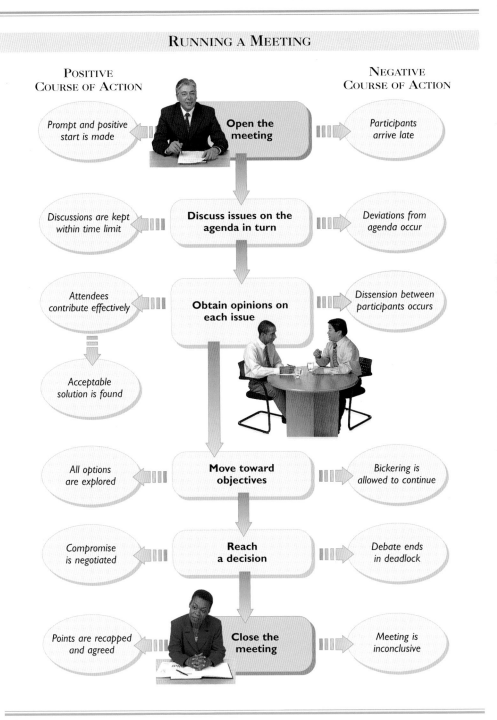

POSITIVE
COURSE OF ACTION

NEGATIVE
COURSE OF ACTION

Prompt and positive
start is made

**Open the
meeting**

Participants
arrive late

Discussions are kept
within time limit

**Discuss issues on the
agenda in turn**

Deviations from
agenda occur

Attendees
contribute effectively

**Obtain opinions on
each issue**

Dissension between
participants occurs

Acceptable
solution is found

All options
are explored

**Move toward
objectives**

Bickering is
allowed to continue

Compromise
is negotiated

**Reach
a decision**

Debate ends
in deadlock

Points are recapped
and agreed

**Close the
meeting**

Meeting is
inconclusive

PREPARING FOR A MEETING

Time spent preparing for a meeting is rarely wasted.
Ensure that the right people attend at the right
time and place and that they reach the right decisions.

INVITING PARTICIPANTS

*Choosing the right people to attend a
meeting may determine whether its
aims are achieved. Each participant should
be attending because they can make a specific
contribution; otherwise, the meeting will not
be making the best use of their time.*

21 Consider how
participants
will work in a
group setting.

22 Consider travel
times before you
schedule a meeting.

23 Rearrange a
meeting if people
cannot attend.

SELECTING ATTENDEES

When you are considering whom to invite,
certain people will probably present themselves as
obvious choices. For example, if a loan is to be
discussed, you should invite someone who can
authorize the agreed amount. Others may be able
to contribute specific skills or advice. Invite
individuals whose communication skills will help
the group work productively and achieve set goals.
If some participants are needed for only part of a
meeting, give them estimated start and finish
times for the relevant items. This will save time
and make the meeting easier to control.

EVALUATING CONTRIBUTIONS

When you have made an initial list of participants, pinpoint the the potential contribution of each person in turn:

- Do they have information to share? For example, a sales manager reporting on customer reactions.
- Can they offer specific advice or information? For example, a production manager.
- Is their professional status is useful? For example, a lawyer in a contract dispute.
- Can they implement agreed action? For example, a finance director at a budget meeting.

 24 List speakers' names by each item on an agenda.

CONSIDERING PARTICIPANTS

PROVIDING INFORMATION
An individual from one part of a company, such as production or sales, may be invited to inform other company members about progress in their department.

OFFERING ADVICE
A person's current involvement with a particular issue, or their past experience, may qualify them to offer helpful advice to other participants.

OFFERING SPECIALIZED EXPERTISE
The presence of a person with specialized skills, either from inside or outside a company, may facilitate discussion.

AUTHORIZING ACTION
Financial decisions in particular, such as signing or negotiating a new contract, may require the presence of a financial director to authorize the action.

NOTIFYING ATTENDEES

One of the hardest parts of organizing a meeting is finding an appropriate time to suit all those you wish to invite. Sometimes the easiest way to set a meeting is to arrange for it to follow an earlier one attended by the same people. Otherwise, e-mail messages and telephone calls can go back and forth until a date is set. If you find that someone cannot make the proposed date, consider whether it is feasible to hold the meeting without them before you rearrange times. Always send written confirmation of the time and place.

POINTS TO REMEMBER

- Attendees should be informed clearly of the date, time, place, and purpose of a meeting.
- Attendees should understand what they will need to contribute to the meeting.
- Background papers should be sent before the meeting to all the participants.
- The location must be suitably equipped and should be an appropriate size.

PREPARING AN AGENDA

The best way to ensure that those attending a meeting are sure about its purpose is to send them a clear agenda well in advance. There are several ways to prepare an agenda, so find and utilize the one best suited to your purposes.

25 Avoid meeting at low-energy times of the day, such as right after lunch.

COMPILING AGENDAS

An agenda for a meeting is essentially a list of items or issues that need to be raised and debated. It should be short, simple, and clear. First, gather all relevant information, then sort out which items need to be discussed and in how much detail. You may find it useful to consult with other participants. If there are many issues to discuss, assign a time limit to each to help ensure that you do not overrun the allotted duration of the meeting. How far in advance you begin to prepare an agenda will depend on how much preparation time is needed.

26 Ensure the chairperson is informed of any agenda changes.

WRITING AN AGENDA ▶
Use this simple agenda as a model when compiling agendas for similar meetings. Number each item, then assign a start time to each for the benefit of any attendees who are not needed for the entire meeting.

Each item is numbered

27 Keep an agenda as short and simple as possible.

Committee Meeting Agenda
July 6th, 11 a.m.
Green Dragon Hotel

1. (11:00) Appoint a chairperson
2. (11:10) Apologies for absence
3. (11:15) Approve last meeting's minutes
4. (11:30) Matters arising from last meeting
5. (11:45) Correspondence
   (12:00) Refreshments
6. (12:15) Finances
7. (12:45) Special business
8. (1:00) Other motions
9. (1:15) Any other business
10. (1:35) Next meeting's details

Agenda is headed with date, time, and location of meeting

Start time is allocated for each item

Details of next meeting are included at end of agenda

28 Try to restrict an agenda to one sheet of paper.

POINTS TO REMEMBER

● An agenda should contain details of the meeting's date, time, place, and purpose.

● An agenda should be as specific as possible about the main purpose of the meeting.

● All participants need to know exactly what is expected of them in a meeting.

● The time devoted to each item should be indicative of its priority.

● Time allocation should err on the generous side. Nobody minds if a meeting ends early, but overrunning is unpopular.

STRUCTURING AN AGENDA

When you come to compile your meeting's agenda, try to order topics logically and group similar items together. This prevents the risk of going over the same ground again and again. Your agenda should start off with "housekeeping" matters, such as the appointment of a chairperson and apologies for any absences, before moving on to approving the minutes of the last meeting (if relevant) and hearing reports from those assigned tasks at the previous meeting. The next items covered at the meeting should be current issues – for example, the latest financial accounts and sales figures – about which the bulk of the discussion is likely to occur. Finally, allow for any other business and plan to set the date, time, and location of the next meeting.

29 Discuss the most important items early in the proceedings, when participants are most alert.

DISTRIBUTING AN AGENDA

Once you have drafted an agenda, send it to the other participants for comments, additions, or approval. If you wish to add or delete items from a formally approved agenda, you will need to obtain the consent of the participants. They will be more likely to agree to a deletion than an addition, unless they have a particular interest in an item you wish to drop. It is not acceptable to present participants with a revised agenda as they arrive at a meeting unless last-minute events have made it necessary – for example, because of illness of the chairperson or a sudden change in financial circumstances. Distribute the final agenda as far as possible in advance of the meeting.

THINGS TO DO

1. Decide which issues need to be raised at the meeting.

2. Send a draft agenda to all attendees, inviting their suggestions for other items.

3. Incorporate any suggestions into the next draft.

4. Recirculate the agenda to all the meeting's attendees, ask for their approval, then make it final.

LOCATING A MEETING

The choice of location is vitally important to the success of a meeting. It is not only a question of comfort; participants must also feel that the place is appropriate to the occasion. This is true for all meetings, small or large, formal or informal.

 30 Consider the cost in time for those needing to travel long distances.

RECOGNIZING YOUR NEEDS

Try to match the location of a meeting to its aims. If one of the objectives of the meeting is to encourage two groups of people to get to know each other better, a relaxed out-of-town atmosphere may be appropriate. By the same token, do not hold a formal meeting in a messy open-plan office. For meetings within your organization, there is still a choice – you must decide whether home, neutral, or away territory is more suited to your needs.

 31 Ensure that there are facilities available for any disabled attendees.

DECIDING ON A SITE

If you are arranging a meeting that requires rental of rooms and other facilities, shop around to compare prices, especially if you are operating on a tight budget. You may find you can negotiate a discount. Locations in the centers of large cities may be convenient for most attendees and be well served by public transportation, but space in a city center will almost certainly be more expensive than a less central equivalent. An out-of-town location will provide fewer distractions for participants, which can be especially valuable if the meeting lasts for more than one day. On the other hand, the amenities of a city may help entice people to a meeting lasting several days. Weigh your priorities, then make your choice of location for your meeting accordingly.

LEGAL CONCERNS

By law, certain people must be invited to certain meetings, such as companies' annual meetings of shareholders – although some unscrupulous companies have been known to hold meetings at inconvenient locations or times to push through unpopular proposals. It is illegal to set a date and time for an AGM that are designed to prevent the shareholders from voting, and it is illegal to stage public meetings in inaccessible places.

ASSESSING ENVIRONMENT

Physical factors play an important part in any type of meeting. Whatever the occasion, aim to make attendees comfortable enough to concentrate, but not so comfortable that they fall asleep. Check that external noise will be kept to a minimum and heating and ventilation are effective but not excessive. Rooms in big hotels often have excellent air conditioning but little natural light, yet this can be vital for maintaining a dynamic atmosphere.

32 Make sure phone calls are diverted away from the meeting room.

CONSIDERING DIFFERENT TYPES OF LOCATION

LOCATION	FACTORS TO CONSIDER
YOUR OFFICE Your work station or a meeting table with a few extra chairs.	● All your reference material is at hand. ● Your authority may be enhanced. ● Telephones may ring or people interrupt.
SUBORDINATE'S OFFICE A subordinate's work space.	● May boost the status or morale of a subordinate. ● Attendees may feel physically uncomfortable if the workspace is small.
ON-SITE MEETING ROOM A company meeting room for the use of staff members.	● Avoids issues of company hierarchy that can arise when using an individual's office. ● Outsiders may interrupt to contact the attendees.
OFF-SITE MEETING ROOM A neutral meeting space outside your organization.	● Ensures neither party dominates on "home" ground. ● Can be useful if secrecy is important. ● May be expensive and be unfamiliar to everyone.
CONFERENCE CENTER A large facility, such as at a university, which is regularly available.	● Has the capacity to accommodate large numbers. ● Can provide technical support and security if required. ● May lack opportunities for small, informal get-togethers.
OUT OF TOWN An office, meeting space, or hotel in another location.	● Convenient if attendees come from all over the world. ● Adds a degree of glamour to an occasion. ● High costs in terms of travel, time, and accommodation.

AVOIDING PITFALLS

There are a number of reasons – some obvious, some less so – why a location may turn out to be a bad choice. When you are inspecting and booking your site, try to anticipate and avoid the following common pitfalls:

- More people attend than expected – there is insufficient room and people are uncomfortable;
- Fewer people attend than expected, leaving an intimidatingly large and empty space to fill;
- Air conditioning is inadequate and the room becomes stuffy, or it is on too high and not accessible for regulation;
- Technical difficulties arise because the light switches and plugs in the meeting room are not checked and labeled;
- There is a lack of services, such as banks or restaurants, at or near the meeting site.

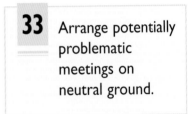

33 Arrange potentially problematic meetings on neutral ground.

POINTS TO REMEMBER

- Unfamiliar locations should be visited at least once before a meeting.
- It is useful for a room to have windows that can be opened or closed as temperatures fluctuate.
- Speakers need to know where thermostats and light switches are located.
- Toilets and other facilities should be clearly marked.
- Seats should be tested for comfort by sitting in them for at least 10 minutes.

34 Ask your support staff to check the availability, schedules, and variations of local public transportation.

CASE STUDY

Following a company's expansion, the accounts department had problems dealing with the sales people, so the accounts manager set up a meeting in a room convenient for the sales department to discuss ways to work together.

However, the room was too small, and more chairs were needed. Due to lack of space, some people had to stand, blocking others' views

of the flip chart the accounts manager was using. The air conditioning was ineffective and the windows did not open, so the room became hot and stuffy. A door was opened, but this let in noise from the office outside. The accounts manager was called away by phone. Several other people then left in annoyance. The manager returned and asked for suggestions, but few responded. No practical solutions were produced.

◀ **CHOOSING THE WRONG LOCATION**

This case shows that, despite every good intention, a poor meeting site actually damaged relations between two teams instead of improving them. More positive results might have been obtained had the two teams met on neutral territory with no interruptions and enough space for all involved in the discussion.

FOCUSING ON ACOUSTICS

A well-structured meeting room does not guarantee a good meeting, but it can increase the chances markedly. Keep in mind your meeting's objectives. The main purpose of most meetings is to share information verbally with others, so good acoustics are essential. Even a handful of people in a small room can have problems hearing each other, but acoustics are especially important for meetings with numerous participants. If there is a visual element – for example, if visual aids are to be used – both acoustics and visibility must be good, and you will need to avoid placing chairs anywhere with a restricted view.

35 Find a room that you are sure will be free from interruptions.

◀ FLOURISHING IN THE RIGHT ATMOSPHERE
A big turnout helps the atmosphere, as do good acoustics, lighting, and seating. If the audience is not distracted, it can pay attention to the speaker, who is encouraged to communicate well.

CASE STUDY

An advertising agency arranged to meet a potential client to discuss a campaign. The client operated from a small, open-plan building a considerable distance away, so the agency suggested using a hotel with conference facilities that was close to the client.

A week before the meeting, a member of the agency visited the hotel to check the room and found a multimedia system and a huge table. He asked for the table to be removed and requested standard audio-visual equipment, since he knew the agency had prepared their presentation using such equipment. On the day of the meeting, the agency executives arrived early to practice their pitch and arrange the seating in a semicircle. The blinds and air conditioning were adjusted and refreshments ordered.

The presentation ran very smoothly, and the agency won the new account.

◀ PROVIDING THE PERFECT LOCATION
As this case illustrates, organizing everything ahead of time plus having a practice run meant that the advertising agency could forestall any potential problems and was able to concentrate on its presentation. In addition, the agency here made a wise decision in rejecting the impressive state-of-the-art hardware in favor of older but more appropriate equipment.

SEATING PARTICIPANTS

The placement of the participants in a meeting can have an enormous impact on the success of that meeting. Consider the seating arrangements in advance and, if necessary, draw up a seating plan to give a meeting the best chance of achieving its goals.

36 Consider several seating plans before choosing the most appropriate one.

MEETING ONE TO ONE

In a one-to-one meeting, the placement of the two individuals can set the tone of the meeting and influence the course of discussion. If you are holding the meeting, influence the degree of formality by arranging the seating appropriately. There are three main examples of one-to-one seating positions to choose from: supporting, collaborating, and confronting. To find out what the other participant perceives the tone of a meeting to be, set four chairs around a table, take your seat before the other person arrives, and watch where he or she sits.

▲ **SUPPORTING**
If you wish to be supportive, sit at right angles to the other person. This helps break down barriers and allows eye contact.

◀ **COLLABORATING**
Sit next to the other person to suggest collaboration. This arrangement implies a similarity of opinions.

◀ **CONFRONTING**
Sit on opposite sides of the table to distance yourself from the other person. This position enables disagreements to be aired more freely.

37 Use a round table for meetings with an informal tone.

SEATING GROUPS

The purpose of a large meeting should determine its seating arrangements. When seating a group of people around a table, there are three basic options using two table shapes. If there is potential for negotiation or confrontation, select a rectangular table at which the two "sides" can sit opposite each other, placing a neutral chairperson in the center of one side. To reinforce a sense of hierarchy in a meeting, seat the chairperson at the head of the table. For more informal, nonhierarchical meetings, choose a round table around which everyone can be seated as equals. If a meeting with a substantial number of people will be held in an auditorium or sizeable room, arrange the seating in rows facing the chairperson.

CULTURAL DIFFERENCES

Hierarchy is more important in some cultures than in others. In parts of Asia, age carries great weight, so the oldest person at a meeting is given the most senior position. Other cultures attach importance to titles, so that a junior vice president would never be seated in a more senior position than a president.

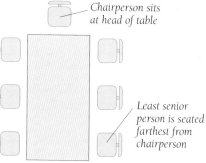

Chairperson sits at head of table

Chairperson sits between team members

Least senior person is seated farthest from chairperson

▲ CONFRONTING OPPOSITION

When you are discussing issues or intending to make decisions, sit parties with opposing points of view on either side of a rectangular table.

▲ INDICATING HIERARCHY

If you wish to indicate hierarchy, put the chairperson at the head of a rectangular table and seat the other attendees in descending order of authority.

DISCUSSING FREELY ▶

Use a round table for a meeting in which open discussion takes precedence over the status of the participants.

38 Make sure all the participants can see and be seen.

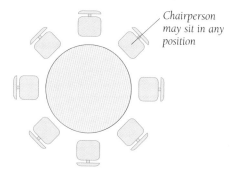

Chairperson may sit in any position

USING TACTICAL SEATING

The significance of seating positions depends on where the chairperson sits. Traditionally, this is at the head of the table, while the seat to the right is a privileged one. However, this need not be the case.

Tactical seating is based on an assumption that participants are influenced by the people they are near to. Decide what you want from a meeting, and arrange the seating to help you achieve this. For controversial issues, split up factions and avoid seating people with violently opposed – or very similar – ideas next to each other. This polarizes opinion and prevents the discussion from spreading. When drawing up a seating plan, base it on your knowledge and research of the attendees' views on the issues being discussed. Eye contact is crucial for indicating to members of your own team which steps you want to take next. Ask yourself who should be able to make eye contact with whom, and seat people accordingly.

39 Seat people an arm's length away from each other.

40 Avoid seating participants in direct sunlight.

▼ **DISPERSING OPPOSITION**
When drawing up a seating plan, base it on the participants' opinions on the most contentious issue being discussed. This will help disperse opposition to the item.

KEY
- 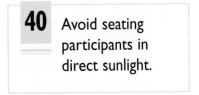 Chairperson
- Undecided
- Supporter
- Opponent
- —— Sightlines

Undecided attendee looks to chairperson for leadership

Opponent sits opposite chairperson to play large part in discussion

Undecided participant can clearly see and hear all points of view

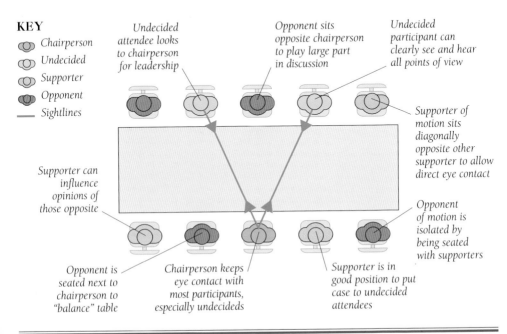

Supporter can influence opinions of those opposite

Supporter of motion sits diagonally opposite other supporter to allow direct eye contact

Opponent of motion is isolated by being seated with supporters

Opponent is seated next to chairperson to "balance" table

Chairperson keeps eye contact with most participants, especially undecideds

Supporter is in good position to put case to undecided attendees

OBSERVING SEATING

When there is no formal seating plan for a meeting, observe where other attendees sit, and select your own seat accordingly. Where someone sits may reveal how they feel about the issues under discussion and what role they wish to play in the meeting. A forceful opponent may choose a commanding position near the chairperson. Sitting in the middle may suggest a wish to participate fully or a desire to dominate the conversation at that part of the table. If you are the chairperson, try to persuade the loudest, most outspoken person to sit directly opposite you.

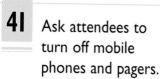

41 Ask attendees to turn off mobile phones and pagers.

▼ INTERPRETING SEATING PATTERNS

There are benefits to be gained from any seat at a meeting table, depending on what you want to achieve. Learn to "read" other attendees' aims from where they sit.

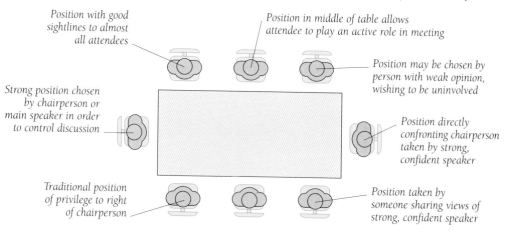

Position with good sightlines to almost all attendees

Position in middle of table allows attendee to play an active role in meeting

Strong position chosen by chairperson or main speaker in order to control discussion

Position may be chosen by person with weak opinion, wishing to be uninvolved

Position directly confronting chairperson taken by strong, confident speaker

Traditional position of privilege to right of chairperson

Position taken by someone sharing views of strong, confident speaker

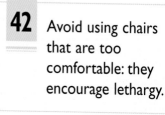

42 Avoid using chairs that are too comfortable: they encourage lethargy.

PRESENTING YOUR CASE

The presentation of your case will be affected by where you sit in relation to your audience. Plan others' seating to benefit your cause. Seating an audience around you implies a collaborative and informal discussion, which may not help you sway opinions. Distancing your audience by standing in front of them, sitting on a platform, or sitting behind a desk will increase your authority and presence but may discourage two-way discussion and make it harder to gauge their mood.

PREPARING PRACTICALITIES

The success of most meetings greatly depends on advance preparation and organization. This includes providing suitable facilities and materials for the occasion – including the meeting rooms, any audio-visual aids, and writing materials.

43 Make sure all audio-visual aids are working before a meeting begins.

THINGS TO DO

1. Check that refreshments have been ordered.
2. Check that the restroom facilities are adequate.
3. Ensure that there is ample parking available.
4. Take copies of background papers in case some participants have lost theirs.
5. Make sure the electrical system is adequate.

ORGANIZING A LOCATION

At your location, you may have only a limited amount of time available to check out the facilities, prepare the seating, set up audio-visual aids such as projectors and screens, and distribute agendas or background papers. If this is the case, consider enlisting extra help for the preparations before the meeting and for clearing up afterward.

When using an on-site meeting room, check the day before the meeting that the room has not been double-booked. Reserve for longer than you need for the meeting to allow for setup and removing any equipment. Check that the seating facilities are adequate for your needs, and make sure the room is neat before and after the meeting.

CHOOSING AUDIO-VISUAL AIDS

Audio-visual (AV) aids are used more and more in large meetings, presentations, and conferences to emphasize the points under discussion.

Such aids can range from basic flip charts to sophisticated rear-projection video screens. Whenever AV aids are required, always rehearse their use before the meeting. Make sure you are familiar with the controls, that the equipment works, and that your aids can be seen from all seats. If necessary, enlist technical support.

44 Beware of sites that overbook to make extra profit.

45 Ensure that special dietary needs are provided for.

PROVIDING WRITING AIDS

The need for speed or accuracy when taking notes at a meeting and the style of the occasion – formal or informal – will influence participants' choice of writing aids. In certain types of meeting (press conferences, for example), attendees may use recorders, laptop computers, or personal organizers to record information. In most meetings, however, notes are still taken on paper.

Provide participants with a notepad and pens or pencils to avoid the potential delays and disturbances that occur when people have to look for their own. Make this an opportunity to gain some free publicity by issuing notepads or pens imprinted with your company's logo, name, address, and telephone number.

PERSONAL ORGANIZER

RECORDER

NOTEPAD AND PEN

▲ **TAKING NOTES**
Provide basic writing materials, such as notepads and pens; attendees may bring their own recorders or organizers.

ORGANIZING BREAKS

In the course of a long meeting, you may want to break for refreshments, even if you are providing water or hot drinks during the meeting. Use breaks to give participants a chance to discuss matters informally in small groups before reconvening. Avoid serving substantial food during breaks; otherwise, attendees may become drowsy.

COFFEE

HOLDING LARGE MEETINGS

At a large public meeting or conference, the organization is as important as the content. Bad planning, technical hitches, and poor facilities will distract from the factual content of the meeting. Attendees are also more likely to remember your message if the event runs smoothly. Check that large numbers of people can enter and leave the room easily, that you have set out enough seating, and that attendees can see any AV displays. Provide a public address system (PA) or separate microphones, loudspeakers, and amplifiers. Ensure that all the speakers know how to adjust and handle the equipment, and provide them with technical or any other necessary assistance.

46 Avoid consuming too much alcohol before a meeting – it often impairs productivity.

ATTENDING A MEETING

It is the responsibility of each participant at a meeting to ensure that it attains its objectives. Prepare in advance and actively contribute to make every meeting productive.

TAKING AN ACTIVE ROLE

As a participant in a meeting, it is vital to be well briefed. Focus on the aims of the meeting by reading the agenda and any previous minutes in advance. Consider your expected role and how you would like to contribute, then prepare accordingly.

47 Work out what you want to say before a meeting begins.

POINTS TO REMEMBER

- Background research is essential for any contribution.
- Contacting other participants before a meeting breaks the ice and allows for a useful exchange of information.
- Personal rivalries between participants must be identified.
- It may be necessary to canvass support on big issues in advance.
- Participants can be sounded out in advance of a meeting.

GATHERING INFORMATION

Carry out some basic but thorough background research before a meeting to help you to make an informed and valid contribution. Gather information by collecting new data – for instance, by talking to colleagues and experts, or reading relevant publications and research material – or by consulting old notes, minutes of meetings, or company records. Your preparation should also include some research on the other attendees. Detailed preparation at this stage will enable you to take an appropriate approach that is carefully targeted at attaining your objectives.

IDENTIFYING OPPOSITION

Before a meeting, try to discover other attendees' views on topics on the agenda, their interests, and whether any view has enough authority behind it to influence the result of the meeting regardless of the discussion. If your views are likely to meet strong resistance, try to identify your opponents and negotiate a compromise in advance, so that neither party has its authority undermined in public. It is important to understand opposing points of view to counter them successfully. You may not win over your opponents, but you should avoid deadlock.

48 Brief other participants about problem issues before a meeting.

Open body language shows willingness to listen

TALKING ▶ ISSUES OVER
It is always useful to share information before a meeting, especially for those with opposing views who may wish to talk over differences. This may help each party tolerate and even accept other opinions.

PREPARING FOR NEGOTIATION

Negotiation is the bargaining that occurs between two parties that each possess something the other wants. The subject may not be a tangible object; it may be support for a particular course of action or assistance in performing a particular task. If you are negotiating, bring a firm goal or objective to the negotiating table – plus a strategy for achieving it. Your strategy should include points of resistance and areas that are open to compromise. To be a successful negotiator, you must be sensitive to the needs and preferences of others. Listening to others will uncover areas of mutual agreement or weakness, which you can then utilize during negotiations. Remember that once each side has outlined its initial demands and concerns, you must both be willing to compromise in order to reach an acceptable settlement.

BEING SEEN AND HEARD

To ensure that your message is getting through to others, you should look and sound the part. Dress appropriately for each meeting, and make sure that you speak clearly and confidently whenever making a contribution to proceedings.

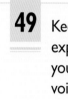

49 Keep your facial expression and your tone of voice positive.

50 Videotape yourself rehearsing to check that you are being clear.

LOOKING THE PART

A professional appearance can gain you extra respect when stating your case, since people tend to make instant judgments based purely on appearance. If you are attending a meeting with another company, find out about its dress code so that you are not the only participant wearing a formal suit while everyone else is in jeans. At a formal meeting, wear a formal suit, especially if you are not known to other people there. Whatever you wear, check that your clothes are clean and pressed, your hair is neat, your nails are clipped and smooth, and your shoes are polished.

Making eye contact shows confidence

Leaning forward indicates alertness and interest

Clothes are smart and neat

Papers are kept in an orderly pile

◀ LOOKING CONFIDENT
This man looks confident and in control. He is well groomed and formally dressed in a well-fitting dark suit, a sober, neat tie, and a crisp, white shirt. His positive body language will leave a good impression.

GAINING CONFIDENCE

Confidence-building is a circular process. If you appear to be confident, people will perceive you as such and are more likely to be convinced by your arguments. Once you feel that other members of the meeting believe you, your confidence will increase. In any verbal communication, it is estimated that your tone of voice has five times more impact, and your body language has eight times more impact, than the actual words that you use to present your argument. Concentrate on speaking clearly and at the right time, as well as on your words and the tone of your voice. Spend at least as much of your preparation time on the quality of these presentational aspects as you do on the actual content of your speech.

POINTS TO REMEMBER

- First impressions count. The opening sentences of an argument should be rehearsed.

- Since you may get only one chance to have your say, the facts need to be right first time.

- Any mistakes that are made while presenting a case should be corrected immediately so the other participants can see that you know your subject.

- Varying voice tones – warm, congratulatory, forceful, or formal – will affect the outcome.

- At the end of a meeting, main points should be summarized.

51 Take a deep breath before starting to speak.

52 If an idea is your own work, take credit for it.

▼ **SPEAKING FLUENTLY**
Remember to put across your points clearly and succinctly. Emphasize the positive aspects of your argument rather than the negative aspects of the opposing viewpoint.

PARTICIPATING STRONGLY

The level of your participation in a meeting will depend very much on its size. If a meeting is small and intimate, you may be able to interject and make points frequently, but always make sure you have something relevant – and preferably interesting – to say. If there is a chairperson, use positive body language to show him or her you would like to speak. In a large gathering, you may get only one chance to participate. Be well prepared so that you can concentrate on your delivery, which should be strong and succinct. In a meeting of any size, if someone tries to interrupt you or prevent you from putting forward your views, look them in the eye, use their name to get their attention, and tell them you have not finished. If they persist, seek support from the chairperson.

Be clear ➤ **Be succinct** ➤ **Be positive**

LISTENING TO OTHERS

It is just as important to listen properly in a meeting as it is to speak – sometimes even more so. Listen to each speaker's words, and consider the meaning behind them. Use clues such as body language and tone of voice to ascertain the strength of a speaker's beliefs.

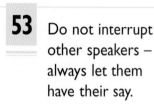

53 Do not interrupt other speakers – always let them have their say.

POINTS TO REMEMBER

- Good listeners look attentive, use eye contact, do not interrupt, and show interest in what is said.
- It is annoying to people who are trying to listen if some participants in a meeting are whispering and fidgeting.
- Irrelevant discussion should be redirected as soon as it starts.
- Listening involves more than just the ears. It is important also to "listen" to people's body language.

LISTENING ATTENTIVELY

When you are in a meeting, try to make the environment conducive to sharing and listening. Look interested in what the person speaking to you is saying – they may need encouragement. Do not interrupt or hurry somebody in the middle of expounding their case. It takes time to develop an argument, and it may not be fully comprehensible until the end. Avoid interrupting speakers, which can make you look foolish if your point is dealt with later. Instead, make a note of questions, then ask them at the end of the presentation.

SHOWING ▶ INTEREST
The woman on the right is a good listener; her body language demonstrates her interest in the conversation.

SPEAKER

Strong eye contact is maintained

LISTENER

Slightly leaning forward indicates enthusiasm

Gently clasped hands indicate a relaxed body

BETRAYING SIGNS OF NEGATIVE BODY LANGUAGE

As the listener, you should try to be aware of the signals you are giving out unconsciously. If you let disbelief, impatience, or cynicism show, this may have a demoralizing effect on a speaker who is trying to convey his or her theories and arguments to you.

SPEAKER

Hand covers facial expression

LISTENER

SPEAKER

LISTENER

Crossed arms form a barrier

▲ **SHOWING DISBELIEF**

The listener's slightly open mouth implies surprise or disbelief at what she hears. She is using her hand to cover her mouth and hide her feelings.

▲ **SHOWING IMPATIENCE**

Leaning back from the speaker indicates that the listener is distancing herself from his views. Her tense body language reveals her impatience.

RESPECTING OTHERS

Do not allow your personal or professional prejudices against individual speakers to deafen you to any good points that they may make – always show respect for them by listening to their comments politely, despite any reservations you have about their ideas. This should serve you well in the long run, since you will be given the same level of respect when your turn comes to speak.

54 Use different phrases to make the same point more interesting.

TAILORING YOUR SPEECH

Listen very carefully to not only the content but also the phrasing of everything that is said in a meeting. You may be surprised to find that the contributions of certain participants are closer to what you had to say than you anticipated, or that they may even lead you to change your plans. If appropriate, tailor your own contribution slightly to reflect what you have heard.

55 Identify any areas of agreement when you are negotiating.

HANDLING PROBLEMS

Problems that arise in small meetings are generally best resolved by using an open and honest approach. In a large meeting, however, problems can be more serious. A firm but fair chairperson who is familiar with procedure should be able to keep order.

56 Take personal responsibility for making every meeting a success.

57 Encourage those at routine meetings to take turns as the chairperson.

SEEING WEAKNESSES

During a meeting that has a chairperson, it is the chairperson's responsibility to maintain a neutral position and keep control. Difficulties arise if a chairperson demonstrates weaknesses, such as showing prejudice or becoming angry. Learn to see these faults so that you can take action and prevent a chairperson from losing control.

HOW A CHAIRPERSON MIGHT ABUSE THE POSITION

SPECIFIC ABUSES	HOW TO RECOGNIZE THEM
BIAS The chairperson defends the needs of one party in a discussion.	You may not recognize bias if it is in your favor, but if a chairperson ignores your attempts to contribute or makes it difficult for you to do so, they may be biased against you.
INDECISION The chairperson does not lead the meeting when a decision is needed.	If a chairperson repeatedly asks for members to summarize their arguments or uses stalling tactics, he or she may not be able to reach or facilitate a decision.
MANIPULATION The chairperson does not allow the facts to speak for themselves.	Continually urging participants to reconsider a matter may be an attempt to manipulate the outcome. However, it could be a conscientious effort to get the right decision.
ANGER The chairperson does not show a calm but assertive demeanor.	Overt displays of anger from a chairperson are easily recognized, but suppressed anger may reveal itself more subtly in tone of voice or posture.

REPRIMANDING A CHAIRPERSON

If a chairperson is abusing his or her power or neglecting duties, you may need to take action – whether the meeting is formal or informal. The best way to do this is to point out what the chairperson's duties are and how those duties are not being fulfilled. State clearly what you expect the chairperson to do differently, and allow him or her the chance to remedy the situation.

58 If you reject a motion, try to find at least one area of agreement.

HOW TO REPRIMAND A CHAIRPERSON

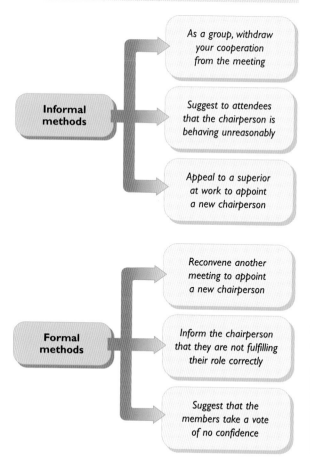

Informal methods

As a group, withdraw your cooperation from the meeting

Suggest to attendees that the chairperson is behaving unreasonably

Appeal to a superior at work to appoint a new chairperson

Formal methods

Reconvene another meeting to appoint a new chairperson

Inform the chairperson that they are not fulfilling their role correctly

Suggest that the members take a vote of no confidence

SOLVING OTHER PROBLEMS

A range of other problems can impede the business of a meeting. Individual members may behave badly, key people may be absent, or vital information may be missing. It is the role of the chairperson to implement an acceptable solution: to restore order in the case of disruptive behavior, to adjourn the meeting if a quorum is not met, or to ask for more information if needed. A solution such as ejecting troublemakers can be quickly implemented by the chairperson alone; gathering information may involve collaborating with attendees.

59 As a chairperson, ensure that all views are heard.

TAKING MINUTES

The minutes of a meeting – short notes detailing its proceedings – are taken by the meeting's secretary as a written record of what was discussed. If you are responsible for taking minutes, ensure that they are accurate and clear.

60 Ensure that the order of minutes follows the order of the agenda.

POINTS TO REMEMBER

● Minutes should be brief; they can be written in note form.

● Prompt delivery of minutes encourages prompt action on issues raised.

● If a meeting's secretary is unclear about an issue, he or she should discuss it with the chairperson.

● Minutes should be entirely understandable to absentees.

WRITING CLEAR MINUTES

In the minutes you should record the time and place of the meeting, the names of attendees (where appropriate), all items presented but not necessarily details of the discussions involved, and all decisions, agreements, or appointments made. During the course of a meeting, make notes from which to write the minutes in full later. Make sure the minutes are unbiased, written in a clear, concise style, and accurate. Accuracy is essential, particularly where minutes may be used as evidence in the case of a later dispute.

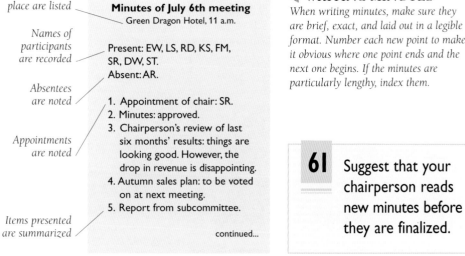

Date and place are listed

Names of participants are recorded

Absentees are noted

Appointments are noted

Items presented are summarized

Minutes of July 6th meeting
Green Dragon Hotel, 11 a.m.

Present: EW, LS, RD, KS, FM, SR, DW, ST.
Absent: AR.

1. Appointment of chair: SR.
2. Minutes: approved.
3. Chairperson's review of last six months' results: things are looking good. However, the drop in revenue is disappointing.
4. Autumn sales plan: to be voted on at next meeting.
5. Report from subcommittee.

continued...

◀ **WRITING MINUTES**
When writing minutes, make sure they are brief, exact, and laid out in a legible format. Number each new point to make it obvious where one point ends and the next one begins. If the minutes are particularly lengthy, index them.

61 Suggest that your chairperson reads new minutes before they are finalized.

DISTRIBUTING AND FOLLOWING UP MINUTES

Once the minutes are complete, make sure that they are distributed quickly to all the relevant people. Compiling the minutes is a meaningless task if the action agreed on at the meeting is not duly followed up. Minutes should indicate clearly the deadlines agreed on for any projects and who is responsible for implementation. After a suitable period but before the next meeting, follow up on the progress of any projects or tasks noted in the minutes, then update the chairperson on their status. If necessary, see that these items are included in the agenda for the next meeting.

THINGS TO DO

1. Make sure the chairperson approves the minutes.
2. Distribute minutes within a day or two of a meeting.
3. Follow up between meetings on issues requiring action.
4. Use the minutes to compile a status report on ongoing issues. Circulate it with the agenda for the next meeting.
5. At each meeting, approve the minutes of the previous meeting and verify their accuracy with the attendees.

THE ROLE OF THE SECRETARY

Coordinating the minutes is the job of the secretary of a meeting. The role of secretary is an important one. The same individual can perform the role at each meeting, or the role can be handled by different people (with the exception of the chairperson, to whom the secretary is directly answerable). If you are asked to take on this role, you can delegate the administrative tasks of composing and typing the minutes as long as you supervise them carefully.

62 Write up the minutes right after a meeting using notes taken in the meeting.

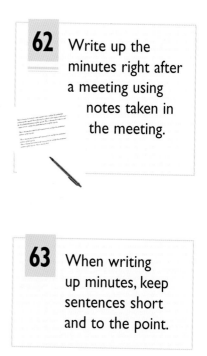

TAKING NOTES ▶
Take detailed notes during a meeting to prepare for the writing of the final minutes.

63 When writing up minutes, keep sentences short and to the point.

EVALUATING YOUR SKILL AS A PARTICIPANT

*E*valuate how well you perform when you attend meetings by responding to the following statements, and mark the options closest to your experience. Be as honest as you can: if your answer is "never," mark Option 1; if it is "always," mark Option 4; and so on. Add your scores together and refer to the Analysis to see how well you scored. Use your answers to identify the areas that most need improvement.

OPTIONS

1 Never

2 Occasionally

3 Frequently

4 Always

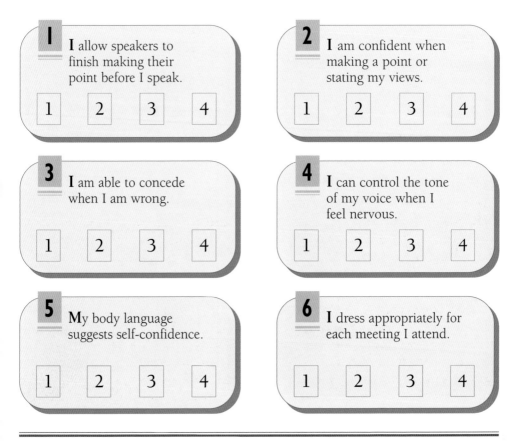

1 I allow speakers to finish making their point before I speak.

1　2　3　4

2 I am confident when making a point or stating my views.

1　2　3　4

3 I am able to concede when I am wrong.

1　2　3　4

4 I can control the tone of my voice when I feel nervous.

1　2　3　4

5 My body language suggests self-confidence.

1　2　3　4

6 I dress appropriately for each meeting I attend.

1　2　3　4

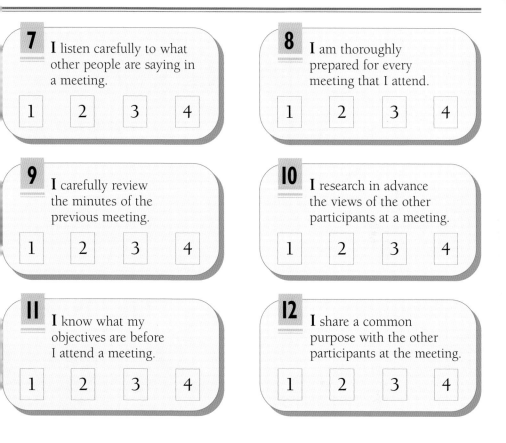

7 I listen carefully to what other people are saying in a meeting.

1 2 3 4

8 I am thoroughly prepared for every meeting that I attend.

1 2 3 4

9 I carefully review the minutes of the previous meeting.

1 2 3 4

10 I research in advance the views of the other participants at a meeting.

1 2 3 4

11 I know what my objectives are before I attend a meeting.

1 2 3 4

12 I share a common purpose with the other participants at the meeting.

1 2 3 4

ANALYSIS

Now that you have completed the self-assessment, add up your total score, then check your ability by reading the corresponding evaluation. Whatever level of skill you have shown at a meeting, it is important to remember that there is always room for improvement. Identify your weakest areas, then refer to the relevant chapters in this section, where you will find practical advice and tips to help you establish and hone your meeting skills.

12–24: Your skills need general attention. Always have a definite purpose when you attend a meeting, and endeavor to achieve it.
25–36: You perform reasonably well in meetings, but certain skills need further development.
37–48: You perform well in meetings, but do not become complacent. Continue to prepare well for each meeting you attend.

CHAIRING A MEETING

Every meeting needs a chairperson to direct the proceedings. As chairperson, you must fulfill the vital role of ensuring the smooth running and successful completion of any meeting.

UNDERSTANDING THE ROLE

A chairperson is the person in charge of running a meeting. He or she has the authority to regulate the meeting and is responsible for enforcing any rules that govern the proceedings, keeping order, and the successful completion of business.

64 Encourage all participants to give opinions by asking open questions.

POINTS TO REMEMBER

● A chairperson is responsible for ensuring that any discussion is relevant to the points on a meeting's agenda.

● A chairperson should repeat any motion proposed by those attending to ensure that everyone has heard and understood it.

● A chairperson can expel anyone who disrupts a meeting.

● A chairperson is responsible for summing up the discussion at the end of a meeting.

USING PERSONAL SKILLS

The ideal chairperson should have a wide range of personal skills. Brush up on these essential skills before chairing any meeting:

● Firmness in running meetings to time and dealing with problems;

● Ability to summarize points succinctly;

● Flexibility when dealing with the different tones and styles of attendees;

● Openness and receptiveness when listening to opinions that you do not share;

● Fair-mindedness in ensuring that all views are aired and given equal consideration.

CHAIRING AN INFORMAL MEETING

Not all informal meetings have an "official" chairperson. Those that do usually appoint one by a vote among participants or via instructions from the meeting's organizers. The role of chairperson here is mainly to keep control and to ensure that every point of view is heard. In general, the chairperson must appear unbiased and cannot fully join in the discussion. However, the chairperson can still exert considerable influence over the outcome of a meeting by allowing detailed coverage of some issues and limited consideration of others. The chairperson also often has a casting vote in the event of it being necessary.

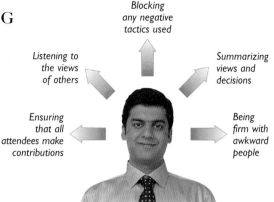

Blocking any negative tactics used

Listening to the views of others

Summarizing views and decisions

Ensuring that all attendees make contributions

Being firm with awkward people

▲ DUTIES OF A CHAIRPERSON

A chairperson can exert enormous influence on the outcome of a formal or informal meeting. It is extremely important that he or she remains neutral throughout the proceedings.

65 Ask a participant to give you honest feedback on your performance as a chairperson.

CHAIRING A FORMAL MEETING

A number of different rules govern the selection of a chairperson for a formal meeting. For example, in the case of a public company, the choice will be controlled by company rules. A government committee, however, will select its chairperson in accordance with statutory regulations. One of the main responsibilities of a chairperson is to ensure that a meeting is properly convened: that is, that the minimum number of people, known as a quorum, is present; that business follows the order of the agenda; and that there is sufficient time to discuss all the items. If these conditions are not met, any decisions taken may not be binding.

THINGS TO DO

1. Open a meeting with a short summary of its purpose and agenda.
2. Allow all parties to express their views on the subject under discussion.
3. Prevent irrelevant debate.
4. Ensure any voting procedure is followed correctly.
5. Cast the deciding vote if necessary.

RESEARCHING ATTENDEES

As chairperson of a meeting, you should familiarize yourself with the people who will be attending. Although it may not be possible to research all attendees of a large meeting, identify whether there are different factions, and be ready to deal with them.

66 Try to get to know newcomers before a meeting takes place.

67 Research any key opinion leaders thoroughly before a meeting.

RECOGNIZING INTERESTS

There is often much at stake in meetings, and discussions can become heated. Pressure groups may dominate public meetings, and there will be vocal supporters and detractors for almost every meeting about a contentious issue, such as a pay review. As chairperson, you must be prepared for any potential problems and be ready to deal with matters calmly, giving all interests a fair say and ensuring a meeting does not get bogged down.

UNDERSTANDING PERSONALITIES

SHY TYPE

Try to gauge if any of the attendees are likely to be nervous and lacking in confidence in a meeting. Take time to chat with them encouragingly beforehand to put them at ease.

DOMINANT TYPE

Domineering participants with strong personalities can be very disruptive at a meeting. They should be clearly identified before a meeting so that you can control them if they start to dominate.

ACCOMMODATING PERSONALITIES

As chairperson of a meeting, you should utilize the personal skills that allow you to recognize and cope with a wide range of personalities. Spend time making inquiries about the personalities of the various participants. Shy attendees may need encouraging to participate in the meeting, while domineering attendees may need to be controlled. Remember that as chairperson you are responsible for ensuring that each participant has a fair say in the discussion.

UNDERSTANDING TACTICS

Before a strategically important meeting, key participants are likely to have planned their strategy for achieving their aims. Find out what these aims are in advance by carefully researching background information on key attendees. You will then be in a better position to anticipate and counter any negative tactics that may be employed to secure these aims. Some of the tactics used by participants may include the following: attempting to change the agenda by shifting the discussion to another subject; undermining less confident participants; and wasting time by avoiding the subject and deferring a final vote.

THINGS TO DO

1. Find out who the key participants will be.

2. Research tactics previously employed by key attendees.

3. Identify possible factions within a meeting.

4. Get to know the various personality types.

5. Familiarize yourself with the opposing views.

ANTICIPATING DISTRACTING TACTICS IN MEETINGS

TACTIC BY PARTICIPANT	COUNTER BY CHAIRPERSON
DIVIDE AND CONQUER This device entails the passing of conflicting information to individuals before a meeting with the intention of creating antagonisms.	**RECAP ON THE FACTS** Find out who is spreading disinformation. Be prepared when in the meeting to reestablish the facts to clear up misapprehensions.
DOMINATION By speaking in a loud voice and interrupting, a dominant person may try to undermine the confidence of less dominant attendees.	**CHALLENGE THE AGGRESSOR** Research who the domineering attendees are, and be prepared to counter them in a meeting with a firm request for orderly conduct.
BLUSTER This time-wasting device involves somebody speaking loudly and at great length about a subject irrelevant to the one under discussion.	**SILENCE THE BLUSTERER** Be prepared to isolate a potential blusterer, and counter the tactic when in a meeting by avoiding eye contact until others have spoken.
ANGER Some people use anger as a tactical weapon in meetings in order to halt the discussion and have the meeting adjourned to a later date.	**STAY CALM** Find out which attendee may use this highly disruptive tactic, and be prepared to calmly expel them from a meeting if necessary.

PACING A MEETING

Pacing a meeting correctly is an important part of the role of chairperson. Always make sure that an agenda is provided and followed and that the speakers have enough time to make their points without allowing the meeting to overrun its schedule.

68 Schedule meetings before lunch – it is more likely they will end on time.

STARTING ON TIME

Always make a point of starting meetings on time. When you are chairing a meeting, arrive at the site well before the planned start time. If some participants are late, start without them. However, if a key contributor is late, it is acceptable to wait for their arrival before beginning or to change the order of the agenda to prevent delays. If starting late is unavoidable, make sure that this is noted in the minutes, along with the reasons for the delay. Do not waste time recapping for late arrivals, unless it is vital that they possess information in order to make a quick decision. Otherwise, leave it to them to find out for themselves what they have missed once the meeting has finished.

69 At the start of a meeting, inform attendees how long it is planned to last.

PICKING UP THE PACE

If the pace of a meeting is flagging, take remedial action to make the most of the rest of the meeting:

● Change position and tone – stand up and speak louder and more quickly to rouse the participants;

● Choose participants known to be lively speakers to address the meeting and generate some momentum;

● Consider skipping inessential items on the agenda – but ensure that all the participants in the meeting are in total agreement with you before taking this course of action;

● Arrange a follow-up meeting to cover any unfinished items if it becomes obvious that parts of the agenda are going to take longer than is practical.

KEEPING TO THE AGENDA

It is important to allocate an overall time limit to complete a meeting's agenda. Research shows that the attention span of most participants picks up for the first 10 to 15 minutes, then dips before rising again as the end of a meeting is anticipated. The ideal meeting length of 45 minutes minimizes loss of attention time. When chairing a meeting, keep things moving briskly by adhering strictly to the agenda, enforcing a strict time limit for each item. This establishes and maintains a sense of urgency and momentum in proceedings.

POINTS TO REMEMBER

- Attendees are usually at their most receptive at the beginning of a meeting.

- The progress of a meeting can be summarized at regular intervals.

- Reminders should be given of how much time is left to complete the agenda.

- Failure to end a meeting on time may antagonize attendees.

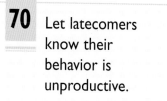

70 Let latecomers know their behavior is unproductive.

USING TIME EFFECTIVELY

It is vital that the chairperson keeps a meeting's purpose clearly in each participant's mind. Do not allow participants to waste time by wandering from the point. If the discussion does begin to stray, bring it back to the main issue by saying, for example, "We are not here to discuss that today – let's get back to the point." Allow time for a brief discussion among the participants before summarizing the debate and, if appropriate, taking a vote on the points raised in the meeting.

PROVIDING BREAKS

Time for breaks and refreshments should always be built into the agenda of a long meeting. These breaks serve several purposes: they allow attendees to discuss matters in small groups, which may help to iron out any awkward differences; they provide the chairperson with useful buffer zones that can be used to extend or shorten a meeting in special circumstances; and they allow bodies and brains to relax. In order to achieve optimum productivity, the maximum time you should allow a meeting to run without breaks is 90 minutes.

▲ REFRESHMENTS

Organize the provision of refreshments during planned breaks. Avoid messy snacks, and discourage eating during the meeting.

CONTROLLING A MEETING

The key to controlling a meeting lies in anticipating problems before they arise. If you learn to interpret the body language of the participants, you can encourage correct behavior, avoid problems, and strive for a positive and successful outcome.

71 Put a stop to any side debates or private conversations.

READING NEGATIVE SIGNS

There are many nonverbal signs that can indicate that individuals are unhappy with the course of a meeting. Frequently checking a watch, gazing out of the window, rustling papers, and yawning all show disinterest. A closed posture – with shoulders hunched and avoidance of eye contact – discourages communication and may indicate lack of interest, but it may also indicate low confidence. Watch for these signs so that you can respond appropriately, perhaps by changing the pace of the meeting.

Posture is closed

▲ **SHOWING NO INTEREST**
A lack of interest in the meeting and a low level of concentration is clearly shown in this attendee's introspective demeanor.

Fists are clenched

Head is lowered

◀ **REVEALING ANGER**
A displeased expression shows that this person is not happy with the way the meeting is going. His fists are clenched, he has lowered his head, and he is glaring aggressively.

Hand is pointing aggressively

72 Defuse anger by inviting participants to express the reasons for their anger.

▲ **BEING ARGUMENTATIVE**
This man has raised his hand to catch the chairperson's eye. His body language denotes a confrontational attitude.

READING POSITIVE SIGNS

There are positive signs that can unequivocally indicate that a person is happy with the progress of a meeting. An open posture with arms and hands relaxed and the body leaning forward or toward the speaker indicates enthusiasm and encourages involvement. Sustained eye contact from an attendee shows that they are focusing their attention on you and have a positive interest in the points you are making. If you can make yourself sensitive to these signs, you will be able to use such positive body language to gauge when one or more of the participants has come to a decision. This can help you establish that the time is right to conclude a discussion or call a vote.

73 Encourage hesitant participants with positive feedback.

74 Watch for positive signs of interest from participants.

Raised eyebrows and slight smile are encouraging

◀ PORTRAYING INTEREST

This participant is showing interest by tilting her head toward the speaker and wearing an open expression.

Posture is alert

SHOWING ▶ ENTHUSIASM

A supportive and focused posture implies that this person is interested in what the speaker is saying.

CULTURAL DIFFERENCES

Seemingly similar expressions of body language "say" slightly different things in different cultures. In the Middle East, for example, a movement of the head upward with a clicking of the tongue means "no." Elsewhere this represents an affirmative nod. Likewise, in India, head-shaking can mean "yes" rather than "no," while expressive hand gestures tend to be used more around the Mediterranean than in northwestern Europe. Familiarize yourself with body language differences when at meetings with business people from different cultural backgrounds.

RECOGNIZING OTHER SIGNALS

As chairperson, watch for the slightest indication of unrest or lack of interest among attendees. Take action to curb disruptive signals – for example, from participants who are trying to dominate the discussion. At other times, you may need to coax introverted or reticent attendees to speak at all. Do not force shy participants to speak if you feel that they will not advance the discussion with their contribution.

Hand is raised to gain attention

◀ **WANTING TO SPEAK**
This woman is trying to contribute to the discussion. Her exaggerated gestures are an attempt to attract the chairperson's attention.

Arms are folded across body

SHYING AWAY ▶
This man does not want to be noticed. His arms are folded, and he avoids making eye contact.

ASSESSING THE MOOD

It is vital that you assess the mood of a meeting correctly when acting as chairperson. The mood can change rapidly from warm and friendly to downright hostile. If the atmosphere is tense, act quickly to improve the situation. For example, if you feel that participants are tiring of a subject, move them on to the next item on the agenda. If you feel that attendees are tiring of the meeting, conclude it by summarizing the discussion and, if necessary, calling for a final vote.

QUESTIONS TO ASK YOURSELF

Q Has everybody had a chance to express their views?

Q Have the procedural rules of the organization been followed?

Q Did you have a firm control of the meeting?

Q Did you encourage people to speak by asking them questions?

75 If someone is due to speak after you, be aware if they become impatient.

KEEPING ORDER

In a formal meeting, maintain control by ensuring that all questions and proposals are addressed through you. Anyone wishing to speak should catch your eye and request permission to "take the floor." In an informal meeting, you can also keep order by acting as a mediator for questions and debate. Do not interrupt a speaker unless they digress, overrun, or try to dominate the meeting.

WORKING TO ONE AIM

It is the responsibility of a chairperson to ensure that individual participants appreciate the interests of the whole group, personal interests are set aside where necessary, and everyone at a meeting is working toward the same aim. Make sure that this happens by firmly controlling those who stray from the purpose of a meeting and by sticking closely to the agenda.

 76 Pick out individuals, then ask them direct questions to stimulate debate.

CULTURAL DIFFERENCES

In Russian meetings, do not be surprised if the chairperson allows angry exchanges or even a walk-out by some participants. These actions are usually a ploy and do not constitute a breakdown. It is common practice for the "protesters" to reenter a meeting and resume the discussion.

COMING TO DECISIONS

A decision can be reached either by taking a vote among participants or by using your controlling authority and making the decision yourself as chairperson. When taking a vote in a smaller meeting, call for a show of hands or a poll. Do this several times if you want a unanimous vote. In a larger meeting, unanimity is unlikely, so agree before you start that a specific number of "yes" votes is enough to carry a motion. Gauge the mood of the meeting, and if you see a consensus in favor of a particular course of action, make the decision without a vote.

STIMULATING DEBATE

If a meeting stalls because the attendees are bored or become sidetracked from the main issue, it is the chairperson's responsibility to restart the discussion and confine it to the subject at hand. In order to do this, try directing open-ended questions to those present, for example, "Let me ask all of you: what would you have done in that situation?" Do not ask questions that require a simple yes or no. When looking for an answer, use your knowledge of the attendees to choose an articulate individual who can respond confidently to your question. Alternatively, try expressing a controversial opinion yourself to provoke further debate: for example, "I think in that situation I would have fired all the staff in the department." Make sure your comment is outrageous enough not to be taken at face value. If even this fails to reignite the discussion, do not waste time – move on to the next item on the agenda.

KEEPING ORDER

*P*roblems of order at a meeting may arise *from breaches of procedure, conflicts of interest, or even willful disruption. As chairperson, you must ensure that the meeting is conducted in an orderly fashion and restore calm if tempers become frayed.*

77 Be aware of the formal disciplinary procedures open to you in meetings.

UNDERSTANDING LIMITS

The nature of a meeting determines the limits or extent of your powers as chairperson and the types of procedure you can use to maintain order. There are two types of meeting: private and public. A private meeting is attended by select members of an organization, such as a company department. The rules of the organization determine the limits of the chairperson's power. A public meeting is open to everyone. If held in a public place, the meeting may be governed by local or statutory law and regulations. If held in a private location, however, the meeting is bound by rules laid down by the meeting's organizers.

HANDLING A BREACH OF ORDER

A breach of order occurs when the strict procedure of a formal meeting is disrupted. Talking out of turn is a common breach. If this occurs, you should halt the debate, look straight at the talkers, and invite them to share their thoughts. If this does not silence them, implement disciplinary procedures, which may culminate in their ejection.

Open hand gesture is an appeal for moderation

Eye contact is directed at principal antagonist

◀ **CALMING THE PROCEEDINGS**
If a discussion between two parties becomes overheated, stand up in order to regain control and pacify them. Your extra height will enable you to exert greater authority. Use a calm, measured tone of voice.

DEFUSING ARGUMENTS

When a debate becomes heated, thoughtless or personal comments may be used as ammunition, leading to increased friction and argument. Defuse arguments by guiding the discussion back to the issues and away from the personalities involved. Mediate to clear up any misunderstandings: "I'm sure Jean did not mean to say…," for example.

78 Enforce a moment's silence to bring a meeting to order following a dispute.

HANDLING SPECIFIC PROBLEMS IN A MEETING

PROBLEMS	POSSIBLE RESPONSES

EXCUSES
Participant makes excuses such as "I forgot" or "That was not my responsibility" when presenting an uncompleted task.

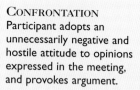

- Remind the participant in front of their peers that they will be expected to perform the task in future.
- Appoint someone to supervise the participant and ensure that they complete the work.
- Transfer the responsibility to someone else.

AMBUSH
Participant makes an attempt to undermine the proceedings so that the meeting does not achieve its specified purpose.

- Isolate the ambusher by drawing attention to their tactics.
- Adjourn the meeting if the participant continually attempts to interrupt discussion.
- In extreme circumstances, eject the ambusher from the meeting.

CONFRONTATION
Participant adopts an unnecessarily negative and hostile attitude to opinions expressed in the meeting, and provokes argument.

- Remind the antagonist of the purpose of the meeting and the need to reach agreement.
- Stick to the facts and encourage participants to discuss these in a calm manner.
- Introduce humor to defuse the situation, but not at the expense of the antagonist.

SERIOUS DISORDER
Participant becomes abusive, unruly, or even physically violent, or causes the meeting to descend into chaos.

- Call for order.
- Ask the participant to leave, or have him or her removed.
- Adjourn the meeting without setting a date to reconvene.

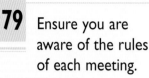

79 Ensure you are aware of the rules of each meeting.

- The rules and regulations that govern a meeting will vary according to the meeting's location and its participants.

- Certain behavior at a meeting, such as slander, may contravene criminal law as well as the meeting's own rules.

- Legal procedures can be used to block, as well as facilitate, the business of a meeting.

- Regulations are effective only when they are enforced properly and followed consistently.

PREVENTING DISRUPTION

When a meeting is disrupted, you must deal with the problem swiftly so that business can continue. The nature of the meeting will determine the most appropriate method of restoring control.

It is easy to control a small informal meeting while maintaining a low profile. If a meeting descends into chaos, you can invoke disciplinary procedures, adjourn until order is restored, or eject the troublemakers in the case of serious disorder. It is difficult to restore order in a large meeting, especially when a disruption has been planned in advance. Take firm control from the outset to establish your authority and discourage trouble.

80 Try to isolate troublemakers in a meeting by getting the majority of participants on your side.

USING LEGAL PROCEDURES

Legal procedures can be used to control or direct the business of any meeting. These procedures reflect the legal powers invested in a chairperson by the rules of a meeting. You must be aware of the legal procedures at your disposal in order to chair a meeting effectively. Your legal control over voting is a very important power, so check your rights with your company lawyers in advance of the meeting. If an acrimonious debate seems to be spinning out of control, you may be able to insist that the matter is resolved by a vote. As chair, you may also have a second or casting vote in cases of deadlock. Legal procedures can be used to govern the behavior of participants at a meeting; rulings may limit certain language or actions. If necessary, institute procedures to bring a meeting to a close.

CULTURAL DIFFERENCES

In Japan the chairperson's role is to achieve a consensus of opinion. This often involves the chairperson withdrawing from the proceedings to allow participants to work their way slowly toward a solution. In the US, however, the chairperson is expected to drive the meeting to an agreement using charisma and force of personality. Power is more obviously wielded to keep order and achieve objectives.

MANAGING A TROUBLEMAKER IN A MEETING

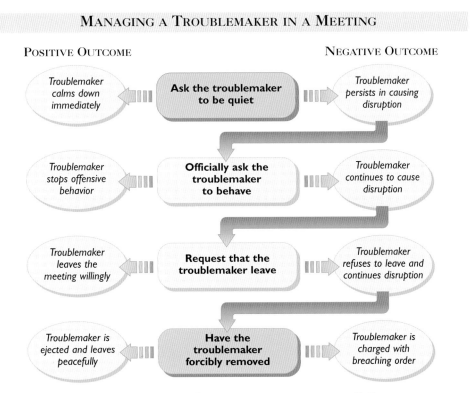

POSITIVE OUTCOME   NEGATIVE OUTCOME

Troublemaker calms down immediately — **Ask the troublemaker to be quiet** — *Troublemaker persists in causing disruption*

Troublemaker stops offensive behavior — **Officially ask the troublemaker to behave** — *Troublemaker continues to cause disruption*

Troublemaker leaves the meeting willingly — **Request that the troublemaker leave** — *Troublemaker refuses to leave and continues disruption*

Troublemaker is ejected and leaves peacefully — **Have the troublemaker forcibly removed** — *Troublemaker is charged with breaching order*

---

81 To change the atmosphere of a meeting, change the subject.

82 Eject any troublemakers only as a last resort.

ADJOURNING A MEETING

If the disorderly conduct of participants leads to their expulsion and a quorum (the minimum number of attendees required for a formal meeting) is no longer present, a meeting may be adjourned. There are specific rules of procedure that can be invoked to adjourn a meeting in the case of a dispute or outbreak of disorder. However, you can use your discretion when deciding on the length of an adjournment. A meeting can be adjourned for a short period, such as half an hour, to allow tempers to cool. Alternatively, if a disruption is more serious, a meeting can be postponed indefinitely – an adjournment *sine die*, (literally, without a day). In this case, no future time or place is set to continue the meeting.

CLOSING A MEETING

When all the items on an agenda have been discussed and any necessary action agreed, it is the duty of the chairperson to bring the proceedings to a close. Ensure that all decisions are recorded accurately and any follow-up procedures are set in motion.

83 Arrange the next meeting while all the participants are present.

THINGS TO DO

1. Conclude Any Other Business.

2. Summarize discussions and recap decisions.

3. Inform participants of the time and location of the next meeting if it has been confirmed.

4. Ensure that any outstanding items are noted for inclusion at the next meeting.

DEALING WITH ANY OTHER BUSINESS

The final item on the agenda of most meetings is Any Other Business (AOB). This gives participants an opportunity to raise issues that could not have been anticipated before the meeting, such as points stimulated by the discussion.

Participants sometimes use AOB tactically to raise controversial issues or to introduce surprise or unexpected items to a meeting. As chairperson, you must decide whether to allow this practice. You may either permit a discussion or vote on the issues raised under AOB, or add the issues to the agenda for the next meeting so that they can be discussed fully before a decision is made.

CASE STUDY

Jim heard that his company's main rival, Digby, was shifting its freight from road to rail. At a company meeting, he suggested doing the same.

Aziz, a partner, said that rail made sense for Digby, which had a lot of business abroad, but for their own domestic business, using the roads was better. Another partner, Frank, said he thought Digby had shifted all its freight to rail and received a special deal as a result. Their fourth partner, Sally, suggested looking at the benefits of a full versus a partial shift to rail. Her motion was seconded and passed. When summing up, the chairperson raised and recapped the subject.

After the meeting, the task of researching the subject was passed to David, a junior colleague. Although he had not attended the meeting, he studied the notes on the motion and then was able to prepare a preliminary report.

◀ **PROPOSING MOTIONS**

Although Jim's proposal was not accepted unequivocally, it led to constructive action. Because it had been recorded in detail as the meeting was being closed, a colleague who had not even been present at the discussion was able to take the matter up and research it thoroughly.

SUMMARIZING DECISIONS

Once participants in a meeting have considered the final item of business, recap on each decision reached, summarizing the discussion leading up to it. This is an opportunity for you to redress the balance of the meeting by giving each of the issues discussed the significance you think they merit. For example, if the most insignificant item on the agenda has inspired the longest, most heated debate, give it scant attention in your summary to indicate the weight you think it deserves. Summing up will also highlight any issues that require further discussion at a future meeting.

84 Ensure decisions are all recorded in writing.

85 Always try to end a meeting on a positive note.

86 Thank everybody for attending and all the speakers for contributing.

CONCLUDING A MEETING

After summarizing the business of a meeting, decide whether you need to meet again, then set a date and time if necessary. You can confirm these details and the location when you circulate a new agenda. The meeting can now be closed. At this point, you should thank all the participants for attending, especially if they have voluntarily given up their time to do so. This is common courtesy, but is also designed to encourage attendance and positive participation at future meetings.

FOLLOWING UP AFTER A MEETING

Your role as chairperson does not cease at the end of a meeting. Your ongoing responsibilities include:
- Approving the minutes;
- Ensuring that the secretary follows up and monitors any action agreed to be undertaken at the meeting;
- Receiving progress reports from the secretary on decisions made at the

meeting, and informing the other participants of advances if necessary;
- Encouraging participants to submit in advance any business they wish to be discussed at the next meeting;
- Setting the agenda for the next meeting, including any items that arose during discussion at the previous meeting or that were missed or not covered fully.

USING FORMAL PROCEDURE

*F*ormal procedure provides a ready-made framework for running a meeting. The use of set procedures can help a meeting achieve its objectives by setting out certain etiquette. Learn to use them properly, and they will help you control any meeting.

ORDER OF PROCEDURE

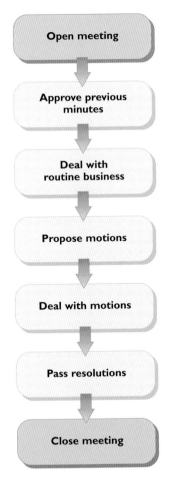

Open meeting

⬇

Approve previous minutes

⬇

Deal with routine business

⬇

Propose motions

⬇

Deal with motions

⬇

Pass resolutions

⬇

Close meeting

OPENING FORMALLY

Before opening a formal meeting, ensure that the following conditions have been met:

- Full and proper notice has been given to all necessary attendees;
- A quorum (the minimum number of people required) is present;
- Both you and the quorum are at the location within a certain time of the scheduled start.

If any of these stipulations are not met, you may adjourn the meeting to another time and place, or delay it for a short time if you have received notification that the missing participants are soon to arrive. If all the criteria have been met, begin the meeting by calling everyone to attention, making any necessary formal introductions, and commencing with the agenda.

SIGNING ▶
A REGISTER
A register of attendees is kept at company AGMs and other formal meetings. Arrivals must sign the register to record their attendance before entering the meeting.

APPROVING MINUTES

Gaining approval for the minutes of the last meeting is one of the first tasks of any regular formal meeting. In general, this process is passed over quickly. As the chairperson, you must ensure that everyone agrees that the decisions have been recorded accurately. Do this by asking for a show of hands from the floor. The value of the minutes as the official record of a meeting is worthless if somebody subsequently claims that events were different from the way they were recorded.

88 Make a tape recording of a formal meeting to help ensure that the minutes are accurate.

DEALING WITH ROUTINE BUSINESS MATTERS

As chairperson of regular meetings, part of your responsibility is to deal with routine business matters – for example, overseeing the appointment of external auditors in an AGM, reviewing your company's financial statements, or considering reports from standing subcommittees with specific areas of responsibility. Raise each routine matter on the agenda and elicit the approval of the attendees as swiftly as possible before moving on to the next point. Record each decision for inclusion in the minutes, then move on to nonroutine matters, which should take up the majority of the meeting.

89 Provide a message-taking service for participants.

90 Deal with routine and administrative matters first.

PROPOSING MOTIONS

In formal meetings, deal with nonroutine business on the agenda through motions – statements of a desire to do something. (In company meetings, the terminology may be different.) Ensure that all motions are made in writing, well in advance of the meeting. Check that they have been proposed and seconded before the meeting begins so that you do not waste time discussing an issue that has no support among the participants and that they appear on the agenda, phrased concisely.

91 Set up an information desk next to the registration area.

92 Stand to exercise your authority at rowdy meetings.

AMENDING A MOTION

Any motion may be amended. Put forward an amendment as you would a motion, discuss and approve it, and then move on to discuss the amended motion. Although advance notice of amendments is required procedurally in formal meetings, they can be made during the course of debate in less formal meetings.

DEALING WITH MOTIONS

Always deal with motions in the order that they appear on the agenda: introduce each motion, then open the discussion to the meeting. In your role as chairperson, it is important for you to keep a tight control on proceedings, direct any debate, and encourage all attendees to participate. If necessary, consider adjourning the meeting to seek further information from expert sources.

As chairperson, you have the power in certain situations to introduce emergency motions on important issues if there has been no time to put forward a motion in advance. It is not, however, possible for you to withdraw a motion from the agenda of a meeting without first obtaining the unanimous consent of all the participants.

Once a motion has been fully debated, you will be required to put it to vote in order to reach an agreement on any action to be taken. It is vital to understand the various voting majorities demanded in different situations for a motion to be passed.

PASSING RESOLUTIONS

Voting on a motion leads to the passing of a resolution – a written indication of action to be taken in the future. As chairperson, take a vote by asking for a show of hands on each motion as you go through the agenda. If there is no dissension, pass the motion and record it as a resolution. This can then be rescinded only if a countermotion is put forward at a subsequent meeting. You have the casting vote in case of a tied result following debate of a motion. When a motion calls for a secret vote, ask for written votes to be placed in a ballot box, and count them at the end of the meeting, announcing the result at a later date. If agreement cannot be reached, amend the original motion and arrange to discuss it in the future.

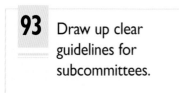

93 Draw up clear guidelines for subcommittees.

94 Avoid using too many formalities – they may inhibit free discussion.

APPOINTING SUBCOMMITTEES

The chairperson is instrumental in appointing any subcommittees needed to take responsibility for issues that require particular consideration. For example, as chairperson of a company board, you may choose to set up a subcommittee to discuss the remuneration package of the directors. Such groups can be a subset of the main committee or experts in a specific field who are drafted in from outside, such as management consultants or industry leaders. In both cases, their function is to assist an existing committee in reaching an informed decision quickly and efficiently.

BRIEFING A ▶
SUBCOMMITTEE
It is important that a subcommittee knows what is required of them. When briefing subcommittee members, provide a clear written report and explain it carefully to them.

CLOSING FORMALLY

Before you can close a meeting formally, a motion that it be ended must be proposed. When this has been seconded and voted on, request a vote by a show of hands from those in favor of the motion. You may choose to ask for a show of hands from those against the motion, which will help you to identify any participants wishing to extend the meeting for further discussion (for example, because they disagree with a particular decision reached during the meeting). As the chairperson, you need not allow everyone who wants to speak to do so, nor should you permit participants to speak for too long. It is at your discretion how long you permit discussions to continue before you formally close the meeting.

95 Refer complex issues to a working party that reports back at a later date.

96 Remember, you have the power to decide when a meeting closes.

SOLVING PROBLEMS IN FORMAL MEETINGS

The problems that arise in large formal meetings can be very different from those that occur at small informal events. As chairperson, you will need to resolve problems and ensure that procedure is followed so that meetings can progress smoothly.

97 Record important meetings on video to use for future reference.

HANDLING PROBLEMS USING FORMAL PROCEDURES

PROBLEMS	CORRECT PROCEDURE
LACK OF A QUORUM The minimum number of participants needed to validate a decision is not present.	Adjourn the meeting, specifying the date on which it must reconvene. Quorum requirements are variable, so they need to be checked.
DISRUPTIVE PARTICIPANTS The attendees behave in a disorderly or disruptive manner and invite expulsion.	Obtain the consent of the other members of the meeting before trying to eject the disruptive participants.
WALKOUT As chairperson, you decide to walk out of a meeting before the agenda is concluded.	The meeting must appoint a new chairperson as quickly as possible; otherwise, it will automatically be terminated.
MERGER OR ACQUISITION PROPOSAL A company's share capital may become unstable when it faces a hostile bid or buyout.	To approve the bid, you must pass special resolutions, which require the approval of a specific percentage of the shareholders.
TAKEOVER BID BY SHAREHOLDERS Shareholders attempt to take over a company by accumulating the majority of the shares.	Check the company's rules to establish correct procedure. If the company is listed on a stock exchange, the exchange's rules apply.
DISSOLVING A COMPANY A company can be dissolved for failing to pay its debts or not fulfilling its original purpose.	Inform the shareholders that they must apply to the courts in order to wind up the company with the correct legal process.

98 Simplify procedural rules wherever possible.

99 Keep calm during demonstrations, and they may defuse themselves.

USING SET PROCEDURES

Always fall back on procedure when a problem arises. Referring to procedure helps you uphold the rights of the participants and manage the meeting effectively. Remember that:

- There are always rules to control an unruly meeting, implement action, or force a resolution;
- Most formal procedures have a basis in law or have been established by a governing body or a meeting of members;
- Most formal procedures are to ensure that all of a company's shareholders are treated equally;
- All participants should have access to the rules governing procedure so that they are aware of their obligations and rights.

ADAPTING PROCEDURES

You are responsible, as chairperson, for ensuring that participants do not exploit procedures to their own advantage. It may be worth simplifying complicated procedures and tightening loopholes to deter abuse. The process for changing rules or procedures depends on the company: you, as chairperson, may be able to do it yourself, or it may require a vote. Some companies in the US have attempted to protect themselves from takeovers by adopting procedures that make acquisition bids prohibitively expensive. A temporary change in rules can ensure smooth running of a meeting, but permanent procedural changes should be made with care. Remember that your role as chairperson is to protect the long-term interests of members.

100 Call a short adjournment if tempers flare.

POINTS TO REMEMBER

- The chairperson is ultimately responsible for the smooth running of a meeting.
- The chairperson should never become involved in an argument.
- Security staff should be on hand at all times but without being too intimidating or overzealous.
- If the tempers of participants erupt, they should be calmed immediately. If they refuse to settle down, they should be removed from the meeting.
- Exits should be left clear for ejecting troublemakers.

101 Discuss in advance with security staff what the procedure is for dealing with troublemakers.

EVALUATING YOUR SKILL AS A CHAIRPERSON

E valuate how well you perform as a chairperson by responding to the following statements, and mark the options that are closest to your experience. Be as honest as you can: if your answer is "never," mark Option 1; if it is "always," mark Option 4; and so on. Add your scores together and refer to the Analysis to see how you scored. Use your answers to identify the areas that need most improvement.

OPTIONS

1 Never

2 Occasionally

3 Frequently

4 Always

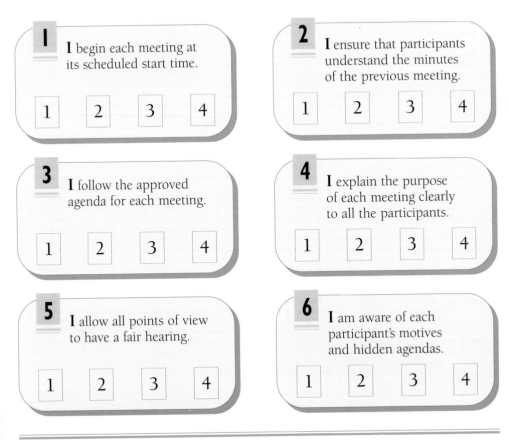

1 I begin each meeting at its scheduled start time.

1   2   3   4

2 I ensure that participants understand the minutes of the previous meeting.

1   2   3   4

3 I follow the approved agenda for each meeting.

1   2   3   4

4 I explain the purpose of each meeting clearly to all the participants.

1   2   3   4

5 I allow all points of view to have a fair hearing.

1   2   3   4

6 I am aware of each participant's motives and hidden agendas.

1   2   3   4

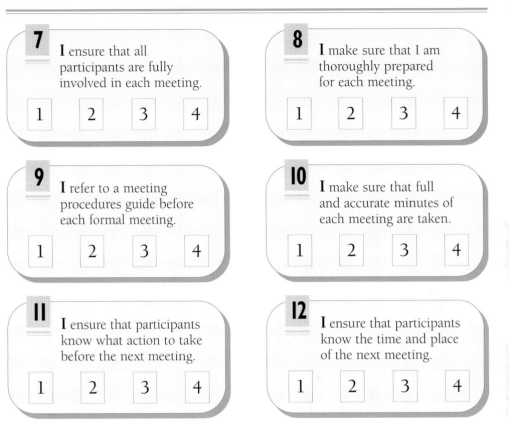

7 I ensure that all participants are fully involved in each meeting.

1   2   3   4

8 I make sure that I am thoroughly prepared for each meeting.

1   2   3   4

9 I refer to a meeting procedures guide before each formal meeting.

1   2   3   4

10 I make sure that full and accurate minutes of each meeting are taken.

1   2   3   4

11 I ensure that participants know what action to take before the next meeting.

1   2   3   4

12 I ensure that participants know the time and place of the next meeting.

1   2   3   4

ANALYSIS

Now you have completed the self-assessment, add up your total score and check your performance by reading the corresponding evaluation. Whatever level of success you have achieved chairing meetings, it is important to remember that there is always room for improvement. Identify your weakest areas, then refer to the chapters in this section where you will find practical advice and tips to help you to hone your skills as a chairperson.

12–24: Your skills as chairperson need considerable improvement; rethink your approach to the role, and take action.
25–36: You have definite strengths but must concentrate on improving weak points.
37–48: The meetings you chair should run smoothly. Since each meeting is different, continue to prepare well.

PRESENTING SUCCESSFULLY

INTRODUCTION

Whether you are a seasoned orator or a novice speaker, you can improve your presentation skills and enhance your credibility through planning, preparation, and practice. This section contains essential information on every aspect of public speaking from researching and writing your presentation material to overcoming tension and dealing with questions from an audience. Practical advice, for example on choosing the right audio-visual aids, will give you the confidence to handle real-life situations professionally and help you develop and perfect your skills. Further vital information is included in the form of 101 concise tips, which appear throughout the section, while a self-assessment exercise allows you to evaluate and chart your progress following each presentation you give.

PREPARING A PRESENTATION

There are two secrets to making a good presentation: preparation and practice. Take the time to prepare properly, and your chances of success will increase enormously.

DEFINING YOUR PURPOSE

What do you want to communicate to your audience? Before you start to prepare your presentation, decide what you want it to achieve. Focus on the purpose of the presentation at every stage to ensure that your preparation is relevant and efficient.

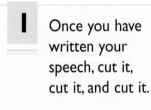

Once you have written your speech, cut it, cut it, and cut it.

POINTS TO REMEMBER

● Your presentation should be relevant, simple, and to the point.

● Your audience will be impressed by the depth and breadth of your knowledge rather than a show of false intellect and wit.

● Your positive attitude, energy, and enthusiasm for the subject will speak volumes. They will be remembered by your audience long after the details of your speech have been forgotten.

CONSIDERING YOUR AIMS

The first points to think about are what you intend to tell your audience and how best to communicate your message. Your strategy will depend on three things: the type of message you wish to deliver, the nature of the audience, and the physical surroundings of the location.

Review the purpose of your presentation, then ask yourself whether it is simple enough or too complex. Think about who might be in your audience and how they might receive your speech. Then ask yourself if this is how you want your speech to be received. If not, modify your purpose.

ASSESSING ABILITIES

Unless you are a trained actor, it is difficult trying to be anyone other than yourself. Concentrate on defining and utilizing your best assets. For example: if you have a good, clear voice, use it to your advantage; if you have a talent for such things, tell a humorous but relevant short anecdote. Next, confront your fears and anxieties about the presentation so that you can make sure that you are prepared for them on the day.

2 Group similar ideas together to establish themes.

SPEAKING ▶
CONFIDENTLY
Use techniques that you are comfortable with in your presentation. This will help you control your nerves once you are standing in front of the audience.

REDUCING YOUR FEARS

COMMON FEARS	PRACTICAL SOLUTIONS
EXCESSIVE NERVES You cannot relax. You forget what you are trying to say and dry up.	Prepare by rehearsing in front of a mirror and, if possible, at the location. Make sure that you can see your notes clearly at all times. Take a deep breath, and smile.
BORED AUDIENCE The audience loses interest and fidgets and talks among themselves.	Ensure that the point you are trying to make is relevant – if not, cut it. Be enthusiastic. Vary the pace of your presentation and maintain eye contact with the audience.
HOSTILE AUDIENCE You are heckled. Questions from the floor are aggressive in tone.	Remain polite and courteous. If your audience has specialized knowledge of your subject, defer to them. Redirect difficult questions back to the audience.
BREAKDOWN OF VISUAL AIDS Equipment fails to work, or you cannot remember how to use it.	Avoid using any technology with which you are not thoroughly familiar. Immediately before the presentation, check all the equipment that you will be using.

KNOWING YOUR AUDIENCE

Find out as much as you can about who will be attending your presentation. Have you invited some of the audience? Does it consist of colleagues? Once you know who will be attending, structure your speech to elicit the best response from them.

3 Make sure that the audience leaves the location feeling informed.

QUESTIONS TO ASK YOURSELF

Q What is the expected size of the audience?

Q What is the average age of the audience?

Q What is the ratio of males to females in the audience?

Q Is the audience well informed about your subject?

Q Has the audience chosen, or been asked, to attend?

Q What do the members of the audience have in common?

Q What prejudices does the audience hold?

Q What is the cultural makeup of the audience?

Q Does everyone or anyone in the audience know you?

4 Always remember to talk *to* your audience, rather than *at* them.

EVALUATING AN AUDIENCE

To communicate your message effectively, you need to take account of the cultural values and opinions held by your audience. Consider how they might react to any sensitive issues raised in your speech, and be aware that this could affect the rest of your presentation. If the audience members are known to hold strong opinions on your chosen subject, be wary of introducing contentious issues without supporting your point of view, and remember that humor can easily cause offense, so use it sparingly in your speech.

FINDING OUT MORE

The primary source of information about your audience will be the organizer of the event at which you are speaking. If your presentation is to be included as part of a conference, ask for a list of the delegates in advance. If you are making a presentation to a potential new client, ask your contacts in the appropriate industry what they can tell you about them. Before addressing a public meeting, take the time to read the local press to see what concerns your audience might have. Use this prior knowledge to your best advantage: a speech that connects directly with members of the audience and shows that you have done your homework will be well received.

BEING ADAPTABLE

The size of the audience will have a significant impact on the way you structure your presentation. With small groups there is plenty of opportunity for two-way interaction – you can answer questions as you go along, or you can ask your audience for their opinions about the questions and issues you are raising. With large groups, the communication is almost entirely one-way, and a very different approach is required by the speaker. It is vital that your material is clear, precise, and easy to follow so that the audience's interest is held throughout.

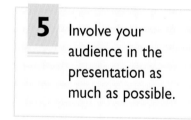

5 Involve your audience in the presentation as much as possible.

ADJUSTING YOUR PRESENTATION TO AUDIENCE SIZE

AUDIENCE SIZE	PRESENTATION STYLES	TECHNIQUES
SMALL AUDIENCE A group of fewer than 15 people is considered a small audience. Most people will be asked to address an audience of this size at some point in their working career.	**FORMAL** Follow formal procedures in committee meetings, sales pitches to prospective clients, and interdepartmental presentations.	● Establish eye contact with each member of the group at an early stage. ● Face your audience at all times – this will help hold their attention.
	INFORMAL Use informality to break the ice when presenting new products to known suppliers and when speaking to colleagues.	● Interact with the audience by soliciting questions. ● Allow individuals to have a say, but keep it brief.
LARGE AUDIENCE A group of 15 or more people constitutes a large audience. It is easier to address this size of audience if you already have previous presenting experience. 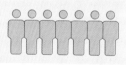	**FORMAL** Follow formal procedures when giving a speech at a conference or at the annual general meeting of a public company.	● Make sure that all of the audience members are able to hear you clearly, especially at the back of the room. ● Link, sum up, emphasize, and repeat main points.
	INFORMAL Use informal procedures when making a spontaneous presentation from the floor at a formal conference.	● Speak slowly, and enunciate at all times. ● Keep your message broad, general, and simple. Go into more detail only if asked.

DEALING WITH LOGISTICS

*O*nly meticulous organization can ensure that your presentation will be effective. Careful planning of the practical details in advance will free you nearer the time to concentrate on perfecting your presentation, rather than dealing with unforeseen hitches.

6 Visit the location in advance to become familiar with its layout.

CONSIDERING KEY POINTS AT THE START

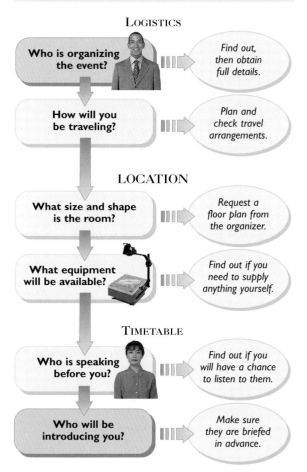

LOGISTICS

| Who is organizing the event? | Find out, then obtain full details. |

| How will you be traveling? | Plan and check travel arrangements. |

LOCATION

| What size and shape is the room? | Request a floor plan from the organizer. |

| What equipment will be available? | Find out if you need to supply anything yourself. |

TIMETABLE

| Who is speaking before you? | Find out if you will have a chance to listen to them. |

| Who will be introducing you? | Make sure they are briefed in advance. |

ORGANIZING YOUR SCHEDULE

At an early stage, think through the event in its entirety. If the site being used is not local, you will need to plan your travel arrangements and organize accommodation well in advance. Try to allow about three hours on the day of the presentation, or the evening before, to prepare yourself for it – both mentally and physically. You should also set aside about an hour to think through your speech and, if possible, rehearse on arrival at the location. Plan what clothes to wear, and ensure they are clean and pressed. If you are the first (or only) speaker, check that any equipment you will be using is in working order.

7 Compile a schedule of preparations for the day.

PLANNING TRAVEL

Calculate your departure time carefully to avoid arriving late at your location and not having sufficient time to prepare. Work backward from the time you want to arrive, adding together travel times, then add at least one hour as a safety factor. Allow for delays and, if traveling by plane, include the time of the trip from the airport. Build enough time into your schedule to rest and to overcome jet lag if you are traveling over a long distance to give your speech.

8 Take work with you to occupy travel time.

ANALYZING TRAVEL REQUIREMENTS

Where is the event taking place? → *Try to combine it with another visit nearby.*

How are you traveling? → *Obtain any medication you need for motion sickness.*

Do you need to allow for jet lag?

How long will the trip take? → *Make an effort to use the time effectively.*

Will you need to find accommodation? → *Make arrangements for expenses.*

MAKING TIME TO PREPARE

The casual, seemingly effortless presentations that are most successful are invariably the result of a great deal of preparation, research, and hard work. A company chairperson's annual speech to shareholders may take several speechwriters weeks of drafting and redrafting before it is of a suitable standard, whereas an induction for new trainees may take considerable work initially but then require only a little last-minute reworking. Start preparing at least four weeks before your presentation to allow time to formulate ideas and gather any necessary reference material. As you gain experience, you may find that you need less time.

9 For every hour of presentation, put aside 10 hours for preparation.

MAKING ITINERARIES AND CHECKLISTS

Even the most organized speakers have many details to consider before giving a speech. Making an itinerary and listing all the materials and props that you require for your presentation are as essential to preparation as rehearsing your speech. The safest way to do this is to make a checklist, noting down points as you think of them. Work through your checklist and try to foresee any potential hitches. If the presentation is being given away from your place of work, make sure that you leave a contact number with your colleagues in case they need to get in touch with you during the day. Be sure they know the time of the presentation, and ask them not to disturb you just before or during it – except in a real emergency.

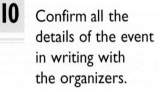 **10** Confirm all the details of the event in writing with the organizers.

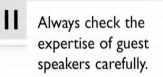 **11** Always check the expertise of guest speakers carefully.

ORGANIZING A PRESENTATION YOURSELF

If you are asked to organize a presentation yourself, there are several important decisions to make early on concerning the location, speakers, and size of audience. Draw up a list of possible locations to compare the advantages and disadvantages of each, bearing in mind costs, location, capacity, and facilities. Select a location to suit the size of your audience and the style of the presentation. Pass on all these details to the other speakers so that they can organize their presentations accordingly. Keep an alternative location in mind in case your first choice is not available on the date you require or falls through after it has been booked. When considering guest speakers, check their credentials thoroughly to ensure that they have the necessary expertise. Give them plenty of notice, and reconfirm the details before the presentation. As with locations, keep alternative speakers in mind.

ORGANIZING A GROUP PRESENTATION

If you are going to organize a group presentation, you need to consider some additional points. The secret of a successful group presentation is to keep a tight hold on the proceedings, since events can easily degenerate into chaos if people speak out of turn. Discuss beforehand the order in which the panel members will speak, and draw up an agenda well in advance so that each member of the panel is aware of this running order. It is important to adhere to this, so appoint a strong chairperson to regulate the proceedings strictly.

When organizing a group presentation, research the background of your chosen speakers carefully – it is vital to have the right balance among the participants. If they are too like-minded, there will be little discussion generated by their speeches; if their ideas clash, they may react to one another with hostility while on the podium. If necessary, build in time for a final question-and-answer session between the panel and audience.

THINGS TO DO

1. Book a location with facilities that can handle group presentations.
2. Check that there are no personal animosities between proposed speakers.
3. Invite the speakers and confirm their attendance.
4. Discuss the running order of the speeches.
5. Draw up a rigid timetable.
6. Appoint a strong individual to act as chairperson.

12 Research your audience before sending invitations to a presentation.

INVITING AN AUDIENCE

When thinking about who should attend a presentation, bear in mind the following points:
● Who would benefit from hearing the information in the presentation?
● What would you like the audience to learn from the presentation?
● How can you reach the target audience?
Planning your publicity is an integral part of the organizational process. Once you have decided on your target audience, ensure that advertising is placed where they will see it – for example, in an appropriate trade publication. The time, date, and location should be clearly visible. Have personal invitations sent to anyone you wish to attend.

KNOWING YOUR LOCATION

If possible, visit your chosen presentation site in advance to check out the layout. If this is not practical, ask the organizers to send you a detailed floorplan showing all the facilities. Consider the lighting, acoustics, seating, and power supply carefully.

13 Assess all details of a location, no matter how minor they may appear.

ASSESSING THE LOCATION

The location will set the mood of your presentation. An informal gathering in a sunny room on a university campus will put an audience in a very different frame of mind than will the sterile conference hall of a large hotel. If you visit the location in advance, note down as many details as possible – including its atmosphere and size. Assess your location at the same time of day as your presentation will be given to make informed decisions about the seating and lighting. Take the opportunity to check out the locations of doorways, power outlets, light switches, and refreshment facilities.

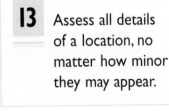

Keep area around doorway clear for easy entry and exit

Position refreshments at the rear of the room to avoid possible distractions

Locate power outlets, and check whether you need extension cords

Lower window blinds to keep out light when projecting visual aids on to screen

14 Locate the light switches so that, if necessary, you can dim the lights to use your visual aids.

▲ ASSESSING THE BASICS

When visiting a location in advance, try to assess whether there are any awkward obstructions that might hide you from the audience. Check the positions of doorways, power outlets, and other facilities, and get a feel for the atmosphere of the room.

15 Decide on the positioning of any visual aids well in advance.

CONSIDERING THE DETAILS

When assessing a location, take careful stock of its features – is it accessible to your audience? Is it near an airport, railroad station, or subway? Is the location on the flight path of a major airport or next to a noisy restaurant? Are there immovable features that could restrict the audience's view? If so, plan your seating around these. Can you control the heating or air conditioning? If so, adjust the temperature to just below what is comfortable, since considerable warmth will be generated by a large number of people being together in one room.

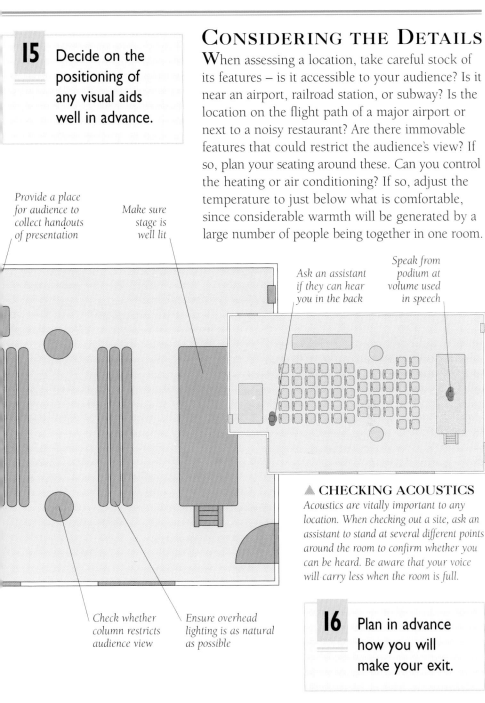

Provide a place for audience to collect handouts of presentation

Make sure stage is well lit

Ask an assistant if they can hear you in the back

Speak from podium at volume used in speech

Check whether column restricts audience view

Ensure overhead lighting is as natural as possible

▲ CHECKING ACOUSTICS

Acoustics are vitally important to any location. When checking out a site, ask an assistant to stand at several different points around the room to confirm whether you can be heard. Be aware that your voice will carry less when the room is full.

16 Plan in advance how you will make your exit.

503

SEATING THE AUDIENCE

It is important to get the right balance when seating your audience. Comfort is an obvious factor to consider, but you must ensure that your audience is not so comfortable that they fall asleep or so uncomfortable that they start fidgeting before you reach the end of your presentation. Ideally, chairs should be upright and of equal size. If you can adjust the seating, place chairs far enough apart to allow people to put their bags and briefcases on the floor beside them. Spacing the chairs out in this way will also prevent the audience from feeling claustrophobic. If you think your audience will want to take notes during your presentation, provide chairs with armrests on which to rest notepads. To ensure that the seats in the front of the auditorium fill up first, remove seats from the rear. Keep a number of accessible spare seats in reserve to put out for any latecomers. Finally, be sure to comply with the location's fire safety regulations with regard to seating arrangements.

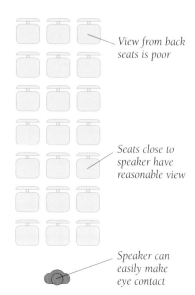

View from back seats is poor

Seats close to speaker have reasonable view

Speaker can easily make eye contact

▲ **PLAN ONE**

A series of straight, narrow rows allows the speaker to make eye contact with all of the audience. However, this layout does not provide a good view or acoustics for people seated at the back of the room.

Audience member seated here has poor view of speaker

Even farthest audience member has good view

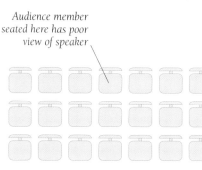

Eye contact with entire audience is difficult

Speaker can see entire audience

▲ **PLAN TWO**

Here an audience of the same size as that in Plan One is seated closer to the speaker. The majority of the audience has a good view of the speaker and is near enough to hear the presentation clearly. The speaker must work hard to make eye contact with everyone.

▲ **PLAN THREE**

This semicircular layout is popular, since it provides the optimum arrangement for acoustics and visibility – but the disadvantage is that it takes up more space than Plans One and Two. The speaker can maintain strong eye contact with all members of the audience.

CHECKING THE LOCATION'S AUDIO-VISUAL FACILITIES

If you intend to use audio-visual elements in your presentation, you must check that the appropriate facilities are available at the location and that they function correctly. Familiarize yourself with each piece of equipment to avoid any delays or mistakes during the presentation. Large rooms will require the use of a basic public address system (PA) consisting of speakers, an amplifier, and one or more microphones. If a PA is not available, you will need to bring and install your own – they can be rented. Make sure is it powerful enough for the entire room. Ensure that there is a screen on which to project any images, checking that the size of the screen is appropriate to the size of the room and that it is in view of the whole audience.

17 Ensure that you know how the public address system functions.

18 Keep spare seats in reserve for any latecomers.

USING A MICROPHONE

A microphone is needed only when you are speaking to a large audience or if you are speaking in the open air. If you need to use one, always test it in advance, making adjustments for volume and background noise. Hand-held or podium microphones tend to restrict movement, so use a wireless hand-held model if you will need to show visual aids. Clip-on microphones allow you to use both hands while presenting your speech, but always be sure to position them correctly; otherwise, they can exaggerate noises such as breathing or turning pages.

On-off switch

Clip attaches to clothing

▲ **CLIP-ON**
A clip-on microphone is attached to clothing and remains at a fixed distance from the mouth.

◀ **HAND-HELD**
A hand-held microphone allows you the freedom to move around but can restrict the use of the hands. It can usually be attached to a podium, adding to its versatility.

CLARIFYING OBJECTIVES

Before you prepare for a presentation, it is important that you think about your objectives. Do you want to entertain the audience, pass on vital information, or inspire them to rush off and take immediate action as a consequence of your speech?

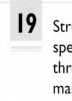

19 Structure your speech around three or four main points.

20 Keep the audience interested by including a few relevant anecdotes.

SETTING THE TONE

The general tone and style of your presentation can reinforce the purpose of your speech. If you want to pass on information, then you need to take a logically consistent, well-structured approach to your subject matter. If your main purpose is to entertain, include some jokes, anecdotes, and funny stories. If you want to inspire the audience, keep the content of your speech positive and pitched at a level at which they can respond personally and emotionally.

ENCOURAGING RESPONSES

Every speaker wants to give a successful and well-received presentation, but many do not know that there are practical methods to achieve this. By structuring your speech in certain ways, you can elicit the response you want from the audience. For example, if you are providing your audience with new information, you may want them to ask questions at the end of your speech. Whet their appetites for the subject not by telling them everything they need to know immediately, but by encouraging them to be inquisitive.

▼ **USING THE THREE E'S**
Each successful presentation has three essential objectives. The first aim is to educate: the audience should learn something from your speech. The second is to entertain: the audience should enjoy your speech. The final element is to explain: all parts of your speech should be clear to your audience.

| Educate | Entertain | Explain |

USING YOUR KNOWLEDGE

The main objective of making a presentation is to relay information to your audience, and nothing is more likely to capture and hold their attention than your enthusiasm for the subject. Do not get too carried away with your preparation – plan to lead your audience with your enthusiasm rather than overwhelm them with it. Authoritative knowledge usually speaks for itself, so there is no need for you to drop names or academic references if you really know your subject. You will gain credibility if you handle audience questions adeptly, so be well informed and well prepared.

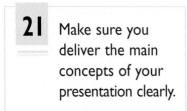

21 Make sure you deliver the main concepts of your presentation clearly.

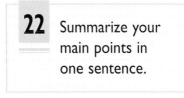

22 Summarize your main points in one sentence.

SELECTING KEY POINTS

Every adult audience has a limited attention span of about 45 minutes. In that time, they will absorb only about a third of what was said and a maximum of seven concepts. Limit yourself to three or four main points, and emphasize them at the beginning of your speech, in the middle, and again at the end to reiterate your message. Try to find a catchy title that sums up your speech, but avoid being too clever or too obscure. "The Role of TQM in BPR" is fine for managers in your company who know that you are intending to talk about the concepts of total quality management and business process reengineering, but it is no use making your title so cryptic that you confuse even the most informed audiences. Your audience will be most open to you if they have a clear idea of the subject of your speech.

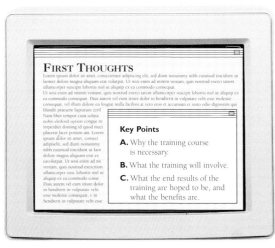

▲ **CHOOSING YOUR MAIN POINTS**
Clarify your ideas by summarizing the main ideas from your notes into succinct points. Limit yourself to three or four points to keep your message simple and memorable.

FINDING MATERIAL

A successful presentation always begins with careful background research. This requires initiative and hard work and can be time-consuming. Allocate sufficient time for your research and explore as many sources as possible, from press clippings to the Internet.

23 Keep your main objectives in mind while researching your material.

A. Why the training course is necessary.

B. What the training will involve.

C. What the end results of the training are hoped to be, and what the benefits are.

▲ **USING YOUR MAIN POINTS**
When you begin your research, keep the three or four main points in mind. As you find material relevant to your speech, organize it into separate files for each main point until you have enough to fill out your presentation.

FINDING SOURCES

A good starting point for research is to review one of the leading books on the subject of your presentation, then look at its bibliography. From there you should be able to find a large amount of relevant reference material. For newspaper or magazine articles, consider using a clipping service, which for a fee will supply you regularly with a package of articles on virtually any subject that you care to name. This will provide you with the free time to explore the many other sources of information available, for example:

● Management reports, government papers, and professional journals;
● Friends, family, and other personal contacts;
● Videos, CD-ROMs, and the Internet.

RESEARCHING MATERIAL

At the beginning of your research, allow yourself enough time to consider thoroughly the advantages and disadvantages of every source of information you intend to use. Be realistic about what you hope to find out from each source, and think about how best to use the information in your speech. Always consult your personal contacts for any leads; there is nothing more frustrating than spending days in a library only to find that a friend of a friend is the greatest living expert on your subject.

24 Try different sources to see which you find the most helpful.

FRESHENING UP YOUR RESEARCH

Be open-minded when starting on your research, and seek out fresh fields of research to enliven your presentation. Do not rely on dusty old books – explore new reference sources on the Internet to glean the latest information on your subject. Your speech will be all the more appealing to the audience if it sounds innovative rather than like a rehash of old information from often-quoted sources. Make the audience feel that you are feeding them new knowledge by providing fresh information around your basic facts and figures.

▲ MAKING GOOD USE OF YOUR TIME
It is important to decide very quickly whether or not a particular avenue of research is worth pursuing. Once you begin to find relevant information, note its source and its main points. Is it the most up-to-date material on the subject? Is the information accurate? Is it giving you any new leads or areas of research? Persevere only with the material that fills your research criteria.

▲ EXPLORING WEB SITES
Each Web site on the Internet holds a wealth of information that can be accessed, saved, or printed out, and used as reference material. One of the chief advantages of this mode of research is that the information Web sites hold is usually more frequently updated than the same information in print.

USING NEW TECHNOLOGY

The Internet brings an international electronic library right onto your desk. Use well-chosen key words to search for relevant reference material from the extraordinary range of information available on the Internet – new sites are springing up daily. The more specific your key words are, the more chance you have of finding the data you require within a reasonable length of time. Store large amounts of material on computerized data bases, which can be purchased as ready-made software packages or designed specifically for your purposes.

 25 Do not ignore a good source just because the information is not immediately accessible to you.

STRUCTURING MATERIAL

The order in which you present the main points of your presentation, and the emphasis each point is given, will affect the message that your audience takes away. Use the most appropriate structure in your speech to give your audience the right message.

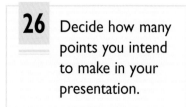

26 Decide how many points you intend to make in your presentation.

CHOOSING A STRUCTURE

There are several ways in which you can present your three or four main points. You may choose to introduce them separately, either one after the other in order of importance, or chronologically, or in any other sequence that makes sense. If you want one particular point to give the strongest impression, present it first, then follow it with supporting points – or any other points that you are making. Alternatively, interweave your points to highlight their equal significance. The structure most commonly used by speakers is to overlap the main points that are being made. This way, an idea can be left open and referred back to in response to subsequent ideas in the presentation.

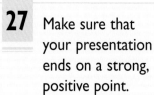

27 Make sure that your presentation ends on a strong, positive point.

▲ MAKING SEPARATE POINTS

Here, ideas that do not necessarily flow into each other can be presented separately and given equal weight. Remember, an audience may assume that the first point has greatest significance.

▲ EMPHASIZING ONE POINT

If one point is of greater significance than the others, put it first and allow it the most time so that you can discuss it fully. Back it up or complement it with your secondary or supporting points.

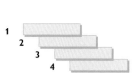

▲ OVERLAPPING POINTS

In practice, the most frequently occurring structure is the one in which each point overlaps and depends to some extent upon the others. The second point must be partially unveiled in order to explain the first, and so on. Each subsequent point can be referred to in relation to the earlier points, linking all the main points together.

MATCHING PRESENTATION STRUCTURE TO MATERIAL

TYPES OF STRUCTURE	PRACTICAL USES
MAKING SEPARATE POINTS Points are presented in a sequence that suits the particular subject.	Formal presentations, such as a serious educational talk or a lecture on management theory, can benefit from this presentation structure. If the audience members are taking notes, the speaker can assist them by summarizing each point after it has been made and providing a brief introduction to lead into the following point.
EMPHASIZING ONE POINT The main point is followed by several other points.	Examples of this type of presentation might include a talk given to staff about the need for improved customer service. The structure is emphatic and is suitable for use when the audience is well informed about the subject matter and can grasp a high level of detail. It is also useful if you want to present another aspect of the same subject.
OVERLAPPING POINTS Points are referred back to or reintroduced for emphasis.	This structure is most suitable for informal talks given in front of a small audience. It is often used in meetings attended by close colleagues who are familiar with the subject matter and can cope with a relatively complex presentation. Overlapping points encourage debate and audience intervention as different ideas present themselves.

USING NARRATIVE

The basic technique of narrative is to give your subject a recognizable beginning, middle, and end. The most common use of this technique is in storytelling. For your presentation to be a success, it is important that you follow this basic format when composing your speech. The introduction to your presentation is the beginning; the middle section consists of your central themes and ideas (using whichever structure you decide best suits your purpose); while the end is formed by your conclusion, referring back to your main themes, and then taking questions from the audience if necessary. Remember that it is important to give the audience clear signals at the beginning and end of each stage of your presentation.

▲ **USING SYMBOLS**
Think laterally when structuring your speech. Choose familiar images to support your ideas, such as a cat to show instinctive behavior. Look outside your original field of research for analogies that illustrate points vividly.

USING AN OUTLINE

It is helpful to prepare a written outline of the material that you wish to present. This will help clarify the structure of your presentation while you are writing it and can be used to jog your memory while you are making the presentation. Think of your three or four main points as A, B, C, and D, and then put subheadings under each one (1, 2, 3). Label any secondary subheadings as i), ii), iii), and so on. When writing these notes, keep them simple so that they are easy to read at a glance.

A. Why training is needed.
  1. Staff benefits from refresher course.
  2. New staff will learn correct procedures.

Main points are labeled alphabetically

B. What training involves.
  1. Improving performance.
    i) Tests of skill level.
    ii) Gaps in knowledge.
  2. Specific details.

Subheadings are labeled with Arabic numerals

C. Expected end results.
  1. Improved efficiency.
  2. Greater productivity.

Secondary subheadings are labeled with Roman numerals

▲ **OUTLINING A STRUCTURE**
Make up a rough outline of the structure you are planning for your presentation, as in the sample above. Use this as a basis from which to expand on your theme while you are researching and preparing your presentation.

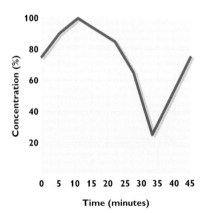

▲ **AUDIENCE ATTENTION SPAN**
This chart shows a typical audience's attention span, based on a 45-minute presentation. Audiences are most alert just after the start of a presentation, reaching a peak at about 10 minutes. Attention fades until 30–35 minutes have passed then increases as the presentation nears its end.

OPENING EFFECTIVELY

It is essential to make a good impression at the beginning of your presentation, and one of the best ways to do this is for you to appear positive and confident. This means you must first be well prepared. Seasoned presenters who prefer not to use notes invariably write out their first sentence or two. That way, they can concentrate more on the impression they are giving and less on the words they are speaking. Plan an effective opening that provides the audience with an outline of the presentation you are about to give, informing them briefly of the points you will be making during your speech. Use anecdotes to break the ice and draw the audience into your speech in a familiar way. Always remember, however, that the audience is not at its most alert at the very beginning of your speech, so save your strongest point for a few minutes into the presentation.

LINKING AND SUMMING UP

It is important to incorporate clear signals into your presentation. Plan a logical flow of ideas and themes to help the audience follow your presentation easily, and introduce new subjects by making clear links between the old and new ideas. Listen to professional speakers on radio and television, and note the techniques they use to link together the points or themes of their speeches and sum up each point before introducing a new one. These links and summaries are as important as the main points themselves, so plan them well.

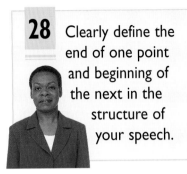

28 Clearly define the end of one point and beginning of the next in the structure of your speech.

USING REPETITION

Recapping information during your presentation is an effective way of reinforcing the main points of your argument. When structuring your speech, build some repetition into its framework at the end of each main point and in the conclusion. However, simply repeating the information you have already delivered in the main body of your speech is not enough. Use different wording to keep the ideas sounding fresh yet familiar.

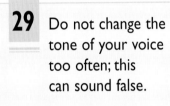

29 Do not change the tone of your voice too often; this can sound false.

ENDING MEMORABLY

Structuring a strong ending to your presentation is as important as planning a good beginning – it is vital to signal to your audience that the end of your speech is approaching. Insert phrases such as "for my final point..." or "in conclusion..." to alert the audience to the fact that you are about to summarize all that you have said. They will be grateful for the opportunity to catch up on any points they may have missed during your speech.

▼ **REINFORCING POINTS**
It is important to reinforce the main points of any presentation. You can do this by first giving the audience a "contents list" of your speech, then discussing the issues you are raising, finishing off with a summary.

| Tell them what you are going to tell them | → | Tell them | → | Tell them what you have told them |

WRITING A PRESENTATION

*I*t is important to be aware that written
material can sound very different when
it is delivered to an audience in spoken form.
Learn to write your prose in a natural oral
style that follows natural speech patterns
and is suitable for verbal presentation.

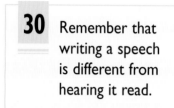

30 Remember that
writing a speech
is different from
hearing it read.

STARTING TO WRITE

Once you have completed all your research and
outlined the structure of your presentation, you
are ready to start writing. Try to imagine your
words as you would like your audience to hear
them. Spend some quiet time alone thinking
about what you will write, then compose a first
draft by writing down – without stopping –
everything that you think you would like to
include. If you are unsure about how to write
for speech, prepare by assessing the difference
between spoken and written language.

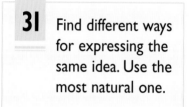

31 Find different ways
for expressing the
same idea. Use the
most natural one.

ADAPTING WRITING STYLES FOR SPEECH

SENTENCE STRUCTURE

GRAMMAR
Try to avoid sentences that are
grammatically correct but sound
stilted when spoken. To sound
direct, use the first and second
person (*I* and *you*) and active verbs.

SYNTAX
Always put the most important or
interesting facts first. Do not begin
a sentence with a subordinate
clause or with any statement that
could be put in parentheses.

SPEAKING RATHER THAN WRITING

Say: "The accounting system I work with," *not*
"The accounting system with which I work."

Say: "You must recognize these ploys for what they are,"
not "It is important that these ploys are recognized..."

Say: "Lower costs and increased output – that's what we
need," *not* "We need to reduce costs and increase output."

Say: "This can make all the difference," *not* "Although this
may seem a minor detail, it can make all the difference..."

STREAMLINING MATERIAL

Once you have produced the first draft of your presentation, you can begin to pare down the material. Read through your draft to ensure that you have prioritized the facts correctly and included all the essential information. Fill in your material with relevant examples to reinforce your main points. Finally, use items of particular interest or appeal, which are not essential but will enhance audience enjoyment of your presentation, to add humor and topicality to your speech.

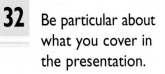

32 Be particular about what you cover in the presentation.

▼ **PRIORITIZING LEVELS OF INFORMATION**
Before you begin, write down every point relevant to the theme of your presentation, then put each in one of these categories.

Must know	Should know	Nice to know

WRITING TO SOUND NATURAL

The best starting point for giving a successful presentation is that you feel confident and relaxed about the words you are delivering, so when you are writing your speech, keep your sentence construction simple. Think about your audience as a single person – this will help to create an atmosphere of intimacy. Speakers who succeed in doing this make every member of the audience feel that the content is directed uniquely at them, which holds their attention. If you are not sure whether you sound natural, tape-record yourself reading a draft of your speech, then listen and amend your text where necessary.

DO'S AND DON'TS

✔ Do use simple, direct sentences.

✔ Do use the pronouns "you" and "I."

✔ Do use active verbs (run, go, do, use, etc.).

✔ Do sprinkle your speech liberally with adjectives.

✔ Do prepare and rehearse phrases to avoid stumbling.

✔ Do include examples and analogies to illustrate your points.

✘ Don't use jargon or inappropriate language.

✘ Don't fill your speech with irrelevant points.

✘ Don't feel that you need to write out the speech word for word.

✘ Don't overwhelm the audience with too much detail.

✘ Don't patronize your audience.

✘ Don't try to imitate someone else's style; it will sound false.

33 Make sure the written structure of your presentation is not too complex, or it may be confusing.

CONDENSING A PRESENTATION INTO NOTES

If you choose to deliver a presentation using notes, begin by writing a full draft of the presentation, including all your main points and the examples you will use to illustrate and explain them. This script is the starting point from which you can begin to condense your prose into notes. Using clearly numbered note cards, pick out the key words and phrases from your script, then write them legibly on one side of the cards. Do not write too much on each card, and keep the information simple and unambiguous.

◀ **PREPARING A DRAFT**
Having decided on the structure of your presentation and then compiled your research material, write (or type) the speech out in full. Edit and reedit this draft until you are satisfied with the flow and pace of the speech.

◀ **PREPARING NOTES**
Extract the major points from the final draft, then write them on numbered cards. Limit your notes to two points per card for clarity.

PACING A SPEECH

Think about what makes a good speech work well. More often than not, it is the timing. The silent parts of a speech – in other words, the pauses – are just as important as the spoken words in communicating the content of the speech, since they provide aural punctuation. When writing your speech, consider how it will sound to your audience. Whether you choose to read the presentation from notes or as a full script, write "pause" wherever you feel a break is necessary – for example, where a point requires emphasis or to mark a break between one clear idea and another. Include these pauses when rehearsing. Using silence takes courage: a scripted pause should last about three seconds – much longer than a pause in your normal speech.

34 Print your speech on one side of the page only, and use a large typeface.

35 Always number the pages of a full, written speech.

PREPARING NOTE CARDS

Regard using notes during a presentation as an insurance against forgetting your speech – you do not need to read from them word for word, but you have the security of knowing that they are there if your mind goes blank. Notes are meant to provide a series of cues to remind you what you want to say and in what order, allowing you to talk to the audience instead of reciting your presentation to them. There are a number of useful techniques you can use if speaking from notes, such as condensing a preprepared outline, writing key sentences, or noting key words – but write out quotations and jokes in full unless you are sure you know them. Use a system of color coding to mark text that you can cut from your speech without compromising the integrity of your message if, for instance, you exceed your allotted time. For example, write essential text in blue ink, and write text that can be cut in green ink.

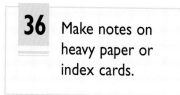

36 Make notes on heavy paper or index cards.

▲ **USING PROMPTS**
Transfer key words and phrases from your presentation onto cards. Be straightforward in what you write down so that you are able to remember the point of each prompt.

PREPARING A WRITTEN SCRIPT

If you choose to use a written script in your presentation, it is essential to arrange it carefully. Use large type and double line-spacing so that the text is easy to read. Set out the headings clearly so that it is easy to keep your place. Use a variety of different styling methods, such as emboldening or italicizing, to highlight the text that you want to emphasize. Finally, print the finished document onto heavy paper and keep a spare copy.

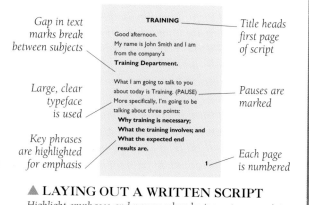

Gap in text marks break between subjects

Large, clear typeface is used

Key phrases are highlighted for emphasis

Title heads first page of script

Pauses are marked

Each page is numbered

▲ **LAYING OUT A WRITTEN SCRIPT**
Highlight emphases and pauses when laying out your script – this will help you speak naturally and confidently to your audience, which is essential for a smooth-running presentation.

USING AUDIO-VISUAL AIDS

Audio-visual (AV) aids can be central to a presentation, since they are often able to illustrate difficult concepts more easily than words. Always ask yourself if using AV aids will contribute to your presentation, and never be tempted to use them unnecessarily.

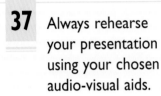

37 Always rehearse your presentation using your chosen audio-visual aids.

USING DIFFERENT AUDIO-VISUAL AIDS

TYPES OF AUDIO-VISUAL AID	EXAMPLES OF AUDIO-VISUAL AID

LOW COMPLEXITY
The advantage of these aids lies in their simplicity; also, no power supply is needed for them to work. Information can be prepared in advance, leaving little to set up on the day. Handouts can be prepared for any size of audience, but boards and flip charts need to be visible and are best for small audiences.

HANDOUTS
Distribute these before giving your presentation, preferably during a break. Make sure that you give the handouts a purpose by referring to them during your presentation.

MEDIUM COMPLEXITY
This group contains some of the most commonly used AV aids, which achieve good effects without involving too much technical hardware. The aids themselves need setting up on the day of your presentation, but the information and any slides used in conjunction with them can be prepared in advance.

SLIDE PROJECTOR
Arrange the slides you need to illustrate your arguments in a carousel prior to your speech. Practice operating the projector before you give your presentation.

HIGH COMPLEXITY
These aids involve the very highest level of technical capability and may require a specialized team to set them up. The impact achieved using high-complexity AV aids can be stunning and well worth the work, but the more complex the AV aid, the more opportunity there is for breakdown or failure.

VIDEO
Use video to show short live-action images or a taped message from a speaker who is not able to attend the presentation in person.

CHOOSING AV AIDS

There is a range of AV aids to suit different types of presentation. Such aids can sometimes distance you from the audience, however, so use them only if they are appropriate and helpful. AV aids have varying levels of complexity; many require a source of electricity, which can lead to problems if the power fails. Others may need to be designed or installed by specialists and may be difficult to use.

38 Pause when you first ask your audience to look at a visual aid.

WRITING BOARD
Use a writing board to illustrate your points in an informal presentation to a small audience. Make sure that your writing is legible to the people sitting at the back of the audience.

FLIP CHART
Prepare any number of sheets in advance, using charts and diagrams to highlight your arguments. Emphasize key points with color, and ensure that the flip chart can be seen by everyone in the audience.

OVERHEAD PROJECTOR
This is the best way of presenting charts and tables. Use a pointer to draw attention to particular graphs or numbers without obscuring the audience's view of the image.

AUDIO SYSTEM
An audio system with headphones is vital if you need to provide simultaneous translation facilities. A microphone, amplifier, and speakers are also handy for large audiences.

MULTIMEDIA
Use CD-ROM packages with moving images and an audio track on a large monitor with speakers. Alternatively, employ a software engineer to create a package to your specific requirements.

COMPUTER GRAPHICS
Software can be used to display graphs, charts, or three-dimensional images on screen. Moving graphics can be used to show how statistics will change over time.

CONSIDERING AUDIENCE SIZE

Different AV aids suit different sizes of audience, but if your resources are limited you can adapt your AV aids to suit any audience. For example, if you are using computer graphics but want to avoid losing definition of images by enlarging them too much, provide each member of the audience with handouts of the computer graphics you are showing on screen. Alternatively, if you are presenting to a large audience, project the images onto several large screens.

◀ **VIEW FROM A SMALL AUDIENCE**
When presenting to a small audience sitting close to you, your visual aids will be clearly visible to everyone – whichever type you choose to use.

39 Number your slides to avoid any confusion.

VIEW FROM A LARGE AUDIENCE ▶
Visual aids that work for a small audience are unlikely to work for a large one. An audience sitting far away may be unable to discern much from them.

PREPARING AV AIDS

All AV aids require considerable preparation, but whereas a writing board can be set up relatively quickly and then used over again, a multimedia demonstration can take a long time to prepare. Generally speaking, the higher the complexity of the AV aid, the more preparation is required.

If you do not have the time, the knowledge, or the creative talent to prepare your own AV aids, enlist somebody to do it for you. Use support staff, a colleague, or an external design agency. Choose your helpers carefully and present them with a tight brief to prevent any misinterpretation regarding the desired final product.

POINTS TO REMEMBER

● Audiences read on-screen material faster than you can speak it, so do not read it out loud for their benefit.

● While one half of the audience will be looking at your visual material, the other half will be looking at you. Stand still when you want the audience to concentrate on visual material.

● If you plan to reuse your AV aids, make sure you arrange to have them gathered up after your presentation.

MAKING AN IMPACT

During your preparation time, you may find that you can make information easier to understand and express abstract ideas more clearly by adding design elements to visual aids. Keep all visual aids simple and uncluttered, and use design elements consistently. Use bold colors – subtleties between pastels do not carry across a crowded room. The sections on a pie diagram can be completely lost if the colors used are not sufficiently contrasting.

When using video, show long segments that illustrate and complement your points, rather than short bursts, which can distract the audience's attention from the essence of your speech.

40 Use cartoons to make serious points lighter.

41 Write notes on the frames of overhead projector slides.

ASSEMBLING TOOLS

Think carefully about which items you may need in order to make proper use of your chosen AV aids. For example:

- A laser pointer to indicate items on screens, writing boards, or flip charts;
- Two sets of chalk or special marker pens to use on writing boards;
- Blank acetate sheets for use with an overhead projector;
- Spare flip chart;
- Extension cord;
- Backup disks and spare cable for multimedia presentations;
- Copies of videos or slides;
- Adapters, if taking electrical equipment abroad.

KNOWING YOUR AV AIDS

By the time you actually come to give your presentation, you should be fully aware of how to operate any high-complexity AV aids you have chosen to augment your subject matter. Even if you do not enjoy working with multimedia or video aids, there are instances in which the effort (and the additional expense of creating them) is worthwhile, even for a small audience.

On rare occasions when using high-complexity AV aids, you may be unlucky enough to experience technical problems. If you do not have the requisite expertise to deal with these hitches, ensure that someone who does will be present at the location to help you out. Always take along a series of low-complexity aids such as handouts as a backup, or be prepared to go without any AV aids at all.

42 Take duplicates of all audio-visual materials that you know you cannot do without in your speech.

REHEARSING

ehearsal is a vital part of preparing for a successful presentation. It is an ideal opportunity to memorize and time your material and to smooth over any rough edges in your delivery. Practice with your AV aids, and allow time for questions at the end.

43 Practice losing your place in your script or notes – and finding it again.

POINTS TO REMEMBER

● You cannot rehearse too much. If you are confident with your material, your audience will have confidence in you.

● The time you will have to speak includes time you will spend using AV aids and answering questions from the audience, so allow for this when rehearsing.

● Rehearsals should rely less and less on the script each time.

● Sample questions should be prepared beforehand so you can practice answering them and estimate timing.

PRACTICING ALOUD

The main point of a rehearsal is to memorize your material and the order in which you are going to present it. This is your best opportunity to fine-tune the content of your speech and to ensure that all your points are delivered with the weight and significance you intend. Start rehearsals by simply reading through your full script. Once you are comfortable with the material, begin to practice in front of the mirror, and switch to notes if you are using them. The first attempt may make you feel slightly nervous and uncomfortable, but your confidence should build with each rehearsal so that you are well prepared when you stand before your real audience and begin your presentation.

DEVELOPING SPONTANEITY

Only when you are freed from slavish reliance on your script or notes can you begin to feel and sound spontaneous. Speaking off the cuff to an audience is a very different discipline to presenting a rehearsed speech. However, it need not be such a daunting task. Develop the trick of apparent "spontaneity" by knowing your subject inside out. In doing this, you give yourself confidence to add details or examples that have not been written into your speech, thus making your presentation sound fresh, off the cuff, and unrehearsed.

44 Practice speaking clearly both in normal tones and at volume.

INVITING FEEDBACK

When you feel ready, begin to practice your speech aloud in front of a friend or colleague, then ask for honest and constructive criticism. Invite your "audience" to point out areas where they feel improvements could be made and to suggest how you can make them. Your audience should bear in mind the context in which the presentation is going to be made, so explain it to them clearly. Try to reproduce the conditions of the presentation, especially the distance between you and the front row of your audience, as closely as possible. That way you can get a sense of how well your voice will carry. Learn to control your voice so that it will sound the same to the audience whether you are presenting in an auditorium or to a small group in a meeting room.

45 Vary the pace of your speech, then decide which pace is most effective.

Use hand gestures that reinforce your message

Audience should watch for any distracting mannerisms

Use notes less as you rehearse and memorize material

Note whether body language of audience indicates interest

◀ **PRACTICING WITH AN AUDIENCE**
Rehearsing in front of a friend will build your confidence. Ask their opinion of both your vocal and physical delivery; enjoy their praise but acknowledge any criticisms or advice for improvement that they might suggest.

PREPARING YOURSELF

It is as important to prepare yourself as it is to prepare your speech. The overall impact of your presentation will be determined as much by how you appear as by what you say.

BELIEVING IN YOURSELF

A positive self-image is all-important for delivering a successful presentation. Identify your strengths, then make the most of them. Except in very rare cases, the audience is as eager as you are for your presentation to be interesting and successful.

 46 An audience is your ally. Its members want to learn from you.

THINKING POSITIVELY

Repeat positive and encouraging thoughts to yourself as you prepare for your presentation and just before it to help boost your confidence and allay any last-minute fears and nerves. For example, try some of the following phrases:

❝ *My presentation is interesting and full of great ideas. The audience will love it.* ❞

❝ *I know my subject inside out. The audience will discover that for themselves early on.* ❞

❝ *The audience is sure to be enthusiastic. My presentation is strong, and I'm well prepared.* ❞

❝ *My rehearsals went really well. I can't wait to see the reaction of the audience.* ❞

VISUALIZING SUCCESS

When preparing for a presentation, train yourself to visualize the scenario positively. Picture an enthusiastic audience loving your successful presentation. You have a message to convey to the audience, and you are being given the perfect opportunity to do so. Imagine your audience taking notes, laughing at any jokes or anecdotes that you may use, and asking interesting and constructive questions at the end. Visualize the body language of the audience's positive response, and imagine yourself making eye contact with members of the audience to encourage the positive rapport developing between you.

47 Behave naturally, and an audience will warm to you.

48 Think of a large audience as if it were a small group.

▼ PICTURING PERFECTION
Increase your confidence by imagining yourself giving a perfect presentation. Visualize the enthusiastic, interested faces of the audience listening to your speech.

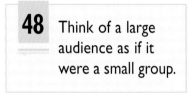

You know your material so well that you do not constantly need to refer to your notes

Audience is interested and attentive

Audience enjoys and applauds your presentation

You look your best and inspire confidence by taking an authoritative stance

ANALYZING APPEARANCE

Your audience will be greatly affected by the way you look, but it is not always easy to judge your own appearance and the impression you are creating. Ask friends or colleagues to comment on your image and to help you adjust it to suit your audience.

> **49** Study yourself in a mirror to see what impression you make.

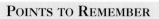

POINTS TO REMEMBER

● A good night's sleep is essential before the day of your presentation.

● A hairbrush, toothbrush, travel iron, clothes brush, and shoe buffer are useful items to take to the location to help you look your best for your presentation.

● Zippers and buttons should be fastened and your shirt should be tucked in before you enter the presentation room.

● If perspiration is a problem, wear a jacket to hide any marks that may appear.

MAKING AN IMPRESSION

First impressions are strong and very hard to change. Think about how quickly you make judgments about people you meet for the first time. Signals can be picked up very quickly from the way people dress, the way they walk, and even from the way they stand. Before you reach the lectern, your audience will have formed an opinion of you based on these first impressions. It is important to decide on the image you want to convey to your audience early on. Making the right first impression may be vital to the success of your presentation, so dress appropriately and walk, speak, and stand with confidence to achieve the right first impression.

KNOWING THE AUDIENCE

Your message will be best received if the audience can identify with you, so it is important always to be aware of the audience's perception of the image you present. If you know a little about your audience, it is easier to decide on the impression that you want to create. Remember, particular styles of dress can communicate specific messages to each different audience. For example, consider how a factory manager will be perceived who addresses the shopfloor workforce wearing a suit in comparison to one dressed in overalls.

> **50** Do not wear anything that may distract the audience.

AVOIDING PITFALLS

Check the clothes that you are going to wear in advance to prevent the problem of needing to wear badly fitting or unlaundered clothes at your presentation. If you want to look your best for the presentation, bring the outfit with you and change into it before you begin your last-minute preparation. Check that changing facilities are available at the location before you arrive.

> **51** Keep your hands out of your pockets during the presentation.

Hair is brushed

Hair is messy

Tie is straight

Tie is loosened

Shirt is wrinkled

Jacket is pressed and hangs well

Shirt sleeves are rolled up

Trousers are pressed with a sharp crease

Trousers need pressing

Shoes are polished

Shoes are inappropriate

▲ LOOKING WELL GROOMED

It is not always necessary to wear a suit, but it is always necessary to look well groomed. Make sure that your clothes are all clean and well pressed, your shoes are polished, and your hair is neat.

▲ LOOKING UNKEMPT

If you do not take time to groom yourself, you will look unprepared and the audience may assume that you are not an expert on your subject. An unkempt appearance may distract people from your message.

ENHANCING BODY IMAGE

As much as two thirds of communication between people is totally nonverbal, transmitted either through hand gestures, facial expressions, or other forms of body language. Good body image begins with posture – the way you hold your skeleton.

52 Make sure your body language reflects what you are saying.

ANALYZING YOUR STANCE

The best posture in which to begin your presentation is upright with the feet slightly apart and the body weight divided equally between them. Your arms should be relaxed by your sides. This is the most noncommittal posture and conveys neutral body language. You can build on this to create different impressions if you understand the ways in which various stances are interpreted. Leaning slightly forward, for example, appears positive and friendly – as if you are involving and encouraging the audience. Leaning backward, however, may appear negative and possibly aggressive.

53 Learn to relax your facial muscles – and smile!

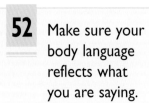

Head is held high and straight

Shoulders are pulled back and level

Back is straight

Stomach is held in

Arms are relaxed and hang by sides

Bottom is held in

Hands are relaxed; fingers are loose

Legs are straight

Knee joints are loose, not locked

Feet are evenly spaced

◀ **STANDING CORRECTLY**
Holding yourself upright and straight not only has physical benefits, such as improved vocal clarity, but can enhance your mental outlook as well. Standing properly increases your stature, which can give you greater self-confidence.

AVOIDING BAD HABITS

To improve your posture and avoid bad habits, practice in front of a mirror or videotape your rehearsal and watch for any unconscious mannerisms. Ask a colleague to watch you practicing and comment on distracting gestures or stances.

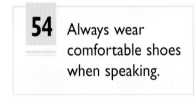

Speaking into podium muffles voice

Eye contact with audience is lost when you look at podium

Slouching looks unprofessional

Standing with your back to an audience detracts from your speech

Visual aid blocked by body

Crossing your legs makes your stance less stable

◀ **BLOCKING THE VIEW**
Avoid the temptation to lean across visual aids as you use them. Prepare them in advance, and use a pointer so you do not block the audience's view.

▲ **BEING UNBALANCED**
Avoid standing on one leg or crossing your legs. These stances are unstable and also lack authority – an unbalanced body can be an indication of an unorganized mind.

IMPROVING YOUR STANCE

The muscles in your body are there to hold the skeleton in an upright position. If you use them correctly, your body language will say "I am a well-balanced, confident person." If your muscles relax too much, your body will slouch. To improve your stance, practice standing in an upright position until you are confident that it looks and feels as natural as your usual relaxed standing position. Imagine that you are taller than you are, or that you are gently being pulled upward by a thread leading from the top of your head, to help achieve and maintain this stance.

54 Always wear comfortable shoes when speaking.

55 Make sure your hair does not fall across your face.

IMPROVING YOUR VOICE

The tone and volume of your voice have a critical effect on a presentation. Understanding how the vocal system works, and how you can control it to manipulate the sound of your voice, is a key part of preparing yourself for a successful presentation.

56 Suck on a mint or piece of hard candy just before you begin to speak.

BREATHING CORRECTLY

Breathe slowly and deeply to improve the flow of oxygen into the body and thus the flow of blood to the brain. This will help you think more clearly, which in turn will help you order your thoughts when speaking in front of an audience. Taking in more oxygen also improves the flow of air to your vocal cords, allowing you to speak clearly, reducing nervousness, and helping you remain calm.

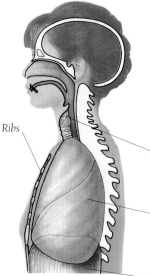

◀ **BREATHING FROM THE DIAPHRAGM**
Learning how to breathe from your diaphragm will give more support to your breathing and strengthen the pitch of your voice.

Ribs

Vocal cords produce sound when they vibrate as air passes over them

Lungs expand and contract with movement of ribs and diaphragm

Diaphragm separates chest from abdomen

57 Consider doing yoga exercises to improve the depth of your breathing.

CONTROLLING YOUR VOICE

Sound is produced when air passes over the vocal cords, making them vibrate. Thus the first requirement for speaking clearly is a good supply of air to the lungs. You can learn to improve your intake of air by practicing a simple breathing exercise (see right). The second requirement is a properly functioning larynx, or voice box, which houses the vocal cords. Make an effort to rest your larynx the day before your presentation by limiting how much you speak.

USING THE RIGHT PITCH

In many languages, the only difference between asking a question and making a statement lies in the intonation. A statement such as "the managing director's office is over there" can be understood as a question if the pitch goes up at the end of the sentence. Your audience should understand the exact meaning of your words, so use intonation and pitch carefully to transmit the right message.

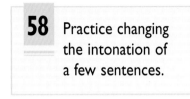

58 Practice changing the intonation of a few sentences.

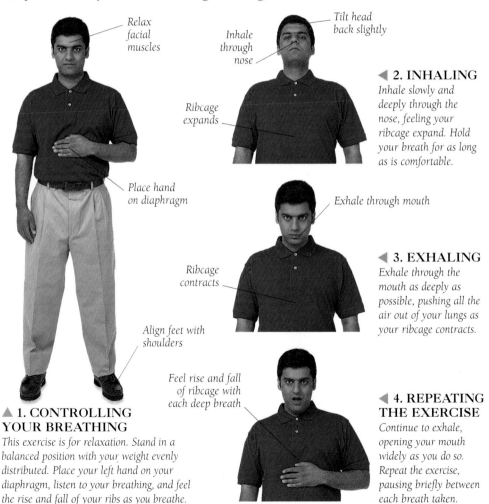

Relax facial muscles

Inhale through nose

Tilt head back slightly

◀ 2. INHALING
Inhale slowly and deeply through the nose, feeling your ribcage expand. Hold your breath for as long as is comfortable.

Ribcage expands

Place hand on diaphragm

Exhale through mouth

◀ 3. EXHALING
Exhale through the mouth as deeply as possible, pushing all the air out of your lungs as your ribcage contracts.

Ribcage contracts

Align feet with shoulders

Feel rise and fall of ribcage with each deep breath

▲ 1. CONTROLLING YOUR BREATHING
This exercise is for relaxation. Stand in a balanced position with your weight evenly distributed. Place your left hand on your diaphragm, listen to your breathing, and feel the rise and fall of your ribs as you breathe.

◀ 4. REPEATING THE EXERCISE
Continue to exhale, opening your mouth widely as you do so. Repeat the exercise, pausing briefly between each breath taken.

531

ELIMINATING TENSION

When you are nervous, your muscles become tense. This is because your body is preparing them in an instinctive way for "fight or flight," the basic choice people face when confronted with danger. Simple exercises can help eliminate this tension.

59 Stretch yourself and imagine that you are taller than you really are.

REDUCING TENSION

Tension building up in your muscles can have some undesirable effects on your body during a presentation. Tension can spoil your posture, making you hunch your shoulders and look defensive. It can also prevent your larynx from functioning smoothly, giving your voice that familiar quiver identified with nervousness. Being tense for any length of time is tiring in itself and can detract from the impact of your presentation. By using a series of simple exercises to help reduce muscular tension, you can make sure that you have more control over your body.

Relieve tension in hand by gripping and relaxing

▲ HAND SQUEEZE
This simple exercise can be done anywhere at any time. Squeeze and release a small rubber ball in your hand. Repeat the exercise several times.

BACK VIEW

Hands join behind head at base of skull

Push head into hands · **FRONT VIEW**

Keep elbow pushed back

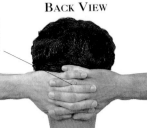

◀ NECK PUSH
To relieve tension in your head and neck, join your hands at the base of your skull, keeping your elbows back. Push your head back into your hands as hard as you can. Hold this stretch for about 10 seconds, release, and repeat.

EXERCISING WHILE SEATED

It is possible to exercise even while you are sitting down – whether at your desk, stuck in a traffic jam, or at home. Follow the simple exercises below to keep your body supple and to help eliminate muscular tension. They do not require a high level of strength or fitness and are most effective when practiced on a daily basis. By taking the time to stretch your body for a couple of minutes each day, you can help prevent the onset of muscle tension and related conditions such as headache, neckache, and backache.

60 Try to relax in an upright position for 10 minutes without moving.

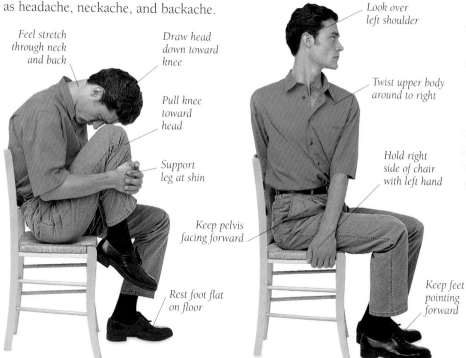

Look over left shoulder

Feel stretch through neck and back

Draw head down toward knee

Twist upper body around to right

Pull knee toward head

Support leg at shin

Hold right side of chair with left hand

Keep pelvis facing forward

Rest foot flat on floor

Keep feet pointing forward

▲ STRETCHING THE BODY

This stretch relieves tension in the neck, back, and hamstrings. Sit facing forward in an upright chair, and pull your right knee toward your chest, supporting it with your hands joined across the shin. Lower your head, then hold the stretch for about 10 seconds. Repeat three times with each leg.

▲ STRETCHING THE SPINE

To relieve tension in your spine and shoulders while sitting down, hold the back of a chair seat with your right hand, turning to hold the right side of the chair with your left hand. Keeping your hips, legs, and feet facing forward, look over your left shoulder. Hold for about 10 seconds, then repeat on the other side.

DELIVERING A PRESENTATION

The keys to good delivery are to be yourself and to be natural. Anything else looks and sounds false – unless you have considerable acting talent.

CONTROLLING NERVES

All but the most experienced of speakers will feel nervous just before making a presentation. Nervousness prevents you from being natural, so you need to do everything you can to control your nerves in order to give the most effective presentation.

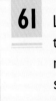

61 List the factors that make you nervous about speaking.

POINTS TO REMEMBER

● Checking that all your props and audio-visual aids have arrived at the location enables you to concentrate on preparing yourself.

● Thorough preparation for your presentation should give you the confidence that everything is going to go right.

● Heavy eating or drinking before a presentation makes you feel and sound sleepy.

● Practice makes perfect.

IDENTIFYING NERVES

To deal with nerves effectively, you need to be able to anticipate and identify the signs of nerves that usually affect you. There are many symptoms; one of the most common is the feeling of having "butterflies" in the stomach. Others signs include dryness of the mouth, a twitch in the corner of an eye, trembling hands, sweaty palms, fidgeting with hair or clothing, and rocking from one side to the other, as well as general tension in various parts of the body. Everyone is affected differently, but it is quite common to experience more than one symptom at a time.

BEING PREPARED

One of the chief causes of nerves is the fear that something will go wrong during a presentation. By reducing the chances of this happening, you can minimize that fear and your nerves will be calmer. The key is to prepare yourself thoroughly, leaving nothing to chance. Every time you think of something you wish to double-check, write it down. Accustom yourself to using a checklist each time you prepare to make a presentation. Some of the points you should remember to check are:

- That the pages of your script or notes are numbered, in case you drop them;
- That your AV aids will be understandable from the back of the room;
- That all the electrical equipment you intend to use is functioning properly;
- That the location and your appearance are confirmed and you have the right date.

62 Smile only when it feels natural to do so. A forced smile always looks false and unconvincing.

CALMING YOURSELF

PREPARATION
Remind yourself how thoroughly you did your preparation, and look through your notes for the presentation.

REHEARSING
Remember the time you spent rehearsing the presentation, and reflect on what you learned during the rehearsals.

RELAXATION
Work through your relaxation exercises five minutes before you begin – and meanwhile, relax!

DEFUSING NERVES

To make a strong, effective presentation, you must be relaxed beforehand. Even if you do not feel tense, about 30 minutes before you are due to speak try to find a quiet place to gather your thoughts and relax. If you know you do have a tendency to feel nervous, try to be positive about these feelings – in time they will become familiar, so welcome their arrival as if they were old friends, and try to use them. Rethink your attack of nerves – and rename it "anticipation."

63 Get a good night's sleep the night before so that you feel alert.

64 Follow the same last-minute routine before each speech.

ESTABLISHING A RITUAL

It can be helpful to follow a ritual in the last few minutes before you begin your presentation. This should come after the preparations described on the previous page and should consist of taking a few moments to gather your thoughts, exercising the facial muscles as shown opposite, and doing a few breathing exercises. This should take your mind off the things that make you nervous. There is also something very comforting in following a sequence of undemanding actions before a stressful event. People who are afraid of flying find it helpful to follow a similar routine during the minutes before their plane takes off.

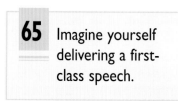 **65** Imagine yourself delivering a first-class speech.

REASSURING YOURSELF

Before your presentation, reassure yourself by running through your last-minute calming ritual, and remind yourself of the following:

- Unless the waiting audience is hostile for some reason, remind yourself that people want to see a successful presentation. In other words, they are on your side.
- Despite the fact that most people are nervous before giving a speech, an audience will assume that you are not.
- You have a message to pass on to your audience – in the form of factual information, personal insights, or both. The audience wants to hear this message; otherwise, they would not have given up the time to come and listen to your presentation. Take heart from this knowledge; use it to your advantage to boost your confidence and counteract your nerves.
- Be wary of being overconfident. This can make you sound like a know-it-all, and there are very few audiences, however interested in a topic, that will warm to such an individual.

POINTS TO REMEMBER

- Nerves can add extra, positive energy to your presentation.
- The audience is more interested in what you are saying than in how you are feeling.
- Your enthusiasm and sincerity will help win over the audience.
- A short exercise regime can help reduce last-minute nerves.
- Time spent relaxing at the last minute helps you concentrate during your presentation.
- The more presentations you make, the more opportunities you have to perfect your skills.

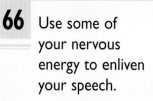 **66** Use some of your nervous energy to enliven your speech.

ELIMINATING TENSION

Take time before you start your presentation to ease the tension that accumulates in the face and upper body. Rid your facial muscles of nervous tension by following the simple exercises shown below. This will help in the articulation of your presentation, since you will be less likely to trip over your tongue or stutter. Repeat all three exercises several times until your face feels relaxed.

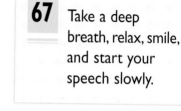

67 Take a deep breath, relax, smile, and start your speech slowly.

Tense forehead muscles

Stretch jaw as wide as possible

Purse lips tightly together

Open eyes wide

▲ **FACIAL SQUEEZE**
Try to squeeze your face as though it is being compressed between your chin and forehead. Start with a frown. Relax and repeat.

▲ **FACIAL SCRUNCH**
Tightly close your eyes, purse your lips, and scrunch up your face as if there is sideways compression. Hold for 30 seconds, then relax.

▲ **MOUTH STRETCH**
Open both your eyes and mouth as wide as possible, stretching the muscles in your face. Repeat two or three times as required.

REDUCING LAST-MINUTE NERVES

Simple last-minute breathing exercises can help you reduce nerves by giving you better control over your body and voice. By concentrating on your breathing, you can also calm your thoughts and dispel feelings of tension and anxiety, enabling you to focus clearly. Follow the exercise on the right, shutting your eyes and taking a series of controlled, deep breaths.

◀ **BREATHING EXERCISE**
Close your eyes. Place one hand on your upper chest, the other on your diaphragm. Breathe in, feeling your diaphragm rise, then breathe out slowly. Repeat several times.

Breathe in through nose

Feel chest remain still as you inhale

Feel diaphragm rise with each inward breath

SPEAKING CONFIDENTLY

The delivery of a presentation has as much impact as the message itself. It is essential to start strongly. After that, use tone of voice, pace, and your body language to enhance your audience's understanding of what you have to say.

68 Scan your notes in small sections, then concentrate on fluent delivery.

Avoid picking up notes when speaking

▲ **OVERCOMING NERVES**
Check the height of the lectern before you start a presentation to ensure it is at a comfortable level. If you feel nervous, it is tempting to hide behind your notes; train yourself to keep them on the lectern.

BEGINNING CONFIDENTLY

Make sure that you are introduced properly to the audience. A good introduction will establish your credibility and can provide the audience with a clear expectation of what you are about to tell them. Find out who will be introducing you, and brief them thoroughly. Make sure that your expertise in the subject of the presentation is mentioned if it would be helpful. Start speaking confidently and at a natural pace, and try to deliver your first few points without referring to your notes. This will reinforce an air of confidence, openness, and authority and at the same time will enable you to establish eye contact with the audience. Try to glance at the whole audience at the start so that they feel involved.

PACING A PRESENTATION

Varying the pace of your delivery will keep the audience interested, but you should avoid speeding up and slowing down just for the sake of it. Remember to pause between your main points, and take the opportunity to make eye contact with the audience. This will also give you a chance to gauge their reactions to your speech. As you progress through the stages of your presentation, speak slowly and emphatically when you want to highlight important points.

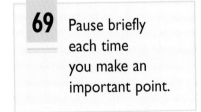

69 Pause briefly each time you make an important point.

USING BODY LANGUAGE

At every moment of your waking life, you are sending out nonverbal signals about your feelings and intentions. It is possible to use this body language in a presentation to help reinforce your message. Keep an open posture at all times, avoiding crossing your arms or creating a barrier between you and the audience. Use hand gestures selectively for emphasis – do not gesture so much that your hands become a distraction. If you are relaxed, your body language will reinforce your message naturally, but using the appropriate gestures can help you disguise your nerves.

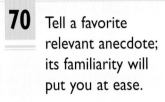

70 Tell a favorite relevant anecdote; its familiarity will put you at ease.

Eye contact establishes positive rapport with audience

Relaxed body language conveys confidence

Open jacket presents an image of honesty

Gaze includes entire audience

Open hand gestures emphasize key points

▲ **SPEAKING AUTHORITATIVELY**
This confident stance suggests a thorough grasp of subject matter and will establish authority and credibility with the audience.

▲ **LOOKING AND FEELING RELAXED**
Once audience rapport has been built, the speaker visibly relaxes and the audience focuses more readily on what is being said.

▲ **USING THE RIGHT GESTURES**
The speaker makes good use of open-handed gestures to emphasize his integrity and draw the entire audience into his presentation.

USING EYE CONTACT

Eye contact is a very powerful tool that establishes a degree of intimacy between people. It is important to establish this intimacy with an audience during a presentation. Sweep your gaze right across the audience, remembering to engage with the people at the very back and far sides as well as those at the front. Although it is tempting to increase the frequency of eye contact with audience members who appear enthusiastic and interested, do not neglect those who appear neutral or negative. Audience members who feel excluded by the speaker are more likely to respond negatively to the speech than those who feel involved.

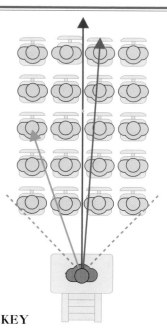

LOOKING AT THE AUDIENCE ▶

Sweep your gaze across the entire audience, remembering to include the back row. Establish initial eye contact with a friendly face, rather than looking over the heads of your audience when speaking.

KEY

71 Make your initial eye contact with someone whom you consider to look approachable.

- – – – *Limit of speaker's sightlines*
- ➔ *Sightline fixed on friendly face in audience*
- ➔ *Sightline fixed on back row of audience*
- ➔ *Sightline fixed on middle distance*

USING GESTURES

Perspective changes in relation to the size of the audience, and you need to adapt your gestures accordingly. Large audiences require greatly exaggerated movements to achieve the same visual effect that a "normal" gesture would for a small audience. For example, a gesture emphasizing two points "on the one hand...and on the other hand..." needs to start from the shoulder, rather than from the elbow or wrist, to have the right visual impact on a large audience. Although gesturing in this exaggerated style may at first feel awkward, it will look natural to the audience.

72 Make eye contact with somebody in the audience at every available opportunity.

DEVELOPING STYLE

As you become more experienced you will be able to use the various tools you have at your disposal – your voice, your demeanor, and the words you use – to create different impressions. Usually you will want to use all the tools at the same time to work toward the single goal of keeping the attention of the audience. For example, if you want to emphasize a point, use concise sentences, stand upright, and raise your voice. To give the audience the impression that you are going to share an exciting revelation with them, lean forward and lower your voice. They will make sure that they hear you because you have made it seem so interesting. These tools are an essential element of any speaker's success, and with practice their use will become second nature. Always use a style that is appropriate to each particular audience – what works well for one group of people may not work at all with another.

73 Repeat key numbers: "15 – one-five – weeks."

74 Do not be afraid to use big gestures and long pauses.

DO'S AND DON'TS

✔ Do use simple, concise language wherever possible for clarity.

✔ Do use eye contact to obtain feedback from the audience. Their body language will reveal their reactions to your presentation.

✔ Do keep pauses specific and emphatic. Use them to allow your audience to absorb what you say.

✔ Do glance at a wall clock to check on the time rather than looking at your watch.

✘ Don't apologize to the audience for your lack of speaking experience.

✘ Don't mumble or hesitate. If you have lost your place, stay calm until you find it.

✘ Don't drop your voice at the end of a each sentence. It will sound as if you are not sure of what you are saying.

✘ Don't lose sight of the message that you are giving, or you will find that you lose your concentration as well as your audience.

LIMITING YOUR SPEECH TIME

Tell your audience how long you will be speaking so they know how long they need to concentrate: "We have only 20 minutes, so let me go straight in…" Later you can remind them again that your eye is still on the clock: "We have only five minutes left, so I'll sum up by saying…" Do not be diverted from your prepared presentation by a member of the audience who wishes to ask a question or appears to disagree with a point you are making. Tell them when you will be answering questions from the floor, then continue your speech.

CLOSING EFFECTIVELY

I*t is vital to have a strong conclusion to your presentation, since this helps form the impression that audience members take away with them. Always reiterate the major points made in your speech to bring them to the attention of the audience again.*

75 Do not leave visual aids on display too long – they distract the audience.

INDICATING THE END

During the course of your presentation, give the audience verbal signals to indicate how many more points you have to make and when the end of your speech is approaching. Use phrases such as: "now the third of my four points…" or "and now, to sum up briefly before I answer your questions…" By informing the audience that the end is near, you will be sure of having their full attention before you summarize your main points. It is important that your summary covers all the major points and ideas from your presentation, so that the audience has a final chance to recap on your subject matter. This gives them a chance to consider any questions that they want to ask you.

THINGS TO DO

1. Tell the audience how many points you want them to take away with them.

2. Make sure you stick to your allocated time.

3. Work out which points can be cut if you exceed your allotted time.

4. If you forget anything, leave it out rather than adding it to the end of your speech.

76 Do not rush off as if you are in a hurry to leave.

77 Always close with a good, strong summary.

LEAVING AN IMPRESSION

It is the final impression that you leave in the minds of your audience that lingers the longest, so make sure that it is a good one. Before delivering the presentation, spend time working on the final sentences of it so that you can deliver them perfectly. Combine pauses, intonation, and verbal devices such as alliteration in your summary to create a memorable "package" for the audience to take away with them. In this way, your message will get across – and your reputation as a speaker will be enhanced.

DRAWING TO A CLOSE

Avoid adopting a dogmatic tone when delivering the conclusion to your presentation. Concentrate on presenting accurate, well-researched facts, and do not be tempted into giving personal opinions on your subject matter. Base your conclusion firmly on the facts you have presented throughout your speech. If your presentation is to be followed by a question-and-answer session, remember that the impact of your own carefully prepared final sentences may be diluted. In such a case, you may choose to accept a series of questions from the audience and then make a short, concise summary speech reiterating your major points.

Use open hand gestures to show enthusiasm

DELIVERING YOUR SUMMARY ▶
As you are about to begin summing up your presentation, move to the front of any visual aids you are using so that the audience can see you clearly. Stand confidently and deliver your closing sentences authoritatively.

78 Use alliteration to make an impact when summing up.

79 Pause between your summary and the question-and-answer session.

FINISHING STRONGLY

It is important to create a strong and memorable finish. To help you to do this, there are several tips that you should bear in mind:

- Encapsulate your presentation in one or two sentences. It is important to be brief when summing up; short, powerful sentences hold the attention of the audience far more effectively than a 10-minute monologue.
- Emphasize key words. Pausing after key words and phrases adds emphasis to them. It is also a good idea to emphasize the word "and" as you approach your final main point.
- Use alliteration. The use of several words beginning with the same letter helps make a summary memorable. Restrict the alliteration to a maximum of three words.

HANDLING AN AUDIENCE

A presentation is made for the benefit of an audience, not for that of the speaker. Be sure that you know how to read an audience's response and how to handle its reactions.

JUDGING THE MOOD

Try to arrive at the location early enough to assess the mood of the audience. Has the audience just come in from the pouring rain? Are they likely to be hostile to what you want to tell them? Has a previous speaker made them laugh?

80 Listen to as many of the previous speakers as you possibly can.

INVOLVING AN AUDIENCE

Judge the mood of your audience – by assessing their reactions to previous speakers, for example. You can then decide on a strategy to deliver your message effectively. If any members of the audience appear bored or drowsy, stimulate them by asking questions that can be answered by a show of hands. "How many of you phoned your office before coming here? Only three? Well then, how many of you *thought* of phoning your office?" If the audience is hostile, you could start the presentation with a joke, but make sure that your body language is giving out positive signals.

81 Let audience members know that you are aware of their feelings.

LOOKING FOR SIGNALS

You will have rehearsed your own body language as part of your preparations for a presentation. Now you need to learn to read the body language of the members of the audience. Watch for signs, and do not expect everyone to be expressing the same thing. Some may be straining forward eagerly to ask a question, while others may be sinking into their seats, wishing they were somewhere else.

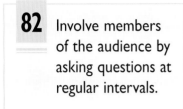

82 Involve members of the audience by asking questions at regular intervals.

Impassive expression

Folded arms form a barrier across body

Crossed legs can suggest negativity

NEGATIVE ▶
POSTURE
This posture – leaning back with arms folded and legs crossed – suggests resistance toward the speakerer.

SPOTTING NEGATIVITY

There is a wide range of ways in which members of an audience can indicate disapproval or hostility. Watch out for people leaning over and criticizing your speech to a neighbor. Alternatively, look for people frowning directly at you with their arms folded or looking in the air as if the ceiling is more interesting than anything you have to say. Remember that looking at one piece of body language in isolation – such as crossed legs – may give a false impression, so look at the whole picture before coming to a conclusion.

SEEING SIGNS OF INTEREST

Stances indicating interest are easy to spot – look for people smiling, nodding, or leaning forward in their seats and watching you intently. The expressions on their faces may reveal faint frowns of concentration. People manifesting any of these signs can probably be won over to your point of view, so make sure that you involve or engage them in your presentation.

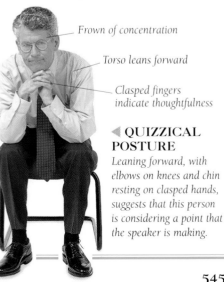

Frown of concentration

Torso leans forward

Clasped fingers indicate thoughtfulness

◀ QUIZZICAL
POSTURE
Leaning forward, with elbows on knees and chin resting on clasped hands, suggests that this person is considering a point that the speaker is making.

READING FACIAL SIGNS

In terms of body language, the face is most expressive. If you are close enough to the members of your audience, you will be able to pick up a multitude of small signals – from the movements of eyebrows and the look in the eyes to the sloping of lips. As with general body language, always remember to read the face as a whole. One sign taken in isolation may not be a true indication of what the person is feeling.

83 Watch for a hand stealthily moving up to stifle a yawn.

Neutral facial expression indicates unformed opinions

Chin resting on hand shows concentration

Crossed legs suggest contemplation

NEUTRAL ▶ POSTURE
This familiar relaxed posture suggests an open mind. This person has yet to be swayed either way by the argument and is willing to hear more.

READING HAND AND ARM GESTURES

Hand and arm movements are helpful in adding to the impact of speech and can tell you a lot about the person using them. During question-and-answer sessions, note the hand and arm gestures of the people asking questions. If you cannot see them clearly, ask individuals to stand up when speaking. The gestures people use have a strong cultural content, so bear this in mind when interpreting body language. For example, if northern Europeans gesticulate emphatically, they are probably agitated, but such gesturing accompanies most conversations among southern Europeans.

DEALING WITH UNFORESEEN CIRCUMSTANCES

Would you know what to do if there were a loud explosion in the middle of your presentation? Or if a member of the audience suddenly had a seizure? Although the chances of such an event are remote, it is as well to go over in your mind the steps you might follow if you were faced with an unexpected incident such as this. Ask yourself if you know where to turn on the lights, where to find a first-aid kit, how to summon medical help, and where the fire exits are. If you do not know where you might find these things, make sure you get this information before your presentation.

USING YOUR EARS

You do not need to have all the lights on to pick up your audience's body language; much of it can be picked up aurally. You can hear the rustle of people fidgeting or the sound of whispering, both of which may indicate that your audience is bored or confused. It is easy to block yourself off when you are concentrating on presenting, but it pays to be alert to noise at all times – it is a valuable clue for judging the mood of your audience.

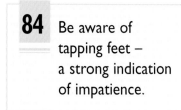

84 Be aware of tapping feet – a strong indication of impatience.

WATCHING LEGS

The position into which someone puts their legs says a lot about their attitude. For example, if an audience member has crossed legs, it may indicate that they are still contemplating your speech. Legs placed together, however, can indicate total agreement. If your audience is seated, movement will be limited and you may be able to see only those in the front row, but their leg movements should give you an indication of how the rest of the audience is reacting to your presentation.

Position of chin on knuckles indicates eagerness to learn

Arrangement of legs indicates alertness

◀ **INTERESTED POSTURE**

This posture expresses interest: the body leans forward and the chin rests on the hand. The leg positions also reinforce the positive stance of the upper body.

Leaning forward demonstrates agreement

AGREEMENT ▶ POSTURE

The relaxed position of the hands, the parallel legs, and the frank, open expression of the face indicate that the listener agrees entirely with your presentation.

NOTICING HABITS

Most people unintentionally reinforce their body language with habitual fidgeting with their personal props, such as glasses, watches, earrings, or cufflinks. Looking at a watch can betray boredom or even impatience, while chewing on a pen or glasses suggests contemplation. On the positive side, sitting still and an absence of any of these habits can often indicate total involvement and agreement with the content of your presentation.

DEALING WITH QUESTIONS

M any a fine presentation has been ruined by poor handling of questions raised by the audience afterward. Learn to deal with difficult and awkward questions during your preparation, and you will handle anything you are asked with confidence.

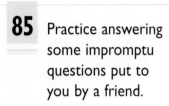

85 Practice answering some impromptu questions put to you by a friend.

86 Remain calm, whatever the tone or intention of the questioner.

POINTS TO REMEMBER

- Question-and-answer sessions can be as important as the main body of the presentation itself.

- It is possible to anticipate most questions when researching presentation material thoroughly.

- Most questions taken from the audience will be intended generally and should not be taken personally.

- Nerves may tempt you to a hasty response. Always think about your answer before you begin to speak.

- Some questions may need clarification from the questioner.

- Questions should always be answered one at a time.

PREPARING WELL

It is important that you go into your presentation fully prepared to answer any questions thrown at you by the audience. The key to this is in careful research and rewriting. Once you have finished drafting your speech, read it through thoroughly several times, note any unanswered questions that it raises, and try to fill in any gaps. Having done this, read your presentation to friends or colleagues, then ask them to raise any questions. Deal with their points, adding extra information as necessary. Be aware that, despite this preparation, someone may raise an awkward point you have not anticipated.

APPEARING CONFIDENT

Just as a good presentation can be ruined by a poor question-and-answer session, a mediocre one can be saved by a confident performance at the end. Answer questions as loudly, clearly, and succinctly as you delivered the presentation. This is especially important if you have needed to sit down or move to another location for questioning. If appropriate, stand up when answering questions, and keep your voice level. Do not fidget with your hands or use negative body language, such as crossing your arms in front of your chest, which will make you appear defensive.

STAYING IN CONTROL

Never allow more than one person to talk at once; otherwise, the occasion may rapidly head out of control. Establish that you can handle only one question at a time: "If we could hear your question first, John, then I'll come back to you, Laura, immediately afterward." Never be drawn into a protracted discussion of minor aspects of your presentation; if matters become too involved, arrange to continue the discussion later.

 87 Say "Good point!" to encourage a questioner who is shy or nervous.

 88 Divert hostile questions back to the questioner or the audience.

HANDLING QUESTIONERS

Questioners come in a variety of guises, so it is important to be able to recognize and deal with them accordingly. Exhibitionists like to try to demonstrate that they know more than you do, while drifters wander around the subject and never seem to ask a direct question. Each requires careful handling. Bring the drifter back to the issue by saying, "That's a good point, and it raises a question about..." Exhibitionists may cause trouble if antagonized, so treat them politely at all times.

TYPES OF QUESTION TO EXPECT FROM AN AUDIENCE

There are certain typical questions that come up over and over in question-and-answer sessions. Learn to recognize these so that you can deal with them successfully:

- The Summary Question: "What you seem to be saying is... Am I right?" This is an effort to recap on proceedings.
- The Straight Question: "Can you tell me about the services you offer in Brazil?" This is a direct appeal for information.
- The Me and Mine Question: "When my mother tried, she found the opposite.

How do you explain that?" Personal experience is used to make a point.
- The Cartesian Question: "How can you say X, yet insist on Y?" Here logic is being used to defeat the speaker.
- The Raw Nerve Question: "When are you going to get back to 1995 levels?" This is an ill-natured dig.
- The Well-Connected Question: "Have you talked to my good friend Bill Clinton about this problem?" Name dropping is used to emphasize power.

ANALYZING QUESTIONS

You have only a brief moment to analyze the nature of each question you are asked. Are you being asked to recap on your presentation? Is it a simple request for further information on your subject matter? Are you being led into a trap? Some people want to make a point rather than ask a question – if their input is positive and reinforces your argument, it is courteous to acknowledge them. However, if the point is irrelevant, thank the speaker and move on to the next question.

GAINING TIME

If you find yourself faced with a particularly difficult question, remain calm and give yourself a little time to think carefully before you reply. When tackling a question that requires careful thought, do not be afraid to refer back to your notes – you will still appear to be in control if you tell the audience what you are doing and why. If absolutely necessary, use a stalling tactic, such as taking a sip of water, coughing, or blowing your nose. This will help you avoid looking as though you are lost for words.

89 Address answers to the whole audience, not just the questioner.

POINTS TO REMEMBER

● Answering questions from the audience can increase your credibility by demonstrating a wider knowledge of your subject.

● The audience needs to know whether you are voicing personal opinions or facts.

● It is crucial not to be drawn into argument with a questioner, regardless of how unacceptable his or her assumptions are.

● All questions should be handled with respect and courtesy.

● Some really difficult questions may need to be researched and answered at a later date.

RESPONDING TO UNANSWERABLE QUESTIONS

There are a number of standard replies you can use in response to difficult questions. If you do not know an answer, try to offer a satisfactory reply to show you have not ignored the question. If a questioner persists, throw the question open to the audience.

❝ I don't know the answer, but I can find out for you. If you leave me your address, I will get back to you. ❞

❝ I'm not sure I know the answer to that one. Perhaps we could discuss it after the session. ❞

❝ I need to think about that one. Could we come back to it later? Next question, please. ❞

❝ There really is no right or wrong answer to that. However, my personal belief is... ❞

DEALING WITH HIDDEN AGENDAS

Beware of loaded questions designed to show up serious weaknesses in an argument, embarrass the speaker, and undermine your case. Questions that have little to do with your presentation may be an attempt by a member of the audience to show off. Alternatively, they may stem from a desire to destroy your credibility by making you appear ill-informed. Try to have a few stock answers at your disposal, such as: "I was not intending to cover that aspect of the subject today," or "That is a separate issue that I do not have time to discuss now," which, though evasive, will ease the pressure on you.

90 Win over your audience with your knowledge.

91 Take care not to patronize your audience.

SPEAKING OFF THE CUFF

On occasions, you may find that somebody in the audience asks a probing question that needs a great deal of discussion about one aspect of your presentation. If this is not of general interest, ask the questioner to contact you after your presentation has finished. However, if you feel that the entire audience would benefit from hearing more detail – and you are sure of your facts – you may chose to launch into an unrehearsed mini-presentation. Keeping it brief, structure your impromptu speech clearly, and present it as fluently as the main body of the presentation.

BEING HONEST WITH THE AUDIENCE

There are going to be times when, for various reasons, you simply do not know the answer to a question. If this happens, be honest with the audience. If you do not know the facts, it is best to admit this right away rather than hedging around the issue. Do not respond with phrases like "I will be covering that point later," because the audience will resent any attempt to fool them, and you may lose credibility.

Assess whether the required reply is purely factual or also a matter of personal opinion. If it is the latter, you are on firmer ground, since you can admit to not knowing the facts but still give a reasonable and considered answer based on past experience or personal opinion.

92 Prepare one or two detailed answers in advance for questions you are sure will be raised.

COPING WITH HOSTILITY

A presentation may occasionally give rise to strong feelings or violently opposed viewpoints among members of the audience. When faced with such a situation, you must be able to cope with both overt outbursts of hostility and a silent reception.

93 Usually, hostility is aimed at your speech, not at you.

94 Avoid prolonged eye contact; it may cause aggravation.

RECOGNIZING DISRUPTERS

Learn to recognize the types of disruptive audience members you may face in order to deal with them more effectively. Attention-seekers may respond to a speech with sarcasm just to make themselves look clever, while others may respond unwittingly to a rhetorical question without intending you any malice. The most serious disruption is likely to be caused by hecklers in the audience – people who disagree with what you are saying and who actively want to cause trouble.

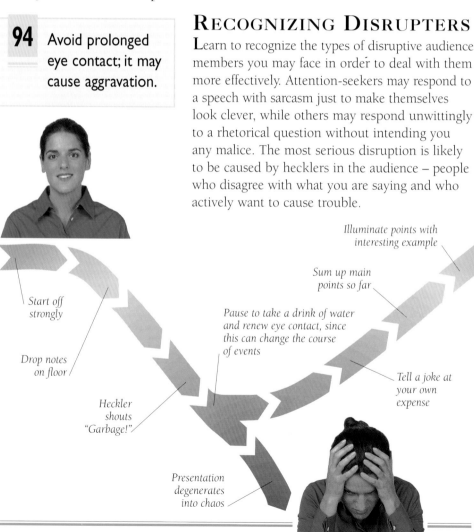

Illuminate points with interesting example

Sum up main points so far

Start off strongly

Pause to take a drink of water and renew eye contact, since this can change the course of events

Drop notes on floor

Tell a joke at your own expense

Heckler shouts "Garbage!"

Presentation degenerates into chaos

DEALING WITH HECKLERS

Hecklers appear in all sorts of situations, harassing speakers with awkward comments and interruptions. To deal with hecklers you must be polite but firm. Your goal should be to get the rest of the audience on your side. This is not always easy, and underestimating hecklers can be costly if you allow them to undermine your presentation. Hecklers often have a genuine concern, which, if not addressed properly and quickly, may be taken up by other members of the audience.

If someone denounces something that you have said, do not enter an argument with them. If you are stating fact rather than opinion, make this clear and present the evidence. If you are stating personal opinion, be frank about it; this is your presentation. Give hecklers an opportunity to speak afterward.

POINTS TO REMEMBER

- Losing your temper will gain you nothing.
- Everyone deserves a fair hearing, even if you cannot agree with their point of view.
- Any points of agreement with hecklers should be emphasized.
- It is important to repeat your case at the end of the presentation.

95 If you are stating facts, back them up with evidence.

Respond well to questions from audience

Conclude with clear summary

▲ KEEPING ON TRACK

This illustration shows two possible courses of a presentation – a negative outcome and positive outcome. Despite a strong start, there may be hecklers and mishaps. This could cause a presentation to end in chaos. To stay on course, stay calm, deal with mishaps as they occur, and move on with composure and aplomb. Hold the audience's interest, and you can make a success of any situation.

DEALING WITH CONFLICT WITHIN AN AUDIENCE

If a serious disagreement between members of an audience disrupts your presentation, remember that you will be assumed by the audience to be the mediator. Defuse the tension by reassuring everyone that they will get a chance to speak, and restore equilibrium as soon as possible. Get everyone back onto the right path by reminding the audience of the presentation's purpose. In all cases, aim to convey to your audience that you are in control. If the situation deteriorates any further, enlist some help from the organizers, or bring the presentation to an end.

96 If you are giving your presentation sitting down, stand up in order to assert your authority.

97 Try to find some common ground with the audience.

98 Guide questioners to other sources of information.

FACING AN UNRESPONSIVE GROUP

Although an unresponsive audience is not necessarily a hostile audience, many people would prefer to deal with outright hostility than silence. In such a situation, it is easy to imagine that the audience has no questions because there is no interest in your talk. This is unlikely to be the case – they are probably just unresponsive people. If a chairperson is present, you should have no worries. He or she will invite questions from the audience and, if there are none, start with questions of their own. If there is no chairperson, try asking the audience a few general, direct questions to encourage them to respond to you.

DEALING WITH HOSTILITY

An audience might be hostile for a number of reasons, including fundamental disagreement with the point of your presentation, anger at a previous speaker, or resentment at having to sit through your speech when they really came to hear someone else. One technique you can use to deal with hostility is to acknowledge it. Try to disarm a hostile audience by being open, then ask them to be fair and nonjudgmental while you give your presentation. Another possibility is to plant a friend or colleague in the audience with a question with which to open the discussion. Your "plant" can ask an apparently awkward question, to which you can respond with a strong, preplanned answer – winning over some audience members.

99 Wait for questions, even if there are none forthcoming.

CULTURAL DIFFERENCES

Sometimes a speaker can unwittingly generate hostility in an audience by making a cultural *faux pas*. When making a presentation, pointing with the index finger to emphasize a remark is considered acceptable by most Westerners. However, many Asians cultures consider this rude, preferring gestures of indication to be made with the whole hand.

100 Tell the truth, because an audience will quickly recognize insincerity, and your authority will be undermined.

DEALING WITH THE MEDIA

If you need to speak at a public meeting or represent your organization at a press conference, it is important to handle the media confidently. Always answer queries calmly, politely, and intelligently, and be careful not to let journalists put words into your mouth.

I have already stated my point of view during my presentation. I don't think I have anything more to add at this juncture...

You have certainly made a valid point, but I prefer to think that...

No, that is not what I am saying at all. I would like to reiterate that what I am actually saying is...

Whereas I appreciate what you are saying, I feel that I must emphasize that...

LEARNING FROM YOUR EXPERIENCE

Dealing with awkward questions and general hostility during a presentation requires skills that can take a long time to develop. Learn from your mistakes, and draw on other situations in life when you have been faced with such difficulties. How did you cope? Did you think the situation through before responding? Did you defuse the situation tactfully? What if an audience resorts to derisive laughter in an attempt to undermine your credibility? The best response in this situation is to employ humor – never use sarcasm, which may only serve to exacerbate the situation.

If you know that your presentation is likely to provoke antagonism – for example, when making an unwelcome speech to shareholders or at a public meeting – try to anticipate the hostility. Practice fielding aggressive comments successfully by asking colleagues to fire difficult questions at you. The more experience you have, the better you will become at responding confidently.

POINTS TO REMEMBER

- Remaining calm when faced with hostility from the audience can help defuse a negative situation.
- Only the question that has been asked should be answered, not one that you would have preferred.
- Answers should be kept relatively short, especially if you know that there are other questioners waiting to be heard.
- There may be a hidden agenda behind aggression or hostility.
- Silence can be used to provoke an audience to ask questions.

 101 Stay relaxed but alert, and enjoy your presentation.

ASSESSING YOUR ABILITY

Remember that practice makes perfect when preparing for a presentation: regard each presentation as a chance to practice for the next. Evaluate your performance by responding to the following statements, then mark the options closest to your experience. Be as honest as you can: if your answer is "never," mark Option 1; if it is "always," mark Option 4; and so on. Add your scores together, then refer to the Analysis to see how you scored. Use your answers to identify the areas that need improving.

OPTIONS

1 Never

2 Occasionally

3 Frequently

4 Always

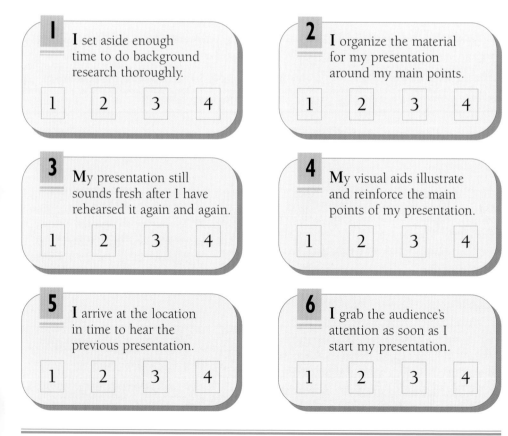

1 I set aside enough time to do background research thoroughly.

1　2　3　4

2 I organize the material for my presentation around my main points.

1　2　3　4

3 My presentation still sounds fresh after I have rehearsed it again and again.

1　2　3　4

4 My visual aids illustrate and reinforce the main points of my presentation.

1　2　3　4

5 I arrive at the location in time to hear the previous presentation.

1　2　3　4

6 I grab the audience's attention as soon as I start my presentation.

1　2　3　4

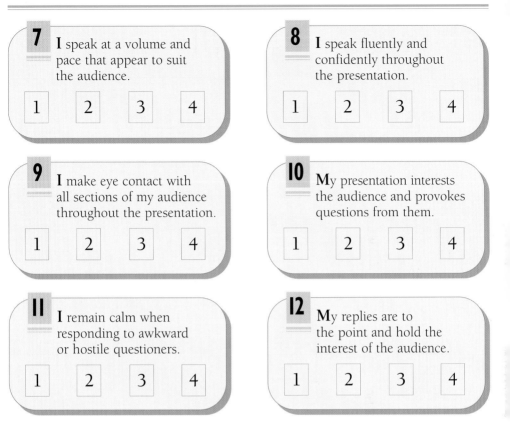

7 I speak at a volume and pace that appear to suit the audience.

1   2   3   4

8 I speak fluently and confidently throughout the presentation.

1   2   3   4

9 I make eye contact with all sections of my audience throughout the presentation.

1   2   3   4

10 My presentation interests the audience and provokes questions from them.

1   2   3   4

11 I remain calm when responding to awkward or hostile questioners.

1   2   3   4

12 My replies are to the point and hold the interest of the audience.

1   2   3   4

ANALYSIS

Now that you have completed the self-assessment, add up your total score and check your performance by reading the corresponding evaluation. Whatever level of success you have achieved during your presentation, it is important to remember that there is always room for improvement. Identify your weakest areas, then refer to the chapters in this section where you will find practical advice and tips to help you establish and hone those skills.

12–24: Use every opportunity to learn from your mistakes, and take more time to prepare and rehearse for each presentation that you give from now on.

25–36: Your presentation skills are generally sound, but certain areas need improvement.

37–48: You have good presentation skills, but do not become complacent. Continue to prepare well.

NEGOTIATING SUCCESSFULLY

INTRODUCTION

Negotiation involves two or more parties who each have something the other wants, reaching an agreement through a process of bargaining. This section explains the principles of this exchange and gives you the confidence and skill to conduct negotiations and achieve a mutually acceptable outcome. Designed for easy access to relevant information, and including 101 practical tips, the section covers the whole process of negotiation from preparation to closing a deal, and it is suitable for novices and seasoned negotiators alike. It includes essential advice on devising a strategy, how to make concessions, what to do when negotiations break down, and how to make use of third parties to resolve deadlock and conflict.

PREPARING FOR A NEGOTIATION

To negotiate successfully you need a game plan – your ultimate aim and a strategy for achieving it. Prepare thoroughly before a negotiation to facilitate the success of your game plan.

DEFINING NEGOTIATION

Negotiation occurs when someone else has what you want and you are prepared to bargain for it – and vice versa. Negotiations take place every day between family members, with shopkeepers, and – almost continuously – in the workplace.

1 To become a good negotiator, learn to "read" the other party's needs.

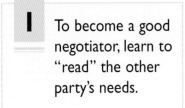

2 Bear in mind that it is almost impossible for a negotiator to do too much preparation.

UNDERSTANDING THE PRINCIPLES

Successful negotiating – an attempt by two people to achieve a mutually acceptable solution – should not result in a winner and a loser. It is a process that ends either with a satisfying conclusion for both sides (win/win), or with failure for both sides (lose/lose). The art of negotiation is based on attempting to reconcile what constitutes a good result for you with what constitutes a good result for the other party. To achieve a situation where both sides win something, you need to be well prepared, alert, and flexible.

RECOGNIZING THE SKILLS

Negotiation is a skill that anyone can learn, and there are plenty of opportunities to practice it once learned. The core skills required for successful negotiations include:

- The ability to define a range of objectives, yet be flexible about some of them;
- The ability to explore the possibilities of a wide range of options;
- The ability to prepare well;
- Interactive competence, the ability to listen to and question other parties; and
- The ability to prioritize clearly.

These proficiencies are useful in everyday life as well as in negotiations. By taking the time to learn them, you will be able to enhance more than just your bargaining abilities.

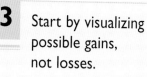

3 Start by visualizing possible gains, not losses.

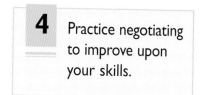

4 Practice negotiating to improve upon your skills.

▼ STUDYING NEGOTIATION
At the start of a commercial negotiation, two teams face each other around a table. Note how each team member's body language is supportive of their partner.

TEAM A

Head is tilted toward partner

TEAM B

Body leans toward partner

Eye contact is maintained with partner

CATEGORIZING TYPES

Different negotiation types require different skills. In business and commerce, each instance of negotiation displays certain characteristics. It may be formal or informal, ongoing or a one-off, depending on who is negotiating for what. The parties involved in a business – such as employees, shareholders, trade unions, management, suppliers, customers, and the government – all have different interests and individual points of view. Whichever group you belong to, you need to reconcile such differences through negotiation: for example, shareholders negotiate with boards of directors over company strategy, unions negotiate with employers over pay and conditions, and governments negotiate with accountants over taxation.

5 Be prepared to compromise when you negotiate.

6 Determine your strategy according to the type of negotiation.

TYPES OF NEGOTIATION IN ORGANIZATIONS

TYPES	EXAMPLES	PARTIES INVOLVED
DAY-TO-DAY/ MANAGERIAL Such negotiations concern internal problems and the working relationship between groups of employees.	● Arranging pay, terms, and working conditions. ● Defining job roles and areas of responsibility. ● Increasing output via, for example, more overtime.	● Management ● Subordinates ● Colleagues ● Trade unions ● Legal advisers
COMMERCIAL The driving factor in these negotiations, which take place between an organization and an external party, is usually financial gain.	● Winning a contract to supply customers. ● Scheduling the delivery of goods and services. ● Agreeing on the quality and price of products.	● Management ● Suppliers ● Customers ● Government ● Trade unions ● Legal advisers
LEGAL These negotiations are usually formal and legally binding. Disputes over precedents can become as significant as the main issues.	● Complying with local authority and national planning laws. ● Communicating with regulators (such as antitrust authorities).	● Local government ● National government ● Regulators ● Management

APPOINTING AGENTS

John F. Kennedy, US President, once said, "Let us never negotiate out of fear, but let us never fear to negotiate." In reality, of course, you may be reluctant to negotiate because you are afraid of an unfamiliar process. If this is the case, you can find someone to negotiate for you. Such people are known as "agents," and they can be assigned as much or as little responsibility as you, the "principal" who employs them, wish to give them in a given negotiation. However, you should always clearly lay out the full extent of that responsibility in advance of the negotiation.

Some common examples of agents include trade union members, who negotiate as agents on behalf of employees, and lawyers, who often negotiate as agents on behalf of all types of stakeholder in an organization, including management, shareholders, and customers.

> **7** Define an agent's responsibilites very clearly.

POINTS TO REMEMBER

- When negotiating, you need to know where you are prepared to give ground – or not.
- A matter under negotiation may be intangible, and therefore must be defined before negotiation can proceed.
- Negotiation implies that you are willing to compromise on the issue under discussion.
- Anything that applies to you as a negotiator applies to the person with whom you are negotiating.

NEGOTIATING IN DAILY LIFE

Domestic situations often involve negotiation. For example, you may agree to take your neighbor's children to school every Monday and Thursday if they take yours on Tuesday and Friday, and you each do alternate Wednesdays. On occasion, negotiated terms may need to be renegotiated. For example, you may have negotiated a price for one vase in a bazaar, but if you buy more than one vase, you should be in a position to renegotiate for a lower price on the first vase. When making an offer on a house, you may need to raise your offer and renegotiate terms if someone else is interested.

▲ **NEGOTIATING WITH REALTORS**
If you are considering buying a house, you will need to discuss terms and conditions of the purchase with a realtor.

UNDERSTANDING THE PRINCIPLE OF EXCHANGE

With a proper understanding of all the processes involved (preparation, proposal, debate, bargaining, and closing), negotiating can create a successful outcome for all parties. Central to this is the principle of exchange: you must give in order to receive.

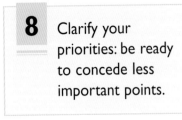

8 Clarify your priorities: be ready to concede less important points.

STAGES OF NEGOTIATION

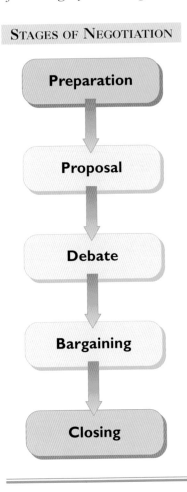

Preparation

Proposal

Debate

Bargaining

Closing

WINNING ON EACH SIDE

The key to negotiation is to realize that all parties need to gain something of value in exchange for any concessions they make. Only then can they all come away feeling successful. Try to achieve this by understanding that what is valued by your party may not be valued by the other. Whereas in a competitive sport victory is valued by both parties – so if one side wins, the other loses – negotiations, in contrast, can end in a win/win conclusion. When trade unions negotiate with a company's management, they may gain more pay for their members, while the management may gain assurances about increased productivity.

CULTURAL DIFFERENCES

Different cultures approach negotiations in very different ways. For example, Europeans and Americans often find the Japanese reluctance to engage in outright confrontation confusing or ambiguous. On the other hand, the Japanese find apparently unequivocal statements or viewpoints unsubtle and difficult to work into a compromise.

BEING FLEXIBLE

Flexibility is a vital characteristic around any negotiating table. The balance of power between the parties fluctuates as negotiations progress. For example, if you are bargaining in a market over a souvenir, you may become less enthusiastic when you discover that the vendor is not able to deliver to your home – anything you buy, you are going to have to take away with you. The vendor should be alert to any such loss of interest, and, in this case, you can expect them to lower their price in order to compensate and to keep you interested.

9 Be flexible – it is a sign of strength, not of weakness.

10 If you agree in haste, you may repent at leisure.

CASE STUDY

Freelance architect John was short of work when Bill, a property developer, asked him to draw up some plans for a warehouse that he was developing on a valuable site. John agreed, and Bill, seeing John was eager to work, offered him half his normal rate of pay. John objected but eventually agreed to do the work for about 60% of his usual rate. It was dull, boring work and involved long trips.

Both parties thought Bill had won and John had lost. After a few weeks, John got a big new contract and began to resent Bill's job. He would do the work in a hurry at the end of the day when he was tired.

When finished, the warehouse had an awkward leak, perhaps the result of John's half-hearted effort. Bill tried unsuccessfully to fix it cheaply. Customers were few, and Bill closed the warehouse after three years.

◀ **EXCHANGING UNSUCCESSFULLY**
In this situation, negotiations led at the beginning to an apparent winner and an apparent loser. However, over time, these positions became reversed as John, the supposed loser, ended up ahead while Bill, the apparent winner, realized that he made an expensive mistake by trying to save money at the outset.

NEGOTIATING A ▶ FAIR EXCHANGE
Both parties in this case can be said to have won. Juan was aware that no more hard cash would be offered by the software company, so they joined in an alliance. Both parties achieved their common aim, which was to minimize their loss if the venture failed and to maximize their profits if it succeeded.

CASE STUDY

Juan was a computer software designer with an idea for a new computer game that he believed would be hugely successful. However, it would take a long time to program it, and he needed to earn a living in the meantime.

He went to see his friend Ellen, an executive at a large computer company. Ellen and her colleagues liked the idea, but offered Juan only $10,000. Juan said it would take him

nine months to develop the game, and, while $10,000 would enable him to survive, it was not sufficient reward.

He suggested that the $10,000 should act as an advance on future profits, and that he and the company share the profits in the ratio 25:75. Eventually, a 20:80 split was agreed upon. The game was launched with a big marketing campaign and was a huge success, making both parties a lot of money.

Identifying Objectives

The first step in planning any form of negotiation is to identify all your objectives. What do you want to get out of the negotiation? Only when you know the answers can you begin to create a plan that will enable you to achieve these goals.

11 Write down all your objectives, then put them in order of priority.

Clarifying Objectives

There is rarely just one objective to a negotiation. You may be buying a chess set in a foreign country, but you also want to take it back to your home country without paying duty and you want to pay by credit card. Therefore, buying the chess set is not your sole objective. Similarly, when unions are negotiating for a pay raise for their members, they may also be looking to reduce excessive working hours or to improve the rate that members will be paid for working at weekends.

Before entering a negotiation, make a list of all your objectives, then put them in your order of priority and identify those that you can live without. When it comes to compromise, you will be aware of which objectives to yield first.

12 Identify issues that are open to compromise and those that are not.

13 Express each objective in a single sentence.

Assigning Different Priorities

For Company	Priority	For Supplier
Price	First	Quality
Time	Second	Price
Quality	Third	Time
Quantity	Fourth	Quantity

CLASSIFYING PRIORITIES

Divide your priorities into three groups:
- Those that are your ideal;
- Those that represent a realistic target;
- Those that are the minimum you must fulfill to feel that the negotiation has not been a failure.

Assign each of them a value. For example, if buying a chess set is your prime objective, give it a value of ten. Paying by credit card may be something that you can yield on, so give it a lower value of two. Finding the chess set in marble may not be crucial but still have a value of, say, seven. Prioritizing in this way ensures that you do not end up compromising on the wrong issues.

14 Abandon any totally unrealistic objectives before you negotiate.

ASSESSING ▶ PRIORITIES

In Anil's case, a decent pension was more important than the other assets of the job; on GUT's side, the expense and trouble of changing the pension fund outstripped the benefits of gaining a talented recruit.

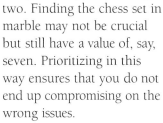

CASE STUDY

Anil was about to accept a new job with Great Universal Technology, who offered him an increased salary and relocation. The only drawback was that GUT, without explanation, said that it was not prepared to include him in its company pension plan but would pay a comparable sum into a new pension plan that he took out on his own. He talked to an accountant and discovered that he would lose out by starting a new fund in this way. Thinking that GUT would be accommodating, he insisted that it sign him on to its own pension plan. GUT withdrew its job offer, saying that to accommodate him would have involved changing the pension plan of everybody else in the company, and that it was not prepared to do this. The negotiation broke down because GUT had not explained the problem fully.

DISTINGUISHING BETWEEN WANTS AND NEEDS

A useful distinction that can help in assigning values to different objectives is that between "wants" and "needs." On the one hand, you may decide that you would like to replace your basic telephone with a sophisticated new telephone with lots of automatic functions. On the other hand, when your computer hard drive breaks down irretrievably, you need that replaced as soon as possible to be able to function properly in the office. So, while you *want* a new phone, you do not need one. What you *need* is a computer hard drive. Understanding the subtlety of this difference is vital to recognizing your opponent's wants and needs around the negotiating table.

PREPARING YOURSELF

Preparing yourself for serious negotiation involves thorough research. You will need to seek out useful information to support your objectives – once you have identified them – and find information that will help you to undermine the other party's case.

> **15** Be sure to gather all key information relevant to a negotiation.

POINTS TO REMEMBER

- Incorrect information is worse than no information at all.
- Companies' annual accounts can be a mine of useful information.
- Your approach should bear in mind what information is available to the other party.
- Too many statistics may only confuse an issue.
- It is worth developing lines of access to information, since they may be useful some day, if not now.

USING PREPARATION TIME

Allowing for preparation time before you start negotiating is vital, as is the constructive use of that time. Allow yourself enough time to complete your research satisfactorily. You may need time to find statistics and case studies to support your arguments and thumbnail sketches of the personalities with whom you will be negotiating. Absorb this information, and use it tactically. For example, if you plan to use complex statistics, prepare an explanation to show how they support your case, rather than undermine the other party by exposing their ignorance of your material.

ASSEMBLING DATA

One valuable use of your preparation time is to acquire in-depth information about the people you will be dealing with and their business. This will be available from both electronic and paper-based sources. Visit a library; search the Internet; talk to others who know the people with whom you are about to negotiate. Look at the company's annual reports, at market research, and at old press releases. A careful scan of such sources can help you come up with telling arguments to support your case, but be absolutely certain of the accuracy of the information you have gleaned.

▲ ASSEMBLING DOCUMENTS

Arrange your data so it is easily accessible. Photocopy key pages of text; use colored pens to highlight points. Time spent checking data is not wasted.

DEVELOPING LOGIC

Having compiled plenty of data, begin to develop a logical argument. You will need to follow through your logic in one of two basic ways:

- Deductively – a conclusion follows from a set of premises. For example, "I am a shareholder in Great Universal Technology. GUT will pay a dividend this quarter of 50 cents per share. Therefore I shall receive a dividend of 50 cents per share this quarter."
- Inductively – a conclusion is drawn from examples based on experience. For example, "Every time someone in GUT has become vice president, they have received a pay raise. I am being made vice president, therefore I will receive a pay raise." If the expected pay raise fails to follow promotion on just one occasion, it undermines the logic.

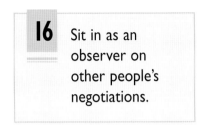

16 Sit in as an observer on other people's negotiations.

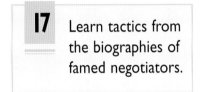

17 Learn tactics from the biographies of famed negotiators.

ANTICIPATING POSSIBLE DIRECTIONS OF A NEGOTIATION

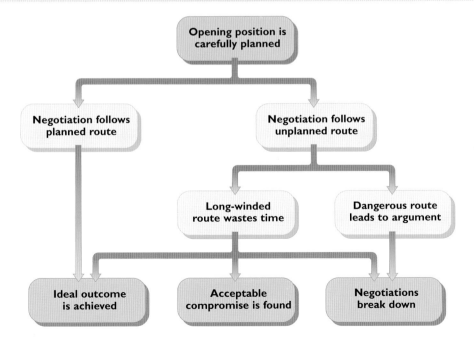

ASSESSING THE OPPOSITION

When preparing your case, it is to your advantage to study the likely strengths and weaknesses of the opposition's negotiating position and to research the background of the individuals who are doing the negotiating. Find out about their negotiating histories.

18 Talk to people who know the other party in the negotiations.

QUESTIONS TO ASK YOURSELF

Q Does the opposition have experienced negotiators?

Q Are there any differences in opinion within the opposition?

Q Does the opposition have the knowledge and facts necessary to achieve its aims?

Q Does the opposition have the power and authority to achieve its aims?

Q Is the opposition under pressure to settle quickly?

LOOKING AT THEIR CASE

Study the opposition's case in the round – that is, look at all aspects of their case. It will have strengths and weaknesses. Aim to expose its major weaknesses in order to undermine its strengths.

Although the logical argument in favor of the opposition's case may be strong, you may be able to counter a logical proposition with, say, a moral objection. For example, if a fish farm wants to use a new type of feed that makes the fish grow 15 percent more rapidly, look for any repercussions of such a fast weight gain. Research may show that the feed makes the bones of the fish so weak that they can barely swim.

ASSESSING STRENGTHS

Since negotiation involves a process of gradual convergence toward agreement or compromise, you need to assess the opposition's starting point and their strengths. Do they have a strong case? Is it logical? Is it morally acceptable? Do they have a strong leader with good negotiating skills? Once you have an idea of the opposition's strong points, assess in what direction they might go once you begin to bargain. How much room do they have to negotiate? Would an adjournment work in their favor, for example, should they want to consult with a higher authority?

19 Be aware that the opposition might have a hidden agenda.

IDENTIFYING OBJECTIVES

Try to identify the opposition's objectives – just as you have identified your own. Make a list of their supposed objectives, and prioritize them. Categorize them according to whether you think they are top, middle, or low priority. Remember that these judgments can only be guesswork and that they need to be tested by observation as the negotiations proceed.

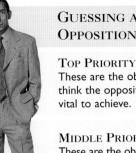

GUESSING AT THE OPPOSITION'S OBJECTIVES

TOP PRIORITY
These are the objectives that you think the opposition considers as vital to achieve.

MIDDLE PRIORITY
These are the objectives that you think the opposition would like to achieve.

LOW PRIORITY
These are the objectives that you think the opposition would regard as bonuses if achieved.

ANALYZING THEIR WEAKNESSES

Just as you need to understand the opposition's strengths, you also must be aware of their weaknesses – both of their case and of their individual skills. For instance, if the opposition consists of a group of people, analyze whether there is any scope to divide and conquer – say, by yielding one point that you know will please some of them but displease others. Research weaknesses in their arguments in advance by looking for morally or politically problematic areas in their case that you could fully exploit. For example, a motion by the sales director of an electrical goods wholesaler to sell off at a high discount some damaged electrical goods raises various ethical and legal problems that could be exploited.

20 Keep testing your own assessment of the opposition against the way they behave during the negotiations.

USING FORMAL SOURCES OF INFORMATION

Carefully examine all formal written information about your opponents. For example, analyze articles printed in trade journals and other allied publications that detail what they have done. They may include invaluable background information about your opponent's present state, history, and current strategic objectives. You can also examine all of the publicly available documentation held by government agencies about an opponent's legal history and financial circumstances.

LEARNING FROM EARLIER ENCOUNTERS

Negotiations often take place between parties who have already dealt with each other over similar issues, such as suppliers renegotiating an annually renewed contract or employees negotiating changes in their terms of employment. If you are negotiating with a known party, analyze the way previous negotiations were handled. Reexamine old minutes or notes and consult with any of your colleagues who were present. Reshape your tactics accordingly, but remember that as you become more familiar with the opposition's modus operandi, so they will be formulating objectives in line with their knowledge of your previous strategies.

POINTS TO REMEMBER

● The balance of power in earlier negotiations may not be the same as it is in the current round.

● The opposing negotiator may have a new job with more authority and more power.

● An opposing negotiator's new job may expose new weaknesses along with strengths.

● The time pressures for both teams may be different.

● The amount of preparation done by each party may be different in any round of a negotiation.

21 If possible, always consult with any members of a previous negotiating team.

22 Research in advance who will be representing the opposition.

FINDING COMMON GROUND

Negotiation involves mapping out ways of finding common ground for agreement or compromise. This goal may be achieved more readily by parties who have previously negotiated and are more likely to understand the concessions that the other side may be willing to make.

For example, if an employee approaches a manager wanting to negotiate a salary increase, he or she may find that the manager's budgetary constraints or a general company ruling prohibit any direct salary increases that year. However, instead of a direct monthly increase, the employee and the manager could discuss and agree on alternative ways of settling on a financial reward that would circumvent these constraints. Both parties could agree on an extra week of annual leave, for example, as an alternative to a pay raise. Such a flexible attitude being shown by both parties, as well as the willingness to seek out common ground, can result in an appropriate compromise being made.

NEGOTIATING WITH MORE THAN ONE GROUP

When the opposition consists of more than one interest group, you should assess whether there are any conflicts between these parties as well as assessing each group and individual as you would normally. Additionally, identify who has the power to make important decisions on behalf of the various groups. If, for example, you are the bidder in a corporate takeover, start by negotiating with the shareholders. In situations where a government body is involved, use a different strategy: address the wider effects of a takeover and use a team that includes lawyers to negotiate and examine all the implications.

CULTURAL DIFFERENCES

Cultural differences exist between races, age groups, and sexes, and you may be able to use these to your advantage. If your opponent is a middle-aged Russian, for example, you may imply that he or she lacks experience of commercial markets. Similarly, a well-educated but young American might be accused of lack of relevant work experience.

USING INFORMAL SOURCES OF INFORMATION

To be proficient at gathering information you must train yourself to think like a detective. Use informal social occasions, business networks, casual encounters, or timely phone calls to the appropriate people to find out how your opponents operate on a day-to-day basis. You can also send someone to their offices to see how they treat their staff and their customers, or invite one of

their long-standing customers to lunch and ask a few discreet questions. Disenchanted ex-employees can also prove to be a mine of useful information, but beware in case they are unwittingly passing on to you misinformation with little basis in reality.

COLLECTING ▶ INFORMATION
Use an informal social occasion with someone who has connections with both parties in the negotiations to acquire as much information about your opponents and their strategies as possible.

CHOOSING A STRATEGY

*O*nce you are clear about your objectives *and have analyzed your opponents' probable objectives, you should be ready to formulate a strategy for achieving your ends. Use the strengths of the personalities in your team to devise your strategy.*

23 Always keep your negotiating strategy simple and flexible.

QUESTIONS TO ASK YOURSELF

Q How will you decide on a strategy and tactics?

Q How many people do you need in your negotiating team?

Q How long will it take you to formulate a strategy?

Q Do all team members need to attend all the negotiations?

Q When can you rehearse your roles and tactics?

CONSIDERING OBJECTIVES

A strategy is an overall policy designed to achieve a number of specified objectives. It is not to be confused with tactics, which are the detailed methods used to carry out a strategy.

Your strategy will depend on several factors including personality, circumstance, and the issue under negotiation. Look carefully at the dynamics of the members of your team in relation to the reasons for and subject of the negotiation, and choose players whose combined strengths and skills can best achieve the team's objectives.

UNDERSTANDING ROLES

Just as every football team needs a quarterback, so every negotiating team requires certain "classic" roles to be filled in order to conclude negotiations successfully. These roles include the Leader, Good Guy, Bad Guy, Hard Liner, and Sweeper. Other roles can also be adopted to suit the circumstances of each particular negotiation you are involved in.

The ideal negotiating team should have between three and five members, and all the key roles should be represented. It is not essential, however, for every role to be filled by a single person – it is common for individual team members to adopt a number of roles that complement each other and reflect their own character traits.

24 Hide short tempers and frustration when negotiating, and never walk out in a rage.

DEFINING ROLES WITHIN TEAMS

ROLES

LEADER
Any negotiating team needs a leader. This may be the person with the most expertise, not necessarily the most senior member of the team.

GOOD GUY
This is the person with whom most members of the opposing team will identify. They may wish that the Good Guy was their only opponent.

BAD GUY
The opposite of the Good Guy, this person's role is to make the opposition feel that agreement could be more easily reached without him or her.

HARD LINER
This member takes a tough line on everything. He or she presents the opposition with complications and is often deferred to by team members.

SWEEPER
This person picks up and brings together all the points of view expressed and then puts them forward as a single cogent case.

RESPONSIBILITIES

- Conducting the negotiation, calling on others occasionally when needed.
- Ruling on matters of expertise – for example, deciding if there is enough money available to finance a takeover bid.
- Orchestrating the other members of the team.

- Expressing sympathy and understanding for the opposition's point of view.
- Appearing to backtrack on a position previously held by their own team.
- Lulling the members of the opposing team into a false sense of security, allowing them to relax.

- Stopping the negotiations from proceeding, if and when needed.
- Undermining any argument or point of view the opposition puts forward.
- Intimidating the opposition and trying to expose their weaknesses.

- Delaying progress by using stalling tactics.
- Allowing others to retreat from soft offers that they might have made.
- Observing and recording the progress of the negotiations.
- Keeping the team focused on the objectives of the negotiations.

- Suggesting ways or tactics to get out of a deadlocked negotiation.
- Preventing the discussion from straying too far from the main issues.
- Pointing out any inconsistencies in the opposition's argument.

Assigning Roles

In negotiation, good strategy involves the appropriate deployment of personnel. You must decide on the roles and responsibilities that you want your team members to assume. Are they better at observing and listening than talking? Have they met any of the opposition before? Are they extroverted? An extroverted member of your team could, for example, play the role of the Good Guy. Allocate roles carefully, since your team must be able to tackle any moves made by the opposition.

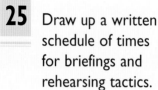

25 Draw up a written schedule of times for briefings and rehearsing tactics.

▼ **REHEARSING ROLES**
When you have selected your team, gather them together for a rehearsal, each member playing out their role. Resolve any gaps or duplication of roles in the team.

Practice using visual aids

Encourage note-taking for reference during the real negotiations

THE IMPORTANCE OF APPEARANCE

Carefully consider your appearance in advance – first impressions count for a lot. Think about the type of negotiation you are entering, and dress accordingly. Power dressing can influence the way that people perceive you and your authority, but it can carry negative connotations of aggression. Encourage your team to dress in the same way, and if you want to appear formal, wear a jacket when you arrive. If in doubt, dress conservatively.

26 Wear clothes that you find comfortable but which are smart and fairly conservative.

27 Practice being silent around a negotiating table.

BRIEFING YOUR TEAM

In order for members of your negotiating team to play particular roles successfully, you must brief them thoroughly. Avoid sending out contradictory messages during negotiations by keeping absent members up to date. For example, if the Leader claims early on that he or she has full authority to agree on a price, make sure that the Hard Liner does not come into the meeting later and, in an attempt to stall for time, assert that head office will need to be consulted for approval on the price. Such an inconsistency can seriously undermine the credibility of your team.

As well as encouraging individual preparation, make sure that the complete team is present for at least one dress rehearsal that uses actual data and visual material where possible. Take notes that can be used afterward to analyze how the team can improve their strategies and tactics.

CASE STUDY

Beth and Kurt were sent to Hong Kong by their employer, an electronics company, to persuade a manufacturer to buy some of its microchips. Before they left, they rehearsed a number of good arguments and decided that Beth was to make the case. In Hong Kong, the factory managers approved of the proposal and seemed happy. However, while Beth was talking, Kurt overheard someone say that "Westerners never accept the first price offered." So when the Chinese put forward their price, expecting it to be rejected, Kurt interrupted. Beth was taken aback, since she thought that the offer price was perfectly reasonable. However, she was pleased to have been interrupted when the Chinese agreed to a price 10% higher than their original offer. Both sides departed happy with the deal.

◀ **WORKING TOGETHER**
In this example of teamwork, Beth was acting as the Leader and Kurt fulfilled the other roles. It would have been much more difficult for a single negotiator, working on his or her own, to have picked up sufficient information to clinch this deal as successfully.

USING AN AGENDA

In certain types of negotiation, it is helpful to draw up an agenda – a written list of issues to be debated. Use an agenda to gain agreement from all the participants, before the negotiating begins, on the areas that are to be discussed or left out altogether.

28 Try to set the agenda – it will influence the rest of the meeting.

POINTS TO REMEMBER

- Items should be allocated a fixed period of time on an agenda.
- A draft agenda should be sent to all parties in advance.
- Typed agendas should have wide margins for making notes.
- Supplementary papers should be distributed with an agenda.
- Agendas can be so important that sometimes their content needs to be negotiated.

DRAFTING AN AGENDA

The items to be discussed on an agenda can become a central part of negotiating strategy, through both the order in which they are to be considered and the time that is given to each. It is therefore sometimes necessary to hold extensive discussions in order to draft an agenda before negotiations begin. Bear in mind when drafting an agenda that it should:

- Formally define what the discussion is about;
- Informally influence the substance of the discussion by prioritizing issues.

WRITING ▶ AN AGENDA

An agenda helps to focus a negotiation on its aims and objectives. Since negotiation is not about airing grievances but achieving solutions, headings should use unchallenging and nonspecific language.

Scheduled times

Close of meeting is indicated

Termination Negotiations
July 24th, 9:00 a.m.
Board Room

1. (9:00) Read minutes of previous meeting.
2. (9:15) Management consultants present case.
3. (9:45) Personnel Director presents case.
   (10:15) Coffee break.
4. (10:30) Financial Director presents case.
5. (11:00) Summing up by Managing Director.
6. (11:30) Discussion.
7. (12:30) Close.

Details of meeting head agenda

Previous decisions are ratified

First speaker sets tone

Specialist participant provides detailed information

AGREEING TO AN AGENDA

If you receive an agenda from the other party, analyze it and adjust your strategy accordingly. The party that sets the agenda is the party with the greatest interest in the meeting and will usually claim the first speaking slot. Thus, you may wish to rearrange the order of speakers to your advantage. If an agenda is relayed to you by phone, ensure you are not thrown off by the informality. Absorb all the information and consult the opposition about changes you wish to make.

29 Arrive a little early for meetings so you will look efficient and relaxed.

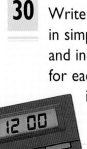

30 Write an agenda in simple language, and include timings for each of the issues under discussion.

SCHEDULING AGENDAS

In some negotiations, a time limit is imposed due to the busy schedules of the people involved. Other negotiations require the parties involved to sit around a table for as long as it takes to reach agreement (in the case of peace treaties, for instance, or of juries in courts of law). Always set a target time for the meeting to end, and schedule the discussion to fit within that time constraint. Remember that most people will become irritable if a meeting overruns its schedule.

RECORDING INFORMATION

Negotiation inevitably involves making concessions that a negotiating team might regret (or at least have second thoughts about). Thus, many people like to record the proceedings on audio cassette. This can be problematic, however, for a number of reasons: it can be difficult to position a tape recorder to pick up all the dialogue; vital parts of the discussion may also be lost if batteries have to be changed; and cassettes rarely last the duration of a negotiation.

If you want to record the meeting in this way, obtain the agreement of the other party in advance. In addition to tape recordings, experienced negotiators always ensure that detailed written minutes of the proceedings are taken.

TAKING NOTES ▶
Use a recorder to take down comments or notes quickly and easily.

CREATING THE RIGHT ATMOSPHERE

The outcome of a negotiating session can be influenced by the environment in which it is held. Create a positive atmosphere for opposing teams from the outset of the proceedings by making the location suitable for the size and nature of the occasion.

31 Do not run a negotiation longer than two hours without a break.

DECIDING ON LOCATION

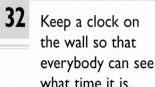

32 Keep a clock on the wall so that everybody can see what time it is.

There are many considerations to take into account when selecting a location, including convenience, neutrality, and facilities. Do you require audio-visual aids or flip charts? Do you need to rent them, and from whom? How long are the facilities reserved? Can you stay overnight nearby if agreement is not reached within one day? Choose a location that fulfills as many of your requirements as possible.

TYPES OF LOCATION FOR NEGOTIATIONS

LOCATION	FACTORS TO CONSIDER
HOME GROUND An office or room in your company building is considered home territory.	● It is easy for you to organize strategic interruptions. ● It is difficult to avoid unplanned interruptions. ● It is easy to call on your own in-house experts for relevant contributions to the negotiations.
NEUTRAL GROUND The office of a third party, or a rented public room, is considered neutral ground.	● Neither party gains the upper hand because of their familiarity with the location. ● Both sides need to "ship in" their experts and any background material they might require.
AWAY GROUND Away ground is an office or room belonging to the other negotiating party.	● Lack of familiarity with the surroundings can be disturbing. ● You have no control of the logistics. ● You can procrastinate by saying that you need to refer the matter back to someone in your office.

ATTENDING TO DETAILS

When hosting a negotiation, take complete control of the situation: manipulate the atmosphere, timing, and the nature of the breaks to increase your advantage. Supply paper and pens for taking notes during the proceedings. Check the bathroom facilities, and make sure that the lighting in the negotiating room is adequate, especially if audio-visual aids are being used. Physical comfort can also be a decisive factor; lower the temperature of the negotiating room by a few degrees, or delay the refreshments, to encourage a quicker decision from your opponents. If proceedings extend over a break, serve refreshments away from the meeting table, and avoid alcoholic drinks.

33 Do not reveal all your tactics at once when negotiating.

◀ **PROVIDING REFRESHMENTS**
Although your team members may lose their appetites during protracted negotiations, they will not lose their thirst. The combination of tension, unfamiliar surroundings, and pressure makes throats dry, so always provide water.

34 If needed, ensure that all parties have access to private phone lines.

35 Take a laptop computer if you need to access company data.

TAKING CONTROL OF AN AWAY-GROUND NEGOTIATION

Some negotiators prefer to visit the opposition on their home territory. Use this ploy to imply a willingness to make an effort and give a positive start to the proceedings. One advantage you may gain by this approach is that you will be able to dictate the time of the meeting to exert maximum pressure on your hosts. If there is no fixed agenda in advance of the negotiation, upon arrival ask your hosts if they mind your setting one. The opposition may be willing to make this concession since you are on their home ground. If you do set the agenda in this way, you must take full advantage of the opportunity – ensure that you build into it the details that you want, and you will start to tip the scales in your favor.

USING SEATING PLANS

The way in which negotiators are seated around a table – whether facing each other in a confrontational manner or seated collaboratively at a round table – can have a marked effect on the tone and even the outcome of a negotiating session.

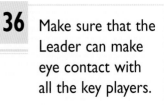

36 Make sure that the Leader can make eye contact with all the key players.

SEATING SMALL TEAMS

For negotiations between small teams, the parties often face each other across a rectangular table. This is the most formal and confrontational arrangement. To undermine the opposition, try to seat your team leader at the head of the table to create the impression that they control the proceedings.

To help soften any hardline attitudes that are hindering negotiations, make the seating as informal as possible, preferably using a round table.

▼ **SEATING YOUR TEAM**
For anything other than extremely formal negotiations, a team of five is the accepted maximum. The "across the table" approach, in which teams sit facing each other, is usual and is favored when negotiators want to emphasize their separate identities. Sit each member of the team where their skills will be of most use and in a way that presents a united front.

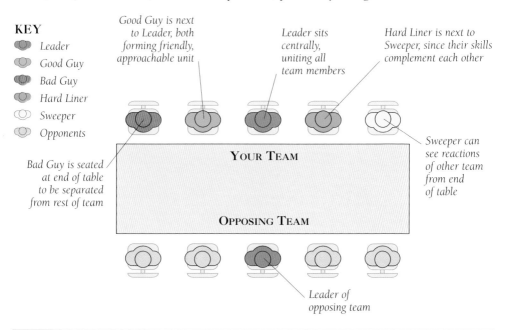

KEY
- 🔵 Leader
- 🔵 Good Guy
- 🔵 Bad Guy
- 🔵 Hard Liner
- ⚪ Sweeper
- ⚪ Opponents

Good Guy is next to Leader, both forming friendly, approachable unit

Leader sits centrally, uniting all team members

Hard Liner is next to Sweeper, since their skills complement each other

Bad Guy is seated at end of table to be separated from rest of team

YOUR TEAM

Sweeper can see reactions of other team from end of table

OPPOSING TEAM

Leader of opposing team

USING SEATING TACTICALLY

When seating any size of team for negotiations, find the most comfortable chairs possible. As an alternative to the traditional or informal seating plan around a table, make it difficult for a visiting team to present a cohesive opposition by seating them among your own team. If possible, seat the most vocal or aggressive member of the visitors' team right next to the leader of your team.

However the teams are seated, eye contact is very important. It helps negotiators read the mood of the opposition and also enables team leaders to get feedback from their own team. The absence of eye contact is disorienting; you may wish to exploit this factor when seating your opponents.

37 Seat your Hard Liner away from your opponent's Hard Liner.

38 Position chairs at an equal distance from each other.

SEATING LARGE TEAMS

If negotiations are between many parties, with only a few representatives of each present (such as at the United Nations or the International Monetary Fund), seat the participants in a large circle, and arrange for individuals to speak from a podium to make their case.

If negotiations are between a few parties, each of which has a large number of representatives, divide the seating into groups, facing each other if possible. This is the way in which national parliaments are often seated and is an arrangement that can be used at either trade union or staff committee negotiations.

INFLUENCING SEATING PLANS

When you arrive at a negotiation hosted by others, ascertain whether there is a prearranged seating plan. If there is no plan, try to seat your team first at the negotiating table so that you can tactically select your positions. Your choice of seats will depend on the dynamics of your team – whether you want to present a united front by sitting together, prefer to divide your opponents by sitting among them, or want to take control at the head of the table.

If you have been allocated seats, try to determine whether there is any logic behind the arrangements. The plan may give clues about the other parties and their views, or your perceived status. Seating may suggest that the talks are expected to be informal, confrontational, or dominated by your hosts. Once you gauge the tone, you can alter your approach accordingly. If you are not happy with the seating arrangements, ask if they can be changed.

CONDUCTING A NEGOTIATION

Plan your opening negotiating moves carefully to establish a positive tone. Then stay alert and be flexible to create and make use of all your opportunities in the course of a negotiation.

JUDGING THE MOOD

Negotiating is as much about listening and observing as it is about talking. You need to be very alert to the mood of the negotiations, since this can change quickly. Being alert involves using all your senses to pick up signals given off by others.

39 Begin any negotiations with uncontroversial, general points.

40 Stress the need for agreement from the outset.

▼ **STUDYING REACTIONS**
Throughout a negotiation, examine the other party's reactions and messages, trying to spot any inconsistencies.

ANTICIPATING THE TONE

Your preparation should help you to anticipate how the opposition will approach the negotiation. Once in the negotiation, try to judge whether you anticipated correctly by noticing nonverbal signals, such as gestures. If you are expecting an aggressive start, try to confirm this by reading signals from the other team – if they appear tense, your suspicions may be correct.

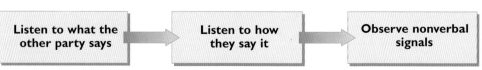

| Listen to what the other party says | Listen to how they say it | Observe nonverbal signals |

READING NONVERBAL SIGNALS

Nonverbal signals include body language, gestures, facial expressions, and eye movements. Learning to read body language among the opposition team will help you compile a true picture of their case – their signals may reinforce or contradict what they are saying. Clear-cut body language includes crossing of arms and legs, which betrays defensiveness, and leaning back on a chair, which expresses boredom. Small gestures and movements, such as hesitating or fidgeting, may indicate lack of conviction; raised eyebrows are a clear sign of surprise. Eye contact is another good source of information: team members may glance at each other when an important point in the negotiation has been reached.

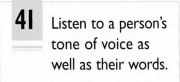

41 Listen to a person's tone of voice as well as their words.

POINTS TO REMEMBER

● Speaking slowly and deliberately indicates that a person feels confident and at ease.

● Smiling unnecessarily and speaking quickly indicates nervousness.

● People who want to leave tend to look and turn their lower bodies toward the exit.

CULTURAL DIFFERENCES

Shaking hands may mean "Goodbye" to one party and "We've struck a deal" to the other. Make sure you understand the cultural rules before offering a handshake. In many Asian cultures, physical contact between the opposite sexes is discouraged. Women should therefore consider carefully whether to shake hands with men, or vice versa.

Direct eye contact is used

Handshake is firm but not overhearty

SETTING THE MOOD ▶
Shaking hands gives clues about the opposition. A confident handshake shows respect and openness; a forceful one indicates dominance; a limp one, passivity.

Making a Proposal

Making a proposal is fundamental to all negotiation. It is vital to decide early on in the planning process whether you wish to speak first or to respond to the proposal from the opposition. This decision is a crucial part of negotiating strategy.

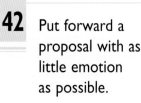

42 Put forward a proposal with as little emotion as possible.

Keeping Options Open

Leave yourself plenty of room for maneuvering when presenting your case. Do not make brash statements that suggest that your position is immovable – make your proposals hypothetical to leave scope for both sides to make concessions at any time. Likewise, do not try to pin down the other party to a fixed position too soon – they need room to maneuver, too. Avoid forcing them into a corner or into making promises at an early stage of the proceedings, since this reduces their options when you come to make concessions later.

43 Do not start speaking until you have something relevant to say.

Do's and Don'ts

✔ Do listen carefully to the other party.

✔ Do leave enough room for maneuvering in your proposals.

✔ Do feel free to reject the first offer received.

✔ Do make conditional offers, such as "If you do this, we'll do that."

✔ Do probe the attitudes of the opposition: "What would be your feelings if…?"

✘ Don't make too many concessions at an early stage.

✘ Don't make your opening offer so extreme that you lose face if you need to back down.

✘ Don't ever say "never."

✘ Don't answer questions directly with a simple "yes" or "no."

✘ Don't make the opposition look foolish.

44 Pay close attention to the proposal of the other party.

45 Use humor when appropriate, but do not try to be too clever.

THINGS TO DO

1. Listen carefully to your opposition – their wishes may be closer to yours than you expect.

2. Be willing to adjust your strategy if you can see a compromise early on in the proceedings.

3. Make your initial offer unrealistic, and compromise from that point onward.

4. Take notes of all the offers made, trying to record them verbatim.

TIMING A PROPOSAL

The outcome of all negotiations depends on the presenting and discussing of proposals made by all parties concerned. These will be expanded and compromised upon until an agreement is reached. There are advantages in letting the other party make the opening proposal, since you may find that there is less distance between their demands and yours than you suspected. If this is the case, adjust your own strategy accordingly. If you decide to make the opening proposal, it will be generally regarded as unrealistic, so make your initial demands greater than you expect to receive, and offer less than you expect to give. If you open with an offer that you think is genuinely fair, there is a danger that the other party will interpret it as being very different from your actual requirements.

PHRASING A PROPOSAL

It is important that you present your initial proposal fluently and with confidence so you are taken seriously by your opponents. While speaking, emphasize the need to reach agreement, saying, for example: "I know that everybody here today is eager to see this project move forward as quickly as possible." When making your proposal, explain the conditions attached before making your initial offer. Summarize your offer briefly and then keep quiet to show that you have finished, allowing the other party time to digest your words.

Posture is open and confident

Direct eye contact is made with other party

MAKING A PROPOSAL ▶
Sit upright in your chair and lean forward slightly. Using positive body language such as this encourages the other party to take both you and your proposal seriously.

RESPONDING TO A PROPOSAL

Try to avoid showing any immediate reaction, favorable or otherwise, when responding to a proposal. Do not be afraid to remain silent while assessing the offer, but be aware that your opposition will be studying you to gauge your reaction.

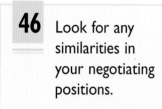

46 Look for any similarities in your negotiating positions.

47 Wait for the other party to finish before responding.

SEEKING CLARIFICATION

When you have heard the other party's offer, do not feel obliged to respond immediately with a counteroffer. Remain as inscrutable as possible while summarizing the proposal as you have understood it. This gives you more time to think about what has been said and also provides an opportunity to confirm that you have understood it correctly. This is the time to focus on any issues that you feel unsure of and to challenge the other party to correct you. For example, "If I grasp what you are saying, we cannot expect to see any goods until next December," or "Can we clarify that you have taken into account the length of time it takes to clear checks in Singapore?" It is crucial that you understand the other party's position completely.

◀ **MAKING YOUR RESPONSE**
Use open body language – making eye contact, sitting upright with hands loosely crossed in front of you – to indicate that you have understood and accepted what has been offered to you. However, do not give away too much – keep the other party guessing about your reactions.

STALLING FOR TIME

Use stalling tactics only if you do not want to respond to your opponent's offer immediately, and then use them sparingly. These are the tactics that you can use without seriously jeopardizing the outcome of your negotiations:

- Interrupt the other party's proposal – but only if you can disguise this as seeking clarification of a point or refocusing the discussion;
- Answer a question with a question, or ask lots of questions – after all, it does no harm to have extra information at your disposal;
- Break off the negotiations for consultation with your colleagues, especially if you have already established that there is an external authority from whom you need to seek feedback.

 48 Always use stalling tactics subtly and sparingly, if at all.

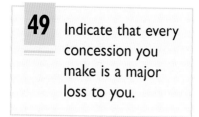 **49** Indicate that every concession you make is a major loss to you.

POINTS TO REMEMBER

- Your position may be damaged if you respond to the other party's proposal too quickly.
- Information should be exchanged as part of a compromise and not merely given away.
- Questions can be asked constantly. The more information you have, the more you can control the negotiations.
- It is a good idea to summarize the other party's proposal.
- Hidden agendas on either side slow down the proceedings and should be guarded against.

50 Ask for a break to consider any new proposals.

PROPOSING ALTERNATIVES

If you decide to make a counteroffer, try to do so immediately after you have completed your assessment of the other team's offer – sometimes it is appropriate to strike while the iron is hot. To become a successful negotiator, learn to recognize that there are alternatives to every situation. Decide what you can offer as a counterproposal by working out which issues are priorities to your opposition. From these, identify the priorities that are least important to you, and incorporate them into your counteroffer. In this way you will appear willing to compromise but will not in fact give away anything of great value to your team.

In a classic example, two brothers are arguing about how to divide the last piece of pie. Each wants the larger slice. Their father suggests that one son cut the pie any way he wants and that the other then choose which piece he wants. Such a piece of lateral thinking can bring a negotiation to a speedy and satisfactory conclusion.

RESPONDING TO PLOYS

Good negotiators need to be able to recognize – and counter – the ploys and tactics that are commonly used by people during negotiation. Identify and resist manipulative tactics as they occur to avoid costly mistakes when negotiating.

51 If you are foiled by a successful ploy, think before you respond.

POINTS TO REMEMBER

- The unexpected introduction of new issues should be avoided.
- Ignoring a ploy will neutralize the intended effect.
- Personal attacks should be deflected with humor rather than allowed to provoke anger.
- Ploys used by the other team should not be taken personally. Be aware that they are used for manipulative purposes.
- Allocating blame for losing ground when the opposing team has employed a successful tactic is a waste of valuable time.

52 Practice your response to a variety of tactics that are often used in negotiation.

UNDERSTANDING PLOYS

It is common during negotiations to encounter tactics employed to enable one party to benefit while conceding as little as possible. These ploys work by creating the perception that your power to get what you want is inferior to that of the other party, thus lowering your resistance to giving the other party its own way.

While you may not choose to use these ploys, it is highly important for you to recognize and counter them so that you remain focused on your objectives and avoid wasting time on distractions.

IDENTIFYING PLOYS

Recognizing the tactics that other parties use to influence negotiations takes practice. To learn how to identify and deal with such ploys without risking expensive mistakes, observe the other parties very carefully and bear in mind that manipulative tactics usually have three main aims:

- To distract your team, allowing the opposition to dominate the discussions;
- To shift the emphasis of the negotiation in order to shape the deal on terms that are purely to the benefit of the opposition;
- To manipulate your team into closing negotiations before you are entirely satisfied with the terms being offered.

COUNTERING TYPICAL TACTICS

TACTICS	COUNTER-TACTICS
MAKING THREATS Warning of unwelcome repercussions if you fail to agree to the terms offered; emphasizing that penalties will be incurred by your side.	Tell the other party that you cannot negotiate under duress and that concessions will be made only if they can prove the merits of the case. Review other options available to you.
OFFERING INSULTS Questioning the performance of your company or your professional competence; criticizing the quality of your product or service.	Stay calm; do not lose your temper or offer insults in return. Restate your position firmly and warn that you will break off negotiations unless the other party is more constructive.
BLUFFING Threatening punitive action without being too specific; making dubious assertions, such as suggesting that competitors can undercut prices.	Call their bluff: refuse to agree to the other party's terms, then wait for a reaction. Question all statements and ask for evidence to support any claims that appear dubious.
USING INTIMIDATION Keeping you waiting; making you sit in an awkward or uncomfortable place; receiving phone calls or visitors during negotiations.	Recognize that these are ploys to make you feel less confident. Do not drop your original terms unless you have gained concessions in return, and do not be coerced into settling.
DIVIDING AND CONQUERING Exploiting potential disagreements among members of your team by appealing to the person most sympathetic to their case.	Brief team members in advance and decide on a position that is acceptable to everyone. Call an adjournment if differences of opinion arise within your team during the meeting.
USING LEADING QUESTIONS Asking you a series of questions that lead you to declare a weakness in your negotiating position; forcing concessions from your side.	Avoid answering questions when you do not understand the intention behind them. Check any claims made by the other party. Attach conditions to any concessions you make.
MAKING EMOTIONAL APPEALS Accusing you of acting unfairly in not agreeing to terms; stressing their sacrifices; claiming to be offended by your lack of trust.	Affirm your commitment to achieving a fair settlement on business terms. Ask questions to test the validity of manipulative claims. Lead the conversation back to discussing the issues.
TESTING THE BOUNDARIES Gaining additional concessions through minor infringements of the terms agreed, resulting in substantial gain over a long period.	Be clear on exactly what you are agreeing to when you reach a settlement. Draw up a clearly worded statement of terms agreed, and hold the other party to these at all times.

DEALING WITH UNHELPFUL BEHAVIOR

Emotional outbursts from attendees can suddenly change the mood of a negotiation. These outbursts may declare indecision, confusion, or aggression, but the most common type is a team member losing their temper. Unhelpful behavior works well as a ploy because it shifts attention from the issue under negotiation to one individual. When this occurs, decide whether it is a ploy or is unintentional, then steer the discussion back on course as quickly as possible. You cannot make a decision if you are not negotiating. Handle these situations well, and people will be less likely to try such ploys again.

 53 Adjourn when an unknown element is introduced into a negotiation.

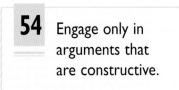 **54** Engage only in arguments that are constructive.

HANDLING PLOYS AND UNHELPFUL BEHAVIOR

PROBLEMS	POSSIBLE SOLUTIONS
CONFUSED NEGOTIATOR	● Use visual aids to clarify complex issues that are causing confusion. ● Put complex proposals in writing, using short, clear sentences. ● Follow a concise step-by-step agenda to prevent further confusion. ● Be prepared to involve a third party to review the issues with a fresh eye.
INDECISIVE NEGOTIATOR	● Proceed slowly and methodically, and be prepared to reiterate points. ● Promise a review of the issues under discussion after a set period of time. ● Adjourn to allow an indecisive negotiator to consult others in their team. ● Try to present the issues in a fresh and original way.
AGGRESSIVE NEGOTIATOR	● Reiterate all the facts, keeping calm and avoiding emotional language. ● Refuse to be drawn into a battle of words, and stay calm at all times. ● State firmly that intimidation, bullying, and threats are unacceptable. ● Suggest an adjournment in the negotiations until tempers cool.
EMOTIONAL NEGOTIATOR	● Do not challenge the motives or integrity of the negotiator. ● Do not interrupt outbursts; wait patiently to make your response. ● Respond to any emotional outburst with rational questioning. ● Adjourn to allow the emotional negotiator to calm down.

ADJOURNING A NEGOTIATION

The natural way to cope with ploys such as emotional outbursts is through an adjournment. But an adjournment may itself be used as a stalling ploy, either by you or your opponent. If an adjournment is called for by one party, the other side must either accept or call off the negotiations.

Adjourn negotiations to allow the opposition to calm down and realize that losing their temper is unlikely to help them achieve their objectives. Alternatively, use an adjournment to review your position and tactics if new issues are introduced unexpectedly. However, be aware that adjournments can delay an agreement and become a disadvantage. If you call for an adjournment, summarize and record the discussion's progress before breaking.

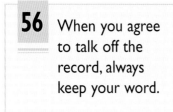

55 Call for an adjournment when a completely new issue is introduced.

56 When you agree to talk off the record, always keep your word.

ADJOURNING FOR INFORMAL DISCUSSION

If formal negotiations have reached a stalemate, it may be helpful to continue the discussion on a different footing. Suggest that you talk off the record, without recording your conversation as part of the official minutes of the meeting and without either party being held to anything discussed. Encourage the other party to talk informally and in confidence about their reservations over making concessions. Move to another room nearby, if one is available, since a different environment may be more conducive to relaxed discussion. If experts disagree on a specific technical matter, suggest that they ask another expert for an independent opinion.

CHATTING IN CONFIDENCE ▶

An informal chat away from the formal table across which parties usually face each other can smooth out negotiations. Use such an opportunity to show an opponent that you are reasonable and approachable.

Understanding Body Language

A lot can be learned about the attitude of the other side in a negotiation from their body language. Watch the eyes, which are the most expressive part of the body, but also pay attention to the rest of the face and the postures of members of the other team.

57 Assign one of your team to detect signals given off by the opposition.

Reading Basic Signs

Eye contact with another person indicates a desire to transmit and receive information. When talking, most people make eye contact with each other that lasts for a few seconds at regular intervals. Recognize that eye contact is one of the most important aspects of body language, but also take into account what your opponents are thinking by "reading" the signs given off by their gestures and their overall postures.

UNDERSTANDING SIGNS ▶
You need only a few seconds to obtain significant feedback about your opponents' initial reactions to what you are saying. Recognize and understand their expressions, and use this knowledge to your advantage. Pinpoint their most receptive listeners, then address your remarks to them.

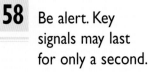

58 Be alert. Key signals may last for only a second.

Open expression shows interest in proceedings

Leaning back implies hostility

Posture suggests attentiveness

Crossed arms indicate disbelief

EXPRESSING OPPOSITION

SHOWING INTEREST

DEALING WITH DUPLICITY

Skilled negotiators can use body language to mislead the other party in a debate. Do not take all body language at face value – it is easy to add a smile to an expression that is otherwise hostile. A person who fulfills the criteria for showing interest may in fact be preparing for a scathing attack. Therefore, always look at an individual's body language in conjunction with that of the members of the other party to get an average reading of the group's mood. It is essential to stay alert, even if you think that the negotiations are proceeding smoothly.

59 Learn to trust your instincts about other people's body language.

Wide eyes and warm expression indicate willingness to be persuaded

Direct eye contact implies positive thoughts

Inattentive gaze means lack of concentration

Open arms imply indecision

Hand on chin shows thoughtfulness

Fiddling with a pen confirms thoughts are elsewhere

MAKING
DECISIONS

LACKING
INTEREST

REMAINING
NEUTRAL

597

ESTABLISHING POSITIONS

The negotiating process can begin in earnest once each team has explored their own position after hearing the other side's proposal. Start to move toward a mutually acceptable agreement once both parties have reassessed their positions.

60 Ask a lot of "how" questions to imply a willingness to compromise.

REINFORCING POSITIONS

After you have heard the other team's proposal, your team may need to reassess its strategy or tactics in order to retain a strong bargaining position. Look for any mutual points of interest between the two sides, and consider the points on which you are prepared to give or concede. Decide whether there are any major differences between the two cases that will require you to prepare a counterproposal in response to the opposition's proposal, or whether you need to make a few minor adjustments to reinforce your current position before beginning the debating stage.

61 Watch for changes in body language, then adjust your tactics accordingly.

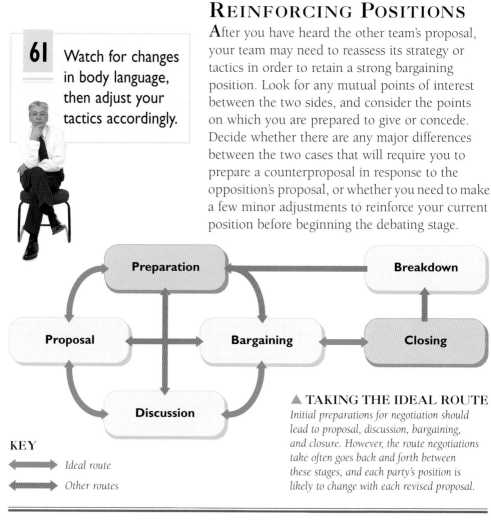

▲ TAKING THE IDEAL ROUTE
Initial preparations for negotiation should lead to proposal, discussion, bargaining, and closure. However, the route negotiations take often goes back and forth between these stages, and each party's position is likely to change with each revised proposal.

KEY
◄► Ideal route
◄► Other routes

READING FACIAL EXPRESSIONS

Most people involuntarily show their emotions in their facial expressions, so watch carefully for a triumphant twitch of the lips or a suppressed yawn. Such signals are particularly valuable at the debating stage, when parties are exploring their positions.

Tense jaw — *Wide eyes*

Head tilted to side — *Steely gaze*

Hand touches ear — *Averted gaze*

▲ **EXASPERATION**
The wide-eyed expression and raised eyebrows convey irritation tinged with frustration. Often, exasperation is experienced when progress is slow.

▲ **BOREDOM**
The tilted head, raised eyebrows, averted gaze, and set mouth all convey boredom. Use a lack of interest to your advantage to move the proceedings forward.

▲ **DISBELIEF**
The unconscious touching of the ear and evasive eye movements suggest that the listener is not convinced by what the other party is telling her.

POINTS TO REMEMBER

● Once you have established your position, use tactics to maintain it.

● Proposals should be revised to accommodate new information from the other party's proposal.

● All possible routes should be explored: "But if we were to do that, then would you…?"

● Always aim for a mutually beneficial outcome.

62 Summarize the assessment of your positions regularly.

DEBATING THE ISSUES

Once both parties have outlined their basic positions, there may be extensive discussion about the underlying assumptions and facts. This debating time is a crucial stage in the negotiating procedure. Use it to search for some common ground and strengthen your case.

Debate can easily become emotional and heated if accusations and counteraccusations are made. Keep every debate calm. If you are frustrated or angry, try not to let it show. Do not score points off the opposition; instead, work to form a bond with them. If they make a mistake, be aware that it strengthens your case, but allow them to retreat without loss of credibility. It may help if you start the discussion on points of mutual agreement before moving on to issues on which you disagree.

STRENGTHENING YOUR POSITION

Gaining the upper hand in negotiations reinforces an argument immediately. Introduce as many relevant points as possible to strengthen your position so that the opposing party is overwhelmed by the strength and thoroughness of your case.

63 Use repetition and positive body language to stress your key points.

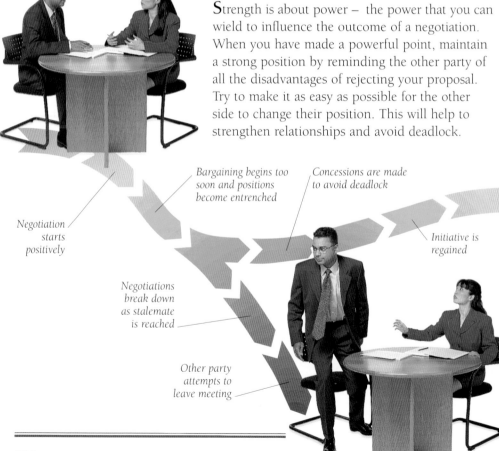

KEEPING THE ADVANTAGE

Strength is about power – the power that you can wield to influence the outcome of a negotiation. When you have made a powerful point, maintain a strong position by reminding the other party of all the disadvantages of rejecting your proposal. Try to make it as easy as possible for the other side to change their position. This will help to strengthen relationships and avoid deadlock.

Bargaining begins too soon and positions become entrenched

Concessions are made to avoid deadlock

Negotiation starts positively

Initiative is regained

Negotiations break down as stalemate is reached

Other party attempts to leave meeting

64 Refer matters to a third party if you need an arbitrator to mediate.

65 Never undermine the dignity of the opposing party.

STAYING IN CONTROL

Negotiating can be a stressful process. Anxiety over the outcome may be heightened by worries about peer pressure and showing yourself in a favorable light. The negotiations may focus on an emotive issue, or you may feel threatened by the opposition's tactics. Never take things personally; otherwise, you may lose control of the situation. Concentrate on the issues and restate your position firmly if necessary. Avoid criticizing an antagonist, and never be tempted to resort to personal insults over the negotiating table.

If you are forced to make concessions to prevent negotiations from breaking down, attach your own conditions. This way, you will not need to give ground without receiving something in return.

Take the long-term view, and remember that compromise can be a constructive tactic to help you reach an agreement.

Agreement is reached

Final points of deal are discussed

▲ CLINCHING A DEAL

This illustration shows two of the possible routes a negotiation can take. Despite a very positive start, the proceedings can be followed by deterioration to the point of breakdown. In this scenario, the negotiators avoid deadlock in their meeting by making concessions and compromising on minor issues in order to reach a mutually satisfactory outcome.

POINTS TO REMEMBER

- Your points should be reiterated in a loud but calm voice – assertively but not aggressively.

- Emphasizing the positive hides the negative; for example, "We may not have made a profit last year, but look at this year's figures."

- Any mistakes should be acknowledged immediately so you can carry on with confidence.

- Appearing arrogant may hinder your chances of reaching an agreement with the other party.

- A deal is made, not won. Opponents should be persuaded that the deal will benefit everyone.

- Your original aims should be firmly fixed in your mind.

WEAKENING THE OTHER PARTY'S POSITION

To achieve a successful outcome in negotiations, strengthen your own position and look for ways to weaken the opposition at the same time. Use one or more of a range of tactics to diminish your opponent's influence in negotiations.

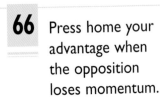

66 Press home your advantage when the opposition loses momentum.

UNDERMINING OPPONENTS

When negotiating, undermine the other party's confidence, and even their credibility, but only by casting doubt on the validity of their information. Continually test the validity of your opponent's case; look for weakness such as errors of logic, misuse of statistics, omissions of fact, and hidden agendas. Avoid the temptation to try to weaken the other party's position by attacking individual personalities. You may face a backlash if the opposition responds in similar vein. Unprovoked attacks are also unlikely to gain you sympathy with a third party if one is called in to mediate or arbitrate.

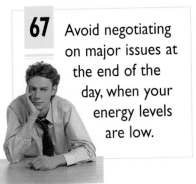

67 Avoid negotiating on major issues at the end of the day, when your energy levels are low.

USING EMOTION

A show of emotion at the negotiating table may convince others of your feelings and the honesty of your argument, helping weaken the other party's position. Use this tactic sparingly, however; repeated displays will be increasingly ineffectual. Emotional outbursts can also backfire unless handled carefully; instead of swaying the opposition, they may inflame tempers and lead to a breakdown in the negotiations.

68 Continually test for weaknesses in the other party's position.

RECOGNIZING ERRORS

An effective way to weaken your opponent's position is to find errors of fact or logic in their proposals. Look out for the selective use of statistics: if you are presented with details that seem too good to be true, ask about the things that are not being talked about. They may be hiding the bad news. If you find flaws, bring them immediately to everybody's attention.

POINTS TO REMEMBER

- Threats may not weaken the opponent – and they may backfire.

- If one party contains employees on strike, they will enter into negotiations having already made an impact on their opposition.

- Teamwork can help maintain pressure on your opponents.

USING TACTICS TO WEAKEN THE OPPOSITION

TYPES OF TACTIC	EXAMPLES OF HOW TO USE TACTICS
FINANCIAL Imposing costs on one or both parties if agreement is not reached.	• Inform the other parties that costs will be incurred if, for example, goods are held in a warehouse until it is possible to resolve a dispute over their ownership. • Point out to the opposition that opportunity costs will occur if the negotiation is prolonged.
LEGAL Using sanctions/injunctions to prevent one party from taking action or to cause delays to proceedings.	• Threaten to pursue a course of legal action, if you have a solid case, and emphasize the cost, both in time and money, to the other party if they lose. • Cause lengthy legal wrangles to effect delays in production and consequently loss of finance to achieve an agreement.
SOCIAL Imposing restrictions by disapproving of a proposed course of action on moral grounds.	• Tell your opponents that their proposals are an insult to the people they are likely to affect. • Demonstrate how unfair suggested proposals are when compared to the treatment that other people receive in similar situations.
HUMILIATION Publicly humiliating one party or individual in the eyes of their peers.	• Humiliate an opposing party in order to damage their image or reputation. This can cause some long-term damage to their credibility but is unlikely to have any drastic effect on the party's business. Be aware that they may seek revenge for the humiliation in the future.
EMOTIONAL Making opponents feel guilty if they do not make any concessions.	• Emotionally blackmail your opponent if they are not giving you enough ground. Note that this tactic can be uneven in its effectiveness. Sometimes, people who feel they have been emotionally manipulated may be even more unwilling to make concessions in the future.

Closing a Negotiation

A negotiation can be brought to a successful conclusion only when both parties have made concessions that are mutually acceptable in order to reach an agreement.

Trading Positions

Trading positions is a delicate process of bargaining whereby each party makes concessions to reach an agreement. However, if you are the weaker party, or your main aim is to minimize your losses, bargaining can be stressful and costly.

69 Offer the smallest concessions first – you may not need to go any further.

70 Make steady eye contact to emphasize that each concession is a serious loss for you.

Making Concessions

When you are forced to make concessions, it is important that you take a long-term view. Try to retain some control of the situation by:

- Judging how much ground you need to yield – put a value on what you are prepared to give so that it can be matched with concessions from the other side;
- Compromising without losing face. For example, if you need to backtrack on a point you had established as your final position, you can say, "Since you have changed your position on…, we may be able to change ours on…"

MAKING HYPOTHETICAL PROPOSALS

Test how flexible your opponents may be by making hypothetical proposals before giving concessions. "If" is the important word in the questions below, which do not commit you to anything yet may help you to identify the issues important to the other party.

If we come up with another million, will you give us the Rome operation and the cargo boat?

If I reduce the price by 20 percent, will you give me firm orders in advance?

If I give you 90 days credit instead of 60, will you give me the interest that you would have paid?

DISCUSSING TERMS

As you near the end of a negotiation, you need to discuss the terms of your agreement. Use your hypothetical proposals to help you work out a basic deal. The terms of the deal will involve the method of payment, the schedule of payment, how long the agreement should stand before being revised, and what to do if any problems arise over implementation of the deal – whether, for example, arbitration should be sought.

71 Do not concede ground unless you receive something in return.

TRADING ▶ SUCCESSFULLY
Here is an example of a successful negotiation. The dealer establishes how much his customer wants to pay, and the customer gets what she wants at a price she can afford.

CASE STUDY
Jane wanted a red carpet she had seen in a store window. She walked into the store and asked how much it was. The dealer did not tell her but knew it cost him $150, and he offered Jane a cup of coffee. Jane began to get defensive and said she really wanted something with more brown in it. "I have lovely brown carpets," said the dealer, offering to show her some. Backtracking again, Jane said she wanted a denser pile, and again the dealer said that he had such a carpet.

So Jane decided to negotiate to get the red carpet. She asked the price again. He told her it was $700. "That is too much," said Jane, starting to walk away. She offered $300. "You can have it for $650," said the dealer. "No, thank you," Jane said, walking toward the door. Believing he would lose a sale, the dealer let Jane buy it for $300, doubling his outlay. Both were happy with the deal.

NEGOTIATING A PACKAGE

As you move toward closing a negotiation and start to discuss terms, try to draw together the various items under negotiation. Group related items together, rather than negotiating for each individually. This gives you scope to make painless concessions: you can yield ground on issues of lesser importance within the package to gain extra leverage for your main objective. For example, do not concentrate only on a new pay deal. Link pay with demands for longer vacations, higher pension contributions, and more generous health benefits. Be prepared to concede on pension and vacation demands to gain your main objective of shorter working hours. Negotiating a package is also a good way of finding out the true priorities of the opposition. Thus, you may be dealing with another party that needs to fill a half-empty cargo ship and so is not too concerned about the price per item of the consignment of goods.

72 Make concessions on a minor issue to lessen intransigence on a major one.

73 Remind the other party of areas of agreement to help break a deadlock.

◆ CONCENTRATING ON ELEMENTS OF A PACKAGE

This pie chart shows an example of the proportions of time spent in a negotiation between employers and staff on various aspects of a pay and benefits package. The most time was spent on salaries – the top priority for the staff. They were prepared to concede to their employer's demands about vacations and pensions to spend more time on their principal aim.

KEY
- Health benefits
- Pensions
- Vacations
- Working hours
- Salaries

Health benefits are of low priority, so little time was spent discussing them

Pensions are a low priority, so they were dealt with quickly

Vacations are a low priority and were dealt with at the same time as pensions

Salaries are the major priority, so they took up most of the discussion

Working hours are a key point for the employees, so they took up considerable negotiation time

AVOIDING REJECTION

The benefit of packaging proposals together is that the least important elements can be rejected without either party losing face, while using hypothetical proposals enables you to refine your negotiations until a compromise is reached. In both cases, you can gain valuable insight into what your opposition is prepared to accept – as well as what they might relinquish – based on their reactions to your bargaining.

Avoid situations in which your final offer will be rejected. This undermines your negotiating position and may make it hard to restore a favorable balance of power in the negotiations. For example, if the other party says, "Your final offer of $400 is totally unacceptable," a response of "What if we raise it to $500?" signals a serious loss of credibility on your part. Prevent outright rejection by refining your package as you edge closer to an agreement.

POINTS TO REMEMBER

● Each party should be clear about their objectives.

● All of your remarks should be fronted with conditions.

● The consequences of failing to agree must be considered.

● As it becomes more difficult to wring concessions out of the other party, it may be time for your final offer to be presented.

● A final offer should be proposed only when the atmosphere is cooperative and receptive.

● The other side must be convinced that your final offer is genuine.

● The other party must be allowed to adjourn for a short period to discuss your offer before they accept or reject it.

RECORDING A DEAL

Once you have successfully completed your negotiations, summarize your agreement in writing and obtain everyone's approval of the summary. This avoids confusion and possible hostility later on. Remember that the summary must clearly record who gets what, how, and when, and the action to be taken. Both parties must sign the agreement. Clarify any ambiguous terminology, such as "adequate," "fair," or "significant," at this stage. If there is not enough time to obtain everybody's written agreement immediately, record the conclusion of the negotiations (either on an electronic notepad, a tape recorder, or in note form),

and have a detailed set of minutes drawn up immediately after the meeting. Send a copy to the other party, and ask for their written confirmation that the minutes represent a true and fair view of the result of the negotiations. Speed in circulating the minutes is essential, because if there is confusion or disagreement over what has been agreed you can reopen negotiations and resolve the problem quickly.

**MAKING ▷
RECORDS**
Take notes or use electronic organizers to record agreements during a negotiation.

Choosing How to Close

As you draw near to completing an agreement, check that all parties share the same understanding of the issues, then confirm what has been agreed and close the negotiation. There are various ways of closing, so select the one that suits your team.

74 Record fully all agreements finalized at a negotiation's close.

Focusing on Issues

Before moving toward closure of a negotiation, it is important to ensure you are clearly focused on the relevant issues and that you have not allowed personal feelings about the other side's negotiating tactics to color your judgment and decisions. Are you holding out for a higher price because you need to make a profit, or just so the other party does not feel they have beaten you down?

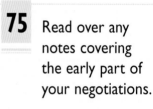

75 Read over any notes covering the early part of your negotiations.

Confirming Terms

At this stage in a negotiation, it is important to be sure that all parties are talking about the same thing. Examine the terminology you are intending to use in your final agreement. If you are drawing up a commercial contract, define any key terms or use easily understood vocabulary. It is vital that your terms are recorded clearly and accurately, since both parties agree to abide by these conditions in the event of a dispute. Reviewing both teams' understanding of the agreement in this way can also highlight previously unnoticed misunderstandings. The close of the negotiations must include ironing out these problems, which may give you or the other party room to negotiate new concessions. For example: "If I'd realized that you meant delivery in New York, I would never have agreed to such high freight costs – let's look at it again."

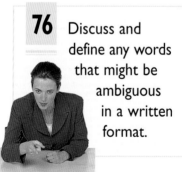

76 Discuss and define any words that might be ambiguous in a written format.

77 Make sure you do not ignore issues in order to speed up negotiations.

Methods of Closing a Negotiation

Methods of Closure	Factors to Consider
Making Concessions that Are Acceptable to All Parties Proposing and accepting concessions that help clinch the deal without jeopardizing your party's position.	● This continuation of the process of trading can break a deadlock. ● The other party may be tempted to try gaining even more concessions. ● Making concessions late in the negotiations may undermine your credibility.
Splitting the Difference Between All Parties Agreeing between all sides involved in the negotiations to move toward the middle ground in order to reach a deal.	● It may be difficult to judge what is a fair split of the difference. ● This is an indication that you are still prepared to make some concessions. ● Neither party will feel that they have won or lost at the end of the negotiations.
Giving One Party a Choice of Two Acceptable Alternatives Encouraging the other party to move forward by offering them two different options from which to choose.	● This suggests that any "final" offer you have already made was not really your last call. ● Finding two options that are equally acceptable to you may not be easy. ● There is no guarantee that the other party will agree to either of the proposals.
Introducing New Incentives or Sanctions Bringing pressure to bear on the other party by introducing new incentives or sanctions.	● The threat of sanctions may increase the opposition's feelings that you are being hostile. ● Introducing new incentives can completely alter the balance of a negotiation. ● This can provide the push necessary to bring the other party to agreement.
Introducing New Ideas or Facts at a Late Stage Bringing new ideas to the meeting table provides an incentive for new discussion and may lead to an agreement.	● This gives the other party room to see new concessions that they could make. ● This may undermine your credibility – you should have introduced the new ideas earlier. ● This may undermine the basis of the negotiation and take you back to square one.
Suggesting an Adjournment when Stalemate Occurs Adjourning allows each side in the negotiations time to consider what will happen if there is no agreement.	● This gives each party an opportunity to consult with outside advisers. ● Circumstances may change the position of the parties during the adjournment. ● It may prove to be too difficult to reconvene a further meeting at another time.

MOVING TO A CLOSE

Having chosen your method of closing, you can now move to execute it – but be aware of any shifts of mood in the other party. Timing your final offer to coincide with an upbeat phase in the talks can make the difference between success and failure.

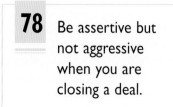

78 Be assertive but not aggressive when you are closing a deal.

TIMING YOUR OFFER

An offer presented at the wrong moment may be rejected, while exactly the same offer – presented at a different moment – is accepted. Make your final offer when the other party is receptive, using all your skills to produce the right atmosphere:

- Praise the other party – "That was an excellent point. I think that in view of that I can offer…"
- Be self-deprecating – "I'm afraid that I've been unable to come up with any bright ideas, but I think we could agree to…"
- Emphasize how far you have come together – "I think we've made really good progress today, and I feel able to offer…"

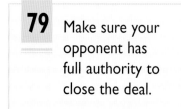

79 Make sure your opponent has full authority to close the deal.

▼ CLOSING A DEAL
When a team of negotiators is about to make a closing move, they will look to their leader to take the first step.

Team leader summarizes and makes final offer

Body language is supportive

Team member backs up leader with data

LEADING UP TO AN OFFER

As you near conclusion, beware of "crying wolf." Earlier in the process, you may have felt a need to imply that certain offers were "final." This tactic is often used, but be careful not to say in so many words that a proposal is final when you know it is not, since this may prevent the other party from believing your "final final offer." Think in advance how to indicate this final final offer. Make it clear that you would prefer not to strike any deal than to compromise any further on the proposed terms.

80 Look at the other party when making your final offer.

81 If you are not satisfied with a deal, do not sign it.

MAKING A FINAL OFFER

Indicate to the other party that you are making your final final offer by choosing the right words, tone of voice, and body language. Create an atmosphere of decisiveness: gather up your papers, stand up, walk about, and generally look as if you intend to leave (in contrast to previous offers, when you may have been leisurely leaning back in your chair, implying that you expected the negotiations to continue). Increase the urgency and firmness of your tone of voice, but do not rush to close the negotiations.

REINFORCING A FINAL OFFER

A carefully selected phrase can indicate that you are about to make your final offer. Use firm, unequivocal language when making your final offer, and reinforce the impact of your words by using a calm, authoritative tone of voice and maintaining steady eye contact.

❝ I have no authority from our head office to make another offer. ❞

❝ I have already gone much further than I intended to go. ❞

❝ This is my final final offer. I have no room whatsoever to move further than this. ❞

❝ I am running out of time. Agree to my proposal, or I will need to leave for another meeting. ❞

Encouraging Closure

When you have made your final offer, the other party may simply accept it as it stands. If they do not, you may be able to nudge them toward making a final offer acceptable to you. Look for points that have not occurred to them – even apparently trivial ones – that could help you reach an agreement. Try to put yourself in the other party's shoes and to understand what might be preventing them reaching an agreement.

 82 Emphasize the common ground you have found during a debate.

Helping the Other Party to Move to a Close

Methods	Results
Emphasizing Benefits Concentrate on explaining to the other party how the proposed deal will be of benefit to them. However, you should avoid mentioning how the same deal will benefit your own side.	● Helps the other party to see advantages in agreeing to a deal that they may not previously have considered. ● Creates the perception of a win/win situation rather than a win/lose situation.
Encouraging and Applauding Welcome any constructive proposal by the other party, no matter how long it takes to emerge. If you do not want to agree to it, you can still reject it later on in the negotiations.	● Creates a positive mood in which to move negotiations toward a close. ● Allows you to avoid criticism of your own counterproposals. ● Avoids antagonizing the other party at what may be a critical point in the debate.
Avoiding a Win/Lose Situation Point out that you are looking for an outcome that is equally acceptable to both parties. Do not push through an acceptance that your opponents will later feel has been forced upon them.	● Avoids confrontation, which is likely to result in increasing hostility and deadlock. ● Fosters a relaxed atmosphere in which constructive discussion can take place. ● Allows counterproposals to be made.
Saving Face Give the other party an escape route by asking hypothetical questions or making hypothetical proposals, such as "How would you feel about...?" or "What if we...?"	● Increases the likelihood of your proposals being given proper consideration by the other party. ● Means the other party feels under less pressure to accept or reject your proposals, but may come to a decision sooner.

WORKING TOWARD COMPROMISE

At every stage of a negotiation, try to create a culture of compromise. By the time you are near closing, the other party should know that you are flexible and are not dogmatic about any issues. If the debate has followed a proper course, an atmosphere of compromise should have developed naturally. Each party will have realized that the other's argument has points in its favor and that each side must compromise at certain points. Even toward the end of the process, try to hold on to a few bargaining chips (minor issues that can be conceded easily) to trade if necessary. Do not respond too hastily to the other party's offers. They may continue to suggest new approaches that you had not considered before.

 83 Try to understand the other party's hesitancy.

 84 Agree on a date to review concessions made to break a deadlock.

POINTS TO REMEMBER

- A little ambiguity may enhance a proposal. There is an old saying: "The wheels of diplomacy turn on the grease of ambiguity."

- A sudden leap forward can make the opposition nervous. It is best to move slowly.

- There is a saying: "It is better to sell the wool than the sheep." Main objectives should not be conceded, but small points can be.

- Phrases that seem to lay down the law, such as "I insist on...," should be avoided.

85 Be polite but persistent. This will gain you respect.

OVERCOMING LAST-MINUTE HESITATION

There is always extra sensitivity on both sides of a negotiating table when a deal looks near to conclusion. The time between reaching a verbal agreement and signing on the dotted line is particularly delicate. Negotiators often get nervous and may try to back out at this stage.

If the other party is hesitant, sympathize with them. Remind them that the deal means changes for you, too, and that you are also nervous about it. If the other party persists in trying to back out, point out to them that this dishonorable behavior will tarnish their reputation, leaving them with an image of unreliability that may affect future negotiations. If you are in a position that allows you to force the deal through despite the objections of the opposition, remember this may well affect future negotiations with the same party.

HANDLING BREAKDOWN

When negotiations break down, immediate action is vital to prevent the situation becoming irretrievable. The longer an acrimonious breakdown is left to fester, the more bitter it becomes and the harder it is to restore a balanced attitude.

86 Avoid the temptation to respond with "an eye for an eye."

▼ LEAVING IN ANGER

Breakdowns often occur when one party stands up in anger and leaves the meeting. If this happens, the other negotiators need to think carefully about how to restore the discussion.

LIMITING DAMAGE

To limit the damage from a breakdown in negotiations, the two parties should reestablish communication as quickly as possible. The best way to do this is in a face-to-face meeting. However, if a breakdown has been very acrimonious, it may be more appropriate to make overtures of reconciliation in writing. E-mails are perfect for this because they are private and fast.

Angry negotiator unwilling to continue discussion

Team member explaining colleague's action

Opposition leader responds angrily to walkout

Opposition team member rises to retrieve situation

HEALING A RIFT

Try to retrieve a breakdown without appealing to outside help. If one member of a team has walked out of a meeting, persuade their colleagues to bring them back. If an entire team leaves, send the individual on your team who has the strongest relationship with them (possibly the Good Guy) to bring them back immediately. Do not allow a breakdown to continue if the consequence of no deal is worse than the last deal that was on the table. If a breakdown cannot be remedied internally, then you may need to call a third party, such as a conciliator, a mediator, or an arbitrator.

87 Do not insist on an apology when order has been restored.

ORCHESTRATING ► A BREAKDOWN

Since one of Joe's objectives was to protect his supply line with Kim's company, walking out was a poor way to deal with a frustrating situation. The future relationship was undermined by Joe's outburst. It would have been better to bring in a third party to mediate.

CASE STUDY
Joe went to Taiwan to reclaim money from Kim's company for a shipment of bicycles that Joe's employer claimed were faulty. Joe knew there were other suppliers happy to provide him with bikes, but he was unwilling to disturb Kim's well-established supply line. Kim had no power to financially compensate Joe; she could only replace the bikes. Joe said that would not be enough to restore his company's reputation with purchasers of faulty goods.
Joe was booked on a plane leaving in three hours and saw nothing to be gained from listening politely to Kim's stonewalling. He stood up angrily and left the room. Kim was embarrassed but did not want to lose face by asking him to return.
Joe now buys his bikes in the US, and Kim's company has suffered as a result.

88 Contact the other party immediately after a walkout.

89 Agree a date for future talks to limit damage.

HANDLING INTENTIONAL BREAKDOWNS

There are occasions when one party actively wants negotiations to break down. If your team comes up with an unexpected bit of information that completely undermines the opposition's case, they may choose to give in on the spot, ask for an adjournment, or manipulate a breakdown in the negotiation. While this is not helpful, they may feel strongly that continuing will be harmful to their case. If this occurs, stay calm and try to amend the situation by effecting a reconciliation.

USING A MEDIATOR

When you have explored all the avenues, and the parties involved in a negotiation have still not reached an agreement, a mediator may be necessary. By agreeing to use a mediator, all parties are expressing a desire to resolve the situation.

 90 View the use of a third party as a positive step, not a failing.

 91 Think twice before using mediation – it is expensive.

ROLE OF A MEDIATOR ▼
The ideal mediator is unbiased, considers all angles, is acceptable to both parties, understands the issues, helps parties to find their own solutions, and prepares recommendations quickly.

UNDERSTANDING THE PROCESS OF MEDIATION

Mediation is the process in which deadlocked parties consider the suggestions of a third party, agreed upon in advance, but are not bound to accept the mediator's recommendations. The mediator acts as a referee between the negotiating parties and tries to find common ground among their agendas. Once some common ground is established, the mediator can begin to find mutually acceptable routes out of the deadlock.

Helps opposing parties understand each other

Helps parties create their own solutions

Considers problem from all angles

Suggests other solutions

Is impartial at all times

Explains issues to each side

CHOOSING A MEDIATOR

A mediator must be acknowledged by both parties as unbiased and must also be sufficiently knowledgable and informed about the points at issue to be able to make sensible recommendations that are relevant to both parties.

It is tempting to appoint a person in a position of authority (a former senior employee with experience in the field or a retired diplomat, for example) as a mediator. Although their authority may influence the final outcome, a mediator's capacity to adjudicate effectively is limited if they do not have the ability to recommend a solution. Consider using a less obvious person to mediate: someone, for example, who can think laterally, who has no preconceptions about the deadlock, and who can come up with a variety of creative suggestions for the best solutions to a stalemate.

92 Ensure mediators act while the parties are still eager to proceed.

93 Consider unconventional suggestions to resolve a deadlock.

DEVELOPING THE ROLE OF NEGOTIATOR-AS-MEDIATOR

You can help the smooth running of a negotiation by adopting a dual role from the very beginning. In the first role, you are a negotiator with specific objectives; in the second role, you are a mediator attempting to reconcile your objectives with those of the other party. In short, try to achieve your own objectives while finding common ground and presenting recommendations that are mutually acceptable to both parties.

It is essential to match a versatile and diplomatic personality to the role of negotiator-as-mediator. Ask yourself if you have a personality that is naturally suited to this dual role: do you look for balance in your life, and do you tend to make "we" statements as opposed to "I" statements? Avoid using forceful or aggressive members of your team in this role – they may be better at holding the floor and making proposals but will need to stand aside if negotiations break down.

BALANCING ▶ ROLES
The role of negotiator-as-mediator requires you to be unbiased to ensure that the best interests of both parties are met.

GOING TO ARBITRATION

If a negotiation breaks down, you can resolve the dispute by using arbitration. This involves introducing a third party to help break the deadlock. Under the rules of arbitration, both sides are required to abide by the final decision given by the arbitrator.

 94 It is worth paying as much as you can afford for good arbitration.

 95 Ensure that you fully understand the process of arbitration.

CHOOSING ARBITRATION

If you need to go to arbitration, there are several options open to you. Use your industry's semi-permanent arbitration bodies or procedures for settling disputes, if it has them. Alternatively, ask an independent tribunal, individual, or professional body to arbitrate for you. However, since this requires the involvement of qualified experts and the establishment of formal agreements, such arbitration is slow and expensive – so make sure that there are no other options available to you.

AN ARBITRATOR'S ROLE ▼
The ideal arbitrator is unbiased, respected by all parties, empowered to enforce judgments, and discreet about findings.

Helps both parties reach their solutions

Adjudicates between both parties

Remains impartial during negotiations

Considers problems that cause deadlock

Is knowledgable about all issues

Reaches decisions enforceable by law

THE ADVANTAGES OF USING AN ARBITRATOR

The arbitrator's role in proceedings is to decide on a fair agreement between the negotiating parties, and then to enforce this ruling. Arbitration effectively bars negotiators from leaving the table without an agreement, although in extreme cases the courts can be asked to implement a decision.

Collect all the information available from both sides in the dispute to enable the arbitrator to assess your case in detail. You will benefit from this process since the arbitration service works independently – the case for each party is heard in confidence, and the final decision is released only to the parties concerned. This is particularly important in commercial disputes – many firms will go to great lengths to avoid the publicity that accompanies the majority of court judgments.

POINTS TO REMEMBER

● Arbitration is appropriate when there are a large number of negotiators whose interests are difficult to disentangle.

● Lawyers and consultants are often the people best placed to act as arbitrators.

● An arbitrator acts similarly to a judge, and decisions can be enforced by a court.

● Arbitrators can decide how their costs are to be divided between the parties in the negotiations.

● Some contracts specify the arbitration procedure that is to be followed in the case of disagreement arising.

96 Choose an arbitrator that both sides can trust completely.

97 If necessary, ask a third party to appoint an arbitrator for you.

USING THE COURTS TO IMPLEMENT DECISIONS

The courts are a last resort for negotiating teams – after they have failed to reach agreement among themselves and if the judgments of independent third parties are not acceptable through either mediation or arbitration. Any legal process is likely to be expensive and to bring the dispute into the public arena. This often exposes negotiators to new and undesirable pressures, so always take legal advice before instituting judicial proceedings. For example, a company with a short-term cash-flow problem should try to reach private rescheduling agreements with its creditors. If these problems end up in court, it is in grave danger of being declared bankrupt, in which case both the company and its creditors could come out with nothing.

Implementing Decisions

Once you have reached an agreement, either independently or with the help of a third party, your final decisions need to be implemented. Draw up a plan of action, then appoint appropriate members of your organization to put this plan into effect.

98 Agree an order in which the action agreed on should be fulfilled.

99 Draw up a final schedule for implementing the action agreed on.

Agreeing on Action

Whenever agreement is reached between parties in a negotiation, the terms should be recorded and signed as an indication of multilateral approval and acceptance. Next, you must agree on how to implement the decisions. You may feel that it is appropriate to appoint a joint team to put the plans into action, or, alternatively, you may prefer to ask an independent party to oversee the project. Decide early on in the planning stage whether you wish for sanctions to be applied if the agreed action is not carried out to your deadlines – such measures can take the form of legal action or financial penalties. Unexpected problems will often arise at the implementation stage of an agreement, so appoint a team leader to monitor the process rigorously.

CASE STUDY

Stefan ran a small design firm and won the contract to refurbish a large office building. He negotiated an agreement on the timing and cost of the work and set a completion deadline of six months.

Knowing that he could not complete the work by himself, Stefan then hired an interior designer to procure the soft furnishings for the building, and an administration assistant to oversee the daily running of the project. This freed him to concentrate on restructuring the building itself.

As the work progressed, it became apparent that Stefan did not have time to deal with the teams of plumbers and electricians working in the building. He handed over this responsibility to his assistant, briefing her very carefully and issuing a schedule of tight deadlines for her to adhere to. The work was completed early and within budget.

◀ **UTILIZING A TEAM WELL**
Once he had negotiated his agreement, Stefan made the best use of the talents of his team by allocating them specific responsibilities. When he rethought his tactics, he briefed his assistant thoroughly and gave her a strict deadline to complete the work on time.

ASSIGNING A TEAM

The people assigned to implement any negotiated agreement may not have taken part in the actual discussions. For them, the provision of clear and accurate information is vital. When appointing a team and allocating specific tasks, pay special attention to the brief. Who is best suited to each task, and who needs to know what? How will team members receive information, and from whom? When will they receive updates, and how long will they be given to act on the information?

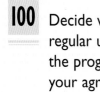

100 Decide who needs regular updates on the progress of your agreement.

101 Make a good last impression. It can be as important as the first one.

SCHEDULING IMPLEMENTATION

A negotiated decision is not considered a success until it has been enforced, so build deadlines and a plan of action into any agreements made around the negotiating table. Check the progress of your plan of action frequently – any slippage in the schedule may affect the agreed package, especially if major concessions were granted on the basis of meeting set targets. If other problems arise, resolve them by holding further negotiations.

◀ REACTING POSITIVELY
Engender good will around a negotiating table by reacting positively and enthusiastically when reaching a final agreement on how to implement decisions. Smile, shake hands, and congratulate each other warmly.

621

ASSESSING YOUR ABILITY

veryone is frequently involved in negotiation at work and at home, but in order to be truly successful at it you need to assess your skills. Evaluate your performance by responding to the following statements, then mark the options that are closest to your experience. Be as honest as you can: if your answer is "never," mark Option 1; if it is "always," mark Option 4; and so on. Add your scores together, then refer to the Analysis to see how you scored. Use your answers to identify which areas need improving.

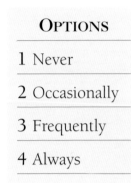

OPTIONS

1 Never

2 Occasionally

3 Frequently

4 Always

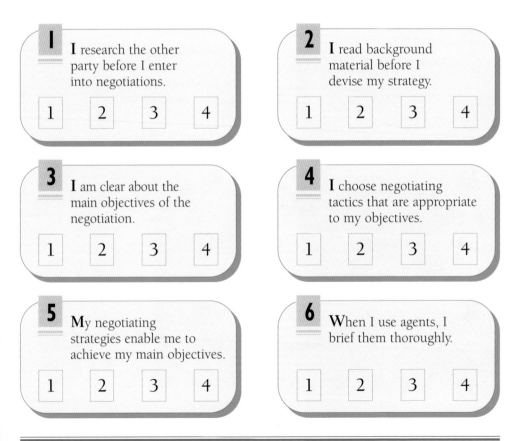

1 I research the other party before I enter into negotiations.

1 2 3 4

2 I read background material before I devise my strategy.

1 2 3 4

3 I am clear about the main objectives of the negotiation.

1 2 3 4

4 I choose negotiating tactics that are appropriate to my objectives.

1 2 3 4

5 My negotiating strategies enable me to achieve my main objectives.

1 2 3 4

6 When I use agents, I brief them thoroughly.

1 2 3 4

7 When I use agents, I aim to give them as much authority as they need.

1   2   3   4

8 I have a flexible attitude toward negotiations.

1   2   3   4

9 I believe negotiations to be an opportunity for both parties to benefit.

1   2   3   4

10 I enter into negotiations determined to reach a satisfactory agreement.

1   2   3   4

11 I communicate my points in plain language.

1   2   3   4

12 I communicate my points logically and clearly.

1   2   3   4

13 I consciously use body language to communicate with the other party.

1   2   3   4

14 I avoid exposing the other party's weaknesses.

1   2   3   4

15 I am polite at all times during the negotiation.

1   2   3   4

16 I create deadlines that are realistic and determined by the negotiation.

1   2   3   4

17 **I** use my instincts to help me understand the other party's tactics.

1   2   3   4

18 **I** have enough power to make decisions when necessary.

1   2   3   4

19 **I** am sensitive to any cultural differences of the other party.

1   2   3   4

20 **I** work well as a member of a negotiating team.

1   2   3   4

21 **I** am able to be objective and put myself in the position of the other party.

1   2   3   4

22 **I** know how to guide the other party into making an offer.

1   2   3   4

23 **I** avoid making the opening offer.

1   2   3   4

24 **I** make progress toward agreement via a series of conditional offers.

1   2   3   4

25 **I** approach my final objectives step by step.

1   2   3   4

26 **I** show emotion only as part of a tactical move.

1   2   3   4

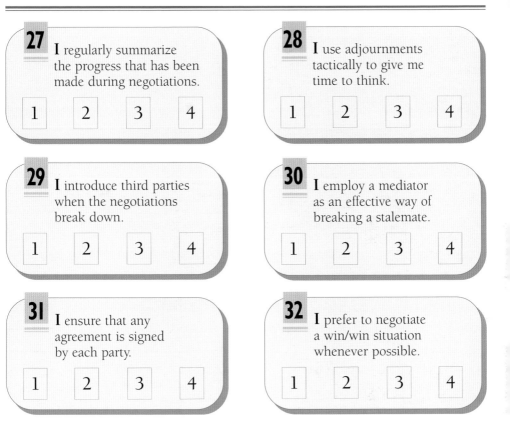

27 I regularly summarize the progress that has been made during negotiations.

| 1 | 2 | 3 | 4 |

28 I use adjournments tactically to give me time to think.

| 1 | 2 | 3 | 4 |

29 I introduce third parties when the negotiations break down.

| 1 | 2 | 3 | 4 |

30 I employ a mediator as an effective way of breaking a stalemate.

| 1 | 2 | 3 | 4 |

31 I ensure that any agreement is signed by each party.

| 1 | 2 | 3 | 4 |

32 I prefer to negotiate a win/win situation whenever possible.

| 1 | 2 | 3 | 4 |

ANALYSIS

Now that you have completed the self-assessment, add up your total score and check your performance by reading the corresponding evaluation. Whatever level of success you have achieved when negotiating, it is important to remember that there is always room for improvement. Identify your weakest areas, then refer to the chapters in this section where you will find practical advice and tips to help you establish and hone your negotiating skills.

32–64: Your negotiating skills are weak. Learn to use and recognize the strategies and tactics essential to successful negotiation.
65–95: You have reasonable negotiating skills, but certain areas need further improvement.
96–128: Your negotiations are successful. Continue to prepare thoroughly for every future negotiation.

INTERVIEWING PEOPLE

INTRODUCTION

Whether it is a major part of your job or a one-time task, interviewing candidates to fill a position can be a complex, time-consuming process that requires careful consideration and planning. This section will help you devise a strategy to eliminate many of the problems involved in interviewing, enabling you to recruit the best candidate every time. Clear information helps you take effective action at each stage of the process, from the initial definition of job requirements and deciding about how to recruit to the conduct of individual interviews. Commonsense advice enables you to evaluate the suitability of an applicant and implement a follow-up procedure. This section also includes 101 concise tips, providing further essential information at a glance, and a self-assessment exercise that lets you chart and evaluate your improvement with each interview you hold.

PREPARING FOR AN INTERVIEW

A job interview rarely lasts longer than an hour, but its consequences may last for years. In order to identify the most suitable candidate for a vacancy, prepare well in advance.

IDENTIFYING OBJECTIVES

An interview is a formal method of exchanging information between people. The interviewer needs to be clear about the purpose of the exchange to ensure that the time is used to give and obtain information that is relevant and revealing.

1 Evaluate every vacancy before calling for interviews.

2 Look for new blood rather than "one of us."

3 Imagine the ideal candidate for a vacant job.

DEFINING THE PURPOSE

The recruitment of new employees is one of the most important tasks a manager will undertake. Meeting candidates face to face provides the best opportunity for gathering information about their skills and experience and, ultimately, matching the right person to the job and to the organization.

In preparing for interviews, remember that your purpose is not only to evaluate the candidates, but also to describe the job accurately so that they can assess whether it is the right one for them. You will also need to represent your organization in the best light possible to attract good-quality candidates.

ASSESSING A VACANCY

Before any employer can set out to find a suitable candidate for a job, it is important that they establish the skills and experience the job requires.

Start by referring to the existing job description. Consider whether the job has changed over time, with the introduction of new technology, for instance. Does it now require different skills? Ask questions about the previous employee to decide if there is anything new that can be brought to the job. Were they suited to the job? Is a similar mix of abilities required in a new employee?

4 Review all job descriptions for your team when a vacancy is created.

ASSESSING JOB RELATIONSHIPS

An interviewer needs to assess how a job will relate to the roles of other employees. Where does it fit into the organizational hierarchy, and what will the role of the new job be within the existing team or department? To whom will the new employee report, and who will report to the new employee?

Bear in mind that there is usually room for some flexibility within an organizational structure. Consider, for instance, whether using new technology would allow a more junior employee to take on the responsibilities of a job previously done by a senior employee

▼ **GATHERING INFORMATION**
Discuss the requirements of a job with the present jobholder and those who work in the same team or department. This may lead to a reallocation of responsibilities among all roles and a reappraisal of the skills needed in a new employee.

INTERVIEWER
The interviewer obtains valuable information about the job from all those who work closely with the jobholder.

PRESENT JOBHOLDER   SUBORDINATE   COLLEAGUE   SUPERIOR

EVALUATING A ROLE

A new vacancy provides you with an opportunity to look closely at a job to evaluate its role within the company. Set aside time to identify specific changes that can be made to improve the job's value to the organization.

Start with the aims of the company. Have there been any directional changes in its goals, and has the job adapted to meet them? Ask other departments what their expectations of the job have been and whether these have been fulfilled.

Consider the assumptions you have about the knowledge and skills you think the job needs. Can you introduce useful new knowledge or skills into the company through the new appointment? Think also about the communication skills that are needed to make the job effective: are closer relationships with clients or other departments needed?

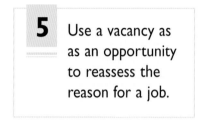

5 Use a vacancy as as an opportunity to reassess the reason for a job.

6 Check whether the qualifications required for a job have changed.

POINTS TO REMEMBER

● Not all vacancies need to be filled.

● Changes in business occur so rapidly that the need for a job may exist only for a short time.

● The best source of information about a job may be the previous jobholder.

● A vacancy can be an opportunity to redefine the responsibilities of a job.

● Currently unfulfilled tasks and duties can be added to a job description.

● It may be possible to reallocate work among current employees.

● Sometimes two people sharing a job can be more productive than one.

▼ REDEFINING A ROLE

This case looks at the way in which the role of librarian has been affected by information technology. Although the role was performed competently by the previous jobholder, a new applicant with updated skills shows how the scope of the job can be extended and improved to the benefit of the organization.

CASE STUDY

For 30 years, Great Universal Technology's library had been presided over by Thelma. In recent years, however, Thelma had become unhappy with the way her profession had changed. Although a proficient typist, she had never become comfortable with the computer, nor to the accelerating pace of corporate life. She decided it was time to retire.

Kevin, an ambitious young employee in the computer maintenance department, made an application for Thelma's job, arguing that the company needed a computer-literate "knowledge manager" – not a librarian. The company needed to be able to access the Internet as well as its own bookshelves. It also needed to bring together information from different departments of the company and to make it accessible to all staff. The chairman, impressed by Kevin's argument, gave him the job.

CONSIDERING CONDITIONS

When a job is vacated, consider whether you need to fill the job in the same way. If part of a job has become obsolete, due to changes in structure, for instance, consider appointing a part-time replacement. Use a jobsharing plan if the role needs different skills or to retain an employee who wants to work part time. If the work occurs only at certain periods, use freelancers or contract workers. Look at your finances: can one expensive employee be replaced by two junior employees, or vice versa?

7 When appropriate, offer flexible working hours.

CREATING A JOBSHARE ▶
Jobsharers who work during different times of the week need to establish a regular handover meeting. Dividing clients or customers between two employees can also create a jobshare.

CONSIDERING A NEW STATUS FOR A JOB

NEW STATUS

UPGRADED OR DOWNGRADED JOB
Senior staff are expensive but can improve the effectiveness of a role. Junior staff can perform routine tasks.

PART-TIME JOB
The employee works for only part of the week for a period and at times agreed with the manager.

JOBSHARE
Two people share responsibility for completing tasks or achieving goals set by their supervisor.

FREELANCE POSITION
A freelancer or contract worker is self-employed. They incur minimal overhead costs for an organization.

REASONS TO REVISE OLD STATUS

● A tight budget forces a reassessment of staff costs, leading to job losses at a junior or senior level.
● A change in emphasis of the responsibilities of a job requires a different level of employee.

● The jobholder cites boredom as a reason for leaving, since the job does not warrant a full-time employee.
● Some tasks have become obsolete or have been reallocated among other employees.

● A valued employee can no longer work full time but wishes to remain with the organization.
● All the skills needed cannot be found in any single person within the organization.

● Expected reorganization means the job is likely to change or become obsolete in the future.
● The job is necessary for a finite period only and therefore is not suitable for a full-time employee.

FINALIZING THE JOB REQUIREMENTS

*O*nce the requirements of a job have
become clear, the responsibilities and
tasks of the position should be detailed in
a job description. The skills and experience
and type of person needed for the position
should then be set out in a job specification.

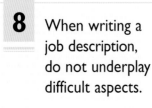

8 When writing a job description, do not underplay difficult aspects.

DEFINING RESPONSIBILITY

Writing an accurate job description helps ensure
that the right information is given when the job
is advertised, ultimately leading to a satisfactory
appointment and preventing misunderstandings.
Include the title of a job and its reporting line in a
description. When describing major responsibilities,
set out in detail what the jobholder is expected
to achieve. Use verbs of action, such as "liaise" or
"develop," to describe day-to-day tasks so that you
are clear about what the employee is going to do.

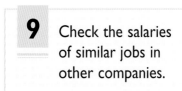

9 Check the salaries of similar jobs in other companies.

▼ **ASSESSING ACCURACY**
*Ask the current jobholder to contribute
toward redefining the job, encouraging them
to be honest about any drawbacks. Discuss
the reworked description with them.*

CHECKING A JOB DESCRIPTION

Check that a job description contains the following elements:

- The job title;
- The reporting line of the job;
- The overall responsibilities of the job, for example "maintaining the store's reputation for attractive window dressing";
- A list of the job's chief tasks and activities, for example "serving customers from 9 a.m. to 5 p.m. on weekdays";
- Details of terms, including pay, and conditions of service.

Key personality characteristics

Experience, training, and technical skill

Special abilities, such as fluency in Tagalog

Education and formal qualifications

Mental and emotional attributes

▲ **DEFINING ATTRIBUTES**
When deciding on the skills you are looking for in your ideal candidate, consider the specific requirements of the job. Break the job into different areas and consider them in turn.

DEFINING SKILLS

Once you have drawn up a revised job description, you can begin to analyze the skills, qualifications, experience, and attributes needed in the person who will fill the job. This will be the job specification. Be as precise as possible: it is useful to specify what is desirable, but also what is the essential minimum, to help you assess the candidates who apply. Be realistic about what you are looking for, and keep other options open. Stating that "a knowledge of statistics is desirable" may not be possible. You may find that all candidates' statistical skills are inadequate and whomever you employ must be sent to a course.

10 Make job titles aspirational. This encourages people to grow into them.

DECIDING HOW TO RECRUIT

*A*fter drawing up a job specification, you need to choose a method of recruitment. The various methods range from advertising in the general press to using a professional headhunter. Whichever method you select will involve at least one interview.

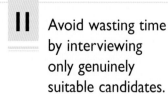

11 Avoid wasting time by interviewing only genuinely suitable candidates.

POINTS TO REMEMBER

- The response to advertisements for jobs in the general press can be overwhelming.
- Headhunters charge a percentage of the salary of the person they are recruiting, so the higher that person's salary, the more hunting they should do.
- Processing responses can be time-consuming, so a candidate should not be interviewed just on the strength of a well-written resume.

RECRUITING INTERNALLY

One way of recruiting is to appoint somebody who already works elsewhere in your organization. Many companies encourage internal recruitment, and some insist that all vacancies be advertised internally before being advertised outside.

It can be easier to interview internal applicants because they already know the company and understand its work culture. However, remember that they were originally recruited for a different job. Why are they suitable for yours? Consider also that internal recruitment may not cut costs overall. The recruit's old job may need to be filled once he or she has moved to your department.

PLACING ADVERTISEMENTS

Where you advertise and what your ad says will determine the type and number of applicants you receive and whether you find the right person for the job. Use trade publications for jobs that require specialized skills. For a more generalized approach, use the general press; some papers allocate different days to particular professions. Advertisements can be costly but usually elicit a huge response. If you lack the time or resources to cope with hundreds of applicants, advertise in a publication with limited circulation. Decide how many times you want the advertisement to appear.

12 If you know of good candidates elsewhere, invite them to apply.

DESIGNING AN ADVERTISEMENT

The design and wording of an advertisement can influence the response you get. Ensure that the layout is eye-catching and clear – size will be dictated by cost and content. Describe the job and be specific about what skills and experience are needed in order to eliminate unsuitable applicants. Always give a closing date for applications.

Relevant qualifications are clearly defined

Company equal-opportunities policy is emphasized

13 Always make sure the advertisements are proofread.

Introduction gives information about level of job

Headline attracts applicants' attention

Dynamic Marketing Manager

James Malcolm Associates, major operators in the computer technology market, are currently looking for a marketing manager to head up a team of three and to report directly to the general manager.

The successful candidate will manage promotion projects, adhere closely to budgets, and contribute toward new business plans for all aspects of our marketing strategy.

The successful candidate will possess a Bachelor's degree, have at least five years' relevant experience, be a team player, and be able to work under pressure.

We are an equal-opportunities employer.

Please send your resume and cover letter to:

Anna Sampson, Personnel Manager
James Malcolm Associates
53 Beech Road
North Brunswick, NJ 08902

Form that application should take is stated

▲ **ATTRACTING THE BEST**
Make the best features of the job prominent. You have only a moment to grab the attention of the perfect applicant!

THE LEGAL ASPECTS OF ADVERTISING

Advertising for recruitment is subject to stringent legal restrictions that vary from country to country, and from state to state in the United States. Keep in mind that your state regulations and procedures relating to employment may be different from the federal statutes and that state laws supercede federal laws. The laws most likely to apply are those of libel and those relating to discrimination on the grounds of gender, race, or age. Do not use sexist terms or refer to "he" or "him" throughout an advertisement. Select your wording carefully to avoid stipulating characteristics that exclude potential applicants of any sex or race or a particular age range, and consider stating that you are an Equal Opportunity Employer in all of your recruiting materials. If in any doubt regarding the legality of your recruiting materials, consult with your personnel office or appropriate government body.

14 Ask for a photograph to remind you of each candidate.

15 Be objective about a recommendation to employ a colleague's relative.

USING RECOMMENDATIONS

There are positive and negative aspects to consider when using personal contacts to help you fill a job vacancy. On the positive side, if a potential recruit comes with a recommendation from someone you trust, it suggests that their skills and experience have, to a degree, been proved in practice. In addition, they may have been briefed by your mutual contact about the work culture within your organization. On the negative side, personal recommendations can be awkward to turn down if you feel the candidate is not right for the job. When a colleague suggests a candidate, assess their skills and abilities objectively and be prepared to reject their application if you consider them unsuitable.

USING LOCAL RESOURCES

Check whether there are any federal or state programs in your area that are aimed at reducing unemployment levels and assisting in training. These programs are often organized on a regional basis to look at specific local needs – both of employers and the unemployed. Local universities or colleges may also employ specialized staff who deal with inquiries from prospective employers. It is a good idea to make contact with both of these resources if you have a vacancy that could be filled by a relatively inexperienced person who is looking for a first job.

Create a database of potential sources of recruits for future reference

Maintain an updated printout of the database

▲ CREATING A LIST OF CONTACTS

Make a list of useful contacts, including individuals, agencies, and advertisers, that you come across while recruiting. You can then use your list every time you need to fill a vacancy.

USING AGENCIES

Recruiting via an agency reduces the extensive amount of time-consuming paperwork involved in sifting through and replying to advertised vacancies. This is particularly relevant if you anticipate a substantial response. For a fee, which can vary according to the seniority of the vacancy, an agency will provide you with a shortlist of candidates from which you make the final selection. If you intend to use a recruitment agency to fill a job, ensure you approach one that can address your specific requirements. You can use professional headhunters to find suitable candidates for a senior vacancy.

16 Record the progress of each recruitment drive to use for reference in the future.

CHOOSING A METHOD OF RECRUITMENT

METHOD	FACTORS TO CONSIDER
RECRUITING INTERNALLY Initially, many employers look to recruit from internal personnel.	● Candidates have an existing track record with the company and are familiar with its way of working. ● You can ask their current manager for references.
PLACING ADVERTISEMENTS Advertisements in relevant media can reach the right candidates.	● You will need to set up a system to process what may be a large response to your advertisement. ● Advertising costs can be high.
USING RECOMMENDATIONS Friends and colleagues can provide contacts with potential candidates.	● Colleagues or acquaintances may have several contacts in the market, providing a good, informal source. ● Rejecting an unsuitable person could be problematic.
USING LOCAL RESOURCES Government agencies and colleges can be a source of recruits.	● For entry-level jobs not requiring work experience, colleges can be a good source of candidates. ● Government programs may involve extensive paperwork.
USING AGENCIES Agencies will shortlist numerous high-caliber candidates for you.	● Agencies have access to a wide range of candidates and can weed out unsuitable ones. ● There is a cost factor attached to using agencies.

SETTING UP A PROCESSING SYSTEM

Once you have decided which recruitment method (or methods) you are going to use, you need to set up an efficient response system that will enable you to deal with applications as quickly and as efficiently as possible, avoiding unnecessary delays.

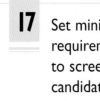

17 Set minimum requirements to screen candidates.

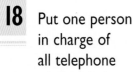

18 Put one person in charge of all telephone applications.

SELECTING A PROCESS

When choosing an appropriate method for processing applications, you should consider a variety of factors. For example, will you need to process numerous application forms? Do you want to see samples of a candidate's work to assess their abilities? Do you want to follow up references before or after the interview? If you expect to receive a resume and an accompanying letter, say so in the job advertisement. Create a process that will initially divide candidates into "for interview," "possible," or "rejected."

IMPLEMENTING A PROCESS

Once the applicants have been sorted into three basic categories, the system for processing applications should include the following stages:
- Preparation of standard letters for rejected candidates – send these out immediately;
- Evaluation of promising candidates;
- Drawing up of a final interview list;
- Scheduling and booking interviews over the phone or by letter, confirming the date and time and stipulating if candidates will be required to take tests.

19 To speed up the process, use standard letters to respond quickly to all applicants.

DELEGATING PROCESSING

It is possible to delegate the processing of applications, but you must ensure that the person to whom you are delegating has been fully briefed. They must:

- Know the stated minimum requirements and be familiar with the job description;
- Have good organizational skills to deal with applications;
- Have time to perform the task;
- Be skilled at communicating over the phone;
- Be able to provide general background information about the company.

COPING WITH A LARGE RESPONSE

If you receive a substantial response to an advertisement, you will need to screen out the most unsuitable candidates to create a manageable number from which to select your shortlist. Do this by setting minimum criteria that all candidates must meet before you process their application any further. These criteria could include minimum educational or professional qualifications, plus a career history that includes relevant experience for a minimum period of time.

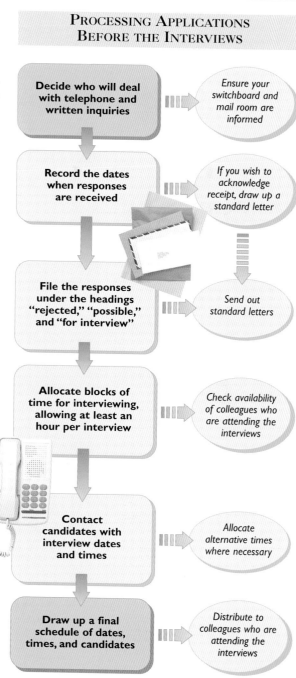

PROCESSING APPLICATIONS BEFORE THE INTERVIEWS

Decide who will deal with telephone and written inquiries → *Ensure your switchboard and mail room are informed*

Record the dates when responses are received → *If you wish to acknowledge receipt, draw up a standard letter*

File the responses under the headings "rejected," "possible," and "for interview" → *Send out standard letters*

Allocate blocks of time for interviewing, allowing at least an hour per interview → *Check availability of colleagues who are attending the interviews*

Contact candidates with interview dates and times → *Allocate alternative times where necessary*

Draw up a final schedule of dates, times, and candidates → *Distribute to colleagues who are attending the interviews*

ASSESSING A RESUME

Although most people are truthful when composing their resume, some may be tempted to omit negative facts or to exaggerate their achievements. Analyze each resume carefully to help select interviewees, then prepare questions to ask them.

20 Note specific points of interest in the resume to discuss later.

 21 Assume a certain amount of creative writing in resumes.

 22 Look for any inconsistencies in the facts provided.

LOOKING AT STRUCTURE

Analyzing the structure of a resume can tell you a lot about a candidate's ability to organize and communicate a set of facts effectively. A well-structured resume will be concise and normally no more than two pages in length. Usually, it will contain educational and career histories in reverse chronological order to emphasize the candidate's most recent activities. Relevant skills are often highlighted. However, there are many ways of presenting a resume, and the most important factor to consider is whether a resume presents information in a logical and easily digestible form.

READING INFORMATION

Once you have looked at the overall structure and style of a resume, examine the information provided. Consider whether the applicant's qualifications and work experience are relevant and meet the required levels you are seeking. Does the candidate have any other useful skills? Does the resume contain any background information that builds up a picture of the candidate's personality? Can you get an idea of the speed and direction of their career track?

 **23** Ask yourself if the format and style of the resume create a positive impression of the applicant.

DEALING WITH GAPS AND INCONSISTENCIES

Breaks in chronology and inconsistencies in the facts provided may be a result of simple error. On the negative side, however, they could provide clues to a candidate's attempt to falsify or hide certain information. You must therefore carefully examine the chronology of the applicant's educational and career achievements and ensure that all dates provided follow a logical sequence. Are there any periods of time unaccounted for? For example, is there a gap from the end of one period of employment to the beginning of the next? Does any other information supplied account for this gap? Do periods of employment overlap with periods in education? Be prepared to give applicants the benefit of the doubt, but compile a list of questions to help clarify inconsistencies.

CHECKLIST

1. Look for gaps in the resume's chronology.

2. If necessary, verify qualifications with relevant institutions.

3. Estimate the average amount of time spent in each job.

4. Judge whether the candidate is making a logical career move.

5. Consider if the style of the resume indicates a well-organized candidate.

Candidate is currently employed

Applicant has experience in dealing with major clients

May 97 – Present
A & B Design. Working on a contract basis with two big clients in the oil industry. In charge of budgets and client relations.

June 1991 – February 1997
First Graphics. Assistant Production Manager in charge of a team of six designers working on corporate literature, including brochures and marketing material. Learned to work to tight deadlines.

Employment dates include specific months

ASSESSING EXPERIENCE ▲
Always concentrate first on the section dealing with career history when assessing a resume to decide whether to shortlist an applicant.

Job title helps interviewer assess experience

Description indicates work skills acquired

CONSIDERING APPLICATIONS

When considering the applications you have received, divide the criteria of the job specification into those that are essential and those that are desirable. Are there other attributes – in terms of personality or physical skills – that you are looking for?

24 Application forms create a level playing field for all candidates.

USING YOUR CRITERIA

Before deciding on candidates to shortlist for interview, take the job specification and divide the criteria into essential and merely desirable. For example, how important is it that the recruit can speak one or more foreign languages? Should they have computer skills, or are you willing to provide training if they do not? Ideal candidates who can fulfill all your criteria will be rare, so you must be prepared to be flexible at the selection stage.

25 Seek the advice of colleagues when considering borderline cases.

CONSIDERING YOUR CRITERIA

INTERVIEWER
By the time you are considering applications, you should have decided which of your criteria are essential and which are merely preferable.

EXAMPLES OF CRITERIA
● Education: What level of educational attainment are you looking for? Would you consider a high-school graduate, or is it essential to have a graduate degree?
● Work experience: Are you looking for specific work skills acquired through employment? Should the applicants bring with them a range of valuable new contacts for your company?
● Information technology skills: Are basic computer skills absolutely essential? Does your company use specific software packages that any new recruit must be thoroughly familiar with, or are you willing to invest in training?
● Communicating and negotiating skills: Should the candidate be an effective communicator and experienced negotiator?
● Travel: Does the candidate need to travel on a regular basis and for prolonged periods?

TALKING TO COLLEAGUES

Before you reject borderline candidates it may be useful to discuss their applications with colleagues whose opinions you trust or who will work with the new person. Objective second opinions may help you decide to interview a seemingly unsuitable candidate who is in fact right for the job. Colleagues may also know of other opportunities for which the candidate could be considered.

DISCUSSING APPLICANTS ▶
Discuss borderline candidates with your workmates. They may highlight some positive qualities that you have missed.

26 Be courteous and positive when replying to all rejected applicants.

REJECTING CANDIDATES

When rejecting a candidate, use a courteous and professional tone. Remember that each applicant is likely to have invested a considerable amount of time and effort in applying for the job. Send a polite letter as soon as possible, thanking each candidate for their interest. Point out that although their application has not been successful this time, you will keep their details on file should any other suitable vacancies arise in the future.

ANALYZING APPLICATION FORMS

Application forms are helpful when it comes to assessing candidates since they put all interviewees on the same footing – each candidate is required to answer the same set of questions. When considering an application form, it is relatively straightforward to compare candidates equally against the criteria and make a selection for interview. You can use the information provided to create a database, which can be used for future reference, and to build up a profile of the range and skills of applicants. This will make it easier for you to select individuals who are skilled in the specific areas in which you are trying to fill vacancies.

SELECTING INTERVIEWEES

O nce you have assessed applicants, you can start to draw up a shortlist of interviewees. Often, only a small number of candidates are suitable – if this is not so, choosing whom to interview from the shortlist can be the hardest part of the exercise.

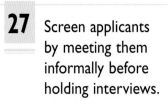

27 Screen applicants by meeting them informally before holding interviews.

USING A MATCHING SHEET

28 Decide if you need to hold written tests to filter out candidates.

One technique for deciding whom to shortlist is to create a "matching sheet" for each candidate. Take a blank sheet of paper and draw two lines down the middle. On one side, list the criteria required for the job; make copies of the sheet and use one per applicant, noting their skills and experience on the blank side. In the center column, check off the items that match for each candidate, then select those with the most checks to interview.

Candidate Name: *Kristin Ward*

Interview Date: *April 23*

Criteria for job		Candidate's experience and skills
Excellent interpersonal skills	✔	*Ran team of three people for 18 months*
Experience of handling management accounts	✔	*Four years of relevant experience*

USING A MATCHING SHEET ▲
This example of part of a matching sheet shows the various criteria required for the job on one side and the skills and experience of the candidate on the other.

Check indicates whether or not candidate matches criteria

Comments detail relevance and quality of candidate's skills and experience

CHECKING ▶
DETAILS
*If you call a candidate
to check their details,
first ask whether it is
convenient for them
to talk to you.*

*Points checked
off as they are
confirmed*

CHECKING DETAILS

If you want to confirm some of the details of a candidate's resume, there are several ways to go about it. You may want to contact their school or university to check details of their education, but be sure that the candidate is aware that you are going to do so at this early stage. Alternatively, telephone the candidate at his or her office. Always remember to check that they can talk freely and are not constrained by being within hearing distance of their current boss or colleagues.

POINTS TO REMEMBER

● Some applicants claim that their current salary is more than it is.

● It is harder to lie in person, even over the telephone, than in a written application.

● If applicable, ask candidates if they are willing to relocate.

● If it is not possible to contact candidates' references immediately, it may initially be necessary to trust what candidates say.

● Although humor is a valuable quality, you should expect a candidate to be serious during the interview.

● Instinctive reactions from speaking to candidates on the phone are worth noting.

ESTABLISHING A SHORTLIST TO INTERVIEW

Your shortlist of candidates selected to interview should not be so long that your impressions of them will blur into one another when interviewing. You need, of course, to include the candidates who appear at this stage to be your first choice plus a reserve or reserves. These should be those with the closest fit to the requirements of the job in terms of their skills and achievements.

On the shortlist, you might want also to include one or two who have exceptional skills in specific areas but who have shortcomings as all-arounders. Depending on the post you are trying to fill, it may be worth interviewing a couple of unconventional candidates. If the job requires making radical changes, the most suitable person is unlikely to be the one who is most familiar with the aspects that need to be revolutionized.

ARRANGING INTERVIEWS

It may be difficult to arrange interviews with all the shortlisted candidates in a short space of time. Many will need to take time off from their current jobs or to travel a considerable distance. Bear this in mind, and be as flexible as possible in scheduling.

29 Be prepared to schedule some interviews outside office hours.

STAGING INTERVIEWS

Before arranging any interviews, clarify how long the whole process will take. The level of vacancy may dictate how many stages you need: for a junior position, one interview may be enough to reach a decision, but for a more senior post you may want to ask some candidates for a second interview. Make arrangements and allow time for any tests that may need to be carried out. Confirm all details of the interviews in writing to the candidates, and send travel instructions to them.

30 Offer refreshments to candidates in order to help put them at ease.

CHOOSING INTERVIEWERS

In certain circumstances, it is desirable to invite specific colleagues to participate in the process of selecting a new employee. In some companies, a member of the personnel department is required to attend all interviews. This is especially valuable if the vacant position is a senior one or if the interviewer is inexperienced. If an employee will be working for more than one person, try to make sure that all those to whom the jobholder will report are present. Consider asking your own superiors if they wish to attend, especially if the position is a key one within your team. If the employee will be working closely with another department, invite one of its representatives to help assess the prospective new team members.

POINTS TO REMEMBER

- Having a colleague join you during the interview can provide a valuable second opinion.

- A perceptive receptionist can offer invaluable insights into candidates' attitudes.

- Candidates should be allowed time to ask questions and perhaps be shown around the office.

- The shorter the shortlist, the shorter the time it is likely to take to fill a position.

- Candidates should not be kept waiting or in an interview longer than necessary. It may be difficult for them to be away from work.

CHOOSING WHO WILL ATTEND THE INTERVIEW

INTERVIEWER		FACTORS TO CONSIDER
	**MANAGER** Another manager for whom the employee will be working.	● Any manager to whom the new employee will report will need to be involved in the selection process to help avoid future dissatisfaction. ● A manager who is a more experienced interviewer than you may suggest useful interviewing techniques and provide a valuable second opinion.
	**COLLEAGUE** A representative of a department with which the employee will work closely.	● Factors pertinent to work that needs to be done with another department will need to be evaluated by a representative of that department. ● A colleague does not have the authority to make the final selection of candidate or to negotiate the terms and conditions of employment.
	SUPERIOR The manager to whom you report who authorizes the appointment.	● Your superior may wish to be involved in the selection process if you are inexperienced. ● The overall "fit" of candidates within the team or department may be best assessed by your superior. ● Your superior may need to meet the candidate before a final offer can be made.

SCHEDULING AND TIMING INTERVIEWS

Make alternative dates and times available for holding interviews in case candidates are unable to attend on suggested days. Schedule interviews with a generous amount of time between them. It can be embarrassing for candidates to bump into their rivals outside. This may make them nervous and unlikely to give their best. Allowing some space between interviews will allow you to spend more time with a candidate if you wish or to run over if there is a delay. It should also mean that you have plenty of time to write up detailed notes on each candidate – a stream of interviewees tends to blur indistinguishably as soon as the interviews are over. Finally, take a brief rest to recharge yourself.

31 Be sure to avoid all interruptions during interviews.

32 Get plenty of rest so that you can be alert during an interview.

LOCATING INTERVIEWS

Give careful thought to the location of interviews: this can have a material effect on the proceedings. Remember that you are interviewing to get the best candidate for the position, but interviewees will find it hard to give their best if they are uncomfortable.

33 Put a "Do not disturb" notice on the door of the interview room.

CHOOSING A LOCATION

You need to decide whether it is best to hold the interview in your workplace or on neutral territory somewhere else. If you use your workplace, do you want to hold it in your own office, or in a more clinical meeting room? If you need privacy or secrecy, then choose neutral ground, such as a hotel room, or the office of a third party. Try to create a relaxing atmosphere with comfortable seats and lighting that is not too harsh.

BEING AWARE OF ▼ THE ATMOSPHERE
While conducting an interview, avoid all distractions and concentrate on putting candidates at ease. This will help them perform at their best.

Candidate feels intimidated due to sitting on a low chair

Computer screen is a distraction

Telephone may ring and interrupt interview

ARRANGING SEATING

There are several different ways to arrange seating at an interview. Sitting face to face is always a more formal option, while sitting side by side creates a more informal, cooperative atmosphere. If you decide on the face-to-face option, remember that people generally prefer to have some kind of solid surface such as a table between them, since sitting with their knees exposed can make interviewees feel even more awkward and vulnerable. Unless it is part of your intentional strategy, do not seat candidates on a chair that is lower than yours – this may make them feel inferior and uncomfortable.

34 Indicate where you would like the interviewee to sit.

35 Provide clear directions to the interview room.

KEY

Interviewer   Candidate

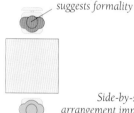

Face-to-face arrangement suggests formality

Side-by-side arrangement implies cooperation

▲ **FORMAL INTERVIEW**

A square or a rectangular table is more formal than a small, round table.

▲ **INFORMAL INTERVIEW**

A large, round table creates an informal atmosphere and can seat more than two people.

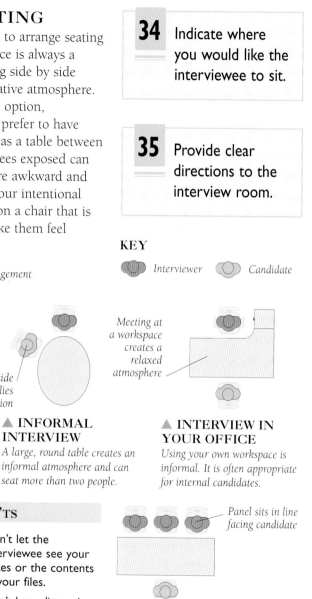

Meeting at a workspace creates a relaxed atmosphere

▲ **INTERVIEW IN YOUR OFFICE**

Using your own workspace is informal. It is often appropriate for internal candidates.

Panel sits in line facing candidate

▲ **PANEL INTERVIEW**

Sitting on opposite sides of a rectangular table is confrontational, which may be appropriate for formal interviews.

DO'S AND DON'TS

✔ Do pull blinds so that nobody gets dazzled.

✔ Do take the phone off the hook during the interview.

✔ Do ensure the room is well ventilated and that neither of you is too hot or too cold.

✘ Don't let the interviewee see your notes or the contents of your files.

✘ Don't hang distracting images on your wall.

✘ Don't offer food. Neither of you can eat and talk properly.

DECIDING ON STRATEGY

The most important decision to make before an interview is what its style should be. Do you want to keep it factual, or do you want to put the candidate under pressure? The answer to this may depend on the job for which you are interviewing.

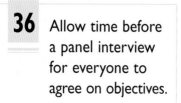

36 Allow time before a panel interview for everyone to agree on objectives.

CONSIDERING YOUR AIMS

Keeping your criteria for the job in mind, consider what you want to achieve in the interview. Select a strategy that will help you. If you know the interviewee's technical skills are right for the job, you may choose to concentrate on their people skills in the interview. Alternatively, you may adopt an aggressive interview style to test the candidate's reactions under pressure.

37 Give all the interviewers full details of all the candidates.

PREPARING AN INTERVIEW STRATEGY

STYLE OF INTERVIEW	HOW TO PREPARE
FACTUAL The main point is to extract factual information. The candidate's personality is less important.	Compile a list of general and specific questions designed to come up with the answers that you need.
SITUATIONAL The aim of a situational interview is to see how the candidate handles key parts of the job.	Prepare open questions such as, "What would you do if...?" Lead interviewees into a full description of the ensuing scenario.
CONFRONTATIONAL Use a confrontational style to gauge how the interviewee behaves under work-related stress.	Plan a confrontation that makes attacks on and insinuations about the interviewee's track record and career progression.
TECHNICAL Use a technical interview to establish that the candidate has the skills that they claim to have.	Set up a practical test, for example selling something to a colleague or manipulating software on your computer.

STRUCTURING INTERVIEWS

Exactly what your interview will consist of depends on your strategy. However, it is usual for interviews to exist as variations of the following:

- An introduction and a "getting to know you" phase where you talk about generalities;
- A question-and-answer session to fill in any gaps in the candidate's resume;
- An investigation of the candidate's character and personal qualities;
- A final stage where the candidate asks questions about the job and its terms and conditions.

You can adapt these to your strategy – for example, you may want to include a technical test. When using aggressive tactics, you might omit the introductory phase.

38 If teamwork is important, set group exercises for the candidates.

39 Structure the interview to suit your strategy.

INTERVIEWING BY PANEL

A panel interview has the advantage of allowing several interviewers to assess a candidate simultaneously. The interplay of their questions can elicit far more than any one line of questioning on its own. Panel interviews also take some of the pressure – and therefore the stress – from the individual interviewer. A decision is reached based on the opinions of several people after conferring. Make sure that the balance of panel members is equal and that no single member dominates the interview. You may choose interviewers based on their areas of expertise, or because they will be working with the successful candidate. Role playing between the panelists is a popular strategy.

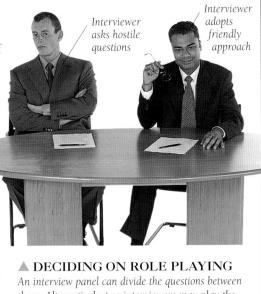

Interviewer asks hostile questions

Interviewer adopts friendly approach

▲ DECIDING ON ROLE PLAYING

An interview panel can divide the questions between them. Alternatively, two interviewers may play the roles of hostile interviewer and friendly interviewer.

PREPARING QUESTIONS

Your main chance to find out information about a candidate comes from asking the right questions in the right way. Phrase questions carefully to obtain the details that you want. Use the interviewee's answers to lead into your next question.

40 Start an interview with easy questions to help relax the candidate.

41 Modify your list of questions for each of the candidates you interview.

QUESTIONS TO ASK AN APPLICANT

Q Why do you want to change jobs at this point?

Q What do you consider your greatest attributes?

Q What have your relationships been like with past employers?

Q What for you has been the highlight of your career so far?

Q What has been the low point of your career so far?

Q What experience do you have with problem-solving?

Q What are your long-term goals, and how do you think you can achieve them here?

UNDERSTANDING HOW TO PHRASE QUESTIONS

You can manipulate a candidate's answers by phrasing your questions in different ways. Open questions are likely to be the most useful in an interview. They encourage the candidate to open up, think, and talk at length, and enable you to observe a candidate's communication skills and elicit detailed information. These questions usually start with words such as "What?", "When?", "Why?", and "How?" – "How did you first become interested in tropical hardwoods?" Open questions may also start with a statement about yourself and then follow with a question – "I once went to the botanical gardens in Sydney. Which gardens have you been to?"

Closed questions lead to a simple affirmative or negative, rather than an in-depth reply. Use them to clarify unclear points, for example, "Can we expect you to begin the job on November 14th?" These questions are also useful for seeking confirmation of details of a candidate's resume.

42 Ask open questions – that is, those that invite more than a simple "yes" or "no" answer.

Understanding Loaded Questions

A loaded question is one that makes the candidate react to a deliberate assumption about them. For example, test how close the candidate is to accepting a job by saying, "When do you think you can go to our Munich office?" If the candidate's response is, "Aren't we jumping the gun?", you know you still have some way to go. However, if he or she seems eager, you can assume that you are near a deal. Avoid asking these questions in an aggressive tone.

Tilted head indicates a lack of trust

Crossed legs and clasped hands imply defensiveness

TAILORING QUESTIONS ▶
When interviewing, avoid asking questions that make the candidate clam up or act defensively. Watch their body language for signs of defensive behavior.

Using a Checklist

It can be useful to have a prepared checklist of questions that you want to ask in an interview. However, do not stick too rigidly to either the order or the content of the list – an interview is a two-way communication. The main purposes of the checklist are to provide the security that comes from knowing that you have covered all the ground and to have a list to refer to if necessary.

43 Use closed questions only if you require a specific response.

Building on Questions

The interviewer's questions must be influenced by the interviewee's answers. Each question should build on the one before to steer the candidate toward providing you with the information you need. "So you decided to take a six-month break?"… "Did you travel immediately?"… "Why did you decide to wait so long before leaving?"… "How long did it take you to get a job when you returned?"… "So you spent two weeks in Asia and five months looking for a job. Is that correct?"

44 Use a candidate's resume and matching sheet to generate interview questions.

HONING LISTENING SKILLS

*A*ttentive listening is one of the most essential abilities of an interviewer. If you appear to be listening, your interviewee will be encouraged to keep talking. Work at keeping your concentration focused and becoming aware of your body language.

45 You have two ears and one mouth – listen twice as much as you talk.

ANALYZING YOUR SKILLS

Most people like the the sound of their own voice yet also believe that they are good listeners. Try this test to find out how good a listener you are. Tape-record a conversation with a colleague, then listen to it objectively. Who talks more? Who talks faster? Do you respond to your colleague's concerns or merely continue what you were saying before you were interrupted? By analyzing the tape, you will be able to hear in which areas you need to improve, as well as in which areas you are strong.

46 Summarize what a candidate is saying to show that you are listening.

**PRACTICING ▼
BODY LANGUAGE**
Learn to use positive body language as part of your preparations. Here, the interviewer is focusing attentively on what the candidate is saying.

Interviewer's expression is open and attentive

Leaning forward indicates interest

AVOIDING BAD HABITS

Even good listeners develop bad habits. Two of the most common ones are "turning off" to information that you are not interested in, and interrupting people before they have finished what they are saying. If you know that you are prone to these habits, make an effort to overcome them. Remember, developing a good listening technique requires awareness, practice, and effort.

47 Keep checking with a candidate that you have understood everything you have been told.

THINGS TO DO

1. Be curious. It helps you listen properly.
2. Ensure you understand a question before answering.
3. Jot down questions as they occur to you, leaving your mind free to listen.
4. Listen to the emotions behind the words.
5. Correct any bad listening habits that you have.

BEING AWARE OF NEGATIVE BODY LANGUAGE

There is a clear distinction between hearing and listening. Make yourself aware of any negative body language you may use when you are not fully concentrating. Once you are aware, you can consciously avoid lapsing into bad habits in an interview.

Interviewer's closed body language implies a closed mind

◀ **BEING DEFENSIVE**
This man is sitting in a defensive position. If you adopt a pose such as this – crossed arms and leaning backward – the candidate will feel you are not receptive to what is said.

Interviewer has chin in hand, indicating contemplation

BEING ▶
INATTENTIVE
This interviewer appears contemplative and unfocused on the interview. This may be interpreted negatively by the interviewee as a lack of enthusiasm in her application.

PREPARING YOURSELF

Just before an interview begins, make a last-minute check that you have all the information you need, that any equipment (such as a tape recorder) is working smoothly, and that you are informed about the subject matter and in a positive frame of mind.

48 Be prepared to answer some questions as well as to ask them.

PREPARING YOUR TOOLS

49 Make a checklist to take into the interview with you.

50 Ask a candidate's permission before taping an interview.

Decide how you are going to keep a record of the interview. Note-taking is the usual method. It is discreet, but it takes up your time and may divert your attention from the interview. If you are going to take notes, use a notepad rather than scribbling in the margins of a resume, which you may later need to show to somebody else. An alternative method is taping an interview. Although this frees you to concentrate on the interview, it may make the interviewee nervous. Always check that your tape recorder has enough batteries and spare tape to last for the duration of the interview.

PRESENTING YOURSELF

Remember that you are an ambassador, selling your organization to a candidate almost as much as they are selling themselves to you. Ensure that you look neat and presentable and are appropriately dressed. If you are recruiting for a laid-back company in which employees usually wear casual clothes, reflect this in your dress. If you are recruiting for a formal organization, dress more soberly.

You will need to be well informed about your company. Gather all the relevant details, and be ready to answer candidates' questions. You may also want to give candidates printed information or copies of the company's annual report.

51 Straighten your clothing and make sure your hair is neat just before starting an interview.

PREPARING YOUR MATERIAL

There is a range of information you should have at your fingertips in an interview, including the following:

- What does the job involve, generally and specifically?
- To whom will the new employee report?
- What salary can you offer, and when will it be reviewed?
- Is there any opportunity (or need) to work overtime?
- What are the prospects for promotion?
- What are the perks that go with the job – such as pension, health insurance, and vacation time?

Interviewer reviews key resume points

Resume and application letter give details of experience

▲ **CHECKING OVER MATERIAL**
Immediately before an interview, take another quick look at a candidate's resume. Make sure that your list of prepared questions will elicit the information you want to obtain.

FOCUSING FOR FIVE MINUTES

Five or ten minutes before a candidate is due to arrive (and you should assume that he or she will be on time, if not a little early), go over their papers. Remind yourself of the questions that you want to ask and the order in which you intend asking them. Focus on the sort of person you are looking for, and try to erase the image of other candidates from your mind. Then relax for a minute or two. Lean back in your chair, arms at your side, and breathe in deeply. Exhale slowly and evenly, and repeat several times. You will feel refreshed and ready for the next candidate.

GETTING ▶ READY
Interviewing can be exhausting. Revitalize yourself between each interview with some slow, deep breaths.

Feel shallow breathing in upper chest

Feel deep breathing in diaphragm

CONDUCTING AN INTERVIEW

Interviews can be nerve-wracking for interviewers as well as candidates. Conduct them in a way that puts both parties at ease to maximize what you glean from your meeting.

OPENING AN INTERVIEW

The first few moments of an interview are vitally important: this is when initial impressions are formed. Whatever your status, greet each candidate with the same politeness and respect you would want to receive if the roles were reversed.

 52 If interviewees arrive early, let them know when you can see them.

CULTURAL DIFFERENCES

Be aware of cultural differences when greeting interviewees: in some cultures, men greet each other with an embrace and a kiss on the cheek; in others, men and women alike simply bow. The handshake, in various forms, is almost universally accepted and is generally the safest option.

GREETING A CANDIDATE

An effective greeting can make all the difference. Stand up when an interviewee arrives, make eye contact, smile, and move forward to give a firm (but not bone-crunching) handshake. Welcome the candidate by name. If there are others in the room, introduce them clearly and repeat their names later on in case the interviewee has forgotten them. Ask the interviewee to sit down, then offer something to drink – this is especially important if the candidate has traveled some distance to meet you. Remember: however nervous you are, the candidate is sure to be more so.

Candidate meets interviewer's eye, suggesting confidence and honesty

Interviewer and candidate shake hands, establishing good will

Interviewer makes direct eye contact

Interviewer leans forward, implying eagerness to meet

Interviewer stands in polite acknowledgment of candidate's arrival

RELAXING A CANDIDATE

There are times in everyone's life when people temporarily lose whatever leadership qualities they may have and wait to be told what to do. Walking into a room to be interviewed is one such occasion. When interviewing, take the initiative in order to help candidates feel at ease. Go through a formal process of asking candidates to sit down and showing them to their seats. Try to avoid embarrassing them. For example, if a candidate misjudges the appropriate level of formality of dress, or spills some coffee, play such matters down when the opportunity arises.

▲ ESTABLISHING AN INSTANT RAPPORT

Create a positive rapport with the candidate by standing to greet him. Lean toward the candidate and make eye contact to encourage him to relax.

 53 Smile, but do not overdo it; this will make you appear nervous.

EVALUATING AN APPLICANT

The most important aim of conducting an interview is to form an impression of a candidate's personality and abilities. To do this, you must supplement the information gained from the resume, so ask perceptive questions and take note of your impressions.

54 Remember that the "best" candidate may just be good at interviews.

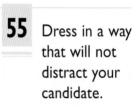

55 Dress in a way that will not distract your candidate.

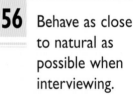

56 Behave as close to natural as possible when interviewing.

CONSIDERING IMPRESSIONS

Before the interview begins in earnest, you will have already formed an impression of the candidate. Be aware of any prejudices that might color your first impression: perhaps you are adversely affected by long hair, by a particular accent, or by a style of dress. Similarly, the interviewee will have formed an opinion about your company. An unfavorable impression is hard to change once formed, so it is your responsibility to give a good impression of yourself and your company.

If possible, start the interview with friendly conversation to make both of you feel at ease. It can be about general subjects such as the weather, your office's location, recent news events, or any subject that you both have in common.

COVERING ALL THE FACTS

Besides getting an overall impression of the candidate's character, you need to check the facts in the resume. Ask detailed questions about education, work experience, and other job-related skills. You may uncover useful things – for example, that the candidate speaks a second language because a parent was born in a foreign country. Interviewees may possess skills that they themselves thought irrelevant but you recognize as having potential.

57 Ask yourself if the candidate is both able and willing to do the job.

LOOKING AT CAREER PROGRESSION

To assess whether candidates are applying for a job to further their careers or whether they want the job for other reasons, ask them how they see their careers developing. If you are interviewing for a company that is often used as a stepping stone by ambitious young people, make sure the candidates' aims relate to the company's aims. Even if people stay with your organization for just a short time, you may benefit enough from their talents to make it worth employing them.

SPOTTING GAPS

If there are gaps in a candidate's employment history, it is important to find out the reasons for them. Remember that not all gaps are the result of involuntary unemployment. They may have occurred because of prolonged illness, travel, taking time off to have children, or looking after ailing parents. Even those gaps that are the result of unemployment may not reflect badly on the candidates themselves. Ask the candidates open-ended questions about any gaps and why they occurred. You may find that they were let go or left a job for good reasons. Focus on how the candidate used the time between periods of paid employment.

 58 Avoid asking personal questions that are irrelevant to the job.

PAYING ATTENTION ▶ TO DETAIL
Look out for career progression or continuity in a particular area of work. Do the candidate's interests reflect any requirements for this job?

ASSESSING ABILITIES

In certain cases, the extent of a candidate's qualifications may be sufficient to gauge his or her ability to do the job, assuming that the qualifications are appropriate and have been kept up to date. In most cases, however, relevant or associated work experience is considered to be a more valuable indication of skill and aptitude. Your job as an interviewer is to assess the candidate's professional, technical, and practical abilities using all the information available to you.

 59 Jot down values for the relevant abilities of a candidate.

ASSESSING A CANDIDATE'S SKILLS

SKILLS	WAYS TO ASSESS SKILLS
ORGANIZATIONAL Does the candidate display signs of being well organized and methodical?	Ask about the candidate's attitude toward being organized. Find out about preferences for filing systems, and ask how the candidate might start to organize a hypothetical project.
ANALYTICAL How well can the candidate analyze business situations, and how quickly can they come up with the best solutions?	Ask for examples of their problem-solving ability. Describe a difficult situation, and ask them to pick out the key points and come up with a potential solution.
DECISION-MAKING How well can the candidate make difficult decisions, and how quickly can they then implement those decisions?	Ask about their previous experience. What difficult decisions have they had to make in the past? How did they reach the decision? How well did they handle the repercussions?
SOCIAL Will the candidate get on well with the superiors, colleagues, and subordinates with whom he or she will be working?	Ask about the candidate's experience of teamwork. Do they prefer to work alone or in a team? Ask them how they would handle a hypothetical problem with a colleague.
COMMUNICATION How efficient is the candidate at communicating clearly and confidently?	Assess the candidate's verbal skills from the interview itself, then ask about written ability. Have they written lengthy reports? Can you see them?

ASSESSING PERSONALITY

The candidate's attitude toward colleagues and the workplace is determined by their personality; their personality also affects their relationships with colleagues and the atmosphere of the workplace.

Try to assess whether a candidate will fit in with the culture of your organization, and find out about the work culture of the candidate's previous companies. For example, a work culture that encourages team spirit will not suit someone who comes from a background of intense internal competition where "creative tension" has been positively encouraged. Has the candidate always worked in small companies where everyone knows what is going on? If yours is a large organization, how will they cope with not knowing the details of company business and decision-making? In addition, think about the balance of current staff. Do you need, for example, a specific personality type such as an extrovert to balance a rather introverted team, or vice versa?

60 Note when a candidate responds with enthusiasm – this can tell you what motivates them.

QUESTIONS TO ASK AN APPLICANT

Q What do you think you could bring to this job?

Q What do you regard as the main achievement in your life?

Q What are you looking for first and foremost in a job?

Q Where do you see yourself in five years' time?

Q How do you handle the pressure of deadlines?

Q Do you like working as part of a team, or do you prefer working on projects alone?

Q How do you think your best friend would describe you?

ACTING AS AN AMBASSADOR

Remember that as you are assessing the candidate, so the candidate is assessing you and the organization for which you work. There is a shortage of potential employees in many areas and, in these cases, you need to work hard to attract high-caliber recruits. This means that when you meet a candidate for the first time, you are acting as an ambassador for your company. Do this by letting the candidate know that you are prepared to go to considerable trouble and expense to find the right person for the job. Show that you are genuinely interested in achieving this and that when they come to work for the company they will be a valued staff member.

61 Give positive feedback to encourage in-depth discussion.

Controlling an Interview

Pace an interview carefully so that you can cover all the necessary ground in the time allocated. You must be able to direct a candidate gently toward another subject if required, or hurry them along politely if they linger too long on a favorite topic.

> **62** Allow a few minutes for small talk before the interview.

Points to Remember

- Talking too much initially may be a symptom of nervousness.
- Initial stuttering and stumbling over words and phrases may also be a sign of nerves.
- Talking directly to the point shows that the candidate is listening to you attentively.
- It is not necessarily a bad sign if a candidate shows some emotion during the interview.

Controlling the Flow of Information

Try to control the flow of information during an interview. For example, give supportive feedback to encourage a candidate to discuss sensitive issues. Say "It must have been very difficult for you to let those people go" to draw out more detail of how the situation was handled. Although you should always try to cover most of your planned questions, do not stick rigidly to them if a candidate has something unexpected to say on a subject that affects their application.

Using Silence Tactically

Use silence tactically during an interview. Do not prolong it to such an extent that it makes the interviewee uncomfortable, but do let it run whenever a candidate is obviously searching for words or thinking about an answer. Note how candidates respond to silence – do they rush to fill the vacuum with hasty, ill-thought-out remarks, or do they have the confidence to take the time that they need to frame a coherent answer to a difficult or complicated question?

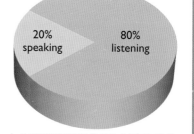

20% speaking

80% listening

▲ LISTENING PROPERLY

Speak for 20 percent of the time in an interview and listen to the candidate speak for the other 80 percent of the session.

HANDLING CANDIDATES

The personalities of candidates who have the same qualifications will vary enormously – one may be seemingly in control, another a bag of nerves. You will be able judge their relative merits only if you know how they all respond to certain situations. Ask all your candidates roughly the same questions – for example, probe their ability to handle crisis situations at work – to see how different their reactions are. If interviewees do become flustered when responding to your questioning, try gently to calm them down; ask another question that leads away from the topic that appears to be causing them discomfort.

63 Respect candidates who can admit that they do not know an answer.

64 If your interviewee becomes flustered, stay calm yourself.

Making direct eye contact reassures interviewee

Hands are raised protectively to face

Facial expression shows distress

Leaning forward shows attentiveness

Open hands help calm interviewee

▲ CALMING A
DISTRESSED CANDIDATE
If someone is having difficulty in explaining a particular point, introduce a new topic and come back to the original point later.

READING BODY LANGUAGE

Learn to read people's body language. It may convey as much about them as their words do. Body language is particularly useful to an interviewer – it is difficult for a candidate to be evasive or dishonest using body language because it is instinctive.

65 Mirror body language to establish a good rapport.

WATCHING A CANDIDATE

66 Train yourself to notice people's body language automatically.

Look at a candidate's body language while he or she is speaking. Do the candidate's words match what they are "saying" with their body? For example, is their posture hunched and defensive even as they are claiming they are "good with people"? In particular, observe the candidate's eyes. Are they averted unconsciously at times when you would expect to have eye contact?

CONTROLLING YOUR BODY LANGUAGE

Be aware of your own body language, and try to avoid giving adverse signals. Certain postures and gestures of the interviewer can give negative signals and may discourage a candidate from continuing to give out information.

Hand stifles yawn

Hands fiddling

Facial expression glazed, with slight smirk

Looking at watch

▲ **BOREDOM**
Yawning during an interview will give the impression of boredom. It may, however, be due to nerves.

▲ **INATTENTION**
Avoid fiddling or looking distracted, since this may indicate that you are preoccupied with other matters.

▲ **IMPATIENCE**
If you often look at your watch a candidate may think you wish to be elsewhere, even if this is not so.

Interviewer's
eye contact
shows interest

Open posture
indicates
concentration

Eye contact shows
self-confidence

Confident posture confirms
self-assurance

Explanatory
hand gestures reveal
relaxed frame of mind

Relaxed sitting
position projects
relaxed atmopshere

Relaxed
legs show
candidate
is at ease

READING POSITIVE SIGNS

A person who is grinning broadly is giving off
a very positive signal, while one whose eyes are
fixed to the floor is giving off a very negative
signal. However, positive signals are not always
so blatant. A confident person will tend to sit
upright, or with their body leaning slightly
forward, even when being interviewed by their
potential future boss. When confident candidates
are not speaking, their legs and arms usually
remain quite still and they tend to make both
frequent and firm eye contact.

Shaking hands with a candidate can give you
an immediate impression of their frame of mind.
If they are relaxed and comfortable, their hands
will be warm and dry. However, cold, sweaty
hands indicate nervousness.

▲ GOOD RAPPORT
*These two people are clearly in tune
with each other: all aspects of their body
language are open, relaxed, and attentive.*

CULTURAL DIFFERENCES

Different cultures have different
norms of body language and
personal space. In some, people
are open and tactile, even with
strangers; in others, people will
feel invaded if you sit or stand too
close. If you are unsure, ask an
experienced colleague for advice.

- Nervousness – and yawning – can be contagious, so it is important to remember that a candidate may be mirroring your own body language.

- A candidate's body language may contradict what he or she is saying verbally.

- Speaking slowly tends to indicate that one is at ease. Speaking quickly may be a sign of being nervous or of great enthusiasm.

READING SUBTLE SIGNS

There are many subtle clues to a person's frame of mind. Pay attention to the position of their body, their arms and legs, and their eyes.

Note, too, their tone of voice. This will strongly affect the way they are perceived. If you are filling a managerial post or a job that involves dealing with the press, for example, bear in mind that someone with a squeaky, high-pitched voice may find it difficult to command attention and respect. On the other hand, they may sound high-pitched on this occasion only because of nerves.

SEEING NERVOUS SIGNALS

Develop your ability to spot nervousness. Common signs include foot-tapping, rubbing the nose or lips with the back of the hand, wringing the hands, fiddling with a writing implement, or tearing up a tissue – if a candidate does any of these, consider the possibility that they may be very nervous. Note, too, if they smile too much, which may indicate an excessive desire to be liked. If an interviewee is unable to establish eye contact – to look you straight in the eye – you can deduce that they are probably ill at ease. But treat such observations as no more than clues to alert you to points to watch for – apparent nervous behavior may have several other explanations.

67 Watch hand movements – they can give a lot away.

Lips are touched in an unconscious form of comfort-seeking

Hands are crossed over body in a defensive manner

Legs are rigid

68 Listen to your candidate's voice: a high pitch may indicate nerves.

◀ **NERVOUS CANDIDATE**
The position of this candidate's feet indicates that he is not at ease. This is further reinforced by the position of his hands: one touching his lips, the other held across his body.

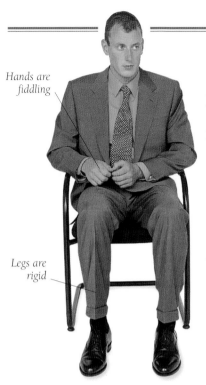

Hands are fiddling

Legs are rigid

SPOTTING EVASIVENESS

Be aware of the signs that candidates are trying to evade a question – either because they do not know how to answer or because their answer might reveal something that they would rather hide. A range of body language may give them away:

- Avoiding eye contact;
- Talking around the question, and including lots of jargon to confuse you;
- Fidgeting, or playing with their hair or with any implement, such as a pen.

◀ **EVASIVE CANDIDATE**
This man's posture shows that he is ill at ease. His body and legs are stiff, and he is fiddling with his hands and looking around him in order to avoid eye contact.

Hand gestures are expansive

Arm is hooked casually over chair arm

RECOGNIZING ARROGANCE

While most candidates at job interviews are nervous and need to be put at ease, a few seem to be overconfident to the extent of being arrogant. They tend to speak rather than listen and to speak at length, giving the impression that they like the sound of their own voice. This behavior may be because they feel they are too good for the job, or perhaps they are overcompensating for lack of self-confidence. Either way, contain such candidates by maintaining a formal interviewing style and asking a series of brisk, difficult questions. They may rise to the challenge – or become defensive.

ARROGANT CANDIDATE ▶
This candidate's body language suggests that he is arrogant. He is sprawled in the chair in an overconfident way, with his legs crossed. His arm gestures are expansive.

Legs are crossed

Using Tests

There are numerous tests available that can be used to estimate a candidate's ability – either their level of intelligence or a specific technical skill. Panel interviews and role-playing are also popular methods of testing the skills of a candidate.

69 Use only tests that have been devised by a reputable source.

Points to Remember

● Tests should not replace face-to-face interviews, but rather they should augment them.

● Personality tests produce a profile of an individual's main characteristics, but they do not tell you whether the candidate is going to be good at the job.

● You can have personality tests tailor-made for your organization or buy them off the shelf.

● With most personality tests, staff need to be specially trained to interpret the results accurately.

Preparing to Use Tests

If you are asking candidates to take any type of test, written or situational, inform them in advance in writing, setting out clearly the criteria by which they will be judged. When deciding which tests to use, choose those that are strictly relevant to the job. Always make sure that they are conducted under the exact conditions stipulated – in some countries legal action can result from a test being improperly conducted. If you intend to hold tests at regular intervals during an employee's time with your organization, that fact should be explained to them at the interview and also be recorded in their job description.

Aptitude Tests

These are relatively simple written tests that measure skills, such as reading, writing, verbal reasoning, and numerical ability. They have a built-in "anticheat" factor, which means they produce a very accurate picture of an individual's abilities. If you receive replies from a large number of apparently suitable candidates, invite them to undergo a series of aptitude tests as a time-efficient way to reduce the list. Make sure you have suitable surroundings in which to conduct the tests, since they should be carried out under controlled conditions.

70 Update the tests that you use at regular intervals.

71 Read test results as a whole, not issue by issue.

PERSONALITY TESTS

The term "personality tests" is used generically to cover a variety of verbal, visual, and written tests. They are based on the belief that personal characteristics are measurable and that the presence or absence of certain traits correlates to success in the workplace and thus suitability for a job. To use such testing effectively, you must first establish a clear idea of the job specification and the type of personality that might fit the vacancy.

 72 Ask for written applications and ask a graphologist to check them.

PSYCHOMETRIC TESTS

 73 Use psychometric tests to support other tests, rather than on their own.

A type of personality test, psychometric tests are widely used to measure the mental ability of candidates under consideration for a job. As an employer, you will probably want to use this method in one of three ways:

● To observe how often a candidate indulges in specific kinds of behavior;
● To discover their powers of self-observation;
● To see how they react in certain set situations.

ANALYZING HANDWRITING

Many major institutions employ graphologists as a matter of course to interpret the characteristics revealed in the handwriting of interviewees. Remember to consider the results of such a test alongside your assessment of a candidate made during an interview, not in isolation.

ANALYZING WRITING ▶
When analyzing a candidate's handwriting, do not attempt to make your own subjective judgments – always rely on careful analysis from an expert graphologist.

Regular rhythm of letters indicates consistency

Upward angled t-bars reveal enthusiasm

Lorem ipsum dolor sit amet, consectetuer adipiscing elit, sed diam nonummy nibh euismod tincidunt ut laoreet dolore magna aliquam erat volutpat. Ut wisi enim ad minim veniam, quis nostrud exerci tation ullamcorper suscipit lobortis nisl ut aliquip ex ea commodo consequat. Duis autem vel eum iriure dolor in hendrerit in vulputate velit esse molestie consequat, vel illum dolore eu feugiat nulla facilisis at vero eros et accumsan accumsan et iusto odio dignissim qui blandit praesent luptatum zzril delenit augue duis dolore te feugait nulla facilisi. Lorem

Starting strokes suggests dependence

Loops in letters show diplomacy

TECHNICAL TESTS

Consider using panel interviews when recruiting for a vacancy that requires a test of a candidate's specialist knowledge, for example in engineering. Decide beforehand on the areas of questioning that each member of the panel will handle – you could concentrate on the candidate's resume, while your colleagues could ask detailed technical questions. The pressure in this kind of interview is unrelenting and often exposes lack of experience.

POINTS TO REMEMBER

● Each interviewer should cover a separate area of questioning.

● Panel interviews are more intimidating for candidates than a one-to-one interview.

● Internal candidates may often be less nervous than external candidates who are competing for the same vacancy.

Technical expert leads questioning on relevant experience

Lead interviewer finds out about resume

Personnel manager checks up on details

▲ **TESTING BY PANEL**
If you take on the role of lead interviewer, keep a tight control on the proceedings and do not let anyone present stray from the object of the test – to find out about the interviewee and his or her knowledge.

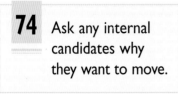

74 Ask any internal candidates why they want to move.

INTELLIGENCE TESTS

The IQ (Intelligence Quotient) test is now mainly used for comparing children of school age. As an employer, you can make use of various more sophisticated means of measuring verbal, abstract, and numerical reasoning, which have been specially prepared for use in the workplace. Great confidence is placed internationally on the GMAT (Graduate Management Admissions Test), which has become a prerequisite for entry into most of the better-quality business schools.

SITUATIONAL TESTS

Putting candidates into a simulated work situation allows you to judge how they might perform on the job. Carry out situational testing in the final stages of the interviewing process, by which time you will have reduced the number of candidates to a shortlist. However, even if the test is very realistic, it will never simulate relationships between individual colleagues that take time to develop and are crucial to personal motivation.

 75 Remember to warn candidates if you are going to test them.

CHOOSING THE APPROPRIATE TEST FOR AN INTERVIEW

TYPE OF TEST	FACTORS TO CONSIDER
APTITUDE Measures general abilities, such as numerical, written, verbal, and reasoning skills.	● This is useful at the very beginning of the selection and interview process. ● This needs to be conducted in a controlled environment, such as a quiet meeting room.
PERSONALITY Measures personality traits. Psychometric tests are often used for this purpose.	● This is appropriate for sensitive jobs such as in the diplomatic service or a customer-complaints department. ● This test is time-consuming and needs to be carried out in a controlled environment.
HANDWRITING Evaluates aspects of personality using characteristics of handwriting (graphology).	● This is useful only in conjunction with other tests as a way of confirming findings from elsewhere. ● Because handwriting may vary in stressful circumstances, several examples need to be taken.
TECHNICAL Tests for technical abilities for jobs, such as machine operation, that require specific skills.	● This is useful at a later stage in the interview process. ● It may be time-consuming and potentially patronizing to those candidates who are able and experienced with all the relevant qualifications.
INTELLIGENCE Compares a young graduate's score to the average score for people of a similar age.	● This may not be appropriate unless some of the interviewees are recent graduates. ● This is helpful where companies are filtering a lot of similarly qualified young applicants for general training.
SITUATIONAL Places candidates in a work situation relevant to the job for which they have applied.	● This is most meaningful for jobs where working relationships are not a top priority. ● It is not useful for initial selection but is appropriate at later stages in the interviewing process.

CLOSING AN INTERVIEW

All interviews should be brought to a polite but unhurried conclusion – even if you believe a candidate to be unsuitable. As an ambassador for your company, the way in which you wrap up the interview will create a lasting impression on the candidate.

 76 Tell candidates how many other interviews you have scheduled.

 77 Keep an open mind throughout an interview.

 78 Give candidates a chance to withdraw their applications.

INVITING QUESTIONS

Toward the end of an interview, ask the candidates if they have any questions. If they have taken the trouble to find information about your organization, they will have at least one interesting question.

Most questions, however, arise spontaneously from issues discussed in the interview. These are often about specific details of the job and its prospects. Take time when preparing to ensure you can answer most of the reasonable questions that may come up. You can learn much about candidates from how they put questions: for example, those who start with phrases such as "I know this is a silly question, but…" may be prone to undermining their own value and are unlikely to present a confident image of your company.

ENCOURAGING QUESTIONS

If a candidate is stumped for questions to ask, and you do not think he is suitable for the job, thank him and close the interview. Otherwise, summarize the points covered in the interview to see if that stimulates a question, or suggest a line of questioning:

❝ *Is there anything more I can tell you about the structure of the department?* ❞

❝ *You seemed concerned about the training involved. Do you want to ask me about that?* ❞

❝ *Are there any aspects of the job that you are not clear on and would like clarifying?* ❞

TYING UP LOOSE ENDS

At the end of an interview, check that you have found out all you need to know about a candidate. Find out how much notice they need to give in order to leave their present job. Let them know when you will contact them if you want them to attend a second interview, and whether this is likely to be by phone or in writing. Tell them, if appropriate, to contact you if they have not heard from you by the specified time. Above all, consider candidates' feelings: be honest and explicit in any instructions or information that you give them.

Handshake is firm and courteous

Interviewer thanks candidate for attending

THANKING A ▶ CANDIDATE
Stand up to signal the end of an interview, thank the candidate for coming to see you, and shake hands. It is polite to do this even if you know they are not suitable for the job.

79 Always preserve the dignity and self-esteem of a candidate.

MAKING A SPONTANEOUS OFFER

You may decide at the end of an interview that you have just met the ideal candidate for the job. Do not risk losing them – ask them immediately if they are genuinely interested in the vacancy, and if they say yes, make them a provisional offer. Although this is not common practice in many businesses, it is often prudent to follow your instincts in certain situations. Make sure, however, that your decision is a rational one and that you have not been carried away by the moment.

ANALYZING AN INTERVIEW

Once the interview is over, assess the information you have gathered. Use this, along with a second interview, to help make your final selection.

RECORDING IMPRESSIONS

After conducting several interviews, they may all begin to blur into each other. Make memory-jogging notes as soon as a candidate has left the room so that you will be able to distinguish the characteristics of one applicant from those of another.

 80 If you are in doubt about an interviewee, trust your instincts.

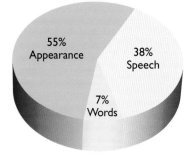

▲ **FIRST IMPRESSIONS**
About 55 percent of our first impressions of a person are formed by their appearance, 38 percent by the way they speak, and a mere 7 percent by the words they use.

55% Appearance

38% Speech

7% Words

NOTING YOUR INSTINCTS

Instincts are a powerful and useful tool and should not be ignored. They are backed by years of subconsciously extracting and compiling information from experience and provide valid pointers to individual characters. Always note your first impressions of every candidate, because at that point your instincts will be working overtime. Although first impressions rely heavily on a candidate's appearance and manner, ask yourself whether you have retained other strong impressions about them. Were you impressed by their posture, or did they have an air of confidence?

AVOIDING BIAS

81 Avoid making biased judgments on any of the candidates.

When analyzing an interview, do not allow your personal prejudices to influence you into making judgments about people based on your notions of class, sex, religion, or race. For example, avoid assuming that someone who went to the same college as you is superior to someone who did not. In addition, beware of a built-in bias in any tests you set the candidates; many have been devised using a single social group as a control.

ASKING OTHER OPINIONS

It is always valuable to get a second opinion. For example, if one of your colleagues has previously interviewed a candidate, share your impressions with the other interviewer as soon as possible, and discuss any areas of disagreement. If you are the sole interviewer, however, it is advisable to ask workmates who may have briefly met the candidate for their impressions. Also ask your reception staff how they found a candidate: were they polite, calm, flustered, or nervous? Add their impressions to your own to build up a more complete picture of the individual.

82 Try to imagine what a candidate is like outside the interview room.

▲ ASKING A ▶
RECEPTIONIST
Check with your reception staff to find out what impression a candidate made on them. Their opinion will add extra useful information to your picture of an individual's personality and suitability for the job.

MAKING A SHORTLIST

Once you have recorded your impressions of each candidate, draw up a shortlist of people for a second interview. Ideally, the shortlist should contain the names of between three and six people that you would like to consider further for the job.

83 Inform candidates before carrying out background checks on them.

CHECKING YOUR NOTES

84 Keep candidates' resumes with your notes, references, and matching sheets.

Read through all your notes again – both those that you took during the interview and the impressions and recollections that you jotted down after the candidate had left. Use different colored markers to underline comments about aspects of the candidate's skills and personality. For example, use blue for computer skills, green for relevant experience, and red for personality traits. This will give you an overall impression of each candidate's strengths and weaknesses. Rate all the candidates in this manner, and select the leading ones for further consideration.

EVALUATING CANDIDATES

Now you need to evaluate the candidates against your ideal candidate. To do this, take a blank matching sheet and divide your criteria into those that the candidate must have and those that would be a welcome bonus. Then use the matching sheets that you have prepared for each candidate in order to see which candidates possess the "must-have" qualities. Eliminate the rest. Look through the remaining list and see how many of the "bonus" qualities each candidate possesses. Weight these (optional) qualities according to their importance for the vacancy, and come up with a ranking of the most suitable candidates.

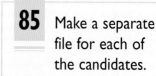

85 Make a separate file for each of the candidates.

86 Do not draw up your shortlist until all candidates have been interviewed.

CHOOSING A SHORTLIST

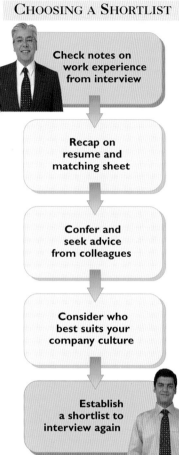

Check notes on
work experience
from interview

⬇

Recap on
resume and
matching sheet

⬇

Confer and
seek advice
from colleagues

⬇

Consider who
best suits your
company culture

⬇

Establish
a shortlist to
interview again

SHORTLISTING THE CANDIDATES

When you have ranked all the suitable candidates, create the shortlist by selecting the top five or six. Keep the shortlist short – it should consist only of those candidates whom you are going to call for a second interview; lengthening it wastes time and resources. Use the shortlist, along with a brief summary of each candidate's main relevant qualities, to show to any other interviewers or senior management, or put it on file after selection for reference when further recruits are needed.

Decide whether to check candidate references at this point or after the second interview. This may be a long process, but is worth doing early – it is very annoying to settle on your final choice only to find that they have a poor track record. Always ask the candidates before you contact their references; some may be current employers, and contact could compromise the candidate's job.

87 Never compromise requirements if nobody is suitable.

READVERTISING AND ALTERING STANDARDS

If none of the applicants are suitable for a job, you have two options. One is to advertise again – perhaps in a different place – in the hope that you attract better candidates. Alternatively, you can alter the specifications of the job – for example, by allocating some aspects to someone else – and then look for someone qualified for this modified job.

POINTS TO REMEMBER

● There is no perfect candidate.

● If the job has a security aspect (for example, working in a bank) it is worth checking candidate references early.

● One aspect of a candidate's personality should not be allowed to carry too much weight.

● Detailed notes from the interview will ease the shortlisting process.

CALLING SUBSEQUENT INTERVIEWS

When inviting candidates for a second interview, there is little point in taking them through the same procedures and questions as on their first visit. Before you can design a different interview for them, however, decide what you want to get out of it.

 88 Offer to pay candidates' travel expenses for their second interviews.

ASSESSING YOUR PURPOSE

You may wish to recall candidates to a second interview for the following reasons:
- To introduce them to other members of the organization;
- To ask them more questions and become better acquainted with them;
- To compare them once again with other shortlisted candidates to determine a "winner";
- To put them through a different set of tests.

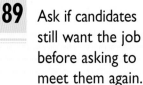 **89** Ask if candidates still want the job before asking to meet them again.

RECALLING CANDIDATES

When you phone candidates to ask them back for another interview, make sure that they are still interested in the position. Remember to be discreet when you recall them and be sensitive to what is potentially an awkward situation at their current workplace. Organizing interview times may be more difficult the second time around because you will probably need to involve more people – either other people in the hiring process, or colleagues, or top management. In addition, you may also want to arrange the interview times close together so it is easy to compare the remaining candidates while they are fresh in your mind.

▲ BEHAVING DISCREETLY
When calling candidates to invite them for a further interview, always make sure that they are able to talk freely.

DECIDING WHICH AREAS TO INVESTIGATE FURTHER

Although there may be specific areas that you feel were insufficiently covered in the first interview, you should use the second interview for testing the candidate against the others on the shortlist. Delve more deeply into each individual's strengths and weaknesses, then compare them with those of the others. It can be appropriate here to look at a candidate's future plans and ambitions. How suitable would he or she be for promotion?

If you are selecting others to assist you in the interview, choose colleagues who can offer specific skills. A director, for example, will have extensive experience in assessing an applicant's potential overall contribution to the company.

 90 Set up a filing system to retain the resumes of all candidates.

 91 Decide which questions each of you will ask during the interview.

CHOOSING INTERVIEWERS FOR THE SECOND ROUND

INTERVIEWERS	FACTORS TO CONSIDER
 **COLLEAGUE** A potentially close coworker of the person to be selected.	● Colleagues understand exactly what is involved in the job and therefore which particular candidate is likely to possess the skills best suited for it. ● Colleagues may need to work closely with the candidate; they should find out whether they are going to get along together.
 **PERSONNEL MANAGER** A specialist in human resources.	● The personnel department tends to have the most skilled interviewers in the organization. ● The personnel department can be objective and systematic about the selection process because it is responsible for processing gains and losses of human resources within the organization.
 **DIRECTOR** Experienced in assessment of potential new recruits.	● The presence of a director flatters a new recruit by showing that the appointment is being considered at boardroom level. ● A member of the board can bring to bear his or her wide experience and understanding of the organization's interests.

MATCHING AN APPLICANT TO A JOB

A subsequent interview may be your last chance to decide which candidate is right for the position. It is important to get the most out of all interviews so that you can compare candidates. Consider conducting a test using a real task to check their skills.

92 Remember that personal references often tend to be rather subjective.

93 Ask candidates for the best time to contact references.

HOLDING SUBSEQUENT INTERVIEWS

Remember that you are looking for someone to be effective in a specific job. It is important that you match the abilities of the candidate to the requirements of the job. If you decide to test interviewees, consider carefully which aspects of the job to test them on, and try to make the test as close to a real work task as possible.

TESTING A ▼
CANDIDATE
Use subsequent interviews to test candidates in a specific work-related area.

Interviewee demonstrates his computer literacy

Interviewer supervises a computer test that she has composed

EVALUATING CANDIDATES' SKILLS

Put the job's top 10 requirements in order from the most to the least important

Give the requirements scores from 10 down to 1

Grade the candidate's skills on a scale of 10 to 1

Add together the two grades for each requirement

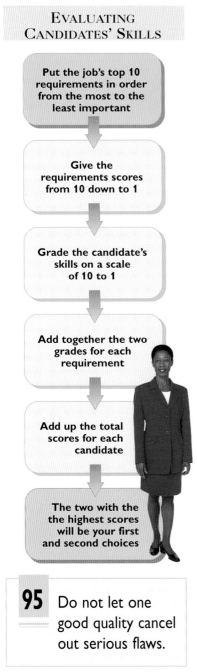

Add up the total scores for each candidate

The two with the the highest scores will be your first and second choices

95 Do not let one good quality cancel out serious flaws.

94 Ask candidates to explain any discrepancies between what they have told you and their references.

CHECKING REFERENCES

If you are checking a candidate's references at this stage, prepare a list of questions to ask the references – for example, questions about the candidate's timekeeping, and their ability to meet deadlines. First, follow up on work-related references, and make sure they are recent. Check how long the reference has known the applicant, and in what capacity. Follow up written references with verbal ones to discuss the applicant's strengths and weaknesses in greater detail. Check with the references on the candidate's interests outside work. What does the declared "charity work" actually involve? Is it a real commitment? How much time does it take up?

MAKING YOUR CHOICE

To select the best applicant for the job, use the chart on the left to make a first and second (backup) choice based on work skills. Compare the candidates' scoring on the job's requirements with your own personal and intuitive feelings about them. This will depend in part on whether you were given satisfactory responses in any areas that you felt needed more questioning. If colleagues were involved in this round of interviews, ask for their opinions and add them to your own. Your final choices should balance technical and personal qualities in the candidates. If you do not have total authority to make the final selection, present your first and second choices to the appropriate manager, then obtain his or her approval of your choice.

MAKING A FINAL OFFER

However pleased and relieved you feel at having found an ideal recruit for your vacancy, spend time attending to the details of the offer. Make the offer verbally, then follow up formally in writing requesting written confirmation of acceptance.

 96 Talk through the details of the job offer with your new recruit.

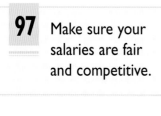 **97** Make sure your salaries are fair and competitive.

98 To avoid confusion, confirm a job offer in writing.

OFFERING A JOB VERBALLY

Begin by offering a job verbally – either on the spot at the end of the second interview or by phone. Outline the benefits package that comes with the position, and allow the candidate time to ask questions. If your verbal offer is rejected, ask if this is negotiable. If the reply is still a refusal, turn your attention to your second choice. In some cases, your chosen candidate may go back to their current employer and ask them to match your offer; in such a case you need to decide if you are willing to negotiate further with the applicant.

CONFIRMING IN WRITING

If your verbal offer is accepted, follow it up as soon as possible with written confirmation of the terms and conditions of the job. An agreement is not binding until a written offer has been accepted in writing. If you are in charge of drafting an offer letter, make sure that it includes:

● Job title, description, and working hours;
● Annual salary;
● The company benefits package;
● Any conditions that the offer is subject to, such as the completion of a medical examination;
● A date by which the prospective employee must sign and return the written job offer to accept the terms and conditions of the job.

HANDLING COUNTEROFFERS

People with skills that are in demand (in financial markets, for example) may play your offer against an offer from their present (or another) company to improve their salary. If you decide to increase your offer in response to this, establish that you will not consider doing so again, and set a deadline for a final acceptance or rejection.

NEGOTIATING A SALARY

Salary negotiations should always be left as late as possible in the interview process. Your priority is to get the best possible candidate at the lowest possible price – in that order. Prepare a strategy for presenting a salary offer, then decide how to bargain if the candidate rejects it. Check that the salary you are offering is comparable to the rest of your field. If not, modify the salary so that it is competitive, but keep the company budget in mind while doing so. Look at other ways of making the package more attractive. Can you offer more benefits instead of more money, such as a company car or complete dental care? Can you offer a salary review after a short period of employment or a non-contributory pension plan? Is there a performance-related bonus plan that the candidate can quickly become part of?

HANDLING THE RESPONSE TO YOUR LETTER

Having sent your offer letter, expect to hear from your chosen candidate within the time limit you set. In most instances, anticipate a positive reply and proceed with organizing a starting date. If, however, you receive a written rejection to your offer, turn again to your previous shortlist. Deal on an individual basis with candidates who respond with further demands; these may be negotiable. For example, if you regard a request for a higher salary instead of a company car to be acceptable, both you and your new recruit will benefit.

Short and concise letter arrives promptly

▼ WRITING QUICKLY

A new recruit will be unwilling to resign from their present job until you send the written offer letter. Do this quickly so that they can complete their notice period and begin the new job at the earliest opportunity.

99 Give the candidate a date by which to reply to your offer.

DEALING WITH UNSUCCESSFUL APPLICANTS

Always notify unsuccessful applicants as soon as possible, especially if they have been shortlisted. If they are curious to know why they have been rejected, it is helpful to give them constructive feedback that might assist them in their future job searches.

 100 Imagine yourself to be the recipient when writing a rejection letter.

POINTS TO REMEMBER

- Business environments change, and yesterday's reject may be tomorrow's hot property.

- Rejected candidates may be suitable to fill vacancies elsewhere in the organization.

- A rejected candidate should be informed if you intend to pass his or her details on to another person or department.

- An applicant's details are confidential even after they have been rejected.

- Everyone is rejected at some time in their lives, but you should be as kind and positive as possible when breaking news of a rejection.

WRITING A ▶ REJECTION LETTER
Failure to send a polite reply as quickly as possible to unsuccessful candidates creates the impression of an ill-mannered and badly managed organization.

REJECTING IN WRITING

It is a matter of courtesy to write to every rejected candidate, letting them know of your decision. Be polite and succinct, thanking each candidate for their interest in the post, and explaining, in general terms, why they were unsuccessful in the application. At this late stage in the recruitment process, the numbers of candidates concerned will not be vast, so try to write individual letters.

Dear Ms. Dartford

Thank you for attending the interview on January 18th for the position of overseas sales manager with TRC.

I regret that in this instance we are unable to offer you the job. We had a very strong response to our advertisement, with a number of first-class applicants for the position, including yourself. While we appreciate your linguistic skills, we feel that your lack of detailed technical knowledge of engineering would be a drawback.

With your permission, we will keep your details on our files for future reference.

Yours sincerely
Doris Fisher
Manager, Human Resources

Thank candidates for attending interviews

Be straightforward in your wording of rejection

Give a valid reason for rejection

Ask if you can keep candidate details on file

KEEPING DETAILS ON FILE

After checking that they are agreeable, keep the details of all relevant job applicants on file. If you have already started a database of such applicants, update it in the light of your interviews. If appropriate, make your colleagues aware of any particularly promising candidates that you have rejected for a post – this may be a cost-effective way of filling another vacancy, since it cuts down on further advertising costs.

101 Show new recruits around your office and introduce them to everybody.

CULTURAL DIFFERENCES

It is common practice in North America to reject unsuccessful applicants in a fairly blunt and straightforward manner, since failure is considered a step to success. In Japan, however, the tone and phrasing of a rejection is very subtle to avoid offending the disappointed candidate.

RESPONDING TO QUERIES

If you receive calls from rejected candidates who would like to know why you have turned them down, always give a reason. Do not be evasive or put them off by saying you will call them back. Deal with them honestly, there and then, since any information and advice that you can give about their performance may be of use to them in their next interview. If the first impression you had of someone was that they looked unkempt, pass that message on, but couch it in polite terms: "Your appearance could benefit from a little attention," is less offensive than "You were a mess."

LETTING DOWN REJECTED CANDIDATES LIGHTLY

Always be polite and constructive when rejecting candidates, either verbally or by letter. Introduce a reassuring phrase or two to soften the blow, but never make feeble excuses.

Your lack of proficiency in German is a drawback, since we expect Germany to become an important market.

We feel that the job needs more line-management experience than you are yet able to bring to it.

You have considerable talents; we would like to keep in touch in case something else comes up.

We have offered the job to a person with a perfect match of skills. You were the next contender.

ASSESSING YOUR ABILITY

P ractice is the most productive way of developing and improving your interviewing technique. Chart your progress and performance as an interviewer by responding to the following statements, then mark the options closest to your experience. Be as honest as you can: if your answer is "never," mark Option 1; if it is "always," mark Option 4; and so on. Add your scores together, then refer to the Analysis to see how you scored. Use your answers to identify the areas that need most improvement.

OPTIONS

1 Never

2 Occasionally

3 Frequently

4 Always

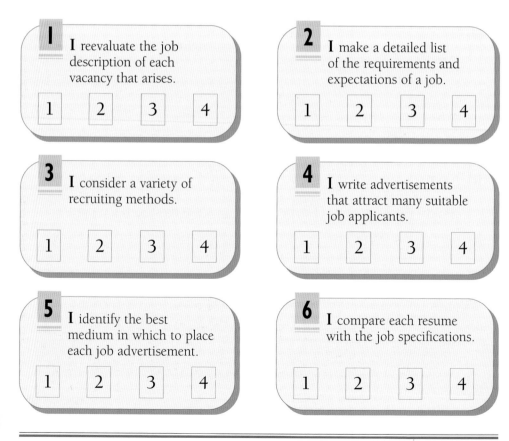

1 I reevaluate the job description of each vacancy that arises.

1   2   3   4

2 I make a detailed list of the requirements and expectations of a job.

1   2   3   4

3 I consider a variety of recruiting methods.

1   2   3   4

4 I write advertisements that attract many suitable job applicants.

1   2   3   4

5 I identify the best medium in which to place each job advertisement.

1   2   3   4

6 I compare each resume with the job specifications.

1   2   3   4

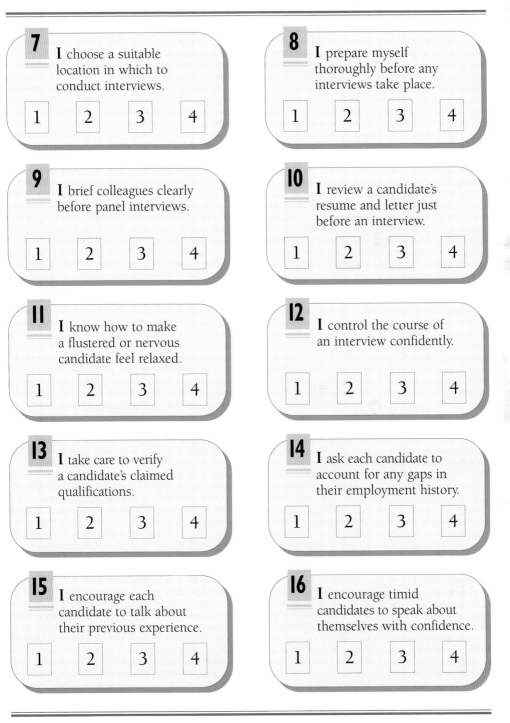

7 I choose a suitable location in which to conduct interviews.

1　2　3　4

8 I prepare myself thoroughly before any interviews take place.

1　2　3　4

9 I brief colleagues clearly before panel interviews.

1　2　3　4

10 I review a candidate's resume and letter just before an interview.

1　2　3　4

11 I know how to make a flustered or nervous candidate feel relaxed.

1　2　3　4

12 I control the course of an interview confidently.

1　2　3　4

13 I take care to verify a candidate's claimed qualifications.

1　2　3　4

14 I ask each candidate to account for any gaps in their employment history.

1　2　3　4

15 I encourage each candidate to talk about their previous experience.

1　2　3　4

16 I encourage timid candidates to speak about themselves with confidence.

1　2　3　4

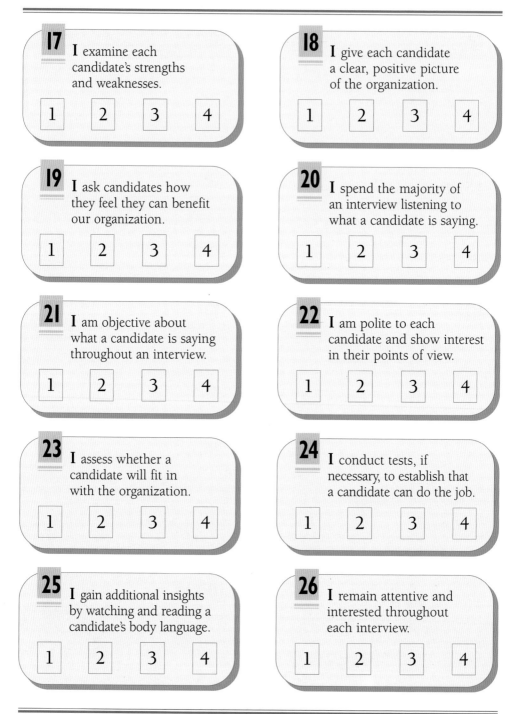

17 I examine each candidate's strengths and weaknesses.

1   2   3   4

18 I give each candidate a clear, positive picture of the organization.

1   2   3   4

19 I ask candidates how they feel they can benefit our organization.

1   2   3   4

20 I spend the majority of an interview listening to what a candidate is saying.

1   2   3   4

21 I am objective about what a candidate is saying throughout an interview.

1   2   3   4

22 I am polite to each candidate and show interest in their points of view.

1   2   3   4

23 I assess whether a candidate will fit in with the organization.

1   2   3   4

24 I conduct tests, if necessary, to establish that a candidate can do the job.

1   2   3   4

25 I gain additional insights by watching and reading a candidate's body language.

1   2   3   4

26 I remain attentive and interested throughout each interview.

1   2   3   4

27 I note down my first impressions immediately after each interview.

| 1 | 2 | 3 | 4 |

28 I ask for a second opinion on all shortlisted candidates.

| 1 | 2 | 3 | 4 |

29 I establish how soon a candidate can join the organization.

| 1 | 2 | 3 | 4 |

30 I conduct negotiations over the salary and benefits package smoothly.

| 1 | 2 | 3 | 4 |

31 I send rejection letters promptly to all unsuccessful applicants.

| 1 | 2 | 3 | 4 |

32 I ensure confidentiality at all times.

| 1 | 2 | 3 | 4 |

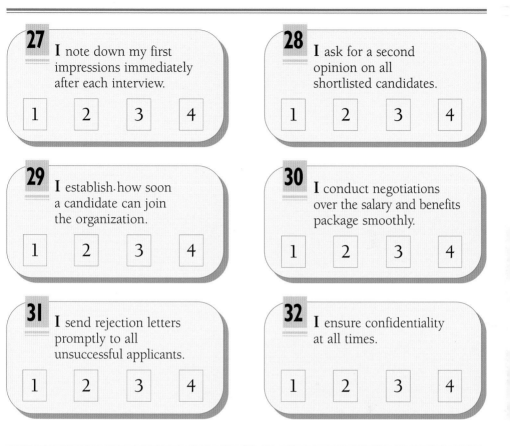

ANALYSIS

Now that you have completed the self-assessment, add up your total score and check your performance by reading the corresponding evaluation. Whatever level of success you have achieved during the interviews, it is important to remember that there is always room for improvement. Identify your weakest areas, then refer to the chapters in this section where you will find practical advice and tips to help you establish and hone your interviewing skills.

32–64: Your skills need improving. Learn from your mistakes and take time to prepare well for every interview that you hold.
65–95: Your interviewing skills are fairly sound, but certain areas still need improvement.
96–128: You have a successful interviewing technique. Continue to look for ways to develop your interviewing style.

MANAGING CHANGE

INTRODUCTION

Change is the single most important element of successful business management today. To remain competitive in increasingly aggressive markets, organizations (and individuals in them) have to adopt a positive attitude to change. Ignoring or trivializing a changing trend can be costly, so this section teaches managers how to be one step ahead of rivals, set trends, and lead change in order to survive. Techniques for planning and implementing change, for example, are explained clearly, to help you maximize potential gain. Practical advice is given on how to achieve the best from staff by using their strengths and involving them at all stages, while 101 tips scattered throughout the section give further vital information. Finally, a self-assessment exercise allows you to evaluate and improve your change-management skills.

UNDERSTANDING CHANGE

Understanding and managing change are the dominant themes of management today. Adapting to the ever-changing present is essential for success in the unpredictable future.

WHY CHANGE?

Change affects every aspect of life; taking a proactive approach to change is the only way to take charge of the future, either as an individual or as an organization. Approach it with an open mind, and learn to develop its positive elements.

1 Write down any changes you would like – and plan for them.

BEING OPEN TO CHANGE

For organizations, change is the way to stay competitive and to grow. For individuals, the opportunities created by change enrich careers and personal lives. You can deal with change in three ways: by resisting, following, or leading. A resister tries to stay put, which is impossible in changing situations; the majority of people and organizations who start by resisting eventually find that they have to follow, trying to catch up. If that fails, they face a competitive disadvantage. Seeking to anticipate and lead change is thus, paradoxically, safer as well as more adventurous.

2 If you find you are resisting change, ask yourself why.

SEEING THE EFFECTS

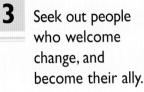

3 Seek out people who welcome change, and become their ally.

Positive aspects of change may be less obvious at first than negative ones. New ventures, expansion, promotions, and booms often bring challenges before delivering gains. Cases such as departmental or factory closings, dismissals, bankruptcies, or deterioration in markets bring difficulties and very few immediate benefits. But, however it appears, approach change positively as potential opportunity. Use it as a stimulus to encourage new ideas and harness enthusiasm for further progress.

CHANGING NATURALLY

People live with change constantly; in a lifetime, everyone goes through personal transformation from infancy to adolescence, young adulthood, middle age, and finally old age. A career path may lead from subordinate to junior management, middle management, and eventually board level or consultancy. Organizations also mature and evolve, with major changes on many levels in policy and practice. For personal satisfaction and career progress, increase your capacity to change.

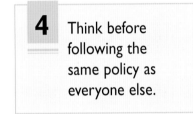

4 Think before following the same policy as everyone else.

▲ **OLD ASSEMBLY LINE**
Mass production revolutionized manufacturing. While still labor intensive, manual work became relatively quick, clean, and less physically demanding, enabling women to work in previously male-dominated areas.

▲ **MODERN ASSEMBLY LINE**
Modern production lines bear only the slightest resemblance to older versions. Technological breakthroughs and economies of scale have radically reduced the ratio of workers to machines.

Understanding the Causes of Change

To deal effectively with increasing rates of change, you need to understand the underlying causes. Specific changes in an organization's internal structure and external markets often derive from wider changes in society, economics, or technology.

> **5** Respond positively to uncertainty rather than avoiding change.

> **6** Cultivate curiosity; try to become the best-informed person you know.

CHANGING MODELS ▼
Office equipment has developed rapidly since the invention of the typewriter. Today's personal computers can perform tasks that were unimaginable 100 years ago.

Social Causes

General trends in society, politics, and demography touch everyone. In recent years these have resulted in upsurges in the youth and consumer markets, a shift in emphasis from community to a more individual-centered society, and aging populations. Businesses are affected by such trends, which influence consumer demand and other economic patterns. Managers need an informed awareness of changes and their reasons. Reading material on social and political issues, and drawing conclusions from what you read and observe, will help you to deal with changing trends and even predict them.

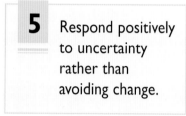

"Golfball" typing head and electric motor were revolutionary

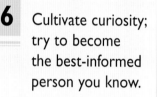

Keys operated type bars manually

MANUAL TYPEWRITER

ELECTRIC TYPEWRITER

ECONOMIC CAUSES

The tides of economics change quite slowly, but with inexorable power. Within their relatively stable trends, however, markets and monetary flows can fluctuate sharply, competitive ways can alter dramatically, and technology and innovation can fracture established patterns. This compels organizations to be ready to adjust to sudden change on any level. But it is also prudent for managers to have basic contingency plans and funds to call on during periods of uncertainty.

7 Master and use new information technology – do not hide from it.

TECHNOLOGICAL CAUSES

At accelerating speed, the revolution in information technology (IT) is having a profound impact on methods of management, manufacturing, service, purchasing, and selling. IT is part of a drive to accomplish current tasks more efficiently (for instance, to better control inventory) and to achieve new purposes (such as space travel). Managers need the former for competitive survival and the latter for competitive success. Try to maintain an informed openness to technological developments, since new technologies that appear irrelevant at first may be tomorrow's essentials.

8 Bear in mind that technology is changing more and more quickly.

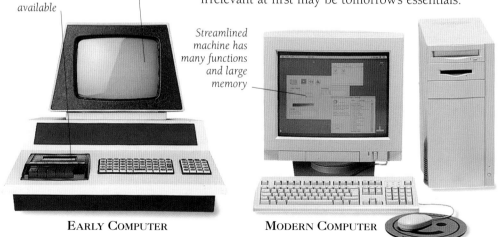

Increased range of functions became available

Screen and processor were added to keyboard

Streamlined machine has many functions and large memory

EARLY COMPUTER   MODERN COMPUTER

701

RECOGNIZING SOURCES OF CHANGE

Change can come from many directions: from superiors or subordinates within an organization, from personal initiative, and from outside. Make sure that you are aware of all the possible sources, and be open to change, wherever it comes from.

9 Welcome change initiatives from all sources.

CHANGING FROM WITHIN

Most changes that occur in an organization are instigated, at least in part, from within. The majority of these changes are minor: for example, requiring a new report or modifying a contract. However, most sizable changes, such as restructuring and acquisitions, are generated from the topmost level, and generally unexpected by subordinate staff. As a manager, you initiate changes yourself, but are also often required to act as a link between different levels of staff. Ensure that the system does not prevent the ideas of subordinates from being heard.

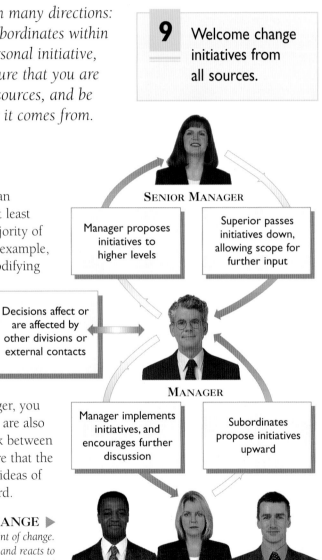

SENIOR MANAGER

Manager proposes initiatives to higher levels

Superior passes initiatives down, allowing scope for further input

Decisions affect or are affected by other divisions or external contacts

MANAGER

Manager implements initiatives, and encourages further discussion

Subordinates propose initiatives upward

SUBORDINATES

FACILITATING CHANGE ▶
The manager is the focal point of change. He receives suggestions and reacts to initiatives from above and below, and works proactively in both directions.

RESPONDING TO RIVALS

The skill of managers is revealed by their response to external change. If a rival manufacturer launches a new product or cuts costs, a passive manager, rather than alter established working practices, ignores the change or denies its significance. A strong manager, on the contrary, seizes the chance to reexamine the market or production processes to better the rival's actions. Better still, proactive managers anticipate competitors and act to instigate winning changes themselves.

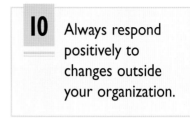

10 Always respond positively to changes outside your organization.

RESPONDING TO CONTEXTS

An organization's markets affect its changes. In fast-moving fields, managers are accustomed to instigating change and are more likely to restructure internally at frequent intervals and be open to experimental practices. The ownership of the organization also influences attitudes to change; in a publicly held company, you may come under pressure from investors to change. However, a private company may allow you to make a risky but brilliant experimental change.

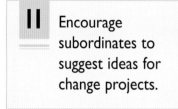

11 Encourage subordinates to suggest ideas for change projects.

LOOKING AT PERSONALITY

Your character affects your propensity to change. A passive, shy, and cautious person is unlikely to become an enthusiastic promoter of change. This is a natural role for a proactive, self-confident risk taker. But change demands followers as well as leaders. Try to discover which personality type best describes each staff member, and use this information to obtain optimum results from your team. Once momentum has been established, each individual can make a contribution in their own way. This becomes evident in crises, when everybody works to the best of their ability to achieve radical change in the interests of survival.

QUESTIONS TO ASK YOURSELF

Q Over the last 12 months, what significant changes have I personally made?

Q Do I try to anticipate external changes and act on my findings?

Q Have I contributed to any internal change programs?

Q Do I listen to ideas for change coming from below?

Q Do I react positively to demands for change?

CATEGORIZING TYPES OF CHANGE

Change divides broadly into gradual and radical forms. Within these, a wide variety of types and combinations occur. Understanding the type you are dealing with will help you to approach change effectively and to interpret others' response to it.

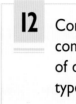 **12** Consider the combined effects of different types of change.

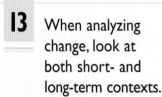 **13** When analyzing change, look at both short- and long-term contexts.

ANALYZING CHANGE

Both gradual and radical change may be either reactive or proactive, according to whether you make the change voluntarily or in response to the pressure of other developments. In practice, change often combines reactive and proactive elements. For instance, a crisis triggers radical reactive change, but you have to decide proactively on the direction of the change in order to maximize the organization's long-term success.

GRADUAL CHANGE

A gradual change is a change that occurs slowly over a prolonged period, at a steady rate or with minor fluctuations in intensity. It can involve many people or just a few, but is most effective as an unending organization-wide program to improve quality of products and processes, reduce costs, and raise productivity. Even small improvements can make powerful savings. Radical change may occur at the same time, either hand in hand with gradual change or independently.

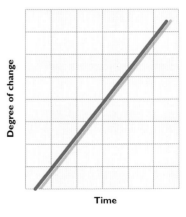

GRADUAL CHANGE ▶
Company-wide changes are implemented at a steady rate over a prolonged period of time.

Degree of change

Time

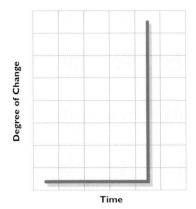

RADICAL CHANGE

A radical change is a sudden, dramatic change with marked effects – for example, reversing company strategy to tap a new market. The change may be commercial or structural, although the two tend to go together; it is often, but not always, large scale. Just as a big, risky stock-market investment has both more to gain and more to lose than a small, cautious one, so successful organizations stand to gain most from radical change. Yet the fact that an organization has been successful up to now may make it hard for people to accept a radical change. Before making radical changes of any kind, plan thoroughly, thinking through the options in detail to minimize risks.

▲ RADICAL CHANGE
After a relatively stable, even stagnant period, one or more major changes are introduced at a single stroke.

CRISIS MANAGEMENT

Managing a crisis inevitably means making radical changes to avert catastrophe. A change is best led by one person or a small group who can make decisions and act rapidly after a quick analysis of critical needs. Nothing is sacrosanct. Closing a treasured head office, for instance, will save money and symbolize change. Full communication with everybody is often a big change. So is the urgency with which a crisis program is pushed through.

14 Learn from crises to prevent them from recurring.

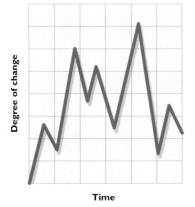

◀ CRISES
In the absence of a comprehensive plan, change shows a roller-coaster pattern. Dramatic action in response to a crisis is followed by a marked fall-off, until the next crisis is triggered.

CULTURAL DIFFERENCES

Japan industrialized extremely quickly; continual, proactive change is part of Japanese culture. Continental Europeans are traditionally reactive, but are starting to instigate change. The British, once conservative, were converted to proactive change by national crises. Americans became more proactive toward change in the 1990s, thanks partly to the microelectronics industry.

CHANGING WITH GROWTH

Growth is change: as an organization expands, change is inevitable. The adjustment may be a gradual process, a series of radical jumps, or most often a combination of the two. Some changes are natural and relatively easy. As people learn new skills, for example, their performance naturally improves with repetition. Other changes may be much more difficult. For instance, as a small business expands, it typically grows beyond the owner's existing management ability. Some owners can accomplish the transformation from proprietor to professional manager successfully, but many do not. All businesses have their limits to growth, which cannot be transcended without considerable change. Plan any growth carefully, keeping it to levels you can cope with. If you do not, the organization – be it large or small – will sooner or later crack under the strain.

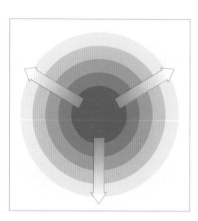

▲ CHANGE THROUGH EXPANSION

As an organization grows, jobs tend to expand in scope as well as number. This means that many people have to adjust to more complex management structures.

CHANGING TO WIN

Many changes in business, both gradual and radical, are driven by a desire to gain advantage and beat the competition. Some advantages – more resources, more customers, and often lower costs – come with growth. But other factors may also help provide a winning edge: technology, service, distribution, productivity, marketing, and financing. They may yield lower costs and prices, too. Any function can hold the key, if you dare to be different. If everyone in your industry is stuck in the same pattern, search for changes that will be welcomed by customers and will enable you to stand out. Prepare for times when only radical change can meet major market or other trends; anticipate and overcome limits to growth; be willing to change anything and everything to enhance your competitive prowess.

QUESTIONS TO ASK YOURSELF

Q What changes would I hope to see in a year's time?

Q What changes have been introduced in the last year, and how successful have they been?

Q Am I keeping up with developments in the market, the industry, and technology?

Q Do I encourage staff to generate ideas for change?

Q What radical changes would make the most difference to this organization?

Q Am I learning continuously – and ensuring that other people do the same?

15 Aim to equal or surpass the best examples you find.

16 Be different and better than the competition if you want to be the winner.

CHANGING INTRINSICALLY

Learning to change may, in many cases, constitute a major change in itself. One of the best ways to establish a new, adaptable way of thinking and working is to develop a "learning organization." This is an organization in which change-oriented thinking becomes a habit for everybody, and so change – gradual and at times radical as well – is always under way, with all processes and systems intrinsically subject to constant review. This kind of approach facilitates the development of the organization and ensures that it is well prepared for crisis management in cases of emergency. For major changes (especially fundamental changes in ways of thinking) to be effective, however, they must extend to everyone and everything. All too often, enormous change is made in parts of an organization, but because other areas are not involved, and have not changed, success is limited.

COMBINING CHANGES

In practice, most change involves a combination of change types, or progression from one sort to another. A process may be largely reactive, as when initial radical response to a crisis gives way to a gradual follow-up program. Or the whole project may be proactive and systematic, as in Total Quality Management (TQM) programs. These introduce various types of needed change simultaneously, covering systems, processes, people, and management. To ensure that change is lasting and effective, there must be practical improvement of operations and at the same time a change in ways of thinking among both managers and staff. This is a challenge for any organization. The task is even more complex because priorities alter with circumstances; reassessing the need for change is a key to changing successfully.

POINTS TO REMEMBER

● Limits to growth must be recognized; growth should not be forced beyond them.

● Changes that give clear competitive advantage are particularly desirable.

● Changes made in isolation will often have disappointing results.

● Valuable changes in thinking by managers and staff will be revealed by changes in behavior.

● In reviewing internal processes and performance, a sense of discontent may be put to constructive use.

● All changes should bring direct or indirect benefits to customers and employees.

Planning Change

Successful change programs always involve
planning – for both the short and the long term.
The clearer the objectives, the better the plan.

Focusing on Goals

*If managers do not know where they are
going, they cannot change to get there.
If they do not know where they are, they
cannot start on the right road. Establish
these start and finish points as a first step
in identifying where changes are needed.*

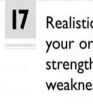

17 Realistically assess
your organization's
strengths and
weaknesses.

18 Keep your vision
statements to one
or two short
sentences.

Assessing Objectives

Most businesses, like most people, have unclear
ambitions or none at all. Forming and clarifying
objectives, either as an organization or as an
individual, can have powerful results – many
companies have turned their fortunes around
merely by focusing their corporate aims. Your
goals should be high but realistic, with the
emphasis on "high;" even the most apparently
far-fetched dreams can sometimes be realized.
Express your dreams in words, then convert those
words into facts and figures, and you will have a
sound basis for planning how to achieve them.

PLANNING CHANGE

EXPRESSING PRINCIPLES

Ambitions expressed in words are known as "visions" – for example, the desire to be the market leader in personal financial services. Visions break down into "missions," such as aiming for a certain ranking in life insurance. Make sure that visions and missions are consistent with long-term "values," the principles on which an organization bases its decisions and actions. Keep these long-term values practical, and make visions, missions, and values as simple and concise as possible, avoiding high-flown language. Being clear about these aims will help to identify changes needed.

IDENTIFYING GAPS

A strategic gap often looms not only between where you are now and where you want to be, but also between your present capabilities and those that your ambitions require. Measure present states ruthlessly; assessing the present is one area in which near-total objectivity and certainty are possible. Then use your judgment to relate the present to your desired ends, working back from future to present. Plotting change in this way, as a means to a predetermined end, is often highly effective, and will help you to measure progress.

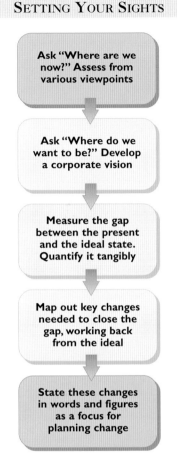

SETTING YOUR SIGHTS

Ask "Where are we now?" Assess from various viewpoints

Ask "Where do we want to be?" Develop a corporate vision

Measure the gap between the present and the ideal state. Quantify it tangibly

Map out key changes needed to close the gap, working back from the ideal

State these changes in words and figures as a focus for planning change

19 Change corporate culture through individuals, not vice versa.

ASSESSING CULTURE

Understanding corporate culture is crucial when planning for change. An organization's long-term aims can be achieved only if staff are in sympathy with them and with each other. Study the corporate culture to see how best to introduce changes, as well as how to encourage personal values to align with organizational ones and develop people's openness to change. Changing corporate culture is notoriously difficult, but positive, lasting change in culture should follow from other changes.

709

IDENTIFYING THE DEMAND FOR CHANGE

Success hinges on pleasing customers; dissatisfied customers will find other suppliers. Unhappy employees – effectively internal "customers" – work poorly or leave. Use surveys to monitor requirements in both groups, then plan changes to satisfy them.

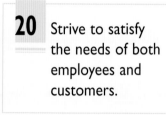

20 Strive to satisfy the needs of both employees and customers.

21 Cherish customers who complain: they tell you what to change.

USING DISSATISFACTION

Make the most of feedback when planning change. Customers are always right: if they believe your product to be inferior, that belief is valid, even if tests prove it false. The same is true of employees, your internal customers. In both cases, use surveys (via questionnaires, focus groups, or interviews) to explore perceptions – dissatisfied people do not always voice their complaints unasked.

ASKING CUSTOMERS

Each product or service has many aspects. Use surveys to find out what matters most to the customers – the results will almost certainly contradict assumptions you might have made.

When carrying out a survey, extend your market research to your competitors, and compare customer opinion about them with customer response to your own organization. This will show where changes are required for greatest impact on customers. Follow up with further surveys after implementing change plans.

MEASURING CUSTOMER ▼ DISSATISFACTION

This pie chart is based on surveys showing the different problems that contributed to customers' dissatisfaction with a telephone service. Bad sales service and faulty equipment accounted for most customer dissatisfaction, so these areas became the main focus of change.

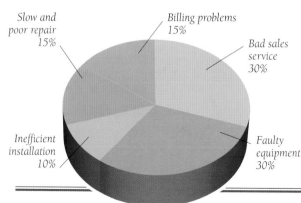

Slow and poor repair 15%

Billing problems 15%

Bad sales service 30%

Inefficient installation 10%

Faulty equipment 30%

ASSESSING QUALITY

Customer requirements for quality are a good basis for starting to plan change. Total Quality Management (TQM) looks at how every element of a business process contributes to the whole. Apply this approach to help identify ways to satisfy customers. At the same time, use quality control methods to run internal checks (such as number of defects per million parts). Remember, there is no point in improving quality on unwanted products, or in making desired products inefficiently.

22 Remember that quality of product depends on quality of process.

ASKING EMPLOYEES

Organizations depend for success on their employees. You need a high level of employee satisfaction if the firm is to perform at its best – dissatisfied employees will soon leave or, worse, perform badly. Conduct surveys, both qualitative and quantitative, among employees as you do among customers, and involve employees in identifying any need for change. This will raise morale and help you improve quality of processes.

23 Use objective measures of customer response.

CONDUCTING A SURVEY

To get the most from a survey – by mail, in person, or by phone – plan thoroughly or use a professional consultant.

● Keep questionnaires short and simple.
● Avoid questions that influence answers.
● Avoid vague measures ("very satisfied") and long scales ("1 to 10").
● Be definite ("Would you use this?"), with few options ("yes," "maybe," "no").
● Make sure you ask appropriate people.
● Be sure that the sample and response rate produce a statistically valid result.

▲ SURVEYING EFFECTIVELY
Prepare questions thoroughly before beginning a survey, and have all necessary equipment at hand. Inefficiency is off-putting for interviewees.

SELECTING ESSENTIAL CHANGES

*C*hange programs must be fully comprehensive if they are to last. But be careful not to overwhelm people with too many specific changes; identify the few significant priority areas in which change will have most impact, and focus on these.

24 Prioritize change in key areas, then focus attention more widely.

POINTS TO REMEMBER

- Change in one area should be supported by change in others.
- The strategic reasons for change should be widely publicized.
- Only change that is people-based will work in the long term.
- Everyone involved in the change program should be consulted.
- Planned changes should not be made all at once.
- Change needs fall into high, medium, and low priorities.

CHOOSING KEY AREAS

Pareto's law holds that roughly 20 percent of activities account for 80 percent of problems: aim to identify and concentrate on these key areas to maximize the impact of change. You can determine your starting point by addressing urgent needs, but do not forget other areas when assessing the most significant aspects, and do not allow the principle "if it ain't broke, don't fix it" to inhibit initiatives; processes that appear to work well may in fact be open to improvement. Bear in mind, too, that an organization's activities are all interdependent, and should not be approached in isolation.

JUSTIFYING CHANGES

Support any proposed changes by making a business case for them. You are not changing for change's sake, but for a purpose. Analyze every aspect to show why and where change is required to reach objectives, the areas in which change is likely to have greatest impact, and what that impact is likely to be. Having fully justified the priorities of your proposals, you can then decide also to make changes in other areas, provided sufficient resources and time are available.

25 Be clear about the purpose of any change you plan to make.

AVOIDING OVERLOAD

One important reason for selecting essential changes is that if you introduce too many new initiatives in close succession, staff may suffer from overload. "Initiative fatigue" reveals itself rapidly in falling performance, high stress levels, low morale, and diminishing return on initiatives. Reversing an initiative, once launched, is extremely difficult, so keep careful control over the number and intensity of planned changes, and consult staff fully.

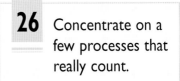

26 Concentrate on a few processes that really count.

▼ TOO MUCH CHANGE
A few changes can make all the difference between a boring work environment and a stimulating one. Too many, however, may leave the workforce overwhelmed.

BORED   STIMULATED   OVERWHELMED

Increasing amount of change

27 Plan a fluid, integrated change program.

MAINTAINING CONTINUITY

Ideally, aim to create an overall program for change, continually renewed, within which many projects move forward simultaneously. It is bad change management to halt one initiative and begin another before the first has had a chance to work; this type of "flavor of the month" approach breeds cynicism and apathy. Prepare well for change, with full consultation, so that people know what will happen and can plan their workload.

CASE STUDY
Henry took over a lagging business and decided on total change. He dropped many products and services, introduced new ones, moved from selling through wholesalers to selling direct to retailers, reorganized sales and marketing into a single team, and replaced half the top management. A major cultural change program, run by consultants, replaced the organization's former hierarchical set-up with a team-centered approach.
Workshops were arranged to facilitate the changes, but the training program was interrupted by severe difficulties with the new products, deliveries, and customers. Sales dropped sharply, further demoralizing the staff, who were already dismayed by uncertainty and rapidly shifting priorities.
Henry was removed, but too late to save the business.

◀ CREATING CHAOS
An old rule states that more than one objective is no objective. To avoid chaos, a change program must focus on a single overriding target, selecting and structuring other changes around it.

EVALUATING COMPLEXITY

To plan and manage change effectively, you need to make realistic estimates of its complexity and whom it will affect directly and indirectly. You then need to break down, quantify, and organize the various components clearly and efficiently.

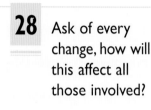

28 Ask of every change, how will this affect all those involved?

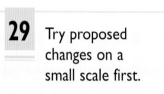

29 Try proposed changes on a small scale first.

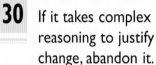

30 If it takes complex reasoning to justify change, abandon it.

BREAKING DOWN CHANGE

Analyzing the complexity of any program requires a logical approach to reduce it to simple elements. List all the areas that will need to be tackled to complete a major change, and group related areas together into projects. Break these projects down into manageable tasks, ready for allocation to different teams. This should give you an idea of the complexity of the change. You may find it valuable to test your methods of analysis and organization on a smaller task before embarking on the main change program itself.

ASSESSING BREADTH

To appreciate the complexity of a planned change, you need to know who will be affected by it. At one extreme, only one person or a small group will be affected. At the other extreme, the whole organization will be involved, and its investors, suppliers, and (very importantly) customers may need to be informed, too. Always bear all three groups in mind when planning a change. Look carefully at each change planned, and list everyone affected. Think whether or not outsiders are involved, and remember that a wide circle of employees and departments must be considered. The more people the change affects, the more complex the change program will be.

POINTS TO REMEMBER

- Everything and everyone that needs to change should be noted.
- Individual responsibilities must be made crystal clear.
- Teams are the prime engines of almost every change.
- Communication with all interested groups is top priority.
- The case for change must be expressed in a short, persuasive, well-supported document.
- The acronym KISS – Keep It Simple, Stupid – represents invaluable advice.

DOVETAILING TASKS

All tasks in a change project need to fit into a master plan in which their schedules are co-ordinated. One way to assess a project is to plot the "critical path" for its completion; work out the order of interdependent tasks to set a framework around which other tasks can fit. Allocate tasks to different teams or individuals so that they can be worked on concurrently, saving time.

▼ **CRITICAL PATH ANALYSIS**
The critical path follows the longest chain of dependent processes – those that can be started only when previous stages are complete: in this case, tasks A1–A5. This path allows leeway in the timing of other tasks (B and C), which take less time to complete but which have to be finished by a certain point in the main path for the project to continue successfully. Missing a deadline can cause ripple effects that disrupt the progress of the critical path tasks.

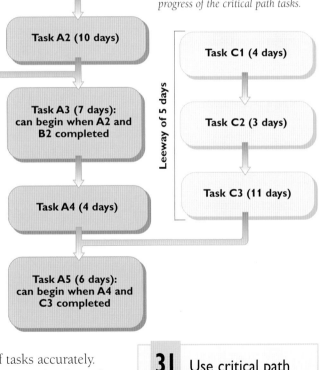

Task B1 (4 days)

Task A1 (2 days)

Leeway of 3 days

Task B2 (5 days)

Task A2 (10 days)

Task C1 (4 days)

QUANTIFYING TASKS

Evaluating a planned change is much easier if you can measure it. Try to establish quantified measures of the current position and improvement sought. Use benchmarking (objective comparison with others, probably the best-performing outsiders) or targets, or both. Make goals as concrete as possible to allow you to assess the size of tasks accurately. Draw together these measurements of tasks and the results of your analyses of tasks and people to give a complete picture of the complexity of the planned change and its components.

Task A3 (7 days): can begin when A2 and B2 completed

Leeway of 5 days

Task C2 (3 days)

Task A4 (4 days)

Task C3 (11 days)

Task A5 (6 days): can begin when A4 and C3 completed

31 Use critical path analysis to help plan tasks.

PLANNING WAYS TO INVOLVE PEOPLE

*T*hose affected by change will vary in their attitudes and needs. Effective change programs should be flexible enough to match this variety. Carefully plan whom to involve in setting change in motion, and in what ways to involve them.

32 Always get your people policies right when planning changes.

33 Use training as a deliberate tool to involve people in change.

CHOOSING A STRATEGY

Different situations require different strategies concerning how much and in what ways to involve people. Whenever possible, involve people fully in developing long-term objectives and planning for change, as well as in implementing plans. But if a situation is uncertain, avoid involving people too early, since this may cause unnecessary anxiety. In general, draw people in through education and communication, although in extreme cases you may need to resort to manipulation or coercion.

CONSIDERING RESPONSES

When selecting a strategy, bear in mind people's potential responses, and consider if you may need to overcome resistance to change. Study your list of people affected, in groups (shop floor, middle management, and so on) as well as individually. Which key people need to be involved? How may people react? Who is likely to be enthusiastic about introducing change? What worries may lead others to resist it? Will people need new skills or training? Specify positives and negatives in detail, and plan and prepare any necessary action with as much care as the change program itself.

QUESTIONS TO ASK YOURSELF

Q Have I involved everyone who should be involved?

Q Do my colleagues and I really believe that involvement is essential for successful change?

Q Has the case for change been communicated and understood?

Q Have people had the necessary training and preparation?

Q Have management layers been kept to a minumum?

DECIDING WHETHER TO INVOLVE PEOPLE

THE SITUATION

A manager is aware that working practices need revision, and can see an appropriate solution. She has to decide how best to plan and introduce the change.

THE SOLUTIONS

Whenever possible, the manager involves staff, setting up informal meetings to develop solutions and plan the changes.

If absolutely necessary in order to maintain confidentiality, the manager plans changes alone, later informing staff of decisions.

CONSULTING PEOPLE

The greater the number of people consulted, the more information will be available for developing change plans. And people involved in identifying needs and planning change will be more prepared for a challenge, willing to work hard, and convinced of management's commitment to the workforce. Change that would cause unease if imposed by managers can be introduced relatively painlessly by ensuring participation in decision-making.

DO'S AND DON'TS

✔ Do invite suggestions from everybody.

✔ Do hold frequent formal and informal meetings.

✔ Do involve teams in planning as well as implementation.

✔ Do manage people's expectations with care.

✘ Don't make offers people cannot refuse.

✘ Don't keep unnecessary secrets or tell any lies.

✘ Don't forget that change should improve business results.

✘ Don't leave anybody out in the cold.

34 Apologize and explain if people feel ill informed.

DELAYING COMMUNICATION

In highly sensitive situations (such as acquisitions and mergers), change cannot be communicated until it is a *fait accompli*. Changes forced from outside – new regulations, for instance – also do not allow involvement until after the event. In such cases, move to involve people as rapidly as possible once the news is out, and explain why you were unable to speak about it earlier.

UNITING THE GROUP

Planning for change is an opportunity to unite the whole organization, which may in turn trigger new ways of thinking and further change. For instance, a holistic Total Quality Management approach involves everybody, individually and in teams. Cooperation across functions and departments binds an organization together as a superteam, encouraging people to use a common change language and aim at common objectives.

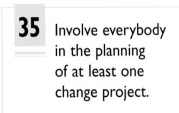

35 Involve everybody in the planning of at least one change project.

36 Give all teams some autonomy in setting their own targets.

WORKING IN TEAMS

Introducing team culture where it has not been the custom can in itself be a powerful force for change. Set up teams to help plan and implement the changes, and establish team targets linked with the overall aims of the organization so that team members can see how their role fits into the wider plan. Make change goals ambitious, specific, and measurable, and maximize potential by giving teams as much autonomy as possible at all times.

▲ **PROVIDING INPUT**
Your experience and knowledge can be invaluable to both senior management and junior staff. Be ready to give tactful advice and input as required.

MAKING A PERSONAL CONTRIBUTION

While it is important to empower and involve others, do not underestimate what you can contribute yourself. Set an example by being open to change, and be ready with advice if either superiors or staff ask for it. Never refuse to contribute, or respond to a question as if it is unimportant. Change is unsettling, but it is also an opportunity to grow; as people progress from producing ideas to actually implementing change, you are their coach, information provider, questioner, challenger, and facilitator.

USING KNOW-HOW

Internal change management often needs extra skills from outside your immediate department. If people elsewhere in your organization have experience of change, or expertise in a particular area, use their knowledge on either a permanent or a temporary basis. Look outside the company, too, even overseas. Many consultants specialize in change management and can play a major role in design and implementation – for a major fee. Shop around before picking a consultant; pay attention to references from former clients, and to the success of the change after the consultant left.

37 Commit any consultants to a clear brief and short timescale.

LEARNING ▶ FROM OTHERS
Encourage people to work together across functions at every stage of the change process. Urge them to share knowledge of equipment, technology, and people skills.

38 If you make promises about change, keep them.

39 Imitate good sports coaches – encourage people to progress.

EMPOWERING PEOPLE

Help people to use their powers and extend themselves, rather than restricting them. Start by initiating immediate practical work, for instance entrusting a team with planning how to improve performance on a key measure. The team will need "enablers" – a steering committee for reporting, monitoring, and backup. Led by this committee, the team will plan its own project and, after completion, identify further change needed, which will become the next project. Real experience of responsibility for projects is a much better means of empowerment than talk. People who achieve change through their own efforts will feel more powerful and be eager to generate more change.

CHOOSING A TIMESCALE

D*ifferent types of change demand very different timescales. As agents for change, managers have to aim for long-term goals and at the same time plan other, smaller changes that take only weeks or days to implement – especially in times of crisis.*

40 Avoid being ruled by financial years; they are purely arbitrary.

41 Aim to introduce one new idea every week.

42 Encourage people to find new ideas for quick-fix changes.

MIXING QUICK AND SLOW

Change projects can last a long time – it is said that it takes ten years to make dedication to customer service irreversible. But short-term fixes with quick results can be essential to gain momentum and sustain enthusiasm. A change strategy should include instant actions with quick, recognizable impact, midterm changes introduced during the current year that may not pay off until the next, and projects to be planned and implemented over the long term. Within each year, combine quick fixes with projects that take several months. In times of crisis, you will have to introduce more quick fixes, and you may find that an organization can absorb more radical change than you thought.

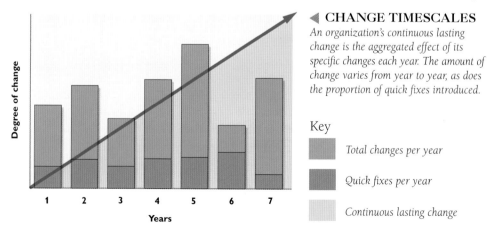

◀ **CHANGE TIMESCALES**
An organization's continuous lasting change is the aggregated effect of its specific changes each year. The amount of change varies from year to year, as does the proportion of quick fixes introduced.

Key

Total changes per year

Quick fixes per year

Continuous lasting change

Degree of change

1 2 3 4 5 6 7

Years

Allotting Time Spans

Each type of change has its appropriate time span. Complete any radical change as swiftly as you can to avoid prolonging upheaval. In a crisis, focus first on short-term solutions, then bring in changes over a longer period to deal with the causes. Continuous change, by definition, needs no set end point; similarly, take a long-term view of organizational development and change aimed at growth. Change for competitive advantage may be fast or slow.

43 To make change easier to accept, plan to introduce it in stages.

THINGS TO DO

1. Think about future change programs before the current one is completed.
2. Seek short-term fixes that sweep away grievances.
3. Set tight timetables and try to keep to them.
4. Build targets for continuous improvement into budgets.

Staggering Change

There is a limit to people's acceptance of the new, and change is usually most palatable when it is broken down into stages. If your research and analysis suggest that people may find a planned change overwhelming if implemented wholesale, stagger the stages so that each does not begin until the previous one has been completed. This is often the most practical course of action. For instance, rather than introduce a change such as redesigning and renaming a chain of stores in a single initiative, "roll out" the plan by proceeding in stages and refining the program as lessons are learned.

Making Quick Changes

To signal that change is on the way, try introducing some of the following:
- Abolish social distinctions between management and staff, such as reserved parking places or separate dining rooms;
- Set up a task force to review rules, forms, reports, and other bureaucratic items, singling out any that can be dropped;
- Shorten chains of command by making reporting structures more flexible and extending the limits within which people at all levels are allowed to take decisions;
- Replace outdated and incompatible office equipment with modern machines.

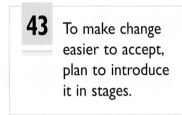

EARLY PERSONAL COMPUTER

Making an Action Plan

O n the basis of the information you have gathered, create a detailed action plan. Keep it clear and concise, making use of visual methods of planning and scheduling. Take into account the opinions of people affected, and review your plan regularly.

44 Ensure that people's views are given full consideration.

Planning Details

Detailed, step-by-step plans are essential for change projects. First plan an outline of the necessary stages, based on your research and analysis. Then fill in the details, using the list of tasks you compiled when evaluating the complexity of the change – updated if necessary. For each task, set down goals, identify a strategy for achieving them, and estimate how long it will take. Apply critical path analysis to decide the order in which tasks should be completed. Give responsibility for each task to specific people, and arrange any training they may require.

Checking Content

Ensure that your overall plan and the plan for each stage answer the following questions:
- Why is change being introduced, and what results are expected?
- What means will be used to reach those results?
- What resources will have to be committed?
- How will the plan be communicated?
- How will behavior have to change?
- Who will lead the program and its parts?
- What stages will it follow, to what timetable?
- How will the program and its progress be measured and monitored?
- What could go wrong; what happens if it does?

ENSURING VIABILITY

Involve people from other departments or disciplines as widely as possible in assessing your plan's viability. Adjust and update the plan in the light of the feedback you receive. Gather feedback on a regular basis, via meetings (large or small), focus groups, and surveys, as appropriate. This will help you and others monitor the suitability of your change plan, and allow you to make adjustments as you go along. Change plans must always be open to reevaluation and amendment.

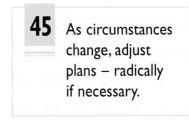

45 As circumstances change, adjust plans – radically if necessary.

46 Make sure that your action plan is properly presented.

BEING CONCISE

When creating a change plan to present to colleagues, make sure that your case for change and your action plan are concise and jargon-free. Avoid marring people's first impressions of the plan by poor presentation or misunderstandings. Describe the program and its purpose succinctly, breaking down the overall objectives into aims specific to units and to individuals. Say concisely what is expected at every stage, and explain how progress will be measured.

Manager explains, answering questions clearly and openly

Colleague takes notes of supplementary points or issues to follow up in future

◀ **EXPLAINING A PLAN**
The manager has prepared for her staff a concise document to describe and justify the project and to outline her action plan. She explains the plan clearly to maximize understanding and useful feedback.

USING PLANNING TOOLS

47 Become proficient in any planning technique you decide to use.

Certain tools are invaluable when planning change as they show complex situations with visual clarity. For example, cause-and-effect diagrams, called "fish bones" because of their shape, show causes that have led to a situation that has to change (the effect). Ask people in different sectors to suggest causes that may have contributed to this need, and analyze each to pinpoint the prime cause or causes.

FISH BONE ▶ DIAGRAM

This diagram shows a completed fish bone. To make one yourself, draw a "spine" and write the situation that needs to change – the effect – at the end. Add "bones" leading into the spine, and label each with a related sector. Write specific possible causes along the relevant bone, and invite people to add further ideas.

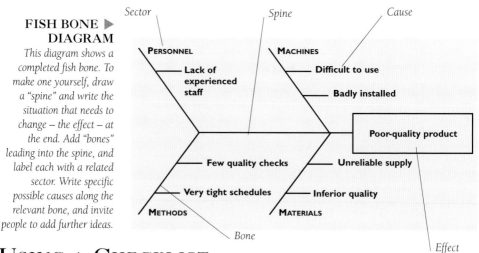

Sector • Spine • Cause

PERSONNEL
— Lack of experienced staff

MACHINES
— Difficult to use
— Badly installed

— Few quality checks

Very tight schedules

METHODS

— Unreliable supply

— Inferior quality

MATERIALS

Poor-quality product

Bone • Effect

USING A CHECKLIST

It is important to be well organized and well informed when planning change; inadequate prior information is a major cause of failed change plans. Use checklists to establish any omissions in your action plan. To create a checklist, hold team analysis sessions, and make a full list of all relevant questions raised. Check off each point on the checklist when you are satisfied that you have devised a workable solution. If any points remain unchecked, conduct further research to fill the gaps – they may prove to be vital. Consult your checklist again after making your initial action plan, and revise it regularly.

48 Go over your checklists at least once a week, updating them.

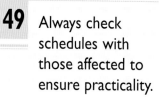

49 Always check schedules with those affected to ensure practicality.

USING A GANTT CHART ▼
This Gantt chart lists tasks on the left and people responsible for them on the right. The timescale of the project is shown across the top in weeks. Mark bars on the chart for each task from start to finish.

CONTINUING RESEARCH
The need to continue your research is often highlighted only after you have created your initial action plan. Omissions or weaknesses in the proposed change plan can become apparent when you look at the action plan in greater detail. To remedy any problems you discover, consult your original research material to find the source of the problem. Work from here, conducting fresh research where necessary, to devise solutions that fit in with the other elements of your action plan, and amend the overall plan accordingly.

Timescale shows length of project

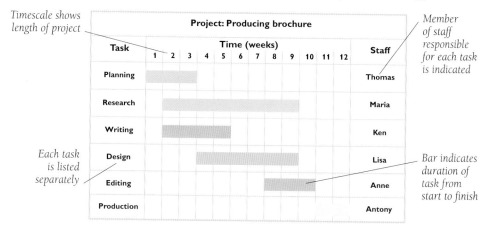

Member of staff responsible for each task is indicated

Each task is listed separately

Bar indicates duration of task from start to finish

POINTS TO REMEMBER
● Cause-and-effect must be confirmed beyond doubt.
● Established work flows can almost always be improved.
● All factors relevant to a plan should be analyzed and charted.
● Change plans need to be built into line management's day-to-day responsibility.
● Effective plans cannot be based on inadequate research.

MAKING A SCHEDULE
When you have made your action plan, schedule it. A Gantt chart is a simple bar chart that gives a visual representation of a schedule, showing what happens when, who is responsible for what, and by what date. To fill in the chart, block in the requisite time for each task over the appropriate dates – it may help to refer back to your critical path analysis. Use the chart to plan and refine schedules, check progress, and anticipate periods that are likely to be particularly busy or allow little leeway for tasks to run late or be delayed.

ANTICIPATING EFFECTS

Having developed an initial change plan, think through its consequences. Check that benefits outweigh disadvantages, assess all the necessary groundwork and requirements for implementing the plan, and prepare contingency plans as backup.

50 Look for big improvements from change projects.

51 Include the prospect of individual and team rewards and recognition in a change plan.

ASSESSING REQUIREMENTS

The greater the change, the less likely it is to fit within existing parameters. For instance, an accounting system or software program that is suitable for one store or office will probably be unable to cope with expansion to a chain of six locations. Use a checklist to assess what you will need. Write down against each change activity the additional resources and skills it will require. Check off each one when you have made preparations to meet that need – and if unexpected needs appear, move immediately to supply them.

ACTING AS LIAISON

The impact of a change program can indirectly affect people outside your immediate department or organization. Make sure that you discuss your initial plan with these people, and work with them as much as possible to assess how the projected changes will affect them, and what you can do to provide for their needs. This may mean amending your basic change plan or adding further elements to accommodate secondary needs. By considering the needs of those even remotely involved with the change program, you can minimize the chance of problems occurring later on. Removing barriers between departments in this way is, for most organizations, a massive change in itself.

QUESTIONS TO ASK YOURSELF

Q Have I ensured that everybody knows what benefits are expected from the change?

Q Does everybody fully understand and accept the case for change?

Q Can I answer everybody's vital question: "What's in it for me?"

Q Will the planned changes genuinely make people's jobs more interesting?

Q What would I want done for me if my job was at stake?

ENSURING IMPROVEMENT

If you are planning to reform specific processes, you should find that people are quite clear about what improvements on current performance to expect. However, if you are embarking on general restructuring, the consequences will often be less tangible. To double-check that the planned changes are likely to bring improvements, refer back to your original written case for change. This should list the issues, explain what would happen without the planned changes, and set out expected gains. Expand on these projections by listing the specific improvements that you anticipate from each reform. Wherever possible, quantify your aims, or link them to measures (such as customer satisfaction) that everyone recognizes as important. This will help to enlist and focus support for the reforms.

52 Never take people's support of action plans for granted.

53 Avoid the temptation to bribe people to change.

BENEFITING EVERYONE

Do not expect individuals to be altruistic. Each person will judge change according to what it promises or threatens for them personally. People rightly expect to benefit as individuals in return for the upheaval of making changes, so plan how to sell the benefits. If people can see nothing but disadvantages, you will not win their support. Make a list of everyone involved in planned changes, noting probable consequences for each person and how they are likely to perceive them. Then think about how best to present the changes and highlight the positive aspects. Emphasize any changes suggested by people themselves, as these are likely to gain support. You may plan to link some changes with higher pay or bonuses for better results, but people will feel most committed to a change project if you create a constructive working atmosphere by making it clear just how the organization's greater success will benefit everyone.

POINTS TO REMEMBER

● The likely consequences of change, inside and outside the organization, need to be considered thoroughly.

● All key managers must fully commit themselves to the change philosophy.

● Vital needs that must be supplied for a project to succeed should be identified and taken care of.

● There needs to be regular liaison between all departments and functions affected by a projected change.

● Everyone should understand the importance of treating others as allies, not enemies.

● People at all levels are fully capable of understanding the business case for change.

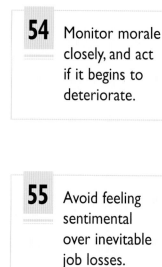

54 Monitor morale closely, and act if it begins to deteriorate.

55 Avoid feeling sentimental over inevitable job losses.

MINIMIZING NEGATIVES

Any change program will have negative effects as well as positive ones. Against your list of benefits, list perceived potential losses, and ensure that the benefits (to the organization and to the majority of individuals) are likely to outweigh them. When discussing the planned change, emphasize that gains (in areas such as customer satisfaction, more interesting jobs, and greater responsibility) will more than compensate for losses (for instance, heavier workloads). If people come to believe fully in the need for improvement at an early stage of planning, the chances are that they will welcome the change program when it is implemented, and will be able to overcome their negative reactions to any disadvantages.

ANTICIPATING ADVERSITY

Dealing with negative aspects of change is a great test of a manager's motivating skills. When there are layoffs, people's living standards, security, sense of community, and self-esteem may suffer. Those kept on may also feel vulnerable about these issues. Prepare people by communicating as fully as possible, so that the need for change is understood, and by making plans for counseling and coaching for new jobs as required. Stress that change will improve people's chances of realizing their individual potential, either by developing a current job or by moving on to a better one. Make sure the plan will deliver on that promise for those who stay. Try to provide support for those who leave.

▼ OUTPLACEMENT COUNSELING
If possible, plan for a counselor to be available to give expert guidance and support to those facing layoffs. This should help them to move on in a positive way, both mentally and financially.

PREPARING CONTINGENCY PLANS

WHAT MAY GO WRONG	HOW TO PREPARE FOR IT
COMMUNICATION Team leaders are unable or unwilling to communicate properly with employees.	Ensure that coaching and seminars are available. If these fail, be prepared to replace the people concerned with new management.
FINANCE Projected cost savings from reforms are disappointingly small or nonexistent.	Develop a backup plan for further changes that will extend and deepen savings, and set up systems for tracing the causes of shortfalls.
IMPLEMENTATION People pay lip service to change, but are hard to wean away from established practices.	Plan to remove old methods once the changes are introduced, so that there is no other option but to use the new methods.
COMMITMENT Feedback and observation suggest that enthusiasm for the changes is waning.	Set up systems for investigating the causes of the disillusionment, and be prepared to revise changes if necessary.
DELAYS The change program begins to fall significantly behind schedule.	Establish checks to detect problems, as well as systems for remedying them and catching up with schedules or rescheduling as necessary.
THIRD PARTIES The program begins to suffer from poor performance by a supplier critical to success.	Prepare for the possibility of setting up a team to study problems, and ensure that consultants are available, should they be required.
TRAINING The training program proves seriously inadequate in either quality or quantity.	Have outside help available to review training and set up new courses to remedy the situation as quickly as possible.
TIMESCALE Superiors, colleagues, and subordinates alike become impatient for results.	Be ready to bring forward projects that will yield immediate payoffs, and make sure that their progress and success are publicized.
INTERDEPARTMENTAL SUPPORT You do not receive enough support from another department – for example, IT.	Arrange for people from other functions to be available for reassignment to work on the change program as needed.
TROUBLESHOOTING Difficult, unforeseen problems arise and threaten to upset the whole plan.	Prepare everyone to treat difficulties as another challenge of change, and be ready to set up task forces to tackle them.

ANTICIPATING RESISTANCE TO CHANGE

Change will always meet with some resistance. You can, however, preempt resistance to a large extent by anticipating and understanding people's reservations. Take steps to accommodate some objections in your plan, and gather evidence to counter others.

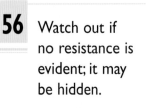

56 Watch out if no resistance is evident; it may be hidden.

ANTICIPATING REACTIONS

Try to see change from other people's points of view and anticipate their fears. Will they feel inadequately informed? Will they fear workload increases, loss of control, loss of status, or loss of jobs? People's reactions to an unexpected change tend to follow a recognized pattern. The initial response is usually negative; passive resistance is followed by active resistance and then further passive feelings, before eventual acceptance. Allow time for these reactions to take their course, and plan presentation and concessions accordingly.

POINTS TO REMEMBER

- Emotion cannot be countered by reason alone, but requires emotional reassurance.
- Once trust is lost, it is very difficult to win back.
- Criticism is not necessarily mere resistance; it may be well founded.
- Once a program is up and running – and working – resistance will dwindle.
- In overcoming resistance, prevention is better than cure.

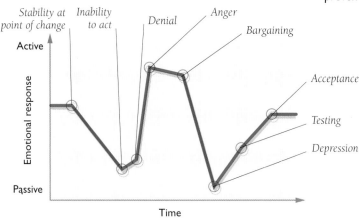

◀ **REACTING NEGATIVELY**
In response to change, people tend to go through a series of emotional reactions. Typically, passivity and denial give way to a fighting impulse, which in turn leads to depression, and finally to acceptance. The duration of this process depends on the particular situation.

BUILDING TRUST

Resistance to change takes three main forms: opposition based on misunderstanding or rational objections; fear of personal consequences; and emotional distrust. Prepare to encounter all these forms of alienation, and plan ways to deal with them. The intensity of negative response will largely depend on the existing degree of trust. So, before introducing a plan, be sure to consult and communicate with everyone as much as possible, to build up trust and prepare people for change.

57 Find allies who will help you to counter critics and conservatives.

DISCUSSING CONTENT

To back change, people need to understand its basis and feel involved in its development. You stand the best chance of forestalling potential resistance if your case for change is factual and watertight. Support your plan with facts and figures. Compare business processes accurately against competition. Be precise about market demands, customer perceptions, and competitive trends. Show why your organization cannot do significantly better without great change. Discuss plans in detail; incorporate any valuable ideas into the action plan, and ensure that people who make suggestions do not feel unimportant or ignored.

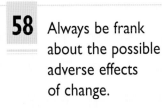

58 Always be frank about the possible adverse effects of change.

▼ SEEKING OPINIONS
When obtaining feedback, even negative opinions contribute to the planning process. Here, colleagues pay attention to one another's views, responding with interest and taking notes on major points.

Explains opinions openly and in detail

Takes notes of feedback and suggestions

Comments on colleagues' opinions

Testing and Checking Plans

Without testing and double-checking, plans will be risky and will almost certainly lead to disappointing results. Use well-designed pilot plans and experiments, together with methodical monitoring, to strengthen and improve your overall planning.

59 Test your plans with experiments in every possible context.

60 Allow for variable factors when reviewing pilot plan results.

Testing Possibilities

Pilot plans – dry runs that test a plan, fully or in part – are ideal for trying out provisional plans without causing disruption to the organization or incurring major risks or expense. You cannot know, for instance, whether manufacturing teams can successfully replace assembly lines until a team is actually operating, but you would not want to introduce teams plant-wide without being sure that they work. A pilot should produce significant payoffs. It also tests and refines planning methods and implementation procedures, and may generate enthusiasm for change by giving people a taste of the consequences.

CASE STUDY

A company's service staff, when visiting customers, usually returned to get parts for major repairs.

The change team believed that altering this system could improve efficiency by 20 percent and serve customers better.

They reviewed the whole system, finding that telephone diagnosis could handle a much larger number of cases than previously thought, thus cutting down on service visits. The change team also proposed halving head-office personnel, altering IT, and introducing measurement methods and incentives to support the changes.

The changes were piloted in three locations; return trips for parts largely vanished, and technicians doubled the number of daily calls. The 20 percent efficiency target was met.

◀ **PILOTING CHANGE**
By using three pilot plans to test new practices, the organization proved their viability and avoided costly mistakes. Proof of viability also helps to minimize skepticism and doubts about a plan.

DOUBLE-CHECKING PLANS

Regular monitoring will lead to modifications and sometimes radical departures from your initial plan. Do not take these as signs of weakness – a healthy change plan should always be adaptable and open to further development. Be sure to check, reassess, and update plans regularly, before and during implementation. In particular, watch out for unexpected side effects and aspects that you may have overlooked earlier. Remember that contingency plans will also need updating, since the likelihood of some complications arising may diminish or unexpected ones may appear.

 61 Analyze shortfalls in performance and find all the reasons for them.

62 Thank people for putting forward useful objections and criticisms.

Plannned cut of 23 percent

Actual cut of 5 percent

◀ **REFINING PLANS**
In many cases, planned cuts are over-ambitious and unrealistic. If, in your enthusiasm, you overlook a key factor, you will probably find that the cut you achieve is much less than you planned.

QUESTIONS TO ASK YOURSELF

Q Have I used pilot plans to raise enthusiasm for change?

Q Does everybody know what is going on at pilot sites?

Q Do I hold a weekly meeting (at least) to review plans?

Q Do I regularly revise contingency plans to eliminate the irrelevant and make new provisions?

Q Do I have a system for tackling major objections?

CHECKING OBJECTIONS

Use objections to help you double-check plans. When a change plan encounters major objections, analyze the reactions from groups and individuals. If you are told that part of the plan will not work, ask for evidence. If none is provided, conduct your own research to see whether the objection is valid, and on what grounds. Once you know the facts, consider whether rejection of this part of the plan would have serious effects, and whether there are alternative courses of action. Where you can find no means of overcoming the objection, develop alternative solutions if possible. Even shelved points can be useful; keep a file of overruled objections, and periodically check their validity.

IMPLEMENTING CHANGE

A change program can be only as good as its execution.
Communicate carefully, monitor progress, and prepare yourself
for possible changes during the course of the program.

COMMUNICATING CHANGE

*To get a project off to a good start,
communication is vital; you can never
communicate too much. Whether or not
people were involved in planning, draw
them in now as quickly and fully as possible,
using a range of communication methods.*

63 Remember that
honesty is not the
best policy; it is
the only policy.

TELLING PEOPLE SOON

Make sure that all aspects of a change plan
are communicated as soon as possible to
everyone affected. Anything short of total
communication will leave some people
unhappily in the dark, at least for a time,
and may create a divide between those
who know and those who do not. Letting
people learn of a major change plan from
outsiders (for instance, suppliers or the
media) is the worst possible introduction
to a program, since it will create an
atmosphere of distrust and anxiety.

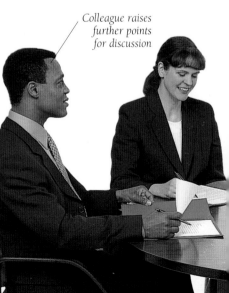

*Colleague raises
further points
for discussion*

GIVING THE FULL PICTURE

Always give people the total picture; if you tell them only what they need to know in order to fulfill their own particular role in a change plan, they may not see the wider significance of their tasks or feel commitment to the plan as a whole. If people know and understand the reasons for change, and how and why the change plan has been formed, they are likely to play their parts with greater enthusiasm and sense of direction. To reinforce this awareness, you can distribute reminders – such as credit-card-size memory aids – that summarize the objectives of a project.

64 Display concise vision statements to reinforce the change message.

DRAWING PEOPLE IN

The best way for everyone to become familiar with change is by action rather than discussion. To some extent, change projects generate their own involvement, since they require people to learn new skills and refurbish existing ones, thus drawing everyone in. But use workshops and meetings, in which managers and staff study the project and its implementation, to inform and involve people fully at every stage of the process.

65 Make training for all the centerpiece of any change program.

Manager expands on points in written plan in response to questions

Colleague follows closely, adding notes to written plan

◀ **BRIEFING PEOPLE**
When communicating change plans to other people, combine written material with verbal explanations, filling in details as required. Hold regular meetings, and encourage others to offer ideas and get involved in the change project.

WAYS TO COMMUNICATE CHANGE

METHODS	WHEN TO USE EACH METHOD
MEDIA Pieces in magazines and newspapers, on your Web site, and on video that signal change.	To create awareness and provide information so that people can keep up to date and think about the change program.
PRESENTATIONS Presentations to large and small groups, supplemented by media as described above.	To sell a large-scale change program and stimulate understanding, support, and involvement from all affected.
TRAINING Training sessions, ranging from management workshops to machine-skills training.	To prepare those affected and back up a forthcoming change program while simultaneously building committed support.
TEAM MEETINGS Full meetings at which people discuss issues, air problems, and suggest solutions.	To advance the change program by involving everyone, allowing them to voice opinions and discuss progress.
TROUBLESHOOTING Regular feedback, team problem-solving, and progress-briefing sessions.	To maintain commitment, solve problems, and advance and monitor the success and failure of the change program.

66 Speak about change plans to as many people individually as you can.

CHOOSING METHODS

You face a wide range of options when revealing change decisions; choose your methods carefully. Use personal communication in preference to written notification, not least because people can ask questions. If some are likely to react badly, you may want to inform people one by one, rather than all together. Ideally, combine a number of methods, such as media, presentations, and team meetings, to enable staff to raise problems or suggestions. In large organizations, groups are often informed in sequence: top management briefs departmental managers, who brief unit managers, who brief unit members.

AVOIDING PITFALLS

Be careful not to create false impressions, whether positive or negative. Promoting excessively high expectations is sure to backfire later; arousing unjustified fears will have an immediate adverse impact. Be realistic, and do not gloss over any less positive facts. You cannot predict how people will react; seek feedback to make sure that the decision to change has been correctly interpreted.

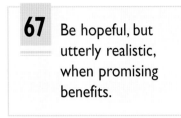

67 Be hopeful, but utterly realistic, when promising benefits.

BREAKING BAD NEWS

Communicating change often involves breaking bad news to people. This may be unexpected or anticipated, but in any case give people the facts as soon as possible – delaying an announcement merely prolongs the agony. Present the case for change with reasoned argument and supporting facts. Whether or not people expect bad news, they will understand rational and considered decisions. If they then disagree with your reasoning, on emotional or intellectual grounds, you need to look into the issues they raise. Consult your contingency plans to help you understand the basis of the problem, and take steps to address it directly.

68 Blame the message, not the messenger or the audience, for bad reactions.

DELIVERING NEWS OF ADVERSE CHANGE

Bad news is bad news, and there is no point in concealing the fact. Try to give positive explanations. Be sympathetic at all times (and apologetic, if need be), but make it clear that the change is unavoidable. Use expressions like the following:

 I'm very sorry that you couldn't be told earlier – this is the first opportunity I've had.

 Nobody wants to make this change, but if we don't, our success will be compromised.

 I would have liked to promote you, but the changed role requires a different set of skills.

 Unfortunately the team's own analysis shows that your department needs major restructuring.

Assigning Responsibility

By their natures, change programmes call for leadership. But they also require inspired, dedicated, and inspiring followers. Whether leaders or followers, "change agents", located in key positions, play an indispensable role in the change process.

69 Put change agents in place before launching a change programme.

Defining Change Agents

A change agent is an enthusiast for change who can pass their enthusiasm on to others, and so takes on pivotal responsibilities in a change programme. Everyone is capable of great reactive change, but a minority are proactive by nature, relishing the challenge of change. In any change programme, but especially a prolonged one where continued enthusiasm is essential, identify potential change agents and place them in strategic positions.

70 Make sure that those leading change support it thoroughly.

Using Change Agents

Change agents are valuable at any level in an organization, and also as outside influences such as consultants. Encourage change agents – especially subordinates in the thick of the action, who are extremely useful as examples and stimuli for others – and give free rein to their ideas. Change agents are often particularly valuable in meetings: they keep discussions going, take the initiative over suggestions and planning, and act as the conduits for delegation and for feedback from those undergoing change.

▼ QUALITIES OF A CHANGE AGENT
An ideal change agent is enthusiastic, restless, and eager for improvements. People with this kind of temperament stimulate eagerness for change in others.

Realistic

Eager for improvement

Effective communicator

Restless

Attentive listener

Good collaborator

Ideas person

DELEGATING CHANGE

Assign active roles in a change programme to various people at all levels, not merely to those you have selected as change agents. Break down every aspect of a programme for change, and entrust each part to a specified person. Designate these roles on the basis of desired outcomes – in other words, suit tasks to the skills and availability of a person rather than being constrained by their job description or rank. Ask yourself, "What final outcome do I expect from a person in this role, and who is capable of achieving it?" Make sure that everyone knows precisely what is expected of them at all times – having a clear role increases involvement. Also, check that everyone is confident about what they are expected to do.

71

Challenge any need for secrecy: avoid keeping information secret unless it is essential to do so.

DO'S AND DON'TS

✔ Do promote comradeship among change agents.

✔ Do give change agents stretching tasks that develop them for future responsibility.

✔ Do encourage people to form and follow up ideas for change.

✔ Do listen to what change agents say about morale and reactions.

✗ Don't assume that older people are too set in their ways to be change agents.

✗ Don't discourage others by singling out change agents for special treatment.

✗ Don't prevent change agents from using their initiative.

✗ Don't create an atmosphere of secrecy for its own sake.

ALLOCATING ROLES

Analyze the changes you want to achieve

Decide who should execute each one

Draw up specific tasks for each person

Discuss these plans with each person

Get feedback to check their commitment

SAFEGUARDING INFORMATION

People involved in a change programme may learn classified or sensitive information. In assigning roles, ensure that change agents understand about confidentiality, yet will keep secrecy to a minimum consistent with security. For example, if careless talk might lead to commercial damage (as with new product plans), security must be absolute. But within an organization, secrets are rarely that sensitive, and refusing to be open will damage morale.

DEVELOPING COMMITMENT

Building up people's support is essential for the success of change projects. Use strong leadership skills to gain and deepen commitment. Set the tone through your own dedicated attitude, and structure meetings and systems to stimulate and involve people.

72 Remind people that change is for everyone, not just a few.

73 Use your own commitment to change as an example for others.

LEADING THE WAY

For a change program to succeed, all levels of management need to be involved along with everyone else. Do not let anyone think that change is just for others and not for them. Lead by example, showing your own commitment to the change philosophy and to this change program; be ready to practice what you preach, and take an active part in discussion and implementation. Your wholehearted personal involvement as a change leader, together with that of your colleagues, provides the best possible example and inspiration to subordinate staff. Make sure that your words and actions reinforce people's awareness of the benefits of the change and their commitment to it.

BEING FLEXIBILE ▼
A person who is flexible and open to new ideas is a good role model for others. To become more flexible, try to develop certain characteristics.

Is able to take a long-term view

Enjoys hearing new and different ideas

Relishes short-term success

Can ride through disappointments and setbacks

Looks forward to personal challenge

Is excited by trying new ventures

Can move quickly to take opportunities

TAKING UP SUGGESTIONS

74 Use regular progress meetings to highlight achievements.

▼ **GETTING FEEDBACK**
A team implementing change meets regularly to discuss progress. Make sure that the whole team is committed to change; take up useful ideas, and give and accept criticism in a positive manner.

Even if a change has been sprung on staff, you can still create a positive, committed atmosphere by involving everyone in implementation. That means being open to suggestions. A change project in which new orders are simply given and followed will not involve people or disarm their resistance. Be seen to listen to and act on people's ideas – this will increase motivation and improve performance. Set up small task forces to tackle specific areas of the plan, and remember that small ideas can be as effective as big ones.

BUILDING DIALOGUE

In a well-run change program, dialogue begins at the beginning, when change is first considered, and never stops. This maximizes commitment from everyone. Treat even resistance as a sign of involvement, and let it play a positive role in the program: objections can provide a springboard for no-holds-barred discussion, and often lead to improvements. As changes progress, encourage dialogue to continue informally, but also set up a regular forum, probably weekly, as an integral part of the process. Here progress can be reported and discussed, and problems and solutions identified.

POINTS TO REMEMBER

- Setting up a special suggestion program works well.
- Moving from following orders to a system of advice and consent is a major change in itself.
- Confronting opposition and opponents is a painful necessity.
- If obstructive ringleaders will not reform, they will have to leave.
- All senior people should develop the habit of talking and listening to everybody.

CHANGING CULTURE

The culture of an organization grows out of the behavior of the people within it, and in turn it influences how they behave. Aim to guide the development of your organization's culture by various means so that it supports your changes.

75 Generate a feel-good factor by redecorating the place.

76 Err on the side of excess when celebrating a major success.

CHANGING ENVIRONMENTS

Environmental changes work practically and symbolically: change is often easier to accept if the physical and structural surroundings also alter. To encourage change within a department, for example, relocate it away from the head office to new premises, reinforcing its sense of autonomy while encouraging initiative, independence, and interest in new ideas. Even a small change such as new decor can make a noticeable difference.

ACKNOWLEDGING SUCCESS

Any process of change takes effort, if only to forget old ways and adopt new methods of working. Special effort deserves a special response. Spare no expense when celebrating the achievements of those who make outstanding contributions – this will encourage everyone. Use presentations, publications, parties, and personal praise and thanks to build an atmosphere of success and progress. But do not trivialize celebrations by holding them too frequently.

▲ **REWARDING ACHIEVEMENT**
When an individual wins an award, his success reflects well on the team. The recognition confirms his sense of achievement and encourages those around him to continue working for change.

WAYS TO INFLUENCE BEHAVIOR

FACTORS	HOW TO USE THEM
GOAL-SETTING	Set personal objectives for people so that they focus their minds on performance; reaching the goals will reinforce their enhanced drive.
PRAISE	Commend people, publicly or privately, to strengthen commitment. Be sure to set high standards, and never ignore mistakes.
ENJOYMENT	Make work fun, with celebrations, outings, posters, awards, and customer visits to stimulate all-around involvement.
ROLES	Allocate temporary or permanent leadership or facilitation roles to encourage people to take a wider view and develop their skills.
REWARDING	Be willing to pay generously for achievement. People may change their behavior radically for significant pay rewards.
CONDITIONS	Move offices, redesign or redecorate them, or use other physical moves to create a fresh atmosphere that affects behavior.
PROCEDURES	Change the way you run meetings or award authority to reinforce new ways of relating to other team members.

LINKING PAY TO EFFORT

People want to feel that their reward will match their efforts; if it does, this will reinforce their commitment to the new ways. In some change projects, links between pay and performance are explicit: a team works to effect improvements, and proof of success lies in savings achieved, which are divided between the organization and the team. However, some experts say that such plans miss the point of change, which is to move to better working systems. People still benefit financially by sharing, as teams and/or individuals, in the organization's growing prosperity.

77 Always attend if celebrations have been arranged.

78 Let teams decide how to share financial rewards.

LIMITING RESISTANCE

T he greatest challenge for managers is to overcome barriers, especially emotional ones, to acceptance of change. While careful planning forestalls many problems, you will still need to interpret and deal effectively with various forms of resistance.

 79 Make people feel their own roles are strategically important.

80 Treat people gently if morale is low during the change cycle.

DETECTING RESISTANCE

Resistance can take many forms, both active and passive. Watch for signs of resistance, and try to interpret them. Consult your change plan to find out what kinds of resistance you anticipated and how you proposed to deal with them. You should be able to tell from the type of resistance what stage a person has reached in their response to change, and whether their prime concerns are rational objections, personal fears, or general emotional distrust of change. This knowledge will help you to choose the best response.

ACTIVE RESISTANCE

If opposition is openly stated and clearly visible, it is active resistance. Opposition to the content of a project will surface in argument and criticism; this may be exaggerated, but deeper objections often lie beneath the surface. Investigate carefully through meetings or troubleshooting sessions. Personal and emotional resistance often combine to reinforce an aggressive attitude. You may notice this in active confrontation in discussions, unofficial opposition meetings, angry memos and e-mails, threats of industrial action, carrying out those threats, and even conspiracies to stop change in its tracks. Avoid hasty reactions to aggression; decide on the best response, and apply it calmly and firmly.

Passive resister leans back and folds arms, suggesting barrier against change

PASSIVE RESISTANCE

During a change program, passive resistance can be just as effective as strident opposition. Successful change requires active collaboration; its absence may be a powerful restraint. Suspect passive resistance if you cannot find people when you want them, if they will not contribute in meetings or even attend them, if they hold back information, if they delay or block messages, or if they seem to block change while paying lip service to it. Be aware that those who are not with you are against you, but do not interpret signs of passive resistance as final. In some cases, resisters will never be converted. In others, resistance merely indicates low points in a cycle of reactions that will eventually end in acceptance.

POINTS TO REMEMBER

- Objectors may have a genuine cause for their concern – resistance is not necessarily misguided or unreasonable.
- The ringleaders of active resistance should be identified and converted or made ineffective.
- Vague reassurances will not counter genuine personal fears.
- People will adjust better if they let off steam rather than having to hide their emotions.
- Resistance is best met with sympathy, without letting the situation become too emotional.

▼ FACING RESISTANCE
You can tell a lot about people's feelings from their body language. An active resister may raise his or her voice and use hand gestures, while a passive resister may lean back and fold his or her arms.

81 Take all resistance seriously, however far-fetched it seems, and deal with it effectively.

Manager leans forward, showing interest in colleague's opinions

Active resister uses gestures to express objections forcefully

COUNTERING ARGUMENTS

Rather than bulldozing through objections that are based on rational arguments, refer to the facts you gathered when originally making the case for change. Turn the change plan into an offer that cannot be refused by stressing the positive potential of change and the negative risks if it is prevented. If anyone is still unconvinced, the first payoffs as you implement the plan should raise enthusiasm and convince people of the wisdom of the new ways.

82 Set up a special suggestion box devoted to the change project.

83 Be sure to investigate silence thoroughly – it is rarely golden.

ENCOURAGING DIRECTNESS

Always encourage people to express concerns openly, and confront those concerns as far as you can. If you ask people in groups, you may find that some leave the talking to others. Deal with this by calling everyone in turn if the group is small enough. With larger groups, call on selected individuals to speak their minds. In cases in which your hands are tied, explain why, express regret about it, and stress positive aspects of the change.

USING MEETINGS

If ringleaders of the opposition emerge, confront them and seek to alter their stance. They may enjoy their roles and be less than willing to relinquish them. Use one-to-one meetings to find a compromise. This must be to both sides' satisfaction, or the ringleader may provoke dissent later. Also hold one-to-one discussions with key people, and anyone who is especially troubled (even if less influential), and set up small groups to tackle specific areas of concern.

Manager shows willingness to listen to rebel's points

Rebel puts his case as emphatically and fully as he wishes

▲ NEGOTIATING WITH A REBEL

Hold private, one-to-one meetings with resistance leaders. Listen sympathetically, then combine direct persuasion, subtle coaxing, and compromise (if possible) to bring them around to the plan.

COMBATING FEARS

Be as straightforward as possible when you are addressing specific fears about the future of individuals. Speak openly about exactly what the change means for people, explain why you are certain that they can cope, and say why personal advantages are likely to outweigh disadvantages. General, vague emotional resistance is most difficult to overcome, since you do not share other people's emotions. Try to counteract negativity by being constantly upbeat and involving people in positive action that will produce quick-fix results – this will help to allay their fears and anxieties.

84 Persuade people that change will always mean opportunity.

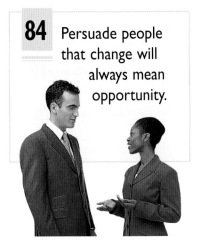

DEALING WITH NEGATIVE REACTIONS TO CHANGE

TYPES OF NEGATIVITY	WHAT TO DO ABOUT THEM
RATIONAL Misunderstanding of details of plan, belief that change is unnecessary, disbelief in planned change's effectiveness, expectation of negative consequences.	● Explain plan with greater clarity and detail. ● Project what would happen if the change program was not introduced. ● Involve everybody in quality-improvement teams to demonstrate effectiveness of managed change. ● Institute a bottom-up program for reorganizing systems and processes.
PERSONAL Fear of job loss, anxiety about the future, resentment at implied criticism of performance, fear of interference from above.	● Stress much-improved job prospects for the future for everyone. ● Present plans for improvements which people are likely to find positive and exciting. ● Accept management responsibility for past failures. ● Present a scenario showing the anticipated benefits of the main changes.
EMOTIONAL Active and/or passive resistance to change in general, lack of involvement, apathy toward initiatives, shock, mistrust of motives behind change.	● Show, with examples, why the old ways no longer work. ● Stage a series of meetings to communicate details of the change agenda. ● Demonstrate that the new policy is not merely a "flavor of the month." ● Explain the reasons for change, and promise involvement. ● Be completely honest, and answer all questions.

CONSOLIDATING CHANGE

The implementation of change is just the beginning.
To ensure a successful change program, develop processes
that constantly review and improve the changes.

MONITORING PROGRESS

Frequent and accurate assessment of progress is essential to ensure that a change program is effective. Simply producing figures at regular intervals is not enough: look at less tangible factors, too, and compare both against planned achievements.

85 Only study or produce statistics that clearly show progress or results.

86 If performance lags, look first at how it is targeted and measured.

MEASURING PERFORMANCE

What you measure is what you get. For example, changing the targets for salespeople from measures based solely on revenue to measures based on profitability has an impact on the way they act to achieve goals and on the actual profit made. Use the financial and nonfinancial internal measures included in your original change plan to focus change and measure its progress over time. Compare actual progress, in terms of product quality and quantity, with planned progress. Make use of external measures, too, such as customer satisfaction, to chart the results of the program.

MAINTAINING A BALANCE

Try to obtain a balanced picture of progress in all the areas that you set out to change. Schedules and measurements should give an indication of concrete achievements, but pay attention also to intangible factors, such as morale. Bear in mind, too, that one achievement may be worth little unless it leads to another – for example, increasing the rate of product development will not bring significant benefit unless it leads to an improvement in market share or profitability. But minimal progress in one sphere may be a worthwhile sacrifice if it means real progress in another, more significant one.

87 Find the few key measures that best judge success.

STUDYING ALL ANGLES OF CHANGE

EXTERNAL
Is customer satisfaction rising? Has the improved quality of the product increased sales?

INTERNAL
Is the organization or department meeting schedules and targets? How is employee morale?

PROCESS
Is quality nearing 100 percent? Can schedules be cut? Are innovations emerging?

RESULT
Is market share up? Is cash flow positive? Are margins and returns as planned?

▼ **KEEPING CUSTOMERS**
A typical survey shows that around 90 percent of customers who see your service as "excellent" remain loyal. Of those who rate it "good," 60 percent stay with you, compared with 25 percent of those who rate it "fair" and none who rate it "poor."

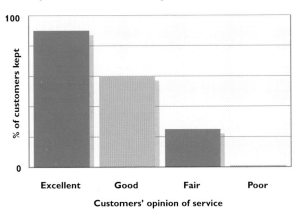

MEASURING RESPONSE

For most companies, sales performance, customer loyalty, and market share are basic hard indicators of the success of a change. But they do not tell why customers buy more or less, and stay or depart. For the answers, conduct surveys comparable to those used when originally planning change, to see what has altered. Even replies given in imprecise terms such as "excellent" or "satisfied" are useful, provided that the sample is statistically valid and that specific questions are asked. If customers rate you "excellent," the chances are that they will stay with you. But a huge gulf separates "excellent" from "good"; avoid combining the two, or results will be very misleading.

REVIEWING ASSUMPTIONS

*C*hange projects should not be set in stone: unless they are open to change themselves, they are unlikely to sustain long-term enthusiasm or to meet changing market needs. Reassessing long-term policies is as crucial for success as the original plan.

 88 Continually check a project's relevance to the changing environment.

 89 Do not abandon failing projects; reorient, revise, and reinforce them.

REASSESSING OBJECTIVES

The objectives of change are not sacred; external developments can invalidate the reasons for a plan. For example, a radical rethink may be turned on its head by developments in technology. The more protracted a change program, the greater the chance that the original plan's aims will no longer be viable. Revise aims every few months to ensure that sufficient progress is being made and that the aims remain relevant to external circumstances.

MAKING IMPROVEMENTS

There is every chance that revisions will strengthen the change process. Plans are based on assumptions and predictions, both of which may prove wrong. Once a plan has been tested by events, its weak points will show up and its successes will show what works and why. Even after the initial thrust of the change program is over, continue to use feedback from everybody concerned to make improvements. These should bring economic benefits and help to sustain staff involvement.

REVISING A PROJECT ▼
Revision of a change program requires data and feedback. Once a program has been implemented, its results should be measured, and opinions and suggestions for amendments obtained from all involved. On the strength of this information, maintain or revise the program as necessary.

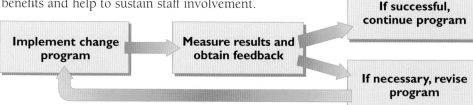

Implement change program → Measure results and obtain feedback → If successful, continue program / If necessary, revise program

REALIGNING PRIORITIES

Managers can be fickle toward change projects. They begin with great enthusiasm, only to cool off as time goes by and other projects catch their attention. When several projects are running at once, each has to fight for attention, and confusion – rather than cooperation – can result. Since projects may well overlap, the consequences are likely to be harmful. Make sure that your frequent progress reviews include an assessment of current attitudes toward and enthusiasm for each change initiative. Use these progress reviews to help realign policies that are no longer appropriate.

90 Avoid change overload; it can ruin the effect of individual projects.

91 Never assume that you know what people think – always ask them.

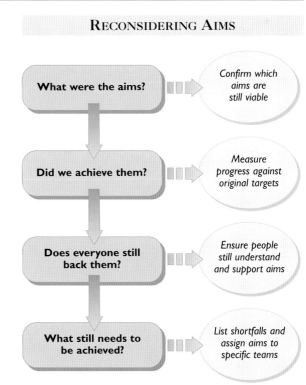

RECONSIDERING AIMS

What were the aims? → Confirm which aims are still viable

Did we achieve them? → Measure progress against original targets

Does everyone still back them? → Ensure people still understand and support aims

What still needs to be achieved? → List shortfalls and assign aims to specific teams

REVIEWING ATTITUDES

All change projects require changes in behavior, which in turn flow from and create changes in attitude. Much effort may have been made to persuade people to support a program, and as it unfolds, attitudes are affected by job experiences, personnel changes, successes, and setbacks. Even if people's behavior complies with the changes, do not assume that all is well: attitudes can become negative, and this may eventually undermine morale. Use trusted people as listening posts, and stage no-holds-barred meetings or interviews. Then revise change programs or restimulate involvement, as necessary, to ensure that people still support the change program and its aims, especially aims that have been revised or replaced.

AVOIDING COMPLACENCY

Success carries a hidden risk. Having achieved excellent results through effective change, organizations easily relapse into complacency. This helps to explain why turnarounds, in which drastic change has moved companies from crisis to strong survival, frequently peter out. The same fate often strikes buyouts, in which a management team, initially inspired into radical action, relaxes once the profits have poured in. The best change programs always look two or three years ahead; to build on success and avoid falling into complacency, ask yourself what comes next. What are the new targets, and how are you going to meet them? What are you doing wrong, and how can you improve? Ask questions like these regularly to keep yourself alert and aware.

92 Keep setting stretching targets to move change forward.

93 Ensure that revised objectives are communicated clearly to everyone.

▼ TRACKING CHANGE

This illustration shows possible positive and negative paths that a change project can follow. The project starts well, with group discussion and planning leading to implementation of new systems. Working practices improve, but without regular reassessment and revision, the new systems become unworkable and fail. However, with regular reviews and amendments, the project's success is ensured.

Project starts strongly, with comprehensive discussion and planning of change

Changes to working systems methodically implemented

BEING REALISTIC

In analyzing success, separate the impact of lasting changes in business systems from the effect of one-time events (such as large layoffs) or external developments. In a very hot summer, anyone can increase ice-cream sales; the important issue is whether your share of the booming market rises, and how your performance compares with the best competition. Similarly the question is not how much money job cuts save, but the productivity of remaining staff. Even if you do well by realistic analysis, higher standards can always be achieved. Concentrate on improving weak areas, rather than just congratulating your team on their strengths.

POINTS TO REMEMBER

- Change projects should be revised and updated regularly to ensure their continued success.
- Effective change managers should always be asked how they intend to repeat the success of their last change program.
- It is best to move leaders of successful projects to new change projects before their personal momentum runs down.
- The pursuit of new change projects should be made a constant managerial priority.

94 Make the most of people who have played a key role in the success of change programs.

Program is reviewed at regular intervals to meet current needs

Program continues unchanged, and eventually degenerates

CHANGING CONTINUALLY

The completion of a change program should not be an end in itself. Because change projects normally have a definite beginning and end, the tendency is to regard the change as complete when a project is over. Special teams that have generated new product breakthroughs, for instance, are often dissolved and their members dispersed. It is more beneficial to examine the procedures and processes that the group followed and to inject the best features and people from them into the rest of the organization. Promote change enthusiasts, and seek new projects that can utilize the lessons of success. Set these projects against a general background of continuous, company-wide improvement, and pave the way for change management to become "the way we do things around here."

MAINTAINING MOMENTUM

*C*hange programs are not unstoppable tides. They change course, stop, and start again. An organization's change momentum will eventually be lost unless there is periodic renewal, both for the specific plan and for those executing it.

95 Agree on people's development objectives, and write them down.

96 Use self-help guides to enhance your development and performance.

REFOCUSING CHANGE

A change program that does not itself change is a contradiction in terms. Think through the details of your change policy regularly, and refocus the program if you see that progress is slowing. One way to refocus is to relaunch the program annually, with fresh mission statements. Consider choosing a theme for each year, such as maximizing quality or improving speed, to focus attention on key issues and renew the thrust of change.

DEVELOPING YOURSELF

Whatever your status within an organization, you will always benefit from developing the range and depth of your own skills as much as those of your colleagues. Maintain the momentum of your personal development along with that of other people and the organization as a whole, and keep abreast of developments in fields that will help you to stay ahead of forthcoming change. Acquire new skills and broaden your horizons: read, listen to the radio, watch television, or use the Internet to tap further sources of information and ideas. Arrange to be sent on training courses that may not be directly related to your job (for example, outward-bound courses that build team skills), learn on the job through trial and error, and take the widest possible interest in any business that is relevant to your organization. Constantly update your knowledge, seek out new ideas, develop your own initiatives, and be eager to plan and implement further change.

GOING OUTWARD-BOUND ▶
Mastering unrelated skills, such as canoeing, can often have a genuine payoff at work. It may, for instance, improve leadership skills, develop confidence, and build team spirit.

UPGRADING BUDGETS

If a change project does not pay for itself, something must be gravely wrong. Investing in improvements should increase profitability, thereby justifying the investment and helping to make continuous change a fundamental part of corporate policy. Review budgets and resources regularly, and upgrade them as necessary to focus change where it can bring most benefit.

97 Set training targets for everybody, including yourself.

DEVELOPING PEOPLE

Change projects change people. Individuals used to following instructions develop independence through directing their own work; managers who have never consulted staff improve their people skills by doing so. Build on these individuals' new skills by helping them look ahead, encouraging career moves, or widening roles. Let people take the initiative in such changes – this, too, will develop them.

98 Make sure that every change program continues to increase profitability.

PROVIDING TRAINING

Education and training "from cradle to grave" is a key element in maintaining the momentum of change. Learning new ways of behaving and working enriches people's jobs and alters their attitudes. Some of the training will need to be technical, related to the specific tasks or techniques required in a job – for instance, mastering statistical methods or new computer software. But remember that people also need training in various interpersonal skills, such as leadership or team building. Whatever courses you offer people, impress on them the principle that everybody can learn new or improved skills at any point in their career. Make this way of thinking part of personal career plans, and see that these plans are followed.

BUILDING ON CHANGE

*C*hange requires great effort. That effort is wasted if changes are abandoned or reversed, or are not the basis for further advances. Successful managers plan for the future as well as the present, and make change part of their organization's culture.

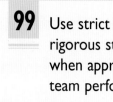

99 Use strict and rigorous standards when appraising team performance.

100 Promote only people dedicated to change.

101 To be successful, plan, implement, revise, update, and build in change.

CONTINUING BENEFITS

A change program at any level is often associated with a particular change leader, but should not be solely dependent upon them. Build positive change into all aspects of the system and culture of an organization in practical and lasting ways – after careful research and planning – so that change programs can continue once the original leader has moved on to a new project. In some cases, however, a new approach may be appropriate, so be open to fresh possibilities, and do not allow success to make you inflexibly committed to the methods and values of the changes you have already implemented.

**BUILDING ▶
ON SUCCESS**
Tom, the team leader, identified the best way to maintain success in the marketplace – continuous change – and repeatedly emphasized it to his team. After he left, the team retained his methods and used their own initiative to continue achieving world-class results.

CASE STUDY
Tom had launched Project World Class with high ambitions. He constantly reminded his team that, unless they continuously adapted, they would lose their advantage and no longer lead the competition or delight customers.
Tom was deservedly promoted to another unit, but he was sure his successors would manage in the same spirit. In fact,

the team maintained the enthusiasm Tom had created – thanks to training, greater job variety, involvement in quality improvement teams, and bonus payments. Many on the team launched and completed change projects using their own initiative.
Because everybody knew their targets and exactly how the team was doing, Tom's aim was achieved: "world-class" performance had become a way of life.

APPLYING SELF-CRITICISM

However good you are, you can always improve. Be sure to highlight your successes and enjoy them, but develop a habit of self-criticism, too – both as an organization and individually. As the best antidote to complacency, adopt a formal system of organizational self-appraisal. Draw up a list of headings, such as "customer satisfaction," "use of resources," and "innovation," and allocate 100 points among these headings according to their importance to you. Next, award your unit or organization a score (for example, 15 out of 20) under each heading, and add up the total; it will fall well short of 100. Then have a harsh critic, perhaps your manager, aggressively challenge your score. This process will reveal shortcomings and continually help renew efforts to improve.

▼ CELEBRATING SUCCESS

It is as important to enjoy the success of a change program as to be aware of and work on its weak points. Do not hesitate to pass on praise and appreciation to staff, and share the fruits of their efforts.

POINTS TO REMEMBER

- New people should be expected to propose new ideas – that is part of their great value.
- Self-criticism must be allied with self-confidence to create a potent mixture.
- If people wholeheartedly support change, they will become its ardent defenders.
- A "court-martial" should be held from time to time to "try" your effectiveness.
- Any setup should be reexamined and improved periodically.

INTEGRATING CHANGES

Always integrate a change program so that each stage builds on its predecessors. For example, a marketing project that relies on next-day delivery has to be integrated with manufacturing change to ensure that orders can be completed on a daily basis. Continue to adapt organizational processes to help keep change alive – all setups eventually outlive their optimum efficiency. To prevent change from stagnating, change people's roles in departments. Move constantly forward, and build each change project onto the last; in this way, the gains from change will continue to benefit individuals and the organization as a whole.

Assessing Your Change-Management Skills

*E*valuate how well you manage the demands of change by responding to the following statements, marking the options closest to your experience. Be as honest as you can: if your answer is "never," mark Option 1; if it is "always," mark Option 4; and so on. Add your scores together, and refer to the Analysis at the end to interpret your score. Use your answers to identify areas that most need improvement.

OPTIONS

1 Never

2 Occasionally

3 Frequently

4 Always

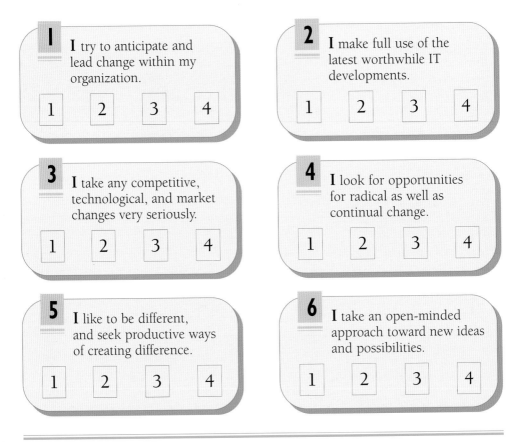

1 I try to anticipate and lead change within my organization.

1 2 3 4

2 I make full use of the latest worthwhile IT developments.

1 2 3 4

3 I take any competitive, technological, and market changes very seriously.

1 2 3 4

4 I look for opportunities for radical as well as continual change.

1 2 3 4

5 I like to be different, and seek productive ways of creating difference.

1 2 3 4

6 I take an open-minded approach toward new ideas and possibilities.

1 2 3 4

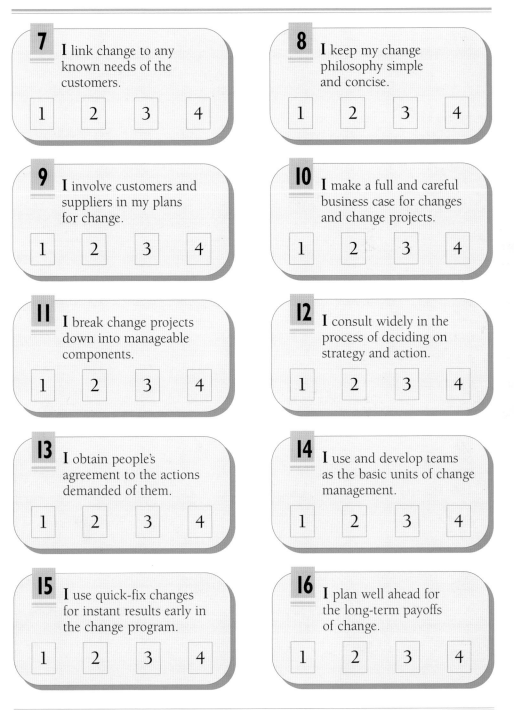

7 I link change to any known needs of the customers.

1　2　3　4

8 I keep my change philosophy simple and concise.

1　2　3　4

9 I involve customers and suppliers in my plans for change.

1　2　3　4

10 I make a full and careful business case for changes and change projects.

1　2　3　4

11 I break change projects down into manageable components.

1　2　3　4

12 I consult widely in the process of deciding on strategy and action.

1　2　3　4

13 I obtain people's agreement to the actions demanded of them.

1　2　3　4

14 I use and develop teams as the basic units of change management.

1　2　3　4

15 I use quick-fix changes for instant results early in the change program.

1　2　3　4

16 I plan well ahead for the long-term payoffs of change.

1　2　3　4

17 **I** am careful not to create overoptimistic or over-pessimistic expectations.

1 2 3 4

18 **I** seize opportunities to reward, celebrate, and encourage successful change.

1 2 3 4

19 **I** make sure everybody knows the answer to "What's in it for me?"

1 2 3 4

20 **I** have effective and adaptable contingency plans available.

1 2 3 4

21 **I** anticipate adverse reactions and plan how to deal with them.

1 2 3 4

22 **I** use well-designed pilots and experiments to test my change plans.

1 2 3 4

23 **I** share relevant information with colleagues and staff as soon as possible.

1 2 3 4

24 **I** work closely with like-minded people who are eager to change.

1 2 3 4

25 **M**y own behavior is flexible and highly adaptable to changing needs.

1 2 3 4

26 **I** encourage people to speak their minds openly and to air their concerns.

1 2 3 4

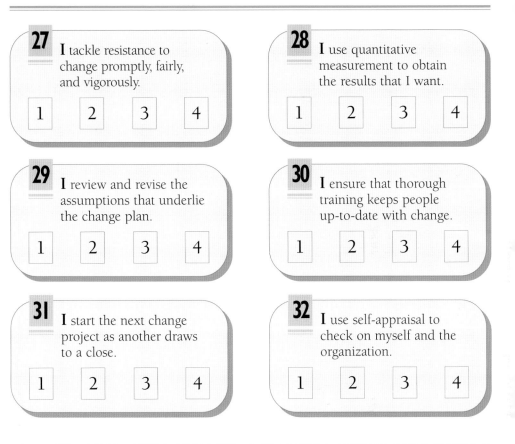

27 I tackle resistance to change promptly, fairly, and vigorously.

| 1 | 2 | 3 | 4 |

28 I use quantitative measurement to obtain the results that I want.

| 1 | 2 | 3 | 4 |

29 I review and revise the assumptions that underlie the change plan.

| 1 | 2 | 3 | 4 |

30 I ensure that thorough training keeps people up-to-date with change.

| 1 | 2 | 3 | 4 |

31 I start the next change project as another draws to a close.

| 1 | 2 | 3 | 4 |

32 I use self-appraisal to check on myself and the organization.

| 1 | 2 | 3 | 4 |

ANALYSIS

Now that you have completed the self-assessment, add up your total score and check your level of skill by reading the corresponding evaluation. However astute your change-management skills may be, it is important to remember that there is always room for improvement. Identify your weakest areas, and refer to the relevant chapters in this section where you will find practical advice and tips to help you to establish and hone those skills.

32–64: You are resisting change or are unsure of its potential benefits. Overcome your fears, and learn to plan for change.

65–95: You understand the need for change – now you must develop your skills to achieve it successfully.

96–128: You are a skilled agent of change, but remember that change is a never-ending process, so keep planning ahead.

MINIMIZING STRESS

INTRODUCTION

S tress is likely to affect all of us at some time in our lives. Learning how to reduce the stress that you encounter as you reach toward your personal goals will allow you to achieve these aims without damaging your health. From relationships to workload to a messy desk, this section offers advice on how to cope with, or avoid, the stress in your daily life. Invaluable information helps you minimize the stress factor in your workplace by analyzing the causes of stress, recognizing its symptoms, and assessing how it is affecting you and others. Throughout the section, 101 useful tips give further vital information, with advice on how to spot warning signals, how to relax, and how to help stressed staff. A self-assessment exercise allows you to plot your own stress levels.

UNDERSTANDING STRESS

Stress has been called "the invisible disease." It is a disease that may affect you, your organization, and any of the people in it, so you cannot afford to ignore it.

WHAT IS STRESS?

On occasion, all of us experience stress. Beneficial stress can help drive a few of us to become Olympic champions, but harmful stress can drive others to despair. A force as powerful as that should always be handled with respect.

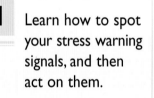 **I** Learn how to spot your stress warning signals, and then act on them.

ANALYZING THE EFFECTS OF STRESS

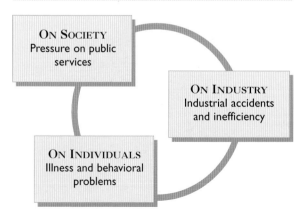

ON SOCIETY
Pressure on public services

ON INDUSTRY
Industrial accidents and inefficiency

ON INDIVIDUALS
Illness and behavioral problems

THE DEFINITION OF STRESS

Stress in individuals is defined as any interference that disturbs a person's healthy mental and physical well-being. It occurs when the body is required to perform beyond its normal range of capabilities. The results of stress are harmful to individuals, families, society, and organizations, which can suffer from "organizational stress."

2 Do not be afraid to talk about situations that you find stressful.

ITS EFFECT ON SOCIETY

The societal costs of stress are already high – and are increasing steadily. Society bears the cost of public services such as healthcare for those made ill by stress, pensions for early retirement brought on by stress, and disability benefits for accidents occurring because of stress. In addition to this, stress often makes people irritable, and this affects the overall quality of everyone's lives.

ITS EFFECT ON COMPANIES

Stress costs industry over $150 billion a year in the US alone through absenteeism and reduced levels of performance by those who are physically present but mentally absent. In the UK, as much as 60 percent of all absenteeism is believed to be caused by stress-related disorders. Anything that can reduce the damaging effects of stress makes workers happier and companies richer.

3 Take a walk when you are stressed – it can help restore your perspective.

ITS EFFECT ON THE BODY

When the human body is placed under physical or psychological stress, it increases the production of certain hormones such as adrenaline and cortisol. These hormones produce marked changes in heart rate, blood-pressure levels, metabolism, and physical activity. Although this physical reaction will help you function more effectively when you are under pressure for short periods of time, it can be extremely damaging to the body in the long run.

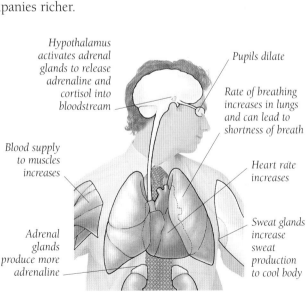

Hypothalamus activates adrenal glands to release adrenaline and cortisol into bloodstream

Pupils dilate

Rate of breathing increases in lungs and can lead to shortness of breath

Blood supply to muscles increases

Heart rate increases

Adrenal glands produce more adrenaline

Sweat glands increase sweat production to cool body

▲ SYMPTOMS OF STRESS
The physical symptoms of stress can affect the whole body, particularly the cardiac and respiratory systems.

767

4 Avoid the habit of taking work home with you every night.

Stress and Mental Health

The incidence of psychological disorders, such as panic attacks and obsessive behavior, increases with the buildup of long-term stress. Worries can reach such a level that they surface as a frightening, painful physical sensation, which can be mistaken for a heart attack. People under prolonged stress are more prone to irrational fears, mood swings, and phobias and may experience fits of depression, anger, and irritability.

Its Effect on Physical Health and Well-being

Long-term stress has been identified as one of the most prevalent causes of numerous common conditions, including high blood pressure and heart disease. It is now commonly thought that prolonged stress can also increase the risk of psychological or psychiatric ailments. Behavioral changes caused by stress, such as the increased and excessive use of alcohol or drugs, are also linked to a marked decline in physical health.

When under an abnormal amount of stress, the risk of dependency on alcohol is very high. Apart from major physical health problems caused by excessive drinking, overconsumption of alcohol can also result in highly strained and therefore stressful personal relationships, both in the home and at work. Alcohol abuse resulting in worker absenteeism is reckoned to cost the US economy more than $100 billion annually.

Prescribed drugs such as tranquilizers, while sometimes useful in the short term to tackle the symptoms of anxiety, can be addictive and have side effects such as loss of concentration, poor coordination, and dizziness. Tranquilizers, by their very nature, are not a cure for stress since they do not deal with its fundamental causes.

Its Effect on Emotions

Those who suffer from stress are far more likely to indulge in destructive behavior, which can have a high cost to themselves, to employers, and to society. Typical symptoms such as mood swings and erratic behavior may alienate colleagues as well as friends and family. In some cases, this can start a vicious circle of decreasing confidence, leading to more serious emotional problems, such as depression.

5 Try to be aware of any changes in your eating and drinking patterns.

ITS EFFECT ON DECISIONS

Suffering from any level of stress can rapidly cause individuals to lose their ability to make sound decisions, especially if their self-confidence fails. This affects health, family, and career alike, since stress in one area of life inevitably affects others. Someone suffering from stress may not heed physical signs of illness, attributing them to the side effects of stress. Faulty decisions made in the workplace and at home may lead to accidents or arguments, financial loss, or even the loss of a job.

6 "Talk truth to power" – do not be afraid to tell your supervisor what really goes on in the office.

POINTS TO REMEMBER

- Stress can be a killer. The Japanese have an officially recognized condition called *karoshi* – death from stress caused by too much work.

- Suffering from stress should not be considered a sign of weakness.

- Stress is infectious. It is stressful to live and work with people who are suffering from stress.

- Stress is produced by high demands in life combined with high constraints and little support from colleagues or family.

- There is no formula guaranteeing a stress-free life, but there are techniques for minimizing stress.

ITS EFFECT ON FAMILIES

Stress can break up homes and families. The high divorce rates in the West are due partly to the rapid increase in stress in the workplace, especially where both partners are working full time. It is difficult to find the energy to be supportive to family and friends if work is very difficult or you are afraid that you may lose your job.

When children are involved, stress can cause a conflict relating to child care and careers. Although we do not yet fully understand the long-term impact of separation or divorce on children, we know that it is not the best way to create a generation of stress-free individuals. This requires a very careful balance of the demands of work and home.

◀ SORTING OUT PRIORITIES
Stress is caused by a failure to balance conflicting demands. Juggling work commitments, social life, and child care may mean that not enough time or energy can be devoted to any one activity.

DEFINING STRESS AT WORK

Changes in working practices, such as the introduction of new technology or the alteration of targets, may cause stress, or stress may be built into an organization's structure. Organizational stress can be measured by absenteeism and quality of work.

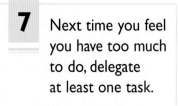 **7** Next time you feel you have too much to do, delegate at least one task.

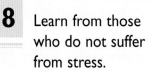 **8** Learn from those who do not suffer from stress.

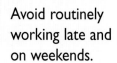 **9** Avoid routinely working late and on weekends.

ORGANIZATIONAL STRESS

Stress affects organizations as well as the individuals within them. An organization with a high level of absenteeism, rapid staff turnover, deteriorating industrial and customer relations, a worsening safety record, or poor quality control is suffering from organizational stress. The causes may range from unclear or overlapping job descriptions to lack of communication to poor working conditions, including "sick building syndrome." This is when a lack of ventilation, insufficient lighting, and inadequate insulation in a building contribute to consistently high levels of illness and absenteeism.

COUNTING THE COST OF WORKPLACE STRESS

Stress causes problems, and these problems cost organizations in different ways:

- Low quality of service. An increase in complaints and lost customers costs time and money. Complaints take time to deal with, and replacement products or services cost money. Loss of customers endangers a company.
- High staff turnover. Both time (for retraining) and money (for recruitment) are spent on replacing unhappy workers.
- Poor reputation. A company with dissatisfied customers will need to pay for changes to restore confidence in its products and services.
- Poor organizational image. A company may recruit only a low-quality – or inexperienced – workforce, since high-fliers are unlikely to be attracted to it.
- Dissatisfied workers. Valuable time is spent in disputes with management over terms and conditions of employment.

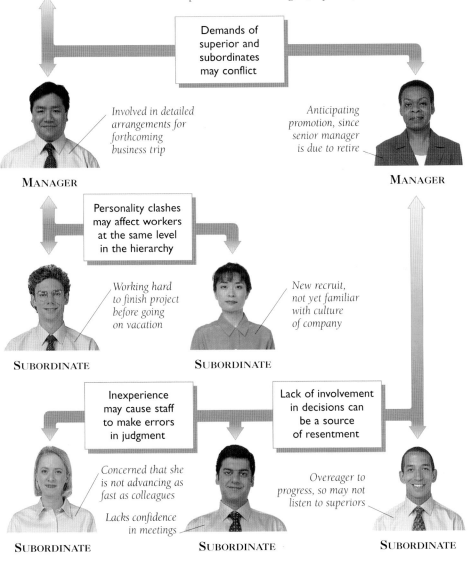

This chart shows one example of the structure of a department in an organization, indicating typical causes of stress that may affect staff at certain levels in the structure and particular causes that are affecting individuals. Stress is contagious: anyone who is not performing well due to stress increases the amount of pressure on their colleagues, superiors, and subordinates.

Anxious about company's annual results

SENIOR MANAGER

Demands of superior and subordinates may conflict

Involved in detailed arrangements for forthcoming business trip

MANAGER

Anticipating promotion, since senior manager is due to retire

MANAGER

Personality clashes may affect workers at the same level in the hierarchy

Working hard to finish project before going on vacation

SUBORDINATE

New recruit, not yet familiar with culture of company

SUBORDINATE

Inexperience may cause staff to make errors in judgment

Lack of involvement in decisions can be a source of resentment

Concerned that she is not advancing as fast as colleagues

Lacks confidence in meetings

SUBORDINATE

Overeager to progress, so may not listen to superiors

SUBORDINATE

SUBORDINATE

RECOGNIZING SYMPTOMS

There is no single symptom that can identify stress – stressed and unstressed people may equally well have heart disease or drink to excess. A common factor in stressed individuals is the presence of a number of symptoms.

> **10** If you suffer from regular headaches or insomnia, see a doctor.

PHYSICAL SIGNS

Some physical symptoms of stress can be life-threatening, such as high blood pressure and heart disease. Less life-threatening physical signs include insomnia, a feeling of constant fatigue, headaches, skin rashes, digestive disorders, ulcers, colitis, loss of appetite, overeating, and cramps. Many of these occur at some point after a stressful event. Other symptoms of stress are more immediate – for example, feelings of nausea, breathlessness, or a dry mouth. All these symptoms, of course, may be caused by factors other than stress. If you or a colleague are naturally prone to headaches, for example, be wary of jumping to inaccurate conclusions about stress levels.

> **11** Make a note of anything that you can find that helps you relax.

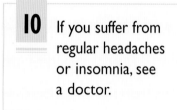

Eyes are bloodshot and puffy

Clothing is disheveled

Posture is slouched

RECOGNIZING ▷ STRESS AT WORK
It is often quite easy to spot signs of stress in the people you work with. Some of the more common symptoms include a marked decline in personal appearance, a quick and fiery temper, changes in eating habits, and a general withdrawal from social activities.

EMOTIONAL SIGNS

The emotional symptoms of stress can include general irritability, acute anxiety attacks, depression, lack of libido, the loss of a sense of humor, and an inability to concentrate on the simplest of routine tasks. Understanding unusual emotional responses and related changes in behavior is the key to recognizing stress in yourself and others. Some of the most common indications of stress are:

- Becoming unnecessarily overemotional or aggressive in conflict situations;
- Loss of interest in personal appearance, other people, social events, or previously enjoyed activities, such as a favorite sport;
- Poor concentration, difficulty in remembering, and an inability to make decisions;
- Sadness, guilt, fatigue, apathy, and a pronounced feeling of helplessness or failure;
- Loss of confidence in personal ability, often coupled with a lack of self-worth.

12 Listen to what your body tells you as objectively as you can.

POINTS TO REMEMBER

- Family, friends, and colleagues often spot signs of stress before the affected individual does.
- Hobbies and interests are healthy mood enhancers; their absence, especially if sudden, may worsen underlying stress.
- Almost everyone has a certain weakness that comes to the fore when they are stressed. For example, many resume smoking even though they "quit" before.

BEHAVIORAL SYMPTOMS

As a temporary relief from stress, many people indulge to excess in eating, smoking, drinking, or spending. Stress can turn an occasional smoker into a chain smoker and the social drinker into an alcoholic. Individuals may not recognize they are overindulging; those who do may go to some lengths to keep their self-destructive behavior from friends, family, and colleagues.

ABUSING STIMULANTS ▶
Sugar, alcohol, nicotine, and caffeine can all help overcome fatigue, anxiety, and tension rapidly – but all too briefly. Used to excess, they heighten the symptoms caused by stress.

Alcohol consumption can creep up imperceptibly

Chocolate provides a short-term sugar high

Caffeine consumption may rise rapidly

Smoking may increase with stress levels

MEASURING STRESS

There are a number of elements that can be quantified and used as approximate measures of stress levels. These elements vary according to whether stress is being measured in an individual, in an organization, or in society itself.

 13 Ask yourself if other people find you stressful to work with.

 14 Keep a diary of the days that you feel highly stressed.

LOOKING AT STATISTICS

One of the most useful sources of information on the level of stress in society is national statistics – for example, the annual rate of heart attacks and suicides. Changes over a period of time in these statistics are particularly significant, since they highlight trends. An increase in heart attacks or suicides usually reflects a major social cause of stress in a country, such as widespread unemployment or economic catastrophe.

MEASURING STRESS IN INDIVIDUALS

Although stress in individuals can be measured to some extent by things like heart rate and the level of adrenaline production, it has more to do with how far "out of sync" an individual is with their usual physical condition. Since everyone has a different heart rate or blood pressure, there is no average statistic to indicate personal stress. Also, different people respond differently to stress. In some, stress can manifest itself in panic attacks, headaches, or stomach problems. Others may suffer a lack of sleep or a loss of self-esteem. There are also thought to be different responses for men and women. Whereas women may become withdrawn or depressed, men are more likely to become aggressive, irritable, or develop addictions.

STRESS STATISTICS

The following statistics attest to some of the effects of stress:
- Stress-related problems are thought to cause half of all premature deaths in the US.
- In the EC, some 10 million people suffer from work-related illness each year.
- In Norway, work-related sickness costs 10 percent of the Gross National Product.
- In the UK, 180 million work days per year are lost through stress in the workplace.

MEASURING STRESS IN ORGANIZATIONS

Companies and other types of organization have certain widely recognized quantitative measures of the level of stress, the most popular of which is the absenteeism figure. This is the percentage of staff absent from work on any one day. However, you cannot deduce that the company with the highest rate of absenteeism is necessarily the most stressed; certain industries are more prone to absenteeism, through injury for example. In fact, many companies suffer from "presenteeism," the presence of disaffected or exhausted workers of no more benefit to the company than absentees. Increasingly, those suffering from stress choose to go to work rather than stay at home.

 15 Treat yourself to something you want but would not normally buy.

 16 Make sure your desk is as near a window as possible.

MEASURING STRESS LEVELS

TYPE OF STRESS	ELEMENTS THAT CAN BE MEASURED
SOCIETAL STRESS This is visible in society as a whole, manifesting itself with a decline in general behavior.	● Unexpected changes in crime figures. ● Unemployment figures, with special regard to inner-city areas in which unemployment may be endemic. ● Educational results, especially in schools in poor rural and run-down inner-city areas. ● Levels of emigration and immigration.
PERSONAL STRESS This causes individuals to suffer a lack of both control and ability to function on a reasonable level.	● Persistent insomnia. ● Rashes, cramps, headaches, or other physical symptoms of unknown origin. ● Changes in eating patterns. ● Marked rise in a personal level of cigarette, alcohol, and drug consumption.
ORGANIZATIONAL STRESS This affects the general morale of an organization, resulting in both financial and personnel problems.	● Unexpected changes in levels of absenteeism among employees. ● Quality of production within the organization, with the emphasis on apparent decline. ● Number of work-related accidents. ● Number of work-related health complaints.

HOW STRESSED ARE YOU?

The first hurdle to beating stress is recognizing its existence – acknowledging that stress is a problem is a vital step toward reducing it. Measure your level of stress regularly by responding to the following statements, then mark the options closest to your experience. Be as honest as you can: if your answer is "never," mark Option 1; if it is "always," mark Option 4; and so on. Add your scores together, then refer to the Analysis to see how you scored. Use your answers to identify the areas that need improving.

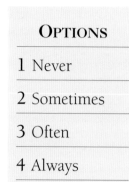

OPTIONS
1 Never
2 Sometimes
3 Often
4 Always

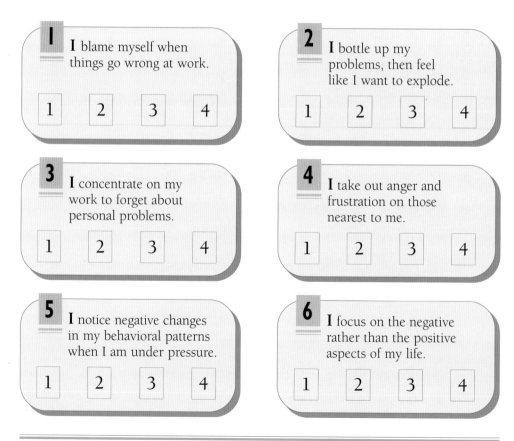

1 I blame myself when things go wrong at work.

1 2 3 4

2 I bottle up my problems, then feel like I want to explode.

1 2 3 4

3 I concentrate on my work to forget about personal problems.

1 2 3 4

4 I take out anger and frustration on those nearest to me.

1 2 3 4

5 I notice negative changes in my behavioral patterns when I am under pressure.

1 2 3 4

6 I focus on the negative rather than the positive aspects of my life.

1 2 3 4

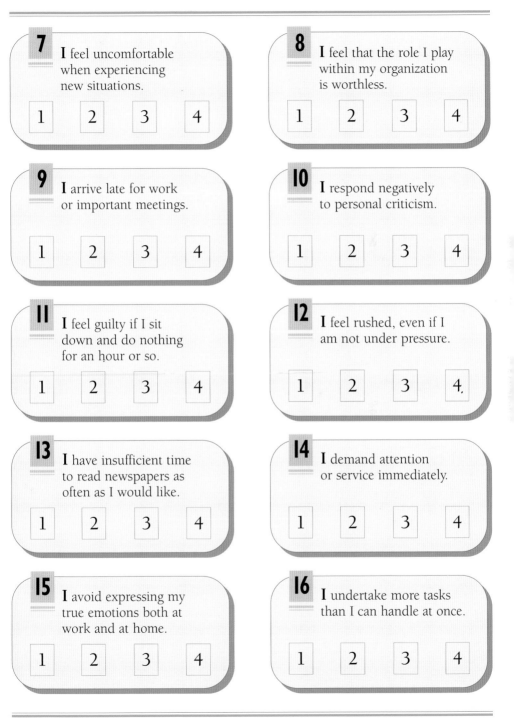

7 **I** feel uncomfortable when experiencing new situations.

1 2 3 4

8 **I** feel that the role I play within my organization is worthless.

1 2 3 4

9 **I** arrive late for work or important meetings.

1 2 3 4

10 **I** respond negatively to personal criticism.

1 2 3 4

11 **I** feel guilty if I sit down and do nothing for an hour or so.

1 2 3 4

12 **I** feel rushed, even if I am not under pressure.

1 2 3 4

13 **I** have insufficient time to read newspapers as often as I would like.

1 2 3 4

14 **I** demand attention or service immediately.

1 2 3 4

15 **I** avoid expressing my true emotions both at work and at home.

1 2 3 4

16 **I** undertake more tasks than I can handle at once.

1 2 3 4

17 I resist taking advice from colleagues and superiors.

1　2　3　4

18 I ignore my own professional or physical limitations.

1　2　3　4

19 I neglect my hobbies and interests because my work takes up all my time.

1　2　3　4

20 I tackle situations before thinking them through thoroughly.

1　2　3　4

21 I am too busy to have lunch with friends and colleagues during the week.

1　2　3　4

22 I put off confronting and resolving difficult situations when they arise.

1　2　3　4

23 People take advantage of me when I do not act assertively.

1　2　3　4

24 I am embarrassed to say when I feel overloaded with work.

1　2　3　4

25 I avoid delegating tasks to other people.

1　2　3　4

26 I deal with tasks before prioritizing my workload.

1　2　3　4

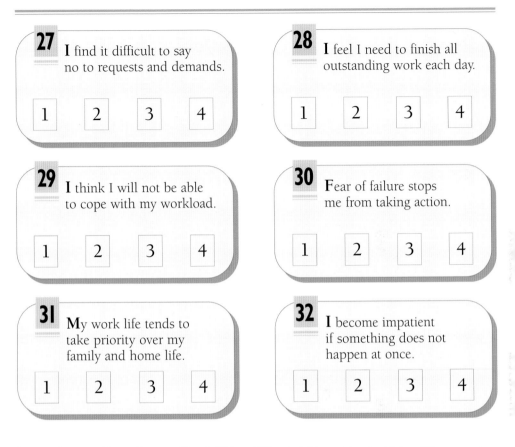

27 I find it difficult to say no to requests and demands.

| 1 | 2 | 3 | 4 |

28 I feel I need to finish all outstanding work each day.

| 1 | 2 | 3 | 4 |

29 I think I will not be able to cope with my workload.

| 1 | 2 | 3 | 4 |

30 Fear of failure stops me from taking action.

| 1 | 2 | 3 | 4 |

31 My work life tends to take priority over my family and home life.

| 1 | 2 | 3 | 4 |

32 I become impatient if something does not happen at once.

| 1 | 2 | 3 | 4 |

ANALYSIS

Now that you have completed the self-assessment, add up your total score and check your stress level by reading the corresponding evaluation. However low your stress level may be, there is always room for improvement. Identify your weakest areas, then refer to the relevant chapters in this section. Here you will find practical advice and tips to reduce your own stress levels and minimize any stress-inducing factors in your work environment.

32–64: You manage your stress level very well. Too little stress can be unstimulating, so strive to achieve the optimum balance between positive and negative stress.
65–95: You have a reasonably safe level of stress, but certain areas need improvement.
96–128: Your level of stress is too high. You need to develop new strategies to help reduce it.

ANALYZING THE CAUSES OF STRESS

Society, the working world, and daily life have changed almost beyond recognition in the past 50 years. These changes have contributed to a major increase in stress.

CHANGING SOCIETIES

Demographic change has been dramatic in recent years. Changes include rapid population growth, migration from rural areas to cities, a rise in the number of elderly people, and the developing role of women. All these changes have increased stress levels.

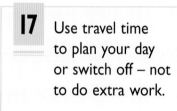

17 Use travel time to plan your day or switch off – not to do extra work.

INCREASING URBANIZATION

The most stressful change in recent decades has been rapid urbanization. In some industrialized countries, such as the Netherlands and Germany, more than 80 percent of the population lives in cities. Stress arises from cramped living conditions, the proximity of millions of other people, and high levels of crime, noise, and air pollution.

◀ **POPULATION INCREASE**
It took thousands of years before our planet boasted one billion people. Now the population increases by over one billion per decade.

AGING POPULATIONS

Life expectancy is increasing – people live longer than ever before. This is due to better diet and a rapid improvement in medical knowledge over the past 200 years. The fall in the birth rate (especially in urban areas) means that the world's industrial nations now have an aging population – an increasing proportion of over-60s. On an individual level, this may be stressful when there is conflict between career plans and long-term care for aging relatives. The cost to society is also increasing as healthcare costs continue to spiral.

▼ **CHANGES IN WORLD POPULATION**
The charts below show how the average age of the world's population changed in a 50-year period. From 1950 to 2000, the population pyramid turns upside down, ending up with the largest slice of the population aged between 50 and 64 years instead of under the age of 30.

KEY

👤 *10 million men*   👤 *10 million women*

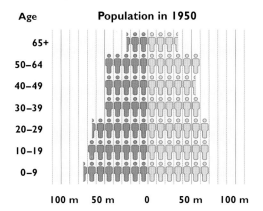

Age	Population in 1950		Age	Estimated population in 2000
65+			65+	
50–64			50–64	
40–49			40–49	
30–39			30–39	
20–29			20–29	
10–19			10–19	
0–9			0–9	

100 m 50 m 0 50 m 100 m   100 m 50 m 0 50 m 100 m

18 Spend an hour or two alone each week, away from work and family.

CHANGING GENDER ROLES

The role of women has changed dramatically over the past 100 years, especially in urban societies. As women make up a greater part of the total labor force, they are judged by the same criteria and put under the same stresses as men. However, women often suffer more stress than their male colleagues because of conflict between work outside the home and work within the home, where they may continue to shoulder the main responsibility for traditional female roles. These changing roles also challenge male identity and work patterns as women take on jobs traditionally held by men.

CHANGING ORGANIZATIONS

In recent years, many companies have launched new products or services while also making cutbacks. Such changes can be vital to a company's survival, but employees may find themselves working harder than ever and facing an uncertain future.

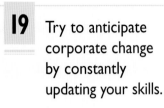

19 Try to anticipate corporate change by constantly updating your skills.

THE LANGUAGE OF CHANGE

ACQUISITION: the purchase by one company of the controlling interest in another.

ALLIANCE: a connection between two organizations for their mutual benefit.

FLATTENING: widening the scope of jobs by compressing organizational hierarchy.

GLOBALIZING: marketing products or services worldwide.

MERGER: the combining of two or more organizations into one.

PRIVATIZING: selling a state-owned firm to the private sector.

QUALITY MANAGING: setting up company systems to monitor product quality.

REENGINEERING: completely rethinking and redesigning organizational processes.

RESTRUCTURING: reorganizing the structure and processes of work within an organization.

RESPONDING TO PRESSURE

The upheaval triggered by the need for cost-cutting and increasing productivity has two main causes:

- Globalization has left local suppliers facing stiff competition and led to aggressive cost-cutting in the marketplace;
- Information technology, including fax machines, e-mail, and video conferencing, has accelerated the speed at which many business transactions can be performed and put pressure on the workforce to be ever more productive.

RETHINKING COMPANIES

New competition and pressures on companies to be more productive have led them to pursue certain strategies that put their workers under stress. Mergers and acquisitions between corporations have been taking place at an increasing rate and, when these occur, they usually bring job losses. This is because they tend to create one large corporation in which key positions at many levels are duplicated, making job cuts inevitable.

20 Adopt new management ideas only if they are useful – never adopt what is merely fashionable.

CHANGING OPERATIONS

In the search for improvement, companies look closely at how they operate – the way production processes work, for example, and ways of keeping track of stock. Many companies have experimented with reengineering their structures and involving employees in controlling product quality and ensuring continuous improvement.

The introduction of robots on to assembly lines has eliminated many manual jobs once required for mass production, so that manufacturing jobs are often relatively isolated with little social contact.

21 Protect your job by drawing attention to the value of your work.

ENCOUNTERING NEW WORK CULTURES

The changes occurring in the workplace in recent years have radically altered the work culture of many companies, large and small. For example, opportunistic takeovers have put old-fashioned organizations into the hands of ambitious and fast-moving entrepreneurs with very different values. Widespread privatization has turned state-owned enterprises into private enterprises, which tend to be more committed to maximizing profit than to maintaining the workforce.

22 Take advantage of training programs to learn as much as you can about new or different work cultures.

REACHING THE LIMITS

All these changes in the workplace – technical, strategic, operational, and cultural – have had profound and far-reaching effects on the employees of the organizations that undergo them. A number of studies have pointed out that, although workers are adaptable, there are limits to the amount of change that human beings can absorb. If organizations keep reaching and exceeding these limits – moving the goalposts – they may find that eventually their workers can no longer tolerate the demands made of them.

23 Identify like-minded colleagues, then work with them to adapt to change.

CHANGING PRACTICES

Change is less stressful when anticipated. Keep abreast of recent developments within your industry, familiarize yourself with new technology, try to gain experience of as many different skills as possible, and maximize the options available to you.

24 Be prepared to change careers at least once in your working life.

25 When learning new technology, start slowly and build confidence.

REASSESSING MARKETS

The ability to anticipate change depends on recognizing shifts in supply and demand in the labor market. This is not easy, if only because the advent of computers has meant that changes occur much more rapidly than in the past. There are, however, a few key communication and computer technologies, including the Internet and multimedia, that are widely available and drive many other developments. Keeping abreast of changes within these technologies can maximize job prospects and minimize stress by giving you the ability to change with the employment market.

UNDERSTANDING NEW TECHNOLOGY

Computers are fundamental to 99 percent of the world's businesses. But many senior managers who are responsible for purchasing hardware and deciding how to use it have scant knowledge of how much it can do. Courses covering all stages are available to help you improve your computer skills – utilize them, since computer literacy is essential for employees at all levels.

◀ **SURFING THE INTERNET**
The advent of e-mail and the World Wide Web on the Internet is rapidly changing the way we all work.

RELOCATING OFFICES

Information technology provides more flexibility in the way we work today by enabling individuals to decide how and where they work. Those whose jobs require little more than a computer and a phone can work as easily in an airport lounge or the back seat of a car as in a traditional office. Many people now choose to work at home. In this way they can work without the usual interruptions while avoiding the cumulative stress of commuting and reducing travel costs. Everyday chores such as shopping and settling bills are increasingly being carried out by computer from home offices.

26 Try to set up an office near other people: isolation can be stressful.

WORKING FROM HOME ▶
Try to locate your home office in a room set aside for that purpose, as far as possible from living and sleeping areas, so you can leave work behind at the end of the day. Many people who work at home convert a spare bedroom into an office.

27 Make sure your home office is separate from your living space.

28 It is never too late to learn a new skill such as computing.

DIVERSIFYING CAREERS

One spin-off from the rapid changes occurring in the workplace is the opportunity to enjoy several different careers during a lifetime. Traditionally, people learned a trade or profession that they then practiced throughout their working life. Today, the demand for skills is changing so fast that this is no longer very likely to happen.

Adaptability and flexibility are vital to minimize the stress of job loss. Anticipate changes, and be prepared for them wherever possible. Retrain if necessary, and look on an unexpected job loss as an "opportunity," allowing you to pursue a new career doing something that really interests you.

Analyzing Jobs

S *ome jobs are intrinsically more stressful than others. Jobs at different levels within the hierarchy of an organization each have their own stress factors. Likely stress levels are an important consideration when deciding if a job is suitable for you.*

29 Assess the stress factors of any new job before you accept it.

Levels of Stress in Different Job Types

Types of Job	Related Causes of Stress
Financial Accountants, stock-market traders, mortgage consultants, bank tellers.	In companies where money is the major product, a high level of stress is a permanent feature. The larger the amounts involved, the greater the stress on the staff.
Sales-Oriented Sales and marketing managers and consultants, advertising executives.	These jobs pressurize workers by continually demanding that they reach targets within certain budgets and deadlines. Salespeople are constantly "on show."
Technological Computer programmers and technicians, statisticians.	Information-technology specialists need to keep abreast of the fastest-changing industry ever. Technicians need to fix hardware and explain complex problems to the uninitiated.
Media Newspaper, magazine, or television journalists, producers, editors.	Periods of calm are interspersed with frantic bursts of activity as media workers hunt for new subject material and are then required to be creative under tight deadlines.
Medical Nurses, doctors, anesthetists, pharmacists, physical therapists.	When people's health and even lives are at stake, there can be enormous pressure to make the right decision quickly. There is great stress in dealing with human distress.
People-Based Personnel managers, social workers, counselors, any managers with a team of staff working under them.	These jobs require skills such as tact and discretion that can make it difficult to socialize with colleagues. It may be necessary to implement job reductions, disciplinary procedures, and other decisions that cause people distress.

STRESS IN MANAGEMENT

Frequently, managers find themselves in isolated positions. They are often caught between trying to satisfy the needs of their staff on the one hand and fulfilling the wishes of their superiors on the other. They also need to make difficult decisions about the future of their staff. Managers require a number of people skills, which may be difficult to define. A feeling that you lack these skills is stressful, as is an inability to delegate, an inability to say "no," a sense of ambiguity about your supposed role, and too much responsibility.

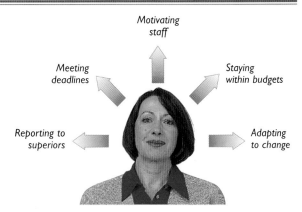

Motivating staff

Meeting deadlines

Staying within budgets

Reporting to superiors

Adapting to change

▲ DEMANDS ON A MANAGER

Too many demands and too much responsibility placed on one person can result in high stress levels. Many managers regard stress as a normal part of working life, but without adequate time for relaxation, stress can lead to illness and even death.

30 Gradually increase the number and complexity of tasks you delegate successfully every day.

Finding little variety in daily tasks

Being uncertain about career prospects

Having no control over workload

Lacking in financial incentives

Feeling the lack of job status

▲ STRESSES ON A CLERICAL WORKER

Many clerical jobs are so repetitive and undemanding that the worker receives very little job satisfaction. There is too little responsibility and therefore a lack of potential for creativity. The boredom and lethargy thus induced can be highly stressful and difficult to shake off.

STRESS AT OTHER LEVELS

Junior white-collar workers may suffer from the stress of too little responsibility and not enough control over a heavy and tedious workload. An employee on a production line may become ill as a result of unstimulating, repetitive work. Stress among manual laborers can often be caused by the physical demands of their jobs, such as dangerous or high-level work on a building site.

ASSESSING RELATIONSHIPS

Poor relationships with colleagues at work can cause stress. Try to analyze relationships that could be improved and identify any problem areas. Is it difficult to control your subordinates, for example, or are superiors distant and unappreciative?

 31 Treat all staff with dignity and respect, regardless of their positions or titles.

 32 Give coworkers a treat to show your appreciation.

EXPERIENCING CHANGE

New organizational structures lay great emphasis on teamwork. The rapid growth of information technology can make middle managers obsolete by reducing their function as communicators of information through an organization. Letting go of such managers and the consequent change in corporate hierarchy are part of a process known as "flattening." Stress in a flattened company can arise because more people find themselves working at a similar level of seniority, and this can lead to greater competition. Employees are working more closely with their colleagues than before, and their roles in a team can often overlap. The success of a smooth-running and happy team depends on cooperation. If this is not present, conflict is likely.

 33 Have lunch with a new colleague to establish a working relationship.

CULTURAL DIFFERENCES

The opportunities for misunderstanding that arise when working with people from other countries can be intensely stressful.

If you do business with a society that is culturally different from yours, familiarize yourself with the values espoused by that society. For example, in Europe and the US, the age of senior staff is regarded as largely irrelevant – in fact, youth is seen as being linked to energy. In East Asia, however, age is respected because it is linked with experience and wisdom. Senior managers may not expect to have dealings on an equal basis with a younger person, and you should always be sensitive to this when negotiating with someone of a different age.

OBSERVING RELATIONSHIPS

Despite corporate restructuring, relationships at work are still largely influenced by hierarchy and by the level of cohesiveness in a group. Factors such as length of service and different skill areas play a crucial role in such work relationships. Look around your office: who goes to whom for help? Who socializes together? Is anybody isolated, and do you know why? Are there any rivalries?

34 Introduce yourself to other people in your company by visiting their offices.

DEALING WITH FELLOW WORKERS

MANAGER
As a manager it is inevitable that you will come into contact with people on all levels. Keep lines of communication open at all times to avoid stressful misunderstandings and any resulting conflict.

SUPERIOR
Is your superior a reader (prefers written reports) or a listener (prefers verbal information)? Communicate in the way they prefer to maintain good relations.

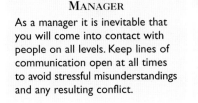

COLLEAGUE
Team members may be competing with you for promotion. If you work together, be aware of any conflict of interest, and do not assume you share the same priorities.

SUBORDINATE
Gain respect from subordinates by treating them as equals. Encourage two-way dialogue so that they know what is going on and can make a positive contribution.

ANALYZING PROBLEMS

Layers of formality at work may make it difficult to confront a relationship problem, but failure to do so means bottling it up, which can be very stressful.

First, you need to identify the basic cause of the problem, then talk to someone who understands the situation and can help. Common problems between people include no feedback on decisions, office politics, uncertainty about roles, unreasonable deadlines, and personality clashes. Once you have analyzed the problem, you can decide on a solution.

35 Share the trip to work with a colleague who lives nearby.

ASSESSING THE WORKPLACE

The structure of an organization and its day-to-day workplace conditions can have a major effect on stress levels. Take a long, hard look at both areas to help identify what is putting you or your colleagues under stress, then work out the best solutions.

36 Always be flexible in your attitudes – you may not know the full story.

37 Play an active part in improving the quality of office life.

38 Do not make major decisions too quickly.

KNOWING YOUR COMPANY

Do you agree with the way your company does business? Do you feel comfortable with its policies, structure, and hierarchy? If the answer to any of these questions is "no," you are in a stress-creating situation. It may seem that the easiest thing to do is just to leave an organization if you dislike its structure, but such a radical move is in itself very stressful. It is better to familiarize yourself with all the information you can about the areas you do not like and to learn the reasons behind the way the company is organized and run. Having armed yourself with all the facts, you can then become involved in suggesting improvements from within.

TREADING ▶ GENTLY
Sharon's attempts to change company policy were vetoed by her boss, putting her in a stressful situation. After learning more about the company, she realized that her original ideas were too radical. She went on to develop successful new products by building on the company's existing strengths.

CASE STUDY
Sharon was appointed the new product development manager at Tiny Tim Toys, makers of quality toys for children. She was faced with a rigid marketing policy and declining sales. The directors constantly rejected her new product ideas, and after several months she became very frustrated.
Under pressure to come up with ideas that the board would find acceptable, she discussed the company's past successes with the sales director, then spoke to the sales representatives to see how the company's products were viewed by toy stores. She then produced a report showing that Tiny Tim Toys was respected by retailers but was seen as unexciting. The board gave Sharon the go-ahead to update its most successful line of toys, and sales figures slowly began to improve.

IMPROVING CONDITIONS

A poor working environment can be a major cause of stress. Not only does it affect the way you do your job, but it can also undermine your health. Assess working conditions using the checklist below. If conditions need improving, make the changes that you can implement, then ask your organization to make it a priority to make further improvements if necessary:

- Are the desks arranged to maximize space?
- Is there noise or other pollution?
- Is there enough natural light?
- Is there enough storage and filing space? Do colleagues put things back where they belong?
- Is the temperature consistently comfortable? Is it controlled artificially? Does the air conditioning work well? Does it make noise?
- Is the office equipment sophisticated enough to deal with the tasks being set?
- Is there a support network in place in case computer, electrical, or other systems fail?

POINTS TO REMEMBER

- Maintaining a pleasant working environment shows the company cares for its employees, giving a better image to visitors.
- Good use of space allows each person some privacy, even within open-plan offices.
- Natural light can lift moods and prevent eye strain.
- Investing in good storage systems cuts down on the time wasted looking for lost papers or files.
- Potted plants improve humidity in dry air-conditioned offices.
- Adjustable chairs help prevent back pain, a major cause of absenteeism among office staff.
- Repairing or replacing faulty office equipment improves efficiency and productivity.

MAKING ▶ CHANGES
If necessary, rearrange the layout of an office to create a more relaxed environment. Try to strike a balance between allowing easy contact and providing privacy. Set aside a table for meetings in a quiet area so that distractions are kept to a minimum.

COPING WITH DAILY LIFE

Many people believe that they have no choice but to work all the hours available. This belief may be reinforced if work is used to escape from other problems. Be aware of your needs, and try to develop a fulfilling private life as well as a career.

39 Attempt to have lunch with your partner or a close friend once a week.

▲ **FORMING CLOSE BONDS**
Building a happy family life and establishing a close circle of friends can prove to be a successful way to avoid stress.

MEASURING STRESS ▶
Research has revealed that the death of a partner is at the top of the list of life's most stressful events. Even positive events such as marriage can cause tremendous stress. Experiencing a number of major life events in a short period of time greatly increases the risk of stress.

DEALING WITH CHANGE

Life events can suddenly disrupt a happy balance between work and home. A change of job is an obvious example; events such as marriage or the death of a parent may also undermine this balance.

When stressful changes occur, take time to reassess your lifestyle. Draw up a list of your priorities. You may know what is important in your life, but you may have difficulty in accepting or seeing the implications. "My children are the most important thing in the world to me," says many a manager who sees them on just one night a week. Use change as a positive way to reorder your life.

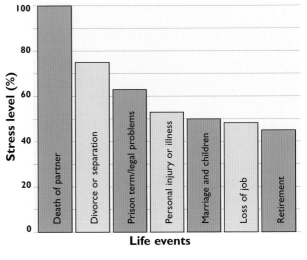

Stress level (%)

Life events: Death of partner, Divorce or separation, Prison term/legal problems, Personal injury or illness, Marriage and children, Loss of job, Retirement

COPING WITH LIFE EVENTS

Aside from death and divorce, there are a number of other life experiences that can cause high stress levels. These include moving, having a baby (for both mother and father), taking a job in a foreign country, and retiring from work. Such events all involve major change, a break in daily routine, and often a series of goodbyes.

To minimize the stress caused by such an event, do not pretend that it has not happened, but try to reduce the uncertainty involved. Visit the foreign job site before you move. Take retirement gradually by working two days a week initially. Take at least a week off work to move. Use up any paid or unpaid leave. Take time and care to say goodbye.

40 Listen carefully to what your children say to you.

41 If you live near your work, walk or cycle to work a few times a week.

▲ COMMUTING BY CAR

If it is important that you arrive somewhere at a specific time, do not travel by road. Today's traffic jams make the car the least reliable form of transportation – as well as the most antisocial. Use an alternative method of transportation where possible.

42 Learn to talk openly about your emotions and feelings with close friends and confidants.

COMMUTING TO WORK

Our daily journeys to and from work are among the most stressful regular events in our lives. Worries about punctuality, traffic jams, and overcrowded trains and buses are experienced on a repeated basis, and over weeks and months this can lead to an accumulation of stress.

Think carefully about whether you can rearrange your travel so that it occurs outside the usual rush hours. If possible, work at home for an hour or two in the morning. Arranging flexible working hours allows you to avoid peak travel times by arriving at work late or early, reducing the stress linked to time pressure and punctuality.

DEALING WITH STRESS AT WORK

Everybody responds to stress in a different way. It is only by understanding the nature of individual responses that you can start fighting stress in yourself and others.

IDENTIFYING ATTITUDES

Organizations, like individuals, differ greatly in their attitudes to stress. Some take a hard-line approach, expecting their employees to be tough enough to handle stress. Others are more caring and helpful in their responses to such problems.

43 Set up a suggestion box so employees can leave ideas for reducing stress.

44 Relieve pressure by discussing work problems openly.

45 Go for a jog or swim at lunchtime to alleviate stress.

KNOWING THE CULTURE

Take note of the predominant attitudes and behavior at work to assess your organization's approach to stress. If stress is an intrinsic part of a job, it is often easier to glamorize it than to change working practices. In certain work cultures, some stress is unavoidable: oil and mining companies expect employees to spend time away from home, and management consulting firms and investment banks expect their staff to work long hours. It is important to be able to identify unacceptable levels of workplace stress; disguising stress can make it harder to deal with the long-term effects.

CASE STUDY

The managing director of a large commercial company often boasted that he spent more time out of the office on business trips than at his desk.

When asked to develop a new product line, he worked day and night to coordinate the efforts of different departments. He flew around the world in search of information and contacts to ensure that the new line would be a success. His free time shrank, his home life suffered, he was constantly tired, and he ate poorly, but, because he knew that his company was depending on him, he continued. He began to experience severe stomach pains and was diagnosed with a peptic ulcer.

The company accepted that his condition was due to the stress of his workload. On his doctor's orders, he took a long vacation. A stress counselor was appointed by the company to help prevent future problems.

◀ **GLAMORIZING STRESS**

This case reflects a common problem. Many high-powered employees accept the heavy workload imposed by their companies and brag about their responsibilities to disguise stress and fears of failure. This company acted well by admitting that it had contributed to an unacceptably high stress level.

ASSESSING COMMITMENT TO STAFF

Some indication of a company's commitment to minimizing stress among its employees can be gleaned from its expenditure on the following:

TRAINING AND DEVELOPMENT

Companies sometimes give a figure for this in their annual accounts. If there is no figure, ask why.

REWARDS AND PROMOTION

A company that appreciates good work may give financial or other incentives, or reward by promotion.

RECRUITMENT AND SELECTION

The company that spends little time on recruitment does not mind if it loses its recruits. Candidates applying for jobs may find that a slow selection procedure or careful checking of references means that the company cares about its staff.

PENSION FUNDS

A company with a generous staff pension plan is probably serious about keeping its employees and looking after their general welfare (including their working conditions) over a long period of time.

CHANGING ATTITUDES

If your organization ignores stress in the workplace, try persuading its decision-makers to take stress seriously by making them aware of the benefits of a new attitude. For example, point out how much money stress can cost in absenteeism, and explain how much other companies have saved – several American companies claim to have reduced absenteeism by up to 60 percent by introducing counseling for staff. Remind employers that productivity usually increases when employees are happy.

46 Challenge racism or sexism within your company.

Devising a Strategy

Any organization should view devising a strategy to reduce stress as a necessary part of the cost of maintaining its most valuable asset – its workforce. The ideal strategy will depend upon the size and resources of the organization.

 47 Think about introducing a pilot program before a full program.

 48 Set up support systems to help stressed staff.

49 Increase investment in staff training where necessary.

THINGS TO DO

1. Identify those employees most at risk from stress.

2. Offer incentives for low absenteeism, being careful not to increase stress.

3. Promote stress awareness in in-house publications.

4. Do not allow anyone to work in-house after 7 p.m.

5. Introduce a no-smoking policy in your office.

Considering Elements

The following elements can be included in an organization's strategy for reducing stress:

- A program to increase the level of awareness throughout the organization of the enormous cost of stress within the workplace;
- A program to help employees identify the symptoms of stress both in themselves and in their colleagues;
- A counseling program to help individuals;
- A system for monitoring absenteeism (the reasons for implementing such a system, and how long it will take to implement, should be explained to all staff);
- Regular feedback reports to staff concerning the progress of the new strategy and any improvements that it brings about;
- A program of stress-preventive measures to improve the overall well-being of employees in the long term, such as the provision of sports facilities, flextime, health insurance, and regular medical checks.

 50 Examine the resources of your company before deciding which strategy to use to deal with stress.

DECIDING ON LEVELS OF CHANGE

When you are devising your strategy, you need to choose a level of intervention: primary, secondary, or tertiary. Each level will bring changes to bear on a different aspect of the stress problem. Primary intervention concerns fundamental change and is rare; secondary intervention combats specific causes of stress; and tertiary intervention is concerned with individual treatment and long-term recovery.

 51 Encourage healthy eating by improving in-house cafeteria lunch menus.

CONSIDERING LEVELS OF INTERVENTION

LEVEL	EXAMPLES	IMPLICATIONS
PRIMARY Involves radical change affecting an entire organization.	● Relocating from urban areas to more rural sites to improve the working environment. ● Redesigning premises, and rebuilding if necessary, to upgrade and modernize facilities.	● Companies must pay relocation expenses and set up support systems to help staff adjust. ● If staff are adversely affected while building work takes place, organizations may be obliged to offer compensation.
SECONDARY Deals with the specific causes of stress by tackling problems directly.	● Improving access to sports facilities to promote the health and fitness of employees. ● Providing an improved diet for staff where in-house cafeteria facilities exist.	● Companies may need to provide showers and changing rooms for those using sports facilities. ● In-house cafeterias should be able to offer a wide choice of meals and provide for those with special dietary requirements.
TERTIARY Provides help on an individual basis for those who suffer from stress.	● Initiating programs to help staff stop smoking or drinking; offering free medical checks. ● Providing free, confidential counseling for employees with personal problems.	● Ongoing support should be provided for staff who are trying to give up smoking or drinking. ● Free counseling services should be made available for as long as individual staff members feel that they require them.

TAKING POSITIVE ACTION

An organization that sets out to take positive action on stress at work must commit itself to the costs involved to reap the full benefits. These benefits can be measured financially as well as in terms of morale and increased productivity.

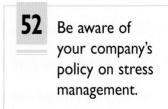

52 Be aware of your company's policy on stress management.

STARTING GRADUALLY

Taking steps to minimize stress involves change, which itself is often stressful. Remember that the costs of a stress-management program can include poor morale if the plan fails. Introduce such programs gradually to ensure that each step achieves its aim. For example, if employees are given free membership at a local gym, monitoring the staff usage will provide a good indication of how popular it is. If the facilities are well used, it might be worthwhile considering providing an on-site company gym, secure in the knowledge that it would not be a waste of money.

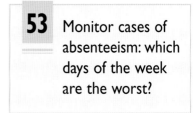

53 Monitor cases of absenteeism: which days of the week are the worst?

ANALYZING THE COSTS OF INTERVENTION

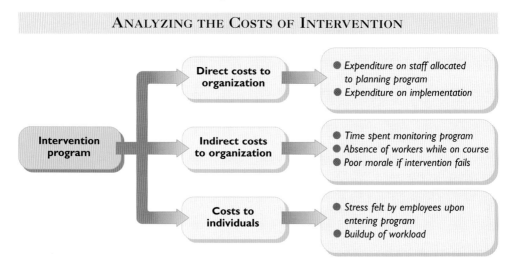

Intervention program

Direct costs to organization
- Expenditure on staff allocated to planning program
- Expenditure on implementation

Indirect costs to organization
- Time spent monitoring program
- Absence of workers while on course
- Poor morale if intervention fails

Costs to individuals
- Stress felt by employees upon entering program
- Buildup of workload

COMMITTING TO CHANGE

Stress management is not a quick-fix solution. To be effective, intervention must extend indefinitely, and the emphasis should gradually shift from cure of stress to prevention. Initially, the aim should be to reduce absenteeism by removing or changing the factors that create stress. Once the drop in absenteeism levels off, the program should aim to prevent it from rising again. So, in the early stages the emphasis should be on change, while later it should be on monitoring and maintaining the well-being of staff.

54 Seek out factual evidence for the effectiveness of any intervention.

MAKING CHANGES ▶

This chief executive focused on shifting the emphasis from speed to quality of work, and building team spirit. These measures increased both job satisfaction and efficiency and thereby reduced stress levels in the workforce.

CASE STUDY

Mudd & Son, a farm machinery manufacturer, appointed a forward-thinking chief executive who discovered problems with absenteeism and low morale among the workers. Employees worked on a piecework system – those who worked quickly were paid more than those who did not.

The chief executive developed a radical plan for change. The piecework system was replaced with single-status employment, in which workers were divided into grades. The better the quality of work, the higher the grade of pay. She also introduced a bonus plan rewarding workers' oustanding achievement.

Signatures of agreement were obtained from all the employees before the changes were implemented. This made the workers feel more like a team and had a positive long-term effect on output.

CASE STUDY

A large electronics company suffered a sharp drop in profit due to a high staff turnover. A team of management consultants was appointed by the directors to investigate the problem; they reported too rigid a management structure and a general lack of communication between staff and management.

Changes to the structure of the company were proposed and implemented. The consultants then suggested that all employees should go on team-building courses involving taking part in a range of outdoor activities.

Despite initial resistance from certain managers, the first course went ahead. Team members noted an increase in trust and understanding during the course. Many managers who attended the course also reported improved working relations with colleagues and junior staff.

◀ BUILDING ON SUCCESS

Here, company structure was found to be the cause of falling profits. Although the fundamental changes introduced to solve the problem met with resistance, the improved relations between staff and management benefited the whole company, lowering stress and ultimately raising profits.

RECLAIMING YOUR DESK

Start with your own desk to reduce stress in the workplace. Mess just makes for stress. Do not fool yourself that a messy desk is acceptable because you know where things are. Do not rely on new technology and the "paperless office" to rescue you.

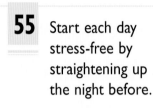

55 Start each day stress-free by straightening up the night before.

POINTS TO REMEMBER

- Papers, files, and books are best stored on shelves and not your desk, leaving more work space.

- Old newspapers should be thrown away – news becomes stale fast.

- Large pieces of paper are best for writing notes. Scraps get lost.

- Records of phone calls are useless if you cannot remember when they occurred, so date notes.

56 Keep an executive toy to play with during breaks.

CLEARING OUT DEBRIS

Some people have a fear of throwing things away and of discovering that they have just disposed of the very thing they need. They therefore hoard every useless or out-of-date note. In most jobs, however, you can safely follow the three-month rule. Anything that has remained unread on your desk for three months is due for a move on to another destination – either to a file for long-term storage or into the wastepaper basket. If you have not organized your desk or done your filing for a long time, you need to be ruthless. Sort papers and notes into three distinct piles:
- Action now – work to be completed today;
- Action later – put the paper in your pending tray and complete the work within a week;
- No action – file it or throw it away.

GETTING ORGANIZED

Equip your desk with an in-box, pending tray, filing tray, and out-box – use a stacking system to save space. Make sure you sort through your pending tray and empty it once a week. Arrange your desk so that those things you use most often are most accessible. Position your computer so you do not need to twist around to use it. The monitor should be directly in front of you.

◀ **DISCARDING WASTE**
It is less stressful to have an empty desk and a full wastepaper basket than the reverse. Putting unwanted paper in the can brings a real sense of achievement. Recycle paper if possible.

IMPROVING SURROUNDINGS

Stress is affected by other visual stimuli, such as the color of our surroundings. Companies use color to create moods – in stores, reception areas, and so on. Do the same for the space around your desk. The color you select will depend on whether you prefer to be soothed or stimulated by your surroundings. Choose whichever shade is easiest for you to live and work with. Add color to your desk with flowers, plants, and family photographs.

57 Try out different room plans before you settle into a new office.

Computer monitor is angled away from harsh light

Desk is brightened up with bunch of flowers

Plant adds touch of greenery to desk

Family photo reminds you of happy times

Boxes are easily reached

Filing cabinet is close at hand

Chair swivels to face computer or writing space

▲ ENHANCING YOUR WORK SPACE

Make your workspace as aesthetically pleasing as your home. After all, you probably spend more waking hours there than you do in your home.

58 When you move to a new work space, spend time thinking how to make it more pleasant.

STUDYING WORK PATTERNS

*S*tress can be insidious and cumulative. *The best way to avoid suffering from it is to learn to anticipate it. By analyzing and pinpointing events and times that regularly cause stress, it is possible to set about preventing further problems from occurring.*

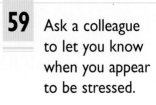

59 Ask a colleague to let you know when you appear to be stressed.

60 Overestimate when calculating the time that a project will take.

RECOGNIZING STRESSFUL TIMES

In the aftermath of a stressful time at work, it is easy to forget just how you managed to cope. In order to analyze stress effectively and make changes, you need to recognize your own patterns and cycles of behavior. To do this, familiarize yourself with those times of year, month, week, and day when you find you are most busy, keep records of the problems you experience, and obtain feedback from colleagues on how you perform when stressed.

ANNUAL WORK PATTERNS

Make up an annual or half-yearly chart to help you analyze annual work patterns. List all the major projects or tasks you need to complete, along with their start and end dates. Draw a line between these two dates for each task, and you will be able to see where the overlaps occur. These mark your busiest times at work and will help you plan ahead, avoiding any bottlenecks and taking vacations to coincide with quiet periods.

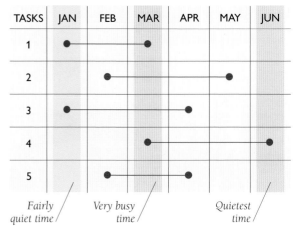

▲ **PREPARING FOR PRESSURE**
This half-yearly chart shows the work pattern of someone whose busiest period is in March. During this time, five major tasks are ending, just beginning, or are in progress.

DAILY WORK PATTERNS

Difficulties in time management and workload prioritization are among the most common causes of stress. Once you have identified where such problems exist, you will be better able to handle them. The best way to do this is to keep a detailed daily stress diary. Prepare a "to do" list of all the tasks you have to perform each day, then use this to analyze how you are coping with your workload. Note down any problems that interfered with or prevented you from completing your tasks. This may take time to produce, but in the long term it will prevent day-to-day stress.

61 Jot down problems on a day-to-day basis, then see if a pattern emerges.

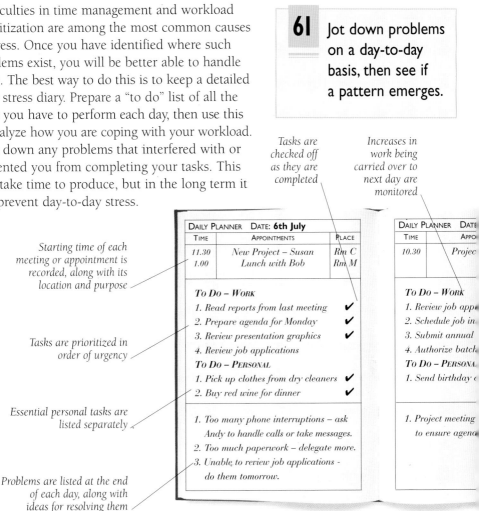

Tasks are checked off as they are completed

Increases in work being carried over to next day are monitored

Starting time of each meeting or appointment is recorded, along with its location and purpose

Tasks are prioritized in order of urgency

Essential personal tasks are listed separately

Problems are listed at the end of each day, along with ideas for resolving them

DAILY PLANNER   DATE: 6th July

TIME	APPOINTMENTS	PLACE
11.30	New Project – Susan	Rm C
1.00	Lunch with Bob	Rm M

TO DO – WORK
1. Read reports from last meeting ✔
2. Prepare agenda for Monday ✔
3. Review presentation graphics ✔
4. Review job applications

TO DO – PERSONAL
1. Pick up clothes from dry cleaners ✔
2. Buy red wine for dinner ✔

1. Too many phone interruptions – ask Andy to handle calls or take messages.
2. Too much paperwork – delegate more.
3. Unable to review job applications - do them tomorrow.

DAILY PLANNER   DATE

TIME	APPO...
10.30	Projec...

TO DO – WORK
1. Review job app...
2. Schedule job in...
3. Submit annual...
4. Authorize batch...

TO DO – PERSONA...
1. Send birthday c...

1. Project meeting to ensure agenc...

▲ USING A STRESS DIARY

The three main reasons for using a stress diary are to record and pinpoint stressful areas, to highlight increases in workload or other potentially stressful developments as they arise, and to have a tool for assigning priorities. Set out your stress diary as shown here, or tailor it to your preferences.

62 Set realistic goals so that you do not feel stressed by too many failures to meet deadlines.

GETTING FEEDBACK

A crucial part of dealing with stress is being able to communicate effectively with the people you spend so much time with – your colleagues. One way of doing this is to ask colleagues for help and advice in response to stressful situations.

If you find yourself under stress, try to make contact with colleagues who are sympathetic and attentive listeners – those who can resist the temptation to interrupt. Even if they are not in a position to offer advice, they can still help by letting you talk through your problems and giving you support and encouragement. Ask for honest feedback about when you appear to be most stressed – do you cope with meetings calmly but appear stressed before a presentation, for example? In return, try to offer support when they are under pressure. Be an attentive listener, and encourage them to talk openly about problems.

63 Never knowingly embarrass people by asking for help they cannot give.

64 Keep negative opinions about your colleagues to yourself.

GAINING ▶ CONFIDANTS
Sharing information bonds people, both in and out of the workplace. You may find that a colleague has a solution to a problem you have been having.

Share a coffee break to encourage an informal atmosphere

Put aside work while talking to colleague

ANALYZING STRESS CYCLES

Once you have analyzed your busy times of the year and recorded your daily workload for a month or so, take an overview to determine your personal daily, monthly, and yearly stress cycles. Bear in mind that the effects of cumulative pressure can increase stress. What may be easy to cope with during a quiet period will feel less possible during a crisis.

Consider which tasks you find particularly stressful – doing a large number of routine tasks may be less stressful than completing an urgent, complex one. Make yearly and daily charts of stress cycles, and use them to help you plan for a regulated stress pattern in the future.

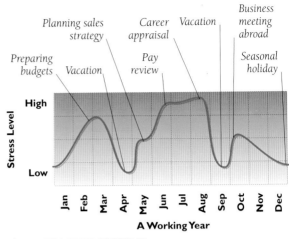

▲ A YEARLY CYCLE
The effects of long-term stress can be serious. The person to whom this chart belongs spends more than five months of the year trying to cope with high level of stress. Periods of low stress occur only when on vacation or spending time away from the office.

▼ A DAILY CYCLE
Although every day is different, a typical pattern usually emerges for most people. Consider whether you can alleviate stress, for example, by delegating more or eliminating unnecessary tasks.

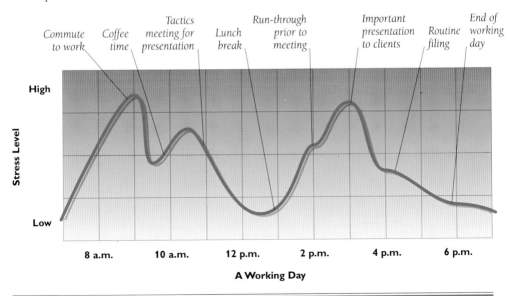

MANAGING TIME

O*ne of the major symptoms of stress in the workplace is the feeling that there are just not enough hours in the day to do everything that needs doing. This feeling can be reduced by organizing time better with the implementation of a few simple systems.*

65 Ask a member of your support staff to field calls if you have urgent work.

66 Try to take a five-minute break from your work every hour or so.

PRIORITIZING OBJECTIVES

In order to manage your time better, you must begin with an assessment of your overall objectives in life. What do you want to achieve – a happy balance of work and family life? Are you actively chasing promotion in your present job? Will you settle for a position in middle management, or do you want the chief executive's office? Once you have decided, work out your long-term priorities, then plan your workload accordingly.

PLANNING TASKS

Divide your workload into three main categories: A, B, and C. Consider any tasks that are both urgent and important as A-tasks, important but slightly less urgent projects as B-tasks, and routine, low-priority jobs as C-tasks. At the end of each working day, plan out what you need to do the next day. Intersperse your important A- and B-tasks with C-tasks, such as filing or background reading, to bring variety into your day and provide relief from the constant pressures of important tasks.

67 Cross each job off your "to do" list when the job is done. It is satisfying to see a list shrink.

ALLOCATING TIME

To make the best use of your time and minimize stress, you need to manage each day carefully. Look at all the tasks you intend to do, and allocate a realistic amount of time to each. When possible, schedule one or more important (category A) tasks in the morning to avoid the pressure of having them in the back of your mind all day. Set out your schedule using a system that works well for you – whether a diary, a computer, or a time planner.

24th

8 a.m.	Read mail and messages (1 hr 20 mins)
9 a.m.	Gather reports for 11 a.m. meeting with BW (40 mins)
10 a.m.	Travel to meeting (45 mins): reread background material
11 a.m.	Meeting with BW (1 hr 15 mins)
12 p.m.	Travel back (45 mins): make notes for 2 p.m. meeting

1 p.m	Lun (1 h
2 p.m	Mee my
3 p.m	Fili (1 h
4 p.m	Pla 4.3(
5 p.m	Ens for

Tuesday: Things to Do

- *Finish report for sales department* (**A**)
- *Prepare for meeting on Wednesday* (**A**)
- *Process invoices* (**B**)
- *Update computer lists* (**B**)
- *Check minutes of meeting for Friday* (**B**)
- *Filing* (**C**)

Urgent tasks (category A) are placed at top of list

◀ **KEEPING TASK LISTS**
Make a list of all the tasks that you have to do. Place them in order of priority, deciding where they rank according to their urgency and their importance.

▲ **RECORDING YOUR DAY**
The time you allocate to a certain task or meeting and the time you spend actually completing it are not always the same. Mark in your diary how long each task takes and the duration of each meeting (including time spent preparing and traveling). Over a period of time, note any habitual discrepancies and build extra time into future schedules to avoid pushing tasks forward, causing them to build up.

RELIEVING STRESS DURING TRAVEL TIME

Many of us spend a lot of time traveling between home and work and for meetings. Traveling can be very stressful – frequent flyers are three times more likely to suffer psychological disorders than most people – so learn a few simple exercises to help you reduce stress while on the move.

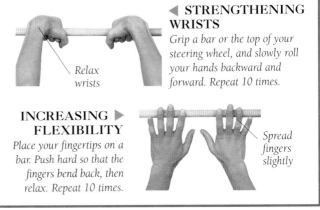

Relax wrists

◀ **STRENGTHENING WRISTS**
Grip a bar or the top of your steering wheel, and slowly roll your hands backward and forward. Repeat 10 times.

INCREASING ▶ **FLEXIBILITY**
Place your fingertips on a bar. Push hard so that the fingers bend back, then relax. Repeat 10 times.

Spread fingers slightly

COMMUNICATING WELL

*O**n average, managers send and receive 178 messages every day of their working lives, while their secretaries handle even more. If this load increases without proper management, it may eventually lead to a communications gridlock.***

68 Do not overload people with information that they do not need.

69 Keep a log of messages that require a reply. Follow them up.

MANAGING INFORMATION

Knowing how to communicate effectively is crucial to the success of organizations everywhere, as well as to your own peace of mind. There is a wide choice of communication tools available for modern businesses, and information can be transmitted efficiently using systems such as e-mail or fax. To minimize stress when using electronic systems, allocate sufficient time to send and reply to letters and messages, or try to delegate these tasks. Keeping on top of correspondence and processing information improves your efficiency at work and reduces stress. Good communication will also encourage a fast response from others.

CASE STUDY

Mary, a departmental manager, needed to decide between two internal candidates for a vacancy. She considered both to be capable but felt that Joe had the edge over Bill.

Instead of just appointing Joe and letting Bill hear the news from other sources, Mary arranged a meeting with Bill before announcing Joe's appointment. Mary felt that a written memo or e-mail, however tactfully composed,

was the wrong way to communicate her final decision to Bill and would intensify any stress that he was feeling. She explained the reasons behind her decision, emphasizing that Bill was a valued employee, that the decision had been difficult, and that Bill would be positively considered for promotion in the future. Since Bill appreciated Mary's honesty and accepted her explanation, he did not feel bitter, undervalued, or resentful toward Joe and Mary.

◀ **COMMUNICATING EFFECTIVELY**
Methods of communication should be tailored to the audience and the situation. In this case, Mary felt that writing a memo was an inappropriate way of informing Bill of the situation. Telling him in a one-to-one meeting that he was valued, and giving him hope of a promotion in the future, helped minimize the stress of not being promoted.

KEEPING UP TO DATE

VIDEO CONFERENCING
People all over the world can participate in the same meeting by using a video link. This saves time and travel expenses.

E-MAIL
Electronic mail allows you to correspond using your computer. It is the fastest and most effective way to send messages and documents worldwide.

INTERNET
An Internet link provides immediate access to information on every imaginable subject (a registration fee may be required). The data can be downloaded and saved onto your computer.

CULTURAL DIFFERENCES

To communicate effectively in business worldwide, it is essential that you are aware of cultural differences. In Britain and the US, for example, you may be able to drop in to see someone "on spec." In Asia, however, where communication in business is less open and more formal, it would be more appropriate to arrange your meeting properly in advance.

WORKING TOGETHER

Communicating with colleagues within a work hierarchy can be stressful. Minimize stress by:
● Communicating and discussing issues face to face whenever possible to establish good working relationships;
● Consulting frequently with colleagues and other teams to get their input;
● Listening to what other people are saying, even if you do not agree with what is said;
● Criticizing people's ideas constructively.

TALKING OPENLY ▶
Face-to-face meetings, such as impromptu meetings between two colleagues, are often more productive than written memoranda.

70 Write faxes and letters early in the day – your communication skills will deteriorate as you tire.

GAINING INNER BALANCE

Although events cannot always be controlled, your reactions to them can be. Learning to respond in a balanced, appropriate fashion to events at work is a key skill in fighting stress. A bad day at the office is just that; it is not life-threatening.

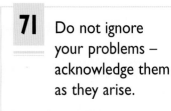

71 Do not ignore your problems – acknowledge them as they arise.

MODIFYING BEHAVIOR

Behavioral patterns deeply embedded in our subconscious often surface in times of stress, even if they are not appropriate for work. For example, if a situation at work makes you feel uncomfortable and you do not take action to change it, you may find that resentment builds up and is reflected in your behavior – you may become angry and intolerant of other people. Learn to find inner balance and overcome inappropriate behavior by analyzing any feelings of unfairness and trying to discover and deal with the root of the problem.

72 Avoid people and situations that tempt you to behave in ways you are not happy with.

SETTING YOUR STANDARDS

A common cause of stress is feeling guilty about doing or not doing something at work. Remember, no one is perfect, so do not ask too much of yourself. If you have very high standards and expectations, it can be difficult to accept that you have made a mistake. Try to regard mistakes as a part of a learning curve – analyze what went wrong, correct the error, and avoid repeating it. Similarly, it can be difficult to refuse work, even when the request is unreasonable. For this reason, it is important to learn to say "no" graciously. To lead a balanced life at work, you need to establish your own priorities, standards, and rights and be willing to take responsibility for your own actions.

YOUR RIGHTS

1. You have the right to make genuine mistakes without feeling guilty.

2. You have the right to refuse other people's excessive demands on your time.

HANDLING ANGER

Gaining inner balance has much to do with controlling anger. Anger is a disabling emotion that produces measurable physical sensations, such as an increase in pulse rate and a rise in blood pressure. An explosion of anger may make you feel better briefly, but it will disguise the real problem by becoming an issue in itself. If you explode unreasonably at a person or in a situation, question the root of it. Make a list of possible reasons: "I am angry because..." To control your anger successfully in the long term, explore what appears after "because."

 73 Exercise can be a short-term solution to anger.

 74 Be honest about your reasons for rejecting a task.

 75 Try not to be pressurized into making important decisions hastily.

THINKING POSITIVELY

In order to obtain a calm, low-stress working environment, train yourself to think positively. A positive outlook and the ability to remain calm under intense pressure are likely to produce positive responses in your colleagues, which in turn will reduce the presence of stress in your team or workplace. In the same way that stress can infect a whole team, it can be eliminated by a conscious group effort to think positively.

LEARNING TO SAY NO

Some people find it difficult to say no; they are afraid of causing offense or think it might be career-threatening. Remember that accepting a task you cannot handle can be damaging. Use the phrases below to say no assertively without being aggressive.

❝ *Let's arrange to meet soon and talk about this in greater detail.* ❞

❝ *I don't think I can give you the answer you're hoping for.* ❞

❝ *I am unable to take on any more commitments at the moment.* ❞

MAKING TIME TO RELAX

When you are under stress, your entire body becomes tense and your posture changes. Make a conscious effort to relax your body while at work so that you can reduce tension and alleviate the damaging effects of your physical response to stress.

76 Practice yoga or a similar exercise routine to help you relax.

Breathe through nose

Place hand on chest

Feel abdomen expand as you breathe

▲ **EXERCISE ONE**
With hands on your chest and abdomen, breathe in and out through the nose, letting your abdomen expand and sink.

RELAXING AT WORK

When you spend several hours sitting at a desk or in long meetings, tension can accumulate in the upper body, particularly around the neck and shoulders, which can cause muscular aches. Follow a simple routine during the day to help you relax, release tension, and renew energy:

● Start by loosening your collar, tie, or scarf, and untying your shoelaces – or take off your shoes;
● Run through the exercises on these pages, concentrating on those you find most helpful;
● Repeat the exercises every couple of hours, rather than waiting until you feel stressed and tense. Remember, it is much easier to work toward preventing stress than to try to cure it.

Let your head fall backward

Draw fingers over collar bone

▲ **EXERCISE TWO**
Loosen your collar and place your hands over your shoulders. Exhale, let your head fall backward, and slowly draw your fingers over your collar bone. Repeat several times.

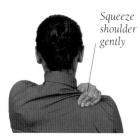

Squeeze shoulder gently

▲ **EXERCISE THREE**
Place your left hand on your right shoulder and squeeze gently. Hold for several seconds, then release. Repeat along the shoulder and arm. Do the same on the opposite side.

Make slow, circular movements

▲ **EXERCISE FOUR**
Place the fingers of both hands at the base of your skull. Apply slow, circular pressure, working gradually down your neck and then out across the shoulders.

TAKING A BREAK FROM WORKING ON SCREEN

Many people spend large amounts of time in front of computer screens. This is especially tiring for the eyes and the surrounding muscles. Take a short break from computer work every hour or so, and move or turn away from the screen. Perform the exercises shown here at regular intervals to reduce tension and prevent eye strain.

Massage gently around eyes

Move thumbs in circular motion

▲ EXERCISE ONE
Close your eyes, relax the muscles in your face, and unclench your jaw. Keeping your fingers together, place the fingertips against your forehead and gently move them in circles around your eyes. Repeat several times in one direction, then repeat in the opposite direction.

EXERCISE TWO ▲
Place your fingertips on your forehead and gently massage the temples with your thumbs.

EXERCISE THREE ▶
Release any tautness in your face by cupping your hands over your eyes and relaxing. Hold this position for several seconds. Do this exercise in darkness, if possible.

Cup hands over eyes

Rest elbow on opposite hand

Gently pull head downward

Roll shoulder backward

▲ EXERCISE FIVE
Support your left elbow on your right hand and drum the fingers of your left hand on your right shoulder blade. Repeat with your right elbow on your left hand.

▲ EXERCISE SIX
Place your hands on the top of your head. Allow your hands to pull your head gently down, then hold the position. Feel the slight stretch in the back of the neck.

▲ EXERCISE SEVEN
Lift your right shoulder and slowly rotate it backward. Repeat the exercise with your left shoulder, then rotate both shoulders together. Keep your arms loose and relaxed.

SEEING STRESS IN OTHERS

Stress can be infectious, so you need to recognize it in others before it affects the people with whom they work (including you). There are many ways of reacting to stress; learn to notice common warning signs so that you have time to decide how to react.

77 Help your stressed colleagues to organize their time better.

78 Ask friends of stressed colleagues to help resolve their problems.

LOOKING FOR SIGNS

The best way to recognize stress in others is to spot changes in behavior. The difference between a bad day and a sign of stress is when the abnormal behavior continues or even deteriorates. For example, the once-prompt man starts arriving late; the woman who was a good listener avoids eye contact; the soft-spoken accountant loses his temper when asked about an unpaid invoice.

NOTICING CHANGING PATTERNS OF BEHAVIOR

NORMAL

TOWARD COLLEAGUES
- Greets colleagues on arrival.
- Has lunch with colleagues.
- Has a friendly manner.
- Asks for opinions.

TOWARD THE ORGANIZATION
- Keeps work space clean and neat.
- Files paperwork in an orderly fashion.
- Knows where to find things.
- Deals with correspondence immediately.

TOWARD OWN APPEARANCE
- Is smartly dressed.
- Wears clean and well-pressed clothes.
- Looks well-groomed.
- Maintains good personal hygiene.

STRESSED

TOWARD COLLEAGUES
- Sits at work in silence.
- Ignores opinions.
- Becomes irritable.
- Lunches alone.

TOWARD THE ORGANIZATION
- Works in a chaotic fashion.
- Scatters papers everywhere.
- Takes 15 minutes to find anything.
- Leaves in-box full of correspondence.

TOWARD OWN APPEARANCE
- Wears clothes unsuited to the job.
- Wears dirty and wrinkled clothing.
- Looks unkempt.
- Does not appear to care about appearance.

- Colleagues may be able to advise on recognizing and dealing with stress within a team; pool your ideas to develop a plan of action.

- Other people's high stress levels can be infectious; try to maintain a level-headed approach to help calm your colleague.

- The best way to help a stressed coworker may be to suggest that they take a break from the project or take a few days off.

ANALYZING TEAM STRESS

Staff who work in teams, brought together to do a particular task, can suffer from specific pressures related to working in a group. For example, if an informal hierarchy develops, some may not approve of the self-appointed leader, or team members may find it stressful to work with people who have different work patterns to their own. Take time to meet teams and individuals so that you are aware of team dynamics and can anticipate problems. You may need to alter working methods and the division of tasks within a team if stress persists.

QUESTIONS TO ASK YOURSELF

Q Will talking to team members highlight any signs of stress?

Q Should staff workloads be reassessed regularly?

Q Can stressed colleagues be encouraged to participate in teamwork by drawing on their specific area of expertise?

Q What is the most likely cause of stress within a team?

EXPLORING REASONS

Once you have noticed some signs of stress in a colleague, you need to start thinking about the reasons for it. Consider as many options as possible – from problems at home to any difficult relationships in the workplace. Remember that the factors that put you under greatest stress may not affect others to the same extent. Once you have pinpointed likely causes, assess whether or how you can help your colleague. Often, only that person can help himself, and all you can do is ensure he is not put under additional pressure.

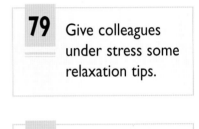

79 Give colleagues under stress some relaxation tips.

80 Offer help only if you have time to follow it up.

AVERTING PRESSURES

You can try to minimize stresses and pressures among those you work with by using open, flexible working practices. The better communication flows, the more likely it is that stress is recognized and defused. Try the following methods of involving people and reducing levels of anxiety:

- Keep staff and colleagues informed about all decisions that may affect them;
- Encourage participation in planning;
- Set aside time each week to ask for comments and suggestions and to give feedback.

ANALYZING PERSONALITY

The effects of stress are closely linked to individual personality. The same level of stress affects different people in different ways, and each person has different ways of coping. Recognizing these personality types means that more focused help can be given.

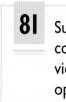

81 Suggest that your colleagues try to view problems as opportunities.

UNDERSTANDING TYPES

Research in the 1960s into the effects of stress on the heart found that some patients with similarities in personality were more prone to heart disease. These people were described as Type A, while those less at risk were classed as Type B. The former are competitive and hard-driving and are likely to seek out positions of responsibility. Whether their health is at risk because they are in high-stress jobs or whether high-risk jobs encourage Type-A behavior is unclear, but these people may need more support.

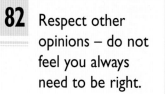

82 Respect other opinions – do not feel you always need to be right.

IDENTIFYING PERSONALITY TYPES A AND B

Listed here are some of the classic traits and behavior patterns associated with personality Types A and B. It is rare to find someone who is a perfect Type A or B – many people exhibit characteristics of both – but those with mostly Type-A traits often cope badly under pressure. If you detect Type-A tendencies in colleagues, they may be at risk from stress and should consider strategies to deal with this.

- Type-A personalities may show the following tendencies: competitiveness; hastiness; aggressiveness; impatience; assertiveness; perfectionism; restlessness; punctuality; seeking attention.
- Type-B personalities may show the following tendencies: noncompetitiveness; placidity; patience; being laid-back; being relaxed; contentment; enjoying routine; tardiness; being happy to work unnoticed.

RECOGNIZING STRATEGIES

Strategies for coping with stress can be divided into two main categories: adaptive and maladaptive. If colleagues exhibit adaptive behavior, they are probably dealing positively with a problem, talking about it, and actively seeking help. If they are behaving maladaptively, they may be causing themselves greater stress by ignoring their problem and trying to carry on as normal. This type of behavior, known as being "in denial," is often associated with competitive, Type-A personalities.

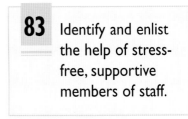

83 Identify and enlist the help of stress-free, supportive members of staff.

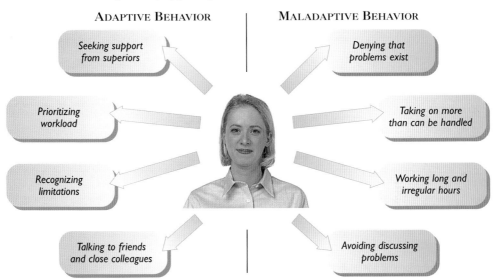

ADAPTIVE BEHAVIOR

Seeking support from superiors

Prioritizing workload

Recognizing limitations

Talking to friends and close colleagues

MALADAPTIVE BEHAVIOR

Denying that problems exist

Taking on more than can be handled

Working long and irregular hours

Avoiding discussing problems

NOTICING CHANGES

When colleagues are adversely affected by stress, their behavior may change dramatically, and negative characteristics may be intensified. For example, a person who normally tends to be impatient – and may be known for "not suffering fools gladly" – may find that this degenerates to a point where they cannot control their temper, leading to explosive and destructive temper tantrums. Watch for such warning signals in your colleagues.

▲ **ASSESSING BEHAVIOR**
Adaptive and maladaptive behaviors are two ways of dealing with stress. The former tends to lead to problems being resolved, while the latter can increase problems.

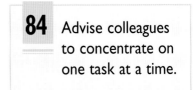

84 Advise colleagues to concentrate on one task at a time.

HELPING OTHERS

O nce you have recognized that someone is under stress and have started to understand the reasons for it, the hardest part begins: making that person aware of what you have observed and encouraging them to take corrective action.

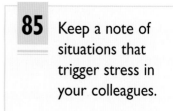

85 Keep a note of situations that trigger stress in your colleagues.

UNDERSTANDING TENSION AREAS

Always be aware of the work your staff needs to cope with on a daily, weekly, monthly, and annual basis. You will then better understand the pressures they may be under at any given time. Tensions may arise as a result of competition between colleagues whose jobs are either very similar or have several overlapping aspects. In most instances, you need not worry about competitive tensions; encourage those directly involved to work things out between themselves. If you become aware that a situation may escalate into a problem, prevent role conflict by defining clearly what is expected of each party.

86 Ensure that staff working together are compatible.

PREVENTING A CONFLICT OF ROLES

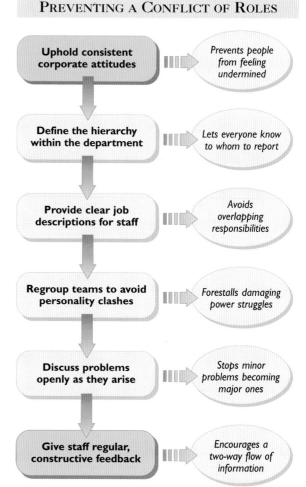

Uphold consistent corporate attitudes — Prevents people from feeling undermined

Define the hierarchy within the department — Lets everyone know to whom to report

Provide clear job descriptions for staff — Avoids overlapping responsibilities

Regroup teams to avoid personality clashes — Forestalls damaging power struggles

Discuss problems openly as they arise — Stops minor problems becoming major ones

Give staff regular, constructive feedback — Encourages a two-way flow of information

ASSESSING RELATIONSHIPS

In many ways, the personal relationships that exist between colleagues are just as important as their professional relationships. As a manager, try to be aware of who gets along with whom. Once you have a clear understanding of the personal relationships around you, you can start to build up teams of people who work well together.

87 List all the people who may be able to help a colleague under stress.

HELPING OTHERS ADMIT TO STRESS

Sometimes a subtle, indirect approach is needed to help others admit to stress. Social relationships can cut across the roles and hierarchies found in the workplace – in some cases it may be appropriate to involve a third party. This is one point where you will find it useful to know who gets on well with whom. A discreet word with the right person can reap great rewards and is a helpful and tactful way – as a first attempt, at least – to bring someone's attention to their own stress levels. This will avoid the person's stress becoming an official issue and may enable them to remedy the situation. A more direct approach may be necessary if this does not work.

88 Encourage staff to be supportive of one another.

BARRIERS TO ADMITTING STRESS

FOR MANAGERS

- Managers may believe that their authority rests to some extent on appearing infallible.
- Managers may not want to admit that they are under stress for fear that it will undermine their leadership.

FOR COLLEAGUES

- Colleagues may not want to expose weaknesses to each other in case they are exploited in the future.
- Friendships may suffer between colleagues who become rivals for the same promotion.

FOR SUBORDINATES

- Subordinates may feel that their careers will suffer if they show signs of stress to staff who have a degree of control over their jobs.
- Subordinates may not want to show signs of weakness to senior staff.

IMPLEMENTING ACTION

Once stress is recognized and acknowledged, devise a strategy to help the sufferer deal with it. Ask both subordinates and colleagues if they have any suggestions on how to reduce their own workload, for example, by delegating some aspects of their role to someone else. Discuss all possible courses of action that can be taken. Always endorse alternative arrangements so that the person under stress does not feel they are letting others down.

 89 Suggest that your meetings should last no longer than half an hour.

FINDING A SOLUTION TO A PROBLEM

Problem → List difficulties → Consider causes → Discuss remedies → Agree on action → Solution

SHARING KNOWLEDGE AND EXPERIENCE

It is sometimes possible to indicate subtly certain courses of action that can be taken to reduce stress levels without suggesting that any one individual member of staff has a problem. For example, everyone knows that time management can cause problems, so it is a good idea to pool your knowledge and ideas on how to streamline the day. Be blatant about introducing time-saving techniques and encourage awareness of stress patterns. Make general statements such as "I couldn't survive without my wallchart," or "I always need at least 15 minutes before I go into a meeting to prepare myself." Make colleagues aware that all brilliant leaders need their crutches. Mention areas that you personally find stressful and share solutions that have been successful for you.

SUPPORTING OTHERS

Occasionally you will need to support others who are in the middle of a stressful situation. Take a calm, logical approach and follow these steps:

- Discuss the problems that the individual is experiencing, then determine the underlying causes of their stress – find out whether their problem is work-related or personal;
- Having analyzed the type of stress from which the person is suffering, discuss what help they would find most useful – this might take the form of work-related help (such as training), emotional help (such as counseling), or medical help (such as treatment for a condition brought on or aggravated by stress);
- Assist the individual in finding the help they need. Be prepared to suggest alternative solutions in case they are unhappy with your initial suggestions and recommendations.

90 Ask colleagues to prioritize tasks in their diaries.

91 When talking with a colleague, banish all interruptions.

▼ **TAKING TIME TO LISTEN**
Any discussion with a stressed colleague or subordinate should take place in confidence in a meeting room. Make as much time available as is necessary.

Sit at right angles to the person under stress to make them feel at ease

Keep body language open to encourage free discussion

Arms forming barrier across chest suggest diffidence

Taking Action at Home

Stress felt at work is guaranteed to affect home life, which will have a detrimental impact on family and friends. Learn to take time off, relax, develop interests, and eat well.

Taking Time Off

Taking stress home from the office has a destructive effect on home life, and vice versa. The two can combine to form a vicious circle with no escape. Remember: to make any stress-reducing action effective, it must be complemented by taking some time off.

92	Plan activities for each weekend. Try not to let the days just drift past.

Making Time for Others

The first step toward reducing stress at home is to allow plenty of time for family matters. Make your family aware that vacations with them are sacred, and show friends that they are worth more than just a quick drink on a Friday night every other month. Make sure that people at work are aware of your commitments to your family – your child's sports day, for example, or a special anniversary – and that they have priority over work issues. Simple things count for a lot: make an effort to have lunch regularly with your partner or time to throw a ball around with your children.

▲ **SPENDING TIME ALONE**
If you do not enjoy your own company, you are condemned to be dependent on others. Learn to enjoy yourself by yourself.

PLANNING AN ANTISTRESS DAY

The world is changing faster than ever, and the speed of these changes is putting us all under unprecedented pressure. It is important that we regularly visit the stability zones – dependable activities such as walking the dog, going for a bicycle ride, reading a book, watering plants, washing the car, or watching a television show full of familiar, predictable characters – that make us feel comfortable with ourselves and convince us that all is well with the world. There is nothing better for recharging flat batteries than a well-planned antistress day. Organize your activities well in advance, take a day off from work, and plan out your time. If you have any children, arrange for them to stay with some relatives or friends, or include them in your plans for your relaxation day.

▲ GETTING EXERCISE
Exercise is a major stress reliever.
Take up a noncompetitive sport,
and build your strength gradually.

MORNING
Make sure that when you wake, you wake naturally. Do not leap out of bed, but savor the prospect of the day ahead. Once you do get up, take a few minutes to do some simple stretching exercises. Drink a glass of water before enjoying a light breakfast, which should include at least one special treat.

AFTERNOON
For some, a noncompetitive day on the golf course might be the most pleasurable thing to follow breakfast. Others may want to set out for some retail therapy – a spot of shopping and a leisurely lunch with a good friend. Try to leave the car at home and walk, ride a bicycle, or use public transportation.

EARLY EVENING
Resist the temptation to read the papers or watch the news on television. In the treatment of stress, no news is good news. A key feature of any antistress day is not knowing what is going on in the rest of the world – it will carry on without you. Read a book, curl up with a video, listen to music, or go to the movies.

NIGHT
Have a leisurely bath, and pamper yourself with body oils. Listen to music while dressing slowly for a relaxed dinner in a restaurant with your partner or a friend. Take a taxi, and do not worry about time. When you get home, have a cup of soothing herbal tea before going to bed and drifting off to sleep.

LEARNING TO RELAX

Relaxing completely is not simply doing nothing: it is a technique that can soon be learned. Take some time out for a few lessons, and you will then find it easy – and pleasurable – to enjoy a regular period of relaxation in your busy daily routine.

BEGINNING TO RELAX

It is not always easy to relax at home, since there are so many demands on our time – telephones ringing, meals to be cooked, clothes to be ironed, and so on. Find a tranquil place in the house, and set aside a period of uninterrupted time to do the simple relaxation exercise shown below. You may choose to try it out first thing in the morning, perhaps before breakfast, or last thing at night, just before you go to bed. Wear some loose, baggy clothes that do not restrict your movement. Place a rug or mat on the floor, along with a cushion, then lie down and begin the exercise.

93 Listen to your favorite comedian. Laughter will help you relax.

94 Avoid eating or drinking heavily just before you go to bed.

Rest arms on floor for support

Tense back muscles

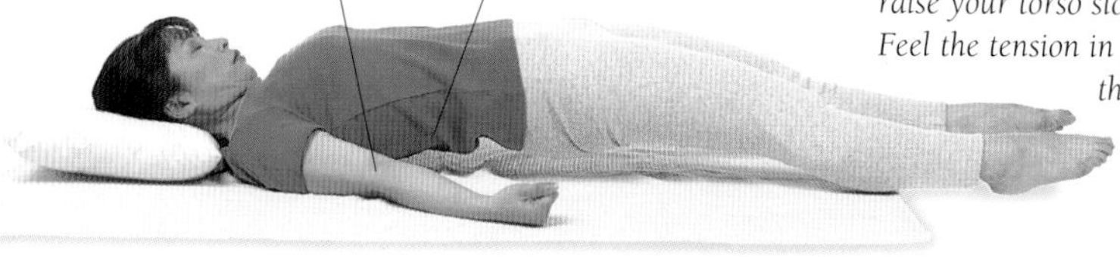

▼ **1. TENSING YOUR BACK MUSCLES**

Lying flat on the floor, stretch your arms out by either side. Use the muscles in your shoulders, back, and buttocks to raise your torso slowly off the ground. Feel the tension in your body, then hold the position for the count of five.

2. RELAXING ▶ YOUR BODY

Slowly lower your back to the floor and relax, breathing slowly and deeply. Repeat as required.

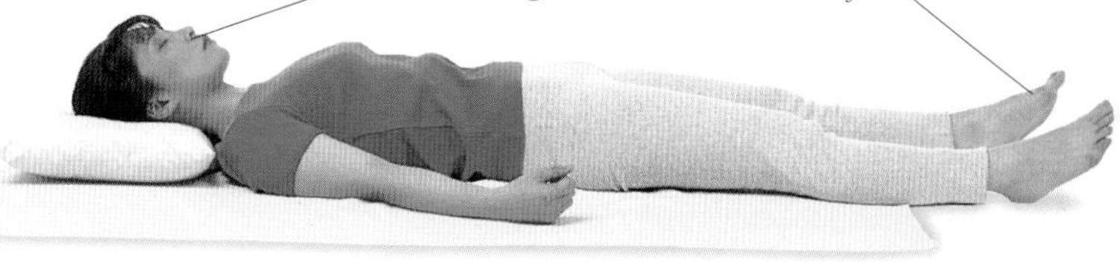

Breathe through nose

Relax feet

LEARNING TO MEDITATE

Meditation has been used for centuries to counteract the effects of stress. Sit on the floor in an upright position with your legs crossed, arms resting on your thighs and palms facing upward. Close your eyes and breathe through your nostrils, focusing on the air coming in and out of your body. Sit for a few minutes, quietly aware of your body. After a while, you will feel the tension start to ease away.

Repeat a word or phrase over and over in your mind

Breathe gently from diaphragm

CALMING DOWN ▷
The goal of meditation is the attainment of a state of calm awareness. If you find it difficult to concentrate at first, persevere, and slowly your mind will clear.

SEEKING HELP

People who have trouble in relaxing may find relaxation therapies helpful. The many systems available include:

ALEXANDER TECHNIQUE: learning how to use the body in everyday tasks to minimize pain, stress, and injury.

AROMATHERAPY: massaging the body with essential oils.

FLOTATION: floating in a water tank filled with a solution of mineral salts.

SHIATSU: using finger pressure on certain areas of the body to relieve stress and tension.

SLEEPING BETTER

Everybody needs a different amount of sleep. For adults, the average is seven to eight hours a night, but many high-achieving people claim to survive on four or five. Stress can cause us to sleep less than we need over a prolonged period and to sleep poorly. To improve the quality of your sleep, make sure you relax before you go to bed. Switch off from all stimulating activities – especially work – at least two hours beforehand. Try meditating. Read some light fiction. Listen to some music, or watch television. Have a warm, milky drink last thing at night, or try an infusion of one of the many herbal plants that are thought to aid sleep, such as chamomile, valerian, or passiflora.

95 When lying down to relax your body, start by relaxing your toes, and work your way upward.

Developing Interests

Finding a balanced lifestyle is essential to our overall well-being. Physical activities such as aerobics or tennis can concentrate the mind and help reduce the outward symptoms of stress, while hobbies such as painting can provide emotional calm.

 96 Join an evening class every year, and start to learn something new.

 97 Ask your company to take corporate membership in a nearby sports club.

Taking Up New Hobbies

Choose an activity that you really enjoy doing to beat stress. The right pastime can be so absorbing that it helps you switch off from everything else and so engrossing that it becomes as refreshing as sleep. A hobby also helps boost self-esteem. After a day at the office when nothing seemed to go right, you can head for your hobby and lose yourself in your skill. Some people's hobbies have even become their livelihoods. Accountants have become avid beekeepers; lawyers have turned to furniture restoration. Hobbies can be portable – many people are able to combine their hobbies with vacations, such as a cycling trip in the Andes, for example, golfing in Portugal, or perhaps a guided tour of the flora and fauna of Australia.

◀ **RELAXING WITH A NEW HOBBY**
Remember that a hobby is meant to be a pleasure, not a chore – go out and paint only when you feel like it. If you cannot find the time to finish that art course, do not worry. Do the best you can, and squeeze enjoyment out of it.

GETTING MORE EXERCISE

Exercise is widely recognized as beneficial in reducing anxiety and improving sleep. However, take care, since those who exercise vigorously while highly stressed are prone to injury. Remember to start gradually and build up to a regular exercise regime. When planning your sporting activities, build in the time that it takes to travel, change, and shower. Some sports, such as tennis and golf, combine physical exercise with social activity – which is in itself a stress minimizer. Brisk walking, swimming, and aerobics classes are all effective in improving the cardiovascular system. The chart below shows the effects of different sports on stamina, flexibility, and strength. Use it to choose one or more sports activities that would suit you.

98 Take a vacation that allows you to pursue a hobby.

99 When taking up a new form of exercise, start with lessons from a qualified instructor.

Key
★ ★ ★ ★ *Excellent effect*   ★ ★ *Beneficial effect*
★ ★ ★ *Very good effect*   ★ *Minimal effect*

CHOOSING THE RIGHT SPORT

ACTIVITY	STAMINA	FLEXIBILITY	STRENGTH
BASKETBALL	★ ★ ★	★ ★ ★ ★	★ ★ ★
BOWLING	★	★ ★	★ ★
CYCLING	★ ★ ★ ★	★ ★	★ ★ ★
GOLF	★ ★	★ ★	★
RUNNING	★ ★ ★ ★	★ ★	★ ★
SOCCER	★ ★ ★	★ ★ ★	★ ★
SQUASH	★ ★ ★ ★	★ ★ ★ ★	★ ★ ★
SWIMMING	★ ★ ★	★ ★ ★	★ ★ ★
TENNIS	★ ★ ★	★ ★ ★	★ ★
WALKING	★ . ★	★	★ ★

IMPROVING DIET

We are what we eat. When we are under stress, we tend to fill ourselves with convenience food, which can be synonymous with "junk." Eating well must be part of any serious program to reduce stress levels. Make a start by minimizing bad habits.

100 Breakfast like a king, lunch like a prince, and dine like a pauper.

REDUCING BAD HABITS

Monitoring what you consume and when may reveal bad habits that have crept into your diet. The one glass of wine with dinner easily becomes most of a bottle, while the pizza once a week becomes a daily meal. Try to adopt a well thought-out and balanced diet, replacing convenience foods with healther alternatives.

Certain foods have been linked with poor overall health. Avoid foods high in saturated fats, such as meat, cheese, butter, and eggs. Use olive oil or sunflower oil for cooking, and steam, bake, or broil food rather than fry it. Eat plenty of oily fish, such as salmon, and try a soy-based meal in place of meat. Reduce your daily intake of caffeine by replacing coffee and tea with water or juice. Drink at least eight glasses of water every day.

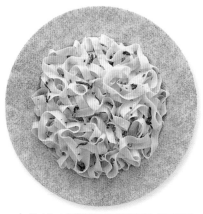

▲ **BALANCING YOUR DIET**
Instead of reheating convenience foods when you come home from work, why not prepare yourself a nutritious plate of pasta? It is just as easy and quick to cook as fast foods and is a much healthier alternative.

DO'S AND DON'TS

✔ Do eat small meals at regular intervals rather than one enormous dinner.

✔ Do determine your optimum weight, and then aim to stick to it.

✔ Do aim for moderation in all things.

✘ Don't snack between meals, especially on sugary foods, which drain the body of valuable nutrients.

✘ Don't keep sweets in the house.

✘ Don't eat a lot of salt, sugar, or white bread.

101 Eat a crisp, raw carrot if you feel the urge to eat between meals.

ESSENTIAL COMPONENTS OF A HEALTHY DIET

COMPONENTS

GOOD SOURCES

VITAMINS AND MINERALS
Vitamins help the body function properly. There is an official recommended daily intake for every vitamin. Minerals, as important to good health as vitamins, consist of some 20 chemical elements.

Vitamins come from many sources: Vitamin C from citrus fruits, tomatoes, melons, strawberries; Vitamin D from green vegetables, oily fish, milk, eggs; Vitamin B1 from meat, yeast, legumes. Leafy vegetables and fish are good sources of minerals.

CARBOHYDRATES
This large group of foodstuffs includes sugars and starches. Nutritionists generally recommend that carbohydrates should make up approximately 55 percent of a typical healthy diet.

Carbohydrates are found in whole-grain bread, candy, cookies, pasta, apples, corn, cereal, baked and red kidney beans, lentils, green peppers, dried apricots, bananas, baked or boiled potatoes, unsalted nuts, dried fruit, brown rice.

PROTEINS FROM PLANTS
The body needs proteins in the form of amino acids for cell growth and repair and to make enzymes for antibodies and hormones. All fruits and vegetables contain a certain amount of these proteins.

Good sources of plant proteins are peas, beans, grains, lentils, seeds, and potatoes. Some plant proteins do not contain all or enough essential amino acids, so vegetarians should try to eat a mixture of nuts or grains and peas or beans.

PROTEINS FROM ANIMALS
Proteins of animal origin provide complete protein. In other words, they contain the whole range of essential amino acids that the human body needs and in the appropriate proportions.

Red meats are a source of animal proteins that are essential for a healthy functioning body. These proteins are also found in other sources, including poultry, fish, eggs, and dairy products such as cheese, butter, milk, and yogurt.

FATS
Fats are a key source of energy – we need fat to function efficiently. A healthy diet should consist of 30 percent fat, but too much can cause serious health problems such as heart disease and obesity.

Fish, chicken, vegetable oils, and avocados are good sources of light polyunsaturated and monosaturated fats. Butter, meats, eggs, cream, and whole milk are high in saturated fat, which is harder for the body to process and less healthy than polyunsaturated or monosaturated fat.

829

INDEX

J

S

ACKNOWLEDGMENTS

AUTHORS' ACKNOWLEDGMENTS

This book owes its existence to the perceptive inspiration of
Stephanie Jackson and Nigel Duffield at Dorling Kindersley, and
I owe more than I can say to the expertise and enthusiasm of
Jane Simmonds and all the editorial and design staff who worked
on the project. I am also greatly indebted to the many colleagues,
friends, and other management luminaries on whose wisdom and
information I have drawn.   *Robert Heller*

The production of this book has called on the skills of many people.
I would like particularly to mention my editors at
Dorling Kindersley, and my assistant Jane Williams.   *Tim Hindle*

PUBLISHER'S ACKNOWLEDGMENTS

Editorial Tracey Beresford, Jennifer Boniello, Marian Broderick, Laaren Brown,
Deirdre Carr, Anna Cheifetz, Felicity Crowe, Michael Downey, Jane Garton,
Christopher Gordon, Jill Hamilton, Adèle Hayward, Sasha Heseltine,
Leonard C. Hort, Emma Lawson, Nicola Munro, Irene Pavitt, Ray Rogers,
Catherine Rubinstein, Nicky Thompson, Victoria Wilks, Anna Youle;
Design Austin Barlow, Helen Benfield, Darren Hill, Jayne Jones, Ian Midson,
Elaine C. Monaghan, Simon Oon, Kate Poole, Adam Powers, Laura Watson,
Nicola Webb; **DTP assistance** Rachel Symons; **Consultants** Josephine Bryan,
Jane Lyle; **Indexer** Sue Lightfoot; **Proofreaders** Helen Partington, David Perry;
Photography Steve Gorton; **Additional photography** Andy Crawford,
Tim Ridley; **Photographers' assistants** Sarah Ashun, Nick Goodall, Lee Walsh;
Illustrators Joanna Cameron, Yahya El-Droubie, Jason Little, Richard Tibbetts;
Picture researchers Victoria Peel, Sam Ruston, Mariana Sonnenberg;
Picture librarians Sue Hadley, Sam Ward.

Models Philip Argent, Marian Broderick, Angela Cameron, Kuo Kang Chen,
Roberto Costa, Felicity Crowe, Patrick Dobbs, Carole Evans, Vosjava Fahkro,
John Gillard, Ben Glickman, Sasha Heseltine, Richard Hill, Zahid Malik,
Maggie Mant, Frankie Mayers, Sotiris Melioumis, Ian Midson, Mutsumi Niwa,
Ted Nixon, Pippa Oakes, Mary-Jane Robinson, Kiran Shah, Lois Sharland,
Lynne Staff, Daniel Stevens, Fiona Terry, Tessa Woodward, Gilbert Wu,
Wendy Yun; **Makeup** Elizabeth Burrage, Lynne Maningley.

Special thanks to the following for their help:

Ron and Chris at Clark Davis & Co. Ltd for stationery and furniture supplies;
Pam Bennett and the staff at Jones Bootmakers, Covent Garden, for the
loan of footwear; Alan Pfaff and the staff at Moss Bros, Covent Garden,
for the loan of the men's suits; David Bailey for his help and time;
Graham Preston and the staff at Staverton for their time and space.

Suppliers Austin Reed, Church & Co, Compaq, David Clulow Opticians,
Elonex, Escada, Filofax, Gateway 2000, Mucci Bags.

PICTURE CREDITS

Key: *b* bottom, *c* center, *l* left, *r* right, *t* top

Ace Photo Library: Andrew Conway 751*bl*, Jigsaw 2 220; **Zephyr
Pictures** 288; **Collections** 792*cl*; **Hulton Getty Picture Collection**
699*bl*; **The Imagebank:** 785*cr*, 793*cl*, David de Lossy 757*cr*; **Pictor
International, London:** 277*tr*, 318*cr*, 331*tr*, 333*tr*; **PowerStock
Photo Library:** 61*br*, 435*br*, 447*cr*, 823*tr*; **Robert Harding Picture
Library:** RW Jones 16–17; **Spicers Limited** 498*cl*, 518*c*, *bc*, 519*tl*, *tr*,
cl, 783; **The Stockmarket:** 699*br*, JM Roberts 780*bl*; **Telegraph
Colour Library:** 282*bl*, 826*bl*, M Malyszko 49*bl*, Terry McCormick
50*br*; **Tony Stone Images:** 84–85, 129*br*, 139*bl*, 140*bl*, 141*tr*,
356–357, 391*br*, 424–425, 434*br*, 492–493, 495*cr*, 509*tr*, 560–561,
565*br*, 621*br*, 628–629, 633*tr*, 663*br*, 764–765, 791*br*, 822*br*, Sean
Arbabi 281*br*, Bruce Ayres 51*bl*, 290*bl*, 349*cr*, Christopher Bissel
293*br*, Sylvain Coffie 43*tr*, David Hanover 69*tl*, Frank Herholdt 4,
Tony Latham 36*br*, Michael Rosenfeld 27*cr*, Loren Santow 339*br*.
Jacket front cover: **Tony Stone Images** *tr*, **Market Photo Agency Inc** *br*.

"Coca-Cola," "Coke," and the Dynamic Ribbon device are registered
trade marks of The Coca-Cola Company and are reproduced with
kind permission from **The Coca-Cola Company**, 67*bl*.

Mind Maps are included on page 35 with the kind permission of
Tony Buzan. For further information contact Buzan Centres Ltd, 54
Parkstone Road, Poole, Dorset BH15 2PX. Tel: 44+(0) 1202 674 676;
Fax: 44+(0) 1202 674 776; e-mail: 101737.1141@compuserve.com

ABOUT ROBERT HELLER

A leading authority in the world of management consulting, Robert Heller was the founding editor of Britain's top management magazine, *Management Today*. He is much in demand as a conference speaker in Europe, North and South America, and the Far East. As editorial director of Haymarket Publishing Group, Robert Heller supervised the launch of several highly successful magazines such as *Campaign*, *Computing*, and *Accountancy Age*. His many acclaimed – and worldwide best-selling – books include *The Naked Manager*, *Culture Shock*, *The Age of the Common Millionaire*, *The Way to Win* (with Will Carling), *The Complete Guide to Modern Management*, and *In Search of European Excellence*.

ABOUT TIM HINDLE

Regular business writer Tim Hindle is the founder of the London-based business language consulting firm, Working Words, which helps international companies compose material in English and communicate their messages clearly to their intended audiences. He has been a contributor to *The Economist* since 1979 and was editor of *EuroBusiness* from 1994 to 1996. As editorial consultant and author, Tim Hindle has produced a number of titles including *Pocket Manager, Pocket MBA*, and *Pocket Finance*, and a biography of Asil Nadir, *The Sultan of Berkeley Square*.